standard catalog of®
FORD

4th Edition

John Gunnell

©2007 Krause Publications

Published by

kp krause publications

An Imprint of F+W Publications

700 East State Street • Iola, WI 54990-0001
715-445-2214 • 888-457-2873
www.krausebooks.com

Our toll-free number to place an order or obtain
a free catalog is (800) 258-0929.

Library of Congress Control Number: 2007924551

ISBN-13: 978-0-89689-615-4
ISBN-10: 0-89689-615-3

Designed by Paul Birling
Edited by Tom Collins

Printed in United States

105 Years of Ford Motor Company

Henry Ford built his first car in the summer of 1896. Charles Ainsley gave $200 for it and Ford used the money to finance his second car. Several attempts to form a car company followed and in June 16, 1903, the Ford Motor Co. was formed. In October of 1908, the Model T arrived. Henry Ford was finished experimenting. The T lasted almost two decades.

By 1926, after building 15 million Model Ts, even Ford had to admit it was outdated. It was followed by the ubiquitous Model A. From 1927-March 1932, five million As were made. Then, the flathead V-8 arrived, offering 65 hp for $460. This car changed it's styling annually, but the flathead V-8 survived through the '50s. In 1935, it outsold Chevrolet, America's best-selling car. The Ford got four-wheel hydraulic brakes in 1939. A six was introduced in 1941.

On May 26, 1943, Henry's son Edsel died. Henry became president of the Ford. When he died in 1947, Ford started moving into the modern age. New postwar envelope body styling was introduced and Ford remained "the car to have" if you were a performance enthusiast.

A big 1954 change was the introduction of Ford's first overhead valve V-8. Another innovation was the T-Bird. A high-water mark in the horsepower race, for all manufacturers including Ford, was 1957. Ford offered a supercharged version of its 312-cid V-8, plus a 340-hp "NASCAR" version.

New for 1958 was the famous "FE" series of 332- and 352-cid V-8s, which grew into the "390" and the awesome "427." The next year was a beauty contest thanks to the 1959 Galaxie — a Fairlane 500 two-door hardtop and with a T-Bird inspired roof.

Through the early '60s, Ford continued on a steady-as-she-goes course, adding the compact Falcon in '60 and mid-size Fairlane in '62. One of the most beautiful cars of the '60s was the '63-1/2 Galaxie 500 fastback. The mid-'64 introduction of the Mustang was historical.

Ford's '65 LTD was a new low-priced car with a luxury image. The big news in '66 was a redesigned Fairlane, now with big-block V-8 power. For 1967, NASCAR allowed mid-size cars to race and Fairlanes took the place of the Galaxies, dominating the big races.

It was the muscle car era and Ford also dominated the streets in the late '60s and early '70s. Then, insurance companies tightened the noose on "Supercar" owners. Experts recognize 1971 as the last year for true high-performance products from Ford until the '80s.

In answer to the growing import threat and new sub-compacts from AMC and Chevy, Ford introduced the Pinto. No automaker offered a more complete line than Ford between 1976 and 1986. Offerings ranged from the sub-compact Pinto through the big Thunderbird. Engines reached all the way up to a 460-cid V-8, which remained available through 1978.

In 1977, the "big 'Bird" was replaced with a modified LTD II. The Torino and Elite soon faded away and the Maverick was about to go too. The Granada became the first American car to offer a standard four-speed (overdrive) gearbox. The big LTD lasted until 1979.

In the '80s the LTD shrunk and the engines shrunk too. The T-Bird was downsized and the Crown Victoria name reappeared, bringing back memories of the sharpest mid-1950s Ford. Every Ford model endured a loss of sales, but so did most other domestic cars. The front-wheel-drive Escort arrived for 1981 carrying a CHV (hemi) engine. It became America's best-selling car. The Granada was slimmed down. The LTD got a small 255-cid V-8 and a six was standard in the T-Bird. Model year 1982 brought a hot Mustang GT and two-seat EXP.

The massive T-Birds of the '70s seemed forgotten as the 10th generation arrived for 1983. This one was loaded with curves and — before long — an optional turbocharged, fuel-injected four-cylinder engine, a close-ratio five-speed and a "quadra-shock" rear suspension.

Not many new models received as much publicity as the front-wheel-drive Taurus, the leader of the 1986 pack. Then, Ford Motor Co. broke records in 1987 with $4.6 billion in net income. New for 1987 was a four-wheel-drive Tempo and a five-liter Thunderbird Sport model. Ford was now the American car sales leader, ahead of Chevrolet's grand total by 66,000 cars. There seemed to be no stopping Ford and in 1989 in realized a 40,000-car sales increase .

A little-changed T-Bird marked its 35th anniversary in 1990. Most other models were also unaltered. In spring, Ford introduced an all-new '92 Crown Victoria. The '95 Contour "world car" replaced the Tempo. The debut of the 1995 Aspire also occurred early in 1994.

The Taurus SHO sedan was offered with V-8 power for the first time in 1996. An all-new '98 Escort ZX2 was made available in "Cool" or "Hot" versions. They featured unique body panels and frameless door glass. There was no '98 T-Bird.

A new Ford Focus was introduced in 2000. It was a sophisticated compact aimed at the worldwide market. In September, at the Henry Ford Museum & Greenfield Village, Ford celebrated a centennial of Ford racing with a very special event.

In 2002, an all-new two-passenger T-Bird based on the Lincoln LS platform arrived. Ford started taking T-Bird orders on Jan. 8, 2001, the day the car made its regular production debut at the Detroit Auto Show. The 2002 Thunderbird captured *Motor Trend* magazine's "Car of the Year" award. However, by the end of 2003, the company announced plans to drop the expensive, slow-selling model by 2005 or 2006. In 2005, Ford designers "nailed it" with a beautiful new "retro" Mustang that looked like a throwback to the '60s. Another hit of the same season was the Ford 500, a good-looking family sedan. Unfortunately, it was the pretty, two-seat T-Bird's last year. The Fusion — a new-generation "World Car" arrived in 2006. For enthusiasts, 2007 was the year of the Mustang Shelby Cobra GT 500 model, which did 0-to-60 in 4.9 seconds and the quarter mile in 13.1 at 115 mph.

Editor's Memo

The Standard Catalog of Ford is one of the cornerstones in this award-winning series of books on the history of automobiles. Rather than the "same old same old," we tried to improve this latest edition for the Ford buff.

To begin with, we decided to make this edition all-Ford so we have more room to give the more collectible Ford models additional coverage. In line with this policy, the Mustang and Thunderbird sections are bigger and more complete.

Next, we eliminated many instances where there were multiple photos of the same model and added photos of models not shown before. In the sections covering cars from the early 1930s to early 1950s, we tried as hard as we could to get a picture of every body style, as used to be featured in automotive historian George Dammann's great old hardcover Crestline books.

For 1955 to 1968 models, we came up with some great new and accurate production records. Believe it or not, the source of these production figures was General Motors! They show how rare some of the cars really were.

Naturally, we updated the Ford and Mustang sections to 2007 and we covered T-Birds until the "end" of the model in 2005. (Like many 'bird buffs, we hope it's not really the end of a great nameplate.)

In any book of this type, certain facts are concrete and certain facts are fluid. Building cars is not an *exact science* and the automakers don't always do what their literature says. This can lead to minor errors in a compilation like this. If you find any, let us know, prove your case and we'll make necessary changes.

At the end of the catalog, we added the latest "ballpark values" on Ford collector cars and ended the book with some listings of contacts helpful to Ford lovers. We hope you find *The Standard Catalog of Ford* to be enjoyable reading.

John "Gunner" Gunnell

standard catalog of®
Ford
Table of Contents

1903 Ford

Ford — Model A — Two-Cylinder: Ford Motor Company was incorporated on June 16, 1903. The company's first car was the Model A, a two-seater runabout capable of a maximum speed of 30 mph. This should not be confused with the better-known Model A of the 1930s. Ford used the Model A name twice. With a weight of just 1,250 pounds, the Model A was an early manifestation of Henry Ford's thinking that that would go into the Model T. As was common with most early automobiles, the Model A had a horse-buggy appearance (without the horse of course). The motor was positioned under the single seat. A detachable rear portion of the body — called a "tonneau" — provided seating for two additional passengers who gained access to their seats through a rear door.

VIN:

Serial numbers were mounted on the dashboard, adjacent to the steering column.

Model A

Model No.	Body/ Style No.	Body Type & Seating	Factory Price	Shipping Weight	Production Total
A	----	Runabout-2P	$ 850	1,250 lbs.	Note 1
A	----	Tonneau-2P	$ 950	------	Note 1

Note 1: Total Model A production was either 670 or 1,708 cars, depending upon the source. referred to. Ford officially uses the 670 figure for 1903 models only. The 1,700 seems to relate to combined 1903-1904 production.

Engine:

Model A: Opposed. Two-cylinder. Cast-iron block. B & S: 4 x 4 in. Displacement: 100.4 cu. in. Brake hp: 8. Valve lifters: mechanical. Carburetor: Schebler (early), Holley.

Chassis:

Wheelbase: 72 inches.

Technical:

Model A: Planetary transmission. Speeds: 2F/1R. Floor controls. Chain drive. Differential, band brakes. Wood-spoke wheels.

History: Introduced July 1903. On June 19, 1903, Barney Oldfield drove the Ford 999 racing car to a new one-mile record time of 59.6 seconds. Calendar year production: 1,708. Model-year production: (1903-1904) 1,700. The president of Ford was John S. Gray.

1903 Ford Model A Runabout (OCW)

1904 Ford

Ford — Model A/Model AC/Model C: These Ford models replaced the Model A in late 1904. Both were powered by a larger engine developing 10 hp. Ford claimed the top speed of both cars was 38 mph. The Model AC was essentially a Model A with the new Model C engine. The Model C had its fuel tank positioned under the hood, while that of the AC was located beneath the seat. Both cars had a longer 78-inch wheelbase than the Model A.

Ford — Model B — Four: The Model B was a drastic shift in direction for Henry Ford. With its four-passenger body, polished wood and brass trim, it was an elegant and expensive automobile. Powered by a 318-cid, 24-hp four, it was capable of a top speed of 40 mph. In place of the dry cell batteries carried by earlier Fords, the Model B was equipped with storage batteries. A 15-gallon fuel tank was also fitted. Other

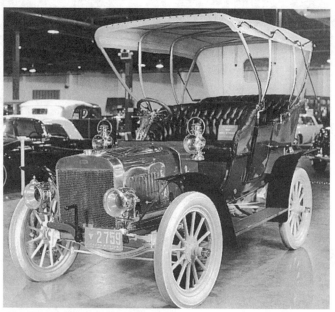

1904 Ford Model B Touring (OCW)

features separating the $2,000 Model B from other Fords was its shaft drive and its rear hub drum brakes.

VIN:

Serial numbers were mounted on the dashboard, adjacent to the steering column.

Model A

Model No.	Body/ Style No.	Body Type & Seating	Factory Price	Shipping Weight	Production Total
A	----	Runabout-2P	$ 850	1,250 lbs.	Note 1
A	----	Tonneau-2P	$ 950	-----	Note 1

Model AC

AC	----	Runabout-2P	$ 850	1,250 lbs.	Note 1
AC	----	Tonneau-2P	$ 950	-----	Note 1

Model C

C	----	Runabout-2P	$ 850	1,250 lbs.	Note 1
C	----	Tonneau-2P	$ 950	-----	Note 1

Model B

B	----	2-dr. Touring-4P	$2,000	1,700 lbs.	Note 1

Note 1: Total production in 1904 was 1,695 cars. Ford reported building a total of 670 model As and 1900 models A and AC altogether. There is no record of Model B production. Other sources show figures that vary from these.

Engines:

Model A: Cylinder layout: opposed. Two. Cast-iron block. B & S: 4 x 4 inches. Displacement: 100.4 cid. Brake hp: 8. Valve lifters: mechanical. Carburetor: Holley.

Model AC/Model C: Two-cylinder. Cast-iron block. B & S: 4-1/4 x 4-1/4 inches. Displacement 120.5 cid. Brake hp: 10. Valve lifters: mechanical. Carburetor: Holley.

Model B: Four-cylinder. Inline. Cast-iron block. B & S: 4-1/4 x 5 inches. Displacement: 283.5 cid. Brake hp; 24. Valve lifters: mechanical.

Carburetor: Holley.

Model A: Wheelbase: 72 in.

Model C/Model AC: Wheelbase: 78 in. Tires: 28 in.

Model B: Wheelbase: 92 in.

Technical:

Model A/AC/C: Planetary transmission. Speeds: 2F/1R. Floor shift controls. Cone clutch. Chain drive. Differential band brakes. Wooden spoke wheels.

Model B: Planetary transmission. Speeds: 2F/1R. Floor shift controls. Cone clutch. Shaft drive. Drum brakes on rear wheels. Wooden spoke wheels.

History:

The Model C and Model AC were introduced September 1904. Calendar-year production: 1,695. Model-year production: (1904-1905) 1,745. The president of Ford was John S. Gray.

1904 Ford Model B touring. [JAC]

1904 Ford Model C Runabout with Tonneau (OCW)

1905 Ford

Ford — Model F — Two-Cylinder: The Ford Models C and B were carried into 1905. The 1905 Model C had light yellow running gear instead of red running gear and wider 3 x 28 wheels. In February 1905, these Fords were joined by the Model F, which was powered by a two-cylinder engine developing approximately 16 hp. The Model F had a wheelbase of 84 inches and was fitted with a green body, cream-colored wheels and cream-colored running gear.

1905 Ford Model C Tonneau Touring (RLC)

Serial numbers were mounted on the dashboard, adjacent to the steering column.

Model C

Model No.	Body/ Style No.	Body Type & Seating	Factory Price	Shipping Weight	Production Total
C	-----	Runabout-2P	$ 800	1,250 lbs.	Note 1
C	-----	Tonneau-2P	$ 950	------	Note 1

Model B

B	----	2-dr. Touring-4P	$2,000	1,700 lbs.	Note 1

Model F

F	-----	2-dr. Touring-4P	$1,000	1,400 lbs.	Note 1
F	-----	2-dr. Coupe-2P	$1,250	------	Note 1

Note 1: Total production for 1905 was 1,599 cars.

Engines:

Model C: Two-cylinder. Opposed. Cast-iron block. B & S: 4-1/4 x 4-1/2 in. Displacement: 120.5 cid. Brake hp: 10. Valve lifters: mechanical. Carburetor: Holley.
Model B: Four-cylinder. Inline. Cast-iron block. B & S: 4-1/4 x 4 in. Displacement: 283.5 cid. Brake hp: 24. Valve lifters: mechanical. Carburetor: Holley.
Model F: Two-cylinder. Opposed. Cast-iron block. B & S: 4-1/2 x 4 in. Displacement: 127 cid. Brake hp: 16. Valve lifters: mechanical. Carburetors: Holley.

Chassis:

Model C: Wheelbase: 78 in. Tires: 28 in.
Model B: Wheelbase: 92 in. Tires: 32 in.
Model F: Wheelbase: 84 in. Tires: 30 in.

Technical:

Model C: Planetary transmission. Speeds: 2F/1R. Floor controls. Cone clutch. Chain drive. Differential band brakes. Wooden spoke wheels. Wheel size: 28 in.
Model B: Planetary transmission. Speeds: 2F/1R. Floor controls. Cone clutch. Shaft drive. Drum brakes on two rear wheels. Wood-spoke wheels. Wheel size: 32 in.
Model F: Planetary transmission. Speeds: 2F/1R. Floor controls. Cone clutch. Chain drive. Differential band brakes. Wood-spoke wheels. Wheel size: 30 in.

Options:

Top. Windshield. Lights.

History:

Introduced February 1905 (Model F). Calendar-year production: 1,599. Model-year production: (1905-1906) 1,599. The president of Ford was John S. Gray.

1905 Ford Model B Tonneau Touring (OCW)

1906 Ford

Ford — Model K — Six: Late in 1905, the Model K Ford debuted. Since Henry Ford was moving close to the final design of the Model T — his "car for the multitudes," it was not surprising that he cared little for the expensive Model K. Along with the Touring model, a Roadster version was offered. It was guaranteed to attain a 60 mph top speed.

Ford — Model N — Four: The $500 Model N, with its front mounted four-cylinder engine, developed over 15 hp. It was capable of going 45 mph. Its styling was highlighted by such features as twin, nickel-plated front lamps and a boattail rear deck. It had an 84-inch wheelbase. Its reputation for reliability represented a solid step forward by Henry Ford and Ford Motor Company in the quest for a low-priced car for the mass market.

Ford — Model F — Two: The Model F was continued into 1906 unchanged.

VIN:

Serial numbers were mounted on the dashboard, adjacent to the steering column.

Model F (Two)

Model No.	Body/ Style No.	Body Type & Seating	Factory Price	Shipping Weight	Production Total
F	-----	2-dr. Touring-4P	$1,100	1,400 lbs.	Note 1

Model K (Six)

| K | ----- | 2-dr. Touring-4P | $2,500 | 2,400 lbs. | Note 1 |
| K | ----- | Runabout-4P | $2,500 | 2,000 lbs. | Note 1 |

Model N (Four)

| N | ----- | Runabout-2P | $ 600 | 800 lbs. | Note 1 |

Note 1: Total production was 2,798 or 8,729, depending on the source. Ford Motor Co. records show both figures.

Engines:

Model F: Two-cylinder. Opposed. Two. Cast-iron block. B & S: 4-1/4 x 4-1/2 in. Displacement: 128 cid. Brake hp: 10. Valve lifters: mechanical. Carburetor: Holley.

Model N: Four-cylinder. Inline. Cast iron block. B & S: 3-3/4 x 3-3/8 in. Displacement: 149 cid. Brake hp: 15-18. Valve lifters: mechanical. Carburetor: Holley.

Model K: Six-cylinder. Inline. Cast-iron block. B & S: 4-1/2 x 4-1/4 in. Displacement: 405 cid. Brake hp: 40. Valve lifters: mechanical. Carburetor: Holley.

Chassis:

Model F: Wheelbase: 84 inches. Tires: 30 in.

Model N: Wheelbase: 84 inches. Tires: 2-1/2 in. wide.

Model K: Wheelbase: 114-120 in.

Technical:

Model F: Transmission: Planetary. Speeds: 2F/1R. Floor shift controls. Cone clutch. Chain drive. Differential band. Wooden spokes. Wheel size: 30 inches.

Model N: Transmission: Planetary. Speeds 2F/1R. Floor controls. Disc clutch. Chain drive.

Model K: Transmission: Planetary. Speeds 2F/1R. Floor shift controls. Disc clutch. Shaft drive.

Options:

Cowl lamps. Bulb horn. Three-inch wheels for Model N ($50).

History:

Henry Ford became president of the Ford Motor Company, following the death of John S. Gray on July 6, 1906. A racing version of the Model K set a new world's 24-hour record of 1,135 miles. It averaged 47.2 mph. The record run took place at Ormond Beach in Florida.

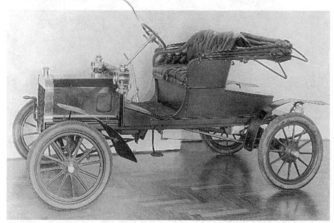

1906 Ford Model N, 4-cyl. runabout (RLC)

1906 Ford Model K Tonneau Touring (RLC)

1907 Ford

Ford — Model N — Four: The Model N was continued unchanged for 1907. As before, it was a handsome automobile with nickel hardware and quarter-circle fenders. Volume production didn't begin until late 1907, when the price rose to $600.

Ford — Model R — Four: The Model R was introduced in February 1907 as a more elaborate version of the Model N. It had footboards in place of the Model N's carriage step. A mechanical lubrication system also replaced the forced-feed oiler of the Model N.

Ford — Model S — Four: The Model S had the same mechanical and appearance features as those of the Model R and also had a single-seat tonneau on the rear.

Ford — Model K — Six: The Model K was unchanged for 1907.

VIN:

Serial numbers were mounted on the dashboard, adjacent to the steering column.

Model N (Four)

Model No.	Body/ Style No.	Body Type & Seating	Factory Price	Shipping Weight	Production Total
N	-----	Runabout-2P	$ 600	1,050 lbs.	-----

Model R (Four)

| R | ----- | Runabout-2P | $ 750 | 1,400 lbs. | Note 1 |

Model S (Four)

| S | ----- | Tonneau-4P | $ 700 | 1,400 lbs. | ------ |
| S | ----- | Roadster-2P | $ 750 | ------ | ------ |

Model K (Six)

| K | ----- | 2-dr. Touring-4P | $2,800 | 2,000 lbs. | ------ |
| K | ----- | Runabout-4P | $2,800 | 2,000 lbs. | ------ |

Note 1: Total production of the Model R was approximately 2,500 cars.

1907 Ford Model K Runabout (OCW)

1907 Ford Model K Touring (OCW)

Engines:

Model N: Four-cylinder. Inline. Cast-iron block. B & S: 3-3/4 x 3-3/8 in. Displacement: 149 cid. Brake hp: 15-18. Valve lifters: mechanical. Carburetor: Holley.

Model R: Four-cylinder. Inline. Cast-iron block. B & S: 3-3/4 x 3-3/8 in. Displacement: 149 cid. Brake hp: 15-18. Valve lifters: mechanical. Carburetor: Holley.

Model S: Four-cylinder. Inline. Cast-iron block. B & S: 3-3/4 x 3-3/8 in. Displacement: 149 cid. Brake hp: 15-18. Valve lifters: mechanical. Carburetor: Holley.

Model K: Six-cylinder. Inline. Cast-iron block. B & S: 4-1/2 x 4-1/4 in. Displacement: 405 cid. Brake hp: 40. Valve lifters: mechanical. Carburetor: Holley.

Chassis:

Model N: Wheelbase: 84 in. Tires: three-inches wide.
Model R: Wheelbase: 84 in. Tires: three-inches wide.
Model S: Wheelbase: 84 in. Tires: three-inches wide.
Model K: Wheelbase: 120 in.

Technical:

Model N: Planetary transmission. Speeds: 2F/1R. Floor controls. Disc clutch. Chain drive.
Model R: Planetary transmission. Speeds: 2F/1R. Floor controls. Disc clutch. Chain drive.
Model S: Planetary transmission. Speeds: 2F/1R. Floor controls. Disc clutch. Chain drive.
Model K: Planetary transmission. Speeds: 2F/1R. Floor controls. Disc clutch. Shaft drive.

History:

Calendar-year production was 6,775 according to some sources and 14,887 according to others. The president of Ford Motor Co. was Henry Ford.

1907 Ford Model S Roadster (OCW)

1908 Ford

Ford — Model N — Four: For the 1908 model year Ford continued to produce the K, N, R, and S models until production of the Model T began in October 1908. The Model N was unchanged. It continued to offer nickel hardware and quarter-circle fenders.

Ford — Model R — Four: The Model R was a more elaborate version of the Model N with footboards and a mechanical lubrication system.

Ford — Model S — Four: The Model S had the same mechanical and appearance features as those of the Model R and also had a single-seat tonneau on the rear.

Ford — Model K — Six: The Model K was unchanged for 1908.

VIN:

Serial numbers were mounted on the dashboard, adjacent to the steering column.

Model N (Four)

Model No.	Body/ Style No.	Body Type & Seating	Factory Price	Shipping Weight	Production Total
N	----	Runabout-2P	$ 600	1,050 lbs.	------
N	----	Landaulette-2P	-----	------	------

Model R (Four)

R	----	Runabout-2P	$ 750	1,400 lbs.	------

Model S (Four)

S	----	Tonneau-4P	$ 750	1,400 lbs.	------
S	----	Roadster-2P	$ 700	------	------

Model K (Six)

K	----	2-dr. Touring-4P	$2,800	2,000 lbs.	------
K	----	Runabout-4P	$2,800	2,000 lbs.	------

Note 1: Total production of the Model R was approximately 2,500 cars.

Engines:

Model N: Four-cylinder. Inline. Cast-iron block. B & S: 3-3/4 x 3-3/8 in. Displacement: 149 cid. Brake hp: 15-18. Valve lifters: mechanical. Carburetor: Holley.

Model R: Four-cylinder. Inline. Cast-iron block. B & S: 3-3/4 x 3-3/8 in. Displacement: 149 cid. Brake hp: 15-18. Valve lifters: mechanical. Carburetor: Holley.

Model S: Four-cylinder. Inline. Cast-iron block. B & S: 3-3/4 x 3-3/8 in. Displacement: 149 cid. Brake hp: 15-18. Valve lifters: mechanical. Carburetor: Holley.

Model K: Six-cylinder. Inline. Cast-iron block. B & S: 4-1/2 x 4-1/4 in. Displacement: 405 cid. Brake hp: 40. Valve lifters: mechanical. Carburetor: Holley.

Chassis:

Model N: Wheelbase: 84 in. Tires: three-inches wide.
Model R: Wheelbase: 84 in. Tires: three-inches wide.
Model S: Wheelbase: 84 in. Tires: three-inches wide.
Model K: Wheelbase: 120 in.

Technical:

Model N: Planetary transmission. Speeds: 2F/1R. Floor controls. Disc clutch. Chain drive.

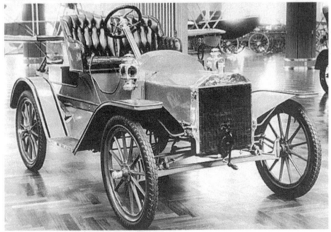

1908 Ford Model S Runabout (RLC)

Model R: Planetary transmission. Speeds: 2F/1R. Floor controls. Disc clutch. Chain drive.

Model S: Planetary transmission. Speeds: 2F/1R. Floor controls. Disc clutch. Chain drive.

Model K: Planetary transmission. Speeds: 2F/1R. Floor controls. Disc clutch. Shaft drive.

History:

Calendar year production was 6,015 according to some sources and 10,202 according to others (including early Model T Fords). The president of Ford Motor Co. was Henry Ford.

1909 Ford

Ford — Early 1909 — Model T: The Model T Ford was introduced in October 1908, and was an entirely new car when compared to Ford's previous models. The engine had four cylinders, cast en bloc with a removable cylinder head, quite unusual for the time. The engine pan was a one-piece steel stamping and had no inspection plate. The chassis featured transverse springs, front and rear, a rear axle housing that was drawn steel rather than a casting. The rear axles were non-tapered, with the hubs being held with a key and a pin and the pin retained by the hub cap. The front axle was a forged "I" beam with spindles that had integral arms. The use of vanadium steel almost throughout made for a stronger, yet lighter, machine that gave the Ford impressive performance for its time. The wheels were 30 in. with 30 x 3 in. tires on the front, and 30 x 3-1/2 in. on the rear. The wheel hub flanges were 5-1/2 in. diameter (compared with 6 in. from 1911 until the end of production in 1927). Windshields and tops were optional equipment on open cars, as were gas headlights, speedometers, robe rails, Prest-O-lite tanks, foot rests, auto chimes, car covers and other accessories that Ford would install at the factory. The radiator was brass, as were any lamps furnished (oil cowl lamps and taillamps were standard equipment). The hood had no louvers and was made of aluminum. The body styles offered were the Touring, the Runabout (a roadster), the Coupe, the Town Car and the Landaulet. The bodies were generally made of wood panels over a wood frame and were offered in red, gray and green. Gray was used primarily on the Runabouts, red on the Touring cars and green on the Town cars and Landaulets. These early cars (first 2,500) were so unique that they are generally considered a separate subject when discussing Model Ts. Essentially, the engines had built-in water pumps and the first 800 cars came with two foot pedals and two control levers (the second lever being for reverse) instead of the usual three pedals and one lever. The front fenders were square tipped, with no "bills."

Ford — Late 1909 — Model T: Beginning about car number 2500, the Model T became more or less standardized. Through most of 1909, the windshields and tops on the open cars remained optional, but more and more were delivered with this equipment, as well as gas headlights, factory installed. By the end of the year, they were standard. Body types and styling continued unchanged. Colors continued as in the early production, except that both green and red Touring cars were produced, along with a mixture of colors in the other models as well. Red was not offered after June 1909. Black was not listed as an available color and only one of the shipping invoices showed black, but early cars extant seem to indicate that black was used. This could be due to oxidation of the top color coat, but black early Fords are an enigma to the Model T student. The one aluminum-paneled touring body, built by Pontiac Body, was discontinued about September 1909. The late 1909 fenders were similar in design to the earlier 1909 fenders, but now had rounded

fronts with small "bills." The engine no longer had the water pump. Instead, it was cooled by thermosyphon action and set the pattern for all later Model T engines.

VIN:

Early 1909: (October 1908 to April 1909) The serial number was between center exhaust ports on side of engine. Starting: 1 (October 1908). Ending: approximately 2500. (The first of the non-water pump engines was 2448, built on April 22, 1909, but there was some mixture of the old and the new in production for a short time.)

Calendar-year engine numbers: 1 to 309, October to December 1908. Car numbers were stamped on a plate on the front seat kick panel and these were the same as the engine numbers. Other numbers stamped on the body sills, etc. were manufacturer's numbers and not an identifying number. [1909] Serial number was behind the timing gear on the lower right side of the engine. Starting: approximately 2501. Ending: approximately 11145. (There is no "break" between the 1909 and 1910 cars, 11146 was the first number assembled in October 1909, the beginning of Ford's fiscal year 1910). 1909 calendar year engine numbers: 310 to 14161 (approximate). Car numbers were stamped on a plate on the front seat kick panel and these were the same as the engine numbers. Other numbers stamped on the body sills, etc. were manufacturer's numbers and not an identifying number.

Model T (Four)

Model No.	Body/Style No.	Body Type & Seating	Factory Price	Shipping Weight	Production Total
T	------	Touring-5P	$ 850	1,200 lbs.	7,728
T	------	Runabout-5P	$ 825	-----	2,351
T	------	Town Car-4P	$1,000	-----	236
T	------	Landaulet-7P	$ 950	-----	298
T	------	Coupe-2P	$ 950	-----	47

Notes: Prices effective October 1, 1908 (at introduction of the Model T). The production totals are for the fiscal year: Oct. 1, 1908 to Sept. 30, 1909.

Engines:

Early 1909: L-head. Four. Cast iron block. B & S: 3-3/4 x 4 in. Displacement.: 176.7 cid. Compression ratio: 4.5:1 (approximate) Brake hp: 22 at 1600 rpm. NACC hp: 22.5. Main bearings: three. Valve lifters: solid. Carburetor: Kingston five-ball, Buffalo. Torque: 83 at 900 rpm. Used only in first 2,500 Model Ts.

Late 1909: L-head. Four. Cast iron block. B & S: 3-3/4 x 4 in. Displacement.: 176.7 cid. Compression ratio: 4.5:1 (approximate) Brake hp: 22 at 1600 rpm. NACC hp: 22.5. Main bearings: three. Valve lifters: solid. Carburetor: Kingston five-ball, Buffalo. Torque: 83 at 900 rpm.

Chassis:

Model T: Wheelbase: 100 in. Overall length: 11 ft. 2-1/2 in. Front tread: 56 in. Rear tread: 56 in. Tires: (front) 30 x 3 front, (rear) 30 x 3-1/2.

Technical:

Early 1909 Model T: (First 800)] Planetary transmission. Speeds: 2F/1R, two pedal controls and two levers on floor. Multiple-disc clutch (24 discs). Torque tube drive. Straight bevel rear axle. Overall ratio: 3.63:1. Brakes: contracting band in transmission. Hand-operated internal expanding in rear wheels. Foot brake stops driveshaft. Parking brake on two rear wheels. Wheel size: 30 in. Clutch and Brakes [through car 800]: Clutch pedal gives low when pressed to

1909 Ford Model T Touring (HFM)

1909 Ford Model T coupe (HAC)

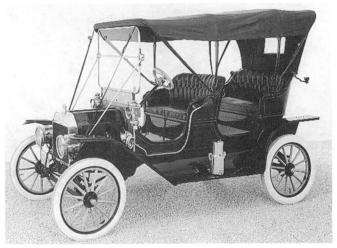

1909 Ford Model T Tourster (OCW)

1910 Ford Model T Touring (OCW)

floor, high when released, neutral in between. Reverse lever puts clutch in neutral and applies reverse brake band. Second lever is the parking brake. [1909-1927] Planetary transmission. Speeds: 2F/1R. Three pedal controls and one lever on floor. Multiple disc clutch (26 discs 1909-1915), (25 discs 1915-1927). Torque tube drive. Straight bevel rear axle. Overall ratio: 3.63:1. Brakes: Contracting band in transmission. Hand-operated internal expanding in rear wheels. Foot brake stops driveshaft. Parking brake on two rear wheels. Wheel size: 30 in. (21 in. optional in 1925, standard in 1926-1927). Drivetrain options: 4.0:1 optional rear axle ratio beginning in 1919. Clutch and Brakes [after car 800]: Clutch pedal gives low when pressed to floor, high when released, neutral in between. Control lever puts clutch in neutral and applies parking brake. Center foot pedal applies reverse. Third (right-hand) pedal is the service brake, applying transmission brake band. Model T Wheels: Standard wheels are wooden spoke with demountable rims, an option beginning in 1919. In 1925, 21 in. wood spoke demountable rim wheels were an option, these became standard in 1926. Beginning January 1926 optional 21 in. wire wheels became available. These became standard on some closed cars in calendar year 1927. In mid-1925 (1926 models) the transmission brake was made about a half-inch wider, and the rear wheel brakes were enlarged to 11 in. with lined shoes. 1909-1925 were seven in. with cast iron shoes (no lining). Springs were transverse semi-elliptic, front and rear. Model T Steering: 3:1 steering gear ratio by planetary gear at top of steering column until mid-1925 when ratio was changed to 5:1.

Options:

Windshield. Headlamps. Tops. Horns. Prest-O-lite tanks (instead of the carbide tank). Robe rails. Tire chains. Top boots. Foot rests. Spare tire carriers. Speedometers. Bumpers. 60-inch front and rear tread.

1910 Ford

Ford — Model T: The 1910 Fords were unchanged from 1909, except for a number of mechanical modifications in the rear axle and the use of one standard color on all models: dark green. The Landaulet and the Coupe were discontinued in 1910 and a new Tourabout (basically a Touring car using two separate seat sections) was added. All body styles except the Roadster and the Tourabout had two doors with the front compartment being open. Only the Coupe came with doors. The Tourabout was similar to the Touring but had two roadster-like seat sections and no doors. All 1910 Model Ts had windshields.

VIN:

The serial number was behind the timing gear on the lower right side of the engine. Starting: 11146 (approximate). Ending: 31532 (approximate). There is no "break" between the 1910 and 1911 cars. 31533 was the first number assembled in October 1910, the beginning of Ford's fiscal year 1911. The first "1911" car built was a torpedo runabout in which the chassis was assembled October 5, and the final assembly occurred October 26. The first "blue" cars were built during October and are presumed to be "1911" models. 1910 calendar year engine numbers: 14162 (approximate) to 34901. Car numbers were stamped on a plate on the front seat kick panel and these were the same as the engine numbers. Other numbers stamped on the body sills, etc. were manufacturer's numbers and not an identifying number.

1910 Ford Model T Runabout (OCW)

Model T (Four)

Model No.	Body/ Style No.	Body Type & Seating	Factory Price	Shipping Weight	Production Total
T	------	Touring-5P	$ 950	1,200 lbs.	16,890
T	------	Tourabout-5P	$ 950	------	------
T	------	Runabout-5P	$ 900	------	1,486
T	------	Town Car-7P	$1,200	------	377
T	------	Landaulet-7P	$1,100	------	2
T	------	Coupe-2P	$1,050	------	187
T	------	Chassis	------	------	108

Notes: Prices effective October 1, 1909. Production was for the fiscal year, Oct. 1, 1909, to Sept. 30, 1910.

Combined production of Touring and Tourabouts was 16,890.

Engine:

Model T: L-head. Four. Cast-iron block. B & S: 3-3/4 x 4 in. Displacement.: 176.7 cid. Compression ratio: 4.5:1 (approximate) Brake hp: 22 at 1600 rpm NACC hp: 22.5. Main bearings: three. Valve lifters: solid. Carburetor: Kingston five-ball, Buffalo (early 1910). Torque: 83 at 900 rpm.

Chassis:

Model T: Wheelbase: 100 in. Overall length: 11 ft. 2-1/2 in. Front tread: 56 in. Rear tread: 56 inches. Tires: (front) 30 x 3 front, (rear) 30 x 3-1/2.

Options:

The many options listed for 1909 were not available in 1910. Standard equipment for the open cars now included the windshield, gas headlamps and carbide generator, speedometer and top with side curtains. Interestingly, the more expensive closed cars (Landaulet, Town Car and Coupe) were equipped with horn and oil lamps only. Headlamps and speedometer were $80 extra.

1911 Ford

Ford — Model T: In approximately January 1911, the Model T Ford was completely restyled. New fenders, a new - but similar - radiator, new wheels, new bodies and, during the year a new engine, front axle and rear axle, made the 1911 Ford almost a new beginning. The bodies were now made with steel panels over a wood framework. A

1911 Ford Model T Touring (OCW)

new standard color of dark blue was used on all models. Body types were the same as offered in 1910. The Tourabout and Landaulet, while listed in the catalogs, were not produced in 1911. The Coupe was phased out and only 45 were built. Two new bodies were offered: the Open Runabout and the Torpedo Runabout. Both of these differed considerably from the other models in that they had curved fenders, a longer hood, a lower seating arrangement, a lower and longer steering column and a gas tank located on the rear deck, behind the seat. The two cars were similar, but not the same. The Open Runabout did not have doors, while the Torpedo Runabout had one door on each side. Near the end of the year - and called a "1912" model - a new Delivery Car was offered. Fender construction was also new, setting a general pattern for the bulk of Model T production until 1926. The new front fenders had larger "bills" than did the 1910 style. Lamps were all brass with gas headlights, and kerosene sidelights and taillights. The rear axle housing was redesigned. The earlier pressed-steel type had gone through a number of modifications in 1909, 1910 and early 1911, but in midyear a new type with a cast-iron center section appeared. The axles were now of taper-end design (perhaps changed before the new housing) and the hub flanges were six inches in diameter. The front axle now used spindles with separate steering arms and the axle ends were modified to accept the new spindles. The front axle remained relatively unchanged in later years.

VIN:

The serial number was behind the timing gear on the lower right side of the engine. Starting: 31533 (approximate). Ending: 70749 (approximate). There is no "break" between the 1911 and 1912 cars. 70750 was the first number assembled in October 1911, the beginning of Ford's fiscal year 1912. 1911 calendar year engine numbers: 34901 to 88900 (approximate). Car numbers were stamped on a plate on the firewall and these might be the same as the engine numbers, Ford now used the engine number to identify all cars. Other numbers stamped on the body sills, etc. were manufacturer's numbers and not an identifying number.

1911 Ford Model T Open Runabout (OCW)

1911 Ford Model T Town Car (HAC)

1911 Ford Model T Touring (OCW)

Model T (Four)

Model No.	Body/ Style No.	Body Type & Seating	Factory Price	Shipping Weight	Production Total
T	------	Touring-5P	$ 780	1,200 lbs.	26,405
T	------	Tourabout-4P	$ 725	------	------
T	------	Runabout-2P	$ 680	------	7,845
T	------	Torpedo Runabout-2P	$ 725	------	------
T	------	Open Runabout-2P	$ 680	------	------
T	------	Town Car-7P	$ 960	------	315
T	------	Landaulet-7P	$1,100	------	0
T	------	Coupe-2P	$ 840	------	45
T	------	Chassis	$ 940	------	248

Notes: Prices effective Oct. 1, 1910. Production is for fiscal year, Oct. 1, 1910, to Sept. 30, 1911. Runabouts were not broken out by types in the production figures.

Engine:

Model T: L-head. Four. Cast-iron block. B & S: 3-3/4 x 4 in. Displacement: 176.7 cid. Compression ratio: 4.5:1 (approximate) Brake hp: 22 at 1600 rpm. NACC hp: 22.5. Main bearings: three. Valve lifters: solid. Carburetor: Kingston five-ball, Holley 4500, Holley H-1 4550. Torque: 83 at 900 rpm.

Chassis:

Model T: Wheelbase: 100 in. Overall length: 11 ft. 2-1/2 in. Front tread: 56 in. Rear tread: 56 inches. Tires: (front) 30 x 3 front, (rear) 30 x 3-1/2.

Note: Thermosyphon. Upper main bearings were now babbited. Valve chambers (two) were now enclosed using steel doors held with one stud/nut each. Inspection plate in the crankcase.

Technical:

Model T: Planetary transmission. Speeds: 2F/1R. Three pedal controls and one lever on floor. Multiple disc clutch. Torque tube drive. Straight bevel rear axle. Overall ratio: 3.63:1. Brakes: Contracting band in transmission. Hand-operated internal expanding in rear wheels. Foot brake stops driveshaft. Parking brake on two rear wheels.

All cars were equipped with headlamps, horn, etc. with no options. Ford Motor Co. even said the warranty, would be voided if any accessories were added.

1912 Ford

Ford — Model T: In approximately January 1912, the Model T was again restyled. However, the appearance was similar to the 1911 cars. The touring car was now supplied with "fore doors" that enclosed the front compartment. These were removable and many have been lost over the years. The metal side panels of the touring were now relatively smooth from top to bottom, eliminating the "step" under the seats, which marked the 1911s. The top support straps now fastened to the windshield hinge, rather than to the front of the chassis as they had in prior years. The torpedo runabout was now based on the standard runabout, and the open runabout was discontinued. While retaining the curved rear fenders, the front fenders were now standard. The hood and steering column were also the same as those used on the other 1912 cars. The front compartment was enclosed in a manner similar to the 1911 torpedo. The "1912" style year lasted only about nine months, an all new "1913" car appeared about September. The only color on record for 1912 was dark blue but the existence of black cars of the era seems to indicate that black was available as well.

VIN:

The serial number was behind the timing gear on the lower right-hand side of the engine until about serial number 100000, then it was moved to just behind the water inlet on the left-hand side of the engine. Also, about this time, the location was again changed to the standard position above the water inlet, with some mixture of locations for a time. Starting: 70750 (approximate). Some records show number 69877 built on September 30, 1911. Ending: 157424 (approximate). There is no break between the 1912 and 1913 cars. Number 157425 was the first number assembled on October 1912, the beginning of Ford's 1913 fiscal year. 1912 calendar-year engine numbers: 88901 to 183563. According to Ford records, engines with numbers B1 and B12247 were built at the Detroit plant beginning October 1912 and October 1913, but no records exist as to the exact dates. Car numbers were stamped on a plate on the firewall. Other numbers were stamped on the body sills, etc., were manufacturer's numbers and not an identifying number. Car numbers no longer agreed with the motor numbers and Ford kept no records of them.

Model T (Four)

Model No.	Body/ Style No.	Body Type & Seating	Factory Price	Shipping Weight	Production Total
T	------	Touring-5P	$ 690	1,200 lbs.	50,598
T	------	Torpedo Runabout-2P	$ 590	------	13,376
T	------	Commercial Roadster-4P	$ 590	------	------
T	------	Town Car-7P	$ 900	------	802
T	------	Delivery Car-2P	$ 700	------	1,845
T	------	Coupe-2P	$ 840	------	19
T	------	Chassis	------	940 lbs.	2,133

Notes: Fiscal year, Oct. 1, 1911, to Sept. 30, 1912. Roadster production figures were combined. The total was 13,376. Coupes and the chassis were not shown in the catalogs.

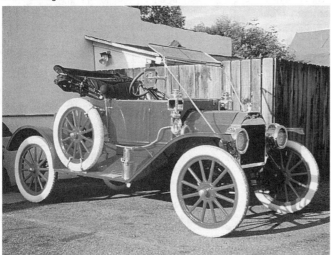

1912 Ford Model T Open Runabout (OCW)

1912 Ford Model T Touring (OCW)

Engine:

Model T: L-head. Four. Cast-iron block. B & S: 3-3/4 x 4 in. Displacement.: 176.7 cid. Compression ratio: 4.5:1 (approximate). Brake hp: 22 at 1600 rpm. NACC hp: 22.5. Main bearings: three. Valve lifters: solid. Carburetor: Kingston six-ball, Holley H-1 4550. Torque: 83 at 900 rpm.

Note: Thermosyphon. Valve chambers (two) now enclosed using steel doors held with one stud/nut each. Inspection plate in the crankcase. Kingston carburetor used in limited quantities and does not appear in any of the Ford parts lists.

Chassis:

Model T: Wheelbase: 100 in. Overall length: 10 ft. 8 in. Front tread: 56 in. Rear tread: 56 in. Tires: (front) 30 x 3 front, (rear) 30 x 3-1/2.

Technical:

Model T: Planetary transmission. Speeds: 2F/1R. Three pedal controls and one lever on floor. Multiple disc clutch. Torque tube drive. Straight bevel rear axle. Overall ratio: 3.63:1. Brakes: Contracting band in transmission. Hand-operated internal expanding in rear wheels. Foot brake stops driveshaft. Parking brake on two rear wheels.

Options:

The basic equipment included three oil lamps (two side and one tail). Windshield. Headlamps. Tops. Horns. Top boots. Speedometers.

1913 Ford

Ford — Model T: In about September of 1912, Ford introduced the second new body to arrive that calendar year and marketed it as a 1913 Model T. The redesigned Model T set the pattern for the next 12 years. Metal side panels now extended from the firewall to the rear of the car. There was one rear door on the left side of the Touring Car and two doors on the right side. The doors were unique in that they extended clear to the splash apron. There was no metal support between the front and rear sections of the body, which proved to be a problem. The bodies flexed so much that the doors opened during driving. The initial solution to the problem was to add a steel reinforcement across the rear door sills. Later, heavier body sills were used. Still later, Ford used both the steel reinforcements and the heavier sills. The bottom section of the windshield on the open cars now sloped rearwards, while the upper section was vertical and folded forward. The fenders followed the pattern of those used on 1911-1912 Model Ts, except that they no longer had the "bills" at the front. Side, tail and headlamps were still oil fired or gas-fired, but they were now made of painted black steel, except for the tops and rims, which were still made of brass. The rear axle housings were again redesigned so that the center section was larger (fatter) and the axle tubes were flared and riveted to the center section. "Made in USA" now appeared on the radiator under the "Ford" name. The same notation appeared on many other parts as well. This may have been done to differentiate from cars built in Canada Ford of Canada first started manufacturing its own engines and other parts in 1913. According to Ford data, the 1913 cars were painted dark blue, with striping on early models. As in earlier models, black body finish is a possibility, but it is not documented in any Ford literature. Body styles offered were the Touring Car, Runabout and Town Car. The Torpedo Roadster, which had a rear-deck-mounted gas tank, was discontinued. (Ford called the regular Runabout a "Torpedo" for several years after this.) The Delivery Car, which had proved to be a sales disaster, was also dropped.

VIN:

The serial number was above the water inlet on the left side of he engine. Starting: 157425 (approximate) October 1912. Some 1913 cars may have been built earlier. Ending: 248735. (There is no break between the 1913 and 1914 cars. The 1914-style Touring was

1913 Ford Model T Touring (HFM)

1914 Ford Model T Touring (OCW)

introduced about August 1913, which could make the ending number around 320000 for 1913 cars.) 1913 calendar-year engine numbers: 183564 to 408347. According to Ford records, engines with numbers B1 and B12247 were built at the Detroit plant between October 1912 and October 1913, but no records exist as to the exact dates. Numbers stamped on the body sills, etc. were manufacturer's numbers and not an identifying number.

Model T (Four)

Model No.	Body/ Style No.	Body Type & Seating	Factory Price	Shipping Weight	Production Total
T	-----	Touring-5P	$ 600	1,200 lbs.	126,715
T	-----	Runaboout-2P	$ 525	------	33,129
T	-----	Town Car-7p	$ 800	------	1,415
T	-----	Delivery Car-2p	$ 625	------	513
T	-----	Coupe-2p	----	------	1
T	-----	Chassis	----	960 lbs.	8,438

Notes: Fiscal year, Oct. 1, 1912, to Sept. 30, 1913. Coupes and the chassis were not shown in the catalogs.

Engine:

Model T: L-head. Four. Cast-iron block. B & S: 3-3/4 x 4 in. Displacement.: 176.7 cid. Compression ratio: 4.0:1. Brake hp: 20 at 1600 rpm. NACC hp: 22.5. Torque: 83 at 900 rpm. Main bearings: three. Valve lifters: solid. Carburetor: Kingston Y (4400), Holley S (4450).

Note: Thermosyphon. Valve chambers (two) now enclosed using steel doors held with one stud/nut each. Inspection plate in the crankcase. Camshaft modified for less power (less overlap in timing). Modified cylinder head for slightly lower compression.

Chassis:

Model T: Wheelbase: 100 in. Overall length: 10 ft. 8 in., chassis and 11 ft. 2-1/2 in., car. Front tread: 56 in. Rear tread: 56 in. Tires: (front) 30 x 3 front, (rear) 30 x 3-1/2. Chassis essentially identical except those after mid-1913 have a longer rear crossmember.

Technical:

Model T: Planetary transmission. Speeds: 2F/1R. Three pedal controls and one lever on floor. Multiple disc clutch. Torque tube drive. Straight bevel rear axle. Overall ratio: 3.63:1. Brakes: Contracting band in transmission. Hand-operated internal expanding in rear wheels. Foot brake stops driveshaft. Parking brake on two rear wheels.

Options:

All cars equipped with headlamps, horn, etc. with no options. Ford even said the warranty would be voided if any accessories were added, although itís doubtful this ever happened.

1914 Ford

Ford — Model T: The 1914 Model Ts looked almost identical to the 1913s, but the doors were now inset into the side panels and the body metal extended across the rear door sills, solving the weakness problem. The windshield, while similar in appearance to the 1913 style, now folded to the rear. The windshield support rods were given a bend to clear the folded section. The fenders were modified and now had embossed reinforcing ribs across the widest part. Later, ribs were added in the apron area of both front and rear fenders. The front fenders had no bill in most 1914 models, but one was added to fenders used late in the year. The front fender iron bracket was secured to the fender with four rivets. Black was now the Ford color, although records in the Ford Archives seem to indicate that Blue was still offered. Interestingly,

1914 Ford Model T Touring

Black was never listed as an available color prior to 1914, in spite of the many seemingly original pre-1914 Black Fords seen today. It is possible that Black was a common color, but there is nothing in the records to prove it. The use of 1913-style black-and-brass lamps continued. The chassis frame was modified and now had a longer rear cross member. This eliminated the use of the forged-metal body brackets used since 1909. A bare chassis was added to the Ford line in 1914. In the fall of the year a Center Door Sedan and a Coupelet (the first "convertible") were introduced, but these were really 1915 models.

VIN:

The serial number was above the water inlet on the left side of the engine. Starting: 348736 (approximate) October 1913. The 1914 cars were built as early as August, which could make the first 1914 cars around serial number 320000. Ending: 670000 (mid-January 1915). The new 1915 Ford was introduced in January at the Highland Park plant, but the 1914 style continued to be built, for a time, at some branches. There is no clear break point in the style years. 1914 calendar-year engine numbers: 408348 to 656063. Numbers stamped on the body sills, etc., were manufacturer's numbers and not an identifying number.

Model T (Four)

Model No.	Body/ Style No.	Body Type & Seating	Factory Price	Shipping Weight	Production Total
T	-----	Touring-5P	$ 550	1,200 lbs.	165,832
T	-----	Runaboout-2P	$ 500	------	35,017
T	-----	Town Car-7p	$ 750	------	1,699
T	-----	Chassis	----	960 lbs.	119

Notes: Fiscal year, Oct. 1, 1913, to July 31, 1914.

Engine:

Model T: L-head. Four. Cast-iron block. B & S: 3-3/4 x 4 in. Displacement.: 176.7 cid. Compression ratio: 4.0:1. Brake hp: 20 at 1600 rpm. NACC hp: 22.5. Torque: 83 at 900 rpm. Main bearings: three. Valve lifters: solid. Carburetor: Kingston Y (4400), Holley G (6040 brass body).

Note: Thermosyphon. Valve chambers (two) now enclosed using steel doors held with one stud/nut each. Inspection plate in the crankcase.

Chassis:

Model T: Wheelbase: 100 in. Overall length: 10 ft. 8 in., chassis and 11 ft. 2-1/2 in., car Front tread: 56 in. Rear tread: 56 in. Tires: (front) 30 x 3 front, (rear) 30 x 3-1/2. The chassis was essentially identical except those after mid-1913 have a longer rear crossmember.

Technical:

Model T: Planetary transmission. Speeds: 2F/1R. Three pedal controls and one lever on floor. Multiple disc clutch. Torque tube drive. Straight bevel rear axle. Overall ratio: 3.63:1. Brakes: Contracting band in transmission. Hand-operated internal expanding in rear wheels. Foot brake stops driveshaft. Parking brake on two rear wheels.

Options:

The basic equipment included three oil lamps. (Two side and one tail.) Windshield. Headlamps. Tops. Horns. Top boots. Speedometers.

1915 Ford

Ford — Model T: The 1915-style open Model Ts were introduced at Ford's Highland Park, Michigan plant in January 1915, but the 1914 style continued to be manufactured in some of the branches until as late as April. The bodies were essentially the same as the 1914 bodies, except for the front cowl section. Instead of the exposed wooden firewall, a new metal cowl curved "gracefully" inward to the hood. The hood and radiator were the same as on earlier Model Ts, except for the use of louvers in the hood side panels. The windshield was now upright, with the top section folding towards the rear. Electric headlights were standard. These were of "typical" size and shape and were commonly seen on Model T Fords through the end of production in 1927. Brass headlight rims were used. The sidelights were now of a rounded style and were interchangeable from side to side. The taillight was similar, but had a red lens in the door and a clear lens on the side towards the license plate. The side lamps and taillights were still kerosene-fired. They had brass tops and rims, but were otherwise painted black. The headlights were powered by the engine magneto. The front fenders again had "bills" and were the same as the late-1914 design. While retaining the same style, later the fenders had revised iron brackets held in place with three rivets. The rear fenders were curved to follow the wheel outline. Neither the front or rear fenders were crowned. A bulb-type horn was standard in 1915. It was mounted under the hood. The hood now had louvers, perhaps so that the horn could be heard. Early in the year, Ford began using a magneto-powered horn on some cars it built and, by October 1915, all Model Ts had the new horn. The Sedan model was unique from other Model Ts. The Sedan body was made of aluminum panels and required special rear fenders and splash aprons. The Sedan gas tank was located under the rear seat and proved to be quite unsatisfactory, because of poor fuel flow. The body was redesigned during the year and was then made of steel panels. Also, the gasoline tank was relocated under the driver's seat. The Coupelet had a folding top, but differed from the Runabout in that the doors had windows and the windshield was like that of the Sedan. It also had a larger turtle deck. The rear axle was redesigned for the last time (except for minor modifications). The center section was cast iron and the axle tubes were straight and inserted into it.

VIN:

The serial number was above the water inlet on the left side of the engine. Starting: 670000 approximate (January 1915). The new 1915 Ford was introduced in January at the Highland Park plant, but the 1914 style continued to be built for a time at some branches. There is no clear

1915 Ford Model T Runabout (OCW)

1915 Ford Model T Touring (AA)

break point in the style years. Ending: 856513 (July 24, 1915, end of fiscal 1915). 1915 calendar-year engine numbers: 656064 to 1028313. Numbers stamped on the body sills, etc. were manufacturer's numbers and not an identifying number.

Model T (Four)

Model No.	Body/ Style No.	Body Type & Seating	Factory Price	Shipping Weight	Production Total
T	-----	3-dr. Touring-5P	$ 490	1,500 lbs.	244,181
T	-----	2-dr. Runabout-2P	$ 440	1,380 lbs.	47,116
T	-----	4-dr. Town Car-7P	$ 690	------	------
T	-----	2-dr. Sedan-5P	$ 975	1,730 lbs.	989
T	-----	2-dr. Coupe-2P	$ 750	1,540 lbs.	2,417
T	-----	Chassis	$ 410	980 lbs.	13,459

Note: Fiscal year, Aug. 1, 1914, to July 31, 1915.

Engine:

Model T: L-head. Four. Cast-iron block. B & S: 3-3/4 x 4 in. Displacement.: 176.7 cid. Compression ratio: 4.0:1. Brake hp: 20 at 1600 rpm. NACC hp: 22.5. Torque: 83 at 900 rpm. Main bearings: three. Valve lifters: solid. Carburetor: Kingston L (6100), Holley G (6040 brass body).

Note: Thermosyphon. Valve chambers (two) now enclosed using steel doors held with one stud/nut each. Inspection plate in the crankcase.

Chassis:

Model T: Wheelbase: 100 in. Overall length: 10 ft. 8 in., chassis and 11 ft. 2-1/2 in., car. Front tread: 56 in. Rear tread: 56 in. Tires: (front) 30 x 3 front, (rear) 30 x 3-1/2. The chassis was essentially identical except those after mid-1913 had a longer rear crossmember.

Technical:

Model T: Planetary transmission. Speeds: 2F/1R. Three pedal controls and one lever on floor. Multiple disc clutch. Torque tube drive. Straight bevel rear axle. Overall ratio: 3.63:1. Brakes: Contracting band in transmission. Hand-operated internal expanding in rear wheels. Foot brake stops driveshaft. Parking brake on two rear wheels.

Options:

The basic equipment included three oil lamps. (Two side and one tail.) Windshield. Headlamps. Tops. Horns. Top boots. Speedometers.

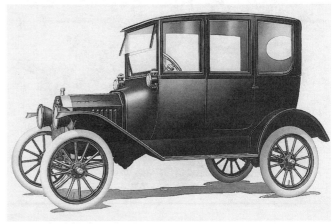

1915 Ford Model T Center door sedan

1916 Ford

Ford — Model T: The 1916 Fords were merely an extension of the 1915s, except for the deletion of the brass trim on the side lamps and taillights. The hood was now made of steel. All Model Ts were now equipped with the magneto horn. "Portholes" were added to the side of the Coupelet in an effort to allow the driver a better side view. The Sedan body was redesigned to now use standard fenders and splash aprons. There was a new gas tank under the driver's seat. The new body was all steel.

VIN:

The serial number was above the water inlet on the left side of the engine. Starting: 856514 (August 1, 1915). Ending: 1362989 (July 25, 1916, end of fiscal 1916). 1916 calendar-year engine numbers: 1028314 to 1614516. Numbers stamped on the body sills, etc. were manufacturer's numbers and not an identifying number.

Model T (Four)

Model No.	Body/Style No.	Body Type & Seating	Factory Price	Shipping Weight	Production Total
T	-----	3-dr. Touring-5P	$ 440	1,510 lbs.	363,024
T	-----	2-dr. Runaboout-2P	$ 390	1,395 lbs.	98,633
T	-----	4-dr. Town Car-7P	$ 640	------	1,972
T	-----	2-dr. Sedan-5P	$ 740	1,730 lbs.	1,859
T	-----	2-dr. Coupe-2P	$ 590	1,060 lbs.	1,174
T	-----	Chassis	$ 410	980 lbs.	13,459
T	-----	Ambulance (military)	-----	------	20,700

Note: Fiscal year, Aug. 1, 1915, to July 30, 1916. Ambulances built for the military.

Engine:

Model T: L-head. Four. Cast-iron block. B & S: 3-3/4 x 4 in. Displacement: 176.7 cid. Compression ratio: 4.0:1. Brake hp: 20 at 1600 rpm. NACC hp: 22.5. Torque: 83 at 900 rpm. Main bearings: three. Valve lifters: solid. Carburetor: Kingston L (6100), Holley G (6040 brass body).
Note: Thermosyphon. Valve chambers (two) now enclosed using steel doors held with one stud/nut each. Inspection plate in the crankcase.

Chassis:

Model T: Wheelbase: 100 in. Overall length: 10 ft. 8 in., chassis and 11 ft. 2-1/2 in. car. Front tread: 56 in. Rear tread: 56 in. Tires: (front) 30 x 3 front, (rear) 30 x 3-1/2. The chassis was essentially identical except those after mid-1913 had a longer rear crossmember.

Technical:

Model T: Planetary transmission. Speeds: 2F/1R. Three pedal controls and one lever on floor. Multiple disc clutch with 25 discs (1916-on). Torque tube drive. Straight bevel rear axle. Overall ratio: 3.63:1. Brakes: Contracting band in transmission. Hand-operated internal expanding brakes in rear wheels. Foot brake stops driveshaft. Parking brake on two rear wheels.

1916 Ford Model T Coupelet (OCW)

1916 Ford Model T Coupelet (OCW)

Options:

The basic equipment included three oil lamps. (Two side and one tail.) Windshield. Headlamps. Tops. Horns. Top boots. Speedometers.

1917 Ford

Ford — Model T: The Model T for 1917 looked like an all-new car, but was actually a rather simple evolution from the 1916 version. The brass radiator and the small hood were gone, as were all bits of brass trim. New curved and crowned fenders appeared. There was also a new black radiator shell, a new hood and a new hood former. The body itself was unchanged. Lamps were the same as 1916. During 1917, the Model T continued to get minor modifications, such as a different mounting base for the windshield and new rectangular cross-section top sockets replacing the oval ones used since 1915. Nickel-plating on the steering gear box, hubcaps and radiator filler neck replaced the earlier brass trim. A new engine pan came out in 1917. It had a larger front section to go with a larger fan pulley. The pulley, however, was not enlarged until about 1920. The "convertible" Coupelet was replaced with a "hardtop" Coupelet. While the top could no longer be folded, the side window posts could be removed and stored under the seat. This gave the car a hardtop look. The Town Car was discontinued during the year. Also during 1917, the Ford Model TT truck chassis was introduced.

VIN:

The serial number was above the water inlet on the left side of the engine. Starting: 1362990 (August 1, 1916). Ending: 2113501 (July 28, 1917, end of fiscal year 1917). 1917 calendar-year engine numbers were 1614517 to 2449179. Numbers stamped on the body sills, etc. were manufacturer's numbers and not an identifying number.

Model T (Four)

Model No.	Body/Style No.	Body Type & Seating	Factory Price	Shipping Weight	Production Total
T	-----	3-dr. Touring-5P	$ 360	1,480 lbs.	583,128
T	-----	2-dr. Runaboout-2P	$ 345	1,385 lbs.	107,240
T	-----	4-dr. Town Car-7P	$ 595	------	2,328
T	-----	2-dr. Sedan-5P	$ 645	1,745 lbs.	7,361
T	-----	2-dr. Coupe-2P	$ 505	1,580 lbs.	7,343
T	-----	Chassis	$ 325	1,060 lbs.	41,165
T	-----	Ambulance (military)	-----	------	1,452

Note: Fiscal year Aug. 1, 1917, to July 30, 1918. Ambulances built for the military.

1917 Ford Model T Runabout (HAC)

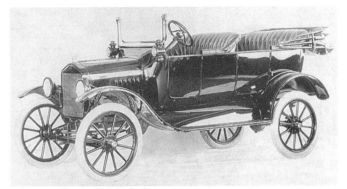

1917 Ford Model T Touring (OCW)

Engine:

Model T: L-head. Four. Cast-iron block. B & S: 3-3/4 x 4 in. Displacement: 176.7 cid. Compression ratio: 4.0:1. Brake hp: 20 at 1600 rpm. NACC hp: 22.5. Torque: 83 at 900 rpm. Main bearings: three. Valve lifters: solid. Carburetor: Kingston L2 (6100), Holley G (6040 iron body). New cylinder head with slightly lower compression and much larger water jacket.

Note: Thermosyphon. Valve chambers (two) now enclosed using steel doors held with one stud/nut each. Inspection plate in the crankcase.

Chassis:

Model T: Wheelbase: 100 in. Overall length: 10 ft. 8 inches, chassis and 11 ft. 2-1/2 in., car. Front tread: 56 in. Rear tread: 56 in. Tires: (front) 30 x 3 front, (rear) 30 x 3-1/2. Chassis essentially identical except those after mid-1913 have a longer rear crossmember.

Technical:

Model T: Planetary transmission. Speeds: 2F/1R. Three pedal controls and one lever on floor. Multiple disc clutch (25 discs 1915-1927). Torque tube drive. Straight bevel rear axle. Overall ratio: 3.63:1. Brakes: Contracting band in transmission. Hand-operated internal expanding in rear wheels. Foot brake stops driveshaft. Parking brake on two rear wheels.

Options:

The basic equipment included three oil lamps (two side and one tail.) Windshield. Headlamps. Tops. Horns. Top boots. Speedometers.

1918 Ford

Ford — Model T: The Model T for 1918 was a continuation of the 1917 line with only very minor changes.

VIN:

Serial number was above the water inlet on the left side of the engine. Starting: 2113502 (August 1, 1917). Ending: 2756251 (July 27, 1918, end of fiscal year 1918). 1918 calendar-year engine numbers: 2449180 to 2831426. Numbers stamped on the body sills, etc. were manufacturer's numbers and not an identifying number.

Model T (Four)

Model No.	Body/ Style No.	Body Type & Seating	Factory Price	Shipping Weight	Production Total
T	-----	3-dr. Touring-5P	$ 360	1,450 lbs.	432,519
T	-----	2-dr. Runabout-2P	$ 345	1,435 lbs.	73,559
T	-----	4-dr. Town Car-7P	$ 595	------	2,142
T	-----	2-dr. Sedan-5P	$ 645	1,715 lbs.	35,697
T	-----	2-dr. Coupe-2P	$ 505	1,580 lbs.	14,771
T	-----	Chassis	$ 325	1,060 lbs.	37,648
T	-----	Ambulance (military)	------	------	2,163
TT	-----	Truck chassis	$ 600	1,450 lbs.	41,105
T	-----	Delivery car	------	------	399
T	-----	Foreign	------	------	24,000

Notes: Fiscal year: Aug. 1, 1917 to July 30, 1918. Ambulances built for the military.

Engine:

Model T: L-head. Four. Cast-iron block. B & S: 3-3/4 x 4 in. Displacement: 176.7 cid. Compression ratio: 4.0:1. Brake hp: 20 at 1600 rpm. NACC hp: 22.5. Torque: 83 at 900 rpm. Main bearings: three. Valve lifters: solid. Carburetor: Kingston L2 (6100), Holley G (6040 iron body). New cylinder head with slightly lower compression and much larger water jacket.

1918 Ford Model T Center Door Sedan (HAC)

Note: Thermosyphon. Valve chambers (two) now enclosed using steel doors held with one stud/nut each. Inspection plate in the crankcase.

Chassis:

Model T: Wheelbase: 100 in. Overall length: 10 ft. 8 inches, chassis and 11 ft. 2-1/2 in., car. Front tread: 56 in. Rear tread: 56 in. Tires: (front) 30 x 3 front, (rear) 30 x 3-1/2. Chassis essentially identical except those after mid-1913 have a longer rear crossmember.

Technical:

Model T: Planetary transmission. Speeds: 2F/1R. Three pedal controls and one lever on floor. Multiple disc clutch (25 discs 1915-1927). Torque tube drive. Straight bevel rear axle. Overall ratio: 3.63:1. Brakes: Contracting band in transmission. Hand-operated internal expanding in rear wheels. Foot brake stops driveshaft. Parking brake on two rear wheels.

Options:

The basic equipment included three oil lamps (two side and one tail.) Windshield. Headlamps. Tops. Horns. Top boots. Speedometers.

1919 Ford

Ford — Model T: In 1919, Model T body styling continued unchanged from 1918, but the Ford was finally given a battery and an electric starter. Beginning as standard equipment on the closed cars only, by mid-1919, a starter became an option on open cars, too. This change required a new engine block, a new transmission cover, new flywheel, etc. The general design of these items was unchanged, except for modifications needed to adapt the starter and generator to the engine. Also available as Ford standard equipment for the first time were wheels with demountable rims. These were standard equipment on closed cars and an option on the open models. When demountable wheels were used, all tires were of the same 30 x 3-1/2 size. With the adoption of electrical equipment came an instrument panel for the first time. Factory-installed instrumentation consisted of only an ammeter. Controls located on the instrument panel included the choke knob and an ignition and light switch. A speedometer was a dealer-installed options. The Model T Coupelet body style was redesigned. While looking the same, its door posts were now integral with the doors and the posts were no longer removable. The rear axle was also modified slightly. The oil filler hole was lowered to reduce the amount of oil that could be put in. This reduced a rear axle oil leaking problem. The center

1919 Ford Model T Touring (OCW)

section of the axle was milled to accept a gasket between the two halves. The front radius rod was redesigned and now fastened below the axle, adding strength to the assembly.

VIN:

The serial number was above the water inlet on the left-hand side of the engine. Starting: 2756252 (August 1, 1918). Ending: 3277851 (July 30, 1919, end of 1919 fiscal year). 1919 calendar-year engine numbers: 2831427 to 3659971. Numbers stamped on the body sills, etc. were manufacturer's numbers and not an identifying number.

Model T (Four)

Model No.	Body/Style No.	Body Type & Seating	Factory Price	Shipping Weight	Production Total
T	-----	3-dr. Touring-5P	$ 525	1,500 lbs.	286,935
T	-----	2-dr. Runaboout-2P	$ 500	1,390 lbs.	48,867
T	-----	2-dr. Sedan-5P	$ 875	1,875 lbs.	24,980
T	-----	2-dr. Coupe-2P	$ 750	1,685 lbs.	11,528
T	-----	4-dr. Town Car-7P	-----	-----	17
T	-----	Chassis	$ 475	1,060 lbs.	47,125
T	-----	Ambulance (military)	-----	-----	2,227
TT	-----	Truck chassis	$ 550	1,477 lbs.	70,816
TT	-----	Truck chassis (pneumatic tires)	-----	-----	399
T	-----	Delivery car	-----	-----	5,847

Notes: Fiscal year: Aug. 1, 1918, to July 30, 1919. Starter optional on open cars at $75. Demountable rims were an additional $25.

Engine:

Model T: L-head. Four. Cast-iron block. B & S: 3-3/4 x 4 in. Displacement: 176.7 cid. Compression ratio: 3.98:1. Brake hp: 20 at 1600 rpm. NACC hp: 22.5. Torque: 83 at 900 rpm. Main bearings: three. Valve lifters: solid. Carburetor: Kingston L4 (6150). Holley NH (6200). New cylinder head with slightly lower compression and much larger water jacket.

Note: Thermosyphon. Valve chambers (two) now enclosed using steel doors held with one stud/nut each. Inspection plate in the crankcase.

Chassis:

Model T: Wheelbase: 100 in. Overall length: 10 ft. 8 in., chassis and 11 ft. 2-1/2 in., car. Front tread: 56 in. Rear tread: 56 in. Tires: (front) 30 x 3 front, (rear) 30 x 3-1/2. 30 x 3-1/2 all around with demountable rims 1919-1925. Chassis essentially identical except those after mid-1913 had a longer rear crossmember.

1919 Ford Model T Runabout (HAC)

1919 Ford Model T Coupe (OCW)

1919 Ford Model T Center Door Sedan (OCW)

Technical:

Model T: Planetary transmission. Speeds: 2F/1R. Three pedal controls and one lever on floor. Multiple disc clutch (25 discs 1915-1927). Torque tube drive. Straight bevel rear axle. Overall ratio: 3.63:1. Brakes: Contracting band in transmission. Hand-operated internal expanding in rear wheels. Foot brake stops driveshaft. Parking brake on two rear wheels.

Options:

All cars equipped with headlamps, horn, etc. Starter ($75). Demountable rims ($25).

Early 1920 Ford

Ford — Model T: The early 1920 Model T Ford was virtually the same car as the 1919 model. In photos, these cars would look identical. An oval-shaped gas tank (located under the driver's seat) replaced the previous round type. This allowed the seat to be lowered.

VIN:

Serial number was above the water inlet on the left side of the engine. Starting: 3277852 (August 1, 1919). Ending: 4233351 (July 31, 1920, end of fiscal year 1920). 1920 calendar-year engine numbers: 3659972 to 4698419. Numbers stamped on the body sills, etc. were manufacturer's numbers and not an identifying number.

Model T (Four)

Model No.	Body/Style No.	Body Type & Seating	Factory Price	Shipping Weight	Production Total
T	-----	3-dr. Touring-5P	$ 575	1,500 lbs.	165,929
T	-----	2-dr. Runaboout-2P	$ 550	1,390 lbs.	31,889
T	-----	2-dr. Sedan-5P	$ 975	1,875 lbs.	81,616
T	-----	2-dr. Coupe-2P	$ 850	1,760 lbs.	60,215
T	-----	Chassis	$ 525	1,060 lbs.	18,173
TT	-----	Truck chassis	$ 660	1,477 lbs.	135,002
TT	-----	Truck chassis (pneumatic tires)	-----	-----	399

Model T (Four) (After in-year price increase)

Model No.	Body/Style No.	Body Type & Seating	Factory Price	Shipping Weight	Production Total
T	-----	3-dr. Touring-5P	$ 675	1,500 lbs.	367,785
T	-----	2-dr. Runaboout-2P	$ 650	1,540 lbs.	63,514
T	-----	2-dr. Sedan-5P	$ 975	1,875 lbs.	-----
T	-----	2-dr. Coupe-2P	$ 850	1,760 lbs.	-----
T	-----	Chassis	$ 620	1,210 lbs.	16,919
TT	-----	Truck chassis	$ 640	1,477 lbs.	-----

Notes: Fiscal year: Aug. 1, 1919, to July 30, 1920.

Engine:

Model T: L-head. Four. Cast-iron block. B & S: 3-3/4 x 4 in. Displacement: 176.7 cid. Compression ratio: 3.98:1. Brake hp: 20 at 1600 rpm. NACC hp: 22.5. Torque: 83 at 900 rpm. Main bearings:

three. Valve lifters: solid. Carburetor: Kingston L4 (6150). Holley NH (6200). New cylinder head with slightly lower compression and much larger water jacket.

Note: Thermosyphon. Valve chambers (two) now enclosed using steel doors held with one stud/nut each. Inspection plate in the crankcase.

Chassis:

Model T: Wheelbase: 100 in. Overall length: 10 ft. 8 inches, chassis and 11 ft. 2-1/2 in., car. Front tread: 56 in. Rear tread: 56 in. Tires: (front) 30 x 3 front, (rear) 30 x 3-1/2. 30 x 3-1/2 all around with demountable rims 1919-1925. Chassis after mid-1913 had a longer rear crossmember.

Technical:

Model T: Planetary transmission. Speeds: 2F/1R. Three pedal controls and one lever on floor. Multiple disc clutch (25 discs 1915-1927). Torque tube drive. Straight bevel rear axle. Overall ratio: 3.63:1. Brakes: Contracting band in transmission. Hand-operated internal expanding in rear wheels. Foot brake stops driveshaft. Parking brake on two rear wheels.

Options:

All cars equipped with headlamps, horn, etc. Starter ($75). Demountable rims ($25).

Late 1920 through 1922 Ford

Ford — Model T: Another new Model T Ford body appeared in the open cars in late 1920. It takes an expert to spot differences in the two cars, but they do exist. The most noticeable variation was a new rear quarter panel. It was now an integral part of the side panel and replaced the two-piece assembly used since 1913. Seat backs were given a more comfortable angle and the result was a far more comfortable car. The chassis frame was modified slightly, the running board support brackets were now pressed steel channels instead of the forged brackets with a tie rod used since 1909. Otherwise the basic car was like the previous models. A new pinion bearing spool was used on the rear axle. The earlier type was an iron casting with enclosed mounting studs. The new spool was a forging and used exposed mounting bolts. Body styles offered during this period were the touring, runabout, coupelet and sedan, in addition to the chassis and the truck chassis.

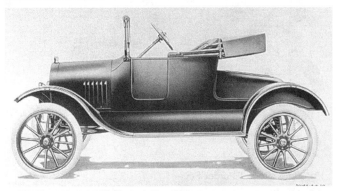

1920 Ford Model T Turtledeck Roadster (RLC)

1921 Ford Model T Turtledeck Roadster (JAC)

VIN:

(1921) Serial number was above the water inlet on the left side of the engine. Starting: 4233352 (August 2, 1920). Ending: 5223135 (July 30, 1921, end of fiscal 1921). 1921 calendar year engine numbers: 4698420 to 5568071. Numbers stamped on the body sills, etc, were manufacturer's numbers and not an identifying number. (1922) Serial number was above the water inlet on the left side of the engine. Starting: 5223136 (August 1, 1921). Ending: 6543606 (September 14, 1922, introduction of first "1923" model). 1922 calendar year engine numbers: 5638072 to 6953071. Numbers stamped on the body sills, etc. were manufacturer's numbers and not an identifying number.

1920-1921 Model T (Four) (Prices effective Sept. 22, 1920)

Model No.	Body/Style No.	Body Type & Seating	Factory Price	Shipping Weight	Production Total
T	-----	3-dr. Touring-5P	$ 440	1,500 lbs.	84,970*
T	-----	3-dr. Touring-5P (electric start and demountable rims)	$ 535	1,650 lbs.	647,300
T	-----	2-dr. Runabout-2P	$ 395	1,390 lbs.	25,918*
T	-----	2-dr. Runabout-2P (electric start and demountable rims)	$ 490	1,540 lbs.	171,745
T	-----	2-dr. Sedan-5P (electric start and demountable rims)	$ 795	1,875 lbs.	179,734
T	-----	2-dr. Coupe-2P (electric start and demountable rims)	$ 745	1,760 lbs.	129,159
T	-----	Chassis	$ 360	1,060 lbs.	13,356*
T	-----	Chassis (electric start and demountable rims)	$ 455	1,210 lbs.	23,536
TT	-----	Truck chassis (pneumatic tires)	$ 545	1,477 lbs.	118,583*
T	-----	Canada and foreign production	-----	-------	42,860*

*Note: Prices Aug. 1, 1920 to Dec. 31, 1921. Ford Motor Co. began calendar year figures in 1921.

1921 Ford Model T Center Door Sedan [JAC]

1921 Ford Model T Touring (OCW)

1921 Model T (Four) (Prices effective June 7, 1921)

T	-----	3-dr. Touring-5P	$ 415	1,500 lbs.	Note 1
T	-----	3-dr. Touring-5P (electric start and demountable rims)	$ 510	1,650 lbs.	Note 1
T	-----	2-dr. Runabout-2P	$ 370	1,390 lbs.	Note 1
T	-----	2-dr. Runabout-2P (electric start and demountable rims)	$ 465	1,540 lbs.	Note 1
T	-----	2-dr. Sedan-5P (electric start and demountable rims)	$ 760	1,875 lbs.	Note 1
T	-----	2-dr. Coupe-2P (electric start and demountable rims)	$ 695	1,760 lbs.	Note 1
T	-----	Chassis	$ 345	1,060 lbs.	Note 1
T	-----	Chassis (electric start and demountable rims)	$ 440	1,210 lbs.	Note 1
TT	-----	Truck chassis (pneumatic tires)	$ 495	1,477 lbs.	Note 1

Note 1 : See chart the top chart for production figures. Ford Motor Co. began calendar year figures in 1921.

1922 Model T (Four) (Prices effective Sept. 2, 1921)

T	-----	3-dr. Touring-5P	$ 355	1,500 lbs.	80,070*
T	-----	3-dr. Touring-5P (electric start and demountable rims)	$ 450	1,650 lbs.	514,333
T	-----	2-dr. Runabout-2P	$ 325	1,390 lbs.	31,923*
T	-----	2-dr. Runabout-2P (electric start and demountable rims)	$ 420	1,540 lbs.	133,433
T	-----	2-dr. Sedan-5P (electric start and demountable rims)	$ 660	1,875 lbs.	146,060
T	-----	2-dr. Coupe-2P (electric start and demountable rims)	$ 595	1,760 lbs.	198,382
T	-----	Chassis	$ 295	1,060 lbs.	15,228*
T	-----	Chassis (electric start and demountable rims)	$ 390	1,210 lbs.	23,313
TT	-----	Truck chassis (pneumatic tires)	$ 445	1,477 lbs.	135,629*

*Note: Production from Jan. 1, 1922 to Dec. 31, 1922 including foreign production.

1922 Model T (Four) (Prices effective Jan. 16, 1922)

T	-----	3-dr. Touring-5P	$ 348	1,500 lbs.	Note 1
T	-----	3-dr. Touring-5P (electric start and demountable rims)	$ 443	1,650 lbs.	Note 1
T	-----	2-dr. Runabout-2P	$ 319	1,390 lbs.	Note 1
T	-----	2-dr. Runabout-2P (electric start and demountable rims)	$ 414	1,540 lbs.	Note 1
T	-----	2-dr. Sedan-5P (electric start and demountable rims)	$ 645	1,875 lbs.	Note 1
T	-----	2-dr. Coupe-2P (electric start and demountable rims)	$ 580	1,760 lbs.	Note 1
T	-----	Chassis	$ 285	1,060 lbs.	Note 1
T	-----	Chassis (electric start and demountable rims)	$ 380	1,210 lbs.	Note 1
TT	-----	Truck chassis (pneumatic tires)	$ 430	1,477 lbs.	Note 1

Note 1: See the production figures in the first 1922 chart.

1922 Model T (Four) (Prices effective Oct. 17, 1922)

T	-----	3-dr. Touring-5P	$ 298	1,500 lbs.	Note 1
T	-----	3-dr. Touring-5P (electric start and demountable rims)	$ 393	1,650 lbs.	Note 1
T	-----	2-dr. Runabout-2P	$ 269	1,390 lbs.	Note 1
T	-----	2-dr. Runabout-2P (electric start and demountable rims)	$ 364	1,540 lbs.	Note 1
T	-----	2-dr. Sedan-5P (electric start and demountable rims)	$ 595	1,875 lbs.	Note 1
T	-----	4-dr. Sedan-5P	$ 725	1,950 lbs.	Note 1
T	-----	2-dr. Coupe-2P (electric start and demountable rims)	$ 530	1,760 lbs.	Note 1
T	-----	Chassis	$ 235	1,060 lbs.	Note 1
T	-----	Chassis (electric start and demountable rims)	$ 330	1,210 lbs.	Note 1
TT	-----	Truck chassis	$ 380	1,477 lbs.	Note 1
TT	-----	Truck chassis (electric start and demountable rims)	$ 475	1,577 lbs.	18,410

Note 1: See the production figures in the first 1922 chart.

Engine:

1920 Model T: L-head. Four. Cast-iron block. B & S: 3-3/4 x 4 in. Displacement: 176.7 cid. Compression ratio: 3.98:1. Brake hp: 20 at 1600 rpm. NACC hp: 22.5. Torque: 83 at 900 rpm. Main bearings: three. Valve lifters: solid. Carburetor: Kingston L4 (6150). Holley NH (6200). New cylinder head with slightly lower compression and much larger water jacket.

Note: Thermosyphon. Valve chambers (two) now enclosed using steel doors held with one stud/nut each. Inspection plate in the crankcase. New lightweight connecting rods.

1921 and 1922 Model T: L-head. Four. Cast-iron block. B & S: 3-3/4 x 4 in. Displacement.: 176.7 cid. Compression ratio: 3.98:1. Brake hp: 20 at 1600 rpm. NACC hp: 22.5. Torque: 83 at 900 rpm. Main bearings: three. Valve lifters: solid. Carburetor: Kingston L4 (6150). Holley NH (6200).

Note: Thermosyphon. Single valve chamber covered with one steel door held with two stud/nuts or bolts. Beginning in 1922 (Serial No. 5530000 - April 1922)

Chassis:

Model T: Wheelbase: 100 in. Overall length: 10 ft. 8 in., chassis and 11 ft. 2-1/2 in., car. Front tread: 56 in. Rear tread: 56 in. Tires: (front) 30 x 3 front, (rear) 30 x 3-1/2. 30 x 3-1/2 all around with demountable rims 1919-1925. Chassis after mid-1913 had a longer rear crossmember.

Technical:

Model T: Planetary transmission. Speeds: 2F/1R. Three pedal controls and one lever on floor. Multiple disc clutch (25 discs 1915-1927). Torque tube drive. Straight bevel rear axle. Overall ratio: 3.63:1. Brakes: Contracting band in transmission. Hand-operated internal expanding in rear wheels. Foot brake stops driveshaft. Parking brake on two rear wheels.

1921 Ford Model T Touring (OCW)

1922 Ford Model T Fordor Sedan (OCW)

1922 Ford Model T Coupe (OCW)

All cars equipped with headlamps, horn, etc. Starter ($75). Demountable rims ($25).

1923 Ford

Ford — Model T: In 1923, open body styles in the Model T lineup were again restyled. They used the same bodies as the 1921-1922 versions, but had a new windshield with a sloping angle and a new "one man" top. These features made the Touring and Runabout look new. The 1923 model was introduced in the fall of 1922 and continued until about June 1923, when another new line of Model Ts appeared. About November 1922, a new Fordor sedan was added to the line. The Fordor body was made of aluminum panels over a wood frame. Instrument panels were now standard on all Model Ts. Cars without and electrical starter had a blank plate where the ammeter would be. The early 1923 cars continued the wooden firewall of all previous Fords. This lasted until early calendar 1923, when the firewall was changed to sheet metal. This took place before the June styling change mentioned above. The starter and generator were standard equipment on all closed cars, as were the demountable wheels. This equipment was optional on the Runabout and Touring car. It was also the last year for the Center Door Sedan and the Coupe with the forward-opening doors.

VIN:

Serial number was above the water inlet on the left side of the engine. Starting: 6543607 (September 22, 1922). Ending: 7927374 (June 30, 1923). 1923 calendar-year engine numbers: 6953072 to 9008371. Numbers stamped on the body sills, etc. were manufacturer's numbers and not an identifying number.

1923 Model T (Four) (Prices effective Oct. 17, 1922)

Model No.	Body/ Style No.	Body Type & Seating	Factory Price	Shipping Weight	Prod. Total
T	—	3 dr. Touring-5P	$ 298	1,500 lbs.	136,441*
T		3 dr. Touring-5P (electric start and demountable rims)	$ 393	1,650 lbs.	792,651
T	—	2 dr. Runabout-2P	$ 269	1,390 lbs.	56,954*
T	---	2 dr. Runabout-2P (electric start and demountable rims)	$ 364	1,540 lbs.	238,638
T		2d Sedan-5P (electric start and demountable rims)	$ 595	1,875 lbs.	96,410
T		4d Sedan-5P (electric start and demountable rims)	$ 725	1,950 lbs.	144,444
T	—	2d Coupe-2P (electric start and demountable rims)	$ 530	1,760 lbs.	313,273
T	—	Chassis	$ 235	1,060 lbs.	9,443*
		Chassis (electric start and demountable rims)	$ 330	1,210 lbs.	42,874
TT		Truck chassis	$ 380	1,477 lbs.	197,057*
TT		Truck chassis (electric start and demountable rims)	$ 475	1,577 lbs.	64,604

Note: Production totals from Jan. 1, 1923 through Dec. 31, 1923 including foreign production.

1923 Ford Model T Touring Car (OCW)

1923 Model T (Four) (Prices effective Oct. 2, 1923)

T	—	3 dr. Touring-5P	$ 295	1,500 lbs.	Note 1
T	—	3 dr. Touring-5P (electric start and demountable rims)	$ 380	1,650 lbs.	Note 1
T	—	2 dr. Runabout-2P	$ 265	1,390 lbs.	Note 1
T	---	2 dr. Runabout-2P (electric start and demountable rims)	$ 350	1,540 lbs.	Note 1
T		2d Sedan-5P (electric start and demountable rims)	$ 590	1,875 lbs.	Note 1
T		4d Sedan-5P (electric start and demountable rims)	$ 685	1,950 lbs.	Note 1
T		2d Coupe-2P (electric start and demountable rims)	$ 525	1,760 lbs.	Note 1
T		Chassis	$ 230	1,060 lbs.	Note 1
T		Chassis (electric start and demountable rims)	$ 295	1,210 lbs.	Note 1
TT		Truck chassis	$ 370	1,477 lbs.	Note 1
TT		Truck chassis (electric start and demountable rims)	$ 435	1,577 lbs.	Note 1

Note 1: See top 1923 chart for production totals.

1923 Model T (Four) (Prices effective Oct. 2, 1923)

T	—	3 dr. Touring-5P	$ 295	1,500 lbs.	Note 1
T	—	3 dr. Touring-5P (electric start and demountable rims)	$ 380	1,650 lbs.	Note 1
T	—	2 dr. Runabout-2P	$ 265	1,390 lbs.	Note 1
T	---	2 dr. Runabout-2P (electric start and demountable rims)	$ 350	1,540 lbs.	Note 1
T	—	2d Sedan-5P (electric start and demountable rims)	$ 590	1,875 lbs.	Note 1
T	—	4d Sedan-5P (electric start and demountable rims)	$ 685	1,950 lbs.	Note 1
T	—	2d Coupe-2P (electric start and demountable rims)	$ 525	1,760 lbs.	Note 1
T	—	Chassis	$ 230	1,060 lbs.	Note 1
T		Chassis (electric start and demountable rims)	$ 295	1,210 lbs.	Note 1
TT	----	Truck chassis	$ 370	1,477 lbs.	Note 1
TT	----	Truck chassis (electric start and demountable rims)	$ 455	1,577 lbs.	Note 1
TT	----	Truck with body	$ 490	------	Note 2

Note 1: See top 1923 chart for production totals.
Note 2: This truck was not listed separately from the chassis figures.

Engine:

Model T: L-head. Four. Cast-iron block. B & S: 3-3/4 x 4 in. Displacement: 176.7 cid. Compression ratio: 3.98:1. Brake hp: 20 at 1600 rpm. NACC hp: 22.5. Torque: 83 at 900 rpm. Main bearings: three. Valve lifters: solid. Carburetor: Kingston L4 (6150). Holley NH (6200).

Note: Thermosyphon. Inspection plate in the crankcase. New lightweight connecting rods.

Chassis:

Model T: Wheelbase: 100 in. Overall length: 10 ft. 8 in., chassis and 11 ft. 2-1/2 in., car. Front tread: 56 in. Rear tread: 56 in. Tires: (front) 30 x 3 front, (rear) 30 x 3-1/2. 30 x 3-1/2 all around with demountable rims 1919-1925.

Technical:

Model T: Planetary transmission. Speeds: 2F/1R. Three pedal controls and one lever on floor. Multiple disc clutch (25 discs). Torque tube drive.

1923 Ford Model T Coupe (OCW)

Straight bevel rear axle. Overall ratio: 3.63:1. Brakes: Contracting band in transmission. Hand-operated internal expanding in rear wheels. Foot brake stops driveshaft. Parking brake on two rear wheels.

Options:

The basic equipment included three oil lamps only (two side and one tail). Options listed included: Windshield. Headlamps. Tops. Horns. Prest-o-lite tanks (instead of the carbide tank). Robe rails. Tire chains. Top boots. Foot rests. Spare tire carriers. Speedometers. Bumpers. No prices were given.

1924 Ford

Ford — Model T: In June of 1923, the Model T lineup was restyled again. Cars built after June, but before calendar-year 1924 began, are commonly called "1923" but Ford referred to them as 1924s. The open-body Model Ts continued with the same body, windshield and top as the earlier 1923s, but a new higher radiator and larger hood altered their appearance noticeably. The front fenders were given a lip on the front of the apron to blend in with a new valance under the radiator. This gave the car a more "finished" look. There was a new coupe with an integral rear turtle deck and doors that opened at the rear. A new Tudor Sedan was also introduced. It had doors at the front of the body, instead of at the center. The Fordor Sedan was the same as the earlier one, except for the new hood and front fenders. The lower body panels were now made of steel instead of aluminum.

VIN:

The serial number was above the water inlet on the left side of the engine. Starting: 7927375 (July 2, 1923). Ending: 10266471 (July 31, 1924). 1924 calendar-year engine numbers: 9008372 to 10994033. Numbers stamped on the body sills, etc. were manufacturer's numbers and not an identifying number.

1923 Model T (Four)   (Prices effective Oct. 30, 1923)

Model No.	Body/ Style No.	Body Type & Seating	Factory Price	Shipping Weight	Prod. Total
T	—	3 dr. Touring-5P	$ 295	1,500 lbs.	99,523*
T		3 dr. Touring-5P (electric start and demountable rims)	$ 380	1,650 lbs.	673,579
T	—	2 dr. Runabout-2P	$ 265	1,390 lbs.	43,317*
T	---	2 dr. Runabout-2P (electric start and demountable rims)	$ 350	1,540 lbs.	220,955
T	—	2d Sedan-5P (electric start and demountable rims)	$ 590	1,875 lbs.	223,203
T	—	4d Sedan-5P (electric start and demountable rims)	$ 685	1,950 lbs.	84,733
T	—	2d Coupe-2P (electric start and demountable rims)	$ 525	1,760 lbs.	327,584
T	—	Chassis	$ 230	1,060 lbs.	3,921*
T	---	Chassis (electric start and demountable rims)	$ 295	1,210 lbs.	43,980
TT	----	Truck chassis	$ 370	1,477 lbs.	127,891*
TT	----	Truck chassis (electric start and demountable rims)	$ 435	1,577 lbs.	32,471
TT	----	Truck with body	$ 490	-------	38,840*
TT	----	Truck with body (electric start and demountable rims)	$ 555	-------	5,649

Note: Production totals from Jan. 1, 1924 through Dec. 31, 1924 including foreign production.

1924 Ford Model T Fordor Sedan (OCW)

1923 Model T (Four)   (Prices effective Dec. 2, 1924)

T	—	3 dr. Touring-5P	$ 290	1,500 lbs.	Note 1
T	—	3 dr. Touring-5P (electric start and demountable rims)	$ 375	1,650 lbs.	Note 1
T	—	2 dr. Runabout-2P	$ 260	1,390 lbs.	Note 1
T	---	2 dr. Runabout-2P (electric start and demountable rims)	$ 345	1,540 lbs.	Note 1
T	—	2d Sedan-5P (electric start and demountable rims)	$ 580	1,875 lbs.	Note 1
T	—	4d Sedan-5P (electric start and demountable rims)	$ 660	1,950 lbs.	Note 1
T	—	2d Coupe-2P (electric start and demountable rims)	$ 520	1,760 lbs.	Note 1
T	—	Chassis	$ 225	1,060 lbs.	Note 1
T	—	Chassis (electric start and demountable rims)	$ 290	1,210 lbs.	Note 1
TT	----	Truck chassis	$ 365	1,477 lbs.	Note 1
TT	----	Truck chassis (electric start and demountable rims)	$ 430	1,577 lbs.	Note 1
TT	----	Truck with body	$ 485	-------	Note 1
TT	----	Truck with body (electric start and demountable rims)	$ 550	-------	Note 1

Note 1: See top chart for 1924 production information.

1924 Model T (Four)   (Price effective Oct. 24, 1924)

TT		Stake body truck	$495	------	Note 2

Note 2: Production figures of this truck were not listed separately. A C truck cab cost $65. The truck rear bed $55 if ordered separately.

Engine:

Model T: L-head. Four. Cast-iron block. B & S: 3-3/4 x 4 in. Displacement: 176.7 cid. Compression ratio: 3.98:1. Brake hp: 20 at 1600 rpm. NACC hp: 22.5. Torque: 83 at 900 rpm. Main bearings: three. Valve lifters: solid. Carburetor: Kingston L4 (6150). Holley NH (6200).
Note: Thermosyphon. Single valve chamber covered with one steel door held with two stud/nuts or bolts.

Chassis:

Model T: Wheelbase: 100 in. Overall length: 10 ft. 8 in., chassis and 11 ft. 2-1/2 in., car. Front tread: 56 in.   Rear tread: 56 in. Tires: (front) 30 x 3 front, (rear) 30 x 3-1/2. 30 x 3-1/2 all around with demountable rims 1919-1925. Chassis essentially identical except those after mid-1913 have a longer rear crossmember.

Technical:

Model T: Planetary transmission. Speeds: 2F/1R. Three pedal controls and one lever on floor. Multiple disc clutch (25 discs 1915-1927). Torque tube drive. Straight bevel rear axle. Overall ratio: 3.63:1. Brakes: Contracting band in transmission. Hand-operated internal expanding in rear wheels. Foot brake stops driveshaft. Parking brake on two rear wheels.

Options:

All cars equipped with headlamps, horn, etc. Starter ($75). Demountable rims ($25).

1924 Ford Model T Roadster (OCW)

1924 Ford Model T Coupe (JAC)

1925 Ford

Ford — Model T: The 1924 Model T line continued until about July of 1925 with no major changes except in upholstery material and construction details. About May 1925 the Roadster Pickup and the Closed Cab truck appeared. A new option introduced late in 1925 was 4.40 x 21-in. "balloon" tires mounted on demountable-rim wooden wheels. The wheels came finished in either black or natural.

VIN:

The serial number was above the water inlet on the left side of the engine. Starting: 10266472 (August 1, 1924, start of fiscal 1925). Ending: 12218728 (July 27, 1925, start of "1926" models). 1925 calendar-year engine numbers: 10994034 to 12990076. Numbers stamped on the body sills, etc. were manufacturer's numbers and not an identifying number.

1925 Ford Model T Coupe (OCW)

1925 Ford Model T Touring (OCW)

1925 Model T (Four) (Prices effective Oct. 24, 1924)

Model No.	Body/ Style No.	Body Type & Seating	Factory Price	Shipping Weight	Prod. Total
T	—	3 dr. Touring-5P	$ 290	1,500 lbs.	64,399*
T		3 dr. Touring-5P (electric start and demountable rims)	$ 375	1,650 lbs.	626,813
T	—	2 dr. Runabout-2P	$ 260	1,390 lbs.	34,206*
T	---	2 dr. Runabout-2P (electric start and demountable rims)	$ 345	1,536 lbs.	264,436
T		2d Sedan-5P (electric start and demountable rims)	$ 580	1,875 lbs.	195,001
T	—	4d Sedan-5P (electric start and demountable rims)	$ 680	1,950 lbs.	81,050
T	—	2d Coupe-2P (electric start and demountable rims)	$ 520	1,760 lbs.	343,969
T	—	Chassis	$ 225	1,060 lbs.	6,523*
T	---	Chassis (electric start and demountable rims)	$ 290	1,210 lbs.	53,450
T	----	2-dr. Roadster pickup	$ 281	1,471 lbs.	33,795 +
T	----	2-dr. Roadster pickup	$ 366	1,621 lbs.	------ +
TT	----	Truck chassis	$ 365	1,477 lbs.	186,810*
TT	----	Truck chassis (electric start and demountable rims)	$ 430	1,577 lbs.	32,471
TT	----	Truck with body	$ 490	-------	192,839*
TT	----	Truck with body (electric start and demountable rims)	$ 555	-------	5,649

Note: Production totals from Jan. 1, 1925 through Dec. 31, 1925 including foreign production.

Note +: Roadster pickups were not separated by electric starter or no starter.

1925 Model T (Four)
(Prices effective Mar. 4, 1925 and unchanged Dec. 31, 1925)

T	—	3 dr. Touring-5P	$ 290	1,500 lbs.	Note 1
T		3 dr. Touring-5P (electric start and demountable rims)	$ 375	1,650 lbs.	Note 1
T	—	2 dr. Runabout-2P	$ 260	1,390 lbs.	Note 1
T	---	2 dr. Runabout-2P (electric start and demountable rims)	$ 345	1,540 lbs.	Note 1
T	—	2d Sedan-5P (electric start and demountable rims)	$ 580	1,875 lbs.	Note 1
T	—	4d Sedan-5P (electric start and demountable rims)	$ 660	1,950 lbs.	Note 1
TT	—	2d Coupe-2P (electric start and demountable rims)	$ 520	1,760 lbs.	Note 1
T	—	Chassis	$ 225	1,060 lbs.	Note 1
T	---	Chassis (electric start and demountable rims)	$ 290	1,210 lbs.	Note 1
T	----	2-dr. Roadster pickup	$ 281	1,471 lbs.	Notes 1,2
T	----	2-dr. Roadster pickup	$ 366	1,621 lbs.	Notes 1,2
TT	----	Truck chassis	$ 365	1,477 lbs.	Note 1
TT	----	Truck chassis (electric start and demountable rims)	$ 430	1,577 lbs.	Note 1
TT	----	Truck with body	$ 485	-------	Note 1
TT	----	Truck with body (electric start and demountable rims)	$ 550	-------	Note 1

Note 1: See top chart for 1924 production information.

Note 2: Roadster pickups were not separated by electric starter or no starter.

1925 Model T (Four)
(Prices effective Mar. 4, 1925 and unchanged Dec. 31, 1925)

TT	-----	Stake body truck	$495	-------	Note 3

Note 3: Production figures of this truck were not listed separately. The C truck cab cost $65. The truck rear bed $55 if ordered separately.

Engine:

Model T: L-head. Four. Cast-iron block. B & S: 3-3/4 x 4 inches. Displacement: 176.7 cid. Compression ratio: 3.98:1. Brake hp: 20 at 1600 rpm. NACC hp: 22.5. Torque: 83 at 900 rpm. Main bearings: three. Valve lifters: solid. Carburetor: Kingston L4 (6150). Holley NH (6200).

Note: Thermosyphon. Single valve chamber covered with one steel door held with two stud/nuts or bolts.

Chassis:

Model T: Wheelbase: 100 in. Overall length: 10 ft. 8 inches, chassis and 11 ft. 2-1/2 in., car. Front tread: 56 in. Rear tread: 56 in. Tires: (front) 30 x 3 front, (rear) 30 x 3-1/2. 30 x 3-1/2 all around with demountable rims 1919-1925. Chassis essentially identical except those after mid-1913 have a longer rear crossmember.

1925 Ford Model T Tudor Sedan (OCW)

Technical:

Model T: Planetary transmission. Speeds: 2F/1R. Three pedal controls and one lever on floor. Multiple disc clutch (25 discs 1915-1927). Torque tube drive. Straight bevel rear axle. Overall ratio: 3.63:1. Brakes: Contracting band in transmission. Hand-operated internal expanding in rear wheels. Foot brake stops driveshaft. Parking brake on two rear wheels.

Options:

All cars equipped with headlamps, horn, etc. Starter ($75). Demountable rims ($25).

1926 Model T

Ford — Model T: About July 1925, an "Improved Ford" marked the first major restyling of the Model T since 1917. New fenders, new running boards, new bodies (except for the Fordor Sedan), new hoods and even a modified chassis made these Fords unique during the era of the Model T. The Touring Car was given a door on the driver's side for the first time since 1911 on U.S. cars (post-1911 Canadian-built Fords had a driver's side door). The Tudor Sedan and the Coupe were actually all-new designs, though similar in style to the 1925 versions. The Fordor Sedan continued the same basic body introduced in late 1922, except for its new cowl, hood, fenders, etc. The chassis had a new and even longer rear crossmember. With a modification of the springs and front spindles, the entire car was lowered about an inch. While sharing basically the same running gear as earlier models, the 1926-1927 cars had 11-inch rear-wheel brake drums, although they were only operated by the "emergency brake" lever. The foot pedals for low speed and braking were larger and the internal transmission brake was made wider for better life and operation. Initially offered in black, the Coupe and the Tudor were later painted a dark green. The Fordor Sedan came in a dark maroon as its standard color. Open cars continued to be finished in black until mid-1926. When the "126" models were introduced in 1925, the standard wheels on the closed cars were the 30 x 3-1/2-inch demountable type. Open cars had 30 x 3-1/2-inch non-demountable wheels. However, by calendar-year 1926, the 21-inch balloon tires were standard on all models. The gasoline tank was now located in the cowl on all models, except the Fordor Sedan, which continued to have it under the driver's seat.

VIN:

The serial number was above the water inlet on the left side of the engine. Starting: 12218729 (July 27, 1925, start of "1926" models).

1926 Ford Model T Fordor Touring (RLC)

Ending: 14049029 (July 30, 1926, end of fiscal year 1926). 1926 calendar-year engine numbers: 12990077 to 14619254. Numbers stamped on the body sills, etc. were manufacturer's numbers and not an identifying number.

1926 Model T (Four) (Prices effective Jan. 1, 1926)

Model No.	Body/ Style No.	Body Type & Seating	Factory Price	Shipping Weight	Prod. Total
T	—	4 dr. Touring-5P	$ 290	1,633 lbs.*	------
T	—	4 dr. Touring-5P (starter and 21-in. demountable wheels)	$ 375	1,738 lbs.	626,813
T	—	2 dr. Runabout-2P	$ 260	1,550 lbs.*	------
T	---	2 dr. Runabout-2P (electric start and demountable rims)	$ 345	1,655 lbs.	342,575
T	—	2d Sedan-5P (electric start and demountable rims)	$ 580	1,972 lbs.	270,331
T	—	4d Sedan-5P (electric start and demountable rims)	$ 660	2,004 lbs.	102,732
T	—	2d Coupe-2P (electric start and demountable rims)	$ 520	1,860 lbs.	288,342
T	—	Chassis	$ 225	1,167 lbs.*	------
T	---	Chassis (electric start and demountable rims)	$ 290	1,272 lbs.	58,223
T	----	2-dr. Roadster pickup	$ 281	------- *	Note 2
T	----	2-dr. Roadster pickup	$ 366	1,736 lbs.	75,406
TT	----	Truck chassis	$ 365	1,477 lbs.	186,810*
TT	----	Truck chassis (electric start and demountable rims)	$ 430	1,577 lbs.	32,471

Note 1(*): Early models had 30 x 3-1/2-in. non-demountable wheels and no starter. They were 10 lbs. lighter.

Note 2: These pickups were only available by special order by calendar year 1926.

1926 Model T (Four)
(Prices effective June 6, 1926 and unchanged Dec. 31, 1926)

T	—	4 dr. Touring-5P (electric start and demountable rims)	$ 380	1,738 lbs.	Note 1
T	---	2 dr. Runabout-2P (electric start and demountable rims)	$ 360	1,655 lbs.	Note 1
T	—	2d Sedan-5P (electric start and demountable rims)	$ 495	1,972 lbs.	Note 1
T	—	4d Sedan-5P (electric start and demountable rims)	$ 545	2,004 lbs.	Note 1
T	—	2d Coupe-2P (electric start and demountable rims)	$ 485	1,860 lbs.	Note 1
T	---	Chassis (electric start and demountable rims)	$ 300	1,272 lbs.	Note 1
T	----	2-dr. Roadster pickup	$ 381	------	Note 2
TT	----	Truck chassis	$ 325	1,477 lbs.	Note 1
TT	----	Truck chassis (electric start and demountable rims)	$ 375	1,577 lbs.	Note 1

Note 1: See top chart for 1924 production information.

Note 2: Roadster pickups were not separated by electric starter or no starter.

1926 Model T Truck Bodies

Model No.	Body Description	Factory Price	Production Total
TT	Open cab	$ 65	Note 3
TT	Closed cab	$ 85	Note 3
TT	Express body	$ 55	Note 3
TT	Platform body	$ 50	Note 3
TT	Express	$ 110	Note 3

Note 3: Chassis production figures are for U.S. and foreign. Body figures are for U.S. only and are included in the chassis count. Starter production is not listed separately.

Engine:

Model T: L-head. Four. Cast-iron block. B & S: 3-3/4 x 4 in. Displacement: 176.7 cid. Compression ratio: 3.98:1. Brake hp: 20 at 1600 rpm. NACC hp: 22.5. Torque: 83 at 900 rpm. Main bearings: three. Valve lifters: solid. Carburetor: Kingston L4 (6150B). Holley NH (6200C), Holley Vaporizer (6250), Kingston Regenerator.

The transmission housing was now on bolts to the rear of the cylinder. The fan was mounted on the water outlet. Later production used nickel-plated head and water connection bolts.

Chassis:

Model T: Wheelbase: 100 in. Overall length: 10 ft. 8 inches, chassis and 11 ft. 2-1/2 in., car. Front tread: 56 in. Rear tread: 56 in. Tires: (front) 30 x 3-1/2, (rear) 30 x 3-1/2. Chassis essentially identical except those after mid-1913 have a much longer rear cross member. Chassis now lowered about an inch by the use of a different front spindle and spring and a deeper crown in the rear crossmember. In mid-1926, the

1926 Ford Model T Fordor Sedan (OCW)

1926 Ford Model T Tudor Sedan (HAC)

rear crossmember was made with a flanged edge and the chassis was made of heavier steel.

Technical:

Model T: Planetary transmission. Speeds: 2F/1R. Three pedal controls and one lever on floor. Multiple disc clutch (25 discs 1915-1927). Torque tube drive. Straight bevel rear axle. Overall ratio: 3.63:1. Brakes: Contracting band in transmission. Hand-operated internal expanding in rear wheels. Foot brake stops driveshaft. Parking brake on two rear wheels. In mid-1925 (1926 models) the transmission brake was made about a half-inch wider, and the rear wheel brakes were enlarged to 11 inches with lined shoes. In January 1926 optional 21-inch wire wheels became available, and these became standard on some closed cars in calendar year 1927.

Options:

All cars built after January 1926 are equipped with headlights, horn, starter and 21-inch demountable rims. Windshield wiper (hand operated) (50 cents).* Vacuum-operated windshield wiper ($3.50). Windshield wings for open cars ($6.50 pair). Gipsy curtains for open cars ($3 per pair). Top boot for open cars ($5). Bumpers front and rear ($15). Wire wheels, set of five ($50) and $35) later in 1926. Rearview mirror for open cars (.75).* Dash lamp for open cars (.60).* Stoplight and switch ($2.50). Shock absorbers ($9 per set). Starter and demountable wheels are standard on all cars. Starter is optional on the truck. Pickup body for runabout, $25.

Note *: Standard on closed cars.

1927 Ford

Ford — Model T: Wire wheels were offered as an option beginning January 1926. In 1926, perhaps as "1927" models (Ford didn't name yearly models consistently), colors were added for the open cars: Gunmetal blue or Phoenix brown. Closed cars were offered in Highland green, Royal maroon, Fawn gray, Moleskin and Drake green. By calendar 1927, any body could be ordered in any standard Ford color. Black could be had on special order on the pickup body, although Commercial green was the standard color. Fenders and running boards were black on all models. By early 1927, many Ford branches were supplying wire wheels as standard equipment on closed cars. Model T production ended in May 1927 although Ford continued building engines through the year, then a few at a time until August 4, 1941.

VIN:

The serial number was above the water inlet on the left side of the engine. Starting: 14049030 (August 2, 1926, start of fiscal 1927). Ending: 15006625 (May 25, 1927, end of Model T Ford car production.)* 1927 calendar year

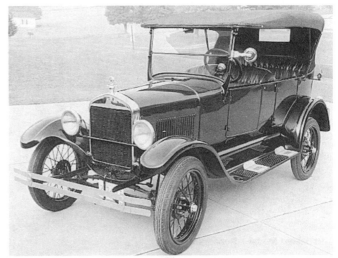

1927 Ford Model T Fordor Touring (OCW)

engine numbers: 14619255 to 15076231.* Numbers stamped on the body sills, etc. were manufacturer's numbers and not an identifying number.

*Most records show 15007032 or 15007033 as the last car but the factory records indicate these numbers were built on May 31, 1927, five days after the car assembly line was stopped. Ford continued building engines through 1927 and at a considerable rate until January 1931 (as many as 12,000 per month after the end of the Model T!). Production averaged about 100 per month in 1931, then dropped to less than 10 and ended, finally, on August 4, 1941, with number 15176888.

1927 Model T (Four)

Model No.	Body/Style No.	Body Type & Seating	Factory Price	Shipping Weight	Production Total
T		4 dr. Touring-5P (electric start and demountable rims)	$ 380	1,738 lbs.	81,181
T	---	2 dr. Runabout-2P (electric start and demountable rims)	$ 360	1,655 lbs.	95,778
T	—	2 dr. Sedan-5P (electric start and demountable rims)	$ 495	1,972 lbs.	78,105
T	—	4 dr. Sedan-5P (electric start and demountable rims)	$ 545	2,004 lbs.	22,930
T	—	2d Coupe-2P (electric start and demountable rims)	$ 485	1,860 lbs.	69,939
T	---	Chassis (electric start and demountable rims)	$ 300	1,272 lbs.	19,280
T	----	2-dr. Roadster pickup	$ 381	1,736 lbs.	28,143
TT	----	Truck chassis	$ 325	1,477 lbs.	83,202
TT	----	Truck chassis (electric start and demountable rims)	$ 375	1,577 lbs.	------

Notes: Production totals are for Jan.1, 1927 through Dec. 31, 1927. Chassis production figures are for U.S. and foreign. Body figures are for U. S. only and are included in the chassis count. Starter production is not listed separately. Model T production ended May 26, 1927 for automobiles. Trucks continued to be produced for some time.

1927 Model T Truck Bodies

Model No.	Body Description	Factory Price	Production Total
TT	Open cab	$ 65	41, 318 (U.S.)
TT	Closed cab	$ 85	------
TT	Express body	$ 55	------
TT	Platform body	$ 50	------
TT	Express	$ 110	------

Engine:

Model T: L-head. Four. Cast-iron block. B & S: 3-3/4 x 4 in. Displacement: 176.7 cid. Compression ratio: 3.98:1. Brake hp: 20 at 1600 rpm. NACC hp: 22.5. Torque: 83 at 900 rpm. Main bearings: three. Valve lifters: solid. Carburetor: Kingston L4 (6150B). Holley NH (6200C), Holley Vaporizer (6250), Kingston Regenerator.

Transmission housing now bolted to the rear of the cylinder. The fan mounted on the water outlet. Later production used nickel-plated head and water connection bolts.

Chassis:

Model T: Wheelbase: 100 in. Overall length: 10 ft. 8 in., chassis and 11 ft. 2-1/2 in., car. Front tread: 56 in. Rear tread: 56 in. Tires: (front) 30 x 3-1/2, (rear) 30 x 3-1/2. Chassis essentially identical except those after mid-1913 have a much longer rear cross member. Chassis now lowered about an inch by the use of a different front spindle and spring and a deeper crown in the rear crossmember. In mid-1926, the rear

1927 Ford Model T Runabout

1927 Ford Model T Tudor Sedan (OCW)

crossmember was made with a flanged edge and the chassis was made of heavier steel.

Technical:

Model T: Planetary transmission. Speeds: 2F/1R. Three pedal controls and one lever on floor. Multiple disc clutch (25 discs 1915-1927). Torque tube drive. Straight bevel rear axle. Overall ratio: 3.63:1. Brakes: Contracting band in transmission. Hand-operated internal expanding in rear wheels. Foot brake stops driveshaft. Parking brake on two rear wheels. In mid-1925 (1926 models) the transmission brake was made about a half-inch wider, and the rear wheel brakes were enlarged to 11 inches with lined shoes. In January 1926 optional 21-inch wire wheels became available, and these became standard on some closed cars in calendar year 1927.

Options:

All cars built after January 1926 were equipped with headlights, horn, starter and 21-inch demountable rims. Hand-operated windshield wiper (50 cents). Vacuum-operated windshield wiper ($2). Windshield wings for open cars ($2.50). Gipsy curtains for open cars ($1.10 per pair). Top boot for open cars ($4). Bumpers front and rear ($15). Wire wheels, set of five ($35). Rearview mirror for open cars (.75). Dash lamp for open cars (.60). Stoplight and switch ($2.50). Shock absorbers ($9 per set).

1928 Ford

Ford — Model A: Reverting to a Model A designation for the "New Ford" suggested a "new beginning." The A designation also symbolized the impact this new automobile had upon Ford Motor Company. The Model A was a far more complex automobile than the Model T. It had approximately 6,800 different parts, compared to less than 5,000 in a Model T. However, there were still similarities. Both cars had four-cylinder L-head engines. Both cars had semi-elliptic front and rear

springs that were mounted transversely. Beyond these points, the Model A moved far away from the heritage of the Model T. Its engine had a water pump and displaced just over 200 cubic inches. With 40 hp, it was virtually twice as powerful as the Model T engine and provided a 65 mph top speed. Superseding the old magneto ignition was a contemporary battery-and-ignition system. The Model T's planetary transmission gave way to a three-speed sliding-gear unit. Other technical advancements found in the Model A included the use of four-wheel mechanical brakes and Houdaille double-acting hydraulic shock absorbers. The styling of the Model A maintained a link with that of the Model T, but with a 103-1/2 inch wheelbase, 4.50 x 21 tires and a higher belt line, the influence of the Lincoln automobile upon the appearance of the new Ford was unmistakable. Full-crown fenders were used and the bodywork of each of the five original models had the body surrounds outlined in contrasting body colors and pinstriping. The Model A's two-piece front and rear bumpers were similar to those used on the 1927 Model T. Its new radiator shell, with its gentle center vee-dip and moderately curved crossbar for the headlights, made it impossible to confuse the two Fords. The first Model A engine was completed on October 20, 1927, and the following day it was installed in the first Model A assembled. From that day (May 25, 1927) Ford announced it would produce a successor to the Model T. Public interest steadily increased to a level that was finally satisfied on December 2, 1927, when the nationwide introduction of the Model A took place. While many industry observers recognized the passing of the Model T as the end of an era, there was equal appreciation for the extraordinary value the Model A represented and an awareness that it was in all ways more than a worthy successor to the "Tin Lizzie."

VIN:

Serial numbers were located on the top side of the frame near the clutch pedal. Starting: October 20-December 31, 1927 - A1, January 1-December 31, 1928 - A5276. Ending: October 20-December 31, 1927 - A5275, January 1-December 31, 1928 - A810122. Engine numbers were located on boss placed on center of left side of block directly below the cylinder head. A prefix letter A was used and a star is found on either end. Starting: October 20-December 31, 1927 - A1, January 1-December 31, 1928 - A5276. Ending: October 20-December 31, 1927 - A5275, January 1-December 31, 1928 - A810122. Model numbers: 1928 models have a date when the body was manufactured stamped on the upper left side of the firewall.

1928 Model A

Model No.	Body/ Style No.	Body Type & Seating	Factory Price	Shipping Weight	Production Total
A	—	2 dr. Roadster-2/4P	$ 480	2,106 lbs.	Note 1
A	---	4 dr. Phaeton-5P	$ 460	2,140 lbs.	Note 1
A	—	2 dr. Business Coupe-2P	$ 550	2,225 lbs.	Note 1
A	---	2 dr. Coupe-2/4P	$ 550	2,265 lbs.	Note 1
A	—	2 dr. Standard Business Roadster-2P	$ 480	2,050 lbs.	Note 1
A	—	4 dr. Business Coupe-2P	$ 525	-------	Note 1
A	—	Tudor-5P	$ 550	2,340 lbs.	Note 1
A	—	Fordor-5P	$ 585	2,386 lbs.	Note 1
A	—	4-dr. Taxi Cab-5PChassis	$ 600	-------	Note 1

Note 1: Body style production was a calendar year record. See list at end of 1931 Model A section.

Engine:

Model A: Inline. L-head. Four. Cast-iron block. B & S: 3-7/8 x 4-1/4 in. Displacement: 200.5 cid. Compression ratio: 4.22:1. Brake hp: 40 at 2200 rpm. SAE hp: 24.03. Torque: 128 lb.-ft. at 1000 rpm. Main bearings: three. Valve lifters: mechanical. Carburetor: Zenith or Holley double venturi.

Chassis:

Model A: Wheelbase: 103.5 in. Front tread: 56 in. Rear tread: 56 in. Tires: 4.50 x 21.

1928 Ford Model A Roadster. (BMHV)

Technical:

Model A: Sliding gear transmission. Speeds: 3F/1R. Floor shift controls. Dry multiple disc clutch. Shaft drive. Three-quarter floating rear axle. Overall ratio: 3.7:1. Mechanical internal expanding brakes on four wheels. Welded wire wheels. Wheel size: 21.

Options:

Single side mount tire. External sun shade. Radiator ornament. Wind vanes. Rearview mirror. Rear luggage rack. Radiator stone guard. Spare tire lock.

1928 Ford Model A Phaeton (JAC)

1928 Ford Model A Town Car w/Joan Crawford (JAC)

1928 Ford Model A Standard Business Roadster (AA)

1928 Ford Model A Business Coupe

1928 Ford Model A Tudor Sedan (RLC)

1928 Ford Model A Fordor Sedan. (JAC)

History:

Introduced December 2, 1927. Innovations: Safety glass installed in all windows. Calendar-year production: 633,594. The president of Ford Motor Co. was Edsel Ford.

1929 Ford

Ford — Model A: The most apparent change made in the 1929 Model A's appearance was the exterior door handles on open models. It also had brighter trim and body paint. With production rapidly increasing, more body styles became available. A Town Car model was introduced on December 13, 1928, followed during 1929 by a wood-bodied station wagon on April 25. Other new styles included a Convertible Cabriolet, several new Fordor Sedans and a Town Sedan. As in 1928, the Model A's base price included many standard equipment features such as a combination tail and stop light, a windshield wiper, front and rear bumpers and a Spartan horn.

VIN:

Serial numbers were located on the top side of frame, near the clutch pedal. Starting: A 810123. Ending: A 2742695. Engine number location: Boss placed on center of left side of block directly below the cylinder head. Starting: A 810123. Ending: A 2724695.

1929 Ford Model A Station Wagon (OCW)

1929 Model A Ford (Four)

Model No.	Body/Style No.	Body Type & Seating	Factory Price	Shipping Weight	Prod. Total
A	—	2 dr. Roadster-2P	$480	2,106 lbs.	Note 1
A	---	4-dr. Station Wagon-5P	$650	2,500 lbs.	Note 1
A	—	2-dr. Convertible-2/4P	$670	2,339 lbs.	Note 1
A	---	2-dr. Sport Coupe-2/4P	$550	2,250 lbs.	Note 1
A	----	2-dr. Roadster-2/4P	$450	2,106 lbs.	Note 1
A	----	2-dr. Business Coupe-2P	$525	2,216 lbs.	Note 1
A	----	4-dr. Phaeton-5P	$460	2,203 lbs.	Note 1
A	----	2-dr. Coupe-2P	$550	2,248 lbs.	Note 1
A	----	4-dr. Town Car-5P	$1,400	2,525 lbs.	Note 1
A	----	4-dr. Taxi Cab-5P	$800	-------	Note 1

Murray Body Sedans

A	----	4-dr. Sedan-5P	$625	2,497 lbs.	Note 1
A	----	4-dr. Town Sedan-5P	$695	2,517 lbs.	Note 1

Briggs Body Sedans

A	----	4-dr. Sedan-5P	$625	2,497 lbs.	Note 1
A	----	4-dr. Sedan-5P	$625	2,419 lbs.	Note 1
A	----	4-dr. Sedan (Long wheelbase)-5P	$625	2,500 lbs.	Note 1
A	----	2-dr. Sedan-5P	$525	2,348 lbs.	Note 1
A	----	4-dr. Town Sedan-5P	$695	2,517 lbs.	Note 1

Note 1: Body style production was recorded only by calendar year. See list at end of 1931 Model A section.

Engine:

Model A: Inline. L-head. Four. Cast-iron block. B & S: 3-7/8 x 4-1/4 in. Displacement: 200.5 cid. Compression ratio: 4.22:1. Brake hp: 40 at 2200 rpm. SAE hp: 24.03. Torque: 128 lb.-ft. at 1000 rpm. Main bearings: three. Valve lifters: mechanical. Carburetor: Zenith or Holley double venturi.

Chassis:

Model A: Wheelbase: 103.5 in. Front tread: 56 in. Rear tread: 56 in. Tires: 4.50 x 21.

Technical:

Model A: Sliding gear transmission. Speeds: 3F/1R. Floor shift controls. Dry multiple disc clutch. Shaft drive. Three-quarter floating rear axle. Overall ratio: 3.7:1. Mechanical internal expanding brakes on four wheels. Welded wire wheels. Wheel size: 21.

Options:

Single side mount tire. External sun shade. Radiator ornament ($3). Wind vanes. Rearview mirror. Rear luggage rack. Radiator stone guard. Spare tire lock.

1929 Ford Model A Rumbleseat Convertible (OCW)

1929 Ford Model A Sport Coupe (AA)

History:

Introduced January 1929. Calendar-year sales: 1,310,147 (registrations). Calendar-year production: 1,507,132. The president of Ford was Edsel Ford. Production of the first million Model A Fords was completed on February 4, 1929. The two-millionth Model A Ford was constructed on July 24, 1929.

1929 Ford Model A Rumbleseat Roadster (HAC)

1929 Ford Model A Standard Business Coupe (HFM)

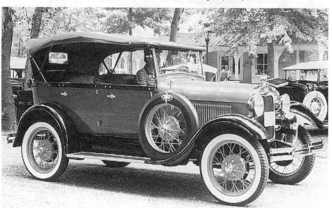

1928 Ford Model A Phaeton (OCW)

1929 Ford Model A Standard Coupe (HFM)

1929 Ford Model A Town Car with driving compartment open (HFM)

1929 Ford Model A Fordor Town Sedan by Murray (JAC)

1929 Ford Model A Town Car with driving compartment closed (OCW)

1929 Ford Model A Tudor Sedan (OCW)

1929 Ford Model A Four-Door Taxi Cab (OCW)

1929 Ford Model A Custom Landaulet (OCW)

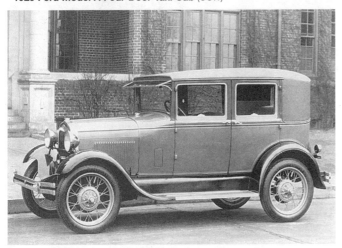

1929 Ford Model A Fordor Sedan by Briggs (OCW)

1929 Ford Model A Sedan Delivery (OCW)

1930 Ford

Ford — Model A: The Model A was given a substantial face-lift for 1930 and it was effective. Larger 4.75 tires on smaller 19-inch wheels resulted in an overall height reduction, which along with wider fenders, a deeper radiator shell and the elimination of the cowl stanchion all were contributors to the Model A's fresh new look. Replacing the older nickel finish for the Ford's exterior bright work was a combination of nickel and stainless steel trim. During the year, a new Victoria body style was introduced, along with a deluxe version of the Phaeton. The Deluxe Roadster and Sport Coupe models included a rumble seat.

VIN:

Serial numbers located on the top side of the frame near the clutch panel. Starting: A 2742696. Ending: A 4237500. Engine numbers were located on a boss on the center of left side of the block, directly below the cylinder head. Starting Engine No: A 2742696. Ending: A 4237500.

1930 Ford Model A (Four)

Model No.	Body/Style No.	Body Type & Seating	Factory Price	Shipping Weight	Production Total
A	35-B	4-dr. Standard Phaeton-5P	$ 440	2,212 lbs.	Note 1
A	40-B	2-dr. Standard Roadster-2P	$ 435	2,155 lbs.	Note 1
A	40-B	2-dr. Deluxe Roadster-2/4P	$ 495	2,230 lbs.	Note 1
A	45-B	2-dr. Standard Coupe-2P	$ 500	2,257 lbs.	Note 1
A	45-B	2-dr. Deluxe Coupe-2/4P	$ 550	2,265 lbs.	Note 1
A	50-B	2-dr. Sport Coupe-2/4P	$ 530	2,283 lbs.	Note 1
A	55-B	Tudor Sedan-5P	$ 490	2,372 lbs.	Note 1
A	68-B	2-dr. Cabriolet-2/4P	$ 645	2,273 lbs.	Note 1
A	150-B	4-dr. Station Wagon-5P	$ 650	2,482 lbs.	Note 1
A	180-A	4-dr. Deluxe Phaeton-5P	$ 645	2,285 lbs.	Note 1
A	190-A	2-dr. Victoria-5P	$ 580	2,375 lbs.	Note 1

Murray Body Sedans

A	155-C	4-dr. Town Sedan-5P	$ 640	2,495 lbs.	Note 1
A	165-C	4-dr. Standard Sedan-5P	$ 580	2,462 lbs.	Note 1

Briggs Body Sedans

A	155-D	4-dr. Town Sedan-5P	$ 650	2,495 lbs.	Note 1
A	165-D	4-dr. Standard Sedan-5P	$ 590	2,462 lbs.	Note 1
A	170-B	4-dr. Two-Window Standard Sedan-5P	$ 590	2,488 lbs.	Note 1
A	170-B	4-dr. Two-Window Sedan-5P	$ 650	2,488 lbs.	Note 1

Note 1: Body style production was recorded only by calendar year. See list at end of 1931 Model A section.

Engine:

Model A: Inline. L-head. Four. Cast-iron block. B & S: 3-7/8 x 4-1/4 in. Displacement: 200.5 cid. Compression ratio: 4.22:1. Brake hp: 40 at 2200 rpm. SAE hp: 24.03. Torque: 128 lbs.-ft. at 1000 rpm. Main bearings: three. Valve lifters: mechanical. Carburetor: Zenith or Holley double venturi.

Chassis:

Model A: Wheelbase: 103.5 in. Front and rear tread: 56 in. Tires: 4.75 x 19.

Technical:

Model A: Sliding gear transmission. Speeds: 3F/1R. Floor shift controls. Dry multiple disc clutch. Shaft drive. Three-quarter floating rear axle. Overall ratio: 3.7:1. Mechanical internal expanding brakes on four wheels. Welded wire wheels. Wheel size: 19 in.

1930 Ford Model A Standard Phaeton (JAC)

Options:

Single side mount ($20). External sun shade. Radiator ornament. Wind vanes. Rearview mirror. Rear luggage rack. Radiator stone guard. Spare tire lock.

1930 Ford Model A Roadster (AA)

1930 Ford Model A Standard Coupe (OCW)

1930 Ford Model A Deluxe Coupe (OCW)

1930 Ford Model A Standard Business Coupe (JAC)

History:

Introduced January 1930. Calendar-year sales: 1,055,097 (registrations). Calendar-year production: 1,155,162. The president of Ford was Edsel Ford. This year Ford Motor Companyís payroll hit $300 million for the year, a record at the time for any U.S. business. In December 1929, Ford announced a $7 per day minimum wage.

1930 Ford Model A Rumbleseat Sport Coupe (OCW)

1930 Ford Model A Tudor Sedan (OCW)

1930 Ford Model A Rumbleseat Convertible (OCW)

1930 Ford Model A Station Wagon (OCW)

1930 Ford Model A Deluxe Phaeton (OCW)

1930 Ford Model A Fordor Town Sedan (JAC)

1930 Ford Model A Standard Fordor Sedan (OCW)

1930 Ford Model A Deluxe Fordor Sedan (OCW)

1930 Ford Model A Deluxe Fordor Two-Window Sedan (OCW)

1930 Ford Model A Budd body **Touring Car** (OCW)

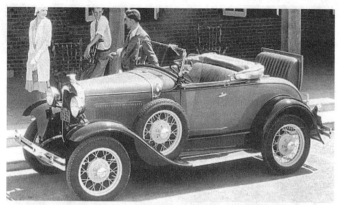

1931 Ford Model A Deluxe Roadster (OCW)

1931 Ford Model A Standard Phaeton

1931 Ford

Ford — Model A: The final year of Model A production brought revised styling, several new body types and on April 14th, production of the 20-millionth Ford, a Fordor sedan. Heading the list of styling changes was a radiator shell with a relief effect, plus running boards fitted with single-piece slash aprons. In addition to the two-and four-door sedans introduced with a smoother roofline, a revamped Cabriolet was also introduced during 1931. However the star attraction was the Convertible Sedan. It had fixed side window frames over which the top rode up or down on a set of tracks. Standard equipment on the Convertible Sedan included a side-mounted spare tire.

VIN:

Serial numbers were located on the top side of the frame, near the clutch pedal. Starting: A 4237501. Ending: A 4849340. Engine numbers were located on a boss on the center of left side of block, directly below the cylinder head. Starting: A 4327501. Ending: A 4849340.

1931 Model A (Four)

Model No.	Body/ Style No.	Body Type & Seating	Factory Price	Shipping Weight	Production Total
A	—	4-dr. Standard Phaeton-5P	$ 435	2,212 lbs.	Note 1
A	---	2-dr. Standard Roadster-2P	$ 430	2,155 lbs.	Note 1
A	—	2-dr. Deluxe Roadster-2/4P	$ 475	2,230 lbs.	Note 1
A	---	2-dr. Standard Coupe-2P	$ 490	2,257 lbs.	Note 1
A	—	2-dr. Deluxe Coupe-2P	$ 525	2,265 lbs.	Note 1
A	—	2-dr. Sport Coupe-2/4P	$ 500	2,283 lbs.	Note 1
A	—	2-dr. Standard Sedan-5P	$ 490	2,462 lbs.	Note 1
A	----	2-dr. Deluxe Sedan-5P	$525	2,488 lbs.	Note 1
A	----	2-dr. Cabriolet-2/4P	$595	2,273 lbs.	Note 1
A	----	4-dr. Station Wagon-4P	$625	2,505 lbs.	Note 1
A	----	2-dr. Deluxe Phaeton-5P	$580	2,265 lbs.	Note 1
A	—	2-dr. Victoria-5P	$580	2,375 lbs.	Note 1
A	—	2-dr. Convertible Sedan-4P	$640	2,335 lbs.	Note 1

Murray Body Sedans

A	----	4-dr. Sedan-5P	$630	2,495 lbs.	Note 1
A	----	4-dr. Standard Sedan-5P	$590	2,462 lbs.	Note 1

Briggs Body Sedans

A	----	4-dr. Standard Sedan-5P	$590	2,462 lbs.	Note 1
A	----	4-dr. Town Sedan-5P	$630	2,495 lbs.	Note 1
A	----	4-dr. Deluxe Sedan-5P	$630	2,488 lbs.	Note 1
A	----	4-dr. Deluxe Two-Window Sedan-4P	$630	2,499 lbs.	Note 1

Note 1: Body style production was recorded only by calendar year. See list in this section.

Engine:

Model A: Inline. L-head. Four. Cast-iron block. B & S: 3-7/8 x 4-1/4 in. Displacement: 200.5 cid. Compression ratio: 4.22:1. Brake hp: 40 at 2200 rpm. SAE hp: 24.03. Torque: 128 lb.-ft. at 1000 rpm. Main bearings: three. Valve lifters: mechanical. Carburetor: Zenith or Holley double venturi.

Chassis:

Model A: Wheelbase: 103.5 in. Front and rear tread: 56 in. Tires: 4.75 x 19.

Technical:

Model A: Sliding gear transmission. Speeds: 3F/1R. Floor shift controls. Dry multiple disc clutch. Shaft drive. Three-quarter floating rear axle. Overall ratio: 3.77:1. Mechanical internal expanding brakes on four wheels. Welded wire wheels. Wheel size: 19 in.

Options:

Single side mount. External sun shade. Radiator ornament. Wind vanes. Rearview mirror. Rear luggage rack. Radiator stone guard. Spare tire lock.

History:

Introduced January 1931. Calendar-year sales 528,581 (registrations). Calendar-year production: 541,615. The president of Ford was Edsel Ford.

Ford Model A Domestic Production Totals: 1927-1931

	1927	1928	1929	1930	1931	Totals
Standard Phaeton	221	47,255	49,818	16,479	4076	117,849
Deluxe Phaeton	—	—	—	3946	2229	6175
Standard Roadster	269	81,937*	191,529	112,901	5,499	392,135
Deluxe Roadster	----	----	----	11,318	52,997	64,315
Sport Coupe	734	79,099	134,292	69,167	19,700	302,992
Standard Coupe	629	70,784	178,982	226,027	79,816	556,238
Deluxe Coupe	—	—	—	28,937	23,067	52,004
Business Coupe	—	37,343	37,644	—	—	74,987
Convertible Cabriolet	—	—	16,421	25,868	11,801	54,090
Standard Tudor	1948	208,562	523,922	376,271	148,425	1,259,128
Deluxe Tudor	—	—	—	—	21,984	21,984
Standard Fordor (two-window)	—	82,349	146,097	5279	—	233,725
Deluxe Fordor (two-window)	—	—	—	12,854	3251	16,105
Standard Fordor (three window)	—	—	53 941	41,133	18,127	113,201
Town sedan	—	—	84,970	104,935	55,469	245,374
Convertible Sedan	—	—	—	—	4864	4864
Victoria	—	—	—	6306	33,906	40,212
Town Car	—	89	913	63	—	1065
Station Wagon	—	5	4954	3510	2848	11,317
Taxi cab	—	264	4576	10	—	4850

* Of these, 51,807 were produced without rumble seat.

1931 Ford Model A Standard Coupe (OCW)

1931 Ford Model A Deluxe Phaeton (OCW)

1931 Ford Model A Deluxe Coupe (OCW)

1931 Ford Model A Victoria (AA)

1931 Ford Model A Rumbleseat Sport Coupe (OCW)

1931 Ford Model A Convertible Sedan (OCW)

1931 Ford Model A Tudor Sedan (OCW)

1931 Ford Model A Fordor Town Sedan (JAC)

1931 Ford Model A Rumbleseat Convertible (OCW)

1931 Ford Model A Standard Fordor Sedan (OCW)

1932 Ford

Ford — Model B — Four: The new 1932 Ford was extremely handsome. Both the front and rear fenders were fully crowned. The soon-to-be classic radiator shell was slightly veed and carried vertical bars. The new Ford's dash carried all instruments and controls within an engine-turned oval placed in the center of a mahogany colored (early) or walnut (late) grained panel. An anti-theft device was incorporated into the key and ignition switch that was mounted on a bracket attached to the steering column. During the model year, Ford incorporated many changes into the design of its new model. One of the most obvious, intended to improve engine cooling, was a switch from a hood with 20 louvers to one with 25. Somewhat overwhelmed by the public's response to Model 18 V-8, the four-cylinder Ford Model B shared the same body as the V-8, minus V-8 emblems on the headlight tie-bars and with Ford lettering rather than V-8 lettering on its hubcaps. All Fords had single transverse leaf springs front and rear. The locating of the rear spring behind the differential and the use of 18-inch wheels gave the '32 Fords a lower overall height than previous models.

Ford — Model 18 — V-8: Once again Henry Ford made automotive history when, on March 31, 1932, he announced the Ford V-8. This type of engine was not a novelty by that time, but when offered at traditional Ford low prices, this new engine was a true milestone. Henry Ford had this 221-cid unit developed in traditional Ford-style extreme secrecy. A small workforce operating under relatively primitive conditions did the work under Henry Ford's close personal supervision. Its early production life was far from tranquil. Hastily rushed into assembly, many of the 1932 engines experienced piston and bearing failures, plus overheating and block cracking. However, these problems were soon overcome and for the next 21 years this V-8 would be powering Ford automobiles. Positioned in the center of the curved headlight tie-bar was Ford's timeless V-8 logo. Apparently sensitive that most of its competitors had longer wheelbases, Ford measured the distance from the center position of the front spring to the center of the rear and claimed it as the V-8's 112-inch wheelbase. Actually its wheelbase was 106 inches.

VIN:

Serial numbers were located on the top side of the frame, near the clutch pedal. Starting: [Model B] AB 5000001 & up. [Model 18] 18-1. Ending: [Model 18] 18-2031126. Prefix "C" indicates Canadian built. Engine numbers located on boss placed on center of left side of block, directly below the cylinder head [Model B]. Starting: [Model B] AB 5000005 & up. [Model 18] 18-1. Ending: [Model 18] 18-2031126.

Ford Model B (Four)

Model No.	Body/Style No.	Body Type & Seating	Factory Price	Shipping Weight	Production Total
B	—	2-dr. Deluxe Roadster-2P	$ 410	2,095 lbs.	948
B	---	2-dr. Deluxe Roadster-2/4P	$ 450	2,102 lbs.	3,719
B	—	4-dr. Phaeton-5P	$ 445	2,238 lbs.	593
B	---	4-dr. Deluxe Phaeton-5P	$ 495	2,268 lbs.	281
B	---	2-dr. Coupe-2P	$ 440	2,261 lbs.	20,342
B	---	2-dr. Sport Coupe-2/4P	$ 485	2,286 lbs.	739
B	---	2-dr. Deluxe Coupe-2/4P	$ 425	2,364 lbs.	968
B	---	2-dr. Sedan-5P	$ 450	2,378 lbs.	36,553
B	---	2-dr. Deluxe Sedan-5P	$ 500	2,398 lbs.	4,077
B	---	4-dr. Sedan-5P	$ 540	2,413 lbs.	4,116
B	---	4-dr. Deluxe Sedan-5P	$ 595	2,432 lbs.	2,620
B	---	2-dr. Cabriolet-2/4P	$ 560	2,295 lbs.	427
B	---	2-dr. Victoria-5P	$ 550	2,344 lbs.	521
B	---	2-dr. Convertible Sedan-5P	$ 600	2,349 lbs.	41

1931 Ford Model A Deluxe Fordor Sedan (OCW)

1931 Ford Model A Taxi (OCW)

1931 Ford Model A Fordor Sedan (20 Millionth)

1931 Ford Model A Station Wagon (OCW)

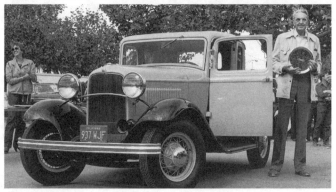

1932 Ford Model B Standard 5-Window Coupe (OCW)

Ford Model 18 (V-8)

18	---	2-dr. Deluxe Roadster-2P	$ 460	2,203 lbs.	520
18	---	2-dr. Deluxe Roadster-2/4P	$ 500	2,308 lbs.	6,893
18	---	4-dr. Phaeton-5P	$ 495	2,369 lbs.	483
18	---	4-dr. Deluxe Phaeton-5P	$ 545	2,375 lbs.	923
18	---	2-dr. Coupe-2P	$ 490	2,398 lbs.	28,904
18	---	2-dr. Sport Coupe-2/4P	$ 535	2,405 lbs.	1,982
18	---	2-dr. Deluxe Coupe-2/4P	$ 575	2,493 lbs.	20,506
18	---	2-dr. Sedan-5P	$ 500	2,508 lbs.	57,930
18	---	2-dr. Deluxe Sedan-5P	$ 550	2,518 lbs.	18,836
18	---	4-dr. Sedan-5P	$ 590	2,538 lbs.	9,310
18	---	4-dr. Deluxe Sedan-5P	$ 645	2,568 lbs.	18,880
18	---	2-dr. Cabriolet-2/4P	$ 610	2,398 lbs.	5,499
18	---	2-dr. Victoria-5P	$ 600	2,483 lbs.	7,241
18	---	2-dr. Convertible Sedan-5P	$ 650	2,480 lbs.	842

Engines:

Model B Four: Inline. L-head. Cast-iron block. B & S: 3-7/8 x 4-1/4 in. Displacement: 200.5 cid. Compression ratio: 4.6:1. Brake hp: 50. Taxable hp: 30. Main bearings: three. Valve lifters: mechanical. Carburetor: Zenith or Holley double-venturi.

Model 18 V-8: 90-degree V. L-head. Cast-iron block. B & S: 3-1/16 x 3-3/4 in. Displacement: 221 cid. Compression ratio: 5.5:1. Brake hp: 65 at 3400 rpm. SAE hp: 30. Torque: 130 lbs.-ft. at 1250 rpm. Main bearings: three. Valve lifters: mechanical. Carburetor: Special Ford Detroit Lubricator downdraft, single barrel, 1-1/2-in. throat.

Chassis:

Model 18: Wheelbase: 106 in. Overall length: 165-1/2-in. Height: 68-5/8-in. Front tread: 55.2 in. Rear Tread: 56.7 in. Tires: 5.25 x 18.

Model B: Wheelbase: 106 in. Overall length: 165-1/2-in. Height: 68-5/8-in. Front tread: 55.2 in. Rear Tread: 56.7 in. Tires: 5.25 x 18.

Technical:

Sliding gear transmission. Speeds: 3F/1R. Floor shift controls. Single dry plate, molded asbestos lining clutch. Shaft drive. Three-quarter floating rear axle. Overall ratio: 4.11:1 (early cars - 4.33:1). Mechanical, rod activated brakes on four wheels. Welded wire, drop center rim wheels. Wheel size: 18 in.

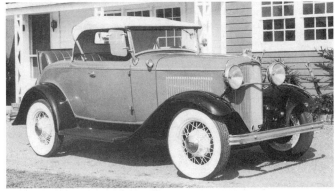

1932 Ford Model B Roadster (OCW)

1932 Ford Model B Deluxe Phaeton (OCW)

Options:

Single side mount tires. Dual side mount tires. Clock. Trunk rack. Leather upholstery. Mirror. Twin taillights. Bedford cord upholstery. Cowl lamps, Standard models.

1932 Ford Model B Standard Tudor Sedan (OCW)

1932 Ford Model B Standard Fordor Sedan (OCW)

1932 Ford Model B Station Wagon (OCW)

1932 Ford Model 18 V-8 Roadster (OCW)

Introduced April 2, 1932. The Ford Model 18 marked the first mass production of a low-priced one-piece 90-degree V-8 engine block. Calendar-year sales: 258,927 (registrations). Calendar-year production: 287,285. The president of Ford was Edsel Ford.

1932 Ford Model 18 V-8 Deluxe Roadster (JAC)

1932 Ford Model 18 V-8 Phaeton (OCW)

1932 Ford Model 18 V-8 Deluxe Phaeton (OCW)

1932 Ford Model 18 V-8 Deluxe three-window coupe (AA)

1932 Ford Model 18 V-8 Deluxe Tudor sedan (OCW)

1932 Ford Model 18 V-8 Deluxe Fordor sedan (OCW)

1932 Ford Model 18 V-8 Cabriolet (PH)

1932 Ford Model 18 V-8 Victoria (BMHV)

1933 Ford

Ford — Model 40 — Standard — Four and V-8: In addition to a longer 112-inch wheelbase and an X-member double-drop frame, the 1933 Ford had valanced front and rear fenders, a new radiator design with vertical bars slanted back to match the rear sweep of the windshield and acorn-shaped headlight shells. Curvaceous one-piece bumpers with a center-dip were used at front and rear. Enhancing the Ford's streamlined appearance were the angled side hood louvers. All models, regardless of body color, were delivered with black fenders and 17-inch wire spoke wheels. Accompanying these exterior revisions was a new dash arrangement with a reshaped engine-tuned panel enclosing the gauges placed directly in front of the driver. A similarly shaped glove box was placed on the passenger's side. As before, the V-8 Fords were identical to the four-cylinder models except for the addition of V-8 trim identification. With its teething problems part of the past, the Ford V-8 by virtue of an improved ignition system, better cooling, higher compression ratio and aluminum cylinder heads, developed 75 hp.

Ford — Model 40 — Deluxe — Four/V-8: Deluxe models had two horns, two taillights and shatter-proof glass all around. They also had rustless steel bullet-style headlight buckets.

1933 Ford V-8 Fordor Deluxe Phaeton (OCW)

1933 Ford V-8 Deluxe Cabriolet (OCW)

VIN:

Serial numbers were located on the top side of the frame near the clutch pedal and also on the left front pillar, the forward portion of left frame member and transmission housing. Starting: (V-8) 18-2031127 & up; (four-cylinder, with prefix "B") 5185849 & up. Engine numbers were located on boss placed on center of left side of block, directly below the cylinder head (four-cylinder); on top of clutch housing (V-8). Starting: (V-8) 18-2031127 & up; (four-cylinder) 5185849 & up.

Ford — Model 40 — Standard (Four)

Model No.	Body/ Style No.	Body Type & Seating	Factory Price	Shipping Weight	Production Total
40	—	2-dr. Roadster-2/4P	$ 425	2,268 lbs.	107
40	---	4-dr. Phaeton-5P	$ 445	2,281 lbs.	457
40	—	2-dr. Three-Window Coupe-2P	$ 440	2,380 lbs.	189
40	---	2-dr. Five-Window Coupe-2P	$ 440	2,220 lbs.	2,148
40	---	2-dr. Sedan-5P	$ 450	2,503 lbs.	2,911
40	---	4-dr. Sedan-5P	$ 510	2,550 lbs.	682

Ford — Model 40 — Deluxe (Four)

40	—	2-dr. Roadster-2/4P	$ 460	2,278 lbs.	101
40	---	2-dr. Cabriolet-2/4P	$ 535	2,306 lbs.	24
40	---	4-dr. Phaeton-5P	$ 495	2,290 lbs.	241
40	—	2-dr. Three-Window Coupe-2P	$ 490	2,220 lbs.	24
40	—	2-dr. Five-Window Coupe-2P	$ 490	2,299 lbs.	28
40	---	2-dr. Victoria-5P	$ 545	2,356 lbs.	25
40	---	2-dr. Sedan-5P	$ 500	2,520 lbs.	85
40	---	4-dr. Sedan-5P	$ 560	2,590 lbs.	179
40	---	4-dr. Station Wagon-5P	$ 590	2,505 lbs.	359

Ford — Model 40 — Standard (V-8)

40	—	2-dr. Roadster-2/4P	$ 475	2,422 lbs.	126
40	---	4-dr. Phaeton-5P	$ 495	2,520 lbs.	232
40	---	2-dr. Three-Window Coupe-2P	$ 490	2,534 lbs.	6,585
40	---	2-dr. Five-Window Coupe-2P	$ 490	2,534 lbs.	31,797
40	---	2-dr. Sedan-5P	$ 500	2,621 lbs.	106,387
40	---	4-dr. Sedan-5P	$ 560	2,675 lbs.	19,602

Ford — Model 40 — Deluxe (V-8)

40	—	2-dr. Roadster-2/4P	$ 510	2,261 lbs.	4,223
40	---	2-dr. Cabriolet-2/4P	$ 585	2,545 lbs.	7,852
40	—	4-dr. Phaeton-5P	$ 545	2,529 lbs.	1,483
40	---	2-dr. Three-Window Coupe-2P	$ 540	2,538 lbs.	15,894
40	---	2-dr. Five-Window Coupe-2P	$ 540	2,538 lbs.	11,244
40	---	2-dr. Victoria-5P	$ 595	2,595 lbs.	4,193
40	---	2-dr. Sedan-5P	$ 550	2,625 lbs.	48,233
40	---	4-dr. Sedan-5P	$ 610	2,684 lbs.	45,443
40	---	4-dr. Station Wagon-5P	$ 640	2,635 lbs.	1,654

Engines:

Model 40 Four: Inline. L-head. Cast-iron block. B & S: 3-7/8 x 4-1/4 in. Displacement: 200.5 cid. Compression ratio: 4.6:1. Brake hp: 50. Taxable hp: 30. Main bearings: three. Valve lifters: mechanical. Carburetor: Zenith or Holley double venturi.

Model 40 V-8: 90 degree V. L-head. Cast-iron block. B & S: 3-1/16 x 3-3/4 in. Displacement: 221 cid. Compression ratio: 6.3:1. Brake hp: 75 at 3800 rpm. Main bearings: three. Valve lifters: mechanical. Carburetor: Detroit Lubricator downdraft, single barrel 1.25-in. throat.

Chassis:

Model 40 V-8: Wheelbase: 112 in. Overall length: 182-9/10 in. Height: 68 in. Front and rear tread: 55-1/5/56-7/10 in. Tires: 5.50 x 17.

Technical:

Sliding gear transmission. Speeds: 3F/1R. Floor shift controls. Single dry plate, woven asbestos lining clutch. Shaft drive. 3/4 floating rear axle. Overall ratio: 4.11:1. Mechanical internal expanding brakes on four wheels. Welded spoke wheels, drop center rims. Wheel Size: 17 in.

Options:

Radio. Heater. Clock. Radio antenna. Greyhound radiator ornament. Trunk. Trunk rack. Twin taillights. Cowl lamps (standard on Deluxe models). Windshield wings. Dual horns (standard on Deluxe models). Whitewall tires. Leather seats. Dual wipers. Steel spare tire cover. Rumble seat (coupes).

History:

Introduced February 9, 1933. Calendar-year sales: 311,113 (registrations). Calendar-year production: 334,969. The president of Ford was Edsel Ford. During 1933 Ford conducted a number of economy runs with the Model 40. Under conditions ranging from the Mojave Desert to the Catskill Mountains the Fords averaged between 18.29 and 22.5 mpg.

1933 Ford V-8 3-Window Deluxe Coupe (OCW)

1933 Ford V-8 Standard 5-Window Coupe (JAC)

1933 Ford V-8 Deluxe 5-Window Coupe (JAC)

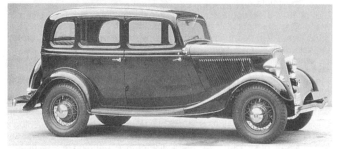
1933 Ford V-8 Deluxe Fordor sedan (OCW)

1933 Ford V-8 Station Wagon (OCW)

1933 Ford V-8 Cantrell Station Wagon (OCW)

1933 Ford V-8 Victoria (OCW)

1934 Ford

Ford — Model 40 — Standard — Four and V-8: Visual changes in 1934 Fords were minor. Different V-8 hubcap emblems (now painted rather than chrome-finished and without a painted surround) were used and the side hood louvers were straight instead of curved. Although the same grille form was continued for 1934 there were changes. The 1934 version had fewer vertical bars and its chrome frame was deeper and flatter. The V-8 grille ornament was placed within an inverted 60-degree triangle and carried a vertical divider. Other exterior alterations included smaller headlight and cowl light shells, two (rather than one) hood handles and three (instead of two) body pin stripes. In addition, the fenders were painted in body color on all models. However, black fenders were available as an option. Closed body models featured front door glass that, prior to lowering vertically into the door, moved slightly to the rear. This was usually referred to as "clear vision" ventilation. The dash panel no longer had an engine-turned panel insert. For 1934 this surface was painted.

Ford — Model 40 — Deluxe — Four and V-8: Deluxe models were easily distinguished from their Standard counterparts by their pin striping, cowl lights, twin horns and two taillights. The principal change in the design of the Ford V-8 consisted of a Stromberg carburetor in place of the Detroit Lubricator unit and a reshaped air cleaner. Ford also offered its four-cylinder engine in all models at a price $50 below that of a corresponding V-8 design. This was the final year for this engine's use in a Ford automobile. The four-cylinder engine was designated Model B; but the cars used the same Model 40 designation as V-8 powered models.

VIN:

Serial numbers were on the top side of the frame, near the clutch panel. The number was also on the left front pillar and forward portion of left frame member and the transmission housing. Starting: 18-451478 and up. Engine numbers were on top of the clutch housing. Starting: 18-457478 and up.

Ford Model 40 Standard (Four)

Model No.	Body/ Style No.	Body Type & Seating	Factory Price	Shipping Weight	Production Total
40	----	2-dr. Five Window Coupe-2P	$ 465	2,220 lbs.	20
40	---	2-dr. Sedan-5P	$ 485	2,503 lbs.	185
40	---	4-dr. Sedan-5P	$ 535	2,590 lbs.	405

Ford Model 40 Deluxe (Four)

40	---	2-dr. Roadster-2/4P	$ 475	2,278 lbs.	----
40	---	4-dr. Phaeton-5P	$ 460	2,281 lbs.	377
40	---	4-dr. Phaeton-5P	$ 510	2,290 lbs.	412
40	---	2-dr. Cabriolet-2/4P	$ 540	2,306 lbs.	12
40	---	2-dr. Three-Window Coupe-2/4P	$ 505	2,220 lbs.	7
40	---	2-dr. Five-Window Coupe-2/4P	$ 505	2,299 lbs.	3
40	---	2-dr. Sedan-5P	$ 525	2,520 lbs.	12
40	---	4-dr. Sedan-5P	$ 575	2,590 lbs.	384
40	---	2-dr. Victoria-5P	$ 560	2,356 lbs.	----
40	---	4-dr. Station Wagon-5P	$ 610	2,505 lbs.	95

Ford Model 40 Standard (V-8)

40 V-8	----	2-dr. Five Window Coupe-2P	$ 515	2,534 lbs.	47,623
40 V-8	---	2-dr. Sedan-5P	$ 535	2,621 lbs.	124,870
40 V-8	----	4-dr. Sedan-5P	$ 585	2,675 lbs.	22,394

Ford Model 40 Deluxe (V-8)

40 V-8	----	2-dr. Roadster-2/4P	$ 525	2,461 lbs.	----
40 V-8	---	4-dr. Phaeton-5P	$ 510	2,520 lbs.	373
40 V-8	----	4-dr. Phaeton-5P	$ 550	2,529 lbs.	3,128
40 V-8	---	2-dr. Cabriolet-2/4P	$ 590	2,545 lbs.	14,496
40 V-8	---	2-dr. Three-Window Coupe-2/4P	$ 555	2,538 lbs.	26,348
40 V-8	---	2-dr. Five-Window Coupe-2/4P	$ 555	2,538 lbs.	26,879
40 V-8	---	2-dr. Sedan-5P	$ 575	2,625 lbs.	121,696
40 V-8	---	4-dr. Sedan-5P	$ 625	2,684 lbs.	102,268
40 V-8	---	2-dr. Victoria-5P	$ 610	2,595 lbs.	20,083
40 V-8	---	4-dr. Station Wagon-5P	$ 660	2,635 lbs.	2,905

Engine:

Ford Four: Inline. L-head. Cast-iron block. B & S: 3-7/8 x 4-1/4 in. Displacement: 200.5 cid. Compression ratio: 4.6:1. Brake hp: 50. Taxable hp: 30. Main bearings: three. Valve lifters: mechanical. Carburetor: Zenith or Holley double venturi.

Ford V-8: 90-degree V. L-head. Cast-iron block. B & S: 3-1/16 x 3-3/4 in. Displacement: 221 cid. C.R.: 6.3:1. Brake hp: 85 at 3800 rpm. Torque: 150 lbs.-ft. at 2200 rpm. Main bearings: three. Valve lifters: mechanical. Carburetor: Stromberg EE-1 two-barrel downdraft.

Chassis:

Wheelbase: 112 in. Overall length: 182.9 in. Height: 68 in. Front tread: 55.2. Rear tread: 56.7 in. Tires: 5.50 x 17.

Technical:

Sliding gear transmission. Speeds: 3F/1R. Floor shift controls. Single dry plate, woven asbestos lining. Shaft drive. 3/4 floating rear axle. Overall ratio: 4.11:1. Mechanical internal expanding brakes on four wheels. Welded spoke drop center rims. Wheel size: 17 in.

Options:

Radio (ash tray or glove box door mounted). Heater. Clock. Cigar Lighter. Radio antenna. Seat covers. Spotlight. Cowl lamps (standard on Deluxe models). Trunk. Whitewalls. Greyhound radiator ornament. Special steel spoke wheels. Oversize balloon tires. Bumper guards. Extra horn, black finish (standard on Deluxe models). Dual windshield wiper. Steel tire cover (standard on Deluxe models). Black painted fenders. Two taillights (standard on Deluxe models).

History:

Introduced January 1934. Calendar-year production: 563,921. The president of Ford was Edsel Ford. In April 1934 Clyde Barrow wrote his famous (or infamous) letter to Henry Ford in which he told Ford "what a dandy car you make." At the Ford press preview, held on Dec. 6, 1933, Ford Motor Co. served alcoholic beverages for the first time. Not since 1930 had the Ford Motor Co. reported a profit. That changed in 1934 with a profit of $3,759,311.

1934 Ford V-8 Cabriolet (JAC)

1934 Ford V-8 5-Window Coupe (OCW)

1934 Ford V-8 5-Window Deluxe Coupe (OCW)

1934 Ford V-8 Deluxe Tudor Sedan (OCW)

1934 Ford V-8 Deluxe Roadster (OCW)

1934 Ford V-8 Fordor Phaeton (OCW)

1934 Ford V-8 Fordor Deluxe Phaeton (OCW)

1934 Ford V-8 Victoria (OCW)

1934 Ford V-8 "Bonnie & Clyde" Sedan (OCW)

1934 Ford V-8 Deluxe Fordor Sedan (OCW)

1934 Ford V-8 Station Wagon (AA)

1935 Ford

Ford — Model 48 — Standard — V-8: Few Ford enthusiasts would dispute Ford's claim of "Greater Beauty, Greater Comfort, and Greater Safety" for its 1935 models. The narrower radiator grille lost its sharply veed base and four horizontal bars helped accentuate the 1935 model's new, lower and more streamlined appearance. The fender outlines were now much more rounded and the side hood louvers received three horizontal bright stripes. In profile, the Ford windshield was seen to be more sharply sloped then previously. No longer fitted were the old cowl lamps, since the parking lamps were integral with the headlights. The headlight shells were painted body color. For the first time, Ford offered a built-in trunk for its Tudor and Fordor Sedan models and all Fords had front-hinged doors front and rear. Standard models had painted windshield and grille trim work, single horns and one taillight.

Ford — Model 48 — Deluxe — V-8: Both Standard and Deluxe models shared a painted dash finish, with the Deluxe Fords having a set of horizontal bars running down the center section. External distinctions were obvious. Deluxe models had bright windshield and grille trim work, as well as dual exposed horns and twin taillights. Added to the Ford model lineup was a Convertible Sedan. No longer available was the Victoria.

VIN:

Serial numbers were located on the left side of the frame near the firewall. Starting: 18-1234357. Ending: 18-2207110. Prefix "C" indicates Canadian built. Engine numbers were located on top of the clutch housing. Starting 18-1234357. Ending 18-2207110.

Ford Model 48 Standard (V-8)

Model No.	Body/Style No.	Body Type & Seating	Factory Price	Shipping Weight	Production Total
48	—	2-dr. Three-Window Coupe-2P	—	2,647 lbs.	—
48	—	2-dr. Five-Window Coupe-2P	$ 520	2,620 lbs.	78,477
48	—	2-dr. Sedan-5P	$ 510	2,717 lbs.	237,833
48	—	4-dr. Sedan-5P	$ 575	2,760 lbs.	49,176
48	—	4-dr. Station Wagon-5P	$ 670	2,896 lbs.	4,536

Ford Model 48 Deluxe (V-8)

Model No.	Body/Style No.	Body Type & Seating	Factory Price	Shipping Weight	Production Total
48	—	4-dr. Phaeton-5P	$ 580	2,667 lbs.	6,073
48	—	2-dr. Roadster-2/4P	$ 550	2,597 lbs.	4,896
48	—	2-dr. Cabriolet-2/4P	$ 625	2,687 lbs.	17,000
48	—	4-dr. Convertible Sedan-4P	$ 750	2,827 lbs.	4,234
48	—	2-dr. Three-Window Coupe-2P	$ 570	2,647 lbs.	31,513
48	—	2-dr. Five-Window Coupe-2P	$ 560	2,643 lbs.	33,065
48	—	2-dr. Sedan-5P	$ 595	2,737 lbs.	84,692
48	—	4-dr. Sedan-5P	$ 635	2,767 lbs.	75,807
48	—	2-dr. Trunk Sedan-5P	$ 595	2,772 lbs.	87,336
48	—	4-dr. Trunk Sedan-5P	$ 655	2,787 lbs.	105,157

Engine:

V-8: 90-degree V. L-head. Cast-iron block. B & S: 3-1/16 x 3-3/4 in. Displacement: 221 cid. Compression ratio: 6.3:1. Brake hp: 85 at 3800 rpm. Torque: 144 lb.-ft. at 2200 rpm. Main bearings: three. Valve lifters: mechanical. Carburetor: Stromberg EE-1, two-barrel downdraft.

Chassis:

Wheelbase: 112 in. Overall length: 182-3/4 in. Height: 64-5/8 in. Front tread: 55-1/2. Rear tread: 58-1/4 in. Tires: 6.00 x 16.

Technical:

Sliding gear transmission. Speeds: 3F/1R. Floor shift controls. Single dry plate, woven asbestos lining clutch. Shaft drive. Three-quarter floating rear axle. Overall ratio: 4.33:1. Mechanical, internal expanding brakes on four wheels. Welded spoke, drop center rims on wheels. Wheel size: 16 in.

Options:

Radio. Heater. Clock. Cigar lighter. Radio antenna. Seat covers. Spotlight. Cowl lamps (standard on Deluxe). Trunk. Luggage rack. Whitewall tires. Greyhound radiator ornament. Special steel spoke wheels. Oversize balloon tires. Bumper guards. Extra horns black finish (standard on Deluxe). Dual windshield wipers. Steel tire cover (standard on Deluxe). Black painted fenders. Two taillights (standard on Deluxe). Banjo type steering wheel. Rumbleseat (coupes and roadsters).

1935 Ford V-8 Standard 5-Window Coupe (OCW)

1935 Ford V-8 Standard 5-Window Coupe (OCW)

1935 Ford V-8 Fordor Deluxe Phaeton (OCW)

1935 Ford V-8 Deluxe Rumbleseat Roadster (JAC)

1935 Ford V-8 Convertible Cabriolet (AA)

1935 Ford V-8 Standard Tudor Sedan (OCW)

1935 Ford V-8 Standard Fordor Sedan (OCW)

1935 Ford V-8 Deluxe Convertible Sedan (OCW)

1935 Ford V-8 Deluxe 3-Window Coupe (OCW)

1935 Ford V-8 Deluxe 5-Window Coupe (OCW)

1935 Ford V-8 Deluxe Tudor sedan (OCW)

1935 Ford V-8 Deluxe Fordor Sedan (OCW)

1935 Ford V-8 Brewster Custom Town Car (OCW)

1935 Ford V-8 Deluxe Fordor Touring Sedan (OCW)

History:

Introduced December 1934. Calendar-year registrations: 826,519. Calendar-year production: 942,439. The president of Ford was Edsel Ford. Ford was America's best selling car for 1935. A Ford convertible sedan paced the 1935 Indianapolis 500. Ford produced its two-millionth V-8 engine in June 1935.

1936 Ford

Ford — Model 68 — Standard — V-8: The 1936 Fords retained the same basic body of the 1935 models, but carried a restyled front end and new rear fenders. The grille, which consisted only of vertical bars, extended further around the hood sides. Standard models had a painted grille, painted windshield molding, one horn and one taillight. Standard and Deluxe models this year shared sheet metal and engines.

Ford — Model 68 — Deluxe — V-8: The dual horns of the Deluxe models were placed behind screens set into the fender catwalks. The Convertible Sedan with its "slant-back" body was superseded by a version with a "trunk-back" styling (incorporating a built-in luggage compartment) during the model year. In place of wire wheels, Ford used new pressed-steel artillery-spoke wheels with large 12-inch painted hubcaps and chrome centers carrying a narrow, stylized V-8 logo. The same design was used on the Ford hood ornament. Design changes for 1936 included a larger capacity radiator, better engine cooling via new hood side louvers and front vents and helical-type gears for first and reverse gears. Previously only the second and third gears were of this design. Early 1936 Ford V-8s had domed aluminum pistons, but they were replaced by steel versions during the year. They also had new insert-type main bearings. Deluxe models featured bright work around the grille, headlights and windshield, as well as dual horns and taillights. Deluxe Fords produced late in the model year also had dual windshield wipers, wheel trim rings, a clock and a rearview mirror as standard equipment.

1936 Ford V-8 Deluxe Phaeton (OCW)

VIN:

Serial numbers were located on the left side of the frame near the firewall. Starting: 18-2207111. Ending: 18-3331856. Prefix "C" indicates Canadian built. Engine numbers were located on top of the clutch housing. Starting: 18-2207111. Ending: 18-3331856.

Ford Model 68 Standard (V-8)

Model No.	Body/ Style No.	Body Type & Seating	Factory Price	Shipping Weight	Production Total
68	—	2-dr. Five-Window Coupe-2P	$ 510	2,599 lbs.	78,534
68	—	2-dr. Sedan-5P	$ 520	2,659 lbs.	174,770
68	—	2-dr. Trunk Sedan-5P	$ 545	2,718 lbs.	—
68	—	4-dr. Sedan-5P	$ 580	2,699 lbs.	31,505
68	—	4-dr. Trunk Sedan-5P	$ 605	2,771 lbs.	—

Ford Model 68 Deluxe (V-8)

Model No.	Body/ Style No.	Body Type & Seating	Factory Price	Shipping Weight	Production Total
68	—	2-dr. Roadster-3P	$ 560	2,561 lbs.	3,862
68	—	4-dr. Phaeton-5P	$ 560	2,561 lbs.	3,862
68	—	2-dr. Cabriolet-5P	$ 625	2,649 lbs.	—
68	—	2-dr. Club Cabriolet-5P	$ 675	2,651 lbs.	4,616
68	ó	2-dr. Five-Window Coupe-2P	$ 510	2,599 lbs.	78,534
68	ó	2-dr. Sedan-5P	$ 520	2,659 lbs.	174,770
68	—	4-dr. Trunk Back Convertible Sedan-5P	$ 780	2,916 lbs.	—
68	—	4-dr. Straight Back Convertible Sedan-5P	$ 760	2,791 lbs.	5,601
68	—	2-dr. Three-Window Coupe-2P	$ 570	2,621 lbs.	21,446
68	—	2-dr. Five-Window Coupe-5P	$ 555	2,641 lbs.	29,938
68	—	2-dr. Sedan-5P	$ 565	2,691 lbs.	20,519
68	—	2-dr. Trunk Sedan-5P	$ 590	2,786 lbs.	125,303
68	—	4-dr. Sedan-5P	$ 625	2,746 lbs.	42,867
68	—	4-dr. Trunk Sedan-5P	$ 650	2,816 lbs.	159,825
68	—	4-dr. Station Wagon-5P	$ 670	3,020 lbs.	7,044

Engine:

Model 68 V-8: 90 degree V. Inline. Cast-iron block. B & S: 3-1/16 x 3-3/4 in. Displacement: 221 cid. Compression ratio: 6.3:1. Brake hp: 85 at 3800 rpm. Taxable hp: 30. Torque: 148 lb.-ft. at 2200 rpm. Main bearings: three. Valve lifters: mechanical. Carburetor: Ford 679510A two-barrel downdraft.

Chassis:

Wheelbase: 112 in. Overall length: 182-3/4 in. Height: 68-5/8 in. Front tread: 55-1/2. Rear tread: 58-1/4 in. Tires: 6.00 x 16.

1936 Ford V-8 Deluxe Roadster (OCW)

1936 Ford V-8 Cabriolet OCW)

1936 Ford V-8 Deluxe Club Cabriolet (OCW)

1936 Ford V-8 Standard Tudor sedan (OCW)

1936 Ford V-8 Trunkback Convertible Sedan (OCW)

1936 Ford V-8 Deluxe Tudor Touring Sedan (OCW)

1936 Ford V-8 Standard five-window Coupe (OCW)

1936 Ford V-8 Deluxe five-window coupe (OCW)

1936 Ford V-8 Standard Fordor sedan (OCW)

1936 Ford V-8 Slantback Convertible Sedan (OCW)

1936 Ford V-8 Deluxe Fordor Touring Sedan (OCW)

Technical:

Sliding gear transmission. Speeds: 3F/1R. Floor shift controls. Single dry plate, molded asbestos lining clutch. Shaft drive. Three-quarter floating rear axle. Overall ratio: 4.33:1. Mechanical, internal expanding brakes on four wheels. Pressed steel wheels, drop center rim. Wheel size: 16 in.

Options:

Radio (five versions from $44.50). Heater ($14). Clock ($9.75). Cigar lighter. Radio antenna. Seat covers. Spotlight. Rumbleseat in Coupe or Roadster ($20). Luggage rack ($7.50). Banjo steering wheel. "Spider" wheel covers ($3.75 early). Wind wings ($10). Combination oil-pressure, gas gauge ($3.75). Dual windshield wipers ($3). Leather upholstery. Electric air horns.

History:

Introduced October 1935. Ford was the overall winner of the 1936 Monte Carlo Rally. Calendar-year registrations: 748,554. Calendar-year production: 791,812. The president of Ford was Edsel Ford.

1936 Ford V-8 Deluxe three-window Coupe (OCW)

1936 Ford V-8 Station Wagon (OCW)

1936 Ford Showroom (OCW)

1937 Ford

Ford — Standard — Model 74 (60-hp) — V-8: The 1937 models were the first Fords to have their headlights mounted in the front fenders and use an all-steel top. The 1937 Ford's styling reflected the strong influence of the Lincoln-Zephyr. The grille with horizontal bars and a center vertical bar cut a sharp vee into the side hood area. As had been the case for many years, the side hood cooling vents reflected the grille's general form. Ford offered Sedans with a "slant-back" or Touring Sedans with a "trunk-back" rear deck. All Ford sedans had access to the trunk area through an external lid. In addition, a new coupe with a rear seat was introduced. All models had a rear-hinged alligator-type hood. Ford introduced a smaller version of its V-8 with a 2-3/5-inch bore and 3-1/5-inch stroke. Its displacement was 136 cid. This 60-hp engine was available only in the Standard Ford bodies, although these were also available with the larger 85-hp V-8 as well. Standard models had painted radiator grilles and windshield frames. A burl mahogany wood grain finish was applied to their interior window trim. Replacing the rod-operated mechanical brake system was a version using a cable linkage.

Ford — Standard — Model 78 (85-hp) — V-8: Standard models with painted radiator grilles and windshield frames were also available in the same body styles with the larger engine. A burl mahogany wood grain finish was applied to their interior window trim. The operation of the 221-cid V-8 was further improved by the use of a higher-capacity water pump, larger insert bearings and cast-alloy steel pistons.

Ford — Deluxe — Model 78 — V-8: Deluxe models had interiors with walnut wood grain window moldings and more exterior trim bright work. There were two matched-tone horns behind the radiator grille, two taillights, two swivel-type interior sun visors, dual windshield wipers and interior lights in coupes and sedans. On the outside, the wheels were dressed up with chrome trim bands. Otherwise, in 1937, the same "speedboat" front end styling was used on all Fords. The hood was hinged at the cowl and opened from the front, a modern feature for 1937. The battery was located on the firewall, below the hood. The V-type slanting windshield used in closed cars could be opened slightly for ventilation.

VIN:

Serial numbers were located on the left side of the frame near the firewall. Starting: (Model 74) 54-6602. (Model 78) 18-3331857. Ending: (Model 74) 54-358334. (Model 78) 18-4186446. Prefix "C" indicates Canadian built. Engine numbers located on top of clutch housing. Starting: (Model 74) 54-6602. (Model 78) 18-3331857. Ending: (Model 74) 54-358334. (Model 78) 18-4186446.

Ford Standard — Model 74 — V-8 (60 hp)

Model No.	Body/ Style No.	Body Type & Seating	Factory Price	Shipping Weight	Production Total
74	—	2-dr. Five-Window Cpe-2P	$ 529	2,275 lbs.	—
74	—	2-dr. Sedan-5P	$ 579	2,405 lbs.	—
74	—	2-dr. Trunk Sedan-5P	$ 604	2,415 lbs.	—
74	—	4-dr. Sedan-5P	$ 639	2,435 lbs.	—
74	—	4-dr. Trunk Sedan-5P	$ 664	2,445 lbs.	—

Ford Standard — Model 78 — V-8 (85 hp)

78	—	2-dr. Five-Window Coupe-2P	$ 586	2,496 lbs.	90,347
78	ó	2-dr. Sedan-5P	$ 611	2,616 lbs.	308,446
78	—	2-dr. Trunk Sedan-5P	$ 636	2,648 lbs.	—
78	—	4-dr. Sedan-5P	$ 671	2,649 lbs.	49,062
78	—	4-dr. Trunk Sedan-5P	$ 696	2,666 lbs.	45,531

Ford Deluxe — Model 78 — V-8 (85 hp)

78	—	2-dr. Roadster-2P	$ 694	2,576 lbs.	1,250
78	—	4-dr. Phaeton-5P	$ 749	2,691 lbs.	3,723
78	—	2-dr. Cabriolet-4P	$ 719	2,616 lbs.	10,184
78	—	2-dr. Club Cabriolet-5P	$ 759	2,636 lbs.	8,001
78	—	4-dr. Sedan-5P	$ 696	2,666 lbs.	45,531
78	—	4-dr. Convertible Sedan-5P	$ 859	2,861 lbs.	4,378
78	—	2-dr. Five-Window Coupe-2P	$ 659	2,506 lbs.	26,738
78	—	2-dr. Five-Window Club Coupe-5P	$ 719	2,616 lbs.	16,992
78	—	2 dr, Sedan-5P	$ 674	2,656 lbs.	33,683
78	—	2-dr. Trunk Sedan-5P	$ 699	2,679 lbs.	—
78	—	4-dr. Sedan-5P	$ 734	2,671 lbs.	22,885
78	—	4-dr. Trunk Sedan-5P	$ 759	2,696 lbs.	98,687
78	—	4-dr. Station Wagon-5P	$ 755	2,991 lbs.	9,304

Engines:

Model 74 60-hp V-8: 90-degree V. Inline. Cast-iron block. B & S: 2-3/5 x 3-1/5 in. Displacement: 136 cid. Compression ratio: 6.6:1. Brake hp 60 at 3600 rpm Taxable hp: 21.6. Torque: 94 lb.-ft. at 2500 rpm. Main bearings: three. Valve lifters: mechanical. Carburetor: Stromberg 922A-9510A two-barrel downdraft.

1937 Ford V-8 Model 74 Standard Tudor Sedan (OCW)

1937 Ford V-8 Model 74 Deluxe five-window Coupe (OCW)

1937 Ford V-8 Model 78 Standard Tudor Sedan (OCW)

1937 Ford V-8 Model 78 Standard Tudor Touring Sedan (OCW)

1937 Ford V-8 Model 78 Standard Fordor Touring Sedan (OCW)

1937 Ford V-8 Model 78 Deluxe Cabriolet (OCW)

Model 78 85-hp V-8: 90-degree V. Inline. Cast-iron block. B & S: 3-1/16 x 3-3/4 in. Displacement: 221 cid. Compression ratio: 6.3:1. Brake hp: 85 at 3800 rpm Taxable hp: 30.01. Torque: 153 lb.-ft. at 2200 rpm. Main bearings: three. Valve lifters: mechanical. Carburetor: Stromberg 67-9510A two-barrel downdraft.

Chassis:

Model 74: Wheelbase: 112 in. Overall length: 179-1/2 in. Height: 68-5/8 in. Front tread: 55-1/2 in. Rear tread: 58-1/4 in. Tires: 5.50 x 16.

Model 78: Wheelbase: 112 in. Overall length: 179-1/2 in. Height: 68-5/8 in. Front tread: 55-1/2 in. Rear tread: 58-1/4 in. Tires: 5.50 x 16.

Technical:

Sliding gear transmission. Speeds: 3F/1R. Floor shift controls. Single dry plate, molded asbestos lining clutch. Shaft drive. Three-quarter floating rear axle. Overall ratio: 4.33:1. Mechanical, internal expanding brakes on four wheels. Pressed steel, drop center rim wheels. Wheel size: 16 in.

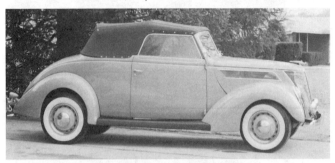
1937 Ford V-8 Model 78 Deluxe Club Cabriolet (OCW)

1937 Ford V-8 Model 78 Deluxe five-window Coupe (AA)

1937 Ford V-8 Model 78 Deluxe five-window Coupe rearview (OCW)

1937 Ford V-8 Model 78 Deluxe Convertible Sedan (OCW)

Fender skirts. Radio. Heater. Clock (mirror clock and glove box clock). Cigar lighter. Radio antenna. Seat covers. Side view mirror. Dual wipers. Sport light. Dual taillights (standard on Deluxe). Fog lamps. Locking gas cap. Glove box lock. Defroster. Draft deflectors. Vanity mirror. Wheel trim bands. Deluxe hubcaps. White sidewall tires. Center bumper guard. Deluxe steering wheel. Sliding glass panels on station wagon ($20).

1937 Ford V-8 Model 78 Deluxe Tudor Sedan (AA)

1937 Ford V-8 Model 78 Deluxe Tudor Touring Sedan (OCW)

1937 Ford V-8 Model 78 Deluxe Fordor Sedan (OCW)

1937 Ford V-8 Model 78 Deluxe Fordor Touring Sedan (OCW)

1937 Ford V-8 Model 78 Deluxe Station Wagon (JAC)

The 1937 Fords were introduced in November 1936. First year for 60 hp V-8. It was the first year for rear fender skirts. Calendar-year sales: 765,933 (registrations). Calendar-year production: 848,608. The president of Ford Motor Co. was Edsel Ford.

1938 Ford

Ford — Standard — Model 81A (85-hp) — V-8: The Standard Fords were also available with the 221-cid V-8. With this engine they were designated part of the Standard Model 81A line.

Ford — Deluxe — Model 81A (85-hp) — V-8: The Deluxe Ford body had a decidedly rounded V-type nose with horizontal grille bars on either side and V-8 insignia mounted in the clear spaces between the grille bars and the horizontal hood louvers. Interior alterations consisted of a new instrument panel with a centrally located radio speaker grille and recessed control knobs. As before, the windshield opening knob was centered high on the dash. The Deluxe model's "banjo" steering wheel had flexible, multiple steel spokes.

Serial numbers were located on the left-hand frame side member near the firewall. Starting: 81A - 18-4186447, 82A - 54-358335 & up. Ending: 81A - 18-4661100. Engine numbers were located on top of the clutch housing. Starting: 81A - 18-4186447, 82A - 54-358335 and up. Ending: 81A - 18-4661100.

Ford Standard Model 82A V-8 (60 hp)

Model No.	Body/ Style No.	Body Type & Seating	Factory Price	Shipping Weight	Production Total
82A	—	2-dr. Five-Window Coupe-2P	$ 595	2,354 lbs.	—
82A	—	2-dr. Sedan-5P	$ 640	2,455 lbs.	—
82A	—	4-dr. Sedan-5P	$ 685	2,481 lbs.	—

Ford Standard Model 81A V-8 (85 HP)

81A	—	2-dr. Five-Window Coupe-2P	$ 625	2,575 lbs.	34,059
81A	—	2-dr. Sedan-5P	$ 665	2,674 lbs.	106,117
81A	—	4-dr. Sedan-5P	$ 710	2,697 lbs.	30,287

Ford Deluxe Model 81A V-8 (85 HP)

81A	-	4-dr. Station Wagon-5P	$ 825	2,981 lbs.	6,944
81A	-	4-dr. Phaeton-5P	$ 820	2,748 lbs.	1,169
81A	-	2-dr. Club Cabriolet-5P	$ 800	2,719 lbs.	6,080
81A	---	2-dr. Cabriolet-3P	$ 770	2,679 lbs.	4,702
81A	---	4-dr. Convertible Sedan-5P	$ 900	2,683 lbs.	2,703
81A	---	2-dr. Five-Window Coupe-3P	$ 685	2,606 lbs.	22,225
81A	---	2-dr. Five-Window Club Coupe-5P	$ 745	2,688 lbs.	7,171
81A	---	2-dr. Sedan-5P	$ 725	2,742 lbs.	101,647
81A	---	4-dr. Sedan-5P	$ 770	2,773 lbs.	92,020

60-hp V-8: 90-degree V. Inline. Cast-iron block. B & S: 2-3/5 x 3-1/5 in. Displacement: 136 cid. Compression ratio: 6.6:1. Brake hp 60 at 3500 rpm Taxable hp: 21.6. Torque: 94 lbs.-ft. at 2500 rpm. Main bearings: three. Valve lifters: mechanical. Carburetor: Chandler-Groves and Stromberg 9221-95101, two-barrel downdraft.

85-hp V-8: 90-degree V. Inline. Cast-iron block. B & S: 3-1/16 x 3-3/4 in. Displacement: 221 cid. Compression ratio: 6.3:1. Brake hp: 85 at 3800 rpm Taxable hp: 30. Torque: 146 lbs.-ft. at 2000 rpm. Main bearings: three. Valve lifters: mechanical. Carburetor: Chandler-Groves and Stromberg 21A-9510A, two-barrel downdraft.

Model 82A: Wheelbase: 112 in. Overall length: 179-1/2 in. Height: 68-5/8 in. Front tread: 55-1/2 in. Rear tread: 58-1/4 in. Tires: 5.50 x 16.

1938 Ford V-8 Model 82A Standard Fordor Sedan (OCW)

Model 81A: Wheelbase: 112 in. Overall length: 179-1/2 in. Height: 68-5/8 in. Front tread: 55-1/2 in. Rear tread: 58-1/4 in. Tires: 6.00 x 16.

Technical:

Sliding gear transmission. Speeds: 3F/1R. Floor shift controls. Single dry plate, molded asbestos lining clutch. Shaft drive. Three-quarter floating rear axle. Overall ratio: 4.33:1. Mechanical, internal expanding brakes on four wheels. Pressed steel, drop center rim wheels. Wheel size: 16 in.

Options:

Fender skirts. Bumper guards. Radio. Heater. Clock (mirror and glove box types). Cigar lighter. Seat covers. Side view mirror. Dual wipers. Sport light. Dual taillights (standard on Deluxe). Fog lights. Locking gas cap. Glove box lock. Defroster. Draft deflectors. Vanity mirror. Wheel trim bands. Deluxe hubcaps (standard on Deluxe). White sidewall tires. Deluxe steering wheel (standard on Deluxe). License plate frame.

1938 Ford V-8 Model 82A Standard five-window Coupe (HAC)

1938 Ford V-8 Model 82A Standard Tudor Sedan (OCW)

1938 Ford V-8 Model 81A Standard Fordor Sedan (OCW)

1938 Ford V-8 Model 81A Deluxe Station Wagon (AA)

History:

Introduced November 1937. Ford secured its second victory in the Monte Carlo Rally. Calendar-year registrations: 363,688. Calendar-year production: 410,048. The president of Ford Motor Co. was Edsel Ford.

1938 Ford V-8 Model 81A Deluxe Cabriolet (OCW)

1938 Ford V-8 Model 81A Deluxe Fordor Sedan (OCW)

1938 Ford V-8 Model 81A Deluxe five-window Coupe (OCW)

1939 Ford

Ford — Standard — Model 922A (60-hp) — V-8: Only four body styles were offered in the Standard series. Standard models carried the general "speedboat" front end styling of the 1938 Ford Deluxe. They had a sharply veed grille with horizontal bars, headlights mounted inboard of the fenders and small side hood louvers. Standard models were not equipped with a banjo-style steering wheel, glove box lock or clock as standard equipment. The smaller 60-hp flathead V-8 was offered only in Standard bodies. A significant 1939 technical development was the adoption by Ford of Lockheed hydraulic brakes.

Ford — Standard — Model 91A (85-hp) — V-8: The Standard Ford models were also available with the larger 85-hp V-8.

Ford — Deluxe — Model 91A (85-hp) — V-8: Deluxe models had a much more modern appearance. Their teardrop-shaped headlights blended smoothly into the leading edges of the front fenders. The radiator grille was set lower in the hood than before. Simple chrome trim replaced the hood louvers and a smoother body profile was featured. Deluxe models had a banjo steering wheel, a locking glove box and a clock as standard equipment.

1939 Ford V-8 Model 922A Standard five-window Coupe (OCW)

1939 Ford V-8 Model 922A Standard Tudor Sedan (OCW)

VIN:

Serial numbers were located on the left side member near the firewall. Starting No.: Model 91A - 18-4661001. Model 922A - 54506501 and up. Ending: 91A - 18-210700. Engine No. location was on top of the clutch housing. Starting: Model 91A - 18-4661001. Model 922A - 54-506501 and up. Ending: Model 91A - 18-5210700.

Ford Standard Model 922A V-8 (60 hp)

Model No.	Body Type & Seating	Factory Price	Shipping Weight	Production Total
922A	2-dr. Five-Window Coupe-2P	$ 599	2,463 lbs.	—
922A	2-dr. Sedan-5P	$ 640	2,608 lbs.	—
922A	4-dr. Sedan-5P	$ 686	2,623 lbs.	—

Ford Standard Model 91A V-8 (85 hp)

91A	2-dr. Five-Window Coupe-2P	$ 640	2,710 lbs.	38,197
91A	2-dr. Sedan-5P	$ 681	2,830 lbs.	124,866
91A	4-dr. Sedan-5P	$ 727	2,850 lbs.	—
91A	4-dr. Station Wagom-5P	$ 840	3,080 lbs.	3,277

Ford Deluxe Model 91A V-8 (85 hp)

91A	2-dr. Convertible-3P	$ 770	2,679 lbs.	4,702
91A	4-dr. Convertible Sedan-5P	$ 900	2,863 lbs.	2,703
91A	2-dr. Five-Window Coupe-2P	$ 685	2,606 lbs.	22,225
91A	2-dr. Sedan-5P	$ 725	2,742 lbs.	101,647
91A	4-dr. Sedan-5P	$ 770	2,773 lbs.	92,020
91A	4-dr. Station Wagom-5P	$ 825	2,981 lbs.	6,944

Engine:

60-hp V-8: 90-degree V. Cast-iron block. B & S: 2-3/5 x 3-1/5 in. Displacement: 136 cid. Compression ratio: 6.6:1. Brake hp 60 at 3500 rpm Taxable hp: 21.6. Torque: 94 lbs.-ft. at 2500 rpm. Main bearings: three. Valve lifters: mechanical. Carburetor: Stromberg 922A-9510A two-barrel downdraft.

85-hp V-8: 90-degree V. Cast-iron block. B & S: 3-1/16 x 3-3/4 in. Displacement: 221 cid. Compression ratio: 6.3:1. Brake hp: 85 at 3800 rpm Taxable hp: 30. Torque: 146 lbs.-ft. at 2000 rpm. Main bearings: three. Valve lifters: mechanical. Carburetor: Chandler-Groves and Stromberg 21A-951A two-barrel downdraft.

Chassis:

Model 922A: Wheelbase: 112 in. Overall length: 179-1/2 in. Height: 68-5/8 in. Front tread: 55-1/2 in. Rear tread: 58-1/4 in. Tires: 5.50 x 16.

Model 91A: Wheelbase: 112 in. Overall length: 179-1/2 in. Height: 68-5/8 in. Front tread: 55-1/2 in. Rear tread: 58-1/4 in. Tires: 6.00 x 16.

Technical:

Sliding gear transmission. Speeds: 3F/1R. Floor shift controls. Single dry plate, molded asbestos lining clutch. Shaft drive. Three-quarter floating rear axle. Overall ratio: 4.33:1. Lockheed hydraulic brakes on four wheels. Pressed steel, drop center rim wheels. Wheel size: 16 in.

Options:

Bumper guards. Radio. Heater. Clock (standard on Deluxe). Seat covers. Side view mirror. Sport light. Fog lamps. Locking gas cap. Draft deflectors. Vanity mirror. Wheel dress up rings (standard on Deluxe). Deluxe hubcaps for Standard. White sidewall tires. License plate frames. Fender skirts.

History:

Introduced November 4, 1938. Lockheed hydraulic brakes. Calendar-year registrations: 481,496. Calendar-year production: 532,152. The president of Ford Motor Co. was Edsel Ford.

1939 Ford V-8 Model 91A Standard five-window Coupe (OCW)

1939 Ford V-8 Model 91A Standard Tudor Sedan (OCW)

1939 Ford V-8 Model 91A Standard Fordor Sedan (OCW)

1939 Ford V-8 Model 91A Standard Station Wagon (OCW)

1939 Ford V-8 Model 91A Deluxe Convertible (OCW)

1939 Ford V-8 Model 91A Deluxe Convertible Sedan (OCW)

1939 Ford V-8 Model 91A Deluxe five-window Coupe (OCW)

1939 Ford V-8 Model 91A Deluxe Tudor Sedan (OCW)

1939 Ford V-8 Model 91A Deluxe Station Wagon (OCW)

1939 Ford V-8 Model 91A Deluxe Fordor Sedan (OCW)

1940 Ford

Ford — Model 02A — Standard (60-hp) — V-8: Standard Fords had a grille and hood similar to those of the 1939 Deluxe models. Their headlight shells were finished in the body color and the integral parking lamp lacked the ribbed surround used on Deluxe models. The vertical grille bars were also painted to match the body color. Deluxe hubcaps had a series of concentric rings surrounding a blue V-8. The Standard dash and steering wheel had a Briarwood Brown finish and the instrument panel had a larger speedometer face. Standard models had front vent windows. This was the final year for availability of the 60-hp V-8 as an option in Standard models only.

Ford — Model 01A — Standard (85-hp) — V-8: As in the past few years, cars with the Standard Ford body were also offered with the larger 85-hp V-8.

Ford — Model 01A — Deluxe (85-HP) — V-8: The 1940 Ford Deluxe body featured extremely handsome styling by Eugene Gregorie. All Fords, including Deluxe models, were fitted with sealed beam headlights and a steering column-mounted shift lever. Deluxe models were distinguished by their chrome headlight trim rings with the parking light cast into its upper surface. The bright Deluxe grille combined a center section with horizontal bars and secondary side grids whose horizontal bars were subdivided into three sections by thicker molding. Hubcaps for these top-level Fords featured bright red "Ford Deluxe" lettering and trim rings finished in the body color. The Deluxe instrument panel was given a maroon-and-sand two-tone finish that matched that of the steering wheel. Only the 85-hp V-8 was available in Deluxe models.

VIN:

Serial numbers were located on the left frame side member near the firewall. Starting: [Model 01A] 18-5210701, [Model 022A] 54-506501 and up. Ending: [Model 01A] 18-5896294. Engine numbers were located on the top of the clutch housing. Starting: [Model 01A] 18-5210701, [Model 022A] 54-506401 and up. Ending: [Model 01A] 18-5896294.

Ford Standard Model 02A V-8 (60 HP)

Model No.	Body/ Style No.	Body Type & Seating	Factory Price	Shipping Weight	Production Total
02A	—	2-dr. Five-Window Coupe-2P	$ 619	2,519 lbs.	—
02A	—	2-dr. Business Coupe-2P	$ 640	2,549 lbs.	—
02A	—	2-dr. Sedan-5P	$ 660	2,669 lbs.	—
02A	—	4-dr. Sedan-5P	$ 706	2,696 lbs.	—

Ford Standard Model 01A V-8 (85 HP)

Model No.	Body/ Style No.	Body Type & Seating	Factory Price	Shipping Weight	Production Total
02A	—	2-dr. Five-Window Coupe-2P	$ 660	2,763 lbs.	33,693
02A	—	2-dr. Business Coupe-2P	$ 681	2,801 lbs.	16,785
02A	—	2-dr. Sedan-5P	$ 701	2,909 lbs.	150,933
02A	—	4-dr. Sedan-5P	$ 747	2,936 lbs.	25,545
02A	—	4-dr. Station Wagon-5P	$ 875	3,249 lbs.	4,469

Ford Deluxe Model 01A V-8 (85 hp)

Model No.	Body/ Style No.	Body Type & Seating	Factory Price	Shipping Weight	Production Total
01A	—	2-dr. Five-Window Coupe-2P	$ 722	2,791 lbs.	27,919
01A	—	2-dr. Business Coupe-2P	$ 742	2,831 lbs.	20,183
01A	—	2-dr. Convertible-5P	$ 849	2,956 lbs.	23,704
01A	—	2-dr. Sedan-5P	$ 765	2,927 lbs.	171,368
01A	—	4-dr. Sedan-5P	$ 747	2,936 lbs.	25,545
01A	—	4-dr. Station Wagon-5P	$ 810	2,966 lbs.	91,756
01A	—	4-dr. Station Wagon-5P	$ 950	3,262 lbs.	8,730

Engine:

60-hp V-8: 90-degree V. Cast-iron block. B & S: 2-3/5 x 3-1/5 in. Displacement: 136 cid. Compression ratio: 6.6:1. Brake hp 60 at 3500 rpm Taxable hp: 21.6. Torque: 94 lbs.-ft. at 2500 rpm. Main bearings: three. Valve lifters: mechanical. Carburetor: Chandler-Groves 922A-9510A two-barrel downdraft.

1940 Ford V-8 Model 02A Standard five-window Coupe (OCW)

1940 Ford V-8 Model 01A Standard Tudor Sedan (OCW)

1940 Ford V-8 Model 01A Standard Station Wagon (OCW)

1940 Ford V-8 Model 01A Deluxe five-window Coupe (OCW)

1940 Ford V-8 Model 01A Deluxe Station Wagon (OCW)

1940 Ford V-8 Model 01A Deluxe Fordor Sedan (OCW)

90-hp V-8: 90-degree V. Cast-iron block. B & S: 3-1/16 x 3-3/4 in. Displacement: 221 cid. Compression ratio: 6.15:1. Brake hp: 85 at 3800 rpm Taxable hp: 30. Torque: 155 lbs.-ft. at 2200 rpm. Main bearings: three. Valve lifters: mechanical. Carburetor: Chandler-Groves 21A-9510A, two-barrel downdraft.

Chassis:

Model 02A: Wheelbase: 112 in. Overall length: 188-1/4 in. Height: 68 in. Front tread: 55-3/4 in. Rear tread: 58-1/4 in. Tires: 5.50 x 16.
Model 01A: Wheelbase: 112 in. Overall length: 188-1/4 in. Height: 68 in. Front tread: 55-3/4 in. Rear tread: 58-1/4 in. Tires: 6.00 x 16.

Technical:

Sliding gear transmission. Speeds: 3F/1R. Floor shift controls. Single dry plate, molded asbestos lining clutch. Shaft drive. Three-quarter floating rear axle. Overall ratio: 4.33:1. Lockheed hydraulic brakes on four wheel. Pressed steel, drop center rim wheels. Wheel size: 16 in.

Options:

Fender skirts. Bumper guards. Radio. Heater. Cigar lighter. Radio antenna. Seat covers. Side view mirror. Right-hand side view mirror. Spotlight. Fog lamps. Locking gas cap. Defroster. Vanity mirror. Deluxe wheel rings (standard on Deluxe). Deluxe hubcaps (standard on Deluxe). White sidewall tires. Gravel deflectors. License plate frame. Two-tone paint.

History:

Introduced in October 1940. Calendar-year sales: 542,755 (registrations). Calendar-year production: 599,175. The president of Ford Motor Co. was Edsel Ford.

1941 Ford

Ford — Special — Series 1GA/11A — Six and V-8: The 1941 Fords had fresh styling and a revamped chassis and were easily recognizable as new models. All versions were mounted on a two-inch-longer wheelbase. The use of a wider body substantially increased the Ford's interior dimensions. Emphasizing the rounder, more curved body form was a new three-piece grille that consisted of a neo-traditional vertical center section with two auxiliary units set low on either side. Running boards were continued, but due to the body's greater width, they were far less noticeable than on earlier Fords. Further accentuating the lower-and-wider nature of the '41 Ford was the position of the headlights, which were set further apart in the fenders. Base cars this year were called "Specials" rather than "Standards." The three Special models were offered only in a Harbor Gray finish. The windshield divider was painted black. The center grille section was, however, chromed. Specials came equipped with a single taillight, only one horn, one windshield wiper and one sun visor. Lacking from their interior were such appointments as armrests, a dome light, a cigarette lighter and a glove box lock. On Monday, June 2, 1941 the following announcement was printed in *Time* magazine: "Last week, for the first time since 1908, auto dealers had for sale a six-cylinder Ford. Expected for months (*Time*, September 9, 1941), the six was not a new car, but a new engine in the V-8 body. It was priced at the old price of the V-8, which was simultaneously raised $15. No official specifications were released, but dealers described the six as a cheaper, more economical (than the V-8), 90-hp L-head engine with three-point suspension." Since the six-cylinder engine arrived so late, some sources say it was available only in Specials. *The Official Blue Book New & Used Car Guide* effective May-June, 1942 indicates that the six was available in all Ford bodies. We also found a Ford ad in the *Motor* show annual for 1941 that incorrectly makes it appear that the six was first announced for 1942 models.

Ford — Deluxe — Series 1GA/11A — Six and V-8: Deluxe series Fords instrument panels were finished in an Ebony grain pattern. Among their standard features were a glove box lock, dual windshield wipers and two interior sun visors. The wheels of these cars were all painted Black. Only the center grille portion was chromed on Deluxe models. Initially, Deluxe Fords were available only with Ford's improved 90-hp V-8 Among its design features were four main bearings, a vibration damper, forged connecting rods, molybdenum-chrome alloy steel valve seat inserts and solid valve lifters. The six-cylinder engine was announced in June and its availability required new hood trim. Prior to the six's introduction the hood molding was a plain trim piece with horizontal liner. With the availability of two engines it now carried either a "6" or a "V-8" logo against the blue background.

Ford — Super Deluxe — Series 1GA/11A — Six and V-8: Super Deluxe Fords were easily identified by the bright trim on the edges of their running boards and their chrome grille sections. Super Deluxe bumpers had ridges along their bottom edge. A March 1941 revision added bright trim to the front and rear fenders, the windshield, the side windows and the rear window. A Super Deluxe script was placed in an inboard position on the left front fender. Bright rear taillight surrounds were installed on Super Deluxe models. In addition, standard features of the Super Deluxe models included a trunk light, a glove box-mounted clock, bright wheel trim rings, twin interior sun visors, dual wipers, a unique license plate guard and plastic Kelobra-grain dashboard trim. The Super Deluxe wheels had either Vermillion or Silver Gray striping. Seven body styles were offered in Super Deluxe form. Initially, all Super Deluxes came with a V-8 engine, but the six-cylinder engine was available after June of 1941.

VIN:

Serial numbers were located on the left frame member, directly behind the front engine mount. Starting: (six-cylinder) IGA-1, (V-8) 18-5986295. Ending: (six-cylinder): IGA-34800, (V-8) 18-6769035. Prefix "C" indicates Canadian built. Engine numbers were located on the top of the clutch housing. Starting: (six-cylinder) IGA-1, (V-8) 18-5986295. Ending: (six-cylinder) IGA-34800, (V-8) 18-6769035.

1941 Ford Six Model 1GA Special Coupe (OCW)

1941 Ford Six Model 1GA Deluxe Tudor Sedan (OCW)

Ford Special Model 1GA (Six)

Model No.	Body/ Style No.	Body Type & Seating	Factory Price	Shipping Weight	Production Total
1GA	---	2-dr. Coupe-2P	$ 684	2,870 lbs.	---
1GA	---	2-dr. Sedan-5P	$ 720	2,975 lbs.	---
1GA	---	4-dr. Sedan-5P	$ 761	3,020 lbs.	---

Ford Deluxe Model 1GA (Six)

1GA	---	2-dr. Five-Window Coupe-2P	$ 715	2,947 lbs.	---
1GA	---	2-dr. Auxiliary Seat Coupe-2/4P	$ 746	2,970 lbs.	---
1GA	---	2-dr. Sedan-5P	$ 756	3,065 lbs.	---
1GA	---	4-dr. Sedan-5P	$ 797	3,100 lbs.	---
1GA	---	4-dr. Station Wagon-5P	$ 946	3,305 lbs.	---

Ford Super Deluxe Model 1GA (Six)

1GA	---	2-dr. Five-Window Coupe-2P	$ 722	2,791 lbs.	---
1GA	---	2-dr. Auxiliary Seat Coupe-2/4P	$ 742	2,831 lbs.	---
1GA	---	2-dr. Sedan Coupe-5P	$ 742	2,831 lbs.	---
1GA	---	2-dr. Convertible-5P	$ 849	2,956 lbs.	---
1GA	---	2-dr. Sedan-5P	$ 765	2,927 lbs.	---
1GA	---	4-dr. Sedan-5P	$ 747	2,936 lbs.	---
1GA	---	4-dr. Station Wagon-5P	$ 810	2,966 lbs.	---

Ford Special Model 11A (V-8)

11A	---	2-dr. Coupe-2P	$ 706	2,878 lbs.	9,823
11A	---	2-dr. Sedan-5P	$ 735	2,983 lbs.	27,189
11A	---	4-dr. Sedan-5P	$ 775	3,033 lbs.	3,838

Ford Deluxe Model 11A (V-8)

11A	---	2-dr. Five-Window Coupe-2P	$ 730	2,953 lbs.	33,598
11A	---	2-dr. Auxiliary Seat Coupe-2/4P	$ 750	2,981 lbs.	12,844
11A	---	2-dr. Sedan-5P	$ 775	3,095 lbs.	177,018
11A	---	4-dr. Sedan-5P	$ 815	3,121 lbs.	25,928
11A	---	4-dr. Station Wagon-5P	$ 965	3,412 lbs.	6,116

Ford Super Deluxe Model 11A (V-8)

11A	---	2-dr. Five-Window Coupe-2P	$ 775	2,969 lbs.	22,878
11A	---	2-dr. Auxiliary Seat Coupe-2/4P	$ 800	3,001 lbs.	10,796
11A	---	2-dr. Sedan Coupe-5P	$ 850	3,052 lbs.	45,977
11A	---	2-dr. Convertible-5P	$ 950	3,187 lbs.	30,240
11A	---	2-dr. Sedan-5P	$ 820	3,110 lbs.	185,788
11A	---	4-dr. Sedan-5P	$ 860	3,146 lbs.	88,053
11A	---	4-dr. Station Wagon-5P	$1,015	3,419 lbs.	9,845

Note: Production totals are combined six-cylinder/V-8 production for series and body style.

Engine:

Ford Six: L-head. Cast-iron block. B & S: 3-3/10 x 4-2/5 in. Displacement: 225.8 cid. Compression ratio: 6.7:1. Brake hp: 90 at 3300 rpm. Taxable hp: 30. Torque: 180 lbs.-ft. at 2000 rpm. Main bearings: four. Valve lifters: mechanical. Carburetor: Ford 1GA-9510A one-barrel.

Ford V-8: 90-degree V. Cast-iron block. B & S: 3-1/16 x 3-3/4 in. Displacement: 221 cid. Compression ratio: 6.15:1. Brake hp: 90 at 3800 rpm Taxable hp: 30. Torque: 156 lbs.-ft. at 2200 rpm. Main bearings: three. Valve lifters: mechanical. Carburetor: Ford 21A-9510A two-barrel downdraft.

Chassis:

All: Wheelbase: 114 in. Overall length: 194.3 in. Height: 68.15 in. Front tread: 55-3/4 in. Rear tread: 58-1/4 in. Tires: 6.00 x 16.

1941 Ford Six Model 1GA Deluxe Station Wagon (OCW)

Technical:

Sliding gear transmission. Speeds: 3F/1R. Floor shift controls. Single dry plate, molded asbestos lining clutch. Shaft drive. Three-quarter floating rear axle. Overall ratio: 3.78:1. Hydraulic brakes on four wheels. Pressed steel, drop center rim wheels. Wheel size: 16 in.

Options:

Fender skirts ($12.50). Radio. Hot air heater ($23). Hot water heater ($20). Clock. Seat covers. Side view mirror. Passenger side mirror. Spotlight. Locking gas cap. Glove compartment lock. Defroster. Vanity mirror. Radio foot control. Wheel trim rings. Deluxe hubcaps. White sidewall tires. Front center bumper guards - front ($3.50). Front center bumper guards - rear ($2.50). Gravel deflector ($1.50).

1941 Ford V-8 Model 11A Deluxe five-window Coupe (OCW)

1941 Ford Six Model 1GA Super Deluxe Convertible (OCW)

1941 Ford V-8 Model 11A Deluxe Tudor Sedan (OCW)

1941 Ford Six Model 1GA Super Deluxe Tudor Sedan (OCW)

1941 Ford V-8 Model 11A Super Deluxe five-window Coupe (AA)

1941 Ford Six Model 1GA Super Deluxe Fordor Sedan (OCW)

1941 Ford V-8 Model 11A Super Deluxe Convertible (OCW)

1941 Ford V-8 Model 11A Special Coupe (OCW)

1941 Ford V-8 Model 11A Super Deluxe Tudor Sedan (OCW)

Introduced September 1941. Calendar-year sales: 602,013 (registrations). Calendar-year production: 600,814. The president of Ford was Edsel Ford. On April 29, 1941, the 29-millionth Ford was constructed.

1941 Ford V-8 Model 11A Super Deluxe Fordor Sedan (OCW)

1941 Ford V-8 Model 11A Super Deluxe Station Wagon (OCW)

1941 Ford V-8 Airport Limousine (OCW)

1942 Ford

Ford — Special Economy Six — Series 2GA — Six: The 1942 Fords were redesigned with fully-concealed running boards plus new front fenders and hood sheet metal. The headlights were flush with the fronts of the fenders and horizontal parking lights were located in the sheet metal above the grille. A new grille design featured a narrow center section in conjunction with side grilles considerably larger and more squared off than previous ones. There were three Special Economy 6 models: a single-cushion Coupe, a Tudor sedan and a Fordor sedan. These cars were offered only with Black finish. This year the lowest-priced Fords also came only with six-cylinder engines. They lacked bumper guards. Black wheel covers were standard and like those on all 1942 models, carried blue Ford script. Common to all 1942 Fords was a revised frame design that was lower by one inch than the 1941 version. All Fords also had lower and wider leaf springs, a two-inch wider tread and dual lateral stabilizer bars. The transition to a wartime economy brought many material substitutes in the 1942 models. Among the more obvious was the use of plastic interior components and the replacement of nickel by molybdenum in valves, gears and shafts. The final 1942 model Fords were produced on February 10, 1942. The new Ford looked larger and more massive. Riding comfort was improved slightly due to the use of longer springs. Larger brake pistons split the braking power 60-40 front and rear, instead of the previous 55-45. The redesigned frame was more rigid. New rubber rear engine mounts were adopted.

Ford — Deluxe — Series 2GA/21A — Six and V-8: The 1942 Ford Deluxe models were equipped with the bumpers used on the 1941 Super Deluxe models. The grille frame was painted in body color.

1942 Ford Six Model 2GA Super Deluxe Tudor Sedan (OCW)

Unique to the Deluxe Ford was its center grille panel with "Deluxe" spelled out vertically, in bright letters, against a blue background. The wheel covers were painted to match body color. The Deluxe instrument panel was finished in Crackle Mahogany grain.

Ford — Super Deluxe — Series 2GA/21A — Six and V-8: The Super Deluxe grille had its bright work accentuated by blue-painted grooves. Used only on these top-of-the-line Fords were front and rear bumpers with ridges along their upper surface. A Super Deluxe script was now positioned just below the left headlight. The taillights on all models were now horizontally positioned, but only those on the Super Deluxe had bright trim plates. Also unique to Super Deluxe Fords was bright trim surrounds for the windshield, rear window and side windows. The wheel covers were painted to match body color and carried three stripes. Wheel trim rings were standard equipment. Interior features included an electric clock, a left-hand front door armrest, a steering wheel with a full-circle horn ring and crank-operated front vent windows. The instrument panel was finished in Sequoia grain. Assist cords were installed on Sedan and Sedan Coupe models.

Serial numbers were located on the left frame member directly behind the front engine mount. Starting: (six-cylinder) IGA-34801, V-8 18-6769036. Ending: (six-cylinder) IGA-227,523, V-8 18-6925878. Prefix "C" indicates Canadian built. Engine numbers were located on top of clutch housing. Starting: (six-cylinder) IGA-34801, V-8 18-6769036. Ending: (six-cylinder) — IGA-227523, V-8 — 18-6925898.

Ford Special Model 1GA (Six)

Model No.	Body/ Style No.	Body Type and Seating	Factory Price	Shipping Weight	Production Total
2GA	77C	2-dr. Coupe-3P	$ 780	2,910 lbs.	1,606
2GA	70C	2-dr. Sedan-6P	$ 815	3,053 lbs.	3,187
2GA	73C	4-dr. Sedan-6P	$ 850	3,093 lbs.	27,189

1942 Ford Six Model 2GA Super Deluxe Station Wagon (OCW)

Ford Deluxe Model 2GA (Six)

2GA	77A	2-dr. Five-Window Coupe-3P	$ 805	2,958 lbs.	-----
2GA	72A	2-dr. Sedan Coupe-6P	$ 865	3,045 lbs.	-----
2GA	70A	2-dr. Sedan-6P	$ 840	3,122 lbs.	-----
2GA	73A	4-dr. Sedan-6P	$ 875	3,141 lbs.	-----
2GA	79A	4-dr. Station Wagon-8P	$1,035	3,400 lbs.	-----

Ford Super Deluxe Model 2GA (Six)

2GA	77B	2-dr. Five-Window Coupe-3P	$ 850	3,030 lbs.	-----
2GA	72B	2-dr. Sedan Coupe-6P	$ 910	3,109 lbs.	-----
2GA	76	2-dr. Convertible-5P	$1,080	3,218 lbs.	-----
2GA	70B	2-dr. Sedan-6P	$ 885	3,136 lbs.	-----
2GA	73B	4-dr. Sedan-6P	$ 920	3,179 lbs.	-----
2GA	79B	4-dr. Station Wagon-8P	$1,115	3,453 lbs.	-----

Ford Deluxe Model 2GA (V-8)

21A	77A	2-dr. Five-Window Coupe-3P	$ 815	2,978 lbs.	5,936
21A	72A	2-dr. Sedan Coupe-6P	$ 875	3,065 lbs.	5,419
21A	70A	2-dr. Sedan-6P	$ 850	3,141 lbs.	27,302
21A	73A	4-dr. Sedan-6P	$ 885	3,161 lbs.	5,127
21A	79A	4-dr. Station Wagon-8P	$1,090	3,460 lbs.	567

Ford Super Deluxe Model 21A (V-8)

21A	77B	2-dr. Five-Window Coupe-3P	$ 860	3,050 lbs.	5,411
21A	72B	2-dr. Sedan Coupe-6P	$ 920	3,120 lbs.	13,543
21A	76	2-dr. Convertible-5P	$1,090	3,238 lbs.	2,920
21A	70B	2-dr. Sedan-6P	$ 895	3,159 lbs.	37,199
21A	73B	4-dr. Sedan-6P	$ 930	3,200 lbs.	24,846
21A	79B	4-dr. Station Wagon-8P	$1,125	3,468 lbs.	5,483

Engines:

Ford Six: L-head. Cast-iron block. B & S: 3-3/10 x 4-2/5 in. Displacement: 225.8 cid. Compression ratio: 6.7:1. Brake hp: 90 at 3300 rpm. Taxable hp: 30. Torque: 180 lbs.-ft. at 2000 rpm. Main bearings: four. Valve lifters: mechanical. Carburetor: Ford 1GA-9510A one-barrel.

Ford V-8: 90-degree V. Cast-iron block. B & S: 3-1/16 x 3-3/4 in. Displacement: 221 cid. Compression ratio: 6.2:1. Brake hp: 96 at 3800 rpm Taxable hp: 30. Torque: 156 lbs.-ft. at 2200 rpm. Main bearings: three. Valve lifters: mechanical. Carburetor: Ford 21A-9510A two-barrel downdraft.

Chassis:

All: Wheelbase: 114 in. Overall length: 194.4 in. Height: 68.15 in. Front Tread: 58 in. Rear Tread: 60 in. Tires: 6.00 x 16.

Technical:

Sliding gear transmission. Speeds: 3F/1R. Floor shift controls. Single dry plate, molded asbestos lining clutch. Shaft drive. Three-quarter floating rear axle. Overall ratio: 3.78:1. Hydraulic brakes on four wheels. Pressed steel, drop center rim wheels. Wheel size: 16 in.

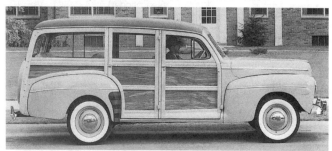

1942 Ford V-8 Model 21A Deluxe Station Wagon (OCW)

1942 Ford V-8 Model 21A Super Deluxe five-window Coupe (PH)

Options:

Fender skirts. Center bumper guards. Radio ($39). Hot air heater ($23). Hot water heater ($20). Clock. Side view mirror. Passenger side mirror. Sport light. Locking gas cap. Fog lights. Seat covers. Defroster. Visor-vanity mirror. Radio foot control. Wheel trim rings. White sidewall tires ($15). Bumper end guards ($2.75 a pair). Oil filter ($6.14). License plate frames.

History:

Introduced September 12, 1941. Calendar-year production 43,407. Model-year production: 160,211. The president of Ford Motor Co. was Edsel Ford.

1942 Ford V-8 Model 21A Super Deluxe Sedan Coupe (OCW)

1942 Ford V-8 Model 21A Super Deluxe Tudor Sedan (OCW)

1942 Ford V-8 Model 21A Super Deluxe Fordor Sedan (OCW)

1946 Ford

Ford — Deluxe — Series 6GA/69A — Six and V-8: All 1946 Fords were, in essence, restyled 1942 models utilizing the same drive train as the prewar models. The grille was restyled with horizontal bars on the outside of the rectangular opening, instead of the flush-mounted grille of the 1942 model. The remainder of the body was virtually the same as the prewar model. The Deluxe series was the base trim level for 1946 and included rubber moldings around all window openings, a horn button instead of a ring, one sun visor and armrests only on the driver's door.

Ford — Super Deluxe — Series 6GA/69A — Six and V-8: The Super Deluxe series was the top trim level for 1946 and included chrome moldings around all windows, a horn ring, two sun visors, armrests on all doors, passenger assist straps on the interior "B" pillars for easier rear seat egress, horizontal chrome trim on the body and leather interior on the convertible models.

1946 Ford Six Model 6GA Deluxe Tudor Sedan (OCW)

1946 Ford Six Model 6GA Super Deluxe Sedan Coupe (OCW)

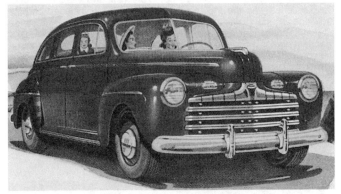

1946 Ford Six Model 6GA Deluxe Fordor Sedan (OCW)

1946 Ford Six Model 6GA Super Deluxe Tudor Sedan (OCW)

Deluxe six-cylinder models began with the designation, "6GA," with production numbers beginning at 1GA-227524 and going to 1GA-326417. Deluxe V-8-powered models began with the designation, "69A", with production numbers beginning at 99A-650280 and going to 99A-1412707. Super Deluxe six-cylinder models began with the same "6GA" designation and used the same production numbers as the Deluxe models. Super Deluxe V-8 models began with the same "69A" designation and used the same production numbers as the Deluxe models.

Ford — Deluxe — Series 6GA (Six)

Model No.	Body/ Style No.	Body Type & Seating	Factory Price	Shipping Weight	Production Total
6GA	77A	2-dr. Coupe-3P	$1,074	3,007 lbs.	------
6GA	70A	2-dr. Sedan-6P	$1,136	3,157 lbs.	-----
6GA	73A	4-dr. Sedan-6P	$1,198	3,167 lbs.	------

Ford —Deluxe — Series 69A (V-8)

6GA	77A	2-dr. Coupe-3P	$1,123	3,040 lbs.	10,760
6GA	70A	2-dr. Sedan-6P	$1,165	3,190 lbs.	74,954
6GA	73A	4-dr. Sedan-6P	$1,248	3,220 lbs.	9,246

Ford — Super Deluxe — Series 6GA (Six)

6GA	77B	2-dr. Coupe-3P	$1,148	3,007 lbs.	------
6GA	72B	2-dr. Sedan Coupe-6P	$1,257	3,107 lbs.	------
6GA	70B	2-dr. Sedan-6P	$1,211	3,157 lbs.	------
6GA	73B	4-dr. Sedan-6P	$1,273	3,207 lbs.	------
6GA	79B	4-dr. Station Wagon-8P	$1,504	3,457 lbs.	------

Ford — Super Deluxe — Series 6GA (V-8)

6GA	77B	2-dr. Coupe-3P	$1,197	3,040 lbs.	12,249
6GA	72B	2-dr. Sedan Coupe-6P	$1,307	3,140 lbs.	70,826
6GA	76	2-dr. Convertible-6P	$1,488	3,240 lbs.	16,359
6GA	71	2-dr. Sportsman-6P	$1,982	3,340 lbs.	723
6GA	70B	2-dr. Sedan-6P	$1,260	3,190 lbs.	163,370
6GA	73B	4-dr. Sedan-6P	$1,322	3,240 lbs.	92,056
6GA	79B	4-dr. Station Wagon-8P	$1,553	3,490 lbs.	16,960

Note 1: Production totals are combined six-cylinder and V-8 production for series and body style.

Ford Six: L-head. Cast-iron block. B & S: 3-3/10 x 4-2/5 in. Displacement: 225.8 cid. Compression ratio: 6.8:1. Brake hp: 90 at 3300 rpm. Taxable hp: 30. Torque: 180 lbs.-ft. at 2000 rpm. Main bearings: four. Valve lifters: mechanical. Carburetor: Holley single-barrel Model 847F.

1946 Ford Six Model 6GA Super Deluxe Fordor Sedan (OCW)

1946 Ford Six Model 6GA Super Deluxe Station Wagon (OCW)

1946 Ford V-8 Model 69A Super Deluxe Convertible (OCW)

1946 Ford V-8 Model 69A Super Deluxe Sportsman Convertible (OCW)

1946 Ford V-8 Model 69A Super Deluxe Tudor Sedan (OCW)

1946 Ford V-8 Model 69A Super Deluxe Fordor Sedan (OCW)

1946 Ford V-8 Model 69A Super Deluxe Station Wagon (OCW)

Ford V-8: L-head. Cast-iron block. B & S: 3.19 x 3.75 in. Displacement: 239 cid. Compression ratio: 6.75:1. Brake hp: 100 at 3800 rpm. Torque: 180 at 2000 rpm. Taxable hp: 32.5. Three main bearings. Solid valve lifters. Crankcase capacity: 5 qt. (add 1 qt. with new oil filter). Cooling system capacity: 22 qt. Carburetor: Holley (Chandler-Groves) Ford No. 59A-9510-A two-barrel downdraft.

Chassis:

Wheelbase: 114 inches. Overall length: 196.2 inches. Tires: 6.00 x 16.

Technical:

Sliding gear transmission. Speeds: 3F/1R. Floor shift controls. Single dry plate, molded asbestos lining clutch. Shaft drive. Three-quarter floating rear axle. Hydraulic brakes on four wheels. Pressed steel, drop center rim wheels. Wheel size: 16 in.

Options:

Fender skirts. Center bumper guards. Radio. Hot air heater. Hot water heater. Clock. Side view mirror. Passenger side mirror. Sport light. Locking gas cap. Fog lights. Seat covers. Defroster. Visor-vanity mirror. Radio foot control. Wheel trim rings. White sidewall tires. Bumper end guards. Oil filter. License plate frames.

The "new" postwar Fords were introduced in dealer showrooms on Oct. 22, 1945.

1947 Ford

Ford — Deluxe — Series 7GA/79A (Six and V-8): The 1947 Fords were slightly changed from the previous year. For example, the red tracer paint on the grille was dropped, a hood-mounted emblem was seen up front and relocated circular parking lights looked attractive. The Deluxe series was the base trim level and included rubber moldings around all window openings, a horn button instead of a ring, one sun visor and armrests only on the driver's door.

Ford — Super Deluxe — Series 7GA/79A (Six and V-8): The Super Deluxe series was the top trim level for 1947 and included chrome moldings around all windows, a horn ring, two sun visors, armrests on all doors, passenger assist straps on the interior "B" pillars for easier rear seat egress, horizontal chrome trim on body and leather interior on the convertible models.

VIN:

Began with the designation "7GA." Production numbers were 71GA-326418 to 71GA-414366, also (beginning 10/3/47) 77HA-0512 to 77HA-9038. Deluxe V-8 models began with the designation, "79A," with the production numbers beginning at 799A-1412708 and going to 799A-2071231. Super Deluxe V-8 models began with the same "79A" designation and used the same production numbers as the Deluxe models.

Ford — Deluxe — Series 7GA (Six)

Model No.	Body/Style No.	Body Type & Seating	Factory Price	Shipping Weight	Factory Price
7GA	77A	2-dr. Coupe-3P	$1,154	3,033 lbs.	-------
7GA	70A	2-dr. Sedan-6P	$1,212	3,183 lbs.	-------
7GA	73A	4-dr. Sedan-6P	$1,270	3,213 lbs.	-------

Ford — Deluxe — Series 79A (V-8)

Model No.	Body/Style No.	Body Type & Seating	Factory Price	Shipping Weight	Factory Price
79A	77A	2-dr. Coupe-3P	$1,230	3,066 lbs.	10,872
79A	70A	2-dr. Sedan-6P	$1,268	3,216 lbs.	44,523
79A	73A	4-dr. Sedan-6P	$1,346	3,246 lbs.	44,563

Ford — Super Deluxe — Series 7GA (Six)

Model No.	Body/Style No.	Body Type & Seating	Factory Price	Shipping Weight	Factory Price
7GA	77B	2-dr. Coupe-3P	$1,251	3,033 lbs.	-----
7GA	72B	2-dr. Sedan Coupe-6P	$1,330	3,133 lbs.	-----
7GA	70B	2-dr. Sedan-6P	$1,309	3,183 lbs.	-----
7GA	73B	4-dr. Sedan-6P	$1,372	3,233 lbs.	-----
7GA	79B	4-dr. Station Wagon-8P	$1,893	3,487 lbs.	-----

Ford — Super Deluxe — Series 7GA (V-8)

Model No.	Body/Style No.	Body Type & Seating	Factory Price	Shipping Weight	Factory Price
7GA	77B	2-dr. Coupe-3P	$1,330	3,066 lbs.	10,872
7GA	72B	2-dr. Sedan Coupe-6P	$1,409	3,166 lbs.	80,830
7GA	76	2-dr. Convertible-6P	$1,740	3,266 lbs.	22,159
7GA	71	2-dr. Sportsman-6P	$2,282	3,366 lbs.	2,274
7GA	70B	2-dr. Sedan-6P	$1,382	3,216 lbs.	132,126
7GA	73B	4-dr. Sedan-6P	$1,440	3,266 lbs.	116,744
7GA	79B	4-dr. Station Wagon-8P	$1,972	3,520 lbs.	16,104

Note 1: Production totals are combined six-cylinder/V-8 production for series and body style.

1947 Ford Six Model 7GA Super Deluxe Tudor Sedan (OCW)

1947 Ford Six Model 7GA Deluxe Coupe (PH)

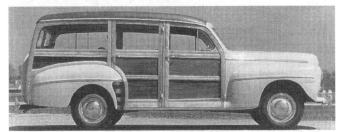

1947 Ford Six Model 7GA Super Deluxe Station Wagon (OCW)

1947 Ford V-8 Model 79A Super Deluxe Sportsman Convertible (OCW)

1947 Ford V-8 Model 79A Super Deluxe Convertible (OCW)

Engines:

Ford Six: L-head. Cast-iron block. B & S: 3-3/10 x 4-2/5 in. Displacement: 225.8 cid. Compression ratio: 6.8:1. Brake hp: 90 at 3300 rpm. Taxable hp: 30. Torque: 180 lbs.-ft. at 2000 rpm. Main bearings: four. Valve lifters: mechanical. Carburetor: Holley single-barrel Model 847F.

Ford V-8: L-head. Cast-iron block. B & S: 3.19 x 3.75 in. Displacement: 239 cid. Compression ratio: 6.75:1. Brake hp: 100 at 3800 rpm. Torque: 180 lbs.-ft. at 2000 rpm. Taxable hp: 32.5. Three main bearings. Solid valve lifters. Crankcase capacity: 5 qt. (add 1 qt. with new oil filter). Cooling system capacity: 22 qt. Carburetor: Holley two-barrel Model 94. Three main bearings.

Chassis:

Wheelbase: 114 in. Overall length: 198.2 in. Tires: 6.00 x 16.

Technical:

Sliding gear transmission. Speeds: 3F/1R. Floor shift controls. Single dry plate, molded asbestos lining clutch. Shaft drive. Three-quarter floating rear axle. Hydraulic brakes on four wheels. Pressed steel, drop center rim wheels. Wheel size: 16 in.

Options:

Fender skirts. Center bumper guards. Radio. Hot air heater. Hot water heater. Clock. Side view mirror. Passenger side mirror. Sport light. Locking gas cap. Fog lights. Seat covers. Defroster. Visor-vanity mirror. Radio foot control. Wheel trim rings. White sidewall tires. Bumper end guards. Oil filter. License plate frames.

History:

The man who put America on wheels, Henry Ford, founder of Ford Motor Co., died at the age of 83 on April 7, 1947.

1948 Ford

Ford — Deluxe — Series 87HA/89A (Six and V-8): The 1948 Fords continued to share the 1946 and 1947 bodies with only slight trim changes. The Deluxe series was the base trim level for 1948 and included rubber moldings around window openings, a horn button instead of horn ring, one sun visor and one armrest only on the driver's door.

Ford — Super Deluxe — Series 87HA/89A (Six and V-8): The Super Deluxe series was the top trim level for 1948 and included chrome moldings around the windows, horn ring, two sun visors, armrests on all doors, passenger assist straps on the interior "B" pillar for easier rear seat egress, horizontal chrome trim on the body and leather interior on the convertible models.

VIN:

Deluxe six-cylinder models began with the designation, "87HA," with production numbers beginning at 87HA-0536 and going to 87HA-73901. Super Deluxe V-8-powered models began with the same "89A" designation and used the same production numbers as the Deluxe models.

Ford — Deluxe — Series 87HA (Six)

Model No.	Body/ Style No.	Body Type & Seating	Factory Price	Shipping Weight	Production Total
87HA	77A	2-dr. Coupe-3P	$1,154	3,033 lbs.	------
87HA	70A	2 dr. Sedan-6P	$1,212	3,183 lbs.	------
87HA	73A	4-dr. Sedan-6P	$1,270	3,213 lbs.	------

Ford — Deluxe — Series 89A (V-8)

89A	77A	2-dr. Coupe-3P	$1,230	3,066 lbs.	5,048
89A	70A	2 dr. Sedan-6P	$1,268	3,216 lbs.	23,356
89A	73A	4-dr. Sedan-6P	$1,346	3,246 lbs.	------

Ford — Super Deluxe — Series 87HA (Six)

87HA	77B	2-dr. Coupe-3P	$1,251	3,033 lbs.	------
87HA	72B	2-dr. Sedan Coupe-6P	$1,330	3,133 lbs.	------
87HA	70B	2 dr. Sedan-6P	$1,309	3,183 lbs.	------
87HA	73B	4-dr. Sedan-6P	$1,372	3,233 lbs.	------
87HA	79B	4-dr. Station Wagon-8P	$1,893	3,487 lbs.	------

Ford — Super Deluxe — Series 89A (V-8):

89A	77B	2-dr. Coupe-3P	$1,330	3,066 lbs.	------
89A	72B	2-dr. Sedan Coupe-6P	$1,409	3,166 lbs.	44,828
89A	76	2-dr. Convertible-6P	$1,740	3,266 lbs.	12,033
89A	71	2-dr. Sportsman-6P	$2,282	3,366 lbs.	28
89A	70B	2 dr. Sedan-6P	$1,382	3,316 lbs.	82,161
89A	73B	4-dr. Sedan-6P	$1,440	3,266 lbs.	71,358
89A	79B	4-dr. Station Wagon-8P	$1,972	3,520 lbs.	8,912

Note 1: Production totals are combined six and V-8 production for the series and body style.

1948 Ford Six Model 87HA Super Deluxe Coupe (OCW)

Engines:

Ford Six: L-head. Cast-iron block. B & S: 3-3/10 x 4-2/5 in. Displacement: 225.8 cid. Compression ratio: 6.8:1. Brake hp: 95 at 3300 rpm. Taxable hp: 30. Torque: 180 lbs.-ft. at 2000 rpm. Main bearings: four. Valve lifters: mechanical. Carburetor: Holley single-barrel Model 847F.

V-8: L-head. Cast-iron block. B & S: 3.19 x 3.75 in. Displacement: 239 cid. Compression ratio: 6.75:1. Brake hp: 100 at 3800 rpm. Torque: 180 at 2000 rpm. Taxable hp: 32.5. Three main bearings. Solid valve lifters. Crankcase capacity: 5 qt. (add 1 qt. with new oil filter). Cooling system capacity: 22 qt. Carburetor: Holley two-barrel Model 94. Three main bearings.

Chassis:

Wheelbase: 114 in. Overall length: 198.2 in. Tires: 6.00 x 16.

Technical:

Sliding gear transmission. Speeds: 3F/1R. Floor shift controls. Single dry plate, molded asbestos lining clutch. Shaft drive. Three-quarter floating rear axle. Hydraulic brakes on four wheels. Pressed steel, drop center rim wheels. Wheel size: 16 in.

Options:

Fender skirts. Center bumper guards. Radio. Hot air heater. Hot water heater. Clock. Side view mirror. Passenger side mirror. Sport light. Locking gas cap. Fog lights. Seat covers. Defroster. Visor-vanity mirror. Radio foot control. Wheel trim rings. White sidewall tires. Bumper end guards. Oil filter. License plate frames.

History:

The actual production run of 1948 Fords, basically retitled 1947 models, ended early, in mid-spring, so retooling could take place for the all-new 1949 Fords. The 1949 Fords were also introduced early, in June 1948.

1948 Ford V-8 Model 89A Super Deluxe Convertible (OCW)

1948 Ford V-8 Model 89A Super Deluxe Sportsman Convertible (OCW)

1948 Ford Six Model 87HA Deluxe Fordor Sedan (OCW)

1948 Ford V-8 Model 89A Super Deluxe Fordor Sedan (AA)

1948 Ford V-8 Model 89A Deluxe Station Wagon (OCW)

1948 Ford V-8 Model 89A Super Deluxe Tudor Sedan (OCW)

1948 Ford V-8 Model 89A Deluxe Fordor Sedan (OCW)

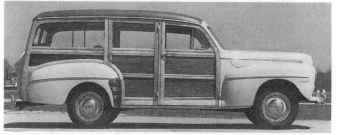

1948 Ford V-8 Model 89A Super Deluxe Station Wagon (OCW)

1949 Ford

Ford — Series 98HA / Series 98BA (Six and V-8): The 1949 model represented the first totally new automobile produced by Ford since 1941. The chassis was of the wishbone type, with longitudinal rear springs replacing the transverse springs used on earlier models. Styling featured a heavy chrome molding curving from the top of the grille down to the gravel deflector, with "FORD" in large block letters mounted above the grille molding. There was a horizontal chrome bar in the center of the grille, extending the full width of the opening, with parking lamps mounted on the ends of the bar. In the center of the bar was a large spinner with either a "6" or "8" designation indicating the type of engine. The body was slab-sided, eliminating the rear fender bulge altogether. A chrome strip near the bottom of the body extended from the front fender openings back to the gas cap. Models for 1949 included the base Ford series and the top line Custom series. The Ford series was the base trim level for 1949 and featured rubber window moldings, a horn button instead of horn ring, one sun visor and an armrest only on the driver's door.

Custom — Series 98A / Series 98BA (Six and V-8): The Custom series was the top trim level for 1949 and included chrome window moldings, a horn ring, two sun visors, passenger assist straps on the interior B pillars for easier rear seat egress and horizontal chrome trim along the lower half of the body.

VIN:

The vehicle identification number was stamped on a plate attached to the front face of the cowl. It was also on the right frame side rail just to the rear of the upper front suspension arm. Ford six-cylinder models began with the designation, "98HA," with production numbers beginning at 98HA-101 and going to 98HA-173310. Custom six-cylinder models began with the same "98HA" designation and used the same production numbers as the Ford series. Ford V-8 models began with the designation, "98BA," with production numbers beginning at 98BA-101 and going to 98BA-948236. Custom V-8 models began with the same "98HA" designation and used the same production numbers as the Ford series.

Ford (Six)

Model No.	Body/ Style No.	Body Type & Seating	Factory Price	Shipping Weight	Production Total
98HA	73A	4-dr. Sedan-6P	$1,472	2,990 lbs.	Note 1
98HA	70A	2-dr. Sedan-6P	$1,425	2,945 lbs.	Note 1
98HA	72A	2-dr. Club Coupe-6P	$1,415	2,925 lbs.	Note 1
98HA	72C	2-dr. Business Coupe-3P	$1,333	2,871 lbs.	Note 1

Ford (V-8)

Model No.	Body/ Style No.	Body Type & Seating	Factory Price	Shipping Weight	Production Total
98HA	73A	4-dr. Sedan-6P	$1,546	3,030 lbs.	44,563
98HA	70A	2-dr. Sedan-6P	$1,499	2,965 lbs.	126,770
98HA	72A	2-dr. Club Coupe-6P	$1,523	2,965 lbs.	4,170
98HA	72C	2-dr. Business Coupe-3P	$1,420	2,911 lbs.	28,946

Custom (Six)

Model No.	Body/ Style No.	Body Type & Seating	Factory Price	Shipping Weight	Production Total
98HA	73B	4-dr. Sedan-6P	$1,559	2,993 lbs.	Note 1
98HA	70B	2-dr. Sedan-6P	$1,511	2,948 lbs.	Note 1
98HA	72B	2-dr. Club Coupe-6P	$1,511	2,928 lbs.	Note 1
98HA	76	2-dr. Convertible-6P	$1,886	3,234 lbs.	Note 1
98HA	79	4-dr. Station Wagon-8P	$2,119	3,523 lbs.	Note 1

Custom (V-8)

Model No.	Body/ Style No.	Body Type & Seating	Factory Price	Shipping Weight	Production Total
98BA	73B	4-dr. Sedan-6P	$1,637	3,093 lbs.	248,176
98BA	70B	2-dr. Sedan-6P	$1,590	3,031 lbs.	433,315
98BA	72B	2-dr. Club Coupe-6P	$1,595	3,003 lbs.	150,254
98BA	76	2-dr. Convertible-6P	$1,948	3,263 lbs.	51,133
98BA	79	2-dr. Station Wagon-6P	$2,107	3,531 lbs.	31,412

Note 1: Production of six and V-8 models of each body style was a combined total.

Engines:

Ford Six: L-head. Cast-iron block. Displacement: 226 cid. B & S: 3.30 x 4.40 in. Compression ratio: 6.6:1. Brake hp: 95 at 3300 rpm. Carburetor: Holley one-barrel Model 847F5S. Four main bearings. Code H.

Custom Six: L-head. Cast-iron block. Displacement: 226 cid. B & S: 3.30 x 4.40 in. Compression ratio: 6.6:1. Brake hp: 95 at 3300 rpm. Carburetor: Holley one-barrel Model 847FS. Four main bearings. Code H.

Ford V-8: L-head. Cast-iron block. Displacement: 239 cid. B & S: 3.19 x 3.75 in. Compression ratio: 6.8:1. Brake hp: 100 at 3600 rpm. Carburetor: Holley two-barrel Model AA-1. Three main bearings. Code B.

Custom V-8: L-head. Cast-iron block. Displacement: 239 cid. B & S: 3.19 x 3.75 inches. Compression ratio: 6.8:1. Brake hp: 100 at 3600 rpm. Carburetor: Holley two-barrel Model AA-1. Three main bearings. Code B.

Chassis:

Ford: Wheelbase: 114 in. Overall length: 196.8 in., car and 208 in., station wagon. Overall width: 72.8 in. Tires: 6.00 x 16, standard, 7.10 x 15, station wagon and 6.70 x 15, optional.

Custom: Wheelbase: 114 in. Overall length: 196.8 in., car and 208 in., station wagon. Overall width: 72.8 in. Tires: 6.00 x 16, standard, 7.10 x 15, station wagon and 6.70 x 15, optional.

Technical:

Ford: The standard Ford transmission was a three-speed manual type with semi-centrifugal-type clutch; three-speed helical gear set and synchronizers for second and third gears. A three-speed manual gearbox with automatic overdrive was optional. The automatic overdrive function cut in at 27 mph and out at 21 mph. Approximate drive ratio was 0.70:1. Rear axle gear ratios with standard transmission: (passenger car) 3.73:1; (station wagon) 3.92:1. Rear axle gear ratio with automatic overdrive: (passenger car) 4.10:1; (station wagon) 4.27:1.

Custom: The standard Ford transmission was a three-speed manual type with semi-centrifugal-type clutch; three-speed helical gear set and synchronizers for second and third gears. A three-speed manual gearbox with automatic overdrive was optional. The automatic overdrive function cut in at 27 mph and out at 21 mph. Approximate drive ratio was 0.70:1. Rear axle gear ratios with standard transmission: (passenger car) 3.73:1; (station wagon) 3.92:1. Rear axle gear ratio with automatic overdrive: (passenger car) 4.10:1; (station wagon) 4.27:1.

Options:

White sidewall tires. Fender skirts. Turn signal indicators. Outside rearview mirror. Full wheel discs. Wheel trim rings.

History:

The 1949 Fords were introduced at the Waldorf-Astoria Hotel in New York City on June 10, 1948, beating General Motors and Chrysler to the punch in the garnering of new-model publicity. Ford also surpassed the million mark in production in 1949 with 1,118,740 units built in the calendar year.

1949 Ford four-door Police Sedan (OCW)

1949 Ford two-door Sedan (OCW)

1950 Ford Custom four-door Sedan (OCW)

1949 Ford Custom two-door Sedan (AA)

1949 Ford two-door Club Coupe (OCW)

1949 Ford Custom two-door Convertible (OCW)

1949 Ford Custom two-door Station Wagon (OCW)

1950 Ford

Deluxe — Series OHA / Series OBA (Six and V-8): That wonderful year 1950. At first glance, the 1950 Ford seemed identical to the 1949 model, but it was said to include "50 improvements for '50." Obvious changes were very modest. Once again a heavy chrome molding curved from the top of the "Air Foil" grille down to the gravel deflector. Instead of the Ford name, a shield-shaped badge now sat above the center of the grille. The horizontal center bar again extended the full width of the opening. In the center was a large spinner with either a "'6" or "8" designation. The center grille bar now wrapped around the body corners. Horizontally ribbed plates, which housed the rectangular parking lights, were now seen between that bar and the bumper. A chrome strip extended from behind the front wheel openings to just above and behind the rear wheel opening. The gas filler cap was now hidden behind a lift-up door on the upper left-hand rear fender. A new finned "knight's helmet" hood ornament was seen. Other changes a three-bladed cooling fan and push-button handles on exterior doors. When a fancy steering wheel was fitted, it included a flat-topped horn ring. The 1950 Fords had similar dimensions to 1949 models. Important selling features for 1950 Fords included an Equa-Flo cooling system, full-pressure engine lubrication, "Deep-Breath" intake manifolding, "Power-Dome" combustion chambers, the use of four-ring pistons, Equa-Poise

engine mountings, a Loadomatic ignition system, a Soft-Action clutch and Black-Light dashboard dials. Dual downdraft carburetion was featured on V-8 models. Ford also promoted Mid-Ship Ride, Lifeguard body construction, Hydra-Coil springs, Magic-Action brakes and Fender-Guard bumpers. Inside, Ford's offered more hip room and more shoulder room than any other car in their price class. The "Jewel Box" interior featured non-sagging front seat springs and special foam rubber seat cushions that were claimed to be more comfortable than ever before. The seats themselves were described as being "Sofa-Wide." Interior fabrics came in a choice of broadcloth or mohair. "You travel first class without extra fare in the Big Ford," said one advertisement. Another ad described this particular model as "A "personal" car with all Ford quality features! Mid Ship Ride! Lifeguard Body! 35% easier-acting King-Size Brakes! And a Deep Deck Locker that holds all the bags and baggage!" The Deluxe series was the base trim level for 1950 Fords and cars in this line had a black rubber windshield gasket, black rubber window moldings, a horn button instead of horn ring, one sun visor and an armrest on the driver's door only. There was no chrome trim around the side windows or windshield. A single chrome body strip without nameplate decorated the body sides. The Deluxe model lineup consisted of the Business Coupe and two- and four-door sedans. (Ford actually described the latter models as the "Tudor" and "Fordor" sedans). A choice of an in-line six-cylinder or flathead V-8 engine was offered.

Custom Deluxe — Series OHA / Series OBA (Six and V-8): The Custom Deluxe series was Ford's top trim level and the cars in this line included chrome window moldings, a chrome horn ring, twin sun visors, armrests on all doors and passenger assist straps on the interior "B" pillars (for easier rear seat egress). The word "Custom" was spelled out in capital letters on the spear-tip-shaped nameplates on the front fenders. Four body styles were offered in the Custom Deluxe six-cylinder lineup. These were the Club Coupe, the Tudor Sedan, the Fordor sedan and the wood-bodied station wagon, which took on the Country Squire name as a running change. Station wagons, required larger-than-usual 7.10 x 15 tires to support the heavier weight of their wood body. The "Country Squire" station wagons included a stowaway center seat, a

1950 Ford Deluxe two-door Sedan (OCW)

1950 Ford Deluxe two-door Business Coupe (OCW)

1950 Ford Deluxe two-door Business Coupe (OCW)

flat-deck loading platform and a rear seat that was easily removable without the use of tools. With the "Level-Loading" tailgate lowered, there was 38.8 square feet of flat deck to handle half a ton of freight with ease. Also available only with a V-8 engine was the Crestliner and the convertible. The 1950 Crestliner was a rare Ford. The Crestliner was released on Sunday, July 9, 1950 as Ford's answer to the popular General Motors hardtops. The distinctive new two-tone Sports Sedan had a black basket weave vinyl top and a striking "Airfoil" paint treatment. It came in Sportsman's Green with a black top and black airfoil side panels or in Coronation Red with a black top and side panels. Ford said the Crestliner's interior trim resembled that of European sports cars. The "Crestliner" name appeared in gold die-cast emblems on each front fender. Completely new full wheel disks with the circular depressions painted black were standard, as were fender skirts and twin side view mirrors. A protective and decorative molding of polished stainless steel extended along the bottom edge of the car. Inside the Crestliner had a two-tone instrument panel with special finish and trim treatments, a 4-spoke airplane type steering wheel and special upholstery and carpeting. The Custom Deluxe convertible was not as rare as the Crestliner. but had special top-down appeal. Said one Ford advertisement, "When the moon looks cool as sherbet, it doesn't take a share of Fort Knox to enjoy it . . . it merely takes a Ford convertible. For no car, yes, _no_ car, has a happier way with your heartstrings for so little money."

VIN:

The vehicle identification number was stamped on a plate attached to the front face of the cowl. It was also on the right frame side rail just to the rear of the upper front suspension arm. The first symbol indicated the engine: H=226-cid six-cylinder, B=239-cid V-8 and P=239-cid police V-8. The second symbol indicated the model year: 0=1950. The third and fourth symbols indicated the assembly plant: AT=Atlanta, Georgia, BF=Buffalo, N.Y., CS=Chester, Pennsylvania, CH=Chicago, Illinois, DL=Dallas, Texas, HM=Highland Park, Michigan, DA=Dearborn, Michigan, LU=Louisville, Kentucky, EG=Edgewater, N.J., KC=Kansas City, Kansas, LB=Long Beach, California, MP=Memphis, Tennessee, NR=Norfolk, Virginia, RH=Richmond, Virginia, SR=Somerville, Massachusetts and SP=Twin Cities, St. Paul, Minnesota. The last six symbols are the sequential production number starting at 100001 and up in each factory.

Deluxe (Six)

Model No.	Body/Style No.	Body Type & Seating	Factory Price	Shipping Weight	Production Total
OHA	D73	4-dr. Sedan-6P	$1,472	3,050 lbs.	Note 1
OHA	D70	2-dr. Sedan-6P	$1,424	2,988 lbs.	Note 1
OHA	D72C	2 dr. Business Coupe-3P	$1,333	2,933 lbs.	Note 1

Deluxe (V-8)

OBA	D73	4-dr. Sedan-6P	$1,545	3,078 lbs.	77,888
OBA	D70	2-dr. Sedan-6P	$1,498	3,026 lbs.	275,360
OBA	D72C	2 dr. Business Coupe-3P	$1,419	2,965 lbs.	35,120

Custom Deluxe (Six)

OHA	C73	4-dr. Sedan-6P	$1,558	3,062 lbs.	Note 1
OHA	C70	2-dr. Sedan-6P	$1,511	2,999 lbs.	Note 1
OHA	C72	2 dr. Club Coupe-6P	$1,511	2,959 lbs.	Note 1
OHA	C79	4-dr. Station Wagon-8P	$2,028	3,491 lbs.	Note 1

Custom Deluxe (V-8)

OBA	C73	4-dr. Sedan-6P	$1,637	3,093 lbs.	247,181
OBA	C70	2-dr. Sedan-6P	$1,590	3,031 lbs.	396,060
OBA	C70C	2-dr. Crestliner-6P	$1,711	3,050 lbs.	8,703
OBA	C72	2 dr. Club Coupe-6P	$1,595	3,003 lbs.	85,111
OBA	C76	2-dr. Convertible-6P	$1,948	3,263 lbs.	50,299
OHA	C79	2-dr. Station Wagon-6P	$2,107	3,531 lbs.	29,017

Note 1: Production of six-cylinder and V-8 models of each body style is a combined total.

Engines:

Custom Six: L-head. Cast-iron block. Displacement: 226 cid. B & S: 3.30 x 4.40 in. Compression ratio: 6.8:1. Brake hp: 95 at 3300 rpm. Carburetor: Holley one-barrel Model 847F5. Four main bearings. Code H.

Custom Deluxe Six: L-head. Cast-iron block. Displacement: 226 cid. B & S: 3.30 x 4.40 in. Compression ratio: 6.8:1. Brake hp: 95 at 3300 rpm. Carburetor: Holley one-barrel Model 847F5. Four main bearings. Code H.

Custom Eight: L-head V-8. Cast-iron block. Displacement: 239 cid. Bore and stroke: 3.19 x 3.75 in. Compression ratio: 6.8:1. Brake hp: 100 at 3600 rpm. Carburetor: Holley two-barrel Model AA-1. Three main bearings. Code B.

Custom Deluxe Eight: L-head V-8. Cast-iron block. Displacement: 239 cid. Bore and stroke: 3.19 x 3.75 in. Compression ratio: 6.8:1. Brake hp: 100 at 3600 rpm. Carburetor: Holley two-barrel Model AA-1. Three main bearings. Code B.

Chassis:

Custom: Wheelbase: 114 in. Overall length: 196.6 in., car and 206 in., station wagon. Overall width: 72.8 in. Tires: 6.00 x 16, standard, 7.10 x 15, station wagon and 6.70 x 15, optional.

Custom Deluxe: Wheelbase: 114 in. Overall length: 196.6 in., car and 206 in., station wagon. Overall width: 72.8 in. Tires: 6.00 x 16, standard, 7.10 x 15, station wagon and 6.70 x 15, optional.

Technical:

Custom: The standard Ford transmission was a three-speed manual type with semi-centrifugal-type clutch; three-speed helical gear set and synchronizers for second and third gears. A three-speed manual gearbox with automatic overdrive was optional. The rear axle gear ratios with standard transmission were: 3.73:1, car and 3.92:1, station

1950 Ford Custom Deluxe Crestliner two-door Sedan (PH)

1950 Ford Custom Deluxe two-door Sedan (OCW)

1950 Ford Custom Deluxe Crestliner two-door Sedan (OCW)

wagon. The rear axle gear ratio with automatic overdrive was: 4.10:1, car and 4.17:1, station wagon.

Custom Deluxe: The standard Ford transmission was a three-speed manual type with semi-centrifugal-type clutch; three-speed helical gear set and synchronizers for second and third gears. A three-speed manual gearbox with automatic overdrive was optional. The rear axle gear ratios with standard transmission were: 3.73:1, car and 3.92:1, station wagon. The rear axle gear ratios with automatic overdrive were: 4.10:1, car and 4.17:1, station wagon.

Options:

White sidewall tires. Fender skirts. Turn signal indicators. Outside rearview mirror. Full wheel discs. Wheel trim rings.

History:

Calendar-year production: 1,187,120 cars. The 1950 Fords were introduced in November of 1949 and the model year closed in November 1950. They had estimated model-year production of 1,209,548 cars. Of these, 897,463 were V-8s and 289,659 were sixes. Calendar-year

1950 Ford Custom Deluxe two-door Club Coupe (AA)

1950 Ford Custom Deluxe two-door Station Wagon (OCW)

1950 Ford Custom Deluxe two-door Convertible (OCW)

1950 Ford "Fashion Car" Interior (OCW)

output was 1,187,120 units, representing 17.79 percent of total industry production. For the second year in a row, the Ford was named "Fashion Car of the Year" by New York's famed Fashion Academy.

1951 Ford

Deluxe — Series 1HA / Series 1BA — Six and V-8: According to the March 26, 1951 issue of *Quick* magazine, "The productive genius of the Ford Motor Co. solved a year-old dilemma." The problem was how to keep children from "liberating" the red-white-and-blue golden lion crests from the hoods of 1950 Fords. It seems that the kids liked to put these on beanies, belts and bikes. Ford's solution was to tell the kids they could write to Ford to get a miniature crest for free. Considering the Ford emblems' popularity among potential future customers, it's no wonder the crest remained on the hood in 1951. Other styling changes were again minor. The new grille featured dual "spinners" that were positioned at the outer edges of the center grille bar. The new front parking lights were round rather than rectangular. The hood ornament looked like an abstract bird, instead of a knight's helmet. At the rear of the car, Ford's "Tell Tale" rear lamps were decorated with jet-style chrome spears that tapered towards the front as they ran down the slab-sided body. Series or model names appeared on a front fender trim plate that looked more like a fin than a spear tip. Squire name in script on the upper front corner of the front doors. The woodie was promoted as a "Double Duty Dandy." Cars with V-8 engines under the hood also had a V-8 emblem on the front fender. Ford offered the coupe, Tudor sedan and Fordor sedan in the Deluxe Six series. These body styles also came as Deluxe Eights. For some reason the coupe cost $87 more with a V-8, while the two- and four-door sedans cost only $75 more with a V-8. Chances are, the Deluxe six coupe was used as a "loss leader" to feature in print ads to get buyers into the showroom. This might explain the larger discount for a six-cylinder version. The "Mileage Maker" in-line six was the same one used in 1950. The optional "Strato-Star" flathead V-8 was also unchanged. Ford engines featured a waterproof ignition system, Loadomatic distributors, and an Equa-Flow cooling system with a Silent-Spin fan, Forced-Feed lubrication, a "Full-Flo" fuel pump, Power-Dome combustion and "Rota-Quiet" valves. A three-speed manual gearbox was standard and overdrive was optional. Ford described its popular overdrive as an automatic fourth gear that reduced engine wear and cut fuel costs up to 15 percent. A fully-automatic transmission was offered for the very first time in 1951, but only in cars with V-8 engines. Ford advertised that the new Ford-O-Matic transmission provided "the magic of liquid-smooth, effortless automatic drive." This unit consisted of a torque converter with a three-speed automatic planetary gear. The five-position Semaphone Drive Selector with an illuminated dial was positioned on the steering column. "The Ford-O-Matic Ford brings you automatic driving at its finest and flexible best," said Ford. "You get flashing getaway . . . instant acceleration . . . plenty of zip for passing and hill climbing . . . and all with real economy." Automatic Ride Control was the name of a new and heavily-advertised Ford feature for 1951. The ad copywriters described it as a "three-way partnership" between the Hydra-Coil front springs, the variable-rate rear leaf springs and the viscous-control

1951 Ford Deluxe two-door Sedan (AA)

1951 Ford Deluxe four-door Sedan (OCW)

telescopic shock absorbers. This system was designed to maintain a level ride and eliminate pitch, jounce and roll. It was advertised as "a new and unique springing system that automatically adjusts spring reaction to road conditions." Ford interiors were highlighted by a new Safety-Glow control panel with knobs and dials that were easy to reach and easy to read. Ignition-key starting was new this year. "Just turn the ignition key to the right - your engine starts. No reaching for a button - no stretching for a starter pedal," Ford explained. The "Chanalited" instrument cluster had all of the gauges located within the speedometer scale for easy readability. The speed indicator incorporated a ring at its end that circled the traveling speed in red and glowed at night. All controls had "Glow-Cup" lighting for night-driving convenience. "Automatic Posture Control" was Ford's trade name for a design in which the entire seat was angled for maximum comfort. Cushioning was by foam rubber over non-sag springs. The seats featured long-wearing Fordcraft fabrics and new harmonized appointments, while "Colorblend" carpeting covered the floor. A "Magic-Air" weather-control system was optional.

Custom Deluxe — Series 1HA / Series 1BA — Six and V-8: Ford offered the Club Coupe, Tudor Sedan, Fordor Sedan and station wagon in the Custom Deluxe Six series and the first two had a chrome body side molding for identification. The wood-paneled wagons did not have room for moldings, but now carried the name "Country Squire" on its front fender. These three body styles came as Custom Deluxe eights as well. The Crestliner Tudor, the convertible and the Victoria hardtop came only with the V-8 engine. The Crestliner, first introduced in 1950, was a special two-door sedan with a vinyl top, extra chrome, a special steering wheel, special two-tone paint and full wheel covers. A special trim plate carried the name Victoria on the hardtop model. It was Ford's first true pillarless hardtop and was aptly described as "the Belle of the Boulevard!" "The car that gives you the smart styling of a convertible with the snugness of a sedan," is how ad copywriters described this convertible-looking model. It featured "Luxury Lounge" interiors that were color-keyed to the finish of the car, which was usually two-toned.

VIN:

The vehicle identification number was stamped on a plate attached to the front face of the cowl. It was also on the right frame side rail just to the rear of the upper front suspension arm. The first symbol indicated the engine: H=226-cid six-cylinder, B=239-cid V-8 and P=239-cid police V-8. The second symbol indicated the model year: 1=1951. The third and fourth symbols indicated the assembly plant: AT=Atlanta, Georgia, BF=Buffalo, N.Y., CS=Chester, Pennsylvania, CH=Chicago, Illinois, DL=Dallas, Texas, HM=Highland Park, Michigan, DA=Dearborn, Michigan, LU=Louisville, Kentucky, EG=Edgewater, N.J., KC=Kansas City, Kansas, LB=Long Beach, California, MP=Memphis, Tennessee, NR=Norfolk, Virginia, RH=Richmond, Virginia, SR=Somerville, Massachusetts and SP=Twin Cities, St. Paul, Minnesota. The last six symbols are the sequential production number starting at 100001 and up in each factory.

Deluxe (Six)

Model No.	Body/Style No.	Body Type & Seating	Factory Price	Shipping Weight	Production Total
1HA	73	4-dr. Sedan-6P	$1,466	3,089 lbs.	Note 1
1HA	70	2-dr. Sedan-6P	$1,417	3,023 lbs.	Note 1
1HA	72C	2-dr. Business Coupe-3P	$1,324	2,960 lbs.	Note 1

Deluxe (V-8)

Model No.	Body/Style No.	Body Type & Seating	Factory Price	Shipping Weight	Production Total
1BA	73	4-dr. Sedan-6P	$1,540	3,114 lbs.	54,265
1BA	70	2-dr. Sedan-6P	$1,492	3,062 lbs.	146,010
1BA	72C	2-dr. Business Coupe-3P	$1,411	2,997 lbs.	20,343

Custom Deluxe (Six)

Model No.	Body/Style No.	Body Type & Seating	Factory Price	Shipping Weight	Production Total
1HA	73	4-dr. Sedan-6P	$1,553	3,089 lbs.	Note 1
1HA	70	2-dr. Sedan-6P	$1,505	3,023 lbs.	Note 1
1HA	72C	2-dr. Club Coupe-6P	$1,505	2,995 lbs.	Note 1
1HA	79	2-dr. Country Squire-8P	------	-------	Note 1
1HA	79	2-dr. Station Wagon-6P	$2,029	3,510 lbs.	Note 1

Custom Deluxe (V-8)

Model No.	Body/Style No.	Body Type & Seating	Factory Price	Shipping Weight	Production Total
1BA	73B	4-dr. Sedan-6P	$1,633	3,114 lbs.	232,691
1BA	70B	2-dr. Sedan-6P	$1,585	3,062 lbs.	317,869
1BA	70C	2-dr. Crestliner-6P	$1,595	3,085 lbs.	8,703
1BA	72C	2-dr. Club Coupe-6P	$1,590	3,034 lbs.	53,263
1BA	60	2-dr. Victoria Hardtop-6P	$1,925	3,188 lbs.	110,286
1BA	76	2-dr. Convertible-6P	$1,949	3,268 lbs.	40,934
1BA	79	2-dr. Country Squire-8P	------	-------	-----
1BA	79	2-dr. Station Wagon-6P	$2,110	3,550 lbs.	29,617

Note 1: Production of six-cylinder and V-8 models of each body style is a combined total.

1951 Ford Custom Deluxe four-door Sedan (PH)

1951 Ford Custom Deluxe two-door Sedan (PH)

Engines:

Custom Six: L-head. Cast-iron block. Displacement: 226 cid. B & S: 3.30 x 4.40 in. Compression ratio: 6.8:1. Brake hp: 95 at 3600 rpm. Carburetor: Holley one-barrel Model 847F5. Four main bearings. Code H.

Custom Deluxe Six: L-head. Cast-iron block. Displacement: 226 cid. B & S: 3.30 x 4.40 in. Compression ratio: 6.8:1. Brake hp: 95 at 3600 rpm. Carburetor: Holley one-barrel Model 847F5. Four main bearings. Code H.

Custom Eight: L-head V-8. Cast-iron block. Displacement: 239 cid. B & S: 3.19 x 3.75 in. Compression ratio: 6.8:1. Brake hp: 100 at 3600 rpm. Carburetor: Holley two-barrel Model AA-1. Three main bearings. Code B.

Custom Deluxe Eight: L-head V-8. Cast-iron block. Displacement: 239 cid. B & S: 3.19 x 3.75 in. Compression ratio: 6.8:1. Brake hp: 100 at 3600 rpm. Carburetor: Holley two-barrel Model AA-1. Three main bearings. Code B.

Chassis:

Custom: Wheelbase: 114 in. Overall length: 196.4 in., car and 208 in., station wagon. Overall width: 72.9 in. Tires: 6.00 x 16, standard, 7.10 x 15, station wagon and 6.70 x 15, optional.

Custom Deluxe: Wheelbase: 114 in. Overall length: 196.4 in., car and 208 in., station wagon. Overall width: 72.9 in. Tires: 6.00 x 16, standard, 7.10 x 15, station wagon and 6.70 x 15, optional.

Technical:

Custom: The standard Ford transmission was a three-speed manual type with semi-centrifugal-type clutch; three-speed helical gear set and synchronizers for second and third gears. A three-speed manual gearbox with automatic overdrive was optional at $92 extra. Two-speed Ford-O-Matic transmission was optional at $159 extra. The rear axle gear ratios with standard transmissions were: 3.73:1, cars and 4.10:1, optional. The rear axle gear ratio with automatic overdrive was 4.10:1. The rear axle gear ratio with Ford-O-Matic automatic transmission was 3.31:1.

Custom Deluxe: The standard Ford transmission was a three-speed manual type with semi-centrifugal-type clutch and three-speed helical gear set and synchronizers for second and third gears. A three-speed manual gearbox with automatic overdrive was optional at $92 extra. Two-speed Ford-O-Matic transmission was optional at $159 extra. The rear axle gear ratios with standard transmission were 3.73:1, car and 4.10:1, optional. The rear axle gear ratio with automatic overdrive was 4.10:1. The rear axle gear ratio with Ford-O-Matic automatic transmission was 3.31:1.

Options:

White sidewall tires. Fender skirts. Turn signal indicators. Outside rearview mirror. Full wheel discs. Wheel trim rings. Ford-O-Matic transmission.

1951 Ford Custom Deluxe two-door Victoria Hardtop (AA)

1951 Ford Custom Deluxe Crestliner two-door Sedan (OCW)

1951 Ford Custom Deluxe Crestliner two-door Sedan (OCW)

1951 Ford Custom Deluxe two-door Club Coupe (AA)

1951 Ford Custom Deluxe two-door Convertible (OCW)

1951 Ford Custom Deluxe two-door Station Wagon (OCW)

1951 Ford Custom Deluxe two-door Country Squire (OCW)

History:

Henry Ford II was president of Ford Motor Company and Earnest R. Breech was executive vice president. C. L. Waterhouse was styling manager. L.O. Crusoe was general manager of Ford Division and L.W. Smead was general sales manager. Although the image of the "shoe box" Ford didn't change much in 1951, Ford general manager L. D. Crusoe was focused on the goal of making Ford the top-selling car brand in America. In addition to offering free replicas of the company's crest to youngsters who might buy Fords tomorrow, he was carefully plotting the course to better future sales with the introduction of modern features like automatic transmission and hardtop styling. Unfortunately, the United States government threw up roadblocks in 1951 by instituting production controls due to the Korean crisis. They held Ford's output to 24 percent below the 1950 figure. Model-year production was 1,013,391 vehicles, which included 753,265 cars with V-8 engines and 147,495 sixes. Calendar-year output was 900,770, giving Ford second place on the sales charts, but only 16.87 percent market share, down from 17.79 the previous year. This year, the sales were lost to Chrysler, which gained market share for all of its divisions. The only GM branch to gain market share in the calendar year was Cadillac. This was a sure sign that the big overhead valve V-8s offered by MoPar and Cadillac had sales appeal. Certainly, Ford was watching this trend as its sights were set in the direction of introducing a new V-8 in the not-too-distant future. In 1951, Ford started new operations at an engine plant in Cleveland, Ohio and a stamping plant in Buffalo, N.Y. The company made aircraft engines, bazooka rockets and medium tanks for the war effort.

1952 Ford

Mainline — Series A2 / Series B2 — Six and V-8: The new Fords introduced to the public on February 1, 1952 were wider, longer, roomier, stronger and more powerful than ever before. Highlighting new-model introductions was the first totally new body for Ford since 1949. The cars were arranged in three different, renamed product lines with each series - Mainline, Customline and Crestline - offering different combinations of body styles, trim and engines. Some body types and all Crestlines were available only with the V-8 engine. Styling-wise, the 1952 Fords featured a new Curva-Lite Safety-View one-piece curved windshield with no center bar, a 48 percent larger full-width rear window, Search-Mount headlights with protruding round parking lights directly below behind "triple spinner" bars, a round three-bladed spinner in the center of the grille bar, a simulated air scoop on the rear quarter panels, a redesigned instrument panel and "Power-Pivot" suspended clutch and brake pedals. This year the gas filler pipe and neck were concealed behind a hinged rear license plate. The Mainline series was the base trim level for 1952. Cars in this line had rubber window moldings, a horn button instead of horn ring, one sun visor and an armrest only on the driver's door. There were four body types in this range: Business Coupe, Tudor Sedan, Fordor Sedan and new all-steel two-door Ranch Wagon. All were available with both engines. The six-cylinder engine was the new overhead-valve "Mileage Maker" Six. Some said this six performed better than the old 239-cid Strato-Star flathead V-8, which was boosted to 110-hp. Of course, any V-8-powered Ford could be "improved" with aftermarket goodies, while there was not nearly as much "hop-up" equipment available for the in-line six. Automatic Power Pilot was the name given to Ford's completely integrated carburetion-ignition-combustion system. It featured a downdraft carburetor that automatically switched to economy jets for idling and a Loadomatic ignition distributor that automatically controlled spark advance. Ford's standard transmission was a three-speed manual-type of the usual design. Three-speed manual with automatic overdrive was a optional. Ford-O-Matic transmission was an option. It featured a torque converter transmission with automatic planetary gear train, a single stage three-element hydraulic torque converter, hydraulic-mechanical automatic controls (with no electrical or vacuum connections), forced-air cooling and power flow through the fluid member at all times. Cars with the automatic transmission had a Ford-O-Matic nameplate on the trunk lid. Others said "Overdrive" in the same spot. A completely new line of custom accessories was brought out by the Ford Motor Company to match 1952 styling.

Customline — Series A2 / Series B2 — Six and V-8: The Customline series was the intermediate trim level for 1952 and included chrome window moldings, a chrome horn ring, two sun visors, armrests on all doors, passenger assist straps on the interior "B" pillars (for easier rear seat egress), a horizontal chrome strip on the front fenders and a chrome opening on the rear quarter panel scoop. Three sixes were offered in Customline trim: the Club Coupe, the Tudor and the Fordor. These were available with a V-8 for $70 more. A four-door Country Sedan station wagon was also offered in the Customline V-8 series.

Crestline — Series B2 — V-8: Crestline was the name of the top-trim-level series for 1952. Crestline models included the Victoria hardtop, the Sunliner convertible and the Country Squire. The latter was now a four-door all-metal station wagon that came with woodgrain side trim appliqués. All three "name" cars were offered only with V-8 engines. This series included all features of the Customline models, plus full wheel covers and additional chrome trim along the bottom of the side windows. The Sunliner included a push-button-operated power soft top. The top-of-the-line Country Squire station wagon was the year's rarest Ford product.

VIN:

The vehicle identification number was stamped on a plate attached to the right front body pillar below the upper hinge opening. It was also stamped on the right frame reinforcement and on the top of the rear frame X-member near the right-hand end. It was also stamped on the top of the second cross member (except on convertibles). The first symbol indicated the engine: A=215-cid six-cylinder, B=239-cid V-8 and P=239-cid police V-8. The second symbol indicated the model year: 2=1952. The third and fourth symbols indicated the assembly plant: AT=Atlanta, Georgia, BF=Buffalo, N.Y., CS=Chester, Pennsylvania, CH=Chicago, Illinois, DL=Dallas, Texas, DA=Dearborn, Michigan, LU=Louisville, Kentucky, EG=Edgewater, N.J., KC=Kansas City, Kansas, LB=Long Beach, California, MP=Memphis, Tennessee, NR=Norfolk, Virginia, RH=Richmond, Virginia, SR=Somerville, Massachusetts and SP=Twin Cities, St. Paul, Minnesota. The last six symbols are the sequential production number starting at 100001 and up in each factory.

1952 Ford Mainline two-door Sedan (OCW)

1952 Ford Mainline two-door Station Wagon (AA)

Mainline (Six)

Model No.	Body/ Style No.	Body Type & Seating	Factory Price	Shipping Weight	Production Total
A2	73A	4-dr. Sedan-6P	$1,530	3,173 lbs.	Note 1
A2	70A	2-dr. Sedan-6P	$1,485	3,070 lbs.	Note 1
A2	72C	2-dr. Business Coupe-3P	$1,389	2,984 lbs.	Note 1
A2	59A	2-dr. Station Wagon-6P	$1,832	3,377 lbs.	Note 1

Mainline (V-8)

Model No.	Body/ Style No.	Body Type & Seating	Factory Price	Shipping Weight	Production Total
A2	73A	4-dr. Sedan-6P	$1,600	3,207 lbs.	41,277
A2	70A	2-dr. Sedan-6P	$1,555	3,151 lbs.	79,931
A2	72C	2-dr. Business Coupe-3P	$1,459	3,085 lbs.	10,137
A2	59A	2-dr. Station Wagon-6P	$1,902	3,406 lbs.	32,566

Customline (Six)

Model No.	Body/ Style No.	Body Type & Seating	Factory Price	Shipping Weight	Production Total
A2	73B	4-dr. Sedan-6P	$1,615	3,173 lbs.	Note 1
A2	70B	2-dr. Sedan-6P	$1,570	3,070 lbs.	Note 1
A2	72B	2-dr. Club Coupe-6P	$1,579	3,079 lbs.	Note 1

Customline (V-8)

Model No.	Body/ Style No.	Body Type & Seating	Factory Price	Shipping Weight	Production Total
B2	73B	4-dr. Sedan-6P	$1,685	3,207 lbs.	188,303
B2	70B	2-dr. Sedan-6P	$1,640	3,151 lbs.	175,762
B2	72B	2-dr. Club Coupe-6P	$1,649	3,153 lbs.	26,550
B2	79C	2-dr. Station Wagon-6P	$2,060	3,617 lbs.	11,927

Crestline (V-8)

Model No.	Body/ Style No.	Body Type & Seating	Factory Price	Shipping Weight	Production Total
B2	60B	2-dr. Victoria Hardtop-6P	$1,925	3,274 lbs.	77,320
B2	76B	2-dr. Convertible-6P	$2,027	3,339 lbs.	22,534
B2	79B	2-dr. Country Squire-8P	$2,186	3,640 lbs.	5,426

Note 1: Production of six-cylinder and V-8 models of each body style is a combined total.

Engines:

Mainline Six: Overhead valve. Cast-iron block. Displacement: 215.3 cid. B & S: 3.56 x 3.60 in. Compression ratio: 7.0:1. Brake hp: 101 at 3500 rpm. Carburetor: Holley one-barrel Model 847F5. Four main bearings. Code A.

Customline Six: Overhead valve. Cast-iron block. Displacement: 215.3 cid. B & S: 3.56 x 3.60 in. Compression ratio: 7.0:1. Brake hp: 101 at 3500 rpm. Carburetor: Holley one-barrel Model 847F5. Four main bearings. Code A.

Mainline Eight: L-head V-8. Cast-iron block. Displacement: 239 cid. B & S: 3.19 x 3.75 in. Compression ratio: 7.2:1. Brake hp: 110 at 3800 rpm. Carburetor: Ford two-barrel Model 8BA. Three main bearings. Code B.

1952 Ford Mainline four-door Sedan (OCW)

1952 Ford Mainline two-door Business Coupe (OCW)

1952 Ford Customline four-door Sedan (OCW)

1952 Ford Customline two-door Sedan (OCW)

Customline Eight: L-head V-8. Cast-iron block. Displacement: 239 cid. B & S: 3.19 x 3.75 in. Compression ratio: 7.2:1. Brake hp: 110 at 3800 rpm. Carburetor: Ford two-barrel Model 8BA. Three main bearings. Code B.

Crestline Eight: L-head V-8. Cast-iron block. Displacement: 239 cid. B & S: 3.19 x 3.75 in. Compression ratio: 7.2:1. Brake hp: 110 at 3800 rpm. Carburetor: Ford two-barrel Model 8BA. Three main bearings. Code B.

Chassis:

Mainline: Wheelbase: 115 in. Overall length: 197.8 in. Overall width: 73.2 in. Tires: 6.00 x 16, standard and 6.70 x 15, optional.
Customline: Wheelbase: 115 in. Overall length: 197.8 in. Overall width: 73.2 in. Tires: 6.00 x 16, standard and 6.70 x 15, optional.
Crestline: Wheelbase: 115 in. Overall length: 197.8 in. Overall width: 73.2 in. Tires: 6.00 x 16, standard and 6.70 x 15. optional.

Technical:

Mainline, Customline and Crestline: The standard transmission was a three-speed manual-type of the usual design. Three-speed manual with automatic overdrive was a $102 option. Ford-O-Matic transmission was a $170 option. Ford-O-Matic featured a torque converter transmission with automatic planetary gear train, single stage three-element hydraulic torque converter, hydraulic mechanical automatic controls with no electrical or vacuum connections, forced air cooling, and power flow through the fluid member at all times. There rear axle gear ratios were: 3.90:1, manual transmission, 4.10:1, overdrive, 3.15:1, optional overdrive, 3.31:1 with Ford-O-Matic and 3.54:1, an option with Ford-O-Matic.

Options:

A completely new line of custom accessories was brought out by the Ford Motor Co. to match 1952 styling. Several interesting additions on the list were a speed governor, turn indicators, illuminated vanity mirror, engine compartment light, five-tube Deluxe radio, seven-tube Custom radio, spring wound clock, electric clock, color-keyed rubber floor mats, wheel discs, wheel trim rings, rear fender skirts, rocker panel trim strips, hand brake signal lamp and Magic Air heater and defroster.

History:

The 1952 Fords were introduced to the public on Feb. 1, 1952. L.D. Crusoe managed to grow Ford Division in 1952, opening nine new parts depots nationwide and starting work on three more new facilities in the East and Midwest. But government restrictions, along with a steel strike and other disputes, held model-year production to 671,725 units. For the calendar-year, Ford built 777,531 cars or 17.93 percent of the industry total. Over 32 percent of cars built this year had Ford-O-Matic gear shifting and over 20 percent of the cars built with manual transmissions had the overdrive option. Ford also led the industry in station wagon production with 32 percent of total industry output for this body style. The Federal-Aid Highway Act of 1952 authorized $25 million for the

interstate highway system on a 50-50 matching basis. These were the first funds authorized specifically for interstate road construction and Ford Motor Company ran a series "American Road" advertisements to support the initiative. The ads touched on the history of American roads from single-file Indian paths, to "Good Roads" movements to modern cloverleaf highways. "We need more of those superb new turnpikes, expressways and superhighways with their overpasses and underpasses, and glittering silver-steel bridges that soar across rivers of the land," one ad suggested. It also pointed out that Ford had put 35 million cars on those roads over the years.

1952 Ford Customline two-door Club Coupe (OCW)

1952 Ford Customline four-door Country Sedan (OCW)

1952 Ford Crestline two-door Victoria Hardtop (OCW)

1952 Ford Crestline two-door Victoria Hardtop (OCW)

1952 Ford Sunliner two-door Convertible (OCW)

1952 Ford Crestline four-door Country Squire (OCW)

1952 Ford interior (OCW)

1953 Ford

Mainline — Series A3 / Series B3 — Six and V-8: Ford held dealer introductions for its 1953 "Golden Jubilee" models on December 12, 1952. The new cars utilized 1952 bodies with moderate trim updating. However, they were said to offer "41 Worth More Features." Selling features for the year included double-seal Magic-Action brakes, push-button door handles, a self-lifting deck lid, "Hull-Tight" body construction, Silent-Doorman two-stage front door checks, Center-Fill fueling, a flight-style control panel, a K-bar frame, high alloy exhaust valves, aluminum pistons and a Safety-Sequence drive selector in cars with Ford-O-Matic transmission. The 1953 grille incorporated a larger horizontal bar with three vertical stripes on either side of a large spinner. The length of this bar was increased and it now wrapped around the front edges of the fenders. The parking lights were horizontal rectangles instead of circles. The Ford crest appeared in the center of the steering wheel hub and contained the words, "50th Anniversary 1903-1953." Ford's Mainline series was the base trim level for 1953 and cars in this line included rubber windshield and rear window moldings, fixed rear vent windows, a horn button instead of a horn ring, one sun visor and an armrest on the driver's door only. Mainline models had no chrome sweep spears on the front and rear fenders. Partial chrome gravel deflectors accented the bulges on the rear quarter panels, just ahead of the rear wheel openings. The Mainline name appeared on the front fenders. The two-door Ranch Wagon, which was part of this series, had no wood-look exterior panels. Body style offerings were identical to those offered in 1952. V-8 power for was $70 additional. Engine choices in 1953 looked identical to those of the previous season. Three-speed manual transmission was again standard. Overdrive was a $108 option. The automatic overdrive function cut in at 27 mph and cut out at 21 mph. Ford-O-Matic automatic transmission was optional. Ford's Automatic Ride Control suspension design was improved for 1953. The new "balanced" system integrated a rubber-cushioned front suspension with variable-rate rear leaf springs and diagonally-mounted telescopic shock absorbers to minimize sidesway on turns. The front tread width was two inches wider than the rear tread width to give better "footing" for easier handling.

1953 Ford Mainline four-door Sedan (OCW)

Customline — Series A3 / Series B3 — Six and V-8: The Customline series was the intermediate trim level for 1953 and included chrome windshield and rear window moldings, a chrome horn half-ring, two sun visors, armrests on all doors and passenger assist straps on interior "B" pillars for easier rear seat egress. A horizontal chrome strip decorated the front fenders just above the wheel opening. Chrome gravel deflectors capped the entire front height of the rear quarter panel scoops. There was another horizontal chrome strip running from the scoop opening, above the rear wheel opening, to the back of the body. The Customline name was on a spear tip at the leading edge of the front fender molding. If a V-8 was installed, an appropriate emblem was placed behind the spear tip. The Country Sedan wagon in this line had four doors, but no exterior woodgrained paneling. Body style offering were again as in 1952.

Crestline — Series B3 — V-8: The Crestline series was the top trim level for 1953 and was again offered only with V-8 engines. This series included all trim in the Customline series, plus wheel covers and additional chrome trim along the bottom of the side windows. The Victoria hardtop, the Sunliner convertible and the Country Squire wood-trimmed wagon were in this series.

VIN:

The vehicle identification number was stamped on a plate attached to the left front body pillar. It was also stamped on the right front frame cross member reinforcement. The first symbol indicated the engine: A=215-cid six-cylinder, B=239-cid V-8 and P=239-cid police V-8. The second symbol indicated the model year: 3=1953. The third symbol indicated the assembly plant: A=Atlanta, Georgia, B=Buffalo, N.Y., C=Chester, Pennsylvania, D=Dallas, Texas, E=Edgewater, N.J., F=Dearborn, Michigan, G=Chicago, Illinois, H=Highland Park, Michigan, K=Kansas City, Kansas, L=Long Beach, California, M=Memphis, Tennessee, N=Norfolk, Virginia, P=Twin Cities, St. Paul, Minnesota, R=Richmond, Virginia, S=Somerville, Massachusetts and U=Louisville, Kentucky. The fourth symbol indicated the body style: C=Convertible, W=Ranch Wagon, X=Country Sedan, Y=Country Squire, V=Victoria, G=All other styles. The last six symbols are the sequential production number starting at 100001 and up in each factory.

Mainline (Six)

Model No.	Body/ Style No.	Body Type & Seating	Factory Price	Shipping Weight	Production Total
A3	73B	4-dr. Sedan-6P	$1,783	3,115 lbs.	Note 1
A3	70A	2-dr. Sedan-6P	$1,734	3,067 lbs.	Note 1
A3	72B	2-dr. Club Coupe-6P	$1,743	3,046 lbs.	Note 1

Mainline (V-8)

B3	73A	4-dr. Sedan-6P	$1,766	3,181 lbs.	66,463
B3	70A	2-dr. Sedan-6P	$1,717	3,136 lbs.	132,995
B3	72C	2-dr. Business Coupe-3P	$1,614	3,068 lbs.	16,280
B3	59A	2-dr. Station Wagon-6P	$2,095	3,408 lbs.	66,976

Customline (Six)

A3	73B	4-dr. Sedan-6P	$1,783	3,115 lbs.	Note 1
A3	70B	2-dr. Sedan-6P	$1,734	3,087 lbs.	Note 1
A3	72B	2-dr. Club Coupe-6P	$1,743	3,046 lbs.	Note 1

Customline (V-8)

B3	73B	4-dr. Sedan-6P	$1,783	3,193 lbs.	374,487
B3	70B	2-dr. Sedan-6P	$1,734	3,133 lbs.	305,433
B3	72B	2-dr. Club Coupe-6P	$1,743	3,121 lbs.	43,999
B3	79B	2-dr. Station Wagon-6P	$2,267	3,539 lbs.	37,743

Crestline (V-8)

B3	60B	2-dr. Victoria Hardtop-6P	$2,120	3,250 lbs.	128,302
B3	76B	2-dr. Convertible-6P	$2,230	3,334 lbs.	40,861
B3	79C	2-dr. Country Squire-6P	$2,403	3,609 lbs.	11,001

Note 1: Production of six-cylinder and V-8 models of each body style is a combined total.

1953 Ford Mainline two-door Sedan (OCW)

1953 Ford Mainline two-door Business Coupe and Sedan (OCW)

1953 Ford Mainline two-door Station Wagon (OCW)

1953 Ford Customline four-door Sedan (AA)

1953 Ford Customline two-door Sedan (OCW)

Engines:

Mainline Six: Overhead valve. Cast-iron block. Displacement: 215.3 cid. B & S: 3.56 x 3.60 in. Compression ratio: 7.0:1. Brake hp: 101 at 3500 rpm. Carburetor: Holley one-barrel Model 1904F. Four main bearings. Code A.

Customline Six: Overhead valve. Cast-iron block. Displacement: 215.3 cid. B & S: 3.56 x 3.60 in. Compression ratio: 7.0:1. Brake hp: 101 at 3500 rpm. Carburetor: Holley one-barrel Model 1904F. Four main bearings. Code A.

Mainline Eight: L-head V-8. Cast-iron block. Displacement: 239 cid. B & S: 3.19 x 3.75 in. Compression ratio: 7.2:1. Brake hp: 110 at 3800 rpm. Carburetor: Ford two-barrel Model 2100. Three main bearings. Code B.

Customline Eight: L-head V-8. Cast-iron block. Displacement: 239 cid. B & S: 3.19 x 3.75 in. Compression ratio: 7.2:1. Brake hp: 110 at 3800 rpm. Carburetor: Ford two-barrel Model 2100. Three main bearings. Code B.

Crestline Eight: L-head V-8. Cast-iron block. Displacement: 239 cid. B & S: 3.19 x 3.75 in. Compression ratio: 7.2:1. Brake hp: 110 at 3800 rpm. Carburetor: Ford two-barrel Model 2100. Three main bearings. Code B.

Chassis:

Mainline: Wheelbase: 115 in. Overall length: 197.8 in. Overall width: 74.3 in. Tires: 6.70 x 15, standard and 7.10 x 15, station wagon.

Customline: Wheelbase: 115 in. Overall length: 197.8 in. Overall width: 74.3 in. Tires: 6.70 x 15, standard and 7.10 x 15, station wagon.

Crestline: Wheelbase: 115 in. Overall length: 197.8 in. Overall width: 74.3 in. Tires: 6.70 x 15, standard and 7.10 x 15, station wagon.

Technical:

Mainline, Customline and Crestline: Three-speed manual transmission was standard. This unit featured a semi-centrifugal-type clutch, three-speed helical gears with synchronizers for second and third gears. Three-speed manual transmission with automatic overdrive was a $108 option. Specifications were the same above with automatic overdrive function cutting in at 27 mph, cutting out at 21 mph. Approximate drive ratio was: 0.70:1. Manual control was provided below the instrument panel. Ford-O-Matic automatic transmission was a $184 option. This was a torque converter-type transmission with automatic planetary gear train, single stage, three-element hydraulic torque converter, hydraulic-mechanical automatic controls and no electrical or vacuum connections. Power was transmitted through the fluid member at all times.

Options:

Power steering ($125). Power brakes ($35). Ford-O-Matic transmission ($184). Overdrive ($108). Six-tube Deluxe radio ($88). Eight-tube Custom radio ($100). Recirculation-type heater ($44). Deluxe heater ($71). Electric clock ($15). Directional signals ($15). Windshield washer ($10). Tinted glass ($23). White sidewall tires ($27).

History:

Introduction of 1953 models took place December 12, 1953. On a model year basis 1,240,000 cars were built, of which 876,300 were estimated to be V-8-powered units. Ford opened a new Technical Service Laboratory at Livonia, Michigan this year. A specially trimmed Sunliner convertible paced the 1953 Indianapolis 500-Mile Race. Master Guide power steering was introduced June 16, 1953. A 1953 Ford Mainliner four-door sedan averaged 27.03 mpg in the Mobilgas Economy Run from Los Angeles to Sun Valley. Business wise, 1953 had a "split personality" at Ford Division. During the first part of the year, auto production was hampered by government limitations, strikes and disputes with parts suppliers. This changed to six-day weeks and overtime during the second half of the year, as Ford's output exploded to a level 52 percent ahead of 1952. By the time the dust cleared, model-year production stood at 1,240,000 cars of which 876,300 were estimated to be V-8-powered units. Six-cylinder model production nearly doubled to 307,887. Calendar-year production climbed steeply to 1,184,187 units or 19.30 percent of industry, although Chevrolet gained nearly four full points of market share compared to just over one point for Ford. Ford-O-Matic transmission grew so popular in 1953 that production schedules had to be expanded. However, due to a 10-week supplier strike at Borg-Warner, which made the Ford automatic, 85 percent of the cars made in June were equipped with stick shift. Nevertheless, 346,939 cars got the automatic. The power steering option released in June was popular enough to go into eight percent of all 1953 Fords made by the end of the year. Ford also upped its production of station wagons to 38 percent of total industry output and made more convertibles (39,945 in the calendar year) than any other automaker. The anniversary year brought several milestones. In May, a specially-trimmed 1953 Ford Sunliner convertible paced the Indianapolis 500-Mile Race. Ford also opened a new Technical Service Laboratory, at Livonia, Michigan, during the year.

1953 Ford Customline four-door Country Sedan (CCC)

1953 Ford Customline two-door Club Coupe (OCW)

1953 Ford Crestline two-door Victoria Hardtop (OCW)

1953 Ford Sunliner two-door Convertible (OCW)

1953 Ford Crestline four-door Country Squire (OCW)

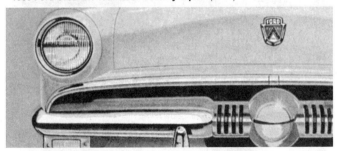

1953 Ford grille detail (OCW)

1953 Ford taillight detail (OCW)

1953 Ford Crestline Victoria interior (OCW)

1954 Ford

Mainline — Series A4 / Series U4 — Six and V-8: Contemporary style was reflected in the '54 Ford's appearance. "Ford brings you tomorrow's clean uncluttered look today," said an advertisement. In truth, this was an easy accomplishment, since barely any changes were made from the cars' 1952 and 1953 styling. The same basic body was used. The modestly-updated grille incorporated a large horizontal bar with large slots on either side of a centrally located spinner. Round parking lights were located in smaller spinners at either end of the horizontal bar. Making news was the availability of a new V-8 engine (promoted as the Ford "Y-8") with *overhead* valves. It was now optional in *all* models. This new engine was rated for nearly 25 percent more power than the 1953 flathead. Ford added many new convenience items to its optional equipment list in 1954. Among them were power windows, four-way power seats and power brakes. Ball joints replaced king pins in the front suspension. Mainline, Customline and Crestline car-lines were offered again and all body styles were available with either engine. This added up to 14 body style and trim combinations times two engines for a total of 28 basic Ford models. Selling features promoted by Ford salesmen of the day were primarily the same ones offered in 1953 and included center-fill fueling, hull-tight body, two-stage door checks, non-sag seats, a K-bar frame, variable-rate rear leaf springs, full-displacement tubular shock absorbers, tailored-to-weight coil front springs, a semi-floating rear axle and hypoid gears. The Mainline series was the base trim level for 1954 and included a Business Coupe, a Tudor Sedan, a Fordor Sedan and a two-door Ranch Wagon with six-passenger seating. These cars had rubber window moldings, a horn button instead of horn ring, a single sun visor and an armrest on the driver's door only. The Mainline name appeared in chrome script on the front fender of the passenger cars, just ahead of the door break line. Station wagons had a Ranch Wagon script plate instead. Small gravel shields were seen on the rear fender "pontoons," just ahead of the rear wheel openings. Naturally, V-8-powered cars had "Y-8" badges just ahead of the front wheel openings. The overhead-valve in-line six was bored out to 223 cid. The new overhead-valve V-8 (or "Y-8") retained the old 239-cubic-inch displacement figure. Transmission options were as in the past.

Customline — Series A4 / Series U4 — Six and V-8: The Customline series was the intermediate trim level for 1954. The Customline Six series offered a Club Coupe, a Tudor Sedan, a Fordor Sedan, a two-door Ranch Wagon with six-passenger seating and a four-door Country Sedan eight-passenger wagon. These cars had chrome window moldings, a chrome half-horn ring, two sun visors, armrests on all doors and passenger assist straps on the interior "B" pillars. On the passenger cars, the Customline name appeared in chrome script on the upper front "corner" of the rear fender pontoon. Two-door Customline wagons had a Ranch Wagon script in the same location and their four-door counterparts had a Country Sedan script there. A sweep spear molding ran from the front to the rear of the car at just-below-headlight level. This trim dipped down in a scalloped V-shape around the upper front corner of the rear fender pontoon. The same small gravel shields used on Mainlines were placed just ahead of the rear wheel openings.

Crestline — Series A4 / Series U4 — Six and V-8: The Crestline series was the top trim level for 1954. This car-line included the exciting new Skyliner hardtop. This model had a tinted, transparent roof panel above the driver's seat. There was also a Fordor sedan, a Victoria two-door hardtop, a Sunliner convertible and the four-door Country Squire eight-passenger wagon with simulated wood-grained trim. The Crestline models were offered with a six-cylinder engine for the first time since the series began in 1950. This series included all of the Customline trim features, plus three chrome hash marks behind the gravel shields, chrome "A" pillar moldings, additional chrome trim along the bottom of the side windows and full wheel covers. The Crestline name appeared on the rear fender pontoon of all models except the wagon, which had Country Squire scripted on the front door instead. On the Victoria, Skyliner and Sunliner models, the model name was engraved in the chrome windowsills along with multiple hash marks. All hardtops had special rear roof pillar trim plates (gold-colored on Skyliners) with medallions.

VIN:

The vehicle identification number was stamped on a plate attached to the left front body pillar below the hinge opening. The first symbol indicated the engine: A=223-cid six-cylinder, U=239-cid V-8 and P=239-cid police V-8. The second symbol indicated the model year: 4=1954. The third symbol indicated the assembly plant: A=Atlanta, Georgia, B=Buffalo, N.Y., C=Chester, Pennsylvania, D=Dallas, Texas, E=Edgewater, N.J., F=Dearborn, Michigan, G=Chicago, Illinois, H=Highland Park, Michigan, K=Kansas City, Kansas, L=Long Beach, California, M=Memphis, Tennessee, N=Norfolk, Virginia, P=Twin Cities, St. Paul, Minnesota, R=Richmond, Virginia, S=Somerville, Massachusetts and U=Louisville, Kentucky. The fourth symbol indicated the body style: C=Sunliner Convertible, F=Skyliner Glasstop, R=Customline Ranch Wagon, W=Mainline Ranch Wagon, T=Crestline Fordor, X=Country Sedan, Y=Country Squire, V=Victoria, G=All other styles. The last six symbols are the sequential production number starting at 100001 and up in each factory.

Mainline (Six)

Model No.	Body/ Style No.	Body Type & Seating	Factory Price	Shipping Weight	Production Total
A4	73A	4-dr. Sedan-6P	$1,701	3,142 lbs.	Note 1
A4	70A	2-dr. Sedan-6P	$1,651	3,086 lbs.	Note 1
A4	72C	2-dr. Business Coupe-3P	$1,548	3,021 lbs.	Note 1
A4	59A	2-dr. Station Wagon-6P	$2,029	3,228 lbs.	Note 1

Mainline (V-8)

Model No.	Body/ Style No.	Body Type & Seating	Factory Price	Shipping Weight	Production Total
U4	73A	4-dr. Sedan-6P	$1,777	3,263 lbs.	55,371
U4	70A	2-dr. Sedan-6P	$1,728	3,207 lbs.	123,329
U4	72C	2-dr. Business Coupe-3P	$1,625	3,142 lbs.	10,665
U4	59A	2-dr. Station Wagon-6P	$2,106	3,459 lbs.	44,315

Customline (Six)

Model No.	Body/ Style No.	Body Type & Seating	Factory Price	Shipping Weight	Production Total
A4	73B	4-dr. Sedan-6P	$1,793	3,155 lbs.	Note 1
A4	70B	2-dr. Sedan-6P	$1,744	3,099 lbs.	Note 1
A4	72B	2-dr. Club Coupe-6P	$1,753	3,080 lbs.	Note 1
A4	59B	2-dr. Station Wagon-6P	$2,122	3,344 lbs.	Note 1
A4	79B	4-dr. Station Wagon-6P	$2,202	3,513 lbs.	Note 1

Customline (V-8)

Model No.	Body/ Style No.	Body Type & Seating	Factory Price	Shipping Weight	Production Total
U4	73B	4-dr. Sedan-6P	$1,870	3,276 lbs.	262,499
U4	70B	2-dr. Sedan-6P	$1,820	3,220 lbs.	293,375
U4	72B	2-dr. Club Coupe-6P	$1,830	3,201 lbs.	33,051
U4	59B	2-dr. Station Wagon-6P	$2,198	3,465 lbs.	36,086
U4	79B	4-dr. Station Wagon-6P	$2,279	3,634 lbs.	43,384

Crestline (Six)

Model No.	Body/ Style No.	Body Type & Seating	Factory Price	Shipping Weight	Production Total
A4	73C	4-dr. Sedan-6P	$1,898	3,159 lbs.	Note 1
A4	60B	2-dr. Victoria Hardtop-6P	$2,055	3,184 lbs.	Note 1
A4	60F	2-dr. Skyliner-6P	$2,164	3,204 lbs.	Note 1
A4	76B	2-dr. Convertible-6P	$2,164	3,231 lbs.	Note 1
A4	79C	2-dr. Country Squire-8P	$2,339	3,563 lbs.	Note 1

Crestline (V-8)

Model No.	Body/ Style No.	Body Type & Seating	Factory Price	Shipping Weight	Production Total
U4	73C	4-dr. Sedan-6P	$1,975	3,280 lbs.	99,677
U4	60B	2-dr. Victoria Hardtop-6P	$2,131	3,305 lbs.	95,464
U4	60F	2-dr. Skyliner-6P	$2,241	3,325 lbs.	13,144
U4	76B	2-dr. Convertible-6P	$2,241	3,352 lbs.	33,685
U4	79C	2-dr. Country Squire-8P	$2,415	3,684 lbs.	12,797

Note 1: Production of six-cylinder and V-8 models of each body style is a combined total.

1954 Ford Mainline two-door Business Coupe (AA)

1954 Ford Mainline two-door Sedan (OCW)

Engines:

Mainline Six: Overhead valve. Cast-iron block. Displacement: 223 cid. B & S: 3.62 x 3.60 in. Compression ratio: 7.2:1. Brake hp: 115 at 3900 rpm. Carburetor: Holley one-barrel Model 1904F. Four main bearings. Code A.

Customline Six: Overhead valve. Cast-iron block. Displacement: 223 cid. B & S: 3.62 x 3.60 in. Compression ratio: 7.2:1. Brake hp: 115 at 3900 rpm. Carburetor: Holley one-barrel Model 1904F. Four main bearings. Code A.

Crestline Six: Overhead valve. Cast-iron block. Displacement: 223 cid. B & S: 3.62 x 3.60 in. Compression ratio: 7.2:1. Brake hp: 115 at 3900 rpm. Carburetor: Holley one-barrel Model 1904F. Four main bearings. Code A.

Mainline Eight: Overhead valve V-8. Cast-iron block. Displacement: 239 cid. B & S: 3.50 x 3.10 in. Compression ratio: 7.2:1. Brake hp: 115 at 3900 rpm. Carburetor: Holley two-barrel Model AA. Four main bearings. Code U.

Customline Eight: Overhead valve V-8. Cast-iron block. Displacement: 239 cid. B & S: 3.50 x 3.10 in. Compression ratio: 7.2:1. Brake hp: 115 at 3900 rpm. Carburetor: Holley two-barrel Model AA. Four main bearings. Code U.

Crestline Eight: Overhead valve V-8. Cast-iron block. Displacement: 239 cid. B & S: 3.50 x 3.10 in. Compression ratio: 7.2:1. Brake hp: 115 at 3900 rpm. Carburetor: Holley two-barrel Model AA. Four main bearings. Code U.

1954 Ford Mainline two-door Station Wagon (OCW)

3 distinctive lines...14 brilliant body styles

1954 Ford Customline four-door Sedan (AA)

1954 Ford Customline two-door Sedan (OCW)

Chassis:

Mainline, Customline and Crestline: Wheelbase: 115 in. Overall length: 198.3 in. Overall width: 73.5 in. Tires: 6.70 x 15, standard and 7.10 x 15, station wagon.

Technical:

Mainline, Customline and Crestline: Three-speed manual transmission was standard equipment. It featured a semi-centrifugal-type clutch, three-speed helical gears and synchronizers for second and third gears. Three-speed with automatic overdrive was optional. Specifications were the same as above with automatic overdrive function cutting in at 27 mph, cutting out at 21 mph. Approximate drive ratio: 0.70:1. Manual control was mounted below the instrument panel. Ford-O-Matic automatic transmission was optional. This was a torque converter-type transmission with automatic planetary gear train, single stage, three-element hydraulic torque converter, hydraulic-mechanical automatic controls with no electrical or vacuum connections and power flow through the fluid member at all times. Rear axle gear ratios: 3.90:1, standard, 4.10:1, with overdrive and 3.31:1 with Ford-O-Matic.

Options:

Automatic overdrive ($110). Ford-O-Matic transmission ($184). Power steering ($134). Power brakes ($41). Radio ($88 to $99). Heater and defroster ($44 to $71). Power windows ($102). Power seat ($64). White sidewall tires ($27 exchange). Note: Power windows were available on Customline and Crestline only.

1954 Ford Customline two-door Club Coupe (OCW)

1954 Ford Customline two-door Ranch Wagon (OCW)

1954 Ford Customline four-door Country Sedan (AA)

1954 Ford Crestline four-door Sedan (PH)

History:

Of the total 1,165,942 Fords built in the 1954 calendar year, industry sources estimate that 863,096 had V-8 engines installed. The 1,000,000th car of the 1954 production run was turned out August 24, 1954. Production of cars built to 1955 specifications began October 25, 1954. Public presentation of the 1954 Ford line was made on January 6, 1954. Of the total 1,165,942 Fords built in the 1954 model year, industry sources estimate that 863,096 had V-8 engines installed. the 1,000,000th Ford of the 1954 production run was turned out August 24, 1954 and in December, Ford announced that it had recorded its best year since 1925.

1954 Ford Crestline two-door Victoria Hardtop (right)

1954 Ford Crestline Skyliner two-door Victoria Hardtop (OCW)

1954 Ford Sunliner two-door Convertible (OCW)

1954 Ford Crestline four-door Country Squire (OCW)

1954 Ford instrument panel detail (OCW)

1954 Ford V-8 engine compartment detail (OCW)

1955 Ford

Mainline — Series A5 / Series U5 — Six and V-8: That wonderful year 1955 brought us 12 months filled with changes. In Great Britain, Anthony Eden took over as Prime Minister after Winston Churchill stepped down. Nikolai Bulganin replaced Georgi Malenkov as premier of the Soviet Union. In Argentina, dictator Juan Peron got the boot after 10 years as President (although he'd return in the 1970s). Ford's 1952 through 1954 styling also got the boot in 1955, but the really big change in Dearborn was a total redesign of the entire Ford line. The new full-size Fords were longer, lower and wider. The cars had a new concave cellular grille, new side trim treatments, a wraparound windshield, Thunderbird Bird-like rear fenders and new series names. Station wagons were now grouped in a separate series. Mainline was the base trim level and included rubber window moldings, a horn button instead of chrome horn ring, one sun visor and an armrest only on the driver's door. These car had a Ford crest on the hood, no series nameplates, no side trim moldings and untrimmed body-color headlight "doors." Just three body styles comprised the Mainline Six offerings. All three models could be had with Ford's famous "Y-block" V-8 for an extra $100. In this case, "Y-8" emblems were placed just ahead of the front wheel openings.

Customline — Series A5 / Series U5 — Six and V-8: The Customline was the intermediate trim level for 1955 and the cars in it included chrome window moldings, a chrome horn half-ring, two sun visors and armrests on all doors. A horizontal chrome strip ran the length of the body from below the headlights to the center of the taillights. A Customline script decorated the front fenders. Only "Tudor" and "Fordor" (in Ford's nomenclature) Sedans remained in the Customline Six series. Both came with a V-8 for $100 more.

Fairlane — Series A5 / Series U5 — Six and V-8: The Fairlane series was the top trim level for 1955 and included chrome window and "A" pillar moldings (hardtops and Sunliner), chrome eyebrows on the headlights and a chrome side sweep molding that dipped on the front doors. The Fairlane name appeared on the hood, below the Ford crest. There were six Fairlane Six models the two-door sedan (called Club Sedan), the four-door sedan (called the Town Sedan), the two-door hardtop (called a Victoria), the Crown Victoria (a two-door hardtop with a tiara-style roof band), the Crown Victoria Skyliner (a hardtop with a transparent forward roof section) and the convertible (called the Sunliner). All could be had with the V-8 for an extra C-Note. The Town Sedan and Club Sedan had rear fender tip scripts. The others had the model name on the door, just behind the dip in the chrome molding.

Station Wagon — Series A5 / Series U5 — Six and V-8: The two-door Ranch Wagon was the base station wagon for six passengers. The Custom Ranch Wagon carried Customline body side moldings. Both of these cars had "Ranch Wagon" scripts on the front fenders. Six- and eight-passenger Country Sedans were offered. The six-passenger had Customline trim with "Country Sedan" on the front fenders, while the eight-passenger had dipping Fairlane sedan trim with "Country Sedan" on the rear fenders. The Country Squire was the top station wagon. It was trimmed on the outside with mahogany-grain panels and blonde fiberglass moldings. The model name was on the rear fenders. All five wagons were available with the six-cylinder engine at prices between $2,043 and $2,991 and a V-8 was $100 additional. See how easy things were back in the "Good Old Days?"

VIN:

The vehicle identification number was stamped on a plate attached to the left front body pillar below the hinge opening. The first symbol indicated the engine: A=223-cid six-cylinder, M=272-cid four-barrel V-8, U=272-cid two-barrel V-8 and P=292-cid police V-8. The second symbol indicated the model year: 5=1955. The third symbol indicated the assembly plant: A=Atlanta, Georgia, B=Buffalo, N.Y., C=Chester, Pennsylvania, D=Dallas, Texas, E=Edgewater, N.J., F=Dearborn, Michigan, G=Chicago, Illinois, K=Kansas City, Kansas, L=Long Beach,

California, M=Memphis, Tennessee, N=Norfolk, Virginia, P=Twin Cities, St. Paul, Minnesota, R=San Jose, California, S=Somerville, Massachusetts and U=Louisville, Kentucky. The fourth symbol indicated the body style: C=Sunliner Convertible, F=Skyliner Glasstop, R=Ranch Wagon, T=Fairlane Tudor/Fordor, V=Victoria Tudor, X=Country Sedan, Y=Country Squire, G=All other styles, W=Special body solid top. The last six symbols were the sequential production number starting at 100001 and up in each factory.

Mainline (Six)

Model No.	Body/ Style No.	Body Type & Seating	Factory Price	Shipping Weight	Production Total
A5	73A	4-dr. Sedan-6P	$1,824	3,106 lbs.	24,132
A5	70A	2-dr. Sedan-6P	$1,778	3,064 lbs.	45,331
A5	70D	2-dr. Business Coupe-3P	$1,677	3,026 lbs.	6,567

Mainline (V-8)

Model No.	Body/ Style No.	Body Type & Seating	Factory Price	Shipping Weight	Production Total
U5	73A	4-dr. Sedan-6P	$1,924	3,216 lbs.	13,583
U5	70A	2-dr. Sedan-6P	$1,878	3,174 lbs.	32,999
U5	70D	2-dr. Business Coupe-3P	$1,777	3,136 lbs.	3,587

Customline (Six)

Model No.	Body/ Style No.	Body Type & Seating	Factory Price	Shipping Weight	Production Total
A5	73B	4-dr. Sedan-6P	$1,916	3,126 lbs.	42,100
A5	70B	2-dr. Sedan-6P	$1,872	3,084 lbs.	55,012

Customline (V-8)

Model No.	Body/ Style No.	Body Type & Seating	Factory Price	Shipping Weight	Production Total
U5	73B	4-dr. Sedan-6P	$2,016	3,236 lbs.	187,089
U5	70B	2-dr. Sedan-6P	$1,972	3,194 lbs.	190,133

Fairlane (Six)

Model No.	Body/ Style No.	Body Type & Seating	Factory Price	Shipping Weight	Production Total
A5	73C	4-dr. Town Sedan-6P	$2,031	3,134 lbs.	3,520
A5	70C	2-dr. Club Sedan-6P	$1,985	3,088 lbs.	1,784
A5	60B	2-dr. Victoria Hardtop-6P	$2,166	3,184 lbs.	556
A5	60F	2-dr. Crown Victoria-6P	$2,273	3,246 lbs.	50
A5	76B	2-dr. Skyliner-6P	$2,343	3,254 lbs.	35
A5	79C	2-dr. Convertible-6P	$2,295	3,248 lbs.	188

Fairlane (V-8)

Model No.	Body/ Style No.	Body Type & Seating	Factory Price	Shipping Weight	Production Total
U5	73C	4-dr. Town Sedan-6P	$2,131	3,268 lbs.	254,680
U5	70C	2-dr. Club Sedan-6P	$2,085	3,222 lbs.	178,086
U5	60B	2-dr. Victoria Hardtop-6P	$2,266	3,318 lbs.	95,439
U5	60F	2-dr. Crown Victoria-6P	$2,373	3,380 lbs.	34,779
U5	76B	2-dr. Skyliner-6P	$2,443	3,388 lbs.	20,000
U5	79C	2-dr. Convertible-6P	$2,395	3,382 lbs.	50,582

Station Wagon (Six)

Model No.	Body/ Style No.	Body Type & Seating	Factory Price	Shipping Weight	Production Total
A5	59A	2-dr. Ranch Wagon-6P	$2,114	3,309 lbs.	14,002
A5	59B	2-dr. Custom Ranch Wagon-6P	$2,180	3,327 lbs.	5,737
A5	79D	4-dr. Country Sedan-6P	$2,227	3,393 lbs.	3,929
A5	79B	4-dr. Country Sedan-8P	$2,358	3,469 lbs.	3,450
A5	79C	4-dr. Country Squire-8P	$2,463	3,471 lbs.	112

Station Wagon (V-8)

Model No.	Body/ Style No.	Body Type & Seating	Factory Price	Shipping Weight	Production Total
U5	59A	2-dr. Ranch Wagon-6P	$2,214	3,443 lbs.	26,614
U5	59B	2-dr. Custom Ranch Wagon-6P	$2,280	3,461 lbs.	39,231
U5	79D	4-dr. Country Sedan-6P	$2,327	3,527 lbs.	51,192
U5	79B	4-dr. Country Sedan-8P	$2,458	3,603 lbs.	47,320
U5	79C	4-dr. Country Squire-8P	$2,563	3,605 lbs.	18,745

Engines:

Base Six: (All) Overhead valve. Cast-iron block. Displacement: 223 cid. B & S: 3.62 x 3.60 in. Compression ratio: 7.5:1. Brake hp: 120 at 4000 rpm. Carburetor: Holley single-barrel. Four main bearings. Code A.

Base V-8 (All): Overhead valve. Cast-iron block. B & S: 3.62 x 3.30 in. Displacement: 272 cid. Compression ratio: 7.60:1. Brake hp: 162 at 4400

1955 Ford Mainline four-door Sedan (OCW)

rpm. Taxable hp: 42.0. Torque: 258 at 2200 rpm. Five main bearings. Solid valve lifters. Crankcase capacity: 5 qt. (add 1 qt. with new oil filter). Cooling system capacity: 19 qt. Carburetor: Holley two-barrel. Code U.

Optional Power-Pack V-8 (All): Overhead valve. Cast-iron block. B & S: 3.62 x 3.30 in. Displacement: 272 cid. Compression ratio: 7.60:1. Brake hp: 182 at 4400 rpm. Taxable hp: 42.0. Torque: 268 at 2600 rpm. Five main bearings. Solid valve lifters. Crankcase capacity: 5 qt. (add 1 qt. with new oil filter). Cooling system capacity: 19 qt. Carburetor: Holley four-barrel. Code M.

Optional Thunderbird V-8 (Manual Transmission): Overhead valve. Cast-iron block. B & S: 3.75 x 3.30 in. Displacement: 292 cid. Compression ratio: 8.1:1. Brake hp: 193 at 4400 rpm. (Taxable hp: 45. Torque: 280 at 2600 rpm. Five main bearings. Solid valve lifters. Crankcase capacity: 5 qt. (add 1 qt. with new oil filter). Cooling system capacity: 19 qt. Carburetor: Holley four-barrel. Code P.

Optional Thunderbird V-8 (Ford-O-Matic Transmission): Overhead valve. Cast-iron block. B & S: 3.75 x 3.30 in. Displacement: 292 cid. Compression ratio: 8.50:1. Brake hp: 198 at 4400 rpm. Taxable hp: 45. Torque: 286 at 2500 rpm. Five main bearings. Solid valve lifters. Crankcase capacity: 5 qt. (add 1 qt. with new oil filter). Cooling system capacity: 19 qt. Carburetor: Holley four-barrel. Code P.

Chassis:

Mainline, Customline and Fairlane: Wheelbase: 115.5 in. Overall length: 198.5 in. Overall width: 75.9 in. Tires: 6.70 x 15 tubeless. Front tread: 58 in. Rear tread: 56 in.

1955 Ford Mainline two-door Business Coupe (OCW)

1955 Ford Mainline two-door Sedan (OCW)

1955 Ford Customline four-door Sedan (OCW)

1955 Ford Fairlane two-door Victoria Hardtop (OCW)

1955 Ford Customline two-door Sedan (AA)

1955 Ford Fairlane two-door Crown Victoria Hardtop (PH)

1955 Ford Fairlane four-door Sedan (OCW)

1955 Ford Fairlane two-door Crown Victoria Hardtop (PH)

1955 Ford Fairlane two-door Club Sedan (OCW)

1955 Ford Sunliner two-door Convertible (OCW)

Station Wagon: Wheelbase: 115.5 in. Overall length: 197.6 in. Overall width: 75.9 in. Tires: 7.10 x 15 tubeless. Front tread: 58 in. Rear tread: 56 in.

Technical:

Mainline, Customline and Fairlane: Three-speed manual was standard equipment. It featured a semi-centrifugal-type clutch, three-speed helical gears and synchronizers for second and third gears. Three-speed with automatic overdrive was optional. Specifications were the same as above with automatic overdrive function cutting in at 27 mph and cutting out at 21 mph. The approximate drive ratio was 0.70:1. Manual control below instrument panel.

Station Wagon: Three-speed manual was standard equipment. It featured a semi-centrifugal-type clutch, three-speed helical gears and synchronizers for second and third gears. Three-speed with automatic overdrive was optional. Specifications were the same as above with automatic overdrive function cutting in at 27 mph and cutting out at 21 mph. Approximate drive ratio: 0.70:1. Manual control below instrument panel.

Options:

Overdrive transmission ($110). Ford-O-Matic automatic transmission ($178). Radio ($99). Heater ($71). Power brakes ($32). Power seat ($64). Power windows ($102). White sidewall tires ($27 exchange). Power steering ($91). Other standard factory and dealer-installed-type options and accessories.

History:

The 1955 Ford was introduced to the public November 12, 1954. Of the total 1,435,002 cars built from October 1954 to September 1955, the majority were V-8s. During the 1955 calendar year, 1,546,762 Ford V-8s and 217,762 sixes were manufactured. Also on a calendar year basis, 230,000 Fords had power steering, 31,800 had power brakes, 22,575 (of all FoMoCo products) had air conditioning, 197,215 cars had overdrive and 1,014,500 cars had automatic transmissions. The 1955 run was the second best in Ford Motor Co. history, behind 1923 when Model Ts dominated the industry. A new factory in Mahwah, N.J., opened this year, to replace one in Edgewater, N.J. A new factory in San Jose, California, replaced a one-third-as-big West Coast plant in Richmond, California. A new factory was also opened in Louisville, Kentucky, replacing a smaller facility in the same city. Robert S. McNamara was vice-president and

1955 Ford two-door Ranch Wagon (OCW)

1955 Ford four-door Country Sedan 8P (OCW)

1955 Ford four-door Country Sedan 6P (OCW)

1955 Ford four-door Country Squire (OCW)

1955 Ford Sunliner trim detail (OCW)

general manager of Ford Division. Ford Motor Company engineering had an experimental turbine-powered vehicle this year. It featured a modified 1955 body shell with an altered grille and exhaust system. This car was actually built in 1954 and had a "4" designation in the prefix code to the assigned serial number, which was from the 1954 production serial number series. The car was scrapped after testing was completed.

1956 Ford

Mainline — Series A6 / Series U6 — Six and V-8: In 1956, Ford re-used its 1955-style body shell. Wheelbase, length, width and height were unchanged. A 12-volt electrical system was adapted for the first time. A wider grille had oblong parking lights at its outer ends. All body side decorations were revamped and the Mainline models finally got body side moldings. Newly-designed taillights featured large, round red lenses with protruding ribbed-chrome center rings. The hood ornament looked like a chrome rocket in a soft tortilla shell. Safety was a popular theme in 1956 and the new Fords featured a completely redesigned instrument panel. A "Lifeguard Safety Package" with dashboard padding, padded sun visors and other ingredients was optional. The steering wheel featured a 2-1/2-inch recessed hub designed to lessen injury to the driver in the event of an accident. Seat belts were also offered for the first time. The Mainline series was the base trim level for 1956. Mainline models built early in the year had rubber window moldings, a horn button instead of horn ring, one sun visor and an armrest on the driver's door only. Later models had bright metal windshield and window molding and a unique molding treatment along the body side. This consisted of two parallel moldings running forward from the taillights, with the longer upper molding curving downwards to a spear tip plate below the rear side window. The lower molding stopped about a foot back and an upward-curving molding connected it with the upper molding near the spear tip. The area between the moldings could be finished in a contrasting color, sometimes matching the roof color. The trunk carried a Ford crest with horizontal chrome bars jutting from either side. Mainline Six models were the same as in 1955. A V-8 was $100 extra in any Mainline model. Ford offered a total of eight engines throughout the model lineup this year. The 223-cid overhead-valve six had another compression ratio boost, which gave it 17 more horsepower. When it came to V-8s, big Fords with manual transmission started with a 272-cid job with a two-barrel carburetor. With Ford-O-Matic, the rating went up. A 292-cid V-8 with a Holley four-barrel was optional. The base Thunderbird V-8 was a dual-exhaust version of the 292. Performance buffs could order a 312-cid Thunderbird Special V-8 with manual transmission or overdrive. By

1956 Ford Mainline two-door Sedan (OCW)

bumping compression up to 9.0:1, Ford made the Thunderbird Special V-8 with Ford-O-Matic transmission attachment even hotter. With two Holley four-barrel carburetors the Thunderbird Special V-8 was top dog except for some rare cars with superchargers.

Customline — Series A6 / Series U6 — Six and V-8: The Customline series was the intermediate trim level and included chrome window moldings, a horn ring, two sun visors, armrests on all doors and passenger assist straps on two-door interior "B" pillars. A constant-width body side molding started on the sides of the front fenders, just behind the headlight hoods, and curved slightly downward, extending past the "Customline" nameplates on the rear doors (or rear quarter panels of four-door models). The rear sections ran from the nameplate to a point just above the taillights. Where the two moldings met there was a "tree branch" effect. Trunk lid identification again consisted of a Ford crest with horizontal chrome bars on either side of the crest. The Tudor Sedan, the Fordor Sedan and a new Victoria Tudor formed the Customline Six series. The $100-more-expensive Customline V-8 models came in the same body styles.

Fairlane — Series A6 / Series U6 — Six and V-8: The Fairlane series was the top trim level for 1956 and included chrome window moldings and chrome "A" pillar moldings on Sunliner convertibles. Fairlane nameplates and crests appeared on the hood and the rear deck lid. Body style nameplates were placed on the front doors. A wide, flared body side molding started on top of the headlight hoods, curved down to dips on the front doors and extended to the rear taillights. Sections to the rear of the "dips" had triple horizontal scoring with eight vertical intersects near the rear. This gave the side trim on the body an "external exhaust pipe" look. The trunk emblem was a black trapezoid with a V-shaped molding on V-8-powered cars. There were seven Fairlane models with a new four-door Victoria hardtop added to the same six body styles offered in 1955. You had to add $100 to get a V-8 engine.

Station Wagon — Series A6 / Series U6 — Six and V-8: Station wagons continued as their own series for 1956. The Ranch Wagon was the base trim level two-door station wagon, while Country Sedans were the intermediate trim level and Country Squires were the top trim level with simulated wood grain exterior paneling. The level of equipment paralleled the Mainline, Customline and Fairlane series of passenger cars. You could get a six-cylinder Ranch Wagon for as little as $2,185 or cough up as much as $2,633 for the V-8 powered "woodie." The all-new Parklane two-door Sport Wagon was not a hardtop like some other non-Ford '56 wagons, but it was decorated with Fairlane side moldings and large chrome trim plates around the front door windows to give it a snazzy, competitive look.

VIN:

The vehicle identification number was stamped on a plate attached to the left front body pillar below the hinge opening. The first symbol indicated the engine: A=223-cid six-cylinder, M=292-cid four-barrel V-8, P=312-cid four-barrel V-8 and U=272-cid two-barrel V-8. The second symbol indicated the model year: 6=1956. The third symbol indicated the assembly plant: A=Atlanta, Georgia, B=Buffalo, N.Y., C=Chester, Pennsylvania, D=Dallas, Texas, E=Edgewater, N.J., F=Dearborn, Michigan, G=Chicago, Illinois, K=Kansas City, Kansas, L=Long Beach, California, M=Memphis, Tennessee, N=Norfolk, Virginia, P=Twin Cities, St. Paul, Minnesota, R=San Jose, California, S=Somerville, Massachusetts and U=Louisville, Kentucky. The fourth symbol indicated the body style: C=Sunliner Convertible, F=Skyliner Glasstop, R=Ranch Wagon, T=Fairlane Tudor/Fordor, V=Victoria Tudor, X=Country Sedan, Y=Country Squire, G=All other styles, W=Special body solid top. The last six symbols are the sequential production number starting at 100001 and up in each factory.

Mainline (Six)

Model No.	Body/ Style No.	Body Type & Seating	Factory Price	Shipping Weight	Production Total
A6	73A	4-dr. Sedan-6P	$1,938	3,127 lbs.	23,403
A6	70A	2-dr. Sedan-6P	$1,892	3,087 lbs.	52,078
A6	70D	2-dr. Business Coupe-3P	$1,791	3,032 lbs.	6,160

Mainline (V-8)

U6	73A	4-dr. Sedan-6P	$1,995	3,238 lbs.	32,081
U6	70A	2-dr. Sedan-6P	$1,992	3,198 lbs.	54,895
U6	70D	2-dr. Business Coupe-3P	$1,891	3,143 lbs.	1,860

Customline (Six)

A6	73B	4-dr. Sedan-6P	$2,043	3,147 lbs.	25,092
A6	70B	2-dr. Sedan-6P	$1,996	3,107 lbs.	29,127
A6	60B	2-dr. Victoria Hardtop-6P	$2,136	3,170 lbs.	1,791

Customline (V-8)

U6	73B	4-dr. Sedan-6P	$2,143	3,258 lbs.	145,603
U6	70B	2-dr. Sedan-6P	$2,096	3,218 lbs.	135,701
U6	60B	2-dr. Victoria Hardtop-6P	$2,236	3,313 lbs.	31,339

Fairlane (Six)

A6	73C	4-dr. Town Sedan-6P	$2,136	3,147 lbs.	3,638
A6	70C	2-dr. Club Sedan-6P	$2,090	3,147 lbs.	1,328
A6	64C	2-dr. Victoria Hardtop-6P	$2,237	3,202 lbs.	727
A6	57A	4-dr. Victoria Hardtop-6P	$2,291	3,297 lbs.	193
A6	64A	2-dr. Crown Victoria-6P	$2,380	3,217 lbs.	103
A6	64B	2-dr. Skyliner-6P	$2,407	3,227 lbs.	Note 1
A6	76B	2-dr. Convertible-6P	$2,402	3,312 lbs.	275

Fairlane (V-8)

U6	73C	4-dr. Town Sedan-6P	$2,190	3,250 lbs.	221,234
U6	70C	2-dr. Club Sedan-6P	$2,014	3,222 lbs.	141,301
U6	64C	2-dr. Victoria Hardtop-6P	$2,337	3,345 lbs.	177,008
U6	57A	4-dr. Victoria Hardtop-6P	$2,391	3,440 lbs.	31,918
U6	64A	2-dr. Crown Victoria-6P	$2,490	3,360 lbs.	9,709
U6	64B	2-dr. Skyliner-6P	$2,507	3,370 lbs.	Note 1
U6	76B	2-dr. Convertible-6P	$2,502	3,455 lbs.	57,872

Station Wagon (Six)

A6	59A	2-dr. Ranch Wagon-6P	$2,227	3,330 lbs.	16,267
A6	59B	2-dr. Custom Ranch Wagon-6P	$2,293	3,345 lbs.	4,272
A6	79D	4-dr. Country Sedan-6P	$2,239	3,420 lbs.	4,770
A6	79B	4-dr. Country Sedan-8P	$2,471	3,485 lbs.	2,248
A6	59C	2-dr. Parklane-6P	$2,471	3,360 lbs.	140
A6	79C	2-dr. Country Squire-8P	$2,576	3,495 lbs.	93

Station Wagon (V-8)

U6	59A	2-dr. Ranch Wagon-6P	$2,327	3,473 lbs.	32,081
U6	59B	2-dr. Custom Ranch Wagon-6P	$2,392	3,488 lbs.	38,045
U6	79D	4-dr. Country Sedan-6P	$2,439	3,563 lbs.	80,604
U6	79B	4-dr. Country Sedan-8P	$2,571	3,628 lbs.	58,000
U6	59C	2-dr. Parklane-6P	$2,571	3,503 lbs.	15,046
U6	79C	2-dr. Country Squire-8P	$2,633	3,638 lbs.	23,128

Note 1: Sources did not separate Crown Victoria Skyliner production. It's likely that the Crown Victoria production numbers above include the 603 Crown Victoria Skyliner Hardtops built. The total of 603 is for sixes and V-8s combined.

Engines:

Base Six: (All): Overhead valve. Cast-iron block. Displacement: 223 cid. B & S: 3.62 x 3.60 in. Compression ratio: 7.5:1. Brake hp: 120 at 4000 rpm. Carburetor: Holley single-barrel. Four main bearings. Code A.

Model U V-8 (Manual transmission): Overhead valve. Cast-iron block. B & S: 3.62 x 3.30 in. Displacement: 272 cid. Compression ratio: 8.40:1. Brake hp: 173 at 4400 rpm. Taxable hp: 42.0. Torque: 260 lbs.-ft. at 2400 rpm. Taxable hp: 42. Five main bearings. Solid valve lifters. Crankcase capacity: 5 qt. (add 1 qt. with new oil filter). Cooling system capacity: 19 qt. Carburetor: Two-barrel. Code U.

1956 Ford Customline four-door Sedan (AA)

1956 Ford Mainline two-door Business Coupe (OCW)

Model U V-8 (Ford-O-Matic): Overhead valve. Cast-iron block. B & S: 3.62 x 3.30 in. Displacement: 272 cid. Compression ratio: 8.40:1. Brake hp: 176 at 4400 rpm. Taxable hp: 42.0. Five main bearings. Solid valve lifters. Crankcase capacity: 5 qt. (add 1 qt. with new oil filter.) Cooling system capacity: 19 qt. Carburetor: Two-barrel. Code U.

Model M Fairlane V-8: Overhead valve. Cast-iron block. B & S: 3.75 x 3.30 in. Displacement: 292 cid. Compression ratio: 8.40:1. Brake hp: 200 at 4600 rpm. Taxable hp: 45. Torque: 285 lbs.-ft. at 2600 rpm. Taxable hp: 45.0. Five main bearings. Solid valve lifters. Crankcase capacity: 5 qt. (add 1 qt. with new oil filter.) Cooling system capacity: 19 qt. Carburetor: Holley 4000 four-barrel. Code M.

Thunderbird V-8: Overhead valve. Cast-iron block. B & S: 3.75 x 3.30 in. Displacement: 292 cid. Compression ratio: 8.40:1. Brake hp: 202 at 4600 rpm. Taxable hp: 45. Torque: 289 lbs.-ft. at 2600 rpm. Taxable hp: 45.0. Five main bearings. Solid valve lifters. Crankcase capacity: 5 qt. (add 1 qt. with new oil filter.) Cooling system capacity: 19 qt. Carburetor: Holley 4000 four-barrel. Code M.

Thunderbird V-8: (Manual transmission or overdrive.) Overhead valve. Cast-iron block. B & S: 3.60 x 3.44 in. Displacement: 312 cid. Compression ratio: 8.4:1. Brake hp: 215 at 4600 rpm. Taxable hp: 45. Torque: 317 lbs.-ft. at 2600 rpm. Five main bearings. Crankcase capacity: 5 qt. (add 1 qt. with new oil filter.) Cooling system capacity: 19 qt. Carburetor: Holley 4000 four-barrel. Code P.

Thunderbird Special V-8: (With Ford-O-Matic.) Overhead valve. Cast-iron block. B & S: 3.60 x 3.44 in. Displacement: 312 cid. Compression ratio: 9.0:1. Brake hp: 225 at 4600 rpm. Taxable hp: 45. Torque: 324 lbs.-ft. at 2600 rpm. Five main bearings. Crankcase capacity: 5 qt. (add 1 qt. with new oil filter.) Cooling system capacity: 19 qt. Carburetor: Holley 4000 four-barrel. Code L.

Thunderbird Special V-8: (With dual four-barrel carburetion.) Overhead valve. Cast-iron block. B & S: 3.60 x 3.44 in. Displacement: 312 cid. Compression ratio: 9.5:1. Brake hp: 260 at unknown rpm. Taxable hp: 45. Torque: unknown. Five main bearings. Crankcase capacity: 5 qt. (add 1 qt. with new oil filter.) Cooling system capacity: 19 qt. Carburetor: Two Holley four-barrel. Code P.

Chassis:

Mainline: Wheelbase: 115.5 in. Overall length: 198.5 in. Overall width: 75.9 in. Tires: 6.70 x 15 tubeless. Front tread: 58 in. Rear tread: 56 in.

Customline: Wheelbase: 115.5 in. Overall length: 198.5 in. Overall width: 75.9 in. Tires: 6.70 x 15 tubeless. Front tread: 58 in. Rear tread: 56 in.

Fairlane: Wheelbase: 115.5 in. Overall length: 198.5 in. Overall width: 75.9 in. Tires: 6.70 x 15 tubeless. Front tread: 58 in. Rear tread: 56 in.

Station Wagon: Wheelbase: 115.5 in. Overall length: 197.6 in. Overall width: 75.9 in. Tires: 7.10 x 15 tubeless. Front tread: 58 in. Rear tread: 56 in.

Technical:

Mainline, Customline, Fairlane and Station Wagon: Three-speed manual transmission with a semi-centrifugal-type clutch, three-speed helical gears and synchronizers for second and third gears standard equipment. Three-speed with automatic overdrive was optional (specifications same as above with automatic overdrive function cutting in at 27 mph, cutting out at 21 mph. Approximate drive ratio: 0.70:1. Manual control below instrument panel.) Ford-O-Matic automatic transmission was optional. This was a torque converter transmission with automatic planetary gear train; single stage, three-element hydraulic torque converter; hydro-mechanical automatic controls with no electric or vacuum connections and power flow through fluid member at all times. Six-cylinder rear axle ratios: (Ford-O-Matic) 3.22:1; (manual transmission) 3.89:1 and (overdrive) 3.89:1. V-8 rear axle ratios: (Ford-O-Matic) 3.22:1; (manual transmission) 3.78:1 and (overdrive) 3.89:1.

1956 Ford Customline two-door Victoria (PH)

1956 Ford Customline two-door Victoria (OCW)

1956 Ford Fairlane four-door Town Sedan (OCW)

1956 Ford Fairlane two-door Club Sedan (OCW)

1956 Ford Fairlane four-door Town Victoria Hardtop (OCW)

1956 Ford Fairlane two-door Club Victoria Hardtop (OCW)

1956 Ford Fairlane two-door Crown Victoria Skyliner Hardtop (OCW)

Automatic overdrive transmission ($110 to $148). Ford-O-Matic transmission ($178 to $215). Power steering for Mainline models ($91). Power steering for other models ($51 to $64). Power seat ($60). Radio ($100). Heater ($85). Power brakes ($32). Thunderbird V-8 for Fairlane ($123). Power brakes ($40). Windshield washers ($10). Wire wheel covers ($35). Power windows ($70). Chrome engine dress-up kit ($25). Rear fender shields. Full wheel discs. White sidewall tires. Continental tire kit. Tinted windshield. Tinted glass. Life-Guard safety equipment. Two-tone paint finish. Front and rear bumper guards. Grille guard package. Rear guard package. Rear mount radio antenna.

History:

Production of 1956 Fords started September 6, 1955. The Parklane station wagon was a Deluxe Fairlane trim level two-door Ranch Wagon. The Crown Victoria Skyliner featured a plexiglass, tinted transparent forward roof, the last year for this type construction. The Sunliner was a two-door convertible. The new Y-block Thunderbird V-8 came with double twin-jet carburetion; integrated automatic choke; dual exhaust; turbo-wedge-shaped combustion chambers and automatic Power Pilot. A 12-volt electrical system and 18-mm anti-fouling spark plugs were adopted this season. Model year sales peaked at 1,392,847 units. Calendar year production hit 1,373,542 vehicles. (Both figures include Thunderbird sales and production). A brand new NBC Television program called "The Ford Show" bowed to the public on October 4, 1956. Many people think the Ford Motor Company-sponsored show was named for its star - Tennessee Ernie Ford. The entertainer had been a big hit in 1955 and 1956 in his own "Tennessee Ernie Ford Show" that aired during daytime hours. The new prime-time evening show increased Ernie's popularity immensely, while selling lots of Fords and Thunderbirds at the same time. Eventually, "The Ford Show" would become the top half-hour variety program in the United States. Ford's trademark closing number was almost always a hymn, gospel or spiritual song. The advertising gurus had flinched when this was proposed, but it turned out to be the winning touch that made the show a big success.

1956 Ford Fairlane two-door Crown Victoria Hardtop (OCW)

1956 Ford Sunliner two-door Convertible (OCW)

1956 Ford two-door Ranch Wagon (OCW)

1956 Ford two-door Custom Ranch Wagon (OCW)

1956 Ford four-door Country Sedan 6P (OCW)

1956 Ford four-door Country Sedan 8P (OCW)

1956 Ford two-door Parklane Sport wagon (OCW)

1956 Ford two-door Parklane Sport wagon (OCW)

1956 Ford four-door Country Squire (OCW)

1957 Ford

Custom — Series A7 / Series U7 — Six and V-8: The 1957 Fords were completely restyled and had several new series designations. They bore only a slight resemblance to 1956 models. Custom models were three inches longer overall and had a one-half-inch longer wheelbase. All models had 14-inch wheels for the first time. The smaller-diameter wheels also contributed to their low-slung lines. Other design changes included a rear-opening hood, streamlined wheel openings and a wraparound windshield with posts that sloped rearward at the bottom. All Fords also sported tail fins, which the automaker described as "high-canted fenders." The big news was the Skyliner model. This car was the world's only true hardtop convertible - or retractable hardtop, depending on how you look at it. A push-button automatic folding mechanism retracted the car's roof into the trunk. Fords in the base Custom car-line had no series nameplates on their fenders. The body side moldings extended from the center side window pillar to the taillights, with a pointed dip on the rear door or fender. Body style offerings consisted of three sedans called the Business Tudor, the Tudor and the Fordor. V-8 versions of each style were $100 additional. This year's base engine was the 223-cid inline six-cylinder. The base V-8 was a 272-cid 190-hp two-barrel version. A 292-cid four-barrel Thunderbird V-8 was optional. Other choices included the 312-cid Thunderbird Special V-8 that came in a 245-hp single four-barrel version, a 270-hp dual four-barrel version, a 285-hp racing version and a 300-hp version (340-hp in NASCAR tune) with a McCulloch/Paxton centrifugal supercharger.

Custom 300 — Series A7 / Series U7 — Six and V-8: The Custom 300 was a new, upper trim level in the short-wheelbase Custom series. Two body styles were available, the Tudor and the Fordor. They had added bright work such as chrome window moldings and a chrome horn ring. Inside there were two sun visors and armrests on all doors. The word F-O-R-D was spelled out in block letters above the grille and a small Ford crest appeared on the trunk lid. There were no series nameplates on the sides of the body. A full-length side molding came with an optional gold aluminum insert that made the smaller, less-expensive Custom 300 look somewhat like a Fairlane 500. The difference was that the rear portion of the molding behind the door dip ran straight to the taillights instead of accenting the tops of the tail fins. This trim lured the author's father into buying a Custom 300 instead of a Fairlane 500, since he felt there wasn't enough difference in the two to justify the Fairlane's higher price. Ford's trim upgrade obviously appealed to buyers of the less-expensive cars. For $100 extra, you could turn your Custom 300 Six into an Eight. (Dad did at least get the V-8!)

Fairlane — Series A7 / Series U7 — Six and V-8: Fairlane was the base trim level for the longer wheelbase Ford series. There were four body styles in this car-line and each was available as a six, at the base price, or as a V-8 for $100 additional. The models available were the two-door Club Sedan, the four-door Town Sedan, the Club Victoria (two-door hardtop) and the Town Victoria (four-door hardtop). These cars had bright Fairlane nameplates on their rear fenders, extra chrome around the roof "C" pillar and bullet-shaped accent panels on the rear fenders - and rear doors of four-door models. The Fairlane name appeared in script on the side of the fenders, above the grille and on the trunk lid. A large, V-shaped Fairlane crest appeared on the trunk lid whenever V-8 engines were added.

Fairlane 500 — Series A7 / Series U7 — Six and V-8: Fairlane 500 was the top trim level in the Fairlane series and included all the trim used on the Fairlane models plus slightly more chrome on the "C" pillars and different side trim. The side trim was a modified version of the Fairlane sweep, which included a gold anodized insert between two chrome strips. It began on the sides of the front fenders, dipping near the back of the front doors, merging into a strip and following the crest of the fins to the rear of the body. Five Fairlane 500s could be had with a six-cylinder engine: Club Sedan, Town Sedan, Club Victoria, Town Victoria and Sunliner convertible. All of these were available with V-8 power for $100 more. A sixth V-8-only model was also offered. This was the Skyliner convertible (retractable hardtop).

Station Wagon — Series A7 / Series U7 — Six and V-8: The Ranch Wagon was the base trim level two-door station wagon for 1957. Country Sedans were the intermediate level with four-door styling. Country Squires were the top trim level, also with four-door styling. The level of equipment paralleled Custom, Custom 300 and Fairlane 500 models of passenger cars.

VIN:

The vehicle identification number was stamped on a plate attached to the left front body pillar below the hinge opening. The first symbol indicated the engine: A=223-cid six-cylinder, B=272-cid V-8, C=292-cid V-8, D=312-cid four-barrel V-8, E=312-cid 2 x four-barrel V-8 and F=312-cid Supercharged V-8. The second symbol indicated the model year: 7=1957. The third symbol indicated the assembly plant: A=Atlanta, Georgia, B=Buffalo, N.Y., C=Chester, Pennsylvania, D=Dallas, Texas, E=Mahwah, N.J., F=Dearborn, Michigan, G=Chicago, Illinois, K=Kansas City, Kansas, L=Long Beach, California, M=Memphis, Tennessee, N=Norfolk, Virginia, P=Twin Cities, St. Paul, Minnesota, R=San Jose, California, S=Somerville, Massachusetts and U=Louisville, Kentucky. The fourth symbol indicated the body style: C=Fairlane 500 Sunliner Convertible, G=Custom and Custom 300 sedans, R=Custom 300 and Ranch Wagon, T=Fairlane Tudor/Fordor, V=Fairlane 500 Victoria Tudor/Fordor, W=Fairlane 500 Skyliner Retractable Hardtop, X=Country Sedan and Y=Country Squire. The last six symbols are the sequential production number starting at 100001 and up in each factory.

1957 Ford Custom two-door Business Sedan (OCW)

1957 Ford Custom 300 four-door Sedan (OCW)

1957 Ford Custom 300 two-door Sedan (AA)

1957 Ford Fairlane four-door Town Sedan (AA)

1957 Ford Custom four-door Sedan (OCW)

1957 Ford Custom two-door Sedan (OCW)

Custom (Six)

Model No.	Body/ Style No.	Body Type & Seating	Factory Price	Shipping Weight	Production Total
A7	73A	4-dr. Sedan-6P	$2,112	3,193 lbs.	37,719
A7	70A	2 dr. Sedan-6P	$2,061	3,150 lbs.	74,477
A7	70A	2-dr. Business Sedan-3P	$1,949	3,141 lbs.	5,242

Custom (V-8)

U7	73A	4-dr. Sedan-6P	$2,212	3,315 lbs.	31,205
U7	70A	2 dr. Sedan-6P	$2,161	3,272 lbs.	42,486
U7	70D	2-dr. Business Sedan-3P	$2,049	3,263 lbs.	1,646

Custom 300 (Six)

A7	73B	4-dr. Sedan-6P	$2,227	3,208 lbs.	33,585
A7	70B	2 dr. Sedan-6P	$2,175	3,163 lbs.	34,242

Custom 300 (V-8)

U7	73B	4-dr. Sedan-6P	$2,327	3,330 lbs.	161,291
U7	70B	2-dr. Sedan-6P	$2,275	3,285 lbs.	126,118

Fairlane (Six)

A7	58A	4-dr. Town Sedan-6P	$2,356	3,315 lbs.	2,304
A7	64A	2-dr. Club Sedan-6P	$2,305	3,270 lbs.	2,199
A7	63B	2-dr. Victoria Hardtop-6p	$2,363	3,305 lbs.	260
A7	57B	4-dr. Victoria Hardtop-6P	$2,427	3,350 lbs.	1,139

Fairlane (V-8)

U7	58A	4-dr. Town Sedan-6P	$2,456	3,437 lbs.	49,756
U7	64A	2-dr. Club Sedan-6P	$2,405	3,392 lbs.	37,644
U7	63B	2-dr. Victoria Hardtop-6p	$2,463	3,427 lbs.	43,867
U7	57B	4-dr. Victoria Hardtop-6P	$2,527	3,472 lbs.	11,556

Fairlane 500 (Six)

A7	58B	4-dr. Town Sedan-6P	$2,403	3,330 lbs.	4,076
A7	64B	2-dr. Club Sedan-6P	$2,351	3,285 lbs.	2,217
A7	63A	2-dr. Victoria Hardtop-6p	$2,389	3,320 lbs.	2,389
A7	57A	4-dr. Victoria Hardtop-6P	$2,474	3,365 lbs.	932
A7	76B	2-dr. Convertible-6P	$2,575	3,475 lbs.	832

Fairlane 500 (V-8)

U7	58B	4-dr. Town Sedan-6P	$2,503	3,452 lbs.	189,086
U7	64B	2-dr. Club Sedan-6P	$2,451	3,407 lbs.	91,536
U7	63A	2-dr. Victoria Hardtop-6P	$2,509	3,442 lbs.	180,813
U7	57A	4-dr. Victoria Hardtop-6P	$2,574	3,487 lbs.	67,618
U7	51A	2-dr. Retractable-6P	$3,012	3,916 lbs.	20,766
U7	76B	2-dr. Convertible-6P	$2,675	3,597 lbs.	76,896

Station Wagon (Six)

A7	59A	2-dr. Ranch Wagon-6P	$2,371	3,394 lbs.	23,924
A7	59B	2-dr. Del Rio Wagon-6P	$2,467	3,401 lbs.	4,981
A7	79D	4-dr. Country Sedan-6P	$2,521	3,464 lbs.	9,007
A7	79B	4-dr. Country Sedan-8P	$2,626	3,553 lbs.	3,830
A7	79E	2-dr. Country Squire-8P	$2,754	3,567 lbs.	245

Station Wagon (V-8)

U7	59A	2-dr. Ranch Wagon-6P	$2,471	3,516 lbs.	36,562
U7	59B	2-dr. Del Rio Wagon-6P	$2,567	3,523 lbs.	41,124
U7	79D	4-dr. Country Sedan-6P	$2,621	3,586 lbs.	128,244
U7	79B	4-dr. Country Sedan-8P	$2,726	3,675 lbs.	45,808
U7	79E	2-dr. Country Squire-8P	$2,854	3,689 lbs.	27,445

Engines:

Base Six: Overhead valve. Cast-iron block. Displacement: 223 cid. B & S: 3.62 x 3.60 in. Compression ratio: 8.6:1. Brake hp: 144 at 4200 rpm. Carburetor: Holley one-barrel. Four main bearings. Code A.

Optional V-8 with manual transmission: Overhead valve. Cast-iron block. B & S: 3.62 x 3.30 in. Displacement: 272 cid. Compression ratio: 8.40:1. Brake hp: 173 at 4400 rpm. Taxable hp: 42.0. Torque: 260 lbs.-ft. at 2400 rpm. Taxable hp: 42. Five main bearings. Solid valve lifters. Crankcase capacity: 5 qt. (add 1 qt. with new oil filter). Cooling system capacity: 19 qt. Carburetor: Two-barrel. Code U.

Optional V-8 with Ford-O-Matic transmission: Overhead valve. Cast-iron block. B & S: 3.62 x 3.30 in. Displacement: 272 cid. Compression ratio: 8.40:1. Brake hp: 176 at 4400 rpm. Taxable hp: 42.0. Five main bearings. Solid valve lifters. Crankcase capacity: 5 qt. (add 1 qt. with new oil filter). Cooling system capacity: 19 qt. Carburetor: Two-barrel. Code U.

Optional Fairlane V-8: Overhead valve. Cast-iron block. B & S: 3.75 x 3.30 in. Displacement: 292 cid. Compression ratio: 8.40:1. Brake hp: 200 at 4600 rpm. Taxable hp: 45. Torque: 285 lbs.-ft. at 2600 rpm. Taxable hp: 45.0. Five main bearings. Solid valve lifters. Crankcase capacity: 5 qt. (add 1 qt. with new oil filter). Cooling system capacity: 19 qt. Carburetor: Holley 4000 four-barrel. Code M.

1957 Ford Fairlane two-door Club Sedan (OCW)

1957Ford Fairlane 500 four-door Town Sedan (PH)

1957 Ford Fairlane 500 Club Victoria two-door hardtop(OCW)

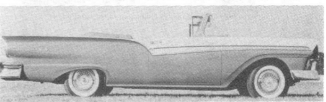

1957 Ford Sunliner two-door Convertible (OCW)

1957 Ford Fairlane two-door Club Victoria Hardtop (OCW)

1957 Ford Skyliner two-door Retractable (OCW)

Optional Thunderbird V-8: Overhead valve. Cast-iron block. B & S: 3.75 x 3.30 in. Displacement: 292 cid. Compression ratio: 8.40:1. Brake hp: 202 at 4600 rpm. Taxable hp: 45. Torque: 289 lbs.-ft. at 2600 rpm. Taxable hp: 45.0. Five main bearings. Solid valve lifters. Crankcase capacity: 5 qt. (add 1 qt. with new oil filter). Cooling system capacity: 19 qt. Carburetor: Holley 4000 four-barrel. Code M.

Optional Thunderbird Special V-8 (Manual or overdrive transmission): Overhead valve. Cast-iron block. B & S: 3.60 x 3.44 in. Displacement: 312 cid. Compression ratio: 8.4:1. Brake hp: 215 at 4600 rpm. Taxable hp: 45. Torque: 317 lbs.-ft. at 2600 rpm. Five main bearings. Crankcase capacity: 5 qt. (add 1 qt. with new oil filter). Cooling system capacity: 19 qt. Carburetor: Holley 4000 four-barrel. Code P.

Optional Thunderbird Special V-8 (Ford-O-Matic transmission): Overhead valve. Cast-iron block. B & S: 3.60 x 3.44 in. Displacement: 312 cid. Compression ratio: 9.0:1. Brake hp: 225 at 4600 rpm. Taxable hp: 45. Torque: 324 lbs.-ft. at 2600 rpm. Five main bearings. Crankcase

capacity: 5 qt. (add 1 qt. with new oil filter). Cooling system capacity: 19 qt. Carburetor: Holley 4000 four-barrel. Code L.

Optional Thunderbird Special V-8 (with dual four-barrel carburetors): Overhead valve. Cast-iron block. B & S: 3.60 x 3.44 in. Displacement: 312 cid. Compression ratio: 9.5:1. Brake hp: 260 at unknown rpm. Taxable hp: 45. Torque: unknown. Five main bearings. Crankcase capacity: 5 qt. (add 1 qt. with new oil filter). Cooling system capacity: 19 qt. Carburetor: Two Holley four-barrel. Code P.

Technical:

Custom, Custom 300, Fairlane, Fairlane 500 and Station Wagon: Three-speed manual transmission (with semi-centrifugal-type clutch, three-speed helical gears and synchronizers for second and third gears) standard. Three-speed with automatic overdrive was optional. Specifications were the same as above with automatic overdrive function cutting in at 27 mph,

1957 Ford Fairlane 500 two-door Club Sedan (OCW)

1957 Ford Fairlane 500 two-door Club Sedan (OCW)

1957 Ford Fairlane 500 Town Victoria four-door hardtop (OCW)

1957 Ford two-door Del Rio Ranch Wagon (OCW)

1957 Ford four-door Country Sedan 6P (OCW)

1957 Ford four-door Country Sedan 8P (PH)

1957 Ford four-door Country Squire (OCW)

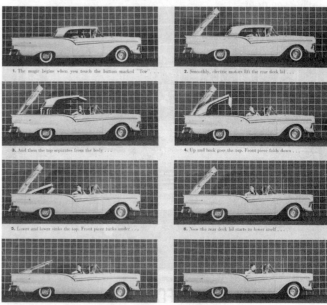

1957 Ford Skyliner (OCW)

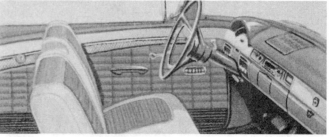

1957 Ford Fairlane 500 interior detail (OCW)

cutting out at 21 mph. Approximate drive ratio: 0.70:1. Manual control below instrument panel. Ford-O-Matic automatic transmission was optional. This was a torque converter transmission with automatic planetary gear train single-stage, three-element hydraulic torque converter hydro-mechanical automatic controls with no electric or vacuum connections and power flow through fluid member at all times. Six-cylinder rear axle ratios: (Ford-O-Matic) 3.22:1 (manual transmission) 3.89:1 and (automatic overdrive) 4.11:1. V-8 rear axle ratios: (Ford-O-Matic) 3.10:1 (manual transmission) 3.56:1 and (automatic overdrive) 3.70:1.

Options:

292-cid V-8 ($439). Ford-O-Matic ($188). Automatic overdrive ($108). Power steering ($68). Radio ($100). Heater and defroster ($85). Power brakes ($38). Fairlane/station wagon 312-cid V-8 engine option ($43). Rear fender shields (skirts). Two-tone paint. Back-up lamps. Large wheel covers (standard on Fairlane 500). White sidewall tires. Continental tire extension kit. Outside rearview mirror. Lifeguard safety equipment package. Oversized tires. Radio antenna. Non-glare mirror.

History:

The introduction of 1957 Fords and Thunderbirds took place in October 1956. The Fairlane 500 Skyliner with retractable hardtop was introduced as a midyear addition to the line. Overdrive or Ford-O-Matic transmission could now be ordered for any car with any engine. Model-year production was 1,655,068 vehicles. Calendar-year sales amounted to 1,522,406 Fords and Thunderbirds. Ford out-produced Chevrolet this season, to become America's number one automaker of 1957 on a model-year-production basis. The name Del Rio was used for a deluxe two-door Ranch Wagon that came with Fairlane level trim.

1958 Ford

Custom 300 — Series A8 / Series U8 — (Six and V-8): The 1958 Fords utilized the same basic body used in 1957 with many new styling ideas. A simulated air scoop hood and honeycomb grille were borrowed from the Thunderbird. Dual headlights and a sculptured rear deck lid created a more futuristic image. Cruise-O-Matic three-speed automatic transmission was offered for the first time, along with 332-cid and 352-cid V-8s. Also new was the one-year-only Ford-Aire air-suspension system for Fairlanes. Custom 300s included chrome window moldings, a horn button instead of a horn ring, one sun visor, an armrest on the driver's door only and a single chrome strip on the body side. This molding began on the side of the front fender, continued horizontally to the back of the front door, then turned down and joined a horizontal chrome strip that continued to the back of the body. A top-of-the-line Styletone trim option duplicated this side trim, except the lower horizontal strip was a double strip with a gold anodized insert. A mid-level Special trim option was also available with a small horizontal chrome strip that turned upward just behind the door. Model offerings were the same as 1957 with prices up $70 to $90. This year adding a V-8 cost $137. The 223-cid six-cylinder engine gained one horsepower. The base Ford V-8 was the 272 with a Holley two-barrel. A new 332-cid Interceptor V-8 came with a two-barrel or four-barrel carburetor. There was also a high-horsepower Interceptor Special V-8 with a single four-barrel carburetor and 10.2:1 compression ratio.

Fairlane — Series A8 / Series U8 — (Six and V-8): The Fairlane model was the entry-level long-wheelbase Ford. It included chrome window moldings (with slightly less chrome around the "C" pillar than Fairlane 500 models) and different side stripe treatments. The initial version had two strips. The lower molding began at the rear of the front wheel opening, then went straight to the back of the front door. From there it began to gradually curve upward. The upper strip began at the front of the fender and went straight back, to the back of the front door. It then began to curve gradually downward, merging with the lower strip directly over the rear wheel opening. A Fairlane script appeared on the rear fenders and directly above the grille opening. Starting at midyear an additional sweep spear of anodized aluminum trim was centered in the panel between the moldings and three "port hole" style trim pieces were added at the rear. The 1957 body styles were carried over. New (and offered only in 1958) was the Ford-Aire suspension system for use in Fairlane series cars and station wagons.

Fairlane 500 — Series A8 / Series U8 — (Six and V-8): The Fairlane 500 models had the top trim level in the Fairlane series. They included all the trim used in the Fairlane models plus slightly more chrome on the "C" pillars and different side trim. The side trim was a double runner chrome strip with a gold anodized insert. The top chrome strip began on the side of the front fender, sloped slightly, and terminated at the top of the rear bumper. The lower molding split from the upper strip where the front door began, dropped in a modified Fairlane sweep and merged with the upper strip at the rear bumper. A Fairlane script appeared

above the grille and on the trunk lid, while the Fairlane 500 script appeared on the rear fenders, above the chrome side trim. This series also had the same styles as last year with similar price differentials.

Station Wagon — Series A8 / Series U8 — (Six and V-8): The Ranch Wagon was the base trim level two-door and four-door station wagons for 1958. The two-door Del Rio wagon also re-appeared. Country Sedans were intermediate level station wagons and Country Squires were the top trim level. You could buy a cheap six-cylinder Ford wagon for under $2,400 or move up a full 12 notches to the V-8-powered Country Squire with a list price approaching $3,000. Ford sure packed a lot of station wagon models into a $600 price spread.

VIN:

Ford's coding system for serial numbers can be broken down, as follows: The first symbol designates the engine type: (A) 223-cid six-cylinder, (B) 332-cid V-8, (C) 292-cid V-8, (G) 332-cid V-8, (H) 352-cid V-8. The second symbol designates the model year: "8" for 1958. The third symbol designates the final assembly plant, as follows: A = Atlanta, B = Buffalo, C = Chester, D = Dallas, G = Chicago, F= Dearborn, E = Mahwah, K = Kansas City, L = Long Beach, M = Memphis, N = Norfolk, R = San Jose, U = Louisville, P = Twin City (St. Paul). The fourth symbol designates body type, as follows: C = Fairlane 500 convertible,

1958 Ford Custom 300 two-door Sedan (OCW)

1958 Ford Fairlane four-door Town Sedan (OCW)

1958 Ford Fairlane 500 two-door Club Sedan (OCW)

G = Custom 300 (two-door and four-door), R = Custom 300 Ranch Wagon, Del Rio, T = Fairlane/Fairlane 500 (two-door and four-door), V = Fairlane/Fairlane 500/Victoria (two-door and four-door), W = Retractable hardtop, X = Country Sedan, Y = Country Squire. The fifth through tenth digits indicate the number of the unit built at each assembly plant, beginning with 100001. Custom 300 six-cylinder models began with the designation "A8" followed by assembly plant code, body type code, and, finally, the unit's production number, according to the final assembly location. Each plant began at 100001 and went up.

Custom 300 (Six)

Model No.	Body/Style No.	Body Type & Seating	Factory Price	Shipping Weight	Production Total
A8	73A	4-dr. Sedan-6P	$2,180	3,222 lbs.	71,306
A8	70A	2-dr. Sedan-6P	$2,126	3,194 lbs.	102,375
A8	70D	2-dr. Business Sedan-3P	$2,038	3,171 lbs.	3,291

Custom 300 (V-8)

A8	73A	4-dr. Sedan-6P	$2,317	3,334 lbs.	92,062
A8	70A	2-dr. Sedan-6P	$2,263	3,306 lbs.	71,066
A8	70D	2-dr. Business Sedan-3P	$2,175	3,283 lbs.	771

Fairlane (Six)

A8	58A	4-dr. Town Sedan-6P	$2,346	3,371 lbs.	8,448
A8	64A	2-dr. Club Sedan-6P	$2,292	3,319 lbs.	9,005
A8	63B	2-dr. Victoria Hardtop-6P	$2,425	3,317 lbs.	1,294
A8	57B	4-dr. Victoria Hardtop-6P	$2,490	3,394 lbs.	215

Fairlane (V-8)

U8	58A	4-dr. Town Sedan-6P	$2,454	3,483 lbs.	49,042
U8	64A	2-dr. Club Sedan-6P	$2,400	3,431 lbs.	29,361
U8	63B	2-dr. Victoria Hardtop-6P	$2,549	3,429 lbs.	15,122
U8	57B	4-dr. Victoria Hardtop-6P	$2,612	3,506 lbs.	5,653

Fairlane 500 (Six)

A8	58A	4-dr. Town Sedan-6P	$2,499	3,379 lbs.	3,694
A8	64B	2-dr. Club Sedan-6P	$2,445	3,307 lbs.	1,311
A8	63A	2-dr. Victoria Hardtop-6P	$2,506	3,317 lbs.	1,766
A8	57A	4-dr. Victoria Hardtop-6P	$2,570	3,414 lbs.	758
A8	76B	2-dr. Convertible-6P	$2,721	3,483 lbs.	581

Fairlane 500 (V-8)

U8	58A	4-dr. Town Sedan-6P	$2,605	3,526 lbs.	102,004
U8	64B	2-dr. Club Sedan-6P	$2,551	3,454 lbs.	32,730
U8	63A	2-dr. Victoria Hardtop-6P	$2,612	3,464 lbs.	78,673
U8	57A	4-dr. Victoria Hardtop-6P	$2,676	3,561 lbs.	35,751
U8	51A	2-dr. Retractable-6P	$3,234	4,069 lbs.	14,713
U8	76B	2-dr. Convertible-6P	$2,845	3,630 lbs.	34,448

Station Wagon (Six)

A8	59A	2-dr. Ranch Wagon-6P	$2,468	3,483 lbs.	19,004
A8	79A	4-dr. Ranch Wagon-6P	$2,522	3,540 lbs.	13,816
A8	59B	2-dr. Del Rio Wagon-6P	$2,574	3,488 lbs.	1,570
A8	79D	4-dr. Country Sedan-6P	$2,628	3,545 lbs.	4,964
A8	79C	4-dr. Country Sedan-8P	$2,735	3,613 lbs.	2,420
A8	79E	4-dr. Country Squire-8P	$2,865	3,650 lbs.	230

Station Wagon (V-8)

U8	59A	2-dr. Ranch Wagon-6P	$2,575	3,620 lbs.	14,997
U8	79A	4-dr. Ranch Wagon-6P	$2,629	3,677 lbs.	19,038
U8	59B	2-dr. Del Rio Wagon-6P	$2,681	3,625 lbs.	11,117
U8	79D	4-dr. Country Sedan-6P	$2,735	3,682 lbs.	63,808
U8	79C	4-dr. Country Sedan-8P	$2,842	3,750 lbs.	18,282
U8	79E	4-dr. Country Squire-8P	$2,972	3,787 lbs.	14,790

Engines:

Base Six: Overhead valve. Cast-iron block. Displacement: 223 cid. B & S: 3.62 x 3.60 in. Compression ratio: 6.6:1. Brake hp: 145 at 4200 rpm. Carburetor: Holley one-barrel. Four main bearings. Code A.

Base V-8: Overhead valve. Cast-iron block. B & S: 3.75 x 3.30 in. Displacement: 292 cid. Compression ratio: 9.10:1. Brake hp: 205 at 4500 rpm. Taxable hp: 45.0. Torque: 295 lbs.-ft. at 2400 rpm. Five main bearings. Solid valve lifters. Crankcase capacity: 5 qt. (add 1 qt. with new oil filter). Cooling system capacity: 19 qt. Carburetor: Holley four-barrel Model R-1281-3A with standard transmission or R-1282-3A with automatic transmission. Code C.

Interceptor V-8: Overhead valve. Cast-iron block. B & S: 4.00 x 3.30 in. Displacement: 332 cid. Compression ratio: 9.50:1. Brake hp:

240 at 4600 rpm. Taxable hp: 51.2. Torque: 360 lbs.-ft. at 2800 rpm. Five main bearings. Valve lifters: hydraulic. Crankcase capacity: 5 qt. (add 1 qt. with new oil filter). Cooling system capacity: 19 qt. Dual exhaust. Carburetor: Holley four-barrel Model R-1406-A with standard transmission or R-1552-A with automatic transmission. Code G.

Interceptor V-8: Overhead valve. Cast-iron block. B & S: 4.00 x 3.30 in. Displacement: 332 cid. Compression ratio: 9.60:1. Brake hp: 265 at 4600 rpm. Taxable hp: 51.2. Torque: 360 lbs.-ft. at 2800 rpm. Five main bearings. Crankcase capacity: 5 qt. (add 1 qt. with new oil filter). Cooling system capacity: 19 qt. Dual exhaust. Carburetor: Holley two-barrel Model R-1406-A with standard transmission or R-1552-A with automatic transmission. Code G.

Thunderbird V-8: Overhead valve. Cast-iron block. B & S: 4.00 x 3.50 in. Displacement: 352 cid. Compression ratio: 10.2:1. Brake hp: 300 at 4600 rpm. Taxable hp: 51.2. Torque: 395 lbs.-ft. at 2800 rpm. Five main bearings. Valve lifters: (early) solid, (late) hydraulic. Crankcase capacity: 5 qt. (add 1 qt. with new oil filter). Cooling system capacity: 19.5 qt. Dual exhaust. Carburetor: Ford-Holley Model B8A-9510-E four-barrel or Carter nos. 2640S-SA-SC four-barrel. Code H.

Police Special V-8: Overhead valve. Cast-iron block. B & S: 4.05 x 3.50 in. Displacement: 361 cid. Compression ratio: 10.50:1. Brake hp:

1958 Ford Fairlane 500 four-door Town Sedan (OCW)

1958 Ford Fairlane 500 Town Victoria four-door hardtop (OCW)

1958 Ford Fairlane 500 Club Victoria two-door hardtop (OCW)

1958 Ford Sunliner two-door Convertible (OCW)

303 at 4600 rpm. Taxable hp: 52.49. Torque: 400 lbs.-ft. at 2800 rpm. Five main bearings. Solid valve lifters. Crankcase capacity: 5 qt. (add 1 qt. with new oil filter). Cooling system capacity (Add 1 qt. for heater): 18.5 qt. Carburetor: (Manual transmission) Holley R-1482-A four-barrel, (Automatic transmission) Holley R-1483-A four-barrel. Engine code: W.

Chassis:

Custom 300: Wheelbase: 116 in. Overall length: 202 in. Overall width: 78 in. Tires: 7.50 x 14.

Fairlane: Wheelbase: 118 in. Overall length: 207 in. Overall width: 78 in. Tires: 7.50 x 14.

Fairlane 500: Wheelbase: 118 in. Overall length: 211 in., Skyliner retractable and 207 in., other Fairlane models. Overall width: 78 in. Tires: 8.00 x 14, Skyliner retractable and 7.50 x 14, other Fairlane 500 models.

Station Wagon: Wheelbase: 116 in. Overall length: 202.7 in. Overall width: 78 in. Tires: 7.50 x 14 and 8.00 x 14, nine-passenger station wagons.

Technical:

Custom 300, Fairlane, Fairlane 500 and Station Wagon: Three-speed manual transmission was standard equipment. It featured semi-centrifugal-type clutch, three-speed helical gears, with synchronizers for second and third gears. Three-speed with automatic overdrive was optional. Specifications were the same as above with automatic overdrive function cutting in at 27 mph, cutting out at 21 mph. Approximate drive ratio: 0.70:1. Manual control below instrument panel. Ford-O-Matic automatic transmission was optional. This was a torque converter transmission with automatic planetary gear train, single-stage, three-element hydraulic torque converter, hydro-mechanical automatic controls with no electrical or vacuum connections and power flow through fluid member at all times. Cruise-O-Matic automatic transmission was also optional. This unit was the same as Ford-O-Matic, except for having three-speeds forward. It was a high-performance automatic transmission with two selective drive ranges for smooth 1-2-3 full-power stabs, or 2-3 gradual acceleration and axle ratio of 2.69:1 for fuel economy. Six-cylinder rear axle ratios: (Ford-O-Matic) 3.22:1, (manual transmission) 3.89:1 and (automatic overdrive) 4.11:1. V-8 rear axle ratios: (Cruise-O-Matic) 2.69:1, (Ford-O-Matic) 3.10:1, (manual transmission) 3.56:1 and (automatic overdrive) 3.70:1.

Options:

Ford-O-Matic ($180). Cruise-O-Matic ($197). Ford-Aire suspension ($156). Overdrive ($108). Power brakes ($37). Power steering ($69). Front power windows ($50), on Custom 300 'business' two-door ($64). Front and rear power windows ($101). Manual four-way adjustable seat ($17). Four-way power adjustable seat ($64). Six-tube radio and antenna ($77). Nine-tube Signal-Seeking radio and antenna ($99). White sidewall tires, four-ply size 7.50 x 14 ($33). White sidewall tires, four-ply, size 6.00 x 14 ($50). Wheel covers ($19 and standard on Fairlane 500). Styletone two-tone paint ($22). Tinted glass ($20). Back-up lights ($10). Custom 300 Deluxe interior trim ($24). Electric clock ($15 and standard on Fairlane 500). Windshield washer ($12). Positive action windshield wiper ($11). Lifeguard safety package with padded

1958 Ford Skyliner two-door Retractable (OCW)

1958 Ford four-door Country Sedan 6P (OCW)

instrument panel and sun visors ($19). Lifeguard safety package, as above, plus two front seat belts ($33). Polar Air Conditioner, includes tinted glass ($271). Select Air Conditioner, includes tinted glass ($395). Interceptor 265-hp V-8 in Custom 300 ($196), in Fairlane ($163). Interceptor Special 300-hp V-8 in Fairlane 500 ($159), in station wagon ($150). Note: Interceptor engine prices are in place of base six-cylinder prices. Automatic overdrive ($108). Heater and defroster ($80). Heater and defroster in Fairlanes and station wagons ($85).

History:

Dealer introductions for 1958 Fords were held November 7, 1957. Dealer introductions for 1958 Thunderbirds were held February 13, 1958. Production at three factories — Memphis, Buffalo and Somerville — was phased out this season. In June 1958, a new plant, having capacity equal to all three aforementioned factories, was opened at Loraine, Ohio. On a model year basis, 74.4 percent of all Fords built in the 1958 run had V-8 power. Sixty-eight percent of these cars had automatic transmission. Model year production of Fords and Thunderbirds totaled 967,945 cars. Calendar-ear sales of Fords and Thunderbirds peaked at 1,038,560 units.

1958 Ford four-door Country Sedan 8P (PH)

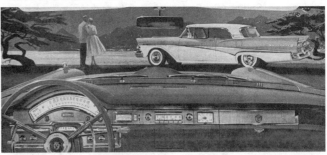

1958 Ford Instrument Panel (OCW)

1958 Ford Del Rio Ranch wagon (OCW)

1958 Ford Country Squire (OCW)

1959 Ford

Custom 300 — Series A9 / Series U9 — (Six and V-8): The 1958 Brussels World's Fair drew 42 million visitors to Hetsel Park, in Brussels, Belgium, to celebrate the theme, "For a more human world." The six-month-long extravaganza involved 4,645 expositors from 51 different nations. Ford Motor Company was one of the participants from the United States and used the fair to launch its redesigned 1959 models. The "Altogether New" '59 Fords were awarded a Gold Medal, at the Fair, by the Comité Francais de L'Elégance, which honored the cars' distinctiveness of style and beautiful proportions. Even now, many Ford enthusiasts and collectors consider the 1959 Fords to be the most beautifully styled Fords ever built. With elegance and understated class, the cars showed remarkably good taste. At a time when other automakers were designing cars that looked capable of interstellar travel or supersonic speeds, Ford exercised great restraint. The designers swept the rear fender feature lines to the back of the car, formed a housing for the back-up lights and curved the lower portion around an oversized taillight for a startling effect. At the front end, a new full-width grille featured an insert with a pattern of "floating" stylized stars. The parking lights were recessed into the bumper. The flat-top front fenders hooded dual headlights. They had a sculptured effect along the sides of the front fender and doors and rolled over the side trim. An exceptionally flat hood characterized these long, low cars. Bright new colors were offered. The Custom 300 series was the base trim level for 1959. These cars wore no series nameplates, but had a Ford crest medallion on the rear deck lid. "Tee Ball" front fender ornaments were optional, as were four "Flying Dart" rear quarter panel ornaments. The side trim consisted of a single molding running back along the front fender/door feature line, then curving upwards the top of the tail fin which it trimmed straight back to the rear of the car. The Business Tudor, Tudor and Fordor were offered as Custom 300 Sixes. All three were available as Custom 300 V-8 models for $110 additional. This year, the big Fords were available with a choice of four engines, starting with the Mileage Maker Six. The 292-cid Thunderbird V-8 had a two-barrel carburetor. Next came the 332-cid Thunderbird Special V-8, also with a two-barrel carb, but a higher 8.9:1 compression ratio. The top option was the 352-cid 300-hp Thunderbird Special with a four-barrel Holley carburetor and even higher compression ratio. Selling features highlighted for '59 included Ford's rugged "Lifeguard" design with a husky frame that spread out a full foot wider around the passenger compartment for greater side-impact protection. Automatic Ride Control teamed a new front suspension with Tyrex tires and the variable-rate rear suspension for a smoother, better-controlled ride. A lighter, simplified version of Ford-O-Matic Drive promised satin-smooth shifting and greater durability.

Fairlane — Series A9 / Series U9 — (Six and V-8): The Fairlane model was the intermediate trim level for 1959 and included the following

1959 Ford Custom 300 four-door Sedan (OCW)

1959 Ford Custom 300 two-door Sedan (OCW)

1959 Ford Custom 300 two-door Business Coupe (OCW)

features that were not standard on Custom 300s: chrome window moldings, a chrome horn ring, two sun visors and armrests on all doors. The Fairlane name appeared on the rear fenders. On these cars, there was a second molding on the front fender and door that flared slightly outwards as it ran rearwards. It ran farther back than the upper molding and a curved piece joined the two. This piece created a bullet-shaped pattern at the front of the rear fender "tube." Painted finish within the two front fender/door moldings was standard and an aluminum insert was optional. The rear deck lid had a bright metal "V" with a gold aluminum insert in the area below the Fairlane name only. Fairlanes included the Tudor Special sedan and Fordor Special sedan.

Fairlane 500 — Series A9 / Series U9 — (Six and V-8): Early in the 1959 model year, Ford's top-of-the-line car was the Fairlane 500. It included all Fairlane trim as well as the aluminum insert between the front moldings. The "Fairlane 500" name appeared at the extreme rear end of the rear fender tubes. In addition, a large, finely-ribbed aluminum panel surrounded the rear wheel opening and ran to the rear bumper. Optional stainless steel fender skirts could be ordered to expand the large expanse of bright metal trim. The rear deck lid was trimmed with a huge chrome V molding that ran from tail fin to tail fin and had the Fairlane 500 name above the center of the "vee." Five Fairlane 500 Sixes were available: the Tudor Special sedan, the Fordor Special sedan, the Tudor Victoria hardtop, the Fordor Victoria hardtop and the Sunliner convertible. The V-8 series offered all of these models for $110 additional, plus the Skyliner retractable hardtop.

Galaxie — Series A9 / Series U9 — (Six and V-8): Shortly after Ford made its new model introductions on Oct. 17, 1958, the Galaxie lineup was introduced. This was a trimmed as a Fairlane 500 sub-series, as it carried the Fairlane 500 name on the deck lid, but the Galaxie name on the rear fender tubes. Like the Fairlane 500 line, the Galaxie series had five six-cylinder cars and six V-8s including the Skyliner. However, some models had different names. The two-door sedan was called the Tudor Club Sedan. The four-door sedan was called the Fordor Town Sedan. The hardtop coupe was called the Club Victoria and the four-door hardtop was called the Town Victoria. The Sunliner and Skyliner names were retained. The difference between the Galaxie and the Fairlane 500 was the styling of the top. Galaxies used the standard top with a Thunderbird style "C" pillar. This combination created one of the best looking cars ever to come out of Dearborn. Galaxies were priced $48 higher than comparable Fairlane 500 models.

Station Wagon — Series A9 / Series U9 — (Six and V-8): The Ranch Wagons were the base trim level two-door and four-door station wagons for 1959. The Del Rio Ranch Wagon was a slightly fancier version of the two-door wagon. It was essentially the two-door Ranch wagon with Country Sedan trim. Country Sedans were the intermediate trim level, comparable to Fairlanes. Country Squires were the top trim level. Their level of equipment paralleled Fairlane 500 and Galaxie models. Again, the 12 wagons were sold with a relatively narrow $500 price spread between the low- and high-end models.

VIN:

Ford's coding system for serial numbers can be broken down, as follows: The first symbol designates the engine type: (A) 223-cid six-cylinder, (B) 332-cid V-8, (C) 292-cid V-8, (H) 352-cid V-8, (J) 430-cid V-8. The second symbol designates the model year: "9" for 1959. The third symbol designates the final assembly plant, as follows: A = Atlanta, C = Chester, D = Dallas, G = Chicago, F= Dearborn, E = Mahwah, H = Loraine, K = Kansas City, L = Long Beach, N = Norfolk, R = San Jose, U = Louisville, P = Twin City (St. Paul). The fourth symbol designates body type, as follows: C = Convertible, G = Custom 300 (two-door and four-door), R = Ranch Wagon, Country Sedan, S = Fairlane 500, Galaxie (two-door and four-door), T = Fairlane (two-door and four-door), V = Fairlane 500 (two-door and four-door), W = Retractable hardtop, Y = Country Squire. The fifth through tenth digits indicate the number of the unit built at each assembly plant, beginning with 100001. Custom 300 six-cylinder models began with the designation "A9" followed by assembly plant code, body type code, and, finally, the unit's production number, according to the final assembly location. Each plant began at 100001 and went up.

Custom 300 (Six)

Model No.	Body/ Style No.	Body Type & Seating	Factory Price	Shipping Weight	Production Total
A9	58E	4-dr. Sedan-6P	$2,180	3,385 lbs.	107,061
A9	64F	2-dr. Sedan-6P	$2,294	3,310 lbs.	120,412
A9	64G	2-dr. Business Tudor-3P	$2,207	3,203 lbs.	3,257

Custom 300 (V-8)

U9	58E	4-dr. Sedan-6P	$2,466	3,486 lbs.	142,492
U9	64F	2-dr. Sedan-6P	$2,412	3,411 lbs.	108,161
U9	64G	2-dr. Business Tudor-3P	$2,325	3,384 lbs.	827

Fairlane (Six)

A9	58A	4-dr. Town Sedan-6P	$2,486	3,415 lbs.	10,564
A9	64A	2-dr. Club Sedan-6P	$2,432	3,332 lbs.	8,197

Fairlane (V-8)

U9	58A	4-dr. Town Sedan-6P	$2,604	3,516 lbs.	54,099
U9	64A	2-dr. Club Sedan-6P	$2,550	3,433 lbs.	26,929

Fairlane 500 (Six)

A9	58B	4-dr. Town Sedan-6P	$2,605	3,417 lbs.	2,118
A9	64B	2-dr. Club Sedan-6P	$2,551	3,338 lbs.	804
A9	63A	2-dr. Victoria Hardtop-6P	$2,612	3,365 lbs.	717
A9	57A	4-dr. Victoria Hardtop-6P	$2,677	3,451 lbs.	414

Fairlane 500 (V-8)

U9	58B	4-dr. Town Sedan-6P	$2,723	3,518 lbs.	33,552
U9	64B	2-dr. Club Sedan-6P	$2,669	3,439 lbs.	9,337
U9	63A	2-dr. Victoria Hardtop-6P	$2,730	3,466 lbs.	23,175
U9	57A	4-dr. Victoria Hardtop-6P	$2,795	3,552 lbs.	8,894

Galaxie (Six)

A9	54A	4-dr. Town Sedan-6P	$2,657	3,405 lbs.	8,314
A9	64H	2-dr. Club Sedan-6P	$2,603	3,338 lbs.	5,609
A9	65A	2-dr. Victoria Hardtop-6P	$2,664	3,377 lbs.	4,312
A9	75A	4-dr. Victoria Hardtop-6P	$2,729	3,494 lbs.	1,216
A9	76B	2-dr. Sunliner-6P	$2,914	3,527 lbs.	1,385

Galaxie (V-8)

U9	54A	4-dr. Town Sedan-6P	$2,775	3,506 lbs.	174,794
U9	64H	2-dr. Club Sedan-6P	$2,721	3,439 lbs.	47,239
U9	65A	2-dr. Victoria Hardtop-6P	$2,782	3,478 lbs.	117,557
U9	75A	4-dr. Victoria Hardtop-6P	$2,847	3,595 lbs.	46,512
U9	76B	2-dr. Sunliner-6P	$3,032	3,628 lbs.	44,483
U9	51A	2-dr. Skyliner-6P	$3,421	4,064 lbs.	12,915

Station Wagon (Six)

A9	59C	2-dr. Ranch Wagon-6P	$2,642	3,590 lbs.	21,540
A9	71H	4-dr. Ranch Wagon-6P	$2,709	3,685 lbs.	25,359
A9	59D	2-dr. Del Rio Wagon-6P	$2,753	3,613 lbs.	1,430
A9	71F	4-dr. Country Sedan-6P	$2,820	3,718 lbs.	6,831
A9	71E	4-dr. Country Sedan-8P	$2,904	3,767 lbs.	3,339
A9	71G	4-dr. Country Squire-8P	$3,033	3,758 lbs.	545

Station Wagon (V-8)

U9	59C	2-dr. Ranch Wagon-6P	$2,760	3,691 lbs.	24,049
U9	71H	4-dr. Ranch Wagon-6P	$2,827	3,786 lbs.	41,979
U9	59D	2-dr. Del Rio Wagon-6P	$2,871	3,714 lbs.	7,233
U9	71F	4-dr. Country Sedan-6P	$2,938	3,819 lbs.	87,770
U9	71E	4-dr. Country Sedan-8P	$3,032	3,868 lbs.	25,472
U9	71G	4-dr. Country Squire-8P	$3,151	3,859 lbs.	23,791

Engines:

Base Six: Overhead valve. Cast-iron block. Displacement: 223 cid. B & S: 3.62 x 3.60 in. Compression ratio: 8.6:1. Brake hp: 145 at 4000 rpm. Carburetor: Holley one-barrel. Four main bearings. Code A.

Base V-8: Overhead valve. Cast-iron block. B & S: 3.75 x 3.30 in. Displacement: 292 cid. Compression ratio: 8.80:1. Brake hp: 200 at 4400 rpm. Taxable hp: 45.0. Torque: 285 lbs.-ft. at 2200 rpm. Five main bearings. Solid valve lifters. Crankcase capacity: 5 qt. (add 1 qt. with new oil filter). Cooling system capacity: 19 qt. Carburetor: Ford two-barrel Model 5752306 and 5752307. Code C.

332 Special V-8: Overhead valve. Cast-iron block. B & S: 4.00 x 3.30 in. Displacement: 332 cid. Compression ratio: 8.90:1. Brake hp: 225 at 4400 rpm. Taxable hp: 51.2. Torque: 325 lbs.-ft. at 2200 rpm. Five main bearings. Hydraulic valve lifters. Crankcase capacity: 5 qt. (add 1 qt. with new oil filter). Cooling system capacity: 19 qt. Carburetor: Holley two-barrel Model R-1843A with standard transmission, R-1844A with automatic transmission or R-1929-AAS as a field service unit. Code B.

Thunderbird 352 Special V-8: Overhead valve. Cast-iron block. B & S: 4.00 x 3.50 in. Displacement: 352 cid. Compression ratio: 10.2:1. Brake hp: 300 at 4600 rpm. Taxable hp: 51.2. Torque: 395 lbs.-ft. at 2800 rpm. Five main bearings. Hydraulic valve lifters. Crankcase capacity: 5 qt. (add 1 qt. with new oil filter). Cooling system capacity: 19.5 qt. Dual exhaust. Carburetor: Ford four-barrel Model 5752304 and 5752305 or Holley four-barrel. Code H.

Thunderbird 430 Special V-8 (Cruise-O-Matic only): Overhead valve. Cast-iron block. B & S: 4.30 x 3.70 in. Displacement: 430 cid.

Compression ratio: 10.0:1. Brake hp: 350 at 4600 rpm. Taxable hp: 51.2. Torque: 490 lbs.-ft. at 2800 rpm. Five main bearings. Hydraulic valve lifters. Crankcase capacity: 5 qt. (add 1 qt. with new oil filter). Cooling system capacity: 19.5 qt. Dual exhaust. Carburetor: Holley four-barrel Model 4160-C. Code J.

Chassis:

Custom 300: Wheelbase: 118 in. Overall length: 208 in. Overall width: 76.6 in. Tires: 7.50 x 14 four-ply tubeless.

Fairlane. Fairlane 500, Galaxie: Wheelbase: 118 in. Overall length: 208 in. and 208.1 in., Skyliner. Overall width: 76.6 in. Tires: 7.50 x 14 four-ply tubeless and 6.00 x 14 four-ply tubeless, Skyliner and Sunliner with automatic transmission.

Station Wagon: Wheelbase: 118 in. Overall length: 208 in. Overall width: 76.6 in. Tires: 7.50 x 14 four-ply tubeless and 6.00 x 14 four-ply tubeless, nine-passenger station wagon.

Technical:

Custom 300: Three-speed manual transmission was standard. It featured a semi-centrifugal-type clutch, three-speed helical gears and synchronizers for second and third gears. Three-speed with automatic overdrive was optional. Specifications were the same as above with automatic overdrive function cutting in at 27 mph, cutting out at 21 mph. Approximate drive ratio: 0.70:1. Manual control below instrument panel. Ford-O-Matic transmission was also optional. This was a torque converter transmission with automatic planetary gear train, single-stage, three-element hydraulic torque converter, hydro-mechanical

1959 Ford Fairlane 500 Town Victoria four-door hardtop (OCW)

1959 Ford Fairlane 500 Club Victoria two-door hardtop (OCW)

1959 Ford Galaxie Club Victoria two-door hardtop (OCW)

1959 Ford Galaxie Sunliner two-door Convertible (OCW)

controls with no electric or vacuum connections and power flow through fluid member at all times. Six-cylinder rear axle gear ratios: (Ford-O-Matic) 3.56:1, (manual transmission) 3.56:1, (optional with automatic overdrive) 3.56:1. V-8 rear axle gear ratios: (Ford-O-Matic with 292-cid V-8) 3.10:1, (Ford-O-Matic with 332/352-cid V-8) 2.91:1, (Cruise-O-Matic with 292-cid V-8) 3.10:1, (Cruise-O-Matic with 332-cid V-8) 2.91:1, (Cruise-O-Matic with 352-cid V-8) 2.69:1, (manual transmission) 3.56:1. Equa-Lock rear axle gear ratios: 3.70:1 or 3.10:1.

Fairlane, Fairlane 500, Galaxie: Three-speed manual transmission was standard. It featured a semi-centrifugal-type clutch, three-speed helical gears and synchronizers for second and third gears. Three-speed with automatic overdrive was optional. Specifications were the same as above with automatic overdrive function cutting in at 27 mph, cutting out at 21 mph. Approximate drive ratio: 0.70:1. Manual control below instrument panel. Ford-O-Matic transmission was also optional. This was a torque converter transmission with automatic planetary gear train, single-stage, three-element hydraulic torque converter, hydro-mechanical controls with no electric or vacuum connections and power flow through fluid member at all times. Six-cylinder rear axle gear ratios: (Ford-O-Matic) 3.56:1, (manual transmission) 3.56:1, (optional with automatic overdrive) 3.56:1. V-8 rear axle gear ratios: (Ford-O-Matic with 292-cid V-8) 3.10:1, (Ford-O-Matic with 332/352-cid V-8) 2.91:1, (Cruise-O-Matic with 292-cid V-8) 3.10:1, (Cruise-O-Matic with 332-cid V-8) 2.91:1, (Cruise-O-Matic with 352-cid V-8) 2.69:1, (manual transmission) 3.56:1. Equa-Lock rear axle gear ratios: 3.70:1 or 3.10:1.

Station Wagon: Three-speed manual transmission was standard. It featured a semi-centrifugal-type clutch, three-speed helical gears and synchronizers for second and third gears. Three-speed with automatic overdrive was optional. Specifications were the same as above with automatic overdrive function cutting in at 27 mph, cutting out at 21 mph. Approximate drive ratio: 0.70:1. Manual control below instrument panel. Ford-O-Matic transmission was also optional. This was a torque converter transmission with automatic planetary gear train, single-stage, three-element hydraulic torque converter, hydro-mechanical controls with no electric or vacuum connections and power flow through fluid member at all times. Six-cylinder rear axle gear ratios: (Ford-O-Matic) 3.56:1, (manual transmission) 3.56:1, (optional with automatic overdrive) 3.56:1. V-8 rear axle gear ratios: (Ford-O-Matic with 292-cid V-8) 3.10:1, (Ford-O-Matic with 332/352-cid V-8) 2.91:1, (Cruise-O-Matic with 292-cid V-8) 3.10:1, (Cruise-O-Matic with 332-cid V-8) 2.91:1, (Cruise-O-Matic with 352-cid V-8) 2.69:1, (manual transmission) 3.56:1. Equa-Lock rear axle gear ratios: 3.70:1 or 3.10:1.

Options:

Ford-O-Matic ($190). Cruise-O-Matic ($231). Automatic overdrive ($108). Power brakes ($43). Power steering ($75). Front and rear power window lifts ($102). Four-Way power seat ($64). Radio and push-button antenna ($59). Signal-seeking radio and antenna ($83). Fresh Air heater and defroster ($75). Recirculating heater and defroster ($48). White sidewall tires, four-ply, 7.50 x 14 ($33), 8.00 x 14 ($50). Wheel covers as option ($17). Styletone two-tone paint ($26). Tinted glass ($26). Back-up lights ($10). Custom 300 and Ranch Wagon Deluxe ornamentation package ($32). Electric clock ($15). Windshield washer

1959 Ford Fairlane 500 Sunliner two-door Convertible (OCW)

1959 Ford Fairlane 500 two-door Skyliner Retractable (OCW)

($14). Two-speed windshield wipers ($7). Lifeguard safety package including padded instrument panel and sun visor ($19), plus pair of front seat safety belts ($21). Polar Air Conditioner, with tinted glass ($271). Select Aire Conditioner, with tinted glass ($404). Heavy-duty 70-amp battery ($6). Equa-Lock differential ($39). Four-way manual seat ($17). Fairlane side molding ($11). Fairlane 500 rocker panel molding ($11). Thunderbird Special 332 cid/225 hp V-8 ($141 over base six). Thunderbird Special 352 cid/300 hp V-8 ($167 over base six). Standard 292-cid two-barrel V-8, all except Skyliner ($118).

History:

Model-year production of Fords and Thunderbird was 1,462,140 units, which was not enough to top Chevrolet's 1,481,071. Fords were 25 percent of the industry's output. Calendar-year output was 1,352,112

1959 Ford Galaxie two-door Skyliner Retractable (OCW)

1959 Ford two-door Ranch Wagon (OCW)

1959 Ford four-door Ranch Wagon (OCW)

1959 Ford four-door Country Sedan 9P (OCW)

1959 Ford four-door Country Sedan 6P (OCW)

1959 Ford four-door Country Squire (OCW)

Fords, 100,757 Falcons, and 75,723 Thunderbirds and that was higher than the calendar-year total of Chevys, Corvettes and Corvairs. As you can see, the calendar-year numbers include 1960 cars built in the fall of 1959. In March 1958, Ford reported it had *reduced* the cost of making an automobile by $94 per unit between 1954 and 1958. On a model year basis, 78.1 percent of all 1959 Fords had V-8 power and 71.7 percent featured automatic transmission.

1960 Ford

Falcon — Series S — (Six): The Falcon was Ford's contribution to the compact-car field. While being nearly three feet shorter overall than the full-size Fords, the Falcon offered an interior spacious enough for occupants more than six-feet tall. The compact station wagon offered more than enough cargo space for the majority of buyers. Falcon styling was simple and ultra-conservative. The body was slab-sided, with just a slightly recessed feature line. Two single headlights were mounted inside the grille opening and the grille itself was an aluminum stamping consisting of horizontal and vertical bars. The name Ford appeared on the hood, in front of the power bulge-type simulated scoop. At the rear, the word Ford, in block letters, appeared between the two round taillights. Standard Falcon equipment included turn signals, a left-hand sun visor and five black tubeless tires.

Falcon Deluxe — Series S — (Six) A Deluxe trim package was a popular $65.80 option for the Falcon.

Fairlane — Series V — (Six and V-8): Fords were totally redesigned from the ground up for 1960. They shared nothing with the previous models except engines and drivelines. While 1960 styling was considered controversial by many, it remains one of the smoothest designs ever to come from the Dearborn drawing boards. The new models were longer, lower and wider than their predecessors and were restrained, especially when compared to some of their contemporaries. All 1960 Fords featured a single chrome strip from the top of the front bumper, sweeping up to the top of the front fender, then back, horizontally along the beltline, to the back of the car. There it turned inward and capped the small horizontal fin. Large semi-circular taillights were housed in an aluminum escutcheon panel below the fins and directly above a large chrome bumper. At the front end, a large, recessed mesh grille housed the dual headlights. In 1960, the Fairlane name was used on the lower-priced full-size models. The Fairlane series contained the word Ford spaced along the recessed section of the full-width hood and

used four cast stripes along the rear quarter panel for trim. The Fairlane series was the base trim level for 1960 and included a Fairlane script on the sides of the front fenders. There were chrome moldings around the windshield and rear windows, two sun visors, armrests on all doors and no extra chrome side trim. Standard Fairlane equipment included electric windshield wipers, an oil-bath air cleaner, an oil filter, dual sun visors, a cigarette lighter and five black tubeless tires

Fairlane 500 — Series V — (Six and V-8): The Fairlane 500 was the intermediate trim level and included all the Fairlane trim plus five "delta wing" chrome stripes on the rear fenders (only on two-door Club Sedans) and the Fairlane crest on the hood. Standard Fairlane 500 equipment included electric windshield wipers, an oil-bath air cleaner, an oil filter, dual sun visors, a cigarette lighter and five black tubeless tires

Galaxie — Series V — (Six and V-8): The Galaxie and Galaxie Special series were the top trim levels for 1960. They included chrome "A" pillar moldings and chrome window moldings. A single chrome strip began near the center of the front door and continued back to the taillights on the side. There was also ribbed aluminum stone shields behind the rear wheels, a Galaxie script on the front fenders, a Galaxie script on the trunk lid and a Ford crest on the hood. Standard Galaxie equipment included electric windshield wipers, an oil-bath air cleaner, an oil filter, dual sun visors, a cigarette lighter, five black tubeless tires, back-up lights and an electric clock.

Galaxie Special — Series V — (Six and V-8): The Galaxie Special series included the Starliner and Sunliner with all the high-level trim, except that the Galaxie script on the trunk lid was replaced with either the Sunliner or Starliner script. Standard Galaxie Special equipment included electric windshield wipers, an oil-bath air cleaner, an oil filter, dual sun visors, a cigarette lighter, five black tubeless tires, back-up lights and an electric clock.

Station Wagon — Series V — (Six and V-8): The Ranch Wagon was the base trim level station wagon. Country Sedans were the intermediate level of station wagons with more trim and equipment. Country Squires were the top trim level. The level of equipment paralleled Fairlane, Fairlane 500 and Galaxie models of passenger cars.

VIN (Falcon):

The VIN for Falcons was die-stamped into the surface of the left-hand brace between the top of the firewall and the left front wheel housing. The first symbol indicates year: 0 = 1960. The second symbol identifies assembly plant, as follows: A=Atlanta, Georgia, C=Chester, Pennsylvania, D=Dallas, Texas, E=Mahwah, New Jersey, F=Dearborn, Michigan, G=Chicago, Illinois, H=Loraine, Ohio, J=Los Angeles, California, K=Kansas City, Kansas, N = Norfolk, Virginia, P=Twin Cities, Minnesota, R=San Jose, S=Pilot Plant, T=Metuchen, New Jersey, U=Louisville, Kentucky, Y=Wixom. The third and fourth symbols identify body series (see second column of tables). The fifth symbol identifies engine code, as follows: S=144-cid six-cylinder, D=144-cid low-compression six-cylinder. The last six digits are the unit's production number, beginning at 100001 and going up, at each of the assembly plants.

VIN (Ford):

The VIN for full-size Fords was die-stamped into the top right-hand of the frame ahead of the front suspension member. The first symbol indicates year: 0 = 1960. The second symbol identifies assembly plant, as follows: A=Atlanta, Georgia, C=Chester, Pennsylvania, D=Dallas, Texas, E=Mahwah, New Jersey, F=Dearborn, Michigan, G=Chicago, Illinois, H=Loraine, Ohio, J=Los Angeles, California, K=Kansas City, Kansas, N = Norfolk, Virginia, P=Twin Cities, Minnesota, R=San Jose, S=Pilot Plant, T=Metuchen, New Jersey, U=Louisville, Kentucky, Y=Wixom, Michigan. The third and fourth symbols identify body series (see second column of tables). The fifth symbol identifies engine code, as follows: V=223-cid six-cylinder, W=292-cid V-8, X=352-cid V-8 with two-barrel carburetor, Y=352-cid V-8 with four-barrel carburetor, T=292-cid export V-8 and G=352-cid export V-8. The last six digits are the unit's production number, beginning at 100001 and going up, at each of the assembly plants.

1960 Ford Falcon two-door Sedan (PH)

1960 Ford Falcon four-door Sedan (PH)

1960 Ford Falcon two-door Station Wagon (PH)

Falcon Standard (Six)

Model No.	Body/Style No.	Body Type & Seating	Factory Price	Shipping Weight	Production Total
S	58A	4-dr. Sedan-6P	$2,042	2,317 lbs.	45,164
S	64A	2-dr. Sedan-6P	$1,980	2,282 lbs.	73,325
S	71A	2-dr. Station Wagon-6P	$2,355	2,275 lbs.	16,272
S	59A	2-dr. Station Wagon-6P	$2,293	2,540 lbs.	14,299

Falcon Deluxe (Six)

Model No.	Body/Style No.	Body Type & Seating	Factory Price	Shipping Weight	Production Total
S	58A	4-dr. Sedan-6P	$2,108	2,317 lbs.	122,732
S	64A	2-dr. Sedan-6P	$2,046	2,282 lbs.	120,149
S	71A	2-dr. Station Wagon-6P	$2,421	2,275 lbs.	30,486
S	59A	2-dr. Station Wagon-6P	$2,245	2,540 lbs.	13,253

Fairlane (Six)

Model No.	Body/Style No.	Body Type & Seating	Factory Price	Shipping Weight	Production Total
B0	32	4-dr. Sedan-6P	$2,386	3,606 lbs.	68,607
B0	31	2-dr. Sedan-6P	$2,332	3,606 lbs.	69,086
B0	32	2-dr. Business Tudor-3P	$2,245	3,507 lbs.	1,458

Fairlane (V-8)

Model No.	Body/Style No.	Body Type & Seating	Factory Price	Shipping Weight	Production Total
V0	32	4-dr. Sedan-6P	$2,499	3,706 lbs.	41,294
V0	31	2-dr. Sedan-6P	$2,445	3,632 lbs.	24,173
V0	32	2-dr. Business Tudor-3P	$2,358	3,607 lbs.	275

Fairlane 500 (Six)

Model No.	Body/Style No.	Body Type & Seating	Factory Price	Shipping Weight	Production Total
B0	42	4-dr. Town Sedan-6P	$2,463	3,610 lbs.	45,626
B0	41	2-dr. Club Sedan-6P	$2,409	3,536 lbs.	43,962

Fairlane 500 (V-8)

Model No.	Body/Style No.	Body Type & Seating	Factory Price	Shipping Weight	Production Total
V0	42	4-dr. Town Sedan-6P	$2,576	3,710 lbs.	107,608
V0	41	2-dr. Club Sedan-6P	$2,522	3,636 lbs.	47,079

Galaxie (Six)

Model No.	Body/Style No.	Body Type & Seating	Factory Price	Shipping Weight	Production Total
B0	52	4-dr. Town Sedan-6P	$2,678	3,634 lbs.	6,783
B0	51	2-dr. Club Sedan-6P	$2,624	3,553 lbs.	6,009
B0	54	4-dr. Victoria-6P	$2,750	3,642 lbs.	1,462

Galaxie (V-8)

Model No.	Body/Style No.	Body Type & Seating	Factory Price	Shipping Weight	Production Total
V0	52	4-dr. Town Sedan-6P	$2,791	3,734 lbs.	98,001
V0	51	2-dr. Club Sedan-6P	$2,737	3,653 lbs.	25,767
V0	54	4-dr. Victoria-6P	$2,863	3,742 lbs.	37,753

Galaxie Special (Six)

Model No.	Body/Style No.	Body Type & Seating	Factory Price	Shipping Weight	Production Total
B0	53	2-dr. Victoria-6P	$2,685	2,672 lbs.	2,672
B0	55	2-dr. Sunliner-6P	$2,935	2,689 lbs.	2,689

Galaxie Special (V-8)

Model No.	Body/Style No.	Body Type & Seating	Factory Price	Shipping Weight	Production Total
V0	53	2-dr. Victoria-6P	$2,798	3,667 lbs.	65,969
V0	55	2-dr. Sunliner-6P	$3,048	3,841 lbs.	42,073

Station Wagon (Six)

Model No.	Body/Style No.	Body Type & Seating	Factory Price	Shipping Weight	Production Total
B0	61	2-dr. Ranch Wagon-6P	$2,661	3,831 lbs.	18,287
B0	62	4-dr. Ranch Wagon-6P	$2,731	3,948 lbs.	21,154
B0	64	4-dr. Country Sedan-6P	$2,827	3,962 lbs.	5,081
B0	66	4-dr. Country Sedan-8P	$2,912	4,008 lbs.	3,409
B0	68	4-dr. Country Squire-8P	$3,042	4,022 lbs.	577

Station Wagon (Six)

Model No.	Body/Style No.	Body Type & Seating	Factory Price	Shipping Weight	Production Total
V0	61	2-dr. Ranch Wagon-6P	$2,774	3,931 lbs.	8,849
V0	62	4-dr. Ranch Wagon-6P	$2,844	4,048 lbs.	22,718
V0	64	4-dr. Country Sedan-6P	$2,940	4,062 lbs.	54,221
V0	66	4-dr. Country Sedan-8P	$3,025	4,108 lbs.	15,868
V0	68	4-dr. Country Squire-8P	$3,155	4,122 lbs.	21,660

Engines:

Falcon Six: Overhead valve. Cast-iron block. Displacement: 144 cid. B & S: 3.50 x 2.50 in. Compression ratio: 8.7:1. Brake hp: 85 at 4200 rpm. Carburetor: Holley one-barrel. Four main bearings. Code S, (D on export models).

Ford Six: Overhead valve. Cast-iron block. Displacement: 223 cid. B & S: 3.62 x 3.60 in. Compression ratio: 8.4:1. Brake hp: 145 at 4000 rpm. Carburetor: Holley single barrel. Four main bearings. Code V.

Base V-8: Overhead valve. Cast-iron block. B & S: 3.75 x 3.30 in. Displacement: 292 cid. Compression ratio: 8.80:1. Brake hp: 185 at 4200 rpm. Taxable hp: 45.0. Torque: 292 at 2200 rpm. Five main bearings. Solid valve lifters. Crankcase capacity: 5 qt. (add 1 qt. with new oil filter). Cooling system capacity: 19 qt. Carburetor: Ford-Holley two-barrel Model COAE-9510-M with standard transmission or COAE-9510-H with automatic transmission. Code W.

Interceptor V-8: Overhead valve. Cast-iron block. B & S: 4.00 x 3.50 in. Displacement: 352 cid. Compression ratio: 8.90:1. Brake hp: 235 at 4400 rpm. Taxable hp: 51.2. Torque: 350 lbs.-ft. at 2400 rpm. Five main bearings. Hydraulic valve lifters. Crankcase capacity: 5 qt. (add 1 qt. with new oil filter). Cooling system capacity: 19.5 qt. Dual exhaust. Carburetor: Ford-Holley two-barrel Model COAE-9510-R with standard transmission or COAE-9510-S with automatic transmission. Code X (Export code G).

Interceptor Special V-8: Overhead valve. Cast-iron block. B & S: 4.00 x 3.50 in. Displacement: 352 cid. Compression ratio: 9.60:1. Brake hp: 300 at 4600 rpm. Taxable hp: 51.2. Torque: 381 lbs.-ft. at 2800 rpm. Five main bearings. Hydraulic valve lifters. Crankcase capacity: 5 qt. (add 1 qt. with new oil filter). Cooling system capacity: 19.5 qt. Dual exhaust. Carburetor: Ford-Holley four-barrel Model COAE-9510-J with standard transmission or COAE-9510-K with automatic transmission. Code Y.

Note: This engine was not mentioned in early 1960 Ford literature. It had an aluminum intake and a Holley carburetor. This engine was not available in cars with power steering or power brakes.

Interceptor Special V-8: Overhead valve. Cast-iron block. B & S: 4.00 x 3.50 in. Displacement: 352 cid. Compression ratio: 10.60:1. Brake hp: 360. Taxable hp: 51.2. Five main bearings. Hydraulic valve lifters. Crankcase capacity: 5 qt. (add 1 qt. with new oil filter). Cooling system capacity: 19.5 qt. Dual exhaust with special header-type exhaust manifolds. Aluminum intake manifold. Dual point distributor. Carburetor: Holley four-barrel. Code Y.

Chassis:

Falcon: Wheelbase: 109.5 in. Overall length: 181.2 in., car and 189 in., station wagon. Overall width: 70 in. Overall height: 54.5 in. Tires: 6.00 x 13, car and 6.50 x 13, station wagon.

Ford: Wheelbase: 119 in. Overall length: 213.7 in. Overall width: 81.5 in. Overall height: 55 in. Tires: 7.50 x 14, most cars and 8.00 x 14, convertible and station wagon.

Options:

Falcon: Heavy-duty battery ($7.60). Deluxe trim package ($65.80). Fresh Air heater/defroster ($67.80). Two-tone paint ($16.80). Manual radio and antenna ($54.05). Safety equipment: padded dash and visors ($19.20). Front seat safety belts ($20.60). Whitewall tires ($28.70). Automatic transmission ($159.40). Wheel covers ($16). Windshield washer ($13.70). Electric windshield wiper ($9.65).

Ford: Standard 185-hp V-8 engine ($113.00). Two-barrel 235-hp V-8 ($147.80). Four-barrel 300-hp V-8 ($177.40). Polar Air conditioning, including tinted glass and V-8 ($270.90). Select Air conditioning, including tinted glass and V-8 ($403.80). Back-up lights ($10.70). Heavy-duty 70-amp battery ($7.60). Equa-Lock differential ($38.60). Electric clock ($14.60). Fresh Air heater/defroster ($75.10). Recirculating heater/defroster ($46.90). Four-way manual seat ($17.00). Rocker panel molding ($14.20). Padded dash and visors ($24.30). Two-tone paint ($19.40). Power brakes ($43.20). Power seat ($63.80). Power steering ($76.50). Front and rear power windows ($102.10). Push-button radio and antenna ($58.50). Front seat belts ($20.60). Tinted glass ($43.00). Cruise-O-Matic ($211.10). Ford-O-Matic with six-cylinder ($179.80). Ford-O-Matic with V-8 ($189.60). Overdrive ($108.40). Wheel covers ($16.60). Windshield washer ($13.70). Two-speed windshield wipers ($9.70). Five 7.50 x 14 black sidewall tires standard all models except convertible, wagons and all models equipped

1960 Ford Falcon four-door Station Wagon (OCW)

1960 Ford Falcon four-door Sedan (PH)

with 235- or 300-hp V-8s (no charge) . Five 7.50 x 14 white sidewall tires for all models using standard 7.50 x 14 black sidewall tires ($32.60 additional). Five 8.00 x 14 black sidewall tires standard on convertibles, wagons and cars with 235-hp or 300-hp V-8 (no charge). Five 8.00 x 14 white sidewall tires on convertibles or wagons or 235- and 300-hp cars having 8.00 x 14 black sidewall tires as standard equipment ($35.70 extra). Five 8.00 x 14 white sidewall tires on other Fords ($49.00).

History:

All three lines of 1960 Fords were introduced to the public on October 8, 1959. Falcon station wagons were added to the new compact series in March 1960. Although Ford did not provide production breakouts by engine type, trade publications recorded that 67.5 percent of all Fords (excluding Thunderbirds and Falcons) had V-8 engines installed. All Falcons were sixes. Automatic transmissions were installed in 67.1 percent of all Fords, 44.5 percent of all Falcons and 97.9 percent of all Thunderbirds built during the model run. Ford's share of the overall automobile market dropped to 22.55 percent this year, compared

1960 Ford Fairlane 500 four-door Town Sedan (OCW)

1960 Ford Galaxie four-door Town Sedan (OCW)

1960 Ford Galaxie Town Victoria four-door hardtop(OCW)

1960 Ford Galaxie Special Starliner two-door hardtop (OCW)

1960 Ford Galaxie Special Sunliner two-door Convertible (PH)

to 27.33 percent in 1959. Model year production peaked at 911,034 Fords and 435,676 Falcons. Model year series production was as follows: (Custom 300) 900, (Fairlane) 204,700, (Fairlane 500) 244,300, (Galaxie) 289,200, (station wagon) 171,800. Just 297,400 six-cylinder Fords were produced for the model year.

1960 Ford Sunliner (OCW)

1960 Ford four-door Country Squire (PH)

1961 Ford

Falcon — Series S/U — (Six): The Falcon continued unchanged from 1961, with the exception of a new convex grille. A new 170-cid six-cylinder engine was added to the lineup and the Futura two-door sedan was added to give a sporty flair to the compact car line. The Futura used the same body shell as the Falcon Tudor Sedan, but it was equipped with a bucket seat interior and a center console. Standard Falcon equipment included turn signals, a left-hand sun visor and five 6.00 x 13 black sidewall tubeless tires. Station wagons used 6.50 x 13 tires.

Fairlane — Series V — (Six and V-8): Model-year 1961 saw the third major restyling of the full-size Ford line in as many years. From the beltline down, the 1961 Fords were completely new. The upper body structure was retained from the 1960 lineup. A full-width concave grille with a horizontal dividing bar highlighted front end styling. The Ford name, in block letters, replaced the crest used in previous years on Fairlane models and the series designation appeared on the front fenders, behind the headlights. The horizontal full-length fin, used in 1960, was replaced with a smaller canted fin, nearly identical in size and shape to the fin used on 1957 and 1958 Custom series cars. Large, round taillights were used once again. A horizontal chrome strip, similar to one used on 1960 models, was used once again. The year 1961 saw the beginning of the great horsepower race of the 1960s, and Ford cracked the magic 400-hp barrier with a new 390-cid V-8. The Fairlane series was the base trim level for 1961 and included chrome moldings around the windshield and rear window, two sun visors, a horn button instead of horn ring, an armrest on all doors and no extra side chrome. Standard equipment included electric windshield wipers, an oil-bath air cleaner, an oil filter, dual sun visors, a cigarette lighter and five tubeless black sidewall tires.

Fairlane 500 — Series V — (Six and V-8): The Fairlane 500 was the intermediate trim level and included all the Fairlane trim plus a chrome horn ring and a single horizontal chrome strip running from the back of

1961 Ford Falcon two-door Sedan (OCW)

the front wheel well to the rear bumper. Standard equipment included electric windshield wipers, an oil-bath air cleaner, an oil filter, dual sun visors, a cigarette lighter and five tubeless black sidewall tires.

Galaxie — (Six and V-8): The Galaxie series was the top trim level for 1961 and included chrome "A" pillar moldings, chrome window moldings, horizontal chrome strip on the side of the body, ribbed aluminum stone shield behind the rear wheel opening, a stamped aluminum escutcheon panel between the taillights (duplicating the pattern of the grille) and either Galaxie, Starliner or Sunliner script on the trunk lid. Standard equipment included electric windshield wipers, an oil-bath air cleaner, an oil filter, dual sun visors, a cigarette lighter, back-up lights, an electric clock and five tubeless black sidewall tires.

Station Wagon — (Six and V-8): The Ranch Wagon was the base trim level station wagon, Country Sedans were the intermediate level and Country Squires were the top trim level. The level of equipment paralleled Fairlane, Fairlane 500 and Galaxie models of passenger cars. Standard equipment on all wagons included electric windshield wipers, an oil-bath air cleaner, an oil filter, dual sun visors, a cigarette lighter and five tubeless black sidewall tires. The Country Squire also had back-up lights and an electric clock. Nine-passenger station wagons also had a power tailgate window.

VIN (Falcon):

The VIN for Falcons was die-stamped into the surface of the left-hand brace between the top of the firewall and the left front wheel housing. The first symbol indicates year: 1=1961. The second symbol identifies assembly plant, as follows: A=Atlanta, Georgia, C=Chester, Pennsylvania, D=Dallas, Texas, E=Mahwah, New Jersey, F=Dearborn, Michigan, G=Chicago, Illinois, H=Lorain, Ohio, J=Los Angeles, California, K=Kansas City, Kansas, N=Norfolk, Virginia, P=Twin Cities, Minnesota, R=San Jose, S=Pilot Plant, T=Metuchen, New Jersey, U=Louisville, Kentucky, Y=Wixom, Michigan. The third and fourth symbols identify body series (see second column of tables). The fifth symbol identifies engine code, as follows: S=144-cid six-cylinder, D=144-cid low-compression six-cylinder, U=170-cid six-cylinder. The last six digits are the unit's production number, beginning at 100001 and going up, at each of the assembly plants. Falcons not built at all Ford plants.

VIN (Ford):

The VIN for full-size Fords was die-stamped into the top right-hand of the frame ahead of the front suspension member. The first symbol indicates year: 1=1961. The second symbol identifies assembly plant, as follows: A=Atlanta, Georgia, C=Chester, Pennsylvania, D=Dallas, Texas, E=Mahwah, New Jersey, F=Dearborn, Michigan, G=Chicago, Illinois, H=Lorain, Ohio, J=Los Angeles, California, K=Kansas City, Kansas, N = Norfolk, Virginia, P=Twin Cities, Minnesota, R=San Jose, S=Pilot Plant, T=Metuchen, New Jersey, U=Louisville, Kentucky, Y=Wixom, Michigan. The third and fourth symbols identify body series (see second column of tables). The fifth symbol identifies engine code, as follows: V=223-cid six-cylinder, W=292-cid V-8, X=352-cid V-8 with two-barrel carburetor, Z=390-cid V-8 with four-barrel carburetor, R=390-cid V-8 low-compression, E=170-cid low-compression six-cylinder, Z=390-cid four-barrel high-horsepower V-8, Z=390-cid dual four-barrel carburetor high-horsepower V-8, Z=390-cid four-barrel police V-8. The last six digits are the unit's production number, beginning at 100001 and going up, at each of the assembly plants. Full-size Fords not built at all Ford plants.

1961 Ford Falcon Futura two-door Sedan (OCW)

1961 Ford Falcon four-door Sedan (PH)

Falcon Standard (Six)

Model No.	Body/ Style No.	Body Type & Seating	Factory Price	Shipping Weight	Production Total
S/U	12	4-dr. Sedan-6P	$2,047	2,289 lbs.	55,437
S/U	11	2-dr. Sedan-6P	$1,985	2,254 lbs.	74,292
S/U	22	4-dr. Station Wagon-6P	$2,341	2,558 lbs.	24,445
S/U	21	2-dr. Station Wagon-6P	$2,298	2,525 lbs.	13,940

Falcon Deluxe (Six)

S/U	12	4-dr. Sedan-6P	$2,125	2,289 lbs.	104,324
S/U	11	2-dr. Sedan-6P	$2,063	2,254 lbs.	75,740
S/U	22	4-dr. Station Wagon-6P	$2,419	2,558 lbs.	63,488
S/U	21	2-dr. Station Wagon-6P	$2,376	2,525 lbs.	18,105

Falcon Futura (Six)

S/U	17	2-dr. Futura Sedan-6P	$2,233	2,322 lbs.	44,470

Fairlane (Six)

B0	32	4-dr. Sedan-6P	$2,390	3,585 lbs.	57,282
B0	31	2-dr. Sedan-6P	$2,336	3,487 lbs.	46,471

Fairlane (V-8)

V0	32	4-dr. Sedan-6P	$2,506	3,683 lbs.	39,425
V0	31	2-dr. Sedan-6P	$2,452	3,585 lbs.	20,329

Fairlane 500 (Six)

B0	42	4-dr. Town Sedan-6P	$2,505	3,593 lbs.	25,911
B0	41	2-dr. Club Sedan-6P	$2,451	3,502 lbs.	16,665

Fairlane 500 (V-8)

V0	42	4-dr. Town Sedan-6P	$2,621	3,961 lbs.	72,738
V0	41	2-dr. Club Sedan-6P	$2,567	3,600 lbs.	25,733

Galaxie (Six)

B0	52	4-dr. Town Sedan-6P	$2,665	3,570 lbs.	11,904
B0	51	2-dr. Club Sedan-6P	$2,611	3,488 lbs.	5,716
B0	54	4-dr. Victoria-6P	$2,737	3,588 lbs.	1,466
B0	57	2-dr. Victoria-6P	$2,672	3,545 lbs.	4,279
B0	53	2-dr. Starliner-6P	$2,672	3,517 lbs.	941
B0	55	2-dr. Sunliner-6P	$2,922	3,694 lbs.	2,764

Galaxie (V-8)

V0	52	4-dr. Town Sedan-6P	$2,781	3,668 lbs.	129,366
V0	51	2-dr. Club Sedan-6P	$2,727	3,586 lbs.	21,997
V0	54	4-dr. Victoria-6P	$2,853	3,686 lbs.	28,846
V0	57	2-dr. Victoria-6P	$2,788	3,643 lbs.	71,038
V0	53	2-dr. Starliner-6P	$2,788	3,615 lbs.	28,728
V0	55	2-dr. Sunliner-6P	$3,038	3,792 lbs.	41,810

Station Wagon (Six)

B0	61	2-dr. Ranch Wagon-6P	$2,661	3,914 lbs.	4,785
B0	62	4-dr. Ranch Wagon-6P	$2,731	3,911 lbs.	13,310
B0	64	4-dr. Country Sedan-6P	$2,827	3,934 lbs.	3,610
B0	66	4-dr. Country Sedan-8P	$2,931	3,962 lbs.	2,848
B0	67	4-dr. Country Squire-6P	$3,016	3,938 lbs.	521
B0	68	4-dr. Country Squire-9P	$3,086	3,966 lbs.	302

Station Wagon (V-8)

V0	61	2-dr. Ranch Wagon-6P	$2,777	3,816 lbs.	7,257
V0	62	4-dr. Ranch Wagon-6P	$2,847	4,009 lbs.	16,982
V0	64	4-dr. Country Sedan-6P	$2,943	4,032 lbs.	42,701
V0	66	4-dr. Country Sedan-8P	$3,047	4,060 lbs.	13,508
V0	67	4-dr. Country Squire-6P	$3,132	4,036 lbs.	16,440
V0	68	4-dr. Country Squire-9P	$3,202	4,064 lbs.	14,355

1961 Ford Fairlane four-door Sedan (OCW)

1961 Ford Falcon Futura two-door Sedan interior detail (OCW)

1961 Ford Galaxie two-door Club Sedan (OCW)

Engines:

Falcon Six: Overhead valve. Cast-iron block. Displacement: 144 cid. B & S: 3.50 x 2.50 in. Compression ratio: 6.7:1. Brake hp: 65 at 4200 rpm. Carburetor: Holley one-barrel. Four main bearings. Code S (Code D, export models).

Falcon Six: Overhead valve. Cast-iron block. Displacement: 170 cid. B & S: 3.50 x 2.94 in. Compression ratio: 8.7:1. Brake hp: 101 at 4400 rpm. Carburetor: Holley one-barrel. Four main bearings. Code U.

Ford Six: Overhead valve. Cast-iron block. Displacement: 223 cid. B & S: 3.62 x 3.60 in. Compression ratio: 6.4:1. Brake hp: 135 at 4000 rpm. Carburetor: Holley one-barrel. Four main bearings. Code V.

Base V-8: Overhead valve. Cast-iron block. B & S: 3.75 x 3.30 in. Displacement: 292 cid. Compression ratio: 8.80:1. Brake hp: 175 at 4200 rpm. Taxable hp: 45.0. Torque: 279 lbs.-ft. at 2200 rpm. Five main bearings. Solid valve lifters. Crankcase capacity: 5 qt. (add 1 qt. with new oil filter). Cooling system capacity: 19 qt. Carburetor: (with PCV) Ford two-barrel Model CIAE-9510-AA with standard transmission or CIAE-9510-AB with automatic transmission, (without PCV) Ford two-barrel Model CIAE-9510-Y with standard transmission or CIAE-9510-Z with automatic transmission. Code W (Code T, export models).

Interceptor V-8: Overhead valve. Cast-iron block. B & S: 4.00 x 3.50 in. Displacement: 352 cid. Compression ratio: 8.90:1. Brake hp: 220 at 4400 rpm. Taxable hp: 51.2. Torque: 336 lbs.-ft. at 2400 rpm. Five main bearings. Hydraulic valve lifters. Crankcase capacity: 5 qt. (add 1 qt. with new oil filter). Cooling system capacity: 19.5 qt. Carburetor: (with PCV) Ford two-barrel Model CIAE-9510-AE with standard transmission or CIAE-9510-AF with automatic transmission, (without PCV) Ford two-barrel Model CIAE-9510-AC with standard transmission or CIAE-9510-AD with automatic transmission. Code X (Code G, export models).

Thunderbird V-8: Overhead valve. Cast-iron block. B & S: 4.05 x 3.78 in. Displacement: 390 cid. Compression ratio: 9.60:1. Brake hp: 300 at 4600 rpm. Taxable hp: 52.49. Torque: 427 lbs.-ft. at 2800 rpm. Five main bearings. Hydraulic valve lifters. Crankcase capacity: 5 qt. (add 1 qt. with new oil filter). Cooling system capacity: 19 qt. Carburetor: Ford four-barrel Model CIAE-9510-AG with standard transmission or CIAE-9510-AH with automatic transmission. Code Z.

Interceptor 390 V-8: Overhead valve. Cast-iron block. Displacement: 390 cid. B & S: 4.05 x 3.78 in. Compression ratio: 9.60:1. Brake hp: 330 at 5000 rpm. Torque: 427 lbs.-ft. at 3200 rpm. Five main bearings. Hydraulic valve lifters. Carburetor: (with PCV) Ford four-barrel Model C2AE-9510-AJ with standard transmission or C2AE-9510-AK with automatic transmission, (without PCV) Ford two-barrel Model C2AE-9510-AG with standard transmission or C2AE-9510-AR with automatic transmission. Cooling system capacity: 20.5 qt. with heater. Crankcase capacity: 5 qt. (add 1 qt. with new oil filter). Dual exhausts. Code Z or Code P (Police).

Thunderbird Special V-8: Overhead valve. Cast-iron block. B & S: 4.05 x 3.78 in. Displacement: 390 cid. Compression ratio: 10.60:1. Brake hp: 375 at 6000 rpm. Taxable hp: 52.49. Torque: 427 lbs.-ft. at 3400 rpm. Five main bearings. Solid valve lifters. Crankcase capacity: 5 qt. (add 1 qt. with new oil filter). Cooling system capacity: 19 qt. Carburetor: Ford four-barrel Model CIAE-9510-AG with standard transmission or CIAE-9510-AH with automatic transmission. Code Q (Early versions may use code Z and export models used code R).

Note: Some cars were delivered with the intake manifold and carburetors in the trunk.

Thunderbird 6V V-8: Overhead valve. Cast-iron block. B & S: 4.05 x 3.78 in. Displacement: 390 cid. Compression ratio: 10.60:1. Brake hp: 401 at 6000 rpm. Taxable hp: 52.49. Torque: 430 lbs.-ft. at 3500 rpm. Five main bearings. Solid valve lifters. Crankcase capacity: 5 qt. (add 1 qt. with new oil filter). Cooling system capacity: 19 qt. Carburetor: Three two-barrel carburetors. Code Q (Early versions may use code Z).

Chassis:

Falcon: Wheelbase: 109.5 in. Overall length: 181.2 in., car and 189 in., station wagon. Front tread: 55 in. Rear tread: 54.5 in. Tires: 6.00 x 13 and 6.50 x 13, station wagon.

Ford: Wheelbase: 119 in. Overall length: 209.9 in. Front tread: 61 in. Rear tread: 60 in. Tires: 7.50 x 14 and 8.00 x 14, station wagon.

Options:

Falcon: Back-up lights ($10.70). Heavy-duty battery ($7.60). Crankcase vent system ($5.70). Deluxe trim package ($78.30). Engine, 170 cid/101 hp ($37.40). Fresh Air heater/defroster ($73.40). Station wagon luggage rack ($35.10). Two-tone paint ($19.40). Manual radio and antenna ($54.05). Safety equipment, including padded dash and visors ($21.89). Front seat belts ($20.60). Electric tailgate windows for station wagons ($29.75). Automatic transmission ($163.10). Wheel covers ($16). Windshield washer ($13.70). Electric windshield wiper ($9.65). Five 6.00 x13 white sidewall tires for sedans ($29.90). Five 6.50 x13 black sidewall tires for sedans ($10.20). Five 6.50 x13 white sidewall tires for sedans ($43.30). Five 6.50 x13 white sidewall tires for wagons ($33). Five 6.50 x13 black sidewall 6-ply tires for wagons ($27.80). Five 6.50 x13 white sidewall 6-ply tires for wagons ($60.90).

Ford: Standard 175-hp V-8 engine ($116.00). Two-barrel, 220-hp V-8 ($148.20). Four-barrel, 300-hp V-8 ($196.70). Polar Air conditioner, including tinted glass ($270.90). Select Aire air conditioner, including tinted glass ($436.00). Back-up lights ($10.70). Heavy-duty, 70-amp battery ($7.60). Crankcase vent system ($5.70). Electric clock ($14.60). Magic-Aire heater/defroster ($75.10). Equa-Lock differential ($38.60). Electric clock ($14.60). Magic-Aire heater/defroster ($75.10). Recirculating heater/defroster ($46.90). Four-way manual seat ($17.00). Rocker panel molding ($16.10). Padded dash and visors ($24.30). Two-tone paint ($22). Power brakes ($43.20). Power seat ($63.80). Power steering ($81.70). Power tailgate window ($32.30). Front and rear power windows ($10210). Push-button radio and antenna ($58.50). Front seat belts ($20.60). Tinted glass ($43.00). Cruise-O-Matic transmission ($212.30). Ford-O-Matic transmission with six-cylinder engine ($179.80). Ford-O-Matic transmission with V-8 engine ($189.60). Overdrive transmission ($108.40). Wheel covers ($18.60). Windshield washer ($13.70). Two-speed windshield wipers ($11.60). Five 7.50 x 14 black sidewall tires standard on all models except wagons and cars equipped

1961 Ford Galaxie four-door Town Sedan (OCW)

1961 Ford Galaxie Club Victoria two-door hardtop (OCW)

1961 Ford Galaxie Special Starliner two-door hardtop (OCW)

with 220- or 300-hp V-8s and air conditioning (no charge). Five 7.50 x 14 white sidewall tires standard on all models equipped with standard 7.50 x 14 tires ($33.90). Five 8.00 x 14 black sidewall tires standard on wagons and cars equipped with 220- or 300-hp V-8s and air conditioning (no charge). Five 8.00 x 14 black sidewall tires standard on other full-size Fords ($15.50). Five 8.00 x 14 white sidewall tires standard on wagons and cars equipped with 220- or 300-hp V-8s and air conditioning ($37). Five 8.00 x 14 white sidewall tires on other full-size Fords ($52.40 extra). Five 8.00 x 14 black sidewall 6-ply tires on wagons ($44.50). Five 8.00 x 14 white sidewall 6-ply tires on wagons ($81.40).

History:

Lee A. Iacocca was in his second season at the Ford helm this year. Calendar year output totaled 1,362,186 cars. Market penetration was up to 24 percent as model year production peaked at 163,600 Fairlanes, 141,500 Fairlane 500s, 349,700 Galaxies, 136,600 station wagons, 73,000 Thunderbirds, 129,700 standard Falcons, 224,500 Deluxe Falcons and 135,100 Falcon station wagons. Dealer introduction dates were September 29, 1960, for Fords and Falcons, November 12, 1960, for Thunderbirds. The full-size line production totals included 201,700 six-cylinder cars, while all Falcons were sixes and all Thunderbirds V-8s.

1961 Ford Galaxie Special Sunliner two-door Convertible (OCW)

1961 Ford four-door Country Squire (OCW)

1962 Ford

Falcon (Six): The Falcon line continued unchanged from the previous year except for the addition of an updated grille. The convex grille bars carried a vertical pattern. A new Galaxie-style top configuration was seen. Standard equipment included turn signals, dual sun visors, front arm rests, an oil filter, a fresh air heater and defroster and five 6.00 x 13 black tubeless tires. Station wagons had 6.50 x 13 4-ply tires.

Falcon Deluxe (Six): There were two separate Falcon lines this year: standard and deluxe series. The latter replaced the Deluxe trim package, which was optional on all 1960 and 1961 Falcons. The Deluxe trim package included all-vinyl trim and aluminum trim panels behind the rear wheel openings. In addition to the equipment on other models, the sporty new Futura two-door sedan included carpets, a cigarette

1962 Ford Falcon Futura Sport Coupe (PH)

lighter, automatic door light switches, chrome door and window frames, a special steering wheel, wheel covers, bucket seats with a console storage department, special interior upholstery and trim and foam-padded rear seats. The new wood-grained Squire station wagon also had a power tailgate window.

Fairlane — (Six and V-8): The big news for 1962 was the introduction of the intermediate-size Fairlane. The new model was nearly 12 inches shorter than the full-size Galaxie, yet was nearly eight inches longer than the compact Falcon. At the time of their introduction, the Fairlanes were compared to the 1949-1950 Fords in length and width. They were nearly identical to the old "shoe box" models, but were considerably lower. No one would ever guess the Fairlane was anything but a Ford. It featured Ford's characteristic round taillights and high-canted fenders, plus a grille that was nearly identical to the Galaxie's. The styling was somewhat similar to that of 1961 full-size Fords, so there was no doubt of the Fairlane's heritage. The Fairlane lineup started with base Fairlane models. The Fairlane introduced the famous 221 series small-block Ford V-8 that used a new thin-wall casting technique that allowed Ford to produce the lightest complete V-8 engine of its time.

Fairlane 500 — (Six and V-8): The Fairlane 500 models were the top trim level and included chrome window moldings, a chrome horn ring, armrests on all doors, simulated chrome inserts on the door upholstery, a two-piece chrome Fairlane sweep with a ribbed aluminum insert and two sun visors. The Sport Coupe two-door sedan, introduced at midyear, included bucket seats and special identification.

Mainliner (Six and V-8): Ford continued its policy of making major annual styling changes in least one car line. The full-size 1962 Fords were restyled and the end result was recognized as one of the cleanest designs to come from Dearborn. Except for one horizontal feature line at the beltline, the body was slab-sided. The model designation was carried in script along the rear fender. Ford continued the tradition of large round taillights throughout the entire line. The model designation was spelled out, in block letters, across the trunk lid. At the front end, a full-width grille carried a horizontal grid pattern and was capped on each end by the dual headlights. The Ford crest was centered at the front of the hood throughout the full-size line. Standard equipment on the low-cost Mainliner models, which were available for fleet sales only, included an oil bath air cleaner, an oil filter, dual sun visors, a cigarette lighter, a foam-padded front seat, a trunk light and five tubeless black sidewall tires. The Mainliner four-door sedan had no ash tray in back of the front seat.

Galaxie (Six and V-8): The taillights on Galaxies were separated by a stamped aluminum escutcheon panel. Standard equipment on the Galaxie models included an oil bath air cleaner, an oil filter, dual sun visors, a cigarette lighter, a foam-padded front seat, a trunk light, carpets and five tubeless black sidewall tires. The Galaxies also had richer upholstery than the Mainliner models.

Galaxie 500 (Six and V-8): Galaxie 500s had all of the same features as regular Galaxies, plus chrome A-pillar moldings, chrome window moldings, a color-keyed horizontal strip at the belt line, chrome rocker panel moldings, chrome quarter panel moldings, chrome strips with a Ford crest at the base of the S-pillar (on the top), back-up lights, special upholstery, special exterior trim, and an electric clock.

Galaxie 500/XL (V-8): Introduced as a midyear addition to the line, the sporty Galaxie 500/XL models included bucket seats with a Thunderbird-styled console in between them and Galaxie 500/XL rear fender nameplates. The hardtop also had special oval badges on the roof sail panels replacing the regular Galaxie 500 crest emblems. Interior trim was also somewhat richer. A new option offered this year was an optional "Starlift" removable convertible top.

Station Wagon (Six and V-8): Ranch wagons compared to Mainliners in their level of equipment and trim, Country Sedans compared to Galaxies in the level of equipment and trim and Country Squires compared to Galaxie 500s in their general level of equipment and trim. Country Squires also had wood-grained exterior paneling and the Country Squire 9-passenger model had a power tailgate window.

1961 Ford Falcon four-door Sedan (OCW)

1962 Ford Galaxie 500 rear view

1962 Ford Falcon Deluxe four-door Sedan (OCW)

VIN (Falcon):

The VIN for Falcons was die-stamped into the surface of the left-hand brace between the top of the firewall and the left front wheel housing. The first symbol indicates year: 2=1962. The second symbol identifies assembly plant, as follows: A=Atlanta, Georgia, D=Dallas, Texas, E=Mahwah, New Jersey, F=Dearborn, Michigan, G=Chicago, Illinois, H=Lorain, Ohio, J=Los Angeles, California, K=Kansas City, Kansas, N=Norfolk, Virginia, P=Twin Cities, Minnesota, R=San Jose, California, S=Pilot Plant, T=Metuchen, New Jersey, U=Louisville, Kentucky, W=Wayne, Michigan, Y=Wixom, Michigan, Z=St. Louis, Mo. The third and fourth symbols identify body series code: 11=two-door, 12=four-door, 17=Tudor Futura, 21=two-door station wagon, 22=four-door station wagon, 26=four-door Squire station wagon. The fifth symbol identifies engine code, as follows: E=170-cid six-cylinder, S=144-cid six-cylinder, D=144-cid low-compression six-cylinder, U=170-cid six-cylinder. The last six digits are the unit's production number, beginning at 100001 and going up, at each of the assembly plants. Falcons not built at all Ford plants.

VIN (Fairlane):

The VIN for Fairlanes was die-stamped into the side of the left-hand front inner fender apron near the top. The first symbol indicates year: 2=1962. The second symbol identifies assembly plant, as follows: A=Atlanta, Georgia, D=Dallas, Texas, E=Mahwah, New Jersey, F=Dearborn, Michigan, G=Chicago, Illinois, H=Lorain, Ohio, J=Los Angeles, California, K=Kansas City, Kansas, N=Norfolk, Virginia, P=Twin Cities, Minnesota, R=San Jose, California, S=Pilot Plant, T=Metuchen, New Jersey, U=Louisville, Kentucky, W=Wayne, Michigan, Y=Wixom, Michigan, Z=St. Louis, Mo. The third and fourth symbols identify body series code: 31=Fairlane two-door Club Sedan, 32=Fairlane four-door Town Sedan, 41=Fairlane 500 two-door Club Sedan, 42=Fairlane 500 four-door Town sedan, 47=Fairlane 500 two-door Sport Coupe. The fifth symbol identifies engine code, as follows: U=170-cid six-cylinder, C=221-cid low-compression export V-8, E=170-cid low-compression export six-cylinder, L=221-cid V-8, F=260-cid V-8. The last six digits are the unit's production number, beginning at 100001 and going up, at each of the assembly plants. Fairlanes not built at all Ford plants.

VIN (Ford):

The VIN for full-size Fords was die-stamped into the top right-hand side rail of the frame ahead of the front suspension member. The first symbol indicates year: 2=1962. The second symbol identifies assembly plant, as follows: A=Atlanta, Georgia, D=Dallas, Texas, E=Mahwah, New Jersey, F=Dearborn, Michigan, G=Chicago, Illinois, H=Lorain, Ohio, J=Los Angeles, California, K=Kansas City, Kansas, N=Norfolk, Virginia, P=Twin Cities, Minnesota, R=San Jose, California, S=Pilot Plant, T=Metuchen, New Jersey, U=Louisville, Kentucky, W=Wayne, Michigan, Y=Wixom, Michigan, Z=St. Louis, Mo. The third and fourth symbols identify body series SG316=Ford Mainliner two-door sedan, SG326=Ford Mainliner four-door sedan, 51=Galaxie two-door Club Sedan, 52=Galaxie four-door Town Sedan, 61=Galaxie 500 two-door

Club Sedan, 62=Galaxie 500 four-door Town sedan, 63=Galaxie 500 two-door Victoria Hardtop, 64=Galaxie 500 four-door Victoria Hardtop, 65=Galaxie 500 Sunliner convertible, 83=Galaxie 500/XL two-door Victoria Hardtop, 85=Galaxie 500/XL Sunliner convertible, 71=two-door Ranch Wagon station wagon, 72=four-door Country Sedan six-passenger station wagon, 74=four-door Country Sedan nine-passenger station wagon, 76=four-door Country Squire six-passenger station wagon, 78=four-door Country Squire nine-passenger station wagon. The fifth symbol identifies engine code, as follows: V=223-cid six-cylinder, W=292-cid two-barrel V-8, X=352-cid two-barrel V-8, Z=390-cid four-barrel V-8, T=292-cid low-compression export two-barrel V-8, R=390-cid low-compression export four-barrel V-8, M=390-cid high-performance V-8 with three two-barrel carburetors, Q=390-cid four-barrel high-performance V-8, P=390-cid four-barrel Police V-8, B=406-cid four-barrel V-8 and G=406-cid low-compression six-cylinder high-performance V-8 with three two-barrel carburetors. The last six digits are the unit's production number, beginning at 100001 and going up, at each of the assembly plants. Full-size Fords not built at all Ford plants.

Falcon Standard (Six)

Model No.	Body/ Style No.	Body Type & Seating	Factory Price	Shipping Weight	Production Total
58A	12	4-dr. Sedan-6P	$2,047	2,279 lbs.	54,804
64A	11	2-dr. Sedan-6P	$1,985	2,243 lbs.	64,266
71A	22	4-dr. Station Wagon-6P	$2,341	2,575 lbs.	23,590
59A	21	2-dr. Station Wagon-6P	$2,298	2,539 lbs.	12,232

Falcon Deluxe (Six)

58B	12	4-dr. Sedan-6P	$2,133	2,285 lbs.	71,237
64B	11	2-dr. Sedan-6P	$2,071	2,249 lbs.	47,825
71B	22	4-dr. Station Wagon-6P	$2,427	2,581 lbs.	43,229
59B	21	2-dr. Station Wagon-6P	$2,384	2,545 lbs.	7,793

Falcon Futura (Six)

64C	17	2-dr. Coupe-6P	$2,232	2,328 lbs.	31,559
62C	17	2-dr. Sport Coupe-6P	$2,273	2,232 lbs.	17,011
71C	26	2-dr. Squire Wagon-6P	$2,603	2,591 lbs.	22,583

Fairlane (Six)

54A	32	4-dr. Sedan-6P	$2,216	2,791 lbs.	27,996
62A	31	2-dr. Sedan-6P	$2,154	2,757 lbs.	23,511

Fairlane (V-8)

54A	32	4-dr. Sedan-6P	$2,319	2,949 lbs.	18,346
62A	31	2-dr. Sedan-6P	$2,257	2,915 lbs.	10,753

Fairlane 500 (Six)

54B	42	4-dr. Town Sedan-6P	$2,304	2,808 lbs.	31,113
62B	41	2-dr. Club Sedan-6P	$2,242	2,774 lbs.	26,533
62C	41	2-dr. Sport Coupe-6P	$2,403	2,842 lbs.	1,659

Fairlane 500 (V-8)

54B	42	4-dr. Town Sedan-6P	$2,407	2,966 lbs.	98,145
62B	41	2-dr. Club Sedan-6P	$2,345	2,932 lbs.	42,091
62C	41	2-dr. Sport Coupe-6P	$2,506	3,002 lbs.	17,969

Mainliner and Galaxie (Six)

54B	52	4-dr. Town Sedan-6P	$2,507	3,581 lbs.	37,994
62B	51	2-dr. Club Sedan-6P	$2,453	3,486 lbs.	26,114

Mainliner and Galaxie (V-8)

54B	52	4-dr. Town Sedan-6P	$2,616	3,692 lbs.	77,600
62B	51	2-dr. Club Sedan-6P	$2,562	3,597 lbs.	28,816

Note: Production includes Mainliner models available for fleet sales only.

Galaxie 500 (Six)

54A	62	4-dr. Town Sedan-6P	$2,667	3,594 lbs.	8,917
62A	61	2-dr. Club Sedan-6P	$2,613	3,484 lbs.	3,510
75A	64	4-dr. Victoria-6P	$2,739	3,585 lbs.	952
65A	63	2-dr. Victoria-6P	$2,674	3,513 lbs.	3,151
76A	65	2-dr. Sunliner-6P	$2,924	3,675 lbs.	2,616

Galaxie 500 (V-8)

54A	62	4-dr. Town Sedan-6P	$2,776	3,705 lbs.	11,904
62A	61	2-dr. Club Sedan-6P	$2,722	3,595 lbs.	165,278
75A	64	4-dr. Victoria-6P	$2,848	3,696 lbs.	29,826
65A	63	2-dr. Victoria-6P	$2,783	3,624 lbs.	84,411
76A	65	2-dr. Sunliner-6P	$3,033	3,786 lbs.	40,030

Galaxie 500/XL (V-8)

65B	64	2-dr. Victoria-6P	$3,056	3,672 lbs.	28,412
76B	65	2-dr. Sunliner-6P	$3,306	3,831 lbs.	13,183

Station Wagon (Six)

71D	71	4-dr. Ranch Wagon-6P	$2,733	3,913 lbs.	13,171
71C	72	4-dr. Country Sedan-6P	$2,829	3,936 lbs.	2,603
71B	74	4-dr. Country Sedan-8P	$2,933	3,954 lbs.	1,774
71A	76	4-dr. Country Squire-6P	$3,018	3,950 lbs.	411
71E	78	4-dr. Country Squire-9P	$3,088	3,967 lbs.	281

Station Wagon (V-8)

71D	71	4-dr. Ranch Wagon-6P	$2,842	4,024 lbs.	20,503
71C	72	4-dr. Country Sedan-6P	$2,938	4,065 lbs.	45,032
71B	74	4-dr. Country Sedan-8P	$3,042	4,067 lbs.	14,788
71A	76	4-dr. Country Squire-6P	$3,127	4,078 lbs.	15,703
71E	78	4-dr. Country Squire-9P	$3,197	4,061 lbs.	15,385

Engines:

Falcon Six: Overhead valve. Cast-iron block. Displacement: 144 cid. B & S: 3.50 x 2.50 in. Compression ratio: 6.7:1. Brake hp: 65 at 4200 rpm. Carburetor: Holley one-barrel. Seven main bearings. Code S.

Falcon Six: Overhead valve. Cast-iron block. Displacement: 170 cid. B & S: 3.50 x 2.94 in. Compression ratio: 8.7:1. Brake hp: 101 at 4400 rpm. Carburetor: Holley one-barrel. Seven main bearings. Code U.

Ford Six: Overhead valve. Cast-iron block. Displacement: 223 cid. B & S: 3.62 x 3.60 in. Compression ratio: 8.4:1. Brake hp: 138 at 4200 rpm. Carburetor: Holley one-barrel. Four main bearings. Code V.

Base Fairlane V-8: Overhead valve. Cast-iron block. Displacement: 221 cid. B & S: 3.50 x 2.87 in. Compression ratio: 8.70:1. Brake hp: 145 at 4400 rpm. Torque: 216 lbs.-ft. at 2200 rpm. Hydraulic valve lifters. Carburetor: Ford two-barrel Model C20E-9510-N with standard transmission or C20E-9510-T with automatic transmission. Cooling system capacity: 14.5 qt. with heater. Crankcase capacity: 4 qt. (add 1 qt. with new oil filter). Code L.

Challenger 260 Fairlane V-8 (mid-year): Overhead valve. Cast-iron block. Displacement: 260 cid. B & S: 3.80 x 2.87 in. Compression ratio: 8.70:1. Brake hp: 164 at 4400 rpm. Torque: 258 lbs.-ft. at 2200 rpm. Five main bearings. Hydraulic valve lifters. Carburetor: Ford two-barrel Model C20F-9510-A. Cooling system capacity: 14.5 qt. with heater. Crankcase capacity: 4 qt. (add 1 qt. with new oil filter). Code F.

Base Ford V-8: Overhead valve. Cast-iron block. Displacement: 292 cid. B & S: 3.75 x 3.30 in. Compression ratio: 8.80:1. Brake hp: 170 at 4200 rpm. Torque: 279 lbs.-ft. at 2200 rpm. Five main bearings. Solid valve lifters. Carburetor: (with PCV) Ford two-barrel Model C2AE-9510-AA with standard transmission or C2AE-9510-AB with automatic transmission, (without PCV) Ford two-barrel Model C2AE-9510-Y with standard transmission or C2AE-9510-Z with automatic transmission.

1962 Ford Falcon Deluxe two-door Sedan (OCW)

1962 Ford Falcon Sports Futura two-door Coupe (OCW)

1962 Ford Falcon Sports Futura interior detail (OCW)

1962 Ford Falcon four-door Squire Station Wagon (OCW)

Cooling system capacity: 16 qt. with heater. Crankcase capacity: 5 qt. (add 1 qt. with new oil filter). Code W.

Interceptor 352 V-8: Overhead valve. Cast-iron block. Displacement: 352 cid. B & S: 4.00 x 3.50 in. Compression ratio: 8.90:1. Brake hp: 220 at 4300 rpm. Torque: 336 lbs.-ft. at 2600 rpm. Five main bearings. Hydraulic valve lifters. Carburetor: (with PCV) Ford two-barrel Model C2AE-9510-AE with standard transmission or C2AE-9510-AF with automatic transmission, (without PCV) Ford two-barrel Model C2AE-9510-AC with standard transmission or C2AE-9510-AD with automatic transmission. Cooling system capacity: 20.5 qt. with heater. Crankcase capacity: 5 qt. (add 1 qt. with new oil filter). Code X.

Interceptor 390 V-8: Overhead valve. Cast-iron block. Displacement: 390 cid. B & S: 4.05 x 3.78 in. Compression ratio: 9.60:1. Brake hp: 300 at 4600 rpm. Torque: 427 lbs.-ft. at 2800 rpm. Five main bearings. Hydraulic valve lifters. Carburetor: (with PCV) Ford four-barrel Model C2AE-9510-AJ with standard transmission or C2AE-9510-AK with automatic transmission. Cooling system capacity: 20.5 qt. with heater. Crankcase capacity: 5 qt. (add 1 qt. with new oil filter). Dual exhaust. Code Z.

Interceptor 390 V-8: Overhead valve. Cast-iron block. Displacement: 390 cid. B & S: 4.05 x 3.78 in. Compression ratio: 9.60:1. Brake hp: 330 at 5000 rpm. Torque: 427 lbs.-ft. at 3200 rpm. Five main bearings. Solid valve lifters. Carburetor: (with PCV) Ford four-barrel Model C2AE-9510-AJ with standard transmission or C2AE-9510-AK with automatic transmission, (without PCV) Ford two-barrel Model C2AE-9510-AG with standard transmission or C2AE-9510-AR with automatic transmission. Cooling system capacity: 20.5 qt. with heater. Crankcase capacity: 5 qt. (add 1 qt. with new oil filter). Dual exhausts. Code P.

390-375 Optional Ford V-8: Overhead valve. Cast-iron block. Displacement: 390 cid. B & S: 4.05 x 3.78 in. Compression ratio: 10.60:1. Brake hp: 375 at 6000 rpm. Torque: 427 lbs.-ft. at 3400 rpm. Five main bearings. Solid valve lifters. Carburetor: Holley Model R-3228A four-barrel. Cooling system capacity: 20.5 qt. with heater. Crankcase capacity: 5 qt. (add 1 qt. with new oil filter). Dual exhausts Code Q.

Thunderbird 406 V-8: Overhead valve. Cast-iron block. Displacement: 406 cid. B & S: 4.13 x 3.78 in. Compression ratio: 11.40:1. Brake hp: 385 at 5800 rpm. Torque: 444 lbs.-ft. at 3400 rpm. Five main bearings. Solid valve lifters. Carburetor: Ford four-barrel Model CIAE-9510-AG with standard transmission or CIAE-9510-AH with automatic transmission. Cooling system capacity: 20.5 qt. with heater. Crankcase capacity: 5 qt. (add 1 qt. with new oil filter). Dual exhausts. Code B.

390-401 Optional Ford V-8: Overhead valve. Cast-iron block. Displacement: 390 cid. B & S: 4.05 x 3.78 in. Compression ratio: 10.60:1. Brake hp: 401 at 6000 rpm. Torque: 430 lbs.-ft. at 3500 rpm. Five main bearings. Solid valve lifters. Carburetor: Holley three two barrels. Cooling system capacity: 20.5 qt. with heater. Crankcase capacity: 5 qt. (add 1 qt. with new oil filter). Dual exhausts. Code M.

Thunderbird Special 406 V-8: Overhead valve. Cast-iron block. Displacement: 406 cid. B & S: 4.13 x 3.78 in. Compression ratio: 11.40:1. Brake hp: 405 at 5800 rpm. Torque: 448 lbs.-ft. at 3500 rpm. Five main bearings. Solid valve lifters. Carburetor: Holley three two-barrel. Cooling system capacity: 20.5 qt. with heater. Crankcase capacity: 5 qt. (add 1 qt. with new oil filter). Dual exhausts. Code G.

Chassis:

Falcon: Wheelbase: 109.5 in. Overall length: 181.1 in. and 189 in., station wagon. Tires: 6.00 x 13, car and 6.50 x 13, station wagon.

Fairlane: Wheelbase: 115.5 in. Overall length: 197.6 in. Tires: 6.50 x 13, Fairlane six, 7.00 x 14, Fairlane V-8 and 7.00 x 13, Fairlane 260 V-8.

Ford: Wheelbase: 119 in. Overall length: 209.3 in. Tires: 7.50 x 14, car and 8.00 x 14, station wagon.

Options:

Falcon and Fairlane: Back-up lights ($11). Heavy-duty battery ($8). Squire bucket seats and console ($120). Crankcase ventilation system ($6). Deluxe trim package ($87). Engine, 170 cid/101 hp ($38). Tinted glass ($27). Windshield tinted glass ($13). Station wagon luggage rack ($39). Two-tone paint ($19). Push-button radio and antenna ($59). Safety equipment, including padded dash and front visors ($22). Seat safety belts ($21). Electric tailgate windows ($30). Automatic transmission ($163). Vinyl trim for sedan (Deluxe trim package required) ($25). Wheel covers ($16). Windshield washer ($14). Electric windshield wiper ($10).

1962 Ford Fairlane two-door Sedan (OCW)

1962 Ford Fairlane 500 four-door Town Sedan (OCW)

1962 Ford Fairlane 500 four-door Town Sedan (OCW)

1962 Ford Fairlane 500 two-door Sports Coupe (OCW)

1962 Ford Galaxie two-door Club Sedan (OCW)

Ford: Polar Air conditioning with V-8 ($271). Select Aire air conditioning with V-8 ($361). Back-up lights, standard Galaxie 500 ($11). Heavy-duty battery, 70-amp ($8). Crankcase ventilation system ($6). Equa-Lock differential ($39). Electric clock, standard Galaxy 500 ($15). Re-circulating heater and defroster ($28 deduct option). Chrome luggage rack ($39). Four-way manual seat ($16). Rocker panel molding ($16). Padded dash and visors ($24). Two-tone paint ($22). Power brakes ($43). Power seat ($64). Power steering ($82). Power tailgate window ($32). Front and rear power windows ($102). Push-button radio and antenna ($59). Front seat belts ($21). Tinted glass ($40). Tinted windshield ($22). Cruise-O-Matic transmission ($212). Ford-O-Matic with six-cylinder ($180). Ford-O-Matic with V-8 ($190). Overdrive transmission ($108). Four-speed manual transmission, 375-hp or 401-hp V-8 required ($188). Vinyl trim, Galaxie 500 except convertible ($26). Deluxe wheel covers ($26). Wheel covers ($19). Windshield washer and wipers, two-speed ($20).

History:

The 1962 Falcon was introduced September 29, 1961. The 1962 Galaxie and station wagon lines appeared the same day. The Fairlane series did not debut until November 16, 1961. Ford announced the introduction of the first transistorized ignition system, for production cars, in March 1962. A total of 30,216 Fairlanes had the 260-cid V-8 installed. A total of 722,647 Galaxies, 386,192 Fairlanes, 381,559 Falcons and 75,536 Thunderbirds were built this year, second only to the record production season 1955. Midyear models included the Galaxie 500/XL hardtop and convertible, the Fairlane 500 Sport Sedan and the Falcon Sport Futura. Lee A. Iacocca was vice-president and general manager of the Ford Division again this year. In a historic move, Ford built 10 Galaxie "factory lightweight" drag racing cars late in model year 1962. This year saw a continuation of the great 1960's horsepower race and to do combat with the General Motors and Chrysler offerings, Ford introduced the famous 406 cid/405 hp V-8. The re-sizing of the Fairlane also brought the introduction of a completely new line of small V-8 engines. At 221 cid, the new base V-8 was the same displacement as the first Ford flathead V-8. It was of thin wall casting design and was the first in a series of lightweight V-8s.

1962 Ford Galaxie 500 two-door Club Sedan (OCW)

1962 Ford Galaxie 500 four-door Town Sedan (OCW)

1962 Ford Galaxie 500 Club Victoria two-door hardtop (OCW)

1962 Ford Galaxie 500 Sunliner two-door Convertible (OCW)

1962 Ford Galaxie 500/XL Club Victoria two-door hardtop (OCW)

1962 Ford Galaxie 500/XL Sunliner two-door convertible (OCW)

1963 Ford

Falcon — Series 06 — (Six and V-8): The Falcon line continued to use the body shell introduced in 1960. A new convex grille featured a full-width horizontal center bar with three full-width horizontal bars above it and four below it. These were intersected by five vertical bars spaced fairly widely apart. This created a grid-work of narrow horizontal openings. The standard models had no body side moldings. The front fenders carried a black oval with a Falcon emblem in it and the "Falcon" name in chrome script just behind the emblems. There was a chrome piece on the front of the simulated hood air scoop and a ribbed chrome piece at the base of the roof pillar. Small "doggie dish" hubcaps were included. The slightly-revised taillight lenses had additional chrome around the inside of the lens. The standard series include two- and four-door sedans. Standard equipment included a six-cylinder 85-hp engine with self-adjusting valves, a three-speed manual transmission, self-adjusting brakes, a full-flow oil filter, a 36,000-mile fuel filter, a fully-aluminized muffler, galvanized main underbody members, a bright-metal windshield molding, a bright-metal rear window molding, parallel-action single-speed electric windshield wipers, two horns, two sun visors, two front arm rests, two coat hooks, a foam-cushioned front seat, a front ash tray, a white vinyl headlining, gold ladder-pattern cloth-and-vinyl seat trim, a color-keyed 3-spoke steering wheel, front seat belt anchors, turn signals with new "safety Amber" lenses and center-fill fueling. A heater was installed during production unless otherwise specified. If deleted, an appropriate price reduction was made. In addition to the above, the following Deluxe Trim items were available for Standard Falcon models at slight additional cost: Bright body side moldings, fender-top ornaments, a choice of red or blue cloth-and-vinyl interior trim, rear arm rests, an ash tray, a cigarette lighter, a chrome horn ring and an automatic dome light. Also introduced at midyear, for all Falcons, was an optional V-8 engine.

1963 Ford Falcon Futura four-door Sedan (OCW)

1963 Ford Falcon Sports Futura two-door Sedan (OCW)

Falcon Futura — Series 10 — (Six and V-8): Ford said that Falcon Futura models had the bold, modern beauty of their Thunderbird cousins. A new body style was a convertible. Standard features included all the equipment that Standard Falcons came with the following additions or replacements: bright-metal side window frames, side body moldings with front fender spear tips and complementary color inserts, fender-top ornaments, "Futura" in block letters and a molding on the rear body panel, a choice of five different "Bar-Line" pattern pleated cloth-and-vinyl interior trims, a chrome-backed rearview mirror, color-keyed carpeting front and rear, a cigarette lighter, rear arm rests, a rear ash tray, a chrome horn ring, an automatic dome light, a Futura molding across the instrument panel, bright inserts in the dashboard control knobs, Futura full wheel covers and a Futura chrome script on the sides of the rear fenders above the body side moldings. Hardtop and convertible models were additions to the lineup. Standard equipment in the convertible included the Falcon 170 Special six with 101 hp, a choice of five pleated all-vinyl interior trims, foam-padded front and rear seat cushions, an electric-hydraulic power-operated convertible top, vinyl 3-ply top material in white, blue or black, added underbody torque boxes, Safety-Yoke door locks, Futura front arm rests, front and rear ash trays and a chrome-backed "floating" windshield mirror.

Falcon Futura Sports — (Six and V-8): This Falcon Futura sub-series contained all of the sporty models, some of which were midyear additions to the lineup. The Futura Sports Sedan, which appeared in the introductory sales catalog, was a two-door sedan that included all regular standard equipment plus foam-cushioned black vinyl bucket front seats, a console, foam-cushioned black bucket-style rear seats, a choice of five pleated all-vinyl interior trims, a unique white whipcord vinyl headlining and special Sports Sedan armrests and ash trays front and rear. A new option for this car was a vinyl roof that came in black or white. In addition to all the features of the Futura convertible, the Futura Sports convertible included bucket front seats, a console and bucket-style rear seat cushions.

Falcon Sprint — (V-8): The Sprint hardtop and Sprint convertible were midyear additions to the lineup. They were created in honor of the Falcon's winning performance in the Monte Carlo Rally. The Sprint models had all the features of the Falcon Futura Sports hardtop and convertible, plus a standard V-8 engine, a tachometer and a special steering wheel.

Falcon Station Wagon — Series 20 — (Six and V-8): Both two- and four-door station wagons were introduced to the Falcon lineup this year. They came in Standard, Futura and Futura Sport trim levels. The Futura versions carried Squire identification and wood-grained exterior trim. The Futura Squire Sport had bucket seats. The sales catalog listed specific station wagon features, which were comparable to the features of the Standard, Futura and Futura Sport trim levels with certain alterations distinct to station wagons.

Fairlane — Series 30 — (Six and V-8): All-new front end styling for the Fairlane was characterized by a concave grille with a cross-hatched insert with chrome ovals in each small opening for a very ornate look. The model lineup was expanded for some series, but the basic series still consisted of two- and four-door sedans. These cars featured the Fairlane name in chrome script on the roof pillar, a ribbed chrome piece

1963 Ford Falcon two-door Sedan (OCW)

1963 Ford Falcon Futura two-door Sedan (OCW)

below the script, a chrome belt line molding with a half spear tip. A ribbed rear beauty panel with crest in the middle, chrome-circled round taillights and "doggie dish" hubcaps with the Ford name embossed in them. Standard features included a choice of "Square-Puff" cloth-and-vinyl upholstery in blue, gold or red, a choice of 11 Diamond Lustre Enamel exterior colors, a bright-metal windshield molding, a white vinyl headlining, a color-keyed 3-spoke steering wheel, dual sun visors, dual coat hooks, front arm rests, a front ash tray, a locking glove box, front seat belt anchors, Safety-Yoke door locks, a foam-cushioned front seat, turn signals with new amber safety lenses in the front bumper, parallel-action single-speed electric wipers, an illuminated trunk (with taillights on), a 101-hp Fairlane Six engine, a three-speed manual transmission, self-adjusting brakes, Zinclad rocker panels and main underbody members, a 6,000-mile full-flow oil filter, a fully-aluminized muffler and a 36,000-mile replaceable fuel filter element.

Fairlane 500 — Series 40 — (Six and V-8): The Fairlane 500 models were the top trim level and included all Fairlane features with the following variations: a choice of "Wheel-Pattern" pleated cloth-and-vinyl interior trims in blue, turquoise, beige, gold or red, a choice of 12 Diamond Lustre enamel exterior colors, bright-metal side window moldings, Fairlane 500 scripts on the roof sail panels, fin-shaped body side moldings with color-keyed inserts, front fender top trim pieces, full wheel covers of a specific design, front and rear arm rests, front and rear ash trays, a cigarette lighter, an automatic dome light, a chrome horn ring and color-keyed carpeting. The Fairlane 500 hardtop also included a "floating" inside rearview mirror. The Fairlane 500 Sports Coupe also included a choice of all-vinyl interior trims in blue, black, red, chestnut or gold, a choice of 13 Diamond Lustre enamel exterior colors, foam-cushioned front bucket seats with a center console, a unique white whipcord vinyl headlining and a bucket-style rear seat. On hardtops the Fairlane 500 script was moved from the roof sail panels to the side of the cowl below the fin-shaped moldings. The sail panels also had T-bird like red, white and blue emblems. The Fairlane 500 Sports coupe had the same wheel covers as other Fairlane 500s. The Fairlane 500 hardtop had three slashes inside the moldings on the front fenders and full wheel covers with tri-bar "spinner" type centers.

Fairlane Station Wagon — (Six and V-8): The Fairlane station wagons came in three four-door models: Ranch Wagon, Custom Ranch Wagon and Squire. Standard Ranch Wagon equipment started with all of the Fairlane sedan features and then included these variations: a choice of "Preline Pattern" vinyl-and-vinyl interior trims in blue and beige, a choice of 11 Diamond Lustre enamel exterior colors, front and rear foam-cushioned seats, a color-keyed cargo area inlay, a roll-down tailgate window with painted molding and a folding second seat. The Custom Ranch Wagon included all Fairlane 500 sedan equipment , a choice of beige pleated "Wheel-Pattern" cloth-and-vinyl interior all-vinyl pleated trim in red, blue or beige, color-keyed vinyl-coated rubber floor coverings, a stowage compartment lock and a bright-metal tailgate molding. The Fairlane Squire also included a choice of beige pleated "Wheel-Pattern" cloth-and-vinyl or pleated all-vinyl interior trims in red, blue or beige, distinctive limed oak fiberglass moldings enclosing walnut-

1963 Ford Falcon Futura two-door Convertible (AA)

1963 Ford Falcon Sprint two-door Hardtop (PH)

1962 Ford Falcon Sprint two-door Convertible (OCW)

1962 Ford Falcon four-door Station Wagon (OCW)

1963 Ford Falcon Deluxe two-door Station Wagon (OCW)

1963 Ford Falcon four-door Squire Station Wagon (OCW)

1963-1/2 Ford Falcon (OCW)

1963 Ford Fairlane two-door Sedan (OCW)

1963 Ford Fairlane 500 four-door Sedan (OCW)

colored steel panels on the body sides and rear, color-keyed carpeting on the passenger floor and a power-operated tailgate window.

Ford 300 — Series 50 — (Six and V-8): Ford styling for '63 was influenced by the Thunderbird. Changes included a flatter roof line and recessed rear window on some models. Up to 36 power combinations were available in big Fords. The four-door sedan had no ash tray in back of the front seat. Crank-operated vent windows, a compliance-link front suspension and Swing-Away steering columns were new features or options this year. The all-new Ford 300 was the newest and lowest-priced of the big Fords. It was offered in two- and four-door sedan models that incorporated the roominess, comfort and convenience of Twice-A-Year Maintenance and all of Ford's service-saving features. The all-new Ford 300 was built to the same high-quality standards as Galaxie models. Buyers of these cars had a choice of three attractive cloth-and-vinyl interior trims in blue, gold or red. Galaxie options and power accessories were available.

Galaxie — Series 50 — (Six and V-8): Galaxie models also came only in two- and four-door sedan models. They had a chrome molding running from the front door to the top of the rear bumper end. Ahead of this was chrome Galaxie script. There were also chrome F-O-R-D block letters on the lip of the hood, chrome fender-top ornaments, red, white and blue crest emblems on the roof sail panels, ribbed chrome pieces at the base of the sail panels and "doggie dish" style hubcaps. Standard equipment included a choice of "Puff-Stripe" cloth-and-vinyl interior trim in blue, beige, gold, turquoise and red, a choice of 11 Diamond Lustre enamel exterior colors, a bright metal windshield molding, a bright metal rear window molding, bright-metal drip rails moldings, Galaxie body trim and side moldings, fender-top ornaments, color-keyed wall-to-wall carpeting, a white vinyl headlining, a color-keyed Lifeguard steering wheel with chrome horn ring, dual sun visors, dual coat hooks, a cigarette lighter, arm rests, front and rear ash trays, an illuminated front ash tray, a locking glove box, a locking luggage compartment, an automatic dome light, front seat belt anchors, Safety-Yoke door locks, a foam-cushioned front seat, crank-adjusted vent windows, turn signals with new safety amber lenses in the front bumper, parallel-action single-speed electric windshield wipers, a step-on parking brake, a 138-hp Mileage Maker Six engine, a Synchro-Smooth Drive three-speed manual transmission, self-adjusting brakes, a full-flow oil filter, a 36,000-mile fuel filter, a fully-aluminized muffler and center-fill fueling.

Galaxie 500 — (Six and V-8): Galaxie 500s had all of the same features as regular Galaxies, plus additional luxury items that varied by body style. The two-and four-door sedans had these extras: a choice of "Gleam" cloth-and vinyl interior trims in blue, beige, chestnut, turquoise, gold, red and black, a choice of 13 Diamond Lustre enamel exterior colors, chrome-like Mylar accents on the seats, doors and side panels, pleated seat fabrics, pleated door panels, pleated side trim panel, deluxe arm rests, front and

1963 Ford Fairlane 500 two-door Hardtop (OCW)

1963 Ford Fairlane four-door Ranch Wagon (OCW)

1963 Ford Fairlane Custom four-door Ranch Wagon (OCW)

rear ash trays, a chrome-backed inside rearview mirror, bright-metal seat side shields, a self-regulating electric clock and back-up lights centered in the taillights. Special exterior body trim included seven has marks on the body sides ahead of the taillights, G-A-L-A-X-I-E block letters on the trunk lip, wider ribbed chrome decorations at the base of the roof side panels, Galaxie 500 scripts and gold badges behind the front wheel openings, full wheel covers with red, white and blue plastic center inserts, double body side moldings (full-length upper and three-quarter lower moldings joined at the rear), and a grille-like rear body trim panel with a crest in its center. The two-and four-door hardtops had these extras: a choice of "Gleam" cloth-and vinyl interior trims in blue, beige, chestnut, turquoise, gold, red and black, a choice of 13 Diamond Lustre enamel exterior colors, chrome-like Mylar accents on the seats, doors and side panels, pleated seat fabrics, pleated door panels, pleated side trim panel, deluxe arm rests, front and rear ash trays, a chrome-backed inside rearview mirror, bright-metal seat side shields, a self-regulating electric clock and back-up lights centered in the taillights. Special exterior body trim included seven has marks on the body sides ahead of the taillights, G-A-L-A-X-I-E block letters on the trunk lip, wider ribbed chrome decorations at the base of the roof side panels, Galaxie 500 scripts and gold badges behind the front wheel openings, full wheel covers with red, white and blue plastic center inserts, double body side moldings (full-length upper and three-quarter lower moldings joined at the rear), and a grille-like rear body trim panel with a crest in its center. The Galaxie 500 convertible had these extras: a choice of pleated all-vinyl interior trims in blue, beige, chestnut, turquoise, gold, red and black, a choice of 13 Diamond Lustre enamel exterior colors, a 3-ply vinyl power-operated top in a choice of white, black or blue, an anti-ballooning top design, a zip-out clear vinyl rear window, a color-keyed and contoured top boot, automatic courtesy lights under the dashboard and a "floating" rearview mirror bonded to the windshield.

Galaxie 500/XL — (V-8): The lively-in-looks Galaxie 500/XL now came in four variations, two-door formal-roof hardtop, two-door fastback hardtop, four-door hardtop and convertible. Standard equipment on the hardtops included everything on Galaxies and Galaxie 500s with the following variations: a choice of all-vinyl interior trims in blue, beige, chestnut, turquoise, gold, red and black, a choice of 13 Diamond Lustre enamel exterior colors, individually-adjusted 100-percent foam-cushioned front bucket seats, a full-length Command Console, an individually-contoured 100-percent full-foam bucket-style rear seat, chrome-like Mylar accents on the seats, doors and side panels, color-keyed wall-to-wall carpeting, a color-keyed instrument panel with full chrome controls, super deluxe front and rear arm rests and ash trays, bright-metal seat side shields and door-lock buttons, bright-metal-accented accelerator and brake pedals, automatic courtesy safety lights in both lower door panels, a 164-hp Galaxie V-8 engine, two-speed Ford-O-Matic Drive transmission with a console-mounted "Sports Stick" and full wheel covers with simulated knock-off spinners. Standard equipment on the Galaxie 500/XL convertible included everything on the Galaxie 500 ragtop, plus a choice of pleated all-vinyl interior trims in blue, Rose Beige, chestnut, turquoise, gold, red or black, a choice of 13 Diamond Lustre enamel exterior colors, individually-adjusted 100-percent foam-cushioned front bucket seats, a full-length Command Console, an individually-contoured 100-percent full-foam bucket-style rear seat, a 3-ply vinyl power-operated top in a choice of white, black or blue, a color-keyed contour-padded top boot with concealed fasteners, color-keyed wall-to-wall carpeting, automatic courtesy safety lights in both lower door panels, a 164-hp Galaxie V-8 engine, two-speed Ford-O-Matic Drive transmission with a console-mounted "Sports Stick" and full wheel covers with simulated knock-off spinners.

1963 Ford Fairlane 500 four-door Ranch Wagon (OCW)

1963 Ford Fairlane Custom four-door Squire Wagon (OCW)

Galaxie Station Wagon — (Six and V-8): Country Sedans compared to Galaxies in the level of equipment and trim and Country Squires compared to Galaxie 500s in their general level of equipment and trim. Country Squires also had wood-grained exterior paneling and the Country Squire 9-passenger model had a power tailgate window.

VIN Falcon:

The VIN for Falcons was die-stamped into the surface of the left-hand brace between the top of the firewall and the left front wheel housing. The first symbol indicates year: 3=1963. The second symbol identifies assembly plant, as follows: A=Atlanta, Georgia, D=Dallas, Texas, E=Mahwah, New Jersey, F=Dearborn, Michigan, G=Chicago, Illinois, H=Lorain, Ohio, J=Los Angeles, California, K=Kansas City, Kansas, N=Norfolk, Virginia, P=Twin Cities, Minnesota, R=San Jose, California, S=Pilot Plant, T=Metuchen, New Jersey, U=Louisville, Kentucky, W=Wayne, Michigan, Y=Wixom, Michigan, Z=St. Louis, Mo. The third and fourth symbols identify body series code: 01=two-door, 02=four-door, 15=convertible, 16=four-door sedan, 17=two-door hardtop, 19=two-door sedan, 21=two-door station wagon, 22=four-door station wagon, 23=two-door Deluxe station wagon, 24=four-door Deluxe station wagon, 26=four-door Squire station wagon. The fifth symbol identifies engine code, as follows: S=144-cid six-cylinder, 2=144-cid six-cylinder, U=170-cid six-cylinder, 4=170-cid six-cylinder, F=260-cid V-8, 8=260-cid V-8 low-compression. The last six digits are the unit's production number, beginning at 100001 and going up, at each of the assembly plants. Falcons not built at all Ford plants.

VIN Fairlane:

The VIN for Fairlanes was die-stamped into the side of the left-hand front inner fender apron near the top. The first symbol indicates year: 3=1962. The second symbol identifies assembly plant, as follows: A=Atlanta, Georgia, D=Dallas, Texas, E=Mahwah, New Jersey, F=Dearborn, Michigan, G=Chicago, Illinois, H=Lorain, Ohio, J=Los Angeles, California, K=Kansas City, Kansas, N=Norfolk, Virginia, P=Twin Cities, Minnesota, R=San Jose, California, S=Pilot Plant, T=Metuchen, New Jersey, U=Louisville, Kentucky, W=Wayne, Michigan, Y=Wixom, Michigan, Z=St. Louis, Mo. The third and fourth symbols identify body series code: 31=Fairlane two-door Club Sedan, 32=Fairlane four-door Town Sedan, 41=Fairlane 500 two-door Club Sedan, 42=Fairlane 500 four-door Town sedan, 43=Fairlane 500 two-door hardtop, 47=Fairlane 500 two-door Sport Coupe. The fifth symbol identifies engine code, as follows: U=170-cid six-cylinder, R=170-cid six-cylinder, T=200-cid six-cylinder, L=221-cid V-8, 3=221-cid V-8, F=260-cid V-8, 8=260-cid V-8 and K=289-cid V-8. The last six digits are the unit's production number, beginning at 100001 and going up, at each of the assembly plants. Fairlanes not built at all Ford plants.

VIN Ford:

The VIN for full-size Fords was die-stamped into the top right-hand side rail of the frame ahead of the front suspension member. The first symbol indicates year: 3=1963. The second symbol identifies assembly plant, as follows: A=Atlanta, Georgia, D=Dallas, Texas, E=Mahwah, New Jersey, F=Dearborn, Michigan, G=Chicago, Illinois, H=Lorain, Ohio, J=Los Angeles, California, K=Kansas City, Kansas, N=Norfolk, Virginia, P=Twin Cities, Minnesota, R=San Jose, California, S=Pilot Plant, T=Metuchen, New Jersey, U=Louisville, Kentucky, W=Wayne, Michigan, Y=Wixom, Michigan, Z=St. Louis, Mo. The third and fourth symbols identify body series 51=Galaxie two-door Club Sedan, 52=Galaxie four-door Town Sedan, 53=Ford 300 two-door sedan, 54=Ford 300 four-door sedan, 61=Galaxie 500 two-door Club Sedan, 62=Galaxie 500 four-door Town sedan, 63=Galaxie 500 two-door Victoria Hardtop, 64=Galaxie 500 four-door Victoria Hardtop, 65=Galaxie 500 Sunliner convertible, 66=Galaxie 500 fastback, 67=Galaxie 500/XL two-door hardtop, 60=Galaxie 500/XL four-door hardtop, 68=Galaxie 500/XL fastback, 69=Galaxie 500/XL two-door convertible, 38=four-door six-passenger station wagon, 48=four-door Custom six-passenger station wagon, 49=four-door Country Squire station wagon, 72=four-door station wagon, 74=four-door station wagon, 76=four-door station wagon

1963 Ford Galaxie two-door Sedan (PH)

and 78=four-door station wagon. The fifth symbol identifies engine code, as follows: V=223-cid six-cylinder, 5=223-cid six-cylinder, E=223-cid six-cylinder, F=260-cid V-8, 8=260-cid V-8, C=289-cid V-8, X=352-cid two-barrel V-8, Z=390-cid four-barrel V-8, 9=390-cid V-8, P=390-cid V-8, B=406-cid V-8, G=406-cid V-8, Q=427-cid V-8, R=427-cid V-8. The last six digits are the unit's production number, beginning at 100001 and going up, at each of the assembly plants. Full-size Fords not built at all Ford plants.

Falcon Standard (Six)

Model No.	Body/ Style No.	Body Type & Seating	Factory Price	Shipping Weight	Production Total
62A	01	2-dr. Sedan-6P	$1,985	2,305 lbs.	68,429
54A	02	4-dr. Sedan-6P	$2,047	2,345 lbs.	59,983

Falcon Standard (V-8)

| 62A | 01 | 2-dr. Sedan-6P | $2,147 | 2,625 lbs. | 2,201 |
| 54A | 02 | 4-dr. Sedan-6P | $2,209 | 2,665 lbs. | 2,382 |

Falcon Futura (Six)

62B	19	2-dr. Sedan-6P	$2,116	2,315 lbs.	15,298
54B	16	4-dr. Sedan-6P	$2,165	2,350 lbs.	28,929
63B	17	2-dr. Hardtop-6P	$2,198	2,455 lbs.	11,124
76A	15	2-dr. Convertible-6P	$2,470	2,655 lbs.	16,091

Falcon Futura (V-8)

62B	19	2-dr. Sedan-6P	$2,278	2,635 lbs.	1,376
54B	16	4-dr. Sedan-6P	$2,327	2,670 lbs.	2,807
63B	17	2-dr. Hardtop-6P	$2,360	2,722 lbs.	6,400
76A	15	2-dr. Convertible-6P	$2,595	2,913 lbs.	2,851

Falcon Futura Sport (Six)

62C	19	2-dr. Sport Coupe-6P	$2,237	2,350 lbs.	9,794
63C	17	4-dr. Sport Hardtop-6P	$2,319	2,490 lbs.	7,449
76B	15	2-dr. Sport Convertible-6P	$2,591	2,690 lbs.	10,690

Falcon Futura Sport (V-8)

62C	19	2-dr. Sport Coupe-6P	$2,399	2,670 lbs.	550
63C	17	4-dr. Sport Hardtop-6P	$2,481	2,757 lbs.	3,523
76B	15	2-dr. Sport Convertible-6P	$2,716	2,948 lbs.	1,560

Falcon Futura Sprint (V-8)

| 63D | 17 | 2-dr. Sprint Hardtop-6P | $2,603 | 2,829 lbs. | 10,479 |
| 76C | 15 | 2-dr. Sprint Convertible-6P | $2,837 | 3,029 lbs. | 4,602 |

Falcon Station Wagon (Six)

| 59A | 21 | 2-dr. Station Wagon-6P | $2,298 | 2,590 lbs. | 7,024 |
| 71A | 22 | 4-dr. Station Wagon-6P | $2,341 | 2,625 lbs. | 17,595 |

Falcon Station Wagon (V-8)

| 59A | 21 | 2-dr. Station Wagon-6P | $2,460 | 2,903 lbs. | 298 |
| 71A | 22 | 4-dr. Station Wagon-6P | $2,503 | 2,938 lbs. | 889 |

Futura Station Wagon (Six)

| 59B | 23 | 2-dr. Station Wagon-6P | $2,384 | 2,605 lbs. | 3,980 |
| 71B | 24 | 4-dr. Station Wagon-6P | $2,427 | 2,645 lbs. | 21,177 |

Futura Station Wagon (V-8)

| 59B | 23 | 2-dr. Station Wagon-6P | $2,546 | 2,918 lbs. | 289 |
| 71B | 24 | 4-dr. Station Wagon-6P | $2,589 | 2,958 lbs. | 2,300 |

Futura Squire Station Wagon (Six)

| 71C | 26 | 4-dr. Station Wagon-6P | $2,603 | 2,645 lbs. | 6,068 |

Futura Squire Station Wagon (V-8)

| 71C | 26 | 4-dr. Station Wagon-6P | $2,765 | 2,958 lbs. | 740 |

Futura Squire Sport (Bucket Seat) Wagon (Six)

| 71D | 26 | 4-dr. Station Wagon-6P | $2,724 | 2,680 lbs. | 1,299 |

Futura Squire Sport (Bucket Seat) Wagon (V-8)

| 71D | 26 | 4-dr. Station Wagon-9P | $2,886 | 2,993 lbs. | 162 |

Fairlane (Six)

| 62A | 31 | 2-dr. Sedan-6P | $2,154 | 2,815 lbs. | 20,347 |
| 54A | 32 | 4-dr. Sedan-6P | $2,216 | 2,855 lbs. | 24,727 |

Fairlane (V-8)

| 62A | 31 | 2-dr. Sedan-6P | $2,257 | 2,947 lbs. | 8,637 |
| 54A | 32 | 4-dr. Sedan-6P | $2,319 | 2,987 lbs. | 19,727 |

Fairlane 500 (Six)

62B	41	2-dr. Sedan-6P	$2,242	2,830 lbs.	11,494
54B	42	4-dr. Sedan-6P	$2,304	2,870 lbs.	20,915
65A	43	2-dr. Hardtop-6P	$2,324	2,850 lbs.	4,610

Fairlane 500 (V-8)

62B	41	2-dr. Sedan-6P	$2,345	2,962 lbs.	23,270
54B	42	4-dr. Sedan-6P	$2,407	3,002 lbs.	83,260
65A	43	2-dr. Hardtop-6P	$2,427	2,982 lbs.	37,031

Fairlane 500 Sport (Six)

65B	47	2-dr. Hardtop-6P	$2,504	2,870 lbs.	1,351

Fairlane 500 Sport (V-8)

65B	47	2-dr. Hardtop-6P	$2,607	3,002 lbs.	26,917

Fairlane Ranch Wagon (Six)

71D	38	4-dr. Station Wagon-6P	$2,525	3,195 lbs.	5,972
71D	38	4-dr. Station Wagon-9P	$2,575	3,210 lbs.	1,180

Fairlane Ranch Wagon (V-8)

71D	38	4-dr. Station Wagon-6P	$2,628	3,327 lbs.	12,691
71D	38	4-dr. Station Wagon-9P	$2,678	3,342 lbs.	4,163

Fairlane Custom Ranch Wagon (Six)

71B	48	4-dr. Station Wagon-6P	$2,613	3,210 lbs.	1,313
71B	48	4-dr. Station Wagon-9P	$2,663	3,225 lbs.	897

Fairlane Custom Ranch Wagon (V-8)

71B	48	4-dr. Station Wagon-6P	$2,716	3,342 lbs.	13,838
71B	48	4-dr. Station Wagon-9P	$2,766	3,357 lbs.	13,564

Fairlane Squire Wagon (Six)

71E	36	4-dr. Station Wagon-6P	$2,781	3,220 lbs.	197
71G	36	4-dr. Station Wagon-9P	$2,831	3,235 lbs.	133

Fairlane Squire Wagon (V-8)

71E	36	4-dr. Station Wagon-6P	$2,884	3,352 lbs.	3,872
71G	36	4-dr. Station Wagon-9P	$2,934	3,367 lbs.	3,781

Ford 300 (Six)

62E	53	2-dr. Sedan-6P	$2,324	3,565 lbs.	13,465
54E	54	4-dr. Sedan-6P	$2,378	3,645 lbs.	19,669

Ford 300 (V-8)

62E	53	2-dr. Sedan-6P	$2,433	3,560 lbs.	12,545
54E	54	4-dr. Sedan-6P	$2,487	3,640 lbs.	24,473

Galaxie (Six)

62B	51	2-dr. Sedan-6P	$2,453	3,575 lbs.	9,677
54B	52	4-dr. Sedan-6P	$2,507	3,665 lbs.	15,977

Galaxie (V-8)

62B	51	2-dr. Sedan-6P	$2,562	3,580 lbs.	20,658
54B	52	4-dr. Sedan-6P	$2,616	3,660 lbs.	66,442

Galaxie 500 (Six)

62A	61	2-dr. Sedan-6P	$2,613	3,605 lbs.	2,023
54A	62	4-dr. Sedan-6P	$2,667	3,685 lbs.	6,603
65A	63	2-dr. Fastback-6P	$2,674	3,620 lbs.	2,561
65A	63	2-dr. Hardtop-6P	$2,674	3,620 lbs.	1,245
75A	64	4-dr. Hardtop-6P	$2,739	3,700 lbs.	620
76A	65	2-dr. Convertible-6P	$2,924	3,775 lbs.	1,512

Galaxie 500 (V-8)

62A	61	2-dr. Sedan-6P	$2,722	3,600 lbs.	19,114
54A	62	4-dr. Sedan-6P	$2,776	3,680 lbs.	199,119
65A	63	2-dr. Fastback-6P	$2,783	3,615 lbs.	97,939
65A	63	2-dr. Hardtop-6P	$2,783	3,615 lbs.	48,488
75A	64	4-dr. Hardtop-6P	$2,848	3,695 lbs.	25,938
76A	65	2-dr. Convertible-6P	$3,033	3,770 lbs.	35,364

Galaxie 500/XL (V-8)

65A	63	2-dr. Fastback-6P	$3,268	3,670 lbs.	33,870
65A	63	2-dr. Hardtop-6P	$3,268	3,670 lbs.	29,713
75A	64	4-dr. Hardtop-6P	$3,333	3,750 lbs.	12,596
76A	65	2-dr. Convertible-6P	$3,518	3,820 lbs.	18,551

Station Wagon (Six)

71C	72	4-dr. Country Sedan-6P	$2,829	3,990 lbs.	4,704
71B	74	4-dr. Country Sedan-8P	$2,933	4,005 lbs.	1,675
71A	76	4-dr. Country Squire-6P	$3,018	4,005 lbs.	301
71E	78	4-dr. Country Squire-8P	$3,088	4,015 lbs.	171

Station Wagon (V-8)

71C	72	4-dr. Country Sedan-6P	$2,938	3,985 lbs.	60,250
71B	74	4-dr. Country Sedan-8P	$3,042	4,000 lbs.	20,575
71A	76	4-dr. Country Squire-6P	$3,127	4,000 lbs.	20,058
71E	78	4-dr. Country Squire-8P	$3,197	4,010 lbs.	19,396

Engines:

Falcon Six: Overhead valve. Cast-iron block. Displacement: 144 cid. B & S: 3.50 x 2.50 in. Compression ratio: 6.7:1. Brake hp: 65 at 4200 rpm. Carburetor: Holley one-barrel. Seven main bearings. Code S.

Falcon Six: Overhead valve. Cast-iron block. Displacement: 170 cid. B & S: 3.50 x 2.94 in. Compression ratio: 8.7:1. Brake hp: 101 at 4400 rpm. Carburetor: Holley one-barrel. Seven main bearings. Code U.

Ford Six: Overhead valve. Cast-iron block. Displacement: 223 cid. B & S: 3.62 x 3.60 in. Compression ratio: 8.4:1. Brake hp: 138 at 4200 rpm. Carburetor: Holley one-barrel. Four main bearings. Code V.

Base Fairlane V-8: Overhead valve. Cast-iron block. Displacement: 221 cid. B & S: 3.50 x 2.87 in. Compression ratio: 8.70:1. Brake hp: 145 at 4400 rpm. Torque: 216 lbs.-ft. at 2200 rpm. Five main bearings. Hydraulic valve lifters. Carburetor: Ford two-barrel C30F-9510-C. Cooling system capacity: 14.5 qt. with heater. Crankcase capacity: 4 qt. (add 1 qt. with new oil filter). Code L. (Export Code 3)

Challenger 260 V-8 (Optional Fairlane and Ford): Overhead valve. Cast-iron block. Displacement: 260 cid. B & S: 3.80 x 2.87 in. Compression ratio: 8.70:1. Brake hp: 164 at 4400 rpm. Torque: 258 lbs.-ft. at 2200 rpm. Five main bearings. Hydraulic valve lifters. Carburetor: Ford two-barrel C30F-9510-E. Cooling system capacity: 14.5 qt. with heater. Crankcase capacity: 4 qt. (add 1 qt. with new oil filter). Code F. (Export code 6).

High-Performance Challenger 289 V-8 (1963-1/2 Fairlane): Overhead valve. Cast-iron block. Displacement: 289 cid. B & S: 4.00 x 2.87 in. Compression ratio: 9.00:1. Brake hp: 195 at 4400 rpm. Torque: 282 lbs.-ft. at 2200 rpm. Five main bearings. Hydraulic valve lifters. Carburetor: Ford two-barrel C30F-9510. Cooling system capacity: 14.5 qt. with heater. Crankcase capacity: 4 qt. (add 1 qt. with new oil filter). Code C.

Interceptor V-8 (Standard in Galaxie 500/XL): Overhead valve. Cast-iron block. Displacement: 352 cid. B & S: 4.00 x 3.50 in. Compression ratio: 8.90:1. Brake hp: 220 at 4300 rpm. Torque: 336 lbs.-ft. at 2600 rpm. Five main bearings. Hydraulic valve lifters. Carburetor: Two-barrel. Cooling system capacity: 20.5 qt. with heater. Crankcase capacity: 5 qt. (add 1 qt. with new oil filter). Code X.

High-Performance C289 V-8 (1963-1/2 Fairlane): Overhead valve. Cast-iron block. Displacement: 289 cid. B & S: 4.00 x 2.87 in. Compression ratio: 10.50:1. Brake hp: 271 at 6000 rpm. Torque: 312 lbs.-ft. at 3400 rpm. Five main bearings. Solid valve lifters. Carburetor: Four-barrel. Cooling system capacity: 14.5 qt. with heater. Crankcase capacity: 4 qt. (add 1 qt. with new oil filter). Code K.

Interceptor 390 V-8: Overhead valve. Cast-iron block. Displacement: 390 cid. B & S: 4.05 x 3.78 in. Compression ratio: 9.60:1. Brake hp: 300 at 4600 rpm. Torque: 427 lbs.-ft. at 2800 rpm. Five main bearings. Hydraulic valve lifters. Carburetor: Ford four-barrel C2AF-9510. Cooling system capacity: 20.5 qt. with heater. Crankcase capacity: 5 qt. (add 1 qt. with new oil filter). Dual exhausts. Code Z.

Interceptor 390 V-8: Overhead valve. Cast-iron block. Displacement: 390 cid. B & S: 4.05 x 3.78 in. Compression ratio: 9.60:1. Brake hp: 330 at 5000 rpm. Torque: 427 lbs.-ft. at 3200 rpm. Five main bearings. Solid valve lifters. Carburetor: Ford four-barrel. Cooling system capacity: 20.5 qt. with heater. Crankcase capacity: 5 qt. (add 1 qt. with new oil filter). Dual exhausts. Code P. (Export code 9)

Thunderbird 406 V-8: Overhead valve. Cast-iron block. Displacement: 406 cid. B & S: 4.13 x 3.78 in. Compression ratio: 11.40:1. Brake hp: 385 at 5800 rpm. Torque: 444 lbs.-ft. at 3400 rpm. Five main bearings. Solid valve lifters. Carburetor: Holley four-barrel. Cooling system capacity: 20.5 qt. with heater. Crankcase capacity: 5 qt. (add 1 qt. with new oil filter). Dual exhausts. Code B.

Thunderbird Special 406 V-8: Overhead valve. Cast-iron block. Displacement: 406 cid. B & S: 4.13 x 3.78 in. Compression ratio: 11.40:1. Brake hp: 405 at 5800 rpm. Torque: 448 lbs.-ft. at 3500 rpm. Five main bearings. Solid valve lifters. Carburetor: Holley three two-barrel. Cooling system capacity: 20.5 qt. with heater. Crankcase capacity: 5 qt. (add 1 qt. with new oil filter). Dual exhausts. Code G.

Note: Export engines have lower compression and less horsepower.

Falcon: Wheelbase: 109.5 in. Overall length: 181.1 in. Tires: 6.00 x 13 four-ply tubeless blackwall (6.50 x 13 four-ply tubeless on station wagons and convertibles).

Fairlane: Wheelbase: 115.5 in. Overall length: 197.6 in. (201.8 in. on station wagons). Tires: 6.50 x 13 four-ply blackwall tubeless (7.00 x 14 four-ply blackwall tubeless on station wagons).

Ford: Wheelbase: 119 in. Overall length: 209.0 in. Tires: 7.50 x 14 four-ply tubeless blackwalls (8.00 x 14 four-ply tubeless blackwalls on station wagons).

Options:

Falcon: Air conditioner ($231.70). Back-up lights ($10.70). Heavy-duty battery ($7.60). Bucket seats and console in Squire station wagon ($120.40). Convenience package ($37.80). 170-cid 101-hp six-cylinder engine ($37.40, but standard in convertible). Tinted glass ($27). Tinted windshield ($12.95). Heater and defroster delete ($73.40 credit). Chrome luggage rack for station wagon ($45.40). Rocker panel molding ($16.10). Two-tone paint ($19.40). Push-button radio and antenna ($58.50). Padded dashboard in convertible ($17.30). Padded dashboard and sun visors, except convertible ($21.80). Safety belts ($16.80). Electric tailgate window in station wagons ($29.75, but standard in Falcon Squire). Five 6.00 x 13 4-ply white sidewall tires on sedans ($29.90). Five 6.50 x 13 4-ply black sidewall tires on sedans ($10.40). Five 6.50 x 13 4-ply white sidewall tires on sedans ($43.50). Five 6.50 x 13 4-ply white sidewall tires on convertibles and station wagons ($33). Five 6.50 x 13 6-ply black sidewall tires on convertibles and station wagons ($28). Five 6.50 x 13 6-ply white sidewall tires on convertibles and station wagons ($61.10). Automatic transmission ($163.10). Four-speed manual transmission ($90.10). Vinyl roof on Futura Sports Sedan ($75.80). Vinyl trim in Futura Sports Sedan ($25). Wheel covers ($16.00, but standard on Futuras). Wire design wheel covers, except Futura ($45.10). Wire design wheel covers on Futuras ($27.40). Two-speed electric wiper washers ($20.10).

Ford and Fairlane: Air conditioner ($231.70 and requires 7.00 tires on Fairlanes). Select Aire air conditioner ($360.90, but standard in Galaxie 500, 500/XL and Squires). Back-up lights ($10.70). Heavy-duty battery ($7.60). Equa-Lock differential ($42.50). Electric clock in Ford 300, Galaxie and Country Sedan wagon ($14.60). Chrome luggage rack for station wagon ($45.40). Rocker panel molding ($16.10). Padded dashboard in convertible ($18.60). Padded dashboard and sun visors, except convertible ($24.30). Tu-Tone paint ($22). Power brakes ($43.20). Full-width power front seat ($63.80, but not available in Fairlane series). Power driver seat only in Galaxie 500/XL ($92.10). Power steering ($81.70). Power tailgate window in Country Sedan six-passenger, Ranch Wagon and Custom Ranch Wagon ($32.30). Front and rear power windows ($102.10). Radio and antenna ($58.50). AM/FM radio and antenna in Fords ($129.30). Safety belts ($16.80). Front bucket seats with console in Fairlane Squire ($120.50). Front bucket seats with console in Galaxie Squire ($141.60). Movable steering column in Ford 300 and all Galaxies ($50 and requires power steering and automatic transmission). Tinted glass ($40.30). Tinted windshield ($21.55). Cruise-O-Matic transmission ($212.30). Ford-O-Matic transmission with six-cylinder ($179.80). Ford-O-Matic transmission with V-8 ($189.60). Overdrive ($108.40). Four-speed manual transmission in all except Galaxie 500/XL ($188 and required V-8 engine with Fairlanes). Four-speed manual transmission in Galaxie 500/XL ($34.80 credit). Vinyl trim in Fairlane 500 and Galaxie 500 ($25.00 and standard in Fairlane Sport Coupe and Galaxie 500/XL). Vinyl trim in Ford 300, Galaxie and Country Sedan ($32.20). Wire design wheel covers, except Fairlane 500 Sports

Coupe and Galaxie 500/XL ($45.10). Wire design wheel covers on Fairlane 500 Sports Coupe and Galaxie 500/XL ($27.40). Deluxe wheel covers ($18.60, but standard on Fairlane Sports Coupe and Galaxie 500/XL). Two-speed electric wiper washers ($20.10).

Tires:

Fairlane: Five 6.50 x 13 4-ply black sidewall tires on six-cylinder sedans and hardtops without air conditioning (standard). Five 7.00 x 13 4-ply black sidewall tires on six-cylinder sedans and hardtops with air conditioning (standard). Five 7.00 x 13 4-ply black sidewall tires on V-8 sedans and hardtops with or without air conditioning (standard). Five 7.00 x 14 4-ply black sidewall tires on station wagons (standard). Ford: Various tire options based on 7.00 x 14, 7.50 x 14, 8.00 x 14, 6.70 x 15 and 7.10 x 15 in 4-ply, 6-ply and Nylon models priced in relation to standard equipment.

History:

The Fairlane 500 Sport Coupe was a two-door pillarless hardtop. The Falcon Sprint was a compact, high-performance V-8-powered Falcon. The Galaxie Fastback was a full-size two-door hardtop with more gently sloping roofline than conventional hardtop, to produce less wind resistance. Ford built 50 Galaxie "factory lightweight" race cars this year. A team of specially prepared 1963 Falcon Sprint hardtops terrorized the European rally circuit, with some very non-Falcon-like performance.

1963 Ford Galaxie 500 Formal two-door hardtop (OCW)

1963 Ford Galaxie 500/XL two-door fastback (PH)

1963 Ford Galaxie 500/XL two-door convertible (AA)

1963 Ford Galaxie two-door Country Sedan 9P (OCW)

1963 Ford Galaxie 500 Sunliner two-door Convertible (OCW)

1963 Ford Galaxie 500 four-door Sedan (OCW)

1963 Ford four-door Country Squire Wagon (OCW)

1964 Ford

Falcon — (Six and V-8): The 1964 Falcons reflected the 'Total Performance' image in their new styling. A more aggressive, angled grille led a completely restyled body. As in 1963, the base trim level was the standard series, and the top trim level was the Futura. The highly sculptured body sides gave the 1964 Falcons a racy appearance and added rigidity to the sheet metal. A convex feature line began on the front fenders, but sloped slightly and increased in width gradually, until it met the taillights. The word "Ford" was spelled out across the hood in block letters and "Falcon" was spelled out in block letters between the taillights. The new grille featured a rectangular design that was angularly recessed and complemented the side profile. As in past years, the Falcons continued to use single headlamps. Standard equipment included a six-cylinder 85-hp engine with self-adjusting valves, a three-speed manual transmission, self-adjusting brakes, a full-flow oil filter, a 36,000-mile fuel filter, a fully-aluminized muffler, galvanized main underbody members, a bright-metal windshield molding, a bright-metal rear window molding, parallel-action single-speed electric windshield wipers, two horns, two sun visors, two front arm rests, two coat hooks, a foam-cushioned front seat, a front ash tray, a white vinyl headlining, gold ladder-pattern cloth-and-vinyl seat trim, a color-keyed 3-spoke steering wheel, front seat belt anchors, and turn signals. A heater was installed during production unless otherwise specified. If deleted, an appropriate price reduction was made. In addition to the above, the following Deluxe Trim items were available for Standard Falcon models at slight additional cost: Bright body side moldings, upgraded cloth-and-vinyl interior trim, rear arm rests, an ash tray, a cigarette lighter, a chrome horn ring and an automatic dome light.

Falcon Futura — (Six and V-8): The Futura series was the top trim level for 1964 Standard features included all the equipment that Standard Falcons came with the following additions or replacements: bright-metal side window frames, two horizontal sloping chrome strips on the body side, four cast "hash marks" on the rear fender in front of the taillights a chrome hood ornament, "Futura" on the front fenders, a choice of five different "Bar-Line" pattern pleated cloth-and-vinyl interior trims, a chrome-backed rearview mirror, color-keyed carpeting front and rear, a cigarette lighter, rear arm rests, a rear ash tray, a chrome horn ring, an automatic dome light, a Futura molding across the instrument panel, bright inserts in the dashboard control knobs, Futura full wheel covers and a Futura chrome script on the sides of the rear fenders above the body side moldings. Hardtop and convertible models were additions to the lineup. Standard equipment in the convertible included the Falcon 170 Special six with 101 hp, a choice of five pleated all-vinyl interior trims, foam-padded front and rear seat cushions, an electric-hydraulic power-operated convertible top, vinyl 3-ply top material in white, blue or black, added underbody torque boxes, Safety-Yoke door locks, Futura front arm rests, front and rear ash trays and a chrome-backed "floating" windshield mirror.

Falcon Futura Sprint — (Six and V-8): This Falcon Futura Sprint sub-series contained two sporty models this year. The Sprint versions of the Futura hardtop and convertible also featured a V-8 engine, bucket seats and wire wheel covers.

1964 Ford Falcon Sprint two-door Hardtop (OCW)

1964 Ford Falcon Sprint two-door Convertible (OCW)

Falcon Station Wagon — (Six and V-8): Both two- and four-door station wagons were again available in the Falcon lineup this year. The Standard wagon came in both body styles. The Deluxe station wagon came only in the four-door model with 78.5 cubic feet of cargo space. Deluxe and Squire versions that were more or less comparable to Falcon, Futura and Sprint variations. The Squire included wood-grained exterior trim. The Deluxe and Squire wagons used a larger six-cylinder engine and the Squire also had a power tailgate window and carpeted floors.

Fairlane — (Six and V-8): The 1964 Fairlane styling featured new sheet metal for the body sides and rear, which seemed to add to the Fairlane's "Total Performance" image. The rear fenders featured a smoother top than in 1963, with a complete absence of fins. The sides were sculptured into a convex shape, which flowed forward from the sides of the taillights and terminated in a chrome scoop. The grille carried the familiar horizontal grid with thin vertical dividers. Standard features included a choice of cloth-and-vinyl upholstery, a choice of Diamond Lustre Enamel exterior colors, a bright-metal windshield molding, a white vinyl headlining, a color-keyed 3-spoke steering wheel, dual sun visors, dual coat hooks, front arm rests, a front ash tray, a locking glove box, front seat belt anchors, Safety-Yoke door locks, a foam-cushioned front seat, turn signals with new amber safety lenses in the front bumper, parallel-action single-speed electric wipers, an illuminated trunk (with taillights on), a 101-hp Fairlane Six engine, a three-speed manual transmission, self-adjusting brakes, Zinclad rocker panels and main underbody members, a 6,000-mile full-flow oil filter, a fully-aluminized muffler and a 36,000-mile replaceable fuel filter element.

Fairlane 500 — (Six and V-8): The Fairlane 500 models were the top trim level and included all Fairlane features with the following variations: a choice of "Wheel-Pattern" pleated cloth-and-vinyl interior trims in blue, turquoise, beige, gold or red, a choice of 12 Diamond Lustre enamel exterior colors, bright-metal side window moldings, Fairlane 500 scripts on the roof sail panels, twin-spear body side moldings running the full length of the body with red, black or white accents between the spears, front fender top trim pieces, full wheel covers of a specific design, front and rear arm rests on all doors, front and rear ash trays, a cigarette lighter, an automatic dome light, a chrome horn ring and color-keyed wall-to-wall carpeting. The Fairlane 500 hardtop also included a "floating" inside rearview mirror. The Fairlane 500 Sports Coupe also included a choice of leather-like all-vinyl interior trims, additional Diamond Lustre enamel exterior colors, foam-cushioned front bucket seats with a center console and

1964 Ford Falcon two-door Sedan (OCW)

1964 Ford Falcon Futura four-door Sedan (OCW)

1964 Ford Falcon Sports Futura two-door Hardtop (OCW)

1962 Ford Falcon four-door Station Wagon (OCW)

1964 Ford Falcon four-door Squire Station Wagon (PH)

1964 Ford Fairlane 500 two-door Sedan

1964 Ford Fairlane 500 two-door Hardtop (OCW)

1964 Ford Fairlane 500 two-door Sports Coupe (OCW)

1964 Ford Fairlane 500 two-door Sports Coupe (OCW)

a upgraded headliner. On Fairlane 500s the model identifying script was on the sides of the cowl above the body. The sail panels also had T-bird like ribbed trim panels and emblems.

Fairlane Station Wagon — (Six and V-8): The Fairlane station wagons came in two four-door models: Ranch Wagon and Custom Ranch Wagon. Standard Ranch Wagon equipment started with all of the Fairlane sedan features and then included these variations: a choice of special vinyl-and-vinyl interior trims, a choice of additional Diamond Lustre enamel exterior colors, front and rear foam-cushioned seats, a color-keyed cargo area inlay, a roll-down tailgate window with painted molding and a folding second seat. The Custom Ranch Wagon included all Fairlane 500 sedan equipment, a choice upgraded cloth-and-vinyl trim, color-keyed vinyl-coated rubber floor coverings, a stowage compartment lock and a bright-metal tailgate molding.

Ford Custom — (Six and V-8): Full-size Fords were completely revamped for 1964. They were recognizable as Ford products only because of their traditional large, round taillights. The grille carried a horizontal grid highlighted with three vertical ribs. The Ford name, in block letters, was seen on all models, but side trim differed considerably. A sheet metal feature line began on the front fender at beltline level. It continued horizontally, to the rear of the car, and dipped down. A lower sheet metal feature line began behind the front wheels and continued, horizontally, toward the rear of the car. There it swept upward and merged with the upper feature line. All models using optional large displacement V-8s earned the engine designation symbol on the lower front fender. Ford said the base-level Custom series cars could fool a buyer because they looked expensive, but weren't. Two- and four-door sedans were available. The four-door sedan had no ash tray in back of the front seat. Crank-operated vent windows, a compliance-link front suspension and Swing-Away steering columns were new features or options this year. Doggie-dish hubcaps were provided. Buyers of these cars had a choice of attractive cloth-and-vinyl interiors. Galaxie options and power accessories were available.

Custom 500 — (Six and V-8): The Custom 500 was the upper trim level of the base-line Custom series and included chrome windshield and rear window moldings, nylon carpeting (instead of the rubber mats used in the Custom models), armrests with ashtrays on all doors, two sun visors and all trim used in the Custom models, plus a single horizontal chrome strip on the exterior body side on the front fender and door and "hash mark" front fender trim plates.

Galaxie 500 — (Six and V-8): The Galaxie 500 was the base Galaxie trim level for 1964 and included all Custom trim, plus chrome fender top ornamentation, chrome window frames, the Ford crest on the roof 'C' pillar and a full-length chrome strip (which split at the rear of the front doors and widened forward of that point with an aluminum insert added). A 'Galaxie 500' script, was included in the aluminum insert near the front inside a sculptured indentation. A stamped aluminum insert also highlighted the rear end treatment and included 'Galaxie 500' in script on the right side of the insert. Two-tone vinyl trim was used on the side of the doors and on the seats. The front floor hump was a third smaller than in 1963, while headroom was increased. Galaxie 500s had all of the same all Custom 500 features, plus additional luxury items that varied by body style. The two-and four-door sedans had these extras: a choice of cloth-and vinyl interior trims in, a choice of additional Diamond Lustre enamel exterior colors, chrome-like Mylar accents on the seats, doors and side panels, pleated seat fabrics, two-tone door panels, deluxe arm

rests, front and rear ash trays, a chrome-backed inside rearview mirror, bright-metal seat side shields, a self-regulating electric clock and back-up lights centered in the taillights. The two-and four-door hardtops also had cloth-and vinyl interior options, Diamond Lustre enamel exterior finish, chrome-like Mylar accents on the seats, doors and side panels, two-tone door panels, deluxe arm rests, front and rear ash trays, a chrome-backed inside rearview mirror, bright-metal seat side shields, a self-regulating electric clock and back-up lights centered in the taillights. The Galaxie 500 Sunliner convertible had all-vinyl interior trims, a choice of Diamond Lustre enamel exterior colors, a 3-ply vinyl power-operated top, an anti-ballooning top design, a zip-out clear vinyl rear window, a color-keyed and contoured top boot, automatic courtesy lights under the dashboard and a "floating" rearview mirror bonded to the windshield.

Galaxie 500/XL — (V-8): The Galaxie 500/XL series now included just three models, two- and four-door hardtops and convertible. These cars included all the trim features of the Galaxie models plus shell-type bucket seats, a console, a floor-mounted transmission shifter, polished door trim panels, dual-lens courtesy/warning lights in the doors, rear reading lights in hardtops and Galaxie 500/XL badges on the body exterior. A 289-cid 195-hp V-8 was standard in all Galaxie 500/XLs.

Galaxie Station Wagon — (Six and V-8): All 1964 full-size Ford station wagons were four-door models. The Country Sedans were the base trim level station wagons for 1964, with the Country Squires being the top trim level. Both were offered in two- and four-door body styles. The trim paralleled the Galaxie 500 and Galaxie 500XL models of passenger cars. Country Squires also had wood-grained exterior paneling and a power tailgate window.

VIN (Falcon):

The VIN for Falcons was die-stamped into the top of the left-hand front inner fender apron. The first symbol indicates year: 4=1964. The second symbol identifies assembly plant, as follows: A=Atlanta, Georgia, D=Dallas, Texas, E=Mahwah, New Jersey, F=Dearborn, Michigan, G=Chicago, Illinois, H=Lorain, Ohio, J=Los Angeles, California, K=Kansas City, Kansas, N=Norfolk, Virginia, P=Twin Cities, Minnesota, R=San Jose, California, S=Pilot Plant, T=Metuchen, New Jersey, U=Louisville, Kentucky, W=Wayne, Michigan, Y=Wixom, Michigan, Z=St. Louis, Mo. The third and fourth symbols identify body series code: 01=two-door sedan, 02=four-door sedan, 11=two-door hardtop with bucket seats, 12=two-door convertible with bucket seats, 13=Sprint two-door hardtop, 14=Sprint two-door convertible, 15=two-door bench-seat convertible, 16=four-door bench-seat sedan, 17=two-door bench-seat hardtop, 19=two-door bench-seat sedan, 21=two-door station wagon, 22=four-door station wagon, 24=four-door Deluxe station wagon, 26=four-door Squire station wagon. The fifth symbol identifies engine code, as follows: S=144-cid six-cylinder, U=170-cid six-cylinder, 4=170-cid six-cylinder, T=200-cid six-cylinder, F=260-cid V-8, G=260-cid V-8 low-compression and K=289-cid V-8. The last six digits are the unit's production number, beginning at 100001 and going up, at each of the assembly plants. Falcons not built at all Ford plants.

VIN (Fairlane):

The VIN for Fairlanes was die-stamped into the side of the left-hand front inner fender apron near the top. The first symbol indicates year: 4=1964. The second symbol identifies assembly plant, as follows: A=Atlanta, Georgia, D=Dallas, Texas, E=Mahwah, New Jersey, F=Dearborn, Michigan, G=Chicago, Illinois, H=Lorain, Ohio, J=Los Angeles, California, K=Kansas City, Kansas, N=Norfolk, Virginia, P=Twin Cities, Minnesota, R=San Jose, California, S=Pilot Plant, T=Metuchen, New Jersey, U=Louisville, Kentucky, W=Wayne, Michigan, Y=Wixom, Michigan, Z=St. Louis, Mo. The third and fourth symbols identify body series code: 31=Fairlane two-door sedan, 32=Fairlane four-door sedan, 41=Fairlane 500 two-door sedan, 42=Fairlane 500 four-door sedan, 43=Fairlane 500 two-door hardtop, 47=Fairlane 500 two-door Sport Coupe, 38=Fairlane four-door six-passenger station wagon, 48=Fairlane Custom four-door six-passenger station wagon. The fifth symbol identifies engine code, as follows: U=170-cid six-cylinder, 4=170-cid low-compression export six-cylinder, T=200-cid six-cylinder, F=260-cid V-8, 6=260-cid low-compression export V-8, C=289-cid two-barrel V-8, 3=289-cid low-compression export two-barrel V-8, K=289-cid four-barrel V-8 and R=427-cid dual four-barrel V-8. The last six digits are the unit's production number, beginning at 100001 and going up, at each of the assembly plants. Fairlanes not built at all Ford plants.

VIN (Ford):

The VIN for full-size Fords was die-stamped into the top right-hand side rail of the frame ahead of the front suspension member. The first symbol indicates year: 4=1964. The second symbol identifies assembly plant, as follows: A=Atlanta, Georgia, D=Dallas, Texas, E=Mahwah, New Jersey, F=Dearborn, Michigan, G=Chicago, Illinois, H=Lorain, Ohio, J=Los Angeles, California, K=Kansas City, Kansas, N=Norfolk, Virginia, P=Twin Cities, Minnesota, R=San Jose, California, S=Pilot Plant, T=Metuchen, New Jersey, U=Louisville, Kentucky, W=Wayne, Michigan, Y=Wixom, Michigan, Z=St. Louis, Mo. The third and fourth symbols identify body series 51=Custom 500 two-door sedan, 52=Custom 500 four-door sedan, 53=Custrom two-door sedan, 54=Custom four-door sedan, 61=Galaxie 500 two-door sedan, 62=Galaxie 500 four-door sedan, 64=Galaxie 500 four-door Victoria Hardtop, 65=Galaxie 500 Sunliner convertible, 66=Galaxie 500 fastback, 60=Galaxie 500/XL four-door hardtop, 68=Galaxie 500/XL fastback, 69=Galaxie 500/XL two-door convertible, 72=four-door six-passenger Country Sedan station wagon, 74=four-door nine-passenger Country Sedan station wagon, 76=four-door Country Squire six-passenger station wagon and 78=four-door Country Squire nine-passenger station wagon. The fifth symbol identifies engine code, as follows: V=223-cid six-cylinder, 5=223-cid Export six-cylinder, B=223-cid Police six, E=223-cid Taxi six-cylinder, C=289-cid two-barrel V-8,

1964 Ford Fairlane four-door Custom Ranch Wagon (OCW)

3=289-cid low-compression export two-barrel V-8, X=352-cid two-barrel V-8, Z=390-cid four-barrel V-8, 9=390-cid V-8, P=390-cid V-8, Q=427-cid V-8, R=427-cid V-8. The last six digits are the unit's production number, beginning at 100001 and going up, at each of the assembly plants. Full-size Fords not built at all Ford plants.

Falcon Standard (Six)

Model No.	Body/ Style No.	Body Style and Seating	Factory Price	Shipping Weight	Production Total
62A	01	2-dr. Sedan-6P	$1,996	2,358 lbs.	61,624
54A	02	4-dr. Sedan-6P	$2,058	2,393 lbs.	50,930

Falcon Standard (V-8)

Model No.	Body/ Style No.	Body Style and Seating	Factory Price	Shipping Weight	Production Total
62A	01	2-dr. Sedan-6P	$2,165	2,713 lbs.	3,228
54A	02	4-dr. Sedan-6P	$2,227	2,748 lbs.	4,224

Falcon Futura (Six)

Model No.	Body/ Style No.	Body Style and Seating	Factory Price	Shipping Weight	Production Total
62B	19	2-dr. Sedan-6P	$2,127	2,367 lbs.	14,682
54B	16	4-dr. Sedan-6P	$2,176	2,402 lbs.	32,097
63B	17	2-dr. Hardtop-6P	$2,209	2,505 lbs.	18,095
76A	15	2-dr. Convertible-6P	$2,481	2,700 lbs.	9.108

Falcon Futura (V-8)

Model No.	Body/ Style No.	Body Style and Seating	Factory Price	Shipping Weight	Production Total
62B	19	2-dr. Sedan-6P	$2,296	2,722 lbs.	2,151
54B	16	4-dr. Sedan-6P	$2,345	2,757 lbs.	5,935
63B	17	2-dr. Hardtop-6P	$2,378	2,809 lbs.	14,513
76A	15	2-dr. Convertible-6P	$2,634	2,982 lbs.	4,112

Falcon Futura Sport (Six)

Model No.	Body/ Style No.	Body Style and Seating	Factory Price	Shipping Weight	Production Total
63C	11	2-dr. Sport Hardtop-6P	$2,325	2,533 lbs.	4,492
76B	12	4-dr. Sport Convertible-6P	$2,591	2,690 lbs.	10,690

Falcon Futura Sport (V-8)

Model No.	Body/ Style No.	Body Style and Seating	Factory Price	Shipping Weight	Production Total
63C	11	2-dr. Sport Hardtop-6P	$2,494	2,837 lbs.	4,115
76B	12	4-dr. Sport Convertible-6P	$2,750	3,010 lbs.	1,256

Falcon Futura Sprint (V-8)

Model No.	Body/ Style No.	Body Style and Seating	Factory Price	Shipping Weight	Production Total
63D/E	13	2-dr. Sprint Hardtop-6P	$2,436	2,803 lbs.	13,830
76D/E	14	4-dr. Sprint Convertible-6P	$2,671	2,976 lbs.	4,278

D=Bucket seats, E=Bench seats

Falcon Station Wagon (Six)

Model No.	Body/ Style No.	Body Style and Seating	Factory Price	Shipping Weight	Production Total
59A	21	2-dr. Station Wagon-6P	$2,326	2,620 lbs.	5,404
71A	22	4-dr. Station Wagon-6P	$2,360	2,655 lbs.	16,007

Falcon Station Wagon (V-8)

Model No.	Body/ Style No.	Body Style and Seating	Factory Price	Shipping Weight	Production Total
59A	21	2-dr. Station Wagon-6P	$2,479	2,975 lbs.	630
71A	22	4-dr. Station Wagon-6P	$2,513	3,010 lbs.	1,772

Deluxe Ranch Wagon (Six)

Model No.	Body/ Style No.	Body Style and Seating	Factory Price	Shipping Weight	Production Total
71B	24	4-dr. Station Wagon-6P	$2,446	2,673 lbs.	15,738

Deluxe Ranch Wagon (V-8)

Model No.	Body/ Style No.	Body Style and Seating	Factory Price	Shipping Weight	Production Total
71B	24	4-dr. Station Wagon-6P	$2,599	3,028 lbs.	4,959

Futura Squire Station Wagon (Six)

Model No.	Body/ Style No.	Body Style and Seating	Factory Price	Shipping Weight	Production Total
71C	26	4-dr. Station Wagon-6P	$2,622	2,675 lbs.	4,304

Futura Squire Station Wagon (V-8)

Model No.	Body/ Style No.	Body Style and Seating	Factory Price	Shipping Weight	Production Total
71C	26	4-dr. Station Wagon-6P	$2,775	3,030 lbs.	2,462

Fairlane (Six)

Model No.	Body/ Style No.	Body Style and Seating	Factory Price	Shipping Weight	Production Total
62A	31	2-dr. Sedan-6P	$2,194	2,805 lbs.	14,777
54A	32	4-dr. Sedan-6P	$2,235	2,857 lbs.	22,233

Fairlane (V-8)

Model No.	Body/ Style No.	Body Style and Seating	Factory Price	Shipping Weight	Production Total
62A	31	2-dr. Sedan-6P	$2,294	2,997 lbs.	5,644
54A	32	4-dr. Sedan-6P	$2,335	3,049 lbs.	14,460

Fairlane 500 (Six)

Model No.	Body/ Style No.	Body Style and Seating	Factory Price	Shipping Weight	Production Total
62B	41	2-dr. Sedan-6P	$2,276	2,820 lbs.	8,760
54B	42	4-dr. Sedan-6P	$2,317	2,872 lbs.	18,791
65A	43	2-dr. Hardtop-6P	$2,341	2,880 lbs.	4,467

Fairlane 500 (V-8)

Model No.	Body/ Style No.	Body Style and Seating	Factory Price	Shipping Weight	Production Total
62B	41	2-dr. Sedan-6P	$2,376	3,012 lbs.	14,687
54B	42	4-dr. Sedan-6P	$2,417	3,064 lbs.	68,128
65A	43	2-dr. Hardtop-6P	$2,441	3,072 lbs.	22,296

Fairlane 500 Sport (Six)

Model No.	Body/ Style No.	Body Style and Seating	Factory Price	Shipping Weight	Production Total
65B	47	2-dr. Hardtop-6P	$2,502	2,904 lbs.	946

Fairlane 500 Sport (V-8)

65B	47	2-dr. Hardtop-6P	$2,602	3,096 lbs.	20,485

Fairlane Ranch Wagon (Six)

71D	38	4-dr. Station Wagon-6P	$2,531	3,207 lbs.	7,324

Fairlane Ranch Wagon (V-8)

71D	38	4-dr. Station Wagon-6P	$2,631	3,399 lbs.	13,656

Fairlane Custom Ranch Wagon (Six)

71B	48	4-dr. Station Wagon-6P	$2,612	3,237 lbs.	2,666

Fairlane Custom Ranch Wagon (V-8)

71B	48	4-dr. Station Wagon-6P	$2,712	3,429 lbs.	22,296

Ford Custom (Six)

62E	53	2-dr. Sedan-6P	$2,361	3,538 lbs.	22,214
54E	54	4-dr. Sedan-6P	$2,415	3,628 lbs.	22,661

Ford Custom (V-8)

62E	53	2-dr. Sedan-6P	$2,470	3,549 lbs.	19,145
54E	54	4-dr. Sedan-6P	$2,524	3,639 lbs.	35,303

Custom 500 (Six)

62B	51	2-dr. Sedan-6P	$2,464	3,571 lbs.	5,785
54B	52	4-dr. Sedan-6P	$2,518	3,671 lbs.	10,256

Custom 500 (V-8)

62B	51	2-dr. Sedan-6P	$2,573	3,582 lbs.	14,834
54B	52	4-dr. Sedan-6P	$2,627	3,682 lbs.	58,572

Galaxie 500 (Six)

62A	61	2-dr. Sedan-6P	$2,624	3,586 lbs.	1,029
54A	62	4-dr. Sedan-6P	$2,678	3,686 lbs.	5,133
63B	63	2-dr. Fastback-6P	$2,685	3,597 lbs.	5,035
57B	64	4-dr. Hardtop-6P	$2,750	3,698 lbs.	710
76A	65	2-dr. Convertible-6P	$2,947	3,798 lbs.	1,034

Galaxie 500 (V-8)

62A	61	2-dr. Sedan-6P	$2,733	3,697 lbs.	12,012
54A	62	4-dr. Sedan-6P	$2,787	3,697 lbs.	193,672
63B	63	2-dr. Fastback-6P	$2,794	3,608 lbs.	201,963
57B	64	4-dr. Hardtop-6P	$2,859	3,709 lbs.	48,532
76A	65	2-dr. Convertible-6P	$3,056	3,779 lbs.	36,277

Galaxie 500/XL (V-8)

63C	63	2-dr. Fastback-6P	$3,233	3,633 lbs.	58,306
57C	64	4-dr. Hardtop-6P	$3,298	3,734 lbs.	14,661
76A	65	2-dr. Convertible-6P	$3,495	3,801 lbs.	15,169

Station Wagon (Six)

71C	72	4-dr. Country Sedan-6P	$2,840	3,990 lbs.	3,813
71B	74	4-dr. Country Sedan-8P	$2,944	4,002 lbs.	1,030
71E	76	4-dr. Country Squire-6P	$3,029	4,004 lbs.	234
71A	78	4-dr. Country Squire-8P	$3,099	4,016 lbs.	121

Station Wagon (V-8)

71C	72	4-dr. Country Sedan-6P	$2,949	4,001 lbs.	64,765
71B	74	4-dr. Country Sedan-8P	$3,053	4,013 lbs.	24,631
71E	76	4-dr. Country Squire-6P	$3,138	4,015 lbs.	23,336
71A	78	4-dr. Country Squire-8P	$3,208	4,027 lbs.	22,999

Engines:

Falcon Six: Overhead valve. Cast-iron block. Displacement: 144 cid. B & S: 3.50 x 2.50 in. Compression ratio: 6.7:1. Brake hp: 65 at 4200 rpm. Carburetor: Holley one-barrel. Seven main bearings. Code S.

Falcon Six: Overhead valve. Cast-iron block. Displacement: 170 cid. B & S: 3.50 x 2.94 in. Compression ratio: 8.7:1. Brake hp: 101 at 4400 rpm. Carburetor: Holley one-barrel. Seven main bearings. Code U.

Ford Six: Overhead valve. Cast-iron block. Displacement: 223 cid. B & S: 3.62 x 3.60 in. Compression ratio: 8.4:1. Brake hp: 138 at 4200 rpm. Carburetor: Holley one-barrel. Four main bearings. Code V.

Challenger 260 V-8 (Optional in Fairlane and Ford): Overhead valve. Cast-iron block. Displacement: 260 cid. B & S: 3.80 x 2.87 in. Compression ratio: 8.8:1. Brake hp: 164 at 4400 rpm. Torque: 258 lbs.-ft. at 2200 rpm. Five main bearings. Hydraulic valve lifters. Carburetor: Two-barrel. Cooling system capacity: 15.5 qt. with heater. Crankcase capacity: 4 qt. (add 1 qt. with new oil filter). Code F.

Challenger 289 V-8: Overhead valve. Cast-iron block. Displacement:

289 cid. B & S: 4.00 x 2.87 in. Compression ratio: 9.00:1. Brake hp: 195 at 4400 rpm. Torque: 282 lbs.-ft. at 2200 rpm. Five main bearings. Hydraulic valve lifters. Carburetor: Ford two-barrel C30F-9510. Cooling system capacity: 16 qt. with heater. Crankcase capacity: 4 qt. (add 1 qt. with new oil filter). Code C.

Challenger 289 V-8 Four Barrel: Overhead valve. Cast-iron block. Displacement: 289 cid. B & S: 4.00 x 2.87 in. Compression ratio: 9.0:1. Brake hp: 210 at 4400 rpm. Torque: 300 lbs.-ft. at 2800 rpm. Five main bearings. Hydraulic valve lifters. Carburetor: Four-barrel. Cooling system capacity: 16 qt. with heater. Crankcase capacity: 4 qt. (add 1 qt. with new oil filter). Code C.

Interceptor V-8 (Base Galaxie 500/XL V-8 and optional in other Fords): Overhead valve. Cast-iron block. Displacement: 352 cid. B & S: 4.00 x 3.50 in. Compression ratio: 9.30:1. Brake hp: 250 at 4400 rpm. Torque: 352 at 2800 rpm. Five main bearings. Hydraulic valve lifters. Carburetor: Four-barrel. Cooling system capacity: 20 qt. with heater. Crankcase capacity: 5 qt. (add 1 qt. with new oil filter). Code X.

High-Performance Challenger 289 V-8: Overhead valve. Cast-iron block. Displacement: 289 cid. B & S: 4.00 x 2.87 in. Compression ratio: 10.50:1. Brake hp: 271 at 6000 rpm. Torque: 312 lbs.-ft. at 3400 rpm. Five main bearings. Solid valve lifters. Carburetor: Four-barrel. Cooling system capacity: 16 qt. with heater. Crankcase capacity: 4 qt. (add 1 qt. with new oil filter). Code K.

Thunderbird 390 V-8 (Optional in Fords): Overhead valve. Cast-iron block. Displacement: 390 cid. B & S: 4.05 x 3.78 in. Compression ratio: 10.0:1. Brake hp: 300 at 4600 rpm. Torque: 427 lbs.-ft. at 2800 rpm. Five main bearings. Hydraulic valve lifters. Carburetor: Four-barrel. Cooling system capacity: 20 qt. with heater. Crankcase capacity: 5 qt. (add 1 qt. with new oil filter). Dual exhausts. Code Z.

Thunderbird Police Special 390 V-8: Overhead valve. Cast-iron block. Displacement: 390 cid. B & S: 4.05 x 3.78 in. Compression ratio: 10.0:1. Brake hp: 330 at 5000 rpm. Torque: 427 lbs.-ft. at 3200 rpm. Five main bearings. Solid valve lifters. Carburetor: Ford four-barrel. Cooling system capacity: 20 qt. with heater. Crankcase capacity: 5 qt. (add 1 qt. with new oil filter). Dual exhausts. Code P.

Thunderbird High-Performance V-8: Overhead valve. Cast-iron block. Displacement: 427 cid. B & S: 4.23 x 3.78 in. Compression ratio: 11.50:1. Brake hp: 410 at 5600 rpm. Torque: 476 lbs.-ft. at 3400 rpm. Five main bearings. Solid valve lifters. Carburetor: Holley four-barrel. Cooling system capacity: 20 qt. with heater. Crankcase capacity: 5 qt. (add 1 qt. with new oil filter). Dual exhausts. Code Q.

Thunderbird Super High Performance V-8: Overhead valve. Cast-iron block. Displacement: 427 cid. B & S: 4.23 x 3.78 in. Compression ratio: 11.50:1. Brake hp: 425 at 6000 rpm. Torque: 480 lbs.-ft. at 3700 rpm. Five main bearings. Solid valve lifters. Carburetor: Two Holley four-barrel. Cooling system capacity: 20 qt. with heater. Crankcase capacity: 5 qt. (add 1 qt. with new oil filter). Dual exhausts. Code R.

Chassis:

Falcon: Wheelbase: 109.5 in. Overall length: 181.1 in., cars and 189 in., wagons. Tires: 6.00 x 13 four-ply tubeless blackwall and 6.50 x 13 four-ply tubeless on station wagons and convertibles).

Fairlane: Wheelbase: 115.5 in. Overall length: 197.6 in. and 201.8 in., station wagons. Tires: 6.50 x 13 four-ply blackwall tubeless and 7.00 x 14 four-ply blackwall tubeless on station wagons.

1964 Ford Custom four-door Sedan

1964 Ford Custom 500 two-door Sedan (OCW)

Ford: Wheelbase: 119 in. Overall length: 209.0 in. Tires: 7.50 x 14 four-ply tubeless blackwalls and 8.00 x 14 four-ply tubeless blackwalls on station wagons.

Options:

Falcon: 170-cid six-cylinder engine ($17). The 260-cid V-8 engine ($170). Ford-O-Matic automatic transmission ($177). Four-speed manual transmission ($92 with six-cylinder, $188 with V-8). AM radio ($58). Two-tone paint ($19). White sidewall tires ($30). Back-up lights ($10). Deluxe trim package for standard sedans ($43). Popular Falcon station wagon options included all those for sedans, plus power tailgate window ($30).

Fairlane: 260-cid V-8 engine ($100). The 289-cid V-8 engine ($145). 390-cid V-8. Ford-O-Matic automatic transmission ($189). Cruise-O-Matic automatic transmission ($189). Four-speed manual transmissions with V-8 engines ($188). AM radio ($58). Power steering ($86). Power tailgate window on station wagons ($32). Luggage rack on station wagons ($45). Two-tone paint ($22). White sidewall tires ($33). Wheel covers ($18). Vinyl roof on two-door hardtops ($75).

Ford: Popular Custom and Galaxie series options included 289-cid V-8 engine ($109). 390-cid V-8 engine ($246). Cruise-O-Matic automatic transmission ($189 or $212). Four-speed manual transmission ($188). Power steering ($86). Power brakes ($43). Power windows ($102). Tinted windshield ($21). AM radio ($58). Vinyl roof on two-door Victorias ($75). Wheel covers ($45). White sidewall tires ($33). Popular station wagon options included the 390-cid V-8 engine ($246). Cruise-O-Matic automatic transmission ($212). Power steering ($86). Power brakes ($43). Power tailgate window ($32). Luggage rack ($45). White sidewall tires ($33). Electric clock ($14). Radio ($58 for AM, $129 for AM/FM).

1964 Ford Galaxie 500 four-door Sedan (OCW)

1964 Ford Galaxie 500 four-door sedan (OCW)

1964 Ford Galaxie 500 four-door hardtop (OCW)

1964 Ford Galaxie 500/XL Convertible shell bucket seat interior (OCW)

1964 Ford Galaxie 500/XL four-door hardtop (OCW)

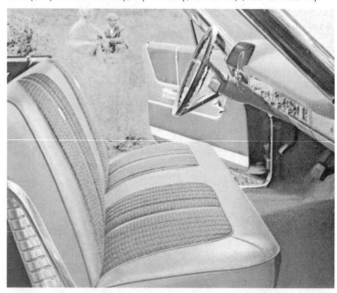

1964 Ford Galaxie 500 four-door hardtop interior (OCW)

1964 Ford Galaxie 500/XL two-door fastback (PH)

1964 Ford Galaxie 500/XL two-door convertible (OCW)

1964 Ford four-door Country Sedan 6P (OCW)

1964 Ford four-door Country Squire Wagon (OCW)

History:

The full-size Fords, Fairlanes and Falcons were introduced September 27, 1963, and the Mustang appeared in dealer showrooms on April 17, 1964. Model-year production peaked at 1,015,697 units. Calendar-year production of 1,787,535 cars was recorded. The entire lineup of 1964 Fords received *Motor Trend* magazine's "Car of the Year" award. Lee A. Iacocca was the chief executive officer of the company this year. Ford introduced the famous Fairlane Thunderbolt drag cars and also the single-overhead cam hemi-engine that Ford tried to use for NASCAR racing. It was disallowed due to insufficient number produced for homologation.

1965 Ford

Falcon — (Six and V-8): Falcons were the base trim level for 1965. While continuing to use the 1964 body shell, trim changes made the 1965 Falcon look considerably different than the previous year. The grille was a thin horizontal bar design, which was divided into two sections by a wider vertical bar at the center. A vertical, three-colored crest was used on the center divider. The round taillights utilized chrome "cross-hairs" for accent, and the optional back-up lights were mounted in the center of the lens. A new Falcon emblem with black, paint-filled Falcon letters was attached to the front fender behind the wheel opening. Standard equipment included chrome windshield and rear window moldings, two horns, two sun visors, armrests on the front doors only, a horn button (instead of a chrome horn ring), a heater and defroster, directional signals, an alternator and five black sidewall tuneless tires.

Falcon Futura — (Six and V-8): The Futura series was the top Falcon trim level for 1965. Futura models included all standard Falcon features and also added armrests front and rear, front and rear ashtrays, dual horns, Futura wheel covers, a chrome hood ornament, a Futura symbol on the front fender behind the wheel well, chrome windshield moldings, chrome rear window moldings, chrome side window moldings, a full-length, spear-type chrome body side molding with either red, white or black painted insert, foam rubber seat cushions and a deluxe steering wheel with a chrome horn ring.

Falcon Station Wagon — (Six and V-8): Both two- and four-door station wagons were again available in the Falcon lineup this year. The Standard wagon came in both body styles. The more deluxe Futura station wagon came only in the four-door model. The Squire included wood-grained exterior trim. The Deluxe and Squire wagons used a more powerful 120-hp six-cylinder engine and the Squire also had a power tailgate window and carpeted floors.

Fairlane — (Six and V-8): The Fairlane was the base trim level for Ford's mid-sized line. The 1965 Fairlane featured new sheet metal below the beltline. This gave it new front, rear and side appearances. The overall length and width were increased. This resulted in the first total restyling of the Fairlane line since its introduction in 1962. The new front end featured a wide horizontal grille and horizontal dual headlights. The hood incorporated a small peak in the center that swept forward over the leading edge and met a similar accent line in the grille. The overall profile was changed and had a higher fender line that traveled farther back and created a more massive look. For the first time since its

1965 Ford Falcon Sports Futura two-door Hardtop (PH)

introduction, the Fairlane's taillights were rectangular instead of circular. They were accented with chrome 'cross-hair' accents across the face of the lens. When ordered, optional back-up lights were mounted in the center of the taillight lens. Standard equipment included chrome windshield moldings, chrome rear window moldings, a deluxe steering wheel with a chrome horn ring, front and rear armrests, a cigarette lighter, a fresh air heater and defroster, seat belts, vinyl coated rubber floor mats, the Fairlane name in block letters at the front of the front fenders, five black sidewall tubeless tires and a 200-cid 120-hp six-cylinder engine.

Fairlane 500 — (Six and V-8): The Fairlane 500 models were the top-level cars in Ford's mid-size or intermediate line and had richer appointments and trim than regular Fairlanes. "F-O-R-D" appeared, in block letters, across the rear escutcheon panel, with two chrome strips between the taillights and a Ford crest in the center of the panel. In addition to the features used on base models, the Fairlane 500s had chrome window moldings, a deluxe steering wheel with a chrome horn ring, and front and rear armrests, special interior upholstery and trim, a Ford crest on the roof "C" pillar, a chrome hood ornament, a single horizontal chrome strip with an aluminum insert and carpeting. The Sports Coupe version of the two-door hardtop also had front bucket seats and special full wheel covers.

Fairlane Station Wagon — (Six and V-8): The Fairlane station wagons came in two four-door models: Fairlane and Fairlane 500. Fairlane Wagon equipment started with all of the Fairlane sedan features and then included these variations: a choice of special vinyl-and-vinyl interior trims, a choice of additional Diamond Lustre enamel exterior colors, front and rear foam-cushioned seats, a color-keyed cargo area inlay, a roll-down tailgate window and a folding second seat. The Custom Ranch Wagon included all Fairlane 500 sedan equipment, a choice upgraded cloth-and-vinyl trim, color-keyed vinyl-coated rubber floor coverings, a stowage compartment lock and a bright-metal tailgate molding.

Custom — (Six and V-8): The new "Total Performance" Ford lineup represented the widest choice of models in Ford Division's history. The 1965 full-size Fords were billed as the 'Newest since 1949.' Luxury and comfort were featured with the big Fords, which used rear coil springs for the first time and featured new interior styling. 'Silent Flow' ventilation systems were standard on four-door hardtops. Completely restyled once again, the full-size Fords possessed incredibly clean styling with sharp, square lines and almost no curves. The new grille featured thin horizontal bars that followed the leading edge contour of the hood and were framed by the new vertical dual headlights. From the side, a single, horizontal feature line divided the less prominent beltline and lower body lines. As in 1964, all full-size Fords carried the engine designation symbol on the front fender behind the front wheel, for the larger, optional V-8 engines. The Custom series was the base trim level full-size Ford for 1965 and included chrome windshield and rear window moldings, two sun visors, a chrome horn ring, armrests on all doors, a MagicAire heater and defroster, the "Custom" name on the front fender, five black sidewall tubeless tires and a 240-cid six-cylinder engine. The taillights were circular lenses in a rectangular housing. The Ford name appeared in block letters across the front of the hood and on the vertical section of the trunk lid.

1965 Ford Falcon Futura two-door Convertible

1965 Ford Falcon four-door Squire Station Wagon (PH)

Custom 500 — (Six and V-8): The Custom 500 was the upper trim level of the base-line Custom series and included all Custom features plus chrome windshield and rear window moldings, nylon carpeting instead of the rubber mats used in the Custom models, armrests, with ashtrays, on all doors, two sun visors and all the trim used in the Custom models, plus a short horizontal chrome strip along the front fender and front door.

Galaxie 500 — (Six and V-8): The Galaxie 500 was the intermediate trim level for 1965 and included all the Custom 500 features, plus a chrome hood ornament, Ford crest in the center of the trunk lid, chrome window frames, the Ford crest on the roof "C" pillar, "Galaxie 500" in block letters at the front of the front fenders, chrome rocker panel trim, hexagonal taillights with chrome 'cross-hairs' trim, back-up lights, an electric clock and special interior upholstery and trim. Two-tone vinyl trim was used on the insides of the doors and on the seats.

Galaxie 500/XL — (V-8): Galaxie 500/XL was the sport trim version of the Galaxie 500 two-door hardtop and two-door convertible. The Galaxie 500/XL models included all Galaxie 500 trim, plus bucket seats, a floor-mounted gearshift lever, polished door trim panels with carpeting on the lower portion of the doors, dual-lens courtesy/warning lights in the door panels, rear reading lights in hardtops, Galaxie 500/XL badges on the body exterior and deluxe wheel covers. The 289-cid 200-hp V-8 and Cruise-O-Matic automatic transmission were standard in both Galaxie 500/XL models.

Galaxie 500 LTD — (V-8): The Galaxie 500 LTD was the new top trim level for 1965. It also offered the two-door hardtop, plus a four-door hardtop. The Galaxie 500 LTDs included all the Galaxie 500/XL trim, plus a 289-cid 200-hp V-8, Cruise-O-Matic automatic transmission, thickly padded seats with 'pinseal' upholstery, simulated walnut appliques on the lower edge of the instrument panel, a Gabardine finish headlining, Gabardine finish sun visors, front and rear door courtesy/warning lights, courtesy lights in the rear roof pillars on the interior, courtesy lights under the instrument panel, a glove box light, an ash tray light and a self regulating clock.

Galaxie Station Wagon — (Six and V-8): The Ranch Wagon was once again the base trim level station wagon for 1965, with the Country Sedans being the intermediate level and the Country Squires being the top trim level. The trim paralleled the Custom 500, Galaxie 500 and Galaxie 500 LTD models of passenger cars.

VIN (Falcon):

The VIN for Falcons was die-stamped into the top of the left-hand front inner fender apron. The first symbol indicates year: 5=1965. The second symbol identifies assembly plant, as follows: A=Atlanta, Georgia, B=Oakville, Ontario, Canada, D=Dallas, Texas, E=Mahwah, New Jersey, F=Dearborn, Michigan, G=Chicago, Illinois, H=Lorain, Ohio, J=Los Angeles, California, K=Kansas City, Kansas, L=Long Beach, California, N=Norfolk, Virginia, P=Twin Cities, Minnesota, R=San Jose, California, S=Pilot Plant, T=Metuchen, New Jersey, U=Louisville, Kentucky, W=Wayne, Michigan, Y=Wixom, Michigan, Z=St. Louis, Mo. The third and fourth symbols identify body series code: 01=two-door sedan, 02=four-door sedan, 11=two-door hardtop with bucket seats, 12=two-door convertible with bucket seats, 15=two-door bench-seat convertible, 16=four-door bench-seat sedan, 27=deluxe, 19=two-door bench-seat sedan, 21=two-door station wagon, 22=four-door station wagon, 24=four-door Deluxe station wagon, 26=four-door Squire station wagon. The fifth symbol identifies engine code, as follows: U=170-cid six-cylinder, 4=170-cid export six-cylinder, T=200-cid six-cylinder, 2=200-

cid export six-cylinder, C=289-cid two-barrel V-8, 3=289-cid export two-barrel V-8 and A=289-cid four-barrel V-8. The last six digits are the unit's production number, beginning at 100001 and going up, at each of the assembly plants. Falcons not built at all Ford plants.

VIN (Fairlane):

The VIN for Fairlanes was die-stamped into the side of the left-hand front inner fender apron near the top. The first symbol indicates year: 5=1965. The second symbol identifies assembly plant, as follows: A=Atlanta, Georgia, B=Oakville, Ontario, Canada, D=Dallas, Texas, E=Mahwah, New Jersey, F=Dearborn, Michigan, G=Chicago, Illinois, H=Lorain, Ohio, J=Los Angeles, California, K=Kansas City, Kansas, L=Long Beach, California, N=Norfolk, Virginia, P=Twin Cities, Minnesota, R=San Jose, California, S=Pilot Plant, T=Metuchen, New Jersey, U=Louisville, Kentucky, W=Wayne, Michigan, Y=Wixom, Michigan, Z=St. Louis, Mo. The third and fourth symbols identify body series code: 31=Fairlane two-door sedan, 32=Fairlane four-door sedan, 41=Fairlane 500 two-door sedan, 42=Fairlane 500 four-door sedan, 43=Fairlane 500 two-door hardtop, 47=Fairlane 500 two-door Sport Coupe, 38=Fairlane four-door six-passenger station wagon, 48=Fairlane Custom four-door six-passenger station wagon. The fifth symbol identifies engine code, as follows: T=200-cid six-cylinder, 2=200-cid export six-cylinder, C=289-cid two-barrel V-8, 3=289-cid export two-barrel V-8 and A=289-cid four-barrel V-8 and K=289-cid four-barrel V-8. The last six digits are the unit's production number, beginning at 100001 and going up, at each of the assembly plants. Fairlanes not built at all Ford plants.

VIN (Ford):

The VIN for full-size Fords was die-stamped into the top right-hand side rail of the frame ahead of the front suspension member. The first symbol indicates year: 5=1965. The second symbol identifies assembly plant, as follows: A=Atlanta, Georgia, B=Oakville, Ontario, Canada, D=Dallas, Texas, E=Mahwah, New Jersey, F=Dearborn, Michigan, G=Chicago, Illinois, H=Lorain, Ohio, J=Los Angeles, California, K=Kansas City, Kansas, L=Long Beach, California, N=Norfolk, Virginia, P=Twin Cities, Minnesota, R=San Jose, California, S=Pilot Plant, T=Metuchen, New Jersey, U=Louisville, Kentucky, W=Wayne, Michigan, Y=Wixom, Michigan, Z=St. Louis, Mo. The third and fourth symbols identify body series 51=Custom two-door sedan, 52=Custom 500 four-door sedan, 53=Custom two-door sedan, 54=Custom four-door sedan, 62=Galaxie 500 four-door sedan, 64=Galaxie 500 four-door Victoria Hardtop, 65=Galaxie 500 Sunliner convertible, 66=Galaxie 500 fastback, 60=Galaxie 500 LTD four-door hardtop, 67=Galaxie 500 LTD fastback, 68=Galaxie 500/XL fastback, 69=Galaxie 500/XL two-door convertible, 72=four-door six-passenger Country Sedan station wagon, 74=four-door nine-passenger Country Sedan station wagon, 76=four-door Country Squire six-passenger station wagon and 78=four-door Country Squire nine-passenger station wagon. The fifth symbol identifies engine code, as follows: V=223-cid six-cylinder, 5=223-cid Export six-cylinder, B=223-cid Police six, E=223-cid Taxi six-cylinder, C=289-cid two-barrel V-8, 3=289-cid low-compression export two-barrel V-8, X=352-cid two-barrel V-8, Z=390-cid four-barrel V-8, 9=390-cid V-8, P=390-cid V-8, R=427-cid V-8. Racing engines: L=427-cid four-barrel V-8 and M=427-cid dual four-barrel V-8. The last six digits are the unit's production number, beginning at 100001 and going up, at each of the assembly plants. Full-size Fords not built at all Ford plants.

1965 Ford Custom two-door sedan (OCW)

1965 Ford Fairlane 500 two-door Sports Coupe (OCW)

1965 Ford Fairlane 500 four-door station wagon (PH)

1965 Ford Galaxie 500 four-door sedan (OCW)

Falcon Standard (Six)

Model No.	Body/Style No.	Body Style and Seating	Factory Price	Shipping Weight	Production Total
62A	01	2-dr. Sedan-6P	$1,997	2,370 lbs.	46,504
54A	02	4-dr. Sedan-6P	$2,038	2,410 lbs.	38,852

Falcon Standard (V-8)

62A	01	2-dr. Sedan-6P	$2,127	2,726 lbs.	3,178
54A	02	4-dr. Sedan-6P	$2,188	2,766 lbs.	5,184

Falcon Futura (Six)

62B	19	2-dr. Sedan-6P	$2,099	2,373 lbs.	9,862
54B	16	4-dr. Sedan-6P	$2,146	2,415 lbs.	28,640
63*	17	2-dr. Hardtop-6P	$2,179	2,395 lbs.	13,723
76*	15	2-dr. Convertible-6P	$2,428	2,675 lbs.	3,944

Falcon Futura (V-8)

62B	19	2-dr. Sedan-6P	$2,248	2,731 lbs.	1,808
54B	16	4-dr. Sedan-6P	$2,295	2,771 lbs.	5,345
63*	17	2-dr. Hardtop-6P	$2,329	2,696 lbs.	14,837
76*	15	2-dr. Convertible-6P	$2,578	2,972 lbs.	3,223

*Suffixes: A=Bench Seat, B=Bucket Seat With Console, H=Bucket Seat Less Console

Falcon Station Wagon (Six)

59A	21	2-dr. Station Wagon-6P	$2,284	2,640 lbs.	4,396
71A	22	4-dr. Station Wagon-6P	$2,317	2,680 lbs.	13,111

Falcon Station Wagon (V-8)

59A	21	2-dr. Station Wagon-6P	$2,433	2,966 lbs.	495
71A	22	4-dr. Station Wagon-6P	$2,467	3,006 lbs.	1,800

Falcon Futura Ranch Wagon (Six)

71B	24	4-dr. Station Wagon-6P	$2,453	2,670 lbs.	9,325

Falcon Futura Ranch Wagon (V-8)

71B	24	4-dr. Station Wagon-6P	$2,558	2,996 lbs.	2,671

Futura Squire Station Wagon (Six)

71C	26	4-dr. Station Wagon-6P	$2,608	2,695 lbs.	3,661

Futura Squire Station Wagon (V-8)

71C	26	4-dr. Station Wagon-6P	$2,714	3,018 lbs.	3,042

Fairlane (Six)

62A	31	2-dr. Sedan-6P	$2,194	2,805 lbs.	14,777
54A	32	4-dr. Sedan-6P	$2,235	2,857 lbs.	22,233

Fairlane (V-8)

62A	31	2-dr. Sedan-6P	$2,294	2,997 lbs.	5,644
54A	32	4-dr. Sedan-6P	$2,335	3,049 lbs.	14,460

Fairlane 500 (Six)

62B	41	2-dr. Sedan-6P	$2,276	2,820 lbs.	8,760
54B	42	4-dr. Sedan-6P	$2,317	2,872 lbs.	18,791
65A	43	2-dr. Hardtop-6P	$2,341	2,880 lbs.	4,467

Fairlane 500 (V-8)

62B	41	2-dr. Sedan-6P	$2,376	3,012 lbs.	14,687
54B	42	4-dr. Sedan-6P	$2,417	3,064 lbs.	68,128
65A	43	2-dr. Hardtop-6P	$2,441	3,072 lbs.	22,296

Fairlane 500 Sport (Six)

65B	47	2-dr. Hardtop-6P	$2,502	2,904 lbs.	946

Fairlane 500 Sport (V-8)

65B	47	2-dr. Hardtop-6P	$2,602	3,096 lbs.	20,485

Fairlane Ranch Wagon (Six)

71D	38	4-dr. Station Wagon-6P	$2,531	3,207 lbs.	7,324

Fairlane Ranch Wagon (V-8)

71D	38	4-dr. Station Wagon-6P	$2,631	3,399 lbs.	13,656

Fairlane Custom Ranch Wagon (Six)

71B	48	4-dr. Station Wagon-6P	$2,612	3,237 lbs.	2,666

Fairlane Custom Ranch Wagon (V-8)

71B	48	4-dr. Station Wagon-6P	$2,712	3,429 lbs.	22,296

Ford Custom (Six)

62E	53	2-dr. Sedan-6P	$2,313	3,275 lbs.	28,094
54E	54	4-dr. Sedan-6P	$2,366	3,378 lbs.	44,278

Ford Custom (V-8)

62E	53	2-dr. Sedan-6P	$2,420	3,319 lbs.	20,940
54E	54	4-dr. Sedan-6P	$2,472	3,422 lbs.	52,115

Custom 500 (Six)

62B	51	2-dr. Sedan-6P	$2,414	3,323 lbs.	6,238
54B	52	4-dr. Sedan-6P	$2,467	3,382 lbs.	13,157

Custom 500 (V-8)

62B	51	2-dr. Sedan-6P	$2,520	3,367 lbs.	13,365
54B	52	4-dr. Sedan-6P	$2,573	3,426 lbs.	58,570

Galaxie 500 (Six)

54A	62	4-dr. Sedan-6P	$2,623	3,393 lbs.	8,417
63B	66	2-dr. Fastback-6P	$2,630	3,351 lbs.	7,099
57B	64	4-dr. Hardtop-6P	$2,708	3,477 lbs.	833
76B	65	2-dr. Convertible-6P	$2,889	3,590 lbs.	1,034

Galaxie 500 (V-8)

54A	62	4-dr. Sedan-6P	$2,730	3,437 lbs.	172,766
63B	66	2-dr. Fastback-6P	$2,737	3,395 lbs.	150,185
57B	64	4-dr. Hardtop-6P	$2,815	3,521 lbs.	49,149
76B	65	2-dr. Convertible-6P	$2,996	3,635 lbs.	30,896

Galaxie 500/XL (V-8)

63C	68	2-dr. Fastback-6P	$3,167	3,556 lbs.	28,141
76B	69	2-dr. Convertible-6P	$3,426	3,704 lbs.	9,849

Galaxie 500 LTD (V-8)

63F	67	2-dr. Fastback-6P	$3,167	3,633 lbs.	58,306
57F	60	4-dr. Hardtop-6P	$3,245	3,611 lbs.	68,038

Ranch Wagon (Six)

71D	71	4-dr. Station Wagon-6P	$2,707	3,819 lbs.	7,889

Custom Ranch Wagon (Six)

71C	72	4-dr. Station Wagon-6P	$2,797	3,849 lbs.	2,661
71B	74	4-dr. Station Wagon-9P	$2,899	3,895 lbs.	1,512

Country Squire Station Wagon (Six)

71E	76	4-dr. Station Wagon-6P	$3,041	3,906 lbs.	245
71A	78	4-dr. Station Wagon-9P	$3,109	3,920 lbs.	179

Ranch Wagon (V-8)

71D	72	4-dr. Station Wagon-6P	$2,813	3,863 lbs.	22,928

Custom Ranch Wagon (V-8)

71C	72	4-dr. Station Wagon-6P	$2,904	3,893 lbs.	57,232
71B	74	4-dr. Station Wagon-9P	$3,005	3,939 lbs.	30,832

Country Squire Station Wagon (V-8)

71E	76	4-dr. Station Wagon-6P	$3,147	3,950 lbs.	24,063
71A	78	4-dr. Station Wagon-9P	$3,216	3,964 lbs.	30,323

Engines:

Falcon Six: Overhead valve. Cast-iron block. Displacement: 144 cid. B & S: 3.50 x 2.50 in. Compression ratio: 6.7:1. Brake hp: 65 at 4200 rpm. Carburetor: Holley one-barrel. Seven main bearings. Code S.

Falcon Six: Overhead valve. Cast-iron block. Displacement: 170 cid. B & S: 3.50 x 2.94 in. Compression ratio: 8.7:1. Brake hp: 101 at 4400 rpm. Carburetor: Holley one-barrel. Seven main bearings. Code U.

Ford Six: Overhead valve. Cast-iron block. Displacement: 223 cid. B & S: 3.62 x 3.60 in. Compression ratio: 8.4:1. Brake hp: 138 at 4200 rpm. Carburetor: Holley one-barrel. Four main bearings. Code V.

Challenger 289 V-8: Overhead valve. Cast-iron block. Displacement: 289 cid. B & S: 4.00 x 2.87 in. Compression ratio: 9.30:1. Brake hp: 200 at 4400 rpm. Torque: 282 lbs.-ft. at 2400 rpm. Five main bearings. Hydraulic valve lifters. Carburetor: Two-barrel. Cooling system capacity: 16 qt. with heater. Crankcase capacity: 4 qt. (add 1 qt. with new oil filter). Code C.

Challenger 289 Four-Barrel V-8: Overhead valve. Cast-iron block. Displacement: 289 cid. B & S: 4.00 x 2.87 in. Compression ratio: 10.0:1. Brake hp: 225 at 4800 rpm. Torque: 305 lbs.-ft. at 3200 rpm. Five main bearings. Hydraulic valve lifters. Carburetor: Four-barrel. Cooling system capacity: 16 qt. with heater. Crankcase capacity: 4 qt. (add 1 qt. with new oil filter). Code A.

Interceptor V-8 (Base Galaxie 500/XL V-8 and optional in other full-size Fords): Overhead valve. Cast- iron block. Displacement: 352 cid. B & S: 4.00 x 3.50 in. Compression ratio: 9.30:1. Brake hp: 250 at 4400 rpm. Torque: 352 lbs.-ft. at 2800 rpm. Five main bearings. Hydraulic valve lifters. Carburetor: Four-barrel. Cooling system capacity: 20.5 qt. with heater. Crankcase capacity: 5 qt. (add 1 qt. with new oil filter). Code X.

Challenger 289 High-Performance Four-Barrel V-8: Overhead valve. Cast-iron block. Displacement: 289 cid. B & S: 4.00 x 2.87 in. Compression ratio: 10.5:1. Brake hp: 271 at 6000 rpm. Torque: 312 lbs.-ft. at 3400 rpm. Five main bearings. Solid valve lifters. Carburetor: Four-barrel. Cooling system capacity: 16 qt. with heater. Crankcase capacity: 4 qt. (add 1 qt. with new oil filter). Code K.

Thunderbird 390 V-8 (Optional in full-size Ford): Overhead valve. Cast-iron block. Displacement: 390 cid. B & S: 4.05 x 3.78 in. Compression ratio: 10.0:1. Brake hp: 300 at 4600 rpm. Torque: 427 lbs.-ft. at 2800 rpm. Five main bearings. Hydraulic valve lifters. Carburetor: Four-barrel. Cooling system capacity: 20.5 qt. with heater. Crankcase capacity: 5 qt. (add 1 qt. with new oil filter). Dual exhausts. Code Z.

Thunderbird Interceptor Special 390 V-8: Overhead valve. Cast-iron block. Displacement: 390 cid. B & S: 4.05 x 3.78 in. Compression ratio: 10.0:1. Brake hp: 330 at 5000 rpm. Torque: 427 lbs.-ft. at 3200 rpm. Five main bearings. Solid valve lifters. Carburetor: Ford four-barrel. Cooling system capacity: 20.5 qt. with heater. Crankcase capacity: 5 qt. (add 1 qt. with new oil filter). Dual exhausts. Code P.

Thunderbird Super-High-Performance V-8: Overhead valve. Cast-iron block. Displacement: 427 cid. B & S: 4.23 x 3.78 in. Compression ratio: 11.50:1. Brake hp: 425 at 6000 rpm. Torque: 480 lbs.-ft. at 3700 rpm. Five main bearings. Solid valve lifters. Carburetor: Two Holley four-barrel. Cooling system capacity: 20.5 qt. with heater. Crankcase capacity: 5 qt. (add 1 qt. with new oil filter). Dual exhausts. Code R.

"SOHC 427" 4V V-8: Overhead valve. Cast-iron block. Hemispherical combustion chambers with overhead valves and overhead camshafts for each engine bank. Displacement: 427 cid. B & S: 4.23 x 3.78 in. Compression ratio: 12.10:1. Brake hp: 616 at 7000 rpm. Five main bearings. Carburetor: Holley four-barrel. Cooling system capacity: 20.5 qt. with heater. Crankcase capacity: 5 qt. (add 1 qt. with new oil filter). Dual exhausts. Code L ($2,500). (This engine was not installed in any Ford production vehicles.)

"SOHC 427" 4V V-8: Overhead valve. Cast-iron block. Hemispherical combustion chambers with overhead valves and overhead camshafts for each engine bank. Displacement: 427 cid. B & S: 4.23 x 3.78 in. Compression ratio: 12.10:1. Brake hp: 657 at 7500 rpm. Five main bearings. Hydraulic valve lifters. Carburetor: Two Holley four-barrel. Cooling system capacity: 20.5 qt. with heater. Crankcase capacity: 5 qt. (add 1 qt. with new oil filter). Dual exhausts. Code M. (This engine was not installed in any Ford production vehicles.)

Chassis:

Falcon: Wheelbase: 109.5 in. Overall length: 181.6 in. and 190 in. on station wagons. Tires: 6.50 x 13 and 7.00 x 13 on station wagons. All tires were four-ply tubeless blackwalls.

1965 Ford Galaxie 500 two-door hardtop (OCW)

1965 Ford Galaxie 500/XL two-door fastback (PH)

Fairlane: Wheelbase: 116 in. Overall length: 198.4 in. and 203.2 in. on station wagons. Tires: 6.94 x 14 four-ply tubeless blackwalls and 7.35 x 14 four-ply tubeless on station wagons.

Ford: Wheelbase: 119 in. Overall length: 210 in. Tires: 7.35 x 15 four-ply tubeless blackwalls and 8.15 x 15 four-ply tubeless on station wagons.

Options:

Falcon: 200-cid six-cylinder engine ($45), or 289-cid V-8 engine ($153). Cruise-O-Matic automatic transmission ($182 or $172 with six-cylinder). Front bucket seats ($69). AM radio ($58). Two-tone paint ($19). White sidewall tires ($30). Sprint package ($222 and $273 on convertibles). Popular Falcon station wagon options included all those of the sedans plus the following: Power tailgate window ($30). Luggage rack ($45).

Fairlane: 289-cid V-8 engine ($108), or high-performance 289-cid V-8 ($430). Cruise-O-Matic automatic. transmission ($190), four-speed manual transmission ($188). AM radio ($58). Power steering ($86). Power tailgate window on station wagons ($32). Luggage rack on station wagons ($45). Two-tone paint ($22). White sidewall tires ($34). Wheel covers ($22). Vinyl roof on two-door hardtops ($76).

Ford: Popular Custom and Custom 500 model options included the 289-cid V-8 engine ($109). Cruise-O-Matic automatic transmission ($189). Power steering ($97). AM radio ($58). Wheel covers ($25). White sidewall tires ($34). Popular Galaxie 500 and Galaxie 500XL options included the 390-cid V-8 engine ($246). Cruise-O-Matic automatic transmission ($190), four-speed manual transmission ($188 - no charge on XLs). Power steering ($97). Power brakes ($43). Power windows ($102). Tinted windshield ($40). Air conditioning ($36). AM radio ($58). Vinyl roof ($76). Wheel covers ($26). White sidewall tires ($34). Popular LTD options included the 390-cid V-8 engine ($137). Power steering ($97). Power brakes ($43). Power windows ($102). Tinted windshield ($40). Air conditioning ($364). AM radio ($72). AM/FM radio ($142). Vinyl roof ($76). White sidewall tires ($34). Popular station wagon options included the 390-cid V-8 engine ($246). Cruise-O-Matic automatic transmission ($190). Power steering ($97). Power brakes ($43). Tinted windows ($40). Power tailgate window ($32). Luggage rack ($45). AM radio ($58). White sidewall tires ($34). Wheel covers ($25). A Borg-Warner T-10 four-speed transmission was replaced, for 1965, with the Ford produced T&C 'top-loader' four-speed.

History:

Model names were dropped for 1965, in favor of designating the car by its actual body style, i.e., "Club Victoria" became "two-door hardtop," and "Sunliner" became "two-door convertible," etc. The 427-cid single-overhead cam engine was installed in the Fairlane Thunderbolt drag cars.

1965 Ford Galaxie 500/XL two-door convertible (OCW)

1965 Ford Galaxie 500 LTD four-door hardtop (PH)

1965 Ford four-door Country Squire Wagon (OCW)

1966 Ford

Falcon — (Six and V-8): The Falcon series received a total restyling for 1966. It had a longer hood, a shorter trunk and rounder lines than in 1965. The two-door hardtops were discontinued for 1966, with the Futura Sports Coupe carrying the sporty image for the year. A Falcon script was located on the front fender behind the front wheel opening. F-O-R-D was spelled out, in block letters, across the front of the hood. F-A-L-C-O-N was spelled out, in block letters, across the vertical section of the trunk lid. Falcon was the base trim level of the compact Falcon line for 1966 and included chrome windshield moldings, chrome rear window moldings, chrome rain gutter moldings, twin horns, dual sun visors, armrests on the front doors only and a standard steering wheel with horn button.

Falcon Futura — (Six and V-8): The Futura series was the top trim level for 1966 and included all the standard Falcon features, plus a cigarette lighter, rear armrests, rear ashtrays, a deluxe steering wheel with a chrome horn ring, nylon carpeting, special Futura moldings, Futura trim, Futura emblems, Futura nameplates and chrome side window frames. In addition, the Falcon Futura Sports Coupe was a sporty version of the two-door sedan that featured the 200-cid 120-hp six-cylinder engine, front bucket seats, special Sports Coupe nameplates and special wheel covers. The Futura convertible also included front bucket seats.

Falcon Station Wagon — (Six and V-8): Only four-door station wagons were available in the Falcon lineup this year. The Standard wagon came in both body styles. The more Deluxe station wagon had richer trim.

Fairlane — (Six and V-8): A major restyling was done to the Fairlane, which included 13 different models. They were longer, lower and wider and featured new front and rear suspensions. The full-width grille featured a horizontal grid with a large divider bar and the Fairlane crest in the center of the grille. The headlights were vertically stacked and angled back at the bottom, for a more aggressive look. A full-length horizontal

1966 Ford Falcon two-door Sedan (OCW)

1966 Ford Falcon standard cloth-and-vinyl interior (OCW)

1966 Ford Falcon Futura two-door Sedan

feature line was used for emphasis and the model designation, in block letters, was located on the rear fender. The taillights were rectangular and featured a chrome ring around the outside and around the centrally located back-up lights. The Fairlane was the base trim level for 1966 and included chrome windshield moldings, chrome rear window moldings, chrome rain gutter moldings, a deluxe steering wheel with a chrome horn ring, front and rear armrests, a cigarette lighter and vinyl-coated rubber floor mats. Engine choices ranged from the 200-cid 120-hp six-cylinder engine up to the mighty 390-cid 335-hp GT V-8 engine. For the first time, three convertibles were added to the lineup of hardtops and sedans.

Fairlane 500 — (Six and V-8) The Fairlane 500 was the intermediate trim level for 1966 and included all the Fairlane trim plus polished aluminum rocker panel moldings, a Fairlane crest in the center of the grille, color-keyed carpets (front and rear) and Fairlane 500 identification, in block letters, on the rear fenders. A Fairlane crest and Fairlane script also appeared on the right-hand vertical section of the trunk lid.

Fairlane 500/XL — (Six and V-8): The Fairlane 500/XL was the sporty version of the Fairlane 500 series and included all the Fairlane 500 features, plus bucket seats, a console, special name plaques, special exterior trim, deluxe wheel covers, red safety lights and white courtesy lights in the door armrests.

Fairlane 500 GT — (V-8): The Fairlane 500/XL was the sporty version of the Fairlane 500 series and included all the Fairlane 500 features, plus bucket seats, a console, special name plaques, special exterior trim, deluxe wheel covers, red safety lights and white courtesy lights in the door armrests.

Fairlane Station Wagon — (Six and V-8): The Fairlane station wagons came in a two-door Ranch Wagon, a four-door Custom Ranch Wagon and four-door Squire models. These were comparable to Fairlane, Fairlane 500 and Fairlane 500/XL cars. Fairlane Wagon equipment started with all of the Fairlane sedan features and then included these variations: a choice of special vinyl-and-vinyl interior trims, a choice of additional Diamond Lustre enamel exterior colors, front and rear foam-cushioned seats, a color-keyed cargo area inlay, a roll-down tailgate window and a folding second seat. The Custom Ranch Wagon included all Fairlane 500 sedan equipment, a choice upgraded cloth-and-vinyl trim, color-keyed vinyl-coated rubber floor coverings, a stowage compartment lock and a bright-metal tailgate molding. The Squire was even richer in trim and appointments than the Custom Ranch Wagon and it had wood trim.

Ford Custom — (Six and V-8): While 1965 and 1966 full-size Fords bear a resemblance to each other, they are quite different cars. The hood is the only interchangeable exterior body component. The 1966 models feature more rounded lines than the previous year's models, even though the feature lines are in the same location. The Custom series is the base trim level and includes chrome windshield moldings, chrome rear window moldings, two sun visors, a deluxe steering wheel with chrome horn ring, armrests on all doors and the Custom name, in script, on the rear fenders. The taillights had square lenses, with centrally-mounted back-up lights surrounded by a chrome bezel. The Ford name appeared, in block letters, across the front of the hood and across the vertical section of the trunk lid.

1966 Ford Falcon Futura Sports all-vinyl interior (OCW)

1966 Ford Falcon four-door Station Wagon (OCW)

1966 Ford Falcon Futura four-door Station Wagon (OCW)

1966 Ford Fairlane four-door sedan

Custom 500 — (Six and V-8): The Custom 500 was the upper trim level of the base line Custom series and included all trim used in the Custom models plus, chrome windshield moldings, chrome rear window moldings, nylon carpeting, armrests with ashtrays on all doors, two sun visors and. There was also a horizontal chrome strip along the side feature line and the designation "500" in a die-cast block, with black-painted background, in front of the Custom script. A small Ford crest was located in the chrome side strip, on the front of the front fenders.

Galaxie 500 — (Six and V-8): The Galaxie 500 was the intermediate trim level for 1966 and included all the Custom trim, plus a chrome hood ornament, the Ford crest in the feature line on the front fender and stamped aluminum rocker panel moldings. A stamped aluminum insert decorated the space between the two chrome strips on the vertical section of the trunk lid and the word F-O-R-D was spelled out in block letters, spaced evenly across it. Two-tone vinyl trim was used on the seats and on the inside of the doors. Simulated wood appliques were used on the instrument panel trim pieces.

Galaxie 500/XL — (V-8): Galaxie 500/XL was the sport trim version of the Galaxie 500 two-door hardtop and two-door convertible and included all Galaxie 500 trim, plus bucket front seats, a floor-mounted shift lever, polished door trim with carpeting on the lower position of the doors, dual-lens courtesy/warning lights in the door panels, rear reading lights (in hardtops) and Galaxie 500/XL badges on the body exterior. The 289-cid 200-hp V-8 and Cruise-O-Matic automatic transmission were standard in both 500/XL body styles.

Galaxie 500/XL 7-Litre — (V-8): The "7-Litre" was a high-performance version of the Galaxie 500/XL and was equipped with the 428-cid 345-hp V-8 engine as standard equipment. It also came with Cruise-O-Matic automatic transmission. A four-speed manual transmission was available as a no-cost option for those who chose to be even more sporting. Along with the 428-cid engine, standard equipment also included a simulated English walnut Sport steering wheel, front bucket seats, a floor-mounted gearshift, low-restriction dual exhaust and a non-silenced air cleaner system. Also standard were power disc brakes.

Galaxie 500 LTD (V-8): The Galaxie 500 LTD was the top trim level for 1966 and included all the Galaxie 500 trim, plus the 289-cid 200-hp V-8 engine, Cruise-O-Matic automatic transmission, thickly padded seats with "pinseal" upholstery, simulated walnut appliqués on the lower edge of the instrument panel, simulated walnut appliqués in the door inserts, a Gabardine finish headliner, Gabardine finish sun visors, front and rear door courtesy/warning lights, courtesy lights on the rear interior roof pillars, courtesy lights under the instrument panel, a glove box light, ashtray lights and a self-regulating clock.

Galaxie Station Wagon (Six and V-8): The Ranch Wagon was the base trim level station wagon for 1966. The Country Sedans were the intermediate level and the Country Squires were the top trim level. The trim paralleled the Custom 500, Galaxie 500 and Galaxie 500 LTD models of passenger cars.

VIN (Falcon):

The VIN for Falcons was die-stamped into the inner fender panel and radiator support at the left side under the hood. The first symbol indicates year: 6=1966. The second symbol identifies assembly plant, as follows: A=Atlanta, Georgia, B=Oakville, Ontario, Canada, C=Ontario, Canada, D=Dallas, Texas, E=Mahwah, New Jersey, F=Dearborn, Michigan, G=Chicago, Illinois, H=Lorain, Ohio, J=Los Angeles, California, K=Kansas City, Kansas, L=Long Beach, California, N=Norfolk, Virginia, P=Twin Cities, Minnesota, R=San Jose, California, S=Pilot Plant, T=Metuchen, New Jersey, U=Louisville, Kentucky, W=Wayne, Michigan, Y=Wixom, Michigan, Z=St. Louis, Mo. The third and fourth symbols identify body series code: 01=two-door sedan, 02=four-door sedan, 11=two-door hardtop with bucket seats, 12=two-door convertible with bucket seats, 14=two-door bucket seat Sport Coupe, 22=four-door station wagon, 24=four-door Deluxe station wagon. The fifth symbol identifies engine code, as follows: U=170-cid six-cylinder, 4=170-cid export six-cylinder, T=200-cid six-cylinder, 2=200-cid export six-cylinder, C=289-cid two-barrel V-8 and 3=289-cid export two-barrel V-8. The last six digits are the unit's production number, beginning at 100001 and going up, at each of the assembly plants. Falcons not built at all Ford plants.

VIN (Fairlane):

The VIN for Fairlanes was die-stamped into the inner fender panel and radiator support at the left side under the hood. The first symbol indicates year: 6=1966. The second symbol identifies assembly plant, as follows: A=Atlanta, Georgia, B=Oakville, Ontario, Canada, C=Ontario, Canada, D=Dallas, Texas, E=Mahwah, New Jersey, F=Dearborn, Michigan, G=Chicago, Illinois, H=Lorain, Ohio, J=Los Angeles, California, K=Kansas City, Kansas, L=Long Beach, California, N=Norfolk, Virginia, P=Twin Cities, Minnesota, R=San Jose, California, S=Pilot Plant, T=Metuchen, New Jersey, U=Louisville, Kentucky, W=Wayne, Michigan, Y=Wixom, Michigan, Z=St. Louis, Mo. The third and fourth symbols identify body series code: 31=Fairlane two-door sedan, 32=Fairlane four-door sedan, 40=Fairlane 500 GT bucket seat two-door hardtop, 44=Fairlane 500 GT bucket seat two-door convertible, 41=Fairlane 500 two-door sedan, 42=Fairlane 500 four-door sedan, 43=Fairlane 500 two-door hardtop, 45=Fairlane 500 two-door convertible, 46=Fairlane 500/XL bucket seat two-door convertible, 47=Fairlane 500/XL two-door bucket-seat hardtop, 38=Fairlane four-door six-passenger station wagon, 48=Fairlane Custom four-door six-passenger station wagon, 49=Fairlane 500 four-door Squire station wagon. The fifth symbol identifies engine code, as follows: T=200-cid six-cylinder, 2=200-cid export six-cylinder, C=289-cid two-barrel V-8, 3=289-cid export two-barrel V-8, Y=390-cid two-barrel V-8, H=390-cid two-barrel V-8 and S=390-cid four-barrel V-8. The last six digits are the unit's production number, beginning at 100001 and going up, at each of the assembly plants. Fairlanes not built at all Ford plants.

VIN (Ford):

The VIN for full-size Fords was die-stamped into an extension tab on the top of the cowl on the right-hand side of the car under the hood. The first symbol indicates year: 6=1966. The second symbol identifies assembly plant, as follows: A=Atlanta, Georgia, B=Oakville, Ontario,

1966 Ford Fairlane 500 two-door Sedan

1966 Ford Fairlane 500 trunk space (OCW)

1966 Ford Fairlane 500 all-vinyl interior (OCW)

1966 Ford Fairlane 500 four-door Sedan (OCW)

1966 Ford Fairlane 500 two-door Hardtop (OCW)

Canada, C=Ontario, Canada, D=Dallas, Texas, E=Mahwah, New Jersey, F=Dearborn, Michigan, G=Chicago, Illinois, H=Lorain, Ohio, J=Los Angeles, California, K=Kansas City, Kansas, L=Long Beach, California, N=Norfolk, Virginia, P=Twin Cities, Minnesota, R=San Jose, California, S=Pilot Plant, T=Metuchen, New Jersey, U=Louisville, Kentucky, W=Wayne, Michigan, Y=Wixom, Michigan, Z=St. Louis, Mo. The third and fourth symbols identify body series 51=Custom 500 two-door sedan, 52=Custom 500 four-door sedan, 53=Custom two-door sedan, 54=Custom four-door sedan, 61=Galaxie 7-Litre two-door fastback, 62=Galaxie 500 two-door convertible, 64=Galaxie 500 four-door Victoria Hardtop, 65=Galaxie 500 Sunliner convertible, 66=Galaxie 500 fastback, 60=Galaxie 500 LTD four-door hardtop, 67=Galaxie 500 LTD fastback, 68=Galaxie 500/XL fastback, 69=Galaxie 500/XL two-door convertible, 71=four-door six-passenger Ranch Wagon, 72=four-door six-passenger Country Sedan station wagon, 74=four-door nine-passenger Country Sedan station wagon, 76=four-door Country Squire six-passenger station wagon and 78=four-door Country Squire nine-passenger station wagon. The fifth symbol identifies engine code, as follows: V=223-cid six-cylinder, 5=223-cid Export six-cylinder, B=223-cid Police six, E=223-cid Taxi six-cylinder, C=289-cid two-barrel V-8, 3=289-cid low-compression export two-barrel V-8, X=352-cid two-barrel V-8, H=390-cid two-barrel V-8, Z=390-cid four-barrel V-8, Q=428-cid four-barrel V-8, 8=428-cid four-barrel V-8, P=428-cid four-barrel V-8, W=427-cid four-barrel V-8 and 4=427-cid four-barrel V-8. The last six digits are the unit's production number, beginning at 100001 and going up, at each of the assembly plants. Full-size Fords not built at all Ford plants.

Falcon Standard (Six)

Model No.	Body/Style No.	Body Style and Seating	Factory Price	Shipping Weight	Production Total
62A	01	2-dr. Sedan-6P	$2,060	2,519 lbs.	32,088
54A	02	4-dr. Sedan-6P	$2,114	2,559 lbs.	26,105

Falcon Standard (V-8)

62A	01	2-dr. Sedan-6P	$2,127	2,726 lbs.	3,178
54A	02	4-dr. Sedan-6P	$2,188	2,766 lbs.	5,184

Falcon Futura (Six)

62A	11	2-dr. Sedan-6P	$2,183	2,527 lbs.	14,604
54A	12	4-dr. Sedan-6P	$2,237	2,567 lbs.	25,033
62C	13	2-dr. Sport Coupe-6P	$2,328	2,597 lbs.	8,898

Falcon Futura (V-8)

62B	11	2-dr. Sedan-6P	$2,315	2,813 lbs.	3,692
54B	12	4-dr. Sedan-6P	$2,369	2,853 lbs.	4,201
62C	13	2-dr. Sport Coupe-6P	$2,434	2,883 lbs.	8,103

Falcon Station Wagon (Six)

71A	22	4-dr. Station Wagon-6P	$2,442	3,037 lbs.	10,484

Falcon Station Wagon (V-8)

71A	22	4-dr. Station Wagon-6P	$2,548	3,236 lbs.	1,999

Falcon Deluxe Station Wagon (Six)

71B	24	4-dr. Station Wagon-6P	$2,553	3,045 lbs.	7,038

Falcon Deluxe Station Wagon (V-8)

71B	24	4-dr. Station Wagon-6P	$2,659	3,244 lbs.	3,938

Fairlane (Six)

62A	31	2-dr. Sedan-6P	$2,240	2,747 lbs.	8,440
54A	32	4-dr. Sedan-6P	$2,280	2,792 lbs.	11,731

Fairlane (V-8)

62A	31	2-dr. Sedan-6P	$2,345	2,916 lbs.	4,258
54A	32	4-dr. Sedan-6P	$2,386	2,961 lbs.	11,774

Fairlane 500 (Six)

62B	41	2-dr. Sedan-6P	$2,317	2,754 lbs.	4,617
54B	42	4-dr. Sedan-6P	$2,357	2,798 lbs.	12,017
63B	43	2-dr. Hardtop-6P	$2,378	2,856 lbs.	7,300
76B	45	2-dr. Convertible-6P	$2,608	3,084 lbs.	1,033

Fairlane 500 (V-8)

62B	41	2-dr. Sedan-6P	$2,423	2,923 lbs.	8,949
54B	42	4-dr. Sedan-6P	$2,463	2,967 lbs.	53,454
63B	43	2-dr. Hardtop-6P	$2,484	3,025 lbs.	65,343
76B	45	2-dr. Convertible-6P	$2,709	3,253 lbs.	8,039

Fairlane 500/XL (Six)

63B	47	2-dr. Hardtop-6P	$2,543	2,884 lbs.	629
76B	46	2-dr. Convertible-6P	$2,768	3,099 lbs.	155

Fairlane 500/XL (V-8)

63C	47	2-dr. Hardtop-6P	$2,649	3,053 lbs.	21,315
76C	46	2-dr. Convertible-6P	$2,709	3,253 lbs.	4,305

Fairlane GT (V-8)

63D	40	2-dr. Hardtop-6P	$2,843	3,335 lbs.	33,015
76D	44	2-dr. Convertible-6P	$3,068	3,500 lbs.	4,327

Fairlane Ranch Wagon (Six)

71D	38	4-dr. Station Wagon-6P	$2,589	3,182 lbs.	3,623

Fairlane Ranch Wagon (V-8)

71D	38	4-dr. Station Wagon-6P	$2,694	3,351 lbs.	8,530

Fairlane Custom Ranch Wagon (Six)

71B	48	4-dr. Station Wagon-6P	$2,665	3,192 lbs.	1,613

Fairlane Custom Ranch Wagon (V-8)

71B	48	4-dr. Station Wagon-6P	$2,770	3,361 lbs.	17,904

Fairlane Squire Wagon (Six)

71E	48	4-dr. Station Wagon-6P	$2,796	3,200 lbs.	771

Fairlane Squire Wagon (V-8)

71E	48	4-dr. Station Wagon-6P	$2,901	3,369 lbs.	10,787

Ford Custom (Six)

62E	53	2-dr. Sedan-6P	$2,380	3,333 lbs.	12,951
54E	54	4-dr. Sedan-6P	$2,432	3,433 lbs.	22,622

Ford Custom (V-8)

62E	53	2-dr. Sedan-6P	$2,487	3,377 lbs.	11,470
54E	54	4-dr. Sedan-6P	$2,539	3,477 lbs.	32,095

Custom 500 (Six)

62B	51	2-dr. Sedan-6P	$2,481	3,375 lbs.	11,882
54B	52	4-dr. Sedan-6P	$2,533	3,444 lbs.	27,164

Custom 500 (V-8)

62B	51	2-dr. Sedan-6P	$2,588	3,419 lbs.	12,454
54B	52	4-dr. Sedan-6P	$2,639	3,488 lbs.	69,771

Galaxie 500 (Six)

54A	62	4-dr. Sedan-6P	$2,677	3,456 lbs.	6,787
63B	66	4-dr. Fastback-6P	$2,685	3,437 lbs.	9,441
57B	64	4-dr. Hardtop-6P	$2,762	3,526 lbs.	727
76A	65	2-dr. Convertible-6P	$2,934	3,633 lbs.	791

Galaxie 500 (V-8)

54A	62	4-dr. Sedan-6P	$2,784	3,500 lbs.	156,769
63B	66	4-dr. Fastback-6P	$2,791	3,481 lbs.	176,790
57B	64	4-dr. Hardtop-6P	$2,869	3,570 lbs.	51,679
76A	65	2-dr. Convertible-6P	$3,041	3,677 lbs.	24,550

Galaxie 500/XL (V-8)

63B	68	2-dr. Fastback-6P	$3,231	3,616 lbs.	22,247
76B	69	2-dr. Convertible-6P	$3,480	3,761 lbs.	5,106

Galaxie 500 LTD (V-8)

63F	67	2-dr. Fastback-6P	$3,201	3,601 lbs.	30,810
57F	60	4-dr. Hardtop-6P	$3,278	3,649 lbs.	66,255

Galaxie 7-Litre (V-8)

63D	67	2-dr. Fastback-6P	$3,621	3,914 lbs.	8,705
76D	60	2-dr. Convertible-6P	$3,872	4,059 lbs.	2,368

Ranch Wagon (Six)

71D	71	4-dr. Station Wagon-6P	$2,793	3,919 lbs.	6,216

Ranch Wagon (V-8)

71D	72	4-dr. Station Wagon-6P	$2,900	3,963 lbs.	27,090

Custom Ranch Wagon (Six)

71C	72	4-dr. Station Wagon-6P	$2,882	3,934 lbs.	1,314
71B	74	4-dr. Station Wagon-9P	$2,999	3,975 lbs.	1,192

Custom Ranch Wagon (V-8)

71C	72	4-dr. Station Wagon-6P	$2,989	3,978 lbs.	50,966
71B	74	4-dr. Station Wagon-9P	$3,105	4,019 lbs.	34,316

Country Squire Station Wagon (Six)

71E	76	4-dr. Station Wagon-6P	$3,182	4,004 lbs.	159
71A	78	4-dr. Station Wagon-9P	$3,265	4,018 lbs.	150

Country Squire Station Wagon (V-8)

71E	76	4-dr. Station Wagon-6P	$3,289	4,048 lbs.	26,184
71A	78	4-dr. Station Wagon-9P	$3,372	4,062 lbs.	40,378

Engines:

Falcon and Fairlane Six: Overhead valve. Cast-iron block. Displacement: 170 cid. B & S: 3.50 x 2.94 in. Compression ratio: 9.1:1. Brake hp: 105 at 4400 rpm. Carburetor: Holley one-barrel. Seven main bearings. Code 4.

1966 Ford Fairlane 500 two-door convertible (OCW)

1966 Ford Fairlane four-door Ranch Wagon (OCW)

1966 Ford Fairlane 500 four-door station wagon (OCW)

Falcon and Fairlane Six: Overhead valve. Cast-iron block. Displacement: 200 cid. B & S: 3.68 x 3.13 in. Compression ratio: 9.2:1. Brake hp: 120 at 4400 rpm. Carburetor: Holley one-barrel. Seven main bearings. Code U.

Ford Six: Overhead valve. Cast-iron block. Displacement: 240 cid. B & S: 4.00 x 3.18 in. Compression ratio: 9.2:1. Brake hp: 150 at 4000 rpm. Carburetor: Holley one-barrel. Seven main bearings. Code V (Police code B and taxi code E).

Challenger 289 V-8: Overhead valve. Cast-iron block. Displacement: 289 cid. B & S: 4.00 x 2.87 in. Compression ratio: 9.30:1. Brake hp: 200 at 4400 rpm. Torque: 282 lbs.-ft. at 2400 rpm. Five main bearings. Hydraulic valve lifters. Carburetor: Two-barrel. Cooling system capacity: 15 qt. with heater. Crankcase capacity: 4 qt. (add 1 qt. with new oil filter). Code C.

Challenger 289 Four-Barrel V-8: Overhead valve. Cast-iron block. Displacement: 289 cid. B & S: 4.00 x 2.87 in. Compression ratio: 10.0:1. Brake hp: 225 at 4800 rpm. Torque: 305 lbs.-ft. at 3200 rpm. Five main bearings. Hydraulic valve lifters. Carburetor: Four-barrel. Cooling system capacity: 15 qt. with heater. Crankcase capacity: 4 qt. (add 1 qt. with new oil filter). Code A.

Interceptor V-8 (Base Galaxie 500XL V-8 and optional in other full-size Fords): Overhead valve. Cast-iron block. Displacement: 352 cid. B & S: 4.00 x 3.50 in. Compression ratio: 9.30:1. Brake hp: 250 at 4400 rpm. Torque: 352 lbs.-ft. at 2800 rpm. Five main bearings. Hydraulic valve lifters. Carburetor: Four-barrel. Cooling system capacity: 20.5 qt. with heater. Crankcase capacity: 5 qt. (add 1 qt. with new oil filter). Code X.

Challenger 289 High-Performance Four-Barrel V-8: Overhead valve. Cast-iron block. Displacement: 289 cid. Bore and stroke: 4.00 x 2.87 inches. Compression ratio: 10.5:1. Brake hp: 271 at 6000 rpm. Torque: 312 at 3400 rpm. Five main bearings. Hydraulic valve lifters. Carburetor: Four-barrel. Cooling system capacity: 15 qt. with heater. Crankcase capacity: 4 qt. (add 1 qt. with new oil filter). Code K.

Thunderbird 390 Two-Barrel V-8 (Optional in full-size Fords): Overhead valve. Cast-iron block. Displacement: 390 cid. B & S: 4.05 x 3.78 in. Compression ratio: 9.5:1. Brake hp: 275 at 4400 rpm. Torque: 405 at 2600 rpm. Five main bearings. Solid valve lifters. Carburetor: Two-barrel. Cooling system capacity: 20.5 qt. with heater. Crankcase capacity: 4 qt. (add 1 qt. with new oil filter). Code Y.

Thunderbird 390 Four-Barrel V-8 (Optional in full-size Fords): Overhead valve. Cast-iron block. Displacement: 390 cid. B & S: 4.05 x 3.78 in. Compression ratio: 10.5:1. Brake hp: 315 at 4600 rpm. Torque: 427 lbs.-ft. at 2800 rpm. Five main bearings. Hydraulic valve lifters. Carburetor: Four-barrel. Cooling system capacity: 20.5 qt. with heater. Crankcase capacity: 4 qt. (add 1 qt. with new oil filter). Dual exhausts. Code Z.

1966 Ford Fairlane 500 four-door Squire station wagon (OCW)

1966 Ford Fairlane 500 two-door convertible (OCW)

1966 Ford Fairlane 500/XL two-door convertible (OCW)

1966 Ford Fairlane 500/XL two-door convertible seats (OCW)

1966 Ford Fairlane 500/XL two-door hardtop (OCW)

1966 Ford Fairlane 500 GTA two-door hardtop (OCW)

Optional Fairlane GT 390 V-8: Overhead valve. Cast-iron block. Displacement: 390 cid. B & S: 4.05 x 3.78 in. Compression ratio: 11.0:1. Brake hp: 335 at 4800 rpm. Torque: 427 lbs.-ft. at 3200 rpm. Five main bearings. Hydraulic valve lifters. Carburetor: Holley four-barrel. Cooling system capacity: 20.5 qt. with heater. Crankcase capacity: 4 qt. (add 1 qt. with new oil filter). Dual exhaust. Code S.

Thunderbird Special V-8: Overhead valve. Cast-iron block. Displacement: 428 cid. B & S: 4.13 x 3.98 in. Compression ratio: 10.50:1. Brake hp: 345 at 4600 rpm. Torque: 462 lbs.-ft. at 2800 rpm. Five main bearings. Hydraulic valve lifters. Carburetor: Four-barrel. Cooling system capacity: 20.5 qt. with heater. Crankcase capacity: 4 qt. (add 1 qt. with new oil filter). Dual exhausts Code Q.

Police Interceptor V-8: Overhead valve. Cast-iron block. Displacement: 428 cid. B & S: 4.13 x 3.98 in. Compression ratio: 10.50:1. Brake hp: 360 at 5400 rpm. Torque: 459 lbs.-ft. at 3200 rpm. Five main bearings. Solid valve lifters. Carburetor: Four-barrel. Cooling system capacity: 20.5 qt. with heater. Crankcase capacity: 4 qt. (add 1 qt. with new oil filter). Dual exhausts. Code P.

Thunderbird High Performance V-8: Overhead valve. Cast-iron block. Displacement: 427 cid. B & S: 4.23 x 3.78 in. Compression ratio: 11.00:1. Brake hp: 410 at 5600 rpm. Torque: 476 lbs.-ft. at 3400 rpm. Five main bearings. Solid valve lifters. Carburetor: Holley four-barrel. Cooling system capacity: 20.5 qt. with heater. Crankcase capacity: 5 qt. (add 1 qt. with new oil filter). Dual exhausts. Code W.

Thunderbird Super-High-Performance V-8: Overhead valve. Cast-iron block. Displacement: 427 cid. B & S: 4.23 x 3.78 in. Compression ratio: 11.50:1. Brake hp: 425 at 6000 rpm. Torque: 480 lbs.-ft. at 3700 rpm. Five main bearings. Hydraulic valve lifters. Carburetor: Two Holley four-barrel. Cooling system capacity: 20.5 qt. with heater. Crankcase capacity: 5 qt. (add 1 qt. with new oil filter). Dual exhausts. Code R.

"SOHC 427" 4V V-8: Overhead valve. Cast-iron block. Hemispherical combustion chambers with overhead valves and overhead camshafts for each engine bank. Displacement: 427 cid. B & S: 4.23 x 3.78 inches. Compression ratio: 12.10:1. Brake hp: 616 at 7000 rpm. Five main bearings. Carburetor: Holley four-barrel. Cooling system capacity: 20.5 qt. with heater. Crankcase capacity: 5 qt. (add 1 qt. with new oil filter). Dual exhaust. Code L. (This engine was available only "over the counter" for $2,500.)

"SOHC 427" 4V V-8: Overhead valve. Cast-iron block. Hemispherical combustion chambers with overhead valves and overhead camshafts for each engine bank. Displacement: 427 cid. B & S: 4.23 x 3.78 in.

Compression ratio: 12.10:1. Brake hp: 657 at 7500 rpm. Five main bearings. Hydraulic valve lifters. Carburetor: Two Holley four-barrel. Cooling system capacity: 20.5 qt. with heater. Crankcase capacity: 5 qt. (add 1 qt. with new oil filter). Dual exhausts. Code M.

Chassis:

Falcon: Wheelbase: 110.9 in and 113 in., station wagons. Overall length: 184.3 in. and 198.7 in., station wagons. Tires: 6.50 x 13 four-ply tubeless blackwall and 7.75 x 14 four-ply tubeless blackwall on station wagons.

Fairlane: Wheelbase: 116 in. and 113 in. on station wagons. Overall length: 197 in. and 199.8 in. on station wagons. Tires: 6.95 x 14 four-ply tubeless blackwall and 7.75 x 14 four-ply tubeless blackwall on station wagons.

Ford: Wheelbase: 119 in. Overall length: 210 in. and 210.9 in. on station wagons. Tires: 7.35 x 15 four-ply tubeless blackwall and 8.45 x 15 four-ply tubeless blackwall on station wagons.

Options:

Falcon: 200-cid six-cylinder engine ($26). The 289-cid V-8 engine ($131). Cruise-O-Matic automatic transmission ($167 with six-cylinder engine, $156 with 289-cid V-8). Power Steering ($84). Power tailgate on station wagons ($44). AM radio ($57). Vinyl roof on two-door models ($74). Wheel covers ($21). White sidewall tires ($32).

Fairlane: 289-cid V-8 engine ($105 and not available on GT). 390-cid V-8 engine ($206 and standard on GT). Cruise-O-Matic automatic transmission ($184 with 289-cid V-8, $214 with 390-cid V-8). Four-speed manual transmission ($183). AM radio ($57). Power steering ($84). Power tailgate window on station wagons ($31). Luggage rack on station wagons ($44). Two-tone paint ($21). White sidewall tires ($33). Wheel covers ($21). Vinyl roof on two-door hardtops ($76)

Ford: Popular Custom and Custom 500 options included the 289-cid V-8 engine ($106). Cruise-O-Matic automatic transmission ($184). Power steering ($94). AM radio ($57). Wheel covers ($22). White sidewall tires ($33). Popular Galaxie 500/Galaxie 500XL/Galaxie 500 7-Litre/Galaxie 500 LTD options included the 390-cid V-8 engine ($101 for two-barrel engine, $153 for four-barrel engine and not available in 7-Litre models). Power steering ($94). Power brakes ($42). Power windows ($99). Tinted windshield ($21). Air conditioning ($353). AM radio ($57). AM/FM radio ($133). Vinyl roof on two-door hardtops ($74), on four-door hardtops ($83). White sidewall tires ($33). Popular station wagon options included all those in the Galaxie 500 models plus power tailgate window ($31). Luggage rack ($44). Third passenger seat ($29).

History:

The full-size Fords were introduced October 1, 1965, and all the Ford lines appeared in dealer showrooms the same day. Model-year production peaked at 2,093,832 units. Calendar-year sales of 2,038,415 cars were recorded. Donald N. Frey was the chief executive officer of the company this year. On a calendar-year sales basis, Ford was the number two maker in America this year and held a 23.71 percent share of total market. Only 237 Ford Motor Co. products, of all types, had 427-cid V-8s installed during the 1966 calendar year. A positive note was the performance of the Ford GT-40 in the European Grand Prix racing circuit. A trio of these cars, running at Le Mans, finished first, second and third. It was the first time American entries had ever captured the championship honors in the prestigious race.

1966 Ford Galaxie 500 four-door hardtop (OCW)

1966 Ford Fairlane 500 GT two-door convertible (OCW)

1966 Ford Galaxie 500 Sunliner two-door Convertible (OCW)

1966 Ford Custom two-door sedan (OCW)

1966 Ford Galaxie 500/XL bucket seat interior (OCW)

1966 Ford Custom 500 four-door Sedan

1966 Ford Galaxie 500 LTD four-door interior (OCW)

1966 Ford Galaxie 500 four-door Sedan (OCW)

1966 Ford Galaxie 500 two-door fastback (OCW)

1966 Ford Galaxie 500/XL two-door convertible (OCW)

1966 Ford Galaxie 500/XL two-door fastback (OCW)

1967 Ford

Falcon — (Six and V-8): The 1967 Ford Falcons were updated but not totally restyled. The most noticeable change in the two years, was the scoop-like indentations behind the front wheel openings, on the front fenders. The grille was nearly identical, with a horizontal and vertical dividing bar being the only difference. Falcon was the base trim level of the compact Falcon line for 1967 and included a 105-hp six-cylinder engine, a heater and defroster, directionals with a lane-change signal, a padded instrument panel, padded sun visors, front and rear seat belts with retractors, an outside rearview mirror, and inside day/night mirror, a dual braking system with a warning light, back-up lights, four-way emergency flashers, two-speed windshield wipers and washers, foam-padded seat cushions and front arm rests. The Falcon also had a chrome windshield molding, a chrome rear window molding, chrome rain gutter moldings, armrests on the front doors only and a horn button. The Falcon name, in script, was located on the rear fender, just ahead of the taillights and, in block letters, across the vertical section of the trunk lid.

Falcon Futura — (Six and V-8): The Futura series was the top trim level for 1967 and included all the standard Falcon features, plus a cigarette lighter, rear armrests, rear ashtrays, a deluxe steering wheel with a chrome horn ring, nylon carpeting, special Futura moldings, Futura trim, Futura emblems, Futura nameplates and chrome side window frames. In addition, the Falcon Futura Sports Coupe was a sporty version of the two-door sedan that featured the 200-cid 120-hp six-cylinder engine, front bucket seats, special Sports Coupe nameplates and special wheel covers. The Futura convertible also included front bucket seats.

Falcon Station Wagon — (Six and V-8): Only four-door station wagons were available in the Falcon lineup this year. The Standard wagon came in both body styles. The standard equipment list was similar to that of the base Falcon. The more Deluxe station wagon had richer trim. Futura wagons also had all-vinyl interior trim

Fairlane — (Six and V-8): The Fairlane was the base trim level for 1967 and included the Fairlane name, in block letters, at the front end. The Fairlane continued to use the body introduced in 1966 with minor trim changes. The new grille was a single aluminum stamping instead of the two grilles used in the previous model and the taillights were divided horizontally by the back-up light, instead of vertically as in 1966. Standard Fairlane equipment included all federally-mandated Ford safety features plus vinyl-covered rubber floor mats, foam-padded cushions, courtesy lights, a heater and defroster, a cigarette lighter, ashtrays, a 200-cid six-cylinder engine and a choice of three cloth-and-vinyl interiors.

Fairlane 500 — (Six and V-8): The Fairlane 500 was the intermediate trim level for 1967 and included all the Fairlane trim plus simulated wood door paneling, carpets and an electric clock. The two-door hardtop and the convertible had a "floating" inside day/night mirror. Sedans and hardtops had a choice of four cloth-and-vinyl interiors, while convertibles have a choice of six all-vinyl trims.

Fairlane 500/XL — (Six and V-8): The Fairlane 500/XL included all features found on Fairlane 500s plus adjustable front bucket seats, a center console, courtesy lights, wheel covers and a choice of seven all-vinyl trims.

1966 Ford Galaxie 500 LTD four-door hardtop (OCW)

1966 Ford Galaxie 500 7-Litre two-door hardtop (OCW)

1966 Ford Galaxie 500 7-Litre two-door convertible (OCW)

1966 Ford four-door Ranch Wagon (OCW)

1966 Ford four-door Country Sedan 6P (OCW)

1967 Ford Falcon two-door Sports Coupe (OCW)

1967 Ford Falcon four-door Futura station wagon (OCW)

1966 Ford four-door Country Squire Wagon (OCW)

Fairlane GT — (V-8): The Fairlane GT included the Fairlane 500/XL features, plus power disc brakes, Wide-Oval sports white tires, GT simulated hood power domes with integral turn indicators, GT stripes, GT fender plaques, a GT black-out grille, deluxe wheel covers, a 289-cid V-8. A left-hand outside rearview mirror and deluxe seat belts .

Fairlane Station Wagon — (Six and V-8): The Fairlane station wagons came in a four-door Fairlane Wagon, a four-door Fairlane 500 Wagon and a four-door Squire model. Fairlane Wagon equipment started with all of the Fairlane sedan features and then included these variations: the Ford Magic Doorgate, foam seat cushions, a heater-and-defroster, a cigar lighter, ash trays, courtesy lighting and a choice of three all-vinyl trims. The Fairlane 500 wagon also had carpeting, an electric clock, a locking stowage compartment and a choice of four pleated all-vinyl trims. The Squire wagon also had simulated wood body trim and as power door gate window.

Ford Custom — (Six and V-8): As in the previous 10 years, Ford continued to restyle at least one of the model lines. The 1967 full-size Fords were completely restyled from the previous year, sharing only drive trains with the 1966 models. The new models were more rounded, with rounder tops and fenders. At the front end, stacked quad headlights were used once again, but the grille was all new. It was a double-stamped aluminum piece featuring horizontal bars divided by five vertical bars. The center portion of the grille projected forward and this point was duplicated in the forward edge of the hood and in the bumper configuration. The body side feature lines were in the same location as the 1966 models, but were somewhat less pronounced. The taillights were vertically situated rectangular units with chrome moldings and chrome cross-hairs surrounding the standard equipment back-up lights. All 1967 Fords are easily recognizable by the energy-absorbing steering wheels used in every model. A large, deeply-padded hub predominated the wheel. Also, all 1967 Fords were equipped with a dual brake master cylinder for the first time. The Custom series was the base trim level Ford for 1967 and included chrome windshield and rear window moldings, a chrome horn ring, nylon carpeting, the Custom name in script on the front fenders and the Ford name, in block letters, spaced across the front of the hood and across the vertical section of the trunk lid. Standard features included a heater and defroster, front and rear seat belts with a reminder light, front seat belt retractors, a non-glare day/night inside rearview mirror, two-speed windshield wipers and washers, back-up lights, Safety-Yoke door latches, emergency flashers, a lane-changing signal, foam seat cushions, courtesy lighting, a cigarette lighter, ash trays, a 240-cid six-cylinder engine, a remote-control outside rearview mirror, a padded dashboard, padded windshield pillars, padded sun visors and three cloth-and-vinyl interior trims.

Custom 500 — (Six and V-8): The Custom 500 was the upper trim level of the base line Custom series and included all the Custom trim plus special Custom 500 exterior trim and choice of four different interior upholstery choices.

Galaxie 500 — (Six and V-8): The Galaxie 500 was the intermediate trim level for 1967 and included all the Custom series trim plus stamped aluminum lower body side moldings, chrome side window moldings, simulated woodgrain appliques on the instrument panel and inner door panels, an electric clock, a trunk light, a glove box light, bright seat side shields and a stamped aluminum trim panel on the vertical section of the trunk lid. The name, Galaxie 500, in block letters, was located on the rear fenders and the Ford crest was located on the trunk lid above the aluminum trim panel. The Galaxie 500 convertible also had a 5-ply

1967 Ford Fairlane 500 four-door Squire station wagon (OCW)

1967 Ford Fairlane 500XL two-door hardtop (OCW)

vinyl power-operated top and a choice of seven all-vinyl interior trims. Hardtops had the same choice of seven all-vinyl interior trims.

Galaxie 500/XL — (V-8): The Galaxie 500XL was the sport trim version of the two-door fastback and two-door convertible and included the 289-cid/200-hp V-8 engine and SelectShift Cruise-O-Matic automatic transmission with a T-bar selector as standard equipment. Also, the model line included individually-adjustable bucket seats, a front Command console with door-ajar warning, bright brake and accelerator pedal trim, courtesy door lights, deluxe wheel covers, a die-cast grille, all Galaxie 500 trim, special ornamentation, automatic courtesy and warning lights in the door panels and chrome trim on the foot pedals. Seven all-vinyl interior trims were available. A four-speed manual gearbox was a no-cost option.

LTD — (V-8): The LTD was the top trim level full-size Ford for 1967 and was considered its own series for the first time since introduced in 1965. LTDs included all the Galaxie 500 trim plus the 289-cid/200-hp V-8 engine and SelectShift Cruise-O-Matic automatic transmission as standard equipment. Other regular features were a Comfort Stream flow-through ventilation system, distinctive LTD trim and ornamentation, special wheel covers, simulated walnut on the instrument panel and door panels, automatic courtesy and warning lights in the doors, deep-foam cushioning in the seating surfaces, pull-down armrests front and rear, color-keyed steering wheel and vinyl top on two-door hardtops. There was a choice of seven all-vinyl trims. A four-speed manual gearbox was a no-cost option.

Galaxie Station Wagon — (Six and V-8): The Ranch Wagon was the base trim level station wagon for 1967, with the Country Sedans being the intermediate level and the Country Squires being the top trim level. The trim paralleled the Custom 500, Galaxie 500 and LTD models of passenger cars. Standard equipment included all standard Ford safety items, a Magic Doorgate, carpeting, foam seats, courtesy lighting, a cigarette lighter, ash trays, a heater and defroster, and a choice of three all-vinyl trims. The Country Sedan also had bright metal exterior trim and a choice of four interiors. The Squire had simulated wood body trim, a power rear window, an electric clock and a choice of six trim options. The Model 72 and Model 74 station wagons also dual facing rear seats, rear bumper steps, a power rear window and power brakes.

VIN (Falcon):

The VIN for Falcons was die-stamped on the top surface of the radiator and the front fender apron support. The first symbol indicates year: 7=1967. The second symbol identifies assembly plant, as follows: A=Atlanta, Georgia, B=Oakville, Ontario, Canada, C=Ontario, Canada, D=Dallas, Texas, E=Mahwah, New Jersey, F=Dearborn, Michigan, G=Chicago, Illinois, H=Lorain, Ohio, J=Los Angeles, California, K=Kansas City, Kansas, N=Norfolk, Virginia, P=Twin Cities, Minnesota, R=San Jose, California, S=Pilot Plant, T=Metuchen, New Jersey, U=Louisville, Kentucky, W=Wayne, Michigan, Y=Wixom, Michigan, Z=St. Louis, Mo. The third and fourth symbols identify body series code: 10=Falcon two-door Club Coupe, 11=Falcon four-door bench seat sedan, 20=Futura two-door Club Coupe with bench seat, 21=Futura four-door sedan with bench seat, 22=Futura two-door hardtop with bucket seats, 12=four-door station wagon, 23=four-door Deluxe station wagon. The fifth symbol identifies engine code, as follows: U=170-cid six-cylinder one-barrel, T=200-cid six-cylinder one-barrel, 2=200-cid export six-cylinder one-barrel, C=289-cid V-8 two-barrel, 3=289-cid export V-8 two-barrel and A=289-cid V-8 four-barrel. The last six digits are the unit's production number, beginning at 100001 and going up, at each of the assembly plants. Falcons were not built at all Ford plants.

1967 Ford Fairlane 500 four-door Sedan (OCW)

1967 Ford Fairlane 500 four-door Sedan (OCW)

VIN (Fairlane):

The VIN for Fairlanes was die-stamped on the top surface of the radiator and the front fender apron support. The first symbol indicates year: 7=1967. The second symbol identifies assembly plant, as follows: A=Atlanta, Georgia, B=Oakville, Ontario, Canada, C=Ontario, Canada, D=Dallas, Texas, E=Mahwah, New Jersey, F=Dearborn, Michigan, G=Chicago, Illinois, H=Lorain, Ohio, J=Los Angeles, California, K=Kansas City, Kansas, N=Norfolk, Virginia, P=Twin Cities, Minnesota, R=San Jose, California, S=Pilot Plant, T=Metuchen, New Jersey, U=Louisville, Kentucky, W=Wayne, Michigan, Y=Wixom, Michigan, Z=St. Louis, Mo. The third and fourth symbols identify body series code: 30=Fairlane two-door sedan, 31=Fairlane four-door sedan, 33=Fairlane 500 two-door sedan with bench seats, 34=Fairlane 500 four-door sedan with bench seats, 35=Fairlane 500 two-door hardtop with bench seats, 36=Fairlane 500 convertible with bench seats, 40=Fairlane 500 XL bucket seat two-door hardtop, 41=Fairlane 500 XL bucket seat two-door convertible, 42=Fairlane 500 GT bucket seat two-door hardtop, 43=Fairlane 500 GT bucket seat two-door convertible, 32=Fairlane four-door six-passenger station wagon, 37=Fairlane 500 four-door six-passenger station wagon, 38=Fairlane 500 four-door Squire station wagon. The fifth symbol identifies engine code, as follows: T=200-cid six-cylinder one-barrel, 2=200-cid export six-cylinder one-barrel, C=289-cid V-8 two-barrel, 3=289-cid export V-8 two-barrel, A=289-cid V-8 four-barrel, K=289-cid four-barrel hi-performance V-8, S=390-cid V-8 four-barrel. The last six digits are the unit's production number, beginning at 100001 and going up, at each of the assembly plants. Fairlanes were not built at all Ford plants.

VIN (Ford):

The VIN for Fords was die-stamped on the top surface of the radiator and the front fender apron support. The first symbol indicates year: 7=1967. The second symbol identifies assembly plant, as follows: A=Atlanta, Georgia, B=Oakville, Ontario, Canada, C=Ontario, Canada, D=Dallas, Texas, E=Mahwah, New Jersey, F=Dearborn, Michigan, G=Chicago, Illinois, H=Lorain, Ohio, J=Los Angeles, California, K=Kansas City, Kansas, N=Norfolk, Virginia, P=Twin Cities, Minnesota, R=San Jose, California, S=Pilot Plant, T=Metuchen, New Jersey, U=Louisville, Kentucky, W=Wayne, Michigan, Y=Wixom, Michigan, Z=St. Louis, Mo. The third and fourth symbols identify body series 50=Custom 500 two-door sedan with bench seat, 51=Custom 500 four-door sedan with bench seat, 52=Custom two-door sedan with bench seat, 53=Custom four-door sedan with bench seat, 54=Galaxie 500 four-door sedan with bench seat, 56=Galaxie 500 four-door hardtop with bench seat, 57=Galaxie 500 two-door with bench seat, 55=Galaxie 500 two-door fastback with bench seat, 58=Galaxie 500/XL two-door hardtop with bucket seats, 59=Galaxie 500/XL two-door convertible with bucket seats, 66=LTD four-door hardtop with bench seat, 62=LTD two-door hardtop with bucket seats and formal roof, 64=LTD four-door sedan, 63=LTD two-door convertible with bucket seats and formal roof, 61=LTD two-door hardtop with bench seat, 3=LTD two-door convertible with bench seat, 70=four-door six-passenger Ranch Wagon, 71=four-door six-passenger Country Sedan station wagon, 72=four-door 10-passenger Country Sedan station wagon, 73=four-door Country Squire six-passenger station wagon and 74=four-door Country Squire 10-passenger station wagon. The fifth symbol identifies engine code, as follows: V=223-cid six-cylinder, 5=223-cid Export six-cylinder, B=223-

cid Police six, E=223-cid Taxi six-cylinder, C=289-cid two-barrel V-8, 3=289-cid low-compression export two-barrel V-8, Y=390-cid two-barrel V-8, H=390-cid two-barrel V-8, Z=390-cid four-barrel V-8, Q=428-cid four-barrel V-8, 8=428-cid four-barrel V-8, 8=428-cid four-barrel V-8, P=428-cid four-barrel V-8, W=427-cid four-barrel V-8 and R=427-cid dual four-barrel V-8. The last six digits are the unit's production number, beginning at 100001 and going up, at each of the assembly plants. Full-size Fords not built at all Ford plants.

Falcon Standard (Six)

Model No.	Body/ Style No.	Body Style and Seating	Factory Price	Shipping Weight	Production Total
62	11	2-dr. Sedan-6P	$2,118	2,520 lbs.	15,352
54A	12	4-dr. Sedan-6P	$2,167	2,551 lbs.	26,105

Falcon Standard (V-8)

Model No.	Body/ Style No.	Body Style and Seating	Factory Price	Shipping Weight	Production Total
62A	11	2-dr. Sedan-6P	$2,249	2,806 lbs.	730
54A	12	4-dr. Sedan-6P	$2,299	2,837 lbs.	1,073

Falcon Futura (Six)

Model No.	Body/ Style No.	Body Style and Seating	Factory Price	Shipping Weight	Production Total
62B	11	2-dr. Sedan-6P	$2,280	2,528 lbs.	4,414
54B	12	4-dr. Sedan-6P	$2,322	2,559 lbs.	7,949
62C	13	2-dr. Sport Coupe-6P	$2,256	2,556 lbs.	2,256

Falcon Futura (V-8)

Model No.	Body/ Style No.	Body Style and Seating	Factory Price	Shipping Weight	Production Total
62B	11	2-dr. Sedan-6P	$2,386	2,814 lbs.	1,872
54B	12	4-dr. Sedan-6P	$2,428	2,845 lbs.	3,305
62C	13	2-dr. Sport Coupe-6P	$2,543	2,842 lbs.	4,797

Falcon Station Wagon (Six)

Model No.	Body/ Style No.	Body Style and Seating	Factory Price	Shipping Weight	Production Total
71A	22	4-dr. Station Wagon-6P	$2,497	3,030 lbs.	3,889

Falcon Station Wagon (V-8)

Model No.	Body/ Style No.	Body Style and Seating	Factory Price	Shipping Weight	Production Total
71A	22	4-dr. Station Wagon-6P	$2,603	3,229 lbs.	1,714

Falcon Deluxe Station Wagon (Six)

Model No.	Body/ Style No.	Body Style and Seating	Factory Price	Shipping Weight	Production Total
71B	24	4-dr. Station Wagon-6P	$2,609	3,062 lbs.	1,691

Falcon Deluxe Station Wagon (V-8)

Model No.	Body/ Style No.	Body Style and Seating	Factory Price	Shipping Weight	Production Total
71B	24	4-dr. Station Wagon-6P	$2,714	3,261 lbs.	2,861

Fairlane (Six)

Model No.	Body/ Style No.	Body Style and Seating	Factory Price	Shipping Weight	Production Total
62A	31	2-dr. Sedan-6P	$2,297	2,747 lbs.	6,948
54A	32	4-dr. Sedan-6P	$2,339	2,782 lbs.	9,461

Fairlane (V-8)

Model No.	Body/ Style No.	Body Style and Seating	Factory Price	Shipping Weight	Production Total
62A	31	2-dr. Sedan-6P	$2,402	2,916 lbs.	3,680
54A	32	4-dr. Sedan-6P	$2,445	2,951 lbs.	10,279

Fairlane 500 (Six)

Model No.	Body/ Style No.	Body Style and Seating	Factory Price	Shipping Weight	Production Total
62B	41	2-dr. Sedan-6P	$2,377	2,755 lbs.	2,934
54B	42	4-dr. Sedan-6P	$2,417	2,802 lbs.	7,149
63B	43	2-dr. Hardtop-6P	$2,439	2,842 lbs.	4,879
76B	45	2-dr. Convertible-6P	$2,664	3,159 lbs.	454

Fairlane 500 (V-8)

Model No.	Body/ Style No.	Body Style and Seating	Factory Price	Shipping Weight	Production Total
62B	41	2-dr. Sedan-6P	$2,482	2,924 lbs.	5,539
54B	42	4-dr. Sedan-6P	$2,522	2,971 lbs.	44,403
63B	43	2-dr. Hardtop-6P	$2,545	3,011 lbs.	65,256
76B	45	2-dr. Convertible-6P	$2,770	3,328 lbs.	4,974

Fairlane 500/XL (Six)

Model No.	Body/ Style No.	Body Style and Seating	Factory Price	Shipping Weight	Production Total
63C	47	2-dr. Hardtop-6P	$2,619	2,870 lbs.	330
76C	46	2-dr. Convertible-6P	$2,843	3,187 lbs.	49

Fairlane 500/XL (V-8)

Model No.	Body/ Style No.	Body Style and Seating	Factory Price	Shipping Weight	Production Total
63C	47	2-dr. Hardtop-6P	$2,724	3,039 lbs.	14,541
76C	46	2-dr. Convertible-6P	$3,064	3,356 lbs.	1,894

Fairlane GT (V-8)

Model No.	Body/ Style No.	Body Style and Seating	Factory Price	Shipping Weight	Production Total
63D	40	2-dr. Hardtop-6P	$2,839	3,301 lbs.	18,670
76D	44	2-dr. Convertible-6P	$3,064	3,607 lbs.	2,117

Fairlane Station Wagon (Six)

Model No.	Body/ Style No.	Body Style and Seating	Factory Price	Shipping Weight	Production Total
71D	38	4-dr. Station Wagon-6P	$2,643	3,198 lbs.	3,057

Fairlane Station Wagon (V-8)

Model No.	Body/ Style No.	Body Style and Seating	Factory Price	Shipping Weight	Production Total
71D	38	4-dr. Station Wagon-6P	$2,748	3,367 lbs.	7,824

Fairlane Squire Wagon (Six)

Model No.	Body/ Style No.	Body Style and Seating	Factory Price	Shipping Weight	Production Total
71E	48	4-dr. Station Wagon-6P	$2,902	3,217 lbs.	425

1967 Ford Fairlane 500XL GTA two-door hardtop (OCW)

1967 Ford Fairlane 500XL GTA two-door convertible (OCW)

Fairlane Squire Wagon (V-8)

71E	48	4-dr. Station Wagon-6P	$3,007	3,386 lbs.	7,923

Ford Custom (Six)

62E	53	2-dr. Sedan-6P	$2,441	3,411 lbs.	7,982
54E	54	4-dr. Sedan-6P	$2,496	3,469 lbs.	13,284

Ford Custom (V-8)

62E	53	2-dr. Sedan-6P	$2,548	3,449 lbs.	10,125
54E	54	4-dr. Sedan-6P	$2,602	3,507 lbs.	28,133

Custom 500 (Six)

62B	51	2-dr. Sedan-6P	$2,553	3,413 lbs.	5,070
54B	52	4-dr. Sedan-6P	$2,595	3,471 lbs.	9,033

Custom 500 (V-8)

62B	51	2-dr. Sedan-6P	$2,659	3,451 lbs.	13,076
54B	52	4-dr. Sedan-6P	$2,701	3,509 lbs.	74,227

Galaxie 500 (Six)

54A	62	4-dr. Sedan-6P	$2,732	3,481 lbs.	2,038
63B	66	2-dr. Fastback-6P	$2,755	3,484 lbs.	2,814
57B	64	4-dr. Hardtop-6P	$2,808	3,552 lbs.	295
76A	65	2-dr. Convertible-6P	$3,003	3,666 lbs.	209

Galaxie 500 (V-8)

54A	62	4-dr. Sedan-6P	$2,838	3,519 lbs.	128,025
63B	66	2-dr. Fastback-6P	$2,861	3,522 lbs.	194,574
57B	64	4-dr. Hardtop-6P	$2,914	3,590 lbs.	56,792
76A	65	2-dr. Convertible-6P	$3,110	3,704 lbs.	18,859

Galaxie 500/XL (V-8)

63C	68	2-dr. Fastback-6P	$3,243	3,594 lbs.	18,174
76B	69	2-dr. Convertible-6P	$3,493	3,794 lbs.	5,161

LTD (V-8)

54B	62	4-dr. Sedan-6P	$3,298	3,562 lbs.	12,491
63F	67	2-dr. Fastback-6P	$3,362	3,632 lbs.	46,036
57F	60	4-dr. Hardtop-6P	$3,369	3,676 lbs.	51,978

Ranch Wagon (Six)

71D	71	4-dr. Station Wagon-6P	$2,836	3,911 lbs.	2,681

Ranch Wagon (V-8)

71D	72	4-dr. Station Wagon-6P	$2,943	3,949 lbs.	21,251

Custom Ranch Wagon (Six)

71C	72	4-dr. Station Wagon-6P	$2,935	3,924 lbs.	523
71B	74	4-dr. Station Wagon-9P	$3,061	4,004 lbs.	445

Custom Ranch Wagon (V-8)

71C	72	4-dr. Station Wagon-6P	$3,042	3,962 lbs.	50,295
71B	74	4-dr. Station Wagon-9P	$3,168	4,042 lbs.	33,932

Country Squire Station Wagon (Six)

71E	76	4-dr. Station Wagon-6P	$3,234	3,971 lbs.	74
71A	78	4-dr. Station Wagon-9P	$3,359	4,011 lbs.	61

Country Squire Station Wagon (V-8)

71E	76	4-dr. Station Wagon-6P	$3,340	4,009 lbs.	25,526
71A	78	4-dr. Station Wagon-9P	$3,466	4,049 lbs.	43,963

Engines:

Falcon and Fairlane Six: Overhead valve. Cast-iron block. Displacement: 170 cid. B & S: 3.50 x 2.94 in. Compression ratio: 9.1:1. Brake hp: 105 at 4400 rpm. Carburetor: Holley one-barrel. Seven main bearings. Code 4.

1967 Ford Galaxie 500XL two-door fastback hardtop (OCW)

Falcon and Fairlane Six: Overhead valve. Cast-iron block. Displacement: 200 cid. B & S: 3.68 x 3.13 in. Compression ratio: 9.2:1. Brake hp: 120 at 4400 rpm. Carburetor: Holley one-barrel. Seven main bearings. Code U.

Ford Six: Overhead valve. Cast-iron block. Displacement: 240 cid. B & S: 4.00 x 3.18 in. Compression ratio: 9.2:1. Brake hp: 150 at 4000 rpm. Carburetor: Holley one-barrel. Seven main bearings. Code V (Police code B and taxi code E).

Challenger 289 V-8: Overhead valve. Cast-iron block. Displacement: 289 cid. B & S: 4.00 x 2.87 in. Compression ratio: 9.30:1. Brake hp: 200 at 4400 rpm. Torque: 282 lbs.-ft. at 2400 rpm. Five main bearings. Hydraulic valve lifters. Carburetor: Two-barrel. Cooling system capacity: 15 qt. with heater. Crankcase capacity: 4 qt. (add 1 qt. with new oil filter). Code C.

Challenger 289 Four-Barrel V-8: Overhead valve. Cast-iron block. Displacement: 289 cid. B & S: 4.00 x 2.87 in. Compression ratio: 10.0:1. Brake hp: 225 at 4800 rpm. Torque: 305 lbs.-ft. at 3200 rpm. Five main bearings. Hydraulic valve lifters. Carburetor: Four-barrel. Cooling system capacity: 15 qt. with heater. Crankcase capacity: 4 qt. (add 1 qt. with new oil filter). Code A.

Challenger 289 Four-Barrel V-8: Overhead valve. Cast-iron block. Displacement: 289 cid. B & S: 4.00 x 2.87 in. Compression ratio: 10.5:1. Brake hp: 271 at 6000 rpm. Torque: 312 lbs.-ft. at 3400 rpm. Five main bearings. Solid valve lifters. Carburetor: Four-barrel. Cooling system capacity: 15 qt. with heater. Crankcase capacity: 4 qt. (add 1 qt. with new oil filter). Code K.

Thunderbird 390 V-8 (Optional in full-size Fords): Overhead valve. Cast-iron block. Displacement: 390 cid. B & S: 4.05 x 3.78 in. Compression ratio: 9.5:1. Brake hp: 275 at 4400 rpm. Torque: 405 lbs.-ft. at 2600 rpm. Five main bearings. Hydraulic valve lifters. Carburetor: Two-barrel. Cooling system capacity: 20.5 qt. with heater. Crankcase capacity: 4 qt. (add 1 qt. with new oil filter). Code Y.

Thunderbird 390 Four-Barrel V-8 (Optional in full-size Fords): Overhead valve. Cast-iron block. Displacement: 390 cid. B & S: 4.05 x 3.78 in. Compression ratio: 10.5:1. Brake hp: 315 at 4600 rpm. Torque: 427 lbs-ft. at 2800 rpm. Five main bearings. Hydraulic valve lifters. Carburetor: Four-barrel. Cooling system capacity: 20.5 qt. with heater. Crankcase capacity: 4 qt. (add 1 qt. with new oil filter). Dual exhausts. Code Z.

Optional Fairlane GT 390 V-8: Overhead valve. Cast-iron block. Displacement: 390 cid. B & S: 4.05 x 3.78 in. Compression ratio: 11.0:1. Brake hp: 335 at 4800 rpm. Torque: 427 lbs.-ft. at 3200 rpm. Five main bearings. Hydraulic valve lifters. Carburetor: Holley four-barrel. Cooling system capacity: 20.5 qt. with heater. Crankcase capacity: 4 qt. (add 1 qt. with new oil filter). Dual exhausts. Code S.

Thunderbird Special V-8: Overhead valve. Cast-iron block. Displacement: 428 cid. B & S: 4.13 x 3.98 in. Compression ratio: 10.50:1. Brake hp: 345 at 4600 rpm. Torque: 462 lbs.-ft. at 2800 rpm. Five main bearings. Hydraulic valve lifters. Carburetor: Four-barrel. Cooling system capacity: 20.5 qt. with heater. Crankcase capacity: 4 qt. (add 1 qt. with new oil filter). Dual exhausts. Code Q.

Police Interceptor V-8: Overhead valve. Cast-iron block. Displacement: 428 cid. B & S: 4.13 x 3.98 in. Compression ratio: 10.50:1. Brake hp: 360 at 5400 rpm. Torque: 459 lbs.-ft. at 3200 rpm. Five main bearings. Solid valve lifters. Carburetor: Holley four-barrel. Cooling system capacity: 20.5 qt. with heater. Crankcase capacity: 4 qt. (add 1 qt. with new oil filter). Dual exhausts. Code P.

Thunderbird High-Performance V-8: Overhead valve. Cast-iron block. Displacement: 427 cid. B & S: 4.23 x 3.78 in. Compression ratio: 11.00:1. Brake hp: 410 at 5600 rpm. Torque: 476 lbs.-ft. at 3400 rpm. Five main bearings. Solid valve lifters. Carburetor: Holley four-barrel. Cooling system capacity: 19.5 qt. with heater. Crankcase capacity: 5 qt. (add 1 qt. with new oil filter). Dual exhausts. Code W.

Thunderbird Super-High-Performance V-8: Overhead valve. Cast-iron block. Displacement: 427 cid. B & S: 4.23 x 3.78 in. Compression ratio: 11.50:1. Brake hp: 425 at 6000 rpm. Torque: 480 lbs.-ft. at 3700 rpm. Five main bearings. Solid valve lifters. Carburetor: Two Holley four-barrel. Cooling system capacity: 19.5 qt. with heater. Crankcase capacity: 5 qt. (add 1 qt. with new oil filter). Dual exhausts. Code R.

"SOHC 427" 4V V-8: Overhead valve. Cast-iron block. Hemispherical combustion chambers with overhead valves and overhead camshafts for each engine bank. Displacement: 427 cid. B & S: 4.23 x 3.78 in. Compression ratio: 12.10:1. Brake hp: 616 at 7000 rpm. Five main bearings. Carburetor: Holley four-barrel. Cooling system capacity: 20.5 qt. with heater. Crankcase capacity: 5 qt. (add 1 qt. with new oil filter). Dual exhausts. Code L. (This engine was available only "over the counter" for $2,500.)

"SOHC 427" 4V V-8: Overhead valve. Cast-iron block. Hemispherical combustion chambers with overhead valves and overhead camshafts for each engine bank. Displacement: 427 cid. B & S: 4.23 x 3.78 in.

1967 Ford Galaxie 500XL two-door convertible (OCW)

1967 Ford LTD two-door fastback hardtop (OCW)

Compression ratio: 12.10:1. Brake hp: 657 at 7500 rpm. Five main bearings. Hydraulic valve lifters. Carburetor: Two Holley four-barrel. Cooling system capacity: 20.5 qt. with heater. Crankcase capacity: 5 qt. (add 1 qt. with new oil filter). Dual exhausts. Code M.

Note: A tunnel-port 427 was available as an over-the-counter kit. It included a special tunnel-port intake manifold and special cylinder heads.

Chassis:

Falcon: Wheelbase: 110.9 in. and 113 in., station wagons. Overall length: 184.3 in. and 197 in., station wagons. Tires: 6.50 x 13 four-ply tubeless blackwall, 7.35 x 14 four-ply tubeless blackwall, Sport Coupe and 7.75 x 14 four-ply tubeless blackwall, station wagons.

Fairlane: Wheelbase: 116 in. and 113 in., station wagons. Overall length: 197 in. and 199.8 in., station wagons. Tires: 6.95 x 14 four-ply tubeless blackwall and 7.15 x 14 four-ply tubeless blackwall, hardtops and station wagons.

Ford: Wheelbase: 119 in. Overall length: 213 in. and 213.9 in., station wagons. Tires: 7.75 x 15 four-ply tubeless blackwall, sedans, 8.15 x 15 four-ply tubeless blackwall, hardtops and 8.45 x 15 four-ply tubeless blackwall, station wagons.

Options:

Falcon: SelectAire air conditioner with V-8 and radio required and tinted glass ($356.09). 42-amp alternator ($10.42). 55-amp alternator ($29.56). High-ratio axle ($2.63). Heavy-duty 55-amp battery ($7.44). Bright window frames on Futura station wagon ($25.91). Courtesy light group including ash tray light, glove box light, trunk or cargo area light and rear door courtesy lamp switches ($14.49, standard on Falcon Sport Coupe). Limited-slip differential ($37.20). Dual-Action tailgate, station wagon only ($45.39). Closed crankcase emission system, exhaust ECS required ($5.19). Exhaust emission control system, not available with 170-cid six teamed with air conditioning ($45.45). Accent stripes and quarter panel peak moldings in standard models ($19.06). Extra-cooling package for Falcon six ($7.44, not available with air conditioning). Extra-cooling package for Falcon V-8 ($10.47, not available with air conditioning). Windshield with tinted band ($30.73). Tinted windshield glass ($21.09). Magic-Aire heater delete, except with air conditioning ($71.85 credit). Chrome luggage rack ($44.44). Outside remote-control mirror ($9.58, standard on Sport Coupe). Right-hand rearview mirror on station wagon ($6.95). Two-tone paint, except station wagon ($18.99). Power brakes ($42.29). Power disc brakes, with V-8s ($97.21). Power steering ($84.47). Power tailgate window ($31.62). Protection group including color-keyed front and rear floor mats, license plate frames and door edge guards on two-door models ($25.28). Protection group including color-keyed front and rear floor mats, license plate frames and door edge guards on two-door models ($29.17). Push-button radio and antenna ($57.44). Deluxe seat belts with warning lights ($10.42 and standard in Sport Coupe). Front shoulder harness ($27.27). Stereosonic tape system ($128.49, but not available with air conditioning teamed with four-speed manual transmission). Heavy-duty suspension on station wagons ($23.38). Cruise-O-Matic Select-Shift automatic transmission with six-cylinder engine ($168.47). Cruise-O-Matic Select-Shift automatic transmission with V-8 engine ($186.80). Four-speed manual transmission with V-8 ($184.02, except not in station wagons). Three-speed manual transmission with 200-cid six-cylinder engine ($32.44, but standard in station wagons). Vinyl roof for Futura models ($74.19). Vinyl trim for Futura models ($24.47, but standard in Sport Coupe and station wagons). Full wheel covers ($21.34, but standard in Sports Coupe). Standard tire equipment was five 6.95 x 14 4-ply-rated black sidewall tires on all models except Sport Coupe and station wagons. Added charge for 6.95 x 14 4-ply-rated whitewalls was $32.47. Added charge for 7.35 x 14 4-ply-rated blackwalls was $14.23. Added charge for 7.35 x 14 4-ply-rated whitewalls was $50.48. Standard tire equipment on Sports Coupe was 7.35 x 14 4-ply-rated blackwall. Added charge for whitewalls was $36.35. Standard tire equipment was five 7.7 x 14 4-ply-rated black sidewall tires on all station wagons. Added charge for 7.75 x 14 4-ply-rated whitewalls was $36.34. Added charge for 7.75 x 14 8-ply-rated blackwalls was $33.45 Added charge for 7.75 x 14 8-ply-rated whitewalls was $69.67. Five 7.35 x 14 (185R) radial tires in blackwall and whitewall styles were a limited-production option, but prices were not available when source information was published.

Ford and Fairlane: Single body side accent stripe on hardtops and convertibles except Fairlanes ($13.90). Body side accent stripe on Fairlane 500, Fairlane 500/XL and Fairlane GT, except station wagons ($13.90). SelectAire air conditioner with V-8 and radio required and tinted glass recommended ($356.09). 42-amp alternator ($10.42, but not available with air conditioner). 55-amp alternator ($21.09, standard with air conditioner, but not available on six with power steering). High-ratio axle ($2.63). Heavy-duty battery ($7.44, but standard with 427- and 428-cid engines). Center console for GT models ($47.92). Limited-slip differential ($41.60 on all except Fairlane but not optional with 427-cid V-8s). Limited-slip differential on Fairlanes ($37.20). Closed crankcase emission system, exhaust ECS required ($5.19). Exhaust emission control system, all models where mandatory ($45.45). Electric clock ($15.59, but standard in Fairlane, Fairlane XL, Fairlane GT, Ford LTD and Ford Squire). 390-cid 320-hp four-barrel V-8 over 289-cid 200-hp V-8 in Fairlane ($158.08 and extra-cost transmission require). 390-cid 270-hp two-barrel V-8 in all ($78.25). 390-cid 31`5-hp four-barrel V-8 in all except Fairlane ($158.08 and extra-cost transmission required). 428-cid 345-hp four-barrel V-8 in all except Fairlane and standard with 7-Litre package ($975.09). 427-cid 410-hp four-barrel V-8 including transistorized ignition, heavy-duty battery, heavy-duty suspension, extra-cooling package, four-speed manual transmission, 8.15 x 15 black nylon tires in all except Fairlane and cars with 7-Litre package ($975.09, not available in station wagons and 4-ply tires required at extra cost). 427-cid 410-hp four-barrel V-8 with 7-Litre Sports package only ($647.51). 427-cid 425-hp dual four-barrel V-8 in all except Fairlane and cars with 7-Litre Sports package ($975.09). 427-cid 425-hp dual four-barrel V-8 with 7-Litre Sports package only ($647.51). Tinted glass in Fairlanes ($30.73). Tinted glass in all except Fairlane ($39.45). Tinted windshield ($21.09). Manually-adjustable load-leveling system for Fords ($42.19). Automatic load-leveling system for Fords ($84.78). Chrome luggage rack for station wagons ($44.44). Adjustable luggage rack for station wagons, except Fairlane ($63.08). Luxury trim package including electric clock, Comfort Stream ventilation and console control panel for Ford XL models ($167.11). Right-hand outside rearview mirror for all station wagons ($6.95). Remote-control left-hand outside rearview mirror ($9.58, but standard on GT). Magic-Aire heater delete, not available with air conditioning, Comfort Stream ventilation option or LTD model ($73.51 credit). Tutone paint for Fairlane and Fairlane 500 two- and four-door sedans and all Fords except convertible or Country Squire ($21.54). Power brakes for all cars except those with 427-cid V-8 ($42.49, but standard in station wagons with dual facing rear seats). Full-width six-way power seat for cars without four-speed manual transmission ($94.75, but not available in Fairlane). Six-way power driver's bucket seat ($84.25, but not available in Fairlane). Driver-only six-way power LTD Twin Comfort Lounge seat, except Fairlane ($84.25). Driver-and-passenger six-way power LTD Twin Comfort Lounge seat, except Fairlanes ($168.40). Power disc brakes, except in station wagons with dual facing rear seats ($97.21). Power disc brakes in station wagons with dual facing rear seats ($54.87). Power steering in Fairlane ($84.47). Power steering in Fords ($94.95). Power tailgate window in Fairlane wagons and Ford Ranch Wagon and Country Sedan ($54.87). Power top on Fairlane convertible ($52.95). Power windows in Galaxie, Galaxie 500, Galaxie 500XL, LTD, Country Squire and Country Sedan with deluxe trim ($99.94). Front push-button power radio antenna for Fairlane ($57.46). Front push-button power radio antenna for Ford, rear speaker required on Galaxie XL and LTD without stereosonic ($57.51). Front power antenna for AM/FM radio in Fords ($133.65 with rear speaker required in Galaxie XL and LTD without stereo). Rear right radio antenna, except Fairlanes and station wagons ($9.50). Rear speaker, except Fairlanes or wagons ($13.22). Deluxe seat belts with warning light ($10.42 and standard on GT). Reclining passenger seat with headrest for Ford Galaxie 500/XL ($44.15). Third facing rear seat for Fairlane station wagons ($29.27). Comfort Lounge seat for Ford LTD models ($116.59). Front shoulder harness ($27.27). Automatic speed control for Fords with V-8s and Cruise-O-Matic ($71.30). Deluxe woodgrain steering wheel for Fairlane ($31.52). Stereosonic tape system for Ford, AM radio required ($128.49). Stereosonic tape for Fairlanes, except cars with four-speed transmission and air conditioning combined ($128.49). Heavy-duty suspension for Fairlane six ($9.58). Heavy-duty suspension for Fairlane V-8 ($13.02, but standard with GT or 390-cid four-barrel V-8). Extra heavy-duty suspension on Ford station wagons ($7.27). Soft Ride suspension on Fords ($23.28, but standard in station wagons with 427-cid V-8). High-speed handling

1967 Ford four-door Country Squire Wagon (OCW)

1967 Ford LTD four-door formal hardtop (OCW)

suspension in Fords, except station wagons ($30.64, but standard in 7 Litre). Tachometer in Fairlanes ($47.92). Cruise-O-Matic transmission with six ($188.18). Cruise-O-Matic transmission with 289-cid V-8 ($197.89, but standard in Galaxie XL and LTD). Cruise-O-Matic transmission with 390-cid/428-cid V-8, in Galaxie XL or LTD only ($34.63). Cruise-O-Matic transmission with 390-cid/428-cid V-8, except in Galaxie XL or LTD ($220.17). Heavy-duty three-speed manual transmission, required with 390-cid four-barrel V-8 ($47.92). Four-speed manual transmission in Fairlane V-8 and other cars with big-block V-8s except Galaxie XL and LTD ($184.62, but not available in station wagons.) Overdrive in Fairlane with 289-cid two-barrel V-8 and other models with 240-cid and 289-cid engines ($116.59). Vinyl roof on four-door sedan and four-door hardtop, except Fairlane ($83.41, but standard on LTDs). Vinyl trim in Galaxie 500 and Fairlane 500 hardtops and sedans ($24.47, but standard in all station wagons). Luxury vinyl trim in LTDs ($24.47). Comfort Stream ventilation system except in Fairlane or with air conditioning ($40.02, but standard in Ford XL and LTD with luxury trim). Deluxe wheel covers on all Fairlanes except XL and Squire ($40.76). Deluxe wheel covers on Fairlane XL and Squire ($19.48). Full wheel covers on all except Galaxie 500/XL, Ford XL, LTD and Squire ($21.34). Styled steel wheel covers, on all Fairlanes except XL, GT and Squire ($56.98). Styled steel wheel covers, on LTD, Squire, Ford XL and with exterior décor group ($35.70). Styled steel 14-inch wheels on all Fairlanes except XL, GT and Squire ($115.11). Styled steel 14-inch wheels on Fairlane XL and Squire ($93.84). Styled steel 14-inch wheels on Fairlane GT ($74.36). Exterior décor group including bright window frames and full wheel covers for Ford Custom, Custom 500 and Ranch Wagon with whitewall tires ($51.82). Protection Group including front and rear floor mats, license plate frames and door edge guards for two-door models ($25.28); for four-door models ($29.17). Courtesy light group including glove box light, ash tray light, trunk light or cargo area light and rear door courtesy switches for Galaxie 500 two-door hardtop and convertible, Ford XL and LTD with parking brake signal and swivel dome lamp switch ($5.09); for all other models except Fairlane ($22.54); for Fairlane with map light ($14.49). Deluxe trim group including Squire-type trim and electric clock for Country Sedans ($108.58). Extra-cooling package for Fairlanes except GT with the 390-cid V-8 ($25.25); for Fairlane GT ($13.58, but standard with air conditioning and the 427-cid engine). Extra-cooling package for all six-cylinder ($9.10); for Fairlane with 289-cid V-8 and Ford V-8 ($10.47). Trailer towing package for Fords except 7-Litre and station wagons, requires 390-cid V-8 with Cruise-O-Matic or 428-cid V-8 ($30.93). Convenience Control Panel includes speed-actuated power door locks, door ajar light, low fuel light, parking brake light and seat belt warning lights on Ford XL ($51.82); on two-door models except Fairlanes and XL ($64.77); on four-door models except Fairlanes ($84.25). 7-Litre Sports Package includes 428-cid V-8, Select Shift Cruise-O-Matic, power disc brakes, extra-heavy-duty suspension, deluxe woodgrain steering wheel, 3.25:1 rear axle ratio, G70-15 whitewall Wide-Oval tires and four-speed manual transmission as a no-cost option ($515.86). Five 7.35 x 14 4-ply-rated Rayon blackwall tires were standard on all convertibles except GTs and all sedans, coupes and hardtops except GTs and 7.35 x 14 4-ply-rated whitewalls were $34.45 additional; 7.75 x 14 4-ply-rated blackwalls were $13.83 additional; 7.75 x 14 4-ply-rated whitewalls were $48.35 additional and F70-14 whitewall Wide-Oval tires were $83.12 additional. Five 7.75 x 14 4-ply-rated Rayon blackwall tires were standard on all station wagons with the 200-cid six or 289-cid V-8 and all convertibles, except GTs, with the 390-cid V-8 and 7.75 x 14 4-ply-rated whitewalls were $34.52 additional; 7.75 x 14 8-ply-rated blackwalls were $33.45 additional on station wagons only; 7.75 x 14 8-ply-rated whitewalls were $68.00 additional on station wagons only and F70-14 whitewall Wide-Oval tires were $82.98 additional on all except station wagons. On all station wagons with the 390-cid V-8 7.75 x 14 8-ply-rated whitewall tires were available for $34.55 extra. Five 7.75 x 14 4-ply-rated Rayon blackwall tires were standard on all Ford Custom, Custom 500 and Galaxie 500 four-door sedans with the standard six or V-8 and 7.75 x 14 4-ply-rated whitewalls were $35.47 additional; 8.15 x 14 4-ply-rated blackwalls were $15.49 additional; 8.15 x 14 4-ply-rated whitewalls were $51,77 additional; 8.45 x 14 4-ply-rated blackwalls were $31.08 additional and 8.45 x 14 4-ply-rated whitewalls were $67.48 additional. Five 7.75 x 14 4-ply-rated Rayon blackwall tires were standard on all Ford Custom, Custom 500 and Galaxie 500 four-door sedans with

the standard six or V-8 and 8.15 x 15 or 205 R15 blackwall or whitewall radials were additional; 8.45 x 15 or 215 R15 blackwall or whitewall radials were additional. (The prices for radial tire options were mot available at the time our source material was published.) Five 8.15 x 15 4-ply-rated Rayon blackwall tires were standard on all Ford Custom, Custom 500 and Galaxie 500 four-door sedans with 390-cid or 428-cid V-8s and 8.15 x 15 4-ply-rated whitewalls were $36.37 additional; 8.45 x 15 4-ply-rated blackwalls were $15.59 additional and 8.45 x 14 4-ply-rated whitewalls were $51.99 additional. Five 7.75 x 14 4-ply-rated Rayon blackwall tires were standard on all Ford Custom, Custom 500 and Galaxie 500 four-door sedans with the standard six or V-8 and 8.15 x 15 or 205 R15 blackwall or whitewall radials were additional; 8.45 x 15 or 215 R15 blackwall or whitewall radials were additional. Note: The prices for radial tire options were mot available at the time our source material was published. Five 8.15 x 15 4-ply-rated Rayon blackwall tires were standard on all Fords with 427-cid V-8s and 8.15 x 15 4-ply-rated Nylon blackwalls were $46.53 additional; 8.15 x 15 4-ply-rated Nylon whitewalls were $82.83 additional; 8.45 x 15 4-ply-rated Nylon blackwalls were $62.22 additional and 8.45 x 14 4-ply-rated Nylon whitewalls were $98.52 additional. On Ford station wagons that came standard with five 8.45 x 15 4-ply-rated Rayon blackwall tires comparable whitewalls were $36.40. These wagons were also available with 215 R15 radial-ply tires in either black sidewall or white sidewall styles. (The prices for radial tire options were mot available at the time our source material was published.)

History:

The 1967 Fords were introduced Sept. 30, 1966. The grand total of assemblies for the 1967 model year was 1,742,311 units. This included 877,128 Fords, 233,688 Fairlanes and 76,500 Falcons. Calendar-year production for all the above lines peaked at 240,712 units. As far as sales and production it was a good year for America's number two automaker. However, vice-president and general manager M.S. McLaughlin did have other things to deal with, such as a 57-day United Auto Worker's strike. It was the longest lasting labor dispute in Ford history and culminated in a three-year contract agreement that included unprecedented wage and benefits packages.

1968 Ford

Falcon — (Six and V-8): The 1968 Falcons again used the same body shell as the previous two years, with only minor trim changes. The most noticeable change in the Falcon was that the taillights were square, instead of the round type used on the car since its introduction in 1960. The grille was a stamped aluminum piece, with a rectangular mesh pattern. The grille was divided by the Falcon crest in the center. The simulated exhaust port, used on the front fender of the 1967 Falcons, was not continued into the year 1968. Standard equipment included a chrome windshield molding, a chrome rear window molding, rain gutter moldings, armrests on the front doors only, a steering wheel horn button, a 170-cid 100-hp six-cylinder engine, a heater and defroster and 6.95 x 14 four-ply tires. The Falcon name, in script, appeared on the rear fenders, just ahead of the taillights and in block letters, across the vertical section of the trunk lid.

Falcon Futura — (Six and V-8): The Futura series was the top trim level for 1968 and included all the standard Falcon features, plus the 200-cid 120-hp six-cylinder engine, a cigarette lighter, front and rear door armrests, front and rear door ashtrays, a deluxe steering wheel with a chrome horn ring, nylon carpeting, special Futura moldings, Futura trim, Futura emblems, Futura nameplates and chrome side window frames. In addition, the Falcon Futura Sports Coupe was a sporty version of the two-door sedan that featured front bucket seats, special Sports Coupe nameplates, a map light, an ash tray, a glove box light, a trunk light, side accent stripes, a driver's side remote-control outside rearview mirror, deluxe seat belts, 7.35 x 14 tires and special wheel covers. The Futura convertible also included front bucket seats.

1968 Ford Falcon Futura two-door Sports Coupe (OCW)

1968 Ford Falcon Futura four-door Sports Coupe (OCW)

Falcon Station Wagon — (Six and V-8): Only four-door station wagons were available in the Falcon lineup this year. The Standard wagon came in both body styles. The standard equipment list was similar to that of the base Falcon. The more Deluxe station wagon had richer trim. Futura wagons also had all-vinyl interior trim. A 200-cid 115-hp six-cylinder engine was used in station wagons, which also had 7.75 x 14 four-ply tires and vinyl seat trim.

Fairlane — (Six and V-8): The Fairlane line was the one chosen for major restyling for the new year. It was undoubtedly one of the nicest looking Fairlanes ever to come out of Detroit. It had a full-width grille, containing horizontally mounted quad headlights, and smooth sides with a single horizontal feature line running front to rear. The taillights were vertically situated rectangular units with a centrally located back-up light. The word Ford was spaced evenly across the trunk lid in block letters. Fairlane was Ford's base trim level for 1968 mid-size models and included a 200-cid 115-hp six-cylinder engine or a 302-cid 210-hp V-8, chrome windshield moldings, chrome rear window moldings; chrome rain gutters, chrome side window frames; a chrome horn ring; front and rear armrests; a cigarette lighter; vinyl-coated rubber floor mats, 7.35 x 14 4-ply-rated tires and the Fairlane name, in script, on the side of the rear fender. The Ford name was spelled out, in block letters, across the front of the hood and across the vertical section of the trunk lid. The top-line Fairlane models for 1968 were called Torinos and Torino GTs, with the Fairlane 500 being demoted to intermediate trim level.

Fairlane 500 — (Six and V-8): The Fairlane 500 was the intermediate trim level for 1968 and included all the Fairlane features, plus special Fairlane 500 trim and moldings, color-keyed carpeting front and rear and a choice of four nylon and vinyl upholsteries. Also included was an aluminum dividing bar, in the center of the vertical portion of the trunk lid, and a horizontal dividing bar, in the center of the grille. The Fairlane 500 name, in script, appeared on the rear fender, just ahead of the taillights.

Fairlane Torino — (Six and V-8): The Fairlane Torino included all features found on Fairlane 500s, plus wheel covers, an electric clock and 7.35 x 14 four-ply-rated black sidewall tires.

Fairlane Torino GT — (V-8): The Fairlane Torino GT included all Fairlane Torino features, plus a vinyl-trimmed bench seat, a GT Handling suspension, Argent Silver styled wheels, chrome wheel trim rings, an electric clock, F70 x 14 Wide-Oval white sidewall tires, GT stripes, a gray-finished grille, GT nameplates and a 302-cid V-8. Power brakes were also a required add-on if the 390-cid four-barrel V-8 was ordered.

Fairlane /Torino Station Wagon — (Six and V-8): The Fairlane station wagons came in a four-door Fairlane Wagon, a four-door Fairlane 500 Wagon and a four-door Fairlane Torino Squire model. Fairlane Wagon equipment started with all of the Fairlane sedan features and then included these variations: the Ford Magic Doorgate, foam seat cushions, a heater-and-defroster, a cigar lighter, ash trays, courtesy lighting and a choice of three all-vinyl trims. The Fairlane 500 wagon also had carpeting, an electric clock, a locking stowage compartment and a choice of four pleated all-vinyl trims. The Fairlane Torino Squire wagon also had simulated wood body trim and as power door gate window.

Ford Custom — (Six and V-8): The 1968 "big" Fords were basically 1967 body shells with updated front ends. The two years look completely different, to be sure, but there is little that changed behind the windshield. The new grille work was less protruding than the 1967 version and offered hidden headlights on the upper lines. It was a honeycomb grille with a single, centrally located vertical dividing bar.

The Ford name, in block letters, and the Ford crest, in a small emblem on the driver's side headlight door, appeared. The rooflines were a little more formal than the previous year and the taillights, although retaining the same shape, were divided horizontally (rather than vertically) by the back-up lights. The large, padded hub used on the steering wheels of all 1967 Fords, was replaced by a more conventional pad covering the entire center spoke. More federally-mandated safety regulations appeared in the form of front and rear fender marker lights. Power-wise, the mighty 427-cid V-8 engine was detuned to 390 hp by limiting carburetion to a single four-barrel and replacing the wild solid-lifter camshaft with a more timid hydraulic rider cam. At midyear, the 427 was discontinued and replaced by the equally famous and powerful Cobra Jet 428 and Super Cobra Jet 428 V-8s. These engines dominated the Super Stock classes at the drag races in 1968, when installed in the light Mustang bodies. The Custom series was the base trim level Ford for 1968 and included chrome windshield moldings, chrome rear window moldings, a chrome horn ring, nylon carpeting, a heater and defroster, body side moldings, the Custom name in script on the rear fenders, the 240-cid six or 302-cid V-8 and 7.75 X 15 four-ply-rated tires. The Ford name, in block letters, appeared across the front of the hood.

Custom 500 — (Six and V-8): The Custom 500 was the upper trim level of the base line Custom series and included all the Custom trim plus special Custom 500 exterior trim and choice of several richer interior upholstery combinations.

Galaxie 500 — (Six and V-8): The Galaxie 500 was the intermediate trim level for 1968 and included all the Custom series trim plus stamped aluminum lower body side moldings, chrome side window moldings, simulated woodgrain appliques on the instrument panel and inner door panels, an electric clock, a trunk light, a glove box light, bright seat side shields and a stamped aluminum trim panel on the vertical section of the trunk lid. The name, Galaxie 500, in block letters, was located on the rear fenders and the Ford crest was located on the trunk lid above the aluminum trim panel. The Galaxie 500 convertible also had a 5-ply vinyl power-operated top and all-vinyl interior trims. The four-door hardtop came with larger 8.15 x 14 four-ply-rated tires.

Ford XL — (V-8): The Ford XL (the Galaxie 500/XL description was dropped) included sport trim versions of the two-door fastback and two-door convertible. New this year was a standard 150-hp six instead of a standard V-8. The 302-cid 210-hp V-8 was available as the base V-8. Other standard features of the Ford XL models included a vinyl bench seat, full wheel covers and an electric clock.

LTD — (V-8): The LTD was the top trim level full-size Ford for 1968. LTDs included all the Ford XL trim plus the 302-cid/210-hp V-8, 8.15 x 15 four-ply-rated black sidewall tires engine, full wheel covers, dual accent striping and an electric clock.

Ford Station Wagon — (Six and V-8): The Ranch Wagon was the base trim level station wagon for 1968 and had the features of the Ford Custom models, plus larger 8.45 x 15 four-ply-rated tires. Also available with Custom 500 level trimmings were the 6- and 9-passenger Ranch Wagons, the latter with dual facing rear seats. They also had the larger-size tires. Clones of those two models with fancier all-vinyl trim were included in the Galaxie 500 line. The two seating variations also came in the LTD series with Country Squire nameplates and trim. The 302-cid 210-hp V-8 was standard equipment in Country Squire wagons.

VIN (Ford):

The VIN for Fords was die-stamped on the top surface of the radiator and the front fender apron support. The first symbol indicates year: 8=1968. The second symbol identifies assembly plant, as follows: A=Atlanta, Georgia, B=Oakville, Ontario, Canada, C=Ontario, Canada, D=Dallas, Texas, E=Mahwah, New Jersey, F=Dearborn, Michigan, G=Chicago, Illinois, H=Lorain, Ohio, J=Los Angeles, California, K=Kansas City, Kansas, N=Norfolk, Virginia, P=Twin Cities, Minnesota, R=San Jose, California, S=Pilot Plant, T=Metuchen, New Jersey, U=Louisville, Kentucky, W=Wayne, Michigan, Y=Wixom, Michigan, Z=St. Louis, Mo. The third and fourth symbols identify body series 50=Custom two-door

1968 Ford Falcon four-door Futura station wagon (OCW)

sedan with bench seat, 51=Custom four-door sedan with bench seat, 52=Custom 500 two-door sedan with bench seat, 53=Custom 500 four-door sedan with bench seat, 54=Galaxie 500 four-door sedan with bench seat, 56=Galaxie 500 four-door hardtop with bench seat, 57=Galaxie 500 two-door with bench seat, 55=Galaxie 500 two-door fastback with bench seat, 58=Galaxie 500/XL two-door hardtop with bucket seats, 60=Ford XL four-door hardtop, 61=Ford XL two-door convertible, 66=LTD four-door hardtop with bench seat, 62=LTD two-door hardtop with bucket seats and formal roof, 64=LTD four-door sedan, 70=four-door six-passenger Ranch Wagon, 71=four-door six-passenger Country Sedan station wagon, 72=four-door 10-passenger Country Sedan station wagon, 73=four-door Country Squire six-passenger station wagon and 74=four-door Country Squire 10-passenger station wagon, 75=Country Squire six-passenger station wagon, 76=Country Squire 10-passenger station wagon, 30=Fairlane two-door hardtop with bench seat, 31=Fairlane four-door sedan with bench seat and formal roof, 33=Fairlane 500 two-door hardtop with bench seat and formal roof, 34=Fairlane 500 four-door sedan with bench seat, 35=Fairlane 500 two-door hardtop with bucket seats, 36=Fairlane 500 two-door convertible with bench seats, 33=Fairlane 500 two-door hardtop with bucket seats and formal roof, 35=Fairlane 500 two-door hardtop with bench seat, 36=Fair 500 convertible with bucket seats, 40=Torino two-door hardtop with bench seat and formal roof, 41=Torino four-door sedan with bench seat, 42=Torino GT two-door hardtop with bucket seats, 44=Torino GT with bucket seats and formal roof, 43=Torino GT convertible with bucket seats, 32=Fairlane four-door station wagon with bench seat, 37=Fairlane 500 four-door station wagon with bench seat, 38=Torino Squire four-door station wagon with bench seat, 10=Standard Falcon two-door club coupe with bench seat, 11-Standard Falcon four-door sedan with bench seat, 20-Falcon Futura two-door club coupe with bench seat, 21=Falcon Futura four-door sedan with bench seat, 22=Falcon Sport Coupe with bucket seats, 12=Falcon four-door station Wagon and 23=Falcon Deluxe four-door station wagon. The fifth symbol identifies engine code, as follows: B=240-cid six-cylinder police engine, C=289-cid two-barrel V-8, E=240-cid six-cylinder taxi engine, F=302-cid two-barrel V-8, J=302-cid four-barrel V-8, N=429-cid four-barrel V-8, P=428-cid four-barrel police V-8, Q-428-cid four-barrel V-8, R=428-cid dual four-barrel Cobra-Jet V-8, S=390-cid four-barrel GT V-8, T=200-cid one-barrel six-cylinder, U=170-cid one-barrel six, V=240-cid six-cylinder, W=427-cid four-barrel V-8, X=390-cid two-barrel premium-fuel V-8, Y=390-cid two-barrel V-8, Z=390-cid four-barrel V-8, 2=200-cid low-compression one-barrel six, 5=240-cid low-compression export six-cylinder, 6=302-cid two-barrel low-compression V-8, 8=428-cid four-barrel low-compression V-8. The last six digits are the unit's production number, beginning at 100001 and going up, at each of the assembly plants. Full-size Fords not built at all Ford plants.

Falcon Standard (Six)

Model No.	Body/Style No.	Body Style and Seating	Factory Price	Shipping Weight	Production Total
62A	11	2-dr. Sedan-6P	$2,252	2,680 lbs.	7,788
54A	12	4-dr. Sedan-6P	$2,301	2,714 lbs.	7,567

Falcon Standard (V-8)

62A	11	2-dr. Sedan-6P	$2,383	2,878 lbs.	466
54A	12	4-dr. Sedan-6P	$2,433	2,912 lbs.	635

Falcon Futura (Six)

62B	11	2-dr. Sedan-6P	$2,419	2,685 lbs.	1,310
54B	12	4-dr. Sedan-6P	$2,456	2,719 lbs.	2,616
62C	13	2-dr. Sport Coupe-6P	$2,541	2,713 lbs.	787

Falcon Futura (V-8)

62A	11	2-dr. Sedan-6P	$2,521	2,685 lbs.	659
54A	12	4-dr. Sedan-6P	$2,562	2,719 lbs.	1,503
62C	13	2-dr. Sport Coupe-6P	$2,647	2,713 lbs.	1,276

Falcon Station Wagon (Six)

71A	22	4-dr. Station Wagon-6P	$2,617	3,123 lbs.	2,040

1968 Ford Fairlane Torino four-door sedan (OCW)

Falcon Station Wagon (V-8)

71A	22	4-dr. Station Wagon-6P	$2,722	3,277 lbs.	1,385

Falcon Deluxe Station Wagon (Six)

71B	24	4-dr. Station Wagon-6P	$2,728	3,123 lbs.	775

Falcon Deluxe Station Wagon (V-8)

71B	24	4-dr. Station Wagon-6P	$2,833	3,277 lbs.	1,606

Fairlane (Six)

65A	31	2-dr. Hardtop-6P	$2,456	3,125 lbs.	15,753
54A	32	4-dr. Sedan-6P	$2,464	3,083 lbs.	8,828

Fairlane (V-8)

65A	31	2-dr. Hardtop-6P	$2,544	3,317 lbs.	28,930
54A	32	4-dr. Sedan-6P	$2,551	3,275 lbs.	9,318

Fairlane 500 (Bench Seats) (Six)

65B	33	2-dr. Formal Hardtop-6P	$2,591	2,983 lbs.	2,723
54B	34	4-dr. Sedan-6P	$2,543	2,927 lbs.	5,142
63B	35	2-dr. Fastback-6P	$2,566	2,969 lbs.	1,269
76B	36	2-dr. Convertible-6P	$2,822	3,129 lbs.	215

Fairlane 500 (Bucket Seats) (Six)

65B	33	2-dr. Formal Hardtop-6P	$2,701	2,983 lbs.	100
63B	35	2-dr. Fastback-6P	$2,676	2,969 lbs.	80
76B	36	2-dr. Convertible-6P	$2,932	3,129 lbs.	11

Fairlane 500 (Bench Seats) (V-8)

65B	33	2-dr. Formal Hardtop-6P	$2,679	3,175 lbs.	28,738
54B	34	4-dr. Sedan-6P	$2,611	3,119 lbs.	37,788
63B	35	2-dr. Fastback-6P	$2,653	3,161 lbs.	27,899
76B	36	2-dr. Convertible-6P	$2,910	3,321 lbs.	3,207

Fairlane 500 (Bucket Seats) (V-8)

65B	33	2-dr. Formal Hardtop-6P	$2,789	3,175 lbs.	1,721
63B	35	2-dr. Fastback-6P	$2,763	3,161 lbs.	3,204
76B	36	2-dr. Convertible-6P	$3,020	3,321 lbs.	328

Fairlane/Torino (Six)

54C	34	4-dr. Sedan-6P	$2,688	2,965 lbs.	502
65C	47	2-dr. Hardtop-6P	$2,710	3,001 lbs.	773

Fairlane/Torino (V-8)

54C	34	4-dr. Sedan-6P	$2,776	3,157 lbs.	17,460
65C	47	2-dr. Hardtop-6P	$2,798	3,193 lbs.	35,191

Fairlane/Torino GT (V-8)

63D	40	2-dr. Fastback-6P	$2,747	3,194 lbs.	23,939
65D	40	2-dr. Formal Hardtop-6P	$2,772	3,208 lbs.	74,135
76D	44	2-dr. Convertible-6P	$3,001	3,352 lbs.	5,310

Fairlane Station Wagon (Six)

71D	38	4-dr. Station Wagon-6P	$2,770	3,422 lbs.	573

Fairlane Station Wagon (V-8)

71D	38	4-dr. Station Wagon-6P	$2,858	3,614 lbs.	14,227

Fairlane 500 Station Wagon (Six)

71B	48	4-dr. Station Wagon-6P	$2,881	3,288 lbs.	2,496

Fairlane 500 Station Wagon (V-8)

71B	48	4-dr. Station Wagon-6P	$2,968	3,480 lbs.	7,694

Fairlane/Torino Station Wagon (Six)

71D	48	4-dr. Station Wagon-6P	$3,032	3,336 lbs.	325

Fairlane/Torino Station Wagon (V-8)

71D	48	4-dr. Station Wagon-6P	$3,119	3,528 lbs.	14,448

Ford Custom (Six)

62E	53	2-dr. Hardtop-6P	$2,584	3,444 lbs.	6,355
54E	54	4-dr. Sedan-6P	$2,642	3,471 lbs.	11,055

Ford Custom (V-8)

62E	53	2-dr. Hardtop-6P	$2,662	3,491 lbs.	9,272
54E	54	4-dr. Sedan-6P	$2,749	3,518 lbs.	27,356

Custom 500 (Six)

62B	51	2-dr. Hardtop-6P	$2,699	3,433 lbs.	1,497
54B	52	4-dr. Sedan-6P	$2,741	3,484 lbs.	3,353

Custom 500 (V-8)

| 62B | 51 | 2-dr. Hardtop-6P | $2,806 | 3,480 lbs. | 6,557 |
| 54B | 52 | 4-dr. Sedan-6P | $2,848 | 3,531 lbs. | 41,493 |

Galaxie 500 (Six)

54A	62	4-dr. Sedan-6P	$2,864	3,489 lbs.	1,108
63B	66	2-dr. Fastback-6P	$2,881	3,507 lbs.	770
65C	66	2-dr. Formal Hardtop-6P	$2,916	3,513 lbs.	592
57B	64	4-dr. Hardtop-6P	$2,936	3,535 lbs.	146
76A	65	2-dr. Convertible-6P	$3,108	3,652 lbs.	72

Galaxie 500 (V-8)

54A	62	4-dr. Sedan-6P	$2,971	3,536 lbs.	109,137
63B	66	2-dr. Fastback-6P	$2,988	3,554 lbs.	76,133
65C	66	2-dr. Formal Hardtop-6P	$3,022	3,560 lbs.	62,139
57B	64	4-dr. Hardtop-6P	$3,043	3,582 lbs.	52,250
76A	65	2-dr. Convertible-6P	$3,215	3,699 lbs.	11,760

Ford XL (Six)

| 63C | 68 | 2-dr. Fastback-6P | $2,985 | 3,581 lbs. | 132 |
| 76B | 69 | 2-dr. Convertible-6P | $3,214 | 3,718 lbs. | 8 |

Ford XL (V-8)

| 63C | 68 | 2-dr. Fastback-6P | $3,092 | 3,608 lbs. | 45,984 |
| 76B | 69 | 2-dr. Convertible-6P | $3,321 | 3,765 lbs. | 6,058 |

Ford LTD (V-8)

54C	62	4-dr. Sedan-6P	$3,135	3,596 lbs.	21,388
65A	67	2-dr. Fastback-6P	$3,153	3,679 lbs.	50,104
57F	60	4-dr. Hardtop-6P	$3,206	3,642 lbs.	56,924

Ranch Wagon (Six)

| 71D | 71 | 4-dr. Station Wagon-6P | $3,000 | 3,898 lbs. | 1,529 |

Ranch Wagon (V-8)

| 71D | 72 | 4-dr. Station Wagon-6P | $3,107 | 3,945 lbs. | 14,250 |

Custom Ranch Wagon (Six)

| 71H | 72 | 4-dr. Station Wagon-6P | $3,063 | 3,908 lbs. | 280 |
| 71J | 74 | 4-dr. Station Wagon-9P | $3,176 | 3,954 lbs. | 193 |

Custom Ranch Wagon (V-8)

| 71H | 72 | 4-dr. Station Wagon-6P | $3,170 | 3,955 lbs. | 15,850 |
| 71J | 74 | 4-dr. Station Wagon-9P | $3,283 | 4,001 lbs. | 11,745 |

Country Sedan (Six)

| 71B | 76 | 4-dr. Station Wagon-6P | $3,181 | 3,917 lbs. | 138 |
| 71C | 78 | 4-dr. Station Wagon-9P | $3,295 | 3,974 lbs. | 83 |

Country Sedan (V-8)

| 71B | 76 | 4-dr. Station Wagon-6P | $3,288 | 3,964 lbs. | 35,895 |
| 71C | 78 | 4-dr. Station Wagon-9P | $3,402 | 4,021 lbs. | 26,885 |

LTD Country Squire (V-8)

| 71E | 76 | 4-dr. Station Wagon-6P | $3,539 | 4,013 lbs. | 29,923 |
| 71A | 78 | 4-dr. Station Wagon-9P | $3,619 | 4,059 lbs. | 52,256 |

Engines:

Falcon (Six): Overhead valve. Cast-iron block. Displacement: 170 cid. B & S: 3.50 x 2.94 in. Compression ratio: 8.7:1. Brake hp: 100 at 4000 rpm. Torque: 158 lbs.-ft. at 2400 rpm. Carburetor: Holley one-barrel. Seven main bearings. Code U.

Falcon, Fairlane and Torino Six: Overhead valve. Cast-iron block. Displacement: 200 cid. B & S: 3.68 x 3.13 in. Compression ratio: 8.8:1. Brake hp: 115 at 3800 rpm. Torque: 190 lbs.-ft. at 2200 rpm. Carburetor: Holley one-barrel. Seven main bearings. Code T.

Ford, Fairlane and Torino Six: Overhead valve. Cast-iron block. Displacement: 240 cid. B & S: 4.00 x 3.18 in. Compression ratio: 9.20:1. Brake hp: 150 at 4000 rpm. Torque: 234 lbs.-ft. at 2200 rpm. Carburetor: Holley one-barrel. Seven main bearings. Code V (Police code B and taxi code E).

Ford, Fairlane and Torino Six: Overhead valve. Cast-iron block. Displacement: 250 cid. B & S: 3.68 x 3.91 in. Compression ratio: 8.50:1. Brake hp: 155 at 4000 rpm. Torque: 240 lbs.-ft. at 1600 rpm. Carburetor: Holley one-barrel. Seven main bearings. Code 5.

Challenger 289 V-8: Overhead valve. Cast-iron block. Displacement: 289 cid. B & S: 4.00 x 2.87 in. Compression ratio: 8.70:1. Brake hp: 195 at 4600 rpm. Torque: 288 lbs.-ft. at 2600 rpm. Five main bearings. Hydraulic valve lifters. Carburetor: Two-barrel. Cooling system capacity:

1968 Ford Fairlane Torino two-door hardtop (PH)

1968 Ford Fairlane Torino four-door Squire station wagon (OCW)

15 qt. with heater. Crankcase capacity: 4 qt. (add 1 qt. with new oil filter). Code C.

302 Two-Barrel V-8: Overhead valve. Cast-iron block. Displacement: 302 cid. B & S: 4.00 x 3.00 in. Compression ratio: 9.00:1. Brake hp: 210 at 4400 rpm. Torque: 300 lbs.-ft. at 2600 rpm. Five main bearings. Hydraulic valve lifters. Carburetor: Two-barrel. Cooling system capacity: 15 qt. with heater. Crankcase capacity: Mid-size and Mustang 4 qt. and (full-Size and Thunderbird) 5 qt. (add 1 qt. with new oil filter). Code F and Export code 6.

302 Four-Barrel V-8: Overhead valve. Cast-iron block. Displacement: 302 cid. B & S: 4.00 x 3.00 in. Compression ratio: 10.00:1. Brake hp: 230 at 4800 rpm. Torque: 310 lbs.-ft. at 2800 rpm. Five main bearings. Hydraulic valve lifters. Carburetor: Two-barrel. Cooling system capacity: 15 qt. with heater. Crankcase capacity: (Mid-size and Mustang) 4 qt. and full-size and Thunderbird 5 qt. (add 1 qt. with new oil filter). Code J.

390 Four-Barrel V-8 (Optional in Ford): Overhead valve. Cast-iron block. Displacement: 390 cid. B & S: 4.05 x 3.78 in. Compression ratio: 9.5:1. Brake hp: 265 at 4400 rpm. Torque: 390 lbs.-ft. at 2600 rpm. Five main bearings. Hydraulic valve lifters. Carburetor: Two-barrel. Cooling system capacity: 20.5 qt. with heater. Crankcase capacity: 5 qt. (add 1 qt. with new oil filter). Code Y.

390 Four-Barrel V-8 (Optional in Ford): Overhead valve. Cast-iron block. Displacement: 390 cid. B & S: 4.05 x 3.78 in. Compression ratio: 10.5:1. Brake hp: 280 at 4400 rpm. Torque: 403 lbs.-ft. at 2600 rpm. Five main bearings. Hydraulic valve lifters. Carburetor: Two-barrel. Cooling system capacity: 20.5 qt. with heater. Crankcase capacity: (Mid-size and Mustang) 4 qt. and full-size and Thunderbird, 5 qt. (add 1 qt. with new oil filter). Dual exhausts. Code X.

390 Four-Barrel V-8 (Optional in Ford): Overhead valve. Cast-iron block. Displacement: 390 cid. B & S: 4.05 x 3.78 in. Compression ratio: 10.5:1. Brake hp: 315 at 4600 rpm. Torque: 427 lbs.-ft. at 2800 rpm. Five main bearings. Hydraulic valve lifters. Carburetor: Four-barrel. Cooling system capacity: 20.5 qt. with heater. Crankcase capacity: (Mid-size and Mustang) 4 qt. and (full-size and Thunderbird), 5 qt. (add 1 qt. with new oil filter). Dual exhausts. Code Z.

Fairlane GT 390 V-8: Overhead valve. Cast-iron block. Displacement: 390 cid. B & S: 4.05 x 3.78 in. Compression ratio: 10.5:1. Brake hp: 325 at 4800 rpm. Torque: 427 lbs.-ft. at 3200 rpm. Five main bearings. Hydraulic valve lifters. Carburetor: Holley four-barrel. Cooling system capacity: 20.5 qt. with heater. Crankcase capacity: (Mid-size and Mustang) 4 qt. and (Full-Size and Thunderbird) 5 qt. (add 1 qt. with new oil filter). Dual exhausts. Code S. (Some literature listed this engine with a 335-hp rating.)

Cobra Jet 428 V-8: Overhead valve. Cast-iron block. Displacement: 428 cid. B & S: 4.13 x 3.98 in. Compression ratio: 10.70:1. Brake hp: 335 at 5600 rpm. Torque: 445 lbs.-ft. at 3400 rpm. Hydraulic valve lifters. Carburetor: Holley four-barrel. Cooling system capacity: 20 qt. with heater. Crankcase capacity: 5 qt. (add 1 qt. with new oil filter). Dual exhausts. Code Q or R.

Thunderbird 428 V-8: Overhead valve. Cast-iron block. Displacement: 428 cid. B & S: 4.13 x 3.98 in. Compression ratio: 10.50:1. Brake hp: 340 at 5400 rpm. Torque: 462 lbs.-ft. at 2800 rpm. Hydraulic valve lifters. Carburetor: Holley four-barrel. Cooling system capacity: 20 qt. with heater. Crankcase capacity: 5 qt. (add 1 qt. with new oil filter). Dual exhausts. Code Q.

1968 Ford Fairlane Torino GT two-door convertible (OCW)

1968 Ford Fairlane Torino GT two-door fastback (OCW)

1968 Ford Galaxie 500 two-door hardtop (OCW)

1968 Ford Galaxie 500 two-door convertible (OCW)

Cobra Jet 428 V-8: Overhead valve. Cast-iron block. Displacement: 428 cid. B & S: 4.13 x 3.98 in. Compression ratio: 10.50:1. Brake hp: 360 at 5400 rpm. Torque: 460 lbs.-ft. at 3200 rpm. Five main bearings. Solid valve lifters. Carburetor: Holley four-barrel. Cooling system capacity: 20 qt. with heater. Crankcase capacity: 5 qt. (add 1 qt. with new oil filter). Dual exhausts. Code P.

Thunder Jet 429 V-8: Overhead valve. Cast-iron block. Displacement: 429 cid. B & S: 4.36 x 3.59 in. Compression ratio: 10.50:1. Brake hp: 360 at 4600 rpm. Torque: 480 lbs.-ft.at 2800 rpm. Five main bearings. Hydraulic valve lifters. Carburetor: Motorcraft four-barrel. Cooling system capacity: 18.6 qt. with heater (T-bird 19.4 qt.). Crankcase capacity: 5 qt. (add 1 qt. with new oil filter). Dual exhausts. Code N.

Thunderbird High Performance V-8: Overhead valve. Cast-iron block. Displacement: 427 cid. B & S: 4.23 x 3.78 in. Compression ratio: 10.90:1. Brake hp: 390 at 4600 rpm. Torque: 460 lbs.-ft. at 3200 rpm. Five main bearings. Hydraulic valve lifters. Carburetor: Holley four-barrel. Cooling system capacity: 20 qt. with heater. Crankcase capacity: 4 qt. (add 1 qt. with new oil filter). Dual exhausts. Code W.

Chassis:

Falcon: Wheelbase: 110.9 in. and 113 in., station wagons. Overall length: 184.3 in. and 198.7 in., station wagons. Tires: 6.95 x 14 four-ply tubeless blackwall and 7.75 x 14 four-ply tubeless blackwall, station wagons.

Fairlane and Torino: Wheelbase: 116 in. and 113 in., station wagons. Overall length: 201 in. and 203.9 in., station wagons. Tires: 7.35 x 14 tubeless blackwall, 7.75 x 14 tubeless blackwall, station wagons and F870-14, GT.

Ford: Wheelbase: 119 in.. Overall length: 213.3 in. and 213.9 in., station wagons. Tires: 7.75 x 15 four-ply tubeless blackwall, 8.15 x 15 four-ply tubeless blackwall, hardtops and 8.45 x 15 four-ply tubeless blackwall, station wagons.

Options:

Falcon: SelectAire air conditioner with V-8 and radio required and tinted glass recommended ($56.09). Rear air deflector for station wagon ($19.48 and luggage rack required). High rear axle ratio ($6.53). Heavy-duty battery ($7.44). Rear window defogger ($21.27 for all models except wagons). Limited-slip differential ($41.60). Station wagon dual-action tailgate ($45.39). 200-cid 115-hp six ($25.91). 289-cid 195-hp two-barrel V-8 ($131.54). 289-cid 195-hp two-barrel V-8 ($105.63). 302-cid 230-hp four-barrel V-8 ($197.68). 302-cid 230-hp four-barrel V-8 ($171.77). Complete tinted glass ($30.73). Adjustable front head rests ($42.02). Chrome luggage rack for station wagon ($44.44). Remote-control outside rearview mirror ($9.58). Two-tone paint, except station wagons ($24.28). Power disc brakes with all models except six-cylinder sedans and Sport Coupes ($64.77). Power steering ($84.47). Power tailgate window for station wagon ($31.62). AM radio ($61.40) AM/FM stereo radio ($181.36). Dual rear radio speakers, except station wagon ($25.91) Front shoulder belt ($23.38). Rear shoulder belt ($23.38) Deluxe seat with warning light ($12.95). Deluxe seat with warning light and front or rear shoulder belts ($15.59). Deluxe seat with warning light and front and rear shoulder belts ($18.22). Heavy-duty suspension for wagons only ($23.38). Select-Shift Cruise-O-Matic transmission with six-cylinder ($171.39). Select-Shift Cruise-O-Matic transmission with V-8 ($189.66). Four-speed manual ($184.02). Vinyl roof on two-door models ($74.19). Vinyl interior trim in Futura ($16.85, standard in station wagons and Falcon Sport Coupe). Full wheel covers ($21.34, standard on Sport Coupe model). Deluxe or Sport wheel covers, Sport

Coupe ($12.95). Deluxe or Sport wheel covers on models other than Sport Coupe ($34.29). 6.95 x 14 4-ply-rated white sidewall tires on cars with five standard 6.95 x 14 4-ply-rated Rayon black sidewall tires except station wagons ($32.47). 7.35 x 14 4-ply-rated black sidewall tires on cars with five standard 6.95 x 14 4-ply-rated Rayon black sidewall tires except station wagons ($52.73). 7.35 x 14 4-ply-rated white sidewall tires on cars with five standard 6.95 x 14 4-ply-rated Rayon black sidewall tires except station wagons ($85.21). 7.75 x 14 4-ply-rated white sidewall tires on station wagons with five standard 7.75 x 14 4-ply-rated Rayon black sidewall tires ($32.52). 7.75 x 14 8-ply-rated black sidewall tires on station wagons with five standard 7.75 x 14 4-ply-rated Rayon black sidewall tires ($33.45). 7.75 x 14 8-ply-rated white sidewall tires on station wagons with five standard 7.75 x 14 4-ply-rated Rayon black sidewall tires ($65.80). Convenience group including seat belt light, door-ajar light, parking brake light and low-fuel light ($32.44). Protection group including front and rear color-keyed floor mats, license plate frames, door edge moldings and glove box lock on two-door models ($25.28). Protection group including front and rear color-keyed floor mats, license plate frames, door edge moldings and glove box lock on four-door models ($29.17). Visibility group including ash tray light, glove box light, trunk or cargo area light, map light, remote-control outside rearview mirror and rear door courtesy light switches ($24.01).

Ford and Fairlane: Single body side accent stripe on Galaxie 500 and Country Sedans ($13.90, not available with body side molding). Body side accent stripe on Fairlane, except Torino and wagons ($13.90, not available with C stripe). SelectAire air conditioner in Fairlane with V-8 other than 427-cid, radio required ($360.30). SelectAire air conditioner in all except Fairlane ($368.72). Rear air deflector for Fairlane station wagons, luggage rack required ($19.48). Heavy-duty alternator ($21.09). Heavy-duty dual-belt alternator for Fords ($21.09, but standard with air conditioner). High-ratio axle ($6.53). Heavy-duty battery ($7.44, but standard with 427- and 428-cid engines). Center console for Fairlanes, bucket seats required ($50,66). Rear window defogger, for all models except convertibles or station wagons ($21.27). Limited-slip differential ($41.60, but not optional with 427-cid V-8s). Electric clock ($15.59, but standard in Torino, Torino GT, LTD, XL and Squire). 390-cid 265-hp two-barrel V-8 for all Fords and Fairlanes ($78.25 over the cost of the base V-8). 390-cid 315-hp in Ford/325-hp in Fairlane four-barrel V-8 over base V-8 ($158.08 and extra-cost transmission required). 428-cid 340-hp four-barrel V-8 in all except Fairlane ($244.77). 427-cid 390-hp four-barrel V-8 for Fairlane two-door hardtops and all Fords includes transistorized ignition, heavy-duty battery, heavy-duty suspension, extra-cooling package, four-speed manual transmission, G70 x 15 black nylon tires ($622.97, not available in Fairlanes with Select Aire, 55-amp alternator, heavy-duty suspension and 4-ply tires required at extra cost). Tinted glass in Fairlanes ($34.97). Tinted glass in all except Fairlane ($42.12). Adjustable front headrests ($42.02). Automatic load-leveling system for Ford V-8s ($89.94). Chrome luggage rack for station wagons ($46.55). Chrome luggage rack for station wagon ($46.55). Adjustable luggage rack for station wagons, except Fairlane ($63.08). Right-hand outside rearview mirror for all except Fairlane ($4,42). Right-hand manual outside rearview mirror, remote style, for all except Fairlanes ($6.95). Remote-control left-hand outside rearview mirror ($9.58, but standard with visibility group). Body side moldings for all full-size Ford and base Fairlane, but not available with Accent ($20.75 and standard on Custom 500 and Squire). Bright window frames for Fairlane 500 four-door sedan ($20.75).Bright window frames for Fairlane 500 four-door wagon ($25.91). TuTone paint for Fairlane and all Fords except convertible and Squire ($26.85). Power disc brakes for all models, required with Fairlane 390 or Ford 427 ($64.77, but standard with GT equipment group). Vacuum

1968 Ford Galaxie XL two-door fastback (PH)

1968 Ford LTD four-door hardtop (PH)

1968 Ford LTD two-door hardtop (PH)

1968 Ford four-door Country Squire Wagon (PH)

door locks for two-doors except base Fairlane ($45.39). Vacuum door locks for four-doors except Fairlane ($68.67). Full-width six-way seats in all except Fairlane ($94.75, but not with four-speed manual transmission). Driver's 6-way seat in all with XL bucket seats and console, except Fairlane ($84.25). Comfort Lounge driver seats in LTD hardtops with Brougham trim ($84.25, but not with four-speed manual transmission). Power steering ($94.95). Power tailgate window in station wagons ($31.62, but standard in Squire and other station wagons with dual facing rear seats). Power windows in all except Custom and Custom 500 ($99.94). AM radio ($61.40). AM/FM radio with two speakers ($181.36). Right rear quarter mounted radio speaker for all Fords except station wagons ($12.95). Dual rear radio speakers for Fairlanes ($25.91, but not available on convertible and station wagon). Dual rear radio speakers for all except Fairlanes with AM/FM radio or tape player ($25.91). Single rear radio speakers for all except Fairlanes with AM radio ($13.22). Stereosonic tape system with two front speakers for all except Fairlane, AM radio required ($133.86, but not available with AM/FM radio). Reflective stripes and paint for Torino GT and XL models ($12.95, but not available with GT equipment group). Front bucket seats for Fairlane 500 hardtops, Fairlane 500 convertible and Torino GT ($110.16). Front bucket seats with console in Ford XL only ($90.68). Rear-facing third seat in Fairlane station wagons, including seat belts ($53.18). Twin Comfort Lounge seat in LTD hardtops with Brougham trim ($77.73). Front shoulder belts ($23.38). Rear shoulder belts in all except convertible ($23.38). Deluxe seat belts with warning light ($12.95). Seat belts with front or rear shoulder belts ($15.59). Seat belts with front and rear shoulder belts ($18.22). Fingertip speed control in cars with V-8 and Cruise-O-Matic transmission, except Fairlanes ($73.83, but not available with 427-cid V-8). Tilt steering wheel for all except Fairlane with power steering plus automatic or four-speed manual transmission ($42.76). Heavy-duty suspension including heavy-duty front and rear springs, heavy-duty front and rear shock absorbers and heavy-duty stabilizer bar for all V-8-powered Fairlanes except 427s ($13.02). Heavy-duty suspension including heavy-duty front and rear springs, heavy-duty front and rear shock absorbers and heavy-duty stabilizer bar for all Fords ($23.38, but standard with 427 V-8). Maximum handling suspension for all V-8-powered Fords except station wagon ($30.64, but standard with GT equipment). 6000-rpm tachometer in Fairlane V-8 ($47.92). Console-mounted 8000-rpm tachometer in all except Fairlane with XL bucket seats and console only ($47.92). Select Shift Cruise-O-Matic transmission in six-cylinder models ($191.13). Select Shift Cruise-O-Matic transmission in models with 302-cid two-barrel V-8 ($200.85). Select Shift Cruise-O-Matic transmission in models with 390-cid two-barrel V-8 ($223.03). Select Shift Cruise-O-Matic transmission in models with 390-, 427- or 428-cid four-barrel V-8s ($233.17). Heavy-duty three-speed manual transmission for all ($79.20 and required on 390-cid V-8 with three-speed transmission). Four-speed manual transmission for Fairlane V-8 without 427 and all other models, except station wagons, with 390- or 428-cid four-barrel V-8 ($184.02). Vinyl roof on two-door Ford hardtops and all Fairlanes except fastbacks or station wagons ($84.99). Vinyl roof on four-door Ford hardtops and LTD four-door sedan ($94.05). Knitted vinyl trim on Fairlane 500 station wagon ($24.53). Vinyl trim in Galaxie 500 and Fairlane 500 models except convertible or station wagon ($16.85, but standard on Galaxie 500 convertible and station wagon). Comfort Stream ventilation system on Fairlanes without air conditioning ($15.59). Comfort Stream ventilation system on all except Fairlane ($40.02, but not available with air conditioning). Full wheel covers on all except GTs ($21.34, but standard on Torino, XL, LTD, Squire and cars with Décor Group option). Deluxe full wheel covers on XL, LTD, Squire and models with Décor Group option ($56.88, but not available with GT equipment). Deluxe wheel covers for all other Fords

($78.35). Deluxe or Sport wheel covers for Torinos ($12.95). Deluxe or Sport wheel covers for Fairlanes other than Torinos ($34.99). Argent styled wheels for Torinos ($17.59, but standard on Torino GT). Argent styled wheels for Fairlanes other than Torinos and GTs ($38.86). Chrome styled wheels for Torinos ($95.31). Chrome styled wheels for Torino GT ($77.73). Chrome styled wheels for Fairlane passenger cars other than Torino/Torino GT ($116.59). Chrome styled wheels for Ford XL, LTD, Squire and cars with Décor group ($35.70). Brougham trim group including luxury seat trim, luxury door trim, front courtesy lights, cut-pile carpet, rear center armrest, bright seat side shields, wood grain ornamentation and deluxe luggage compartment trim for LTD models except Squire ($112.69). Convenience group including door ajar light, low fuel light, parking brake light and seat belt warning light for Torino, GT and Fords except XL convertible ($32.44). Convenience group including door ajar light, low fuel light, parking brake light, seat belt warning light and electric clock for Fairlane, except Torino and Torino GT ($47.92). Exterior décor group including bright window frames and full wheel covers for Ford Custom, Custom 500 and Ranch Wagon with whitewall tires ($51.82). Extra-cooling package including viscous-drive fan or flex-blade fan, fan shroud and extra-cooling radiator in Fairlane with 302-cid two-barrel V-8 ($12.95, but standard in Fairlanes with air conditioning). Extra-cooling package including viscous-drive fan or flex-blade fan, fan shroud and extra-cooling radiator in Fairlane with 390-cid V-8 except Torino GT ($25.25, but standard in Fairlanes with air conditioning). Extra-cooling package including viscous-drive fan or flex-blade fan, fan shroud and extra-cooling radiator in Torino GT with 390-cid V-8 ($13,58, but standard with air conditioning). Extra-cooling package including viscous-drive fan or flex-blade fan, fan shroud and extra-cooling radiator in six-cylinder or V-8 Fords ($12.95, but not available with air conditioning). GT Equipment Group including power disc brakes, Maximum Handling suspension, high-ratio rear axle, simulated mag wheel covers, non-reflective GT tape stripes, GT ornamentation and G70 x 15 Wide-Oval white sidewall tires for XL models with 390- or 428-cid engines ($204.64). GT Handling Suspension including extra-heavy-duty rear springs, heavy-duty front and rear shock absorbers and heavy-duty front and rear stabilizer bars for Fairlane hardtops and convertibles with 427-cid four-barrel V-8 and Torino GT ($30.64). Protection Group including front and rear floor mats, license plate frames and door edge guards for two-door models ($25.28); for four-door models ($29.17). Trailer towing package for Fords except 7-Litre and station wagons, requires 390-cid V-8 with Cruise-O-Matic or 428-cid V-8 ($30.93). Visibility group including ashtray light, glove box light, trunk or cargo area lights, rear door courtesy switches, remote-control mirror and map light for Fairlanes ($24.01). Visibility group including brake-on light and remote-control mirror for Galaxie 500 two-door hardtops and convertible, XL and LTDs ($14.64). Visibility group for all other models including ashtray light, glove box light, trunk or cargo area lights, rear door courtesy switches, remote-control mirror, map light, brake-on light and remote-control mirror ($24.01). Tires for all Fairlane sedans, hardtops and convertibles, with 200-cid six or 302-cid two-barrel V-8 using five 7.35 x 14 four-ply blackwall rayon tires as standard equipment: 7.35 x 14 four-ply whitewall ($34.35); F70 x 14 Wide Oval whitewall ($64.43); 7.35 x 14 or 185 R14 radial blackwalls ($38.53); 7.35 x 14 or 185 R14 radial whitewalls ($73.64); F70 x 14 Wide Oval whitewall radials ($103.44 and GT suspension required). Tires for all Fairlane sedans, hardtops and convertibles, except Torino GTs, with 390-cid V-8s or wagons with 200-cid six or 302-cid two-barrel V-8 using five 7.35 x 14 four-ply blackwall rayon tires as standard equipment: 7.75 x 14 four-ply whitewall ($34.52); 7.75 x 14 eight-ply blackwall ($33.45 on wagons only); 7.75 x 14 eight-ply whitewall ($68.00 on wagons only); F70 x 14 Wide Oval whitewall ($50.13, not available on wagons); F70 x 14 Wide Oval whitewall radials

($89.14, not available on wagons, GT Handling suspension required). Extra charge for 7.75 x 14 eight-ply-rated whitewalls on station wagons with 390-cid V-8 having 7.75 x 14 eight-ply-rated blackwall rayon tires as standard equipment ($34.55). Extra charge for FR70 x 14 eight-ply-rated whitewall nylon Wide-Oval tires on GT models without 427-cid V-8 with standard F70 x 14 whitewall Wide-Oval tires ($39.11). Tires for all Fords except Galaxie 500 four-door hardtop, LTD and station wagons with 240-cid six or 302-cid V-8 using five 7.75 x 15 four-ply blackwall rayon tires as standard equipment: 7.75 x 14 four-ply whitewall ($35.47); 8.15 x 15 four-ply blackwall ($15.49); 8.15 x 15 four-ply whitewall ($51.77); 8.45 x 15 four-ply blackwall ($31.08); G70 x 15 Wide Oval nylon whitewall ($85.09); 8.15 x 15 or 205 R15 radial blackwalls ($54.02); 8.15 x 15 or 205 R15 radial whitewalls ($90.41); 8.45 x 15 or 215 R15 radial blackwalls ($69.60); 8.45 x 15 or 215 R15 radial whitewalls ($106.00); 8.45 x 15 four-ply-rated whitewalls ($67.48). Tires for Fords, except station wagons, with 302-cid two-barrel V-8, 390-cid V-8 or 428-cid V-8 using five 8.15 x 15 four-ply blackwall rayon tires as standard equipment, plus convertibles with air conditioning and Galaxie 500 four-door hardtop with 240-cid six or 302-cid V-8 using same tires: 8.15 x 15 four-ply whitewall ($36.37); 8.45 x 15 four-ply blackwall ($15.59); 8.45 x 15 four-ply whitewall ($51.89); G70 x 15 Wide Oval nylon whitewall ($69.82); 8.15 x 15 or 205 R15 radial blackwalls ($38.75); 8.15 x 15 or 205 R15 radial whitewalls ($75.14); 8.45 x 15 or 215 R15 radial blackwalls ($54.34); 8.45 x 15 or 215 R15 radial whitewalls ($90.83). Tire options for Ford models having five 8.45 x 15 four-ply-rated blackwall rayon tires as standard equipment and all wagons and LTD hardtops with 390- or 428-cid V-8s with air conditioning: extra charge for 8.45 x 15 whitewalls ($36.40); 8.45 x 15 or 215 R15 blackwall radials ($39.00); 8.45 x 15 or 215 R15 whitewall radial ($75.39).

History:

Ford products captured over 20 checkered flags in NASCAR stock car racing during 1968, with Ford driver David Pearson taking the overall championship. In USAC competition, Ford pilot A.J. Foyt was the top driver of the year. Benny Parsons and Cale Yarborough also made Ford racing history this year, driving Fairlanes and Torinos in ARCA contests. A specially-trimmed Torino convertible paced the 52nd Indianapolis 500-Mile race. The new Fords were introduced to the public on Sept. 22, 1967. In Europe, Ford GT-40s competed in the international class races, attempting to repeat the success of 1966, when similar machines finished first, second and third at Le Mans. Early in 1968, Semon E. "Bunkie" Knudsen became the chief executive officer of Ford Motor Co. Knudsen had held a similar position with Pontiac and Chevrolet during some of the most exciting years in automotive history.

1969 Ford

Falcon — 6 and V-8: The Falcons were the base trim level for 1969 and included chrome windshield, rear window and rain gutter molding. Armrests were on the front doors only and a horn button was used instead of the chrome ring found on the more trimmed Futuras. The Falcon name, in script, appeared on the rear fenders and on the vertical section of the trunk lid on the passenger side. Falcons continued to use the same body style as in the previous three years, with no major changes in either sheet metal or trim. An optional V-8, new safety steering wheel and redesigned side marker lamps were the most noticeable revisions from the past. A full-width anodized aluminum grille helped impart a "big car" appearance.

Futura — 6 and V-8: The Futura series was the top trim level for the 1969 Falcons and included all the standard Falcon features plus a cigarette lighter, armrests and ash trays on all doors, a chrome horn ring, nylon carpeting, special Futura moldings, trim, emblems and nameplates and chrome side window frames. The Futura Sports Coupe offered front bucket seats, special nameplates, a map light, glove box and trunk lights plus 7.35 x 14 tires, a side chrome accent stripe, polished aluminum rocker panel moldings and wheel well trim, a remote-control outside driver's mirror and deluxe seat belts.

Maverick — 6: The Maverick was introduced during the 1969 model year on April 17, 1969 as a 1970 model. It used a Falcon chassis and 170-cid

1969 Galaxie 500XL fastback hardtop

1969 Custom 500 four-door sedan

1969 Galaxie 500 convertible

six-cylinder engine to power the only body style available, a two-door sedan. Mavericks featured a sloped hatchback style and boasted about their 10.4 cubic-feet of trunk space. Ford Motor Co. positioned the Maverick as a car that attempted to fill a gap between compacts and imports. Priced at $1,995, Ford said it was "the car of the '70s at 1960s prices." The company also mentioned the car's long service intervals including 6,000 miles between oil changes and 108,000 miles of service intervals over nine years in the owner's manual. Ford advertising said the Maverick "pinches pennies, not people." To emphasize the original nature of the car, the first year color choices included names like Original Cinnamon, Hulla Blue, Freudian Gilt, Thanks Vermillion and Anti-Establish Mint. The Maverick came with Tartan plaid cloth and vinyl seat trim, a fully-padded two-spoke steering wheel with a half horn ring, door-activated courtesy light, a three-speed blower with heater, lighted controls, suspended accelerator, clutch and brake pedals, curved side glass without window vents, coat hooks, cowl induction, flip-type rear quarter windows, a full-width storage tray, a luggage compartment mat and a center fuel filler door. Mavericks would go on to be made in both Mexico and Brazil. There even were Shelby Maverick versions made by Shelby of Mexico.

Fairlane — 6 and V-8: The Fairlane was the base trim level for 1969 and included a chrome windshield and rear window moldings, chrome rain gutters and side window frames, a chrome horn ring, front and rear armrests, vinyl-coated rubber floor mats and the Fairlane name, in script, on the passenger side of the escutcheon panel. The Ford name was spelled out in block letters across the front of the hood and on the vertical section of the trunk lid. Performance was the key word in the Fairlane lineup for 1969. Visually all models, except four-door sedans, looked fast. And most of them were. When equipped with the Cobra Jet 428, the Fairlanes were awesome as well as beautiful. They shared the same body as the 1968 models, with only minor trim updating. The taillights were revised slightly and were squarer than in 1968. The grille was revised slightly, with a more prominent center dividing bar for 1969. At midyear, the Torino Talladega Special was released in extremely limited quantities, just enough to qualify the body style for use in NASCAR racing. The Talladega front end was extended several inches and used a flat grille, mounted at the front of the opening, rather than several inches back, as on standard models. Also, the rear bumper from a standard Fairlane was used up front, because it was more aerodynamic than the original front bumper. All Torino Talladega Specials were equipped with the Cobra Jet 428 engine and offered a choice of either Select Shift Cruise-O-Matic automatic transmission, or the bulletproof "top-loader" four-speed manual gearbox. The Fairlane 500 was the intermediate trim level for 1969 and included all Fairlane trim plus special 500 trim and moldings, color-keyed carpeting in the front and rear plus a choice of four nylon and vinyl upholsteries. Also included was an aluminum trim panel in the center of the rear escutcheon panel, between the taillights. The Fairlane 500 name, in script, appeared on the rear fender, just in front of the taillights.

Torino — 6 and V-8: The Fairlane Torino was the top trim level for 1969 and included all the Fairlane 500 trim plus a polished aluminum rocker panel molding, special emblems and trim inside and out and a Torino crest on the "C" pillars on the two-door hardtop and four-door sedan versions. The Fairlane Torino GT was the sporty version of the Fairlane 500 series and included all the Fairlane 500 features plus the 302-cid, 220 hp V-8, bucket seats and console, special name plaques and exterior trim, styled steel wheels, lower body striping on two-door hardtop and two-door convertible versions and a body stripe "C" on the two-door fastback Sportsroof version. A high-performance version, the Torino Cobra, was also offered. It included the 428-cid, 335-hp V-8, four-speed manual transmission and F70-14 wide oval tires as standard equipment.

1969 Galaxie 500XL GT convertible

1969 LTD Formal two-door hardtop

1969 LTD Country Squire station wagon

1969 Fairlane 500 convertible

Custom and Custom 500 — 6 and V-8: The 1969 full-size Fords were totally restyled and shared nothing with the previous year's offering. The lines of the new models were even rounder than previous editions. They looked more luxurious and luxury was highly promoted. Velour interiors and vinyl tops were the order of the day in the LTD lineup. All full-size Fords shared the same body lines, with the LTD receiving its own front end treatment, segregating it from Customs and Galaxies. The Custom series was the base trim level and included chrome windshield and rear window moldings, a chrome horn ring, nylon carpeting, the Custom name, in script, on the rear fender just in front of the rear marker light, the Ford name in block letters across the rear escutcheon panel and a single horizontal chrome strip along the center of the body. The Custom 500 was the upper trim level of the base Custom series and included all the Custom trim plus special Custom 500 exterior trim and choices of four different upholsteries on the interior..

Galaxie 500 and Galaxie 500XL — 6 and V-8: The Galaxie 500 was the intermediate trim level for 1969 and included all the Custom series trim plus stamped aluminum lower body moldings and pleated interior trim. The Galaxie 500XL was the sport trim version of the Galaxie 500. It came in the two-door fastback coupe style Ford Motor Co. called the "Sportsroof" plus a convertible version. Standard equipment included bucket seats, wheel covers, die-cast grille, retractable headlights, pleated, all-vinyl interior trim and five vertical "hash marks" on the forward portion part of the front fenders. The 500XL also carried all of the standard Galaxie 500 trim.

LTD — (V-8): The LTD was the top level 1969 full-size Ford and included all the Galaxie 500 trim plus the 302-cid, 220-hp V-8, Select Shift Cruise-O-Matic automatic transmission, an electric clock, bright exterior moldings and dual accent paint stripes. The LTD station wagons also had simulated wood grain appliqués on their bodies. All LTDs also came with retractable headlights and die-cast grilles.

VIN: Falcon, Maverick, Fairlane and Ford:

The serial number code was broken down in this manner. The first symbol indicated the year: 9 = 1969. The second symbol identified the assembly plant: A = Atlanta, Georgia; B = Oakville, Ontario, Canada, E = Mahwah, New Jersey, F = Dearborn, Michigan, G =Chicago, Illinois, H = Loraine, Ohio, J = Los Angeles, California, K = Kansas City, Missouri, N = Norfolk, Virginia, P = Twin Cities (Minneapolis and St. Paul), Minnesota, R = San Jose, California, S = Allen Park Pilot Plant, T = Metuchen, New Jersey, U = Louisville, Kentucky, W = Wayne, Michigan, X = St. Thomas, Ontario, Canada, Y = Wixom. Michigan and Z = St. Louis, Missouri. The third and fourth symbols identified the body type and series: 91 = Maverick. The fifth symbol identified the engine code: F = 302-cid V-8; G = 302-cid Boss V-8 with four-barrel carb; H = 351-cid V-8; K = 429-cid V-8; L = 250-cid six-cylinder; M = 351-cid V-8 with four-barrel carb; N = 429-cid V-8 with four-barrel carb; Q = 428-cid V-8 with four-barrel carb; R = 428-cid Super Cobra Jet V-8 with four-barrel carb; S = 390-cid V-8 with four-barrel carb; T = 200-cid six-cylinder; U = 170-cid six-cylinder; V = 240-cid six-cylinder; Y = 390-cid V-8; Z = 429-cid Boss V-8 with four-barrel carb. The last six digits were the unit's production number, beginning at 100001.

The 1969 Ford data plate could be read as follows. After the vehicle ID number was the body type: 62A = two-door sedan. The next space was for color coding: M=White. In the second row was the trim code: 1Y = Light Nugget vinyl. The next space in row two was the axle ratio code: 5 = 2.83:1. Space three in row two was the transmission code: W = C4 automatic. The final space designated the district or special equipment code. Ford Motor Co. used 44 of these codes in 1969 including 37 U. S. districts, one for Ford of Canada (83) and six other codes such as 83 = government and 84 = home office.

Falcon (6)

Model No.	Body/ Style No.	Body Type & Seating	Factory Price	Shipping Weight	Production Total
----	54A	4-dr. Sedan-6P	$2,316	2,735 lbs.	----
----	62A	2-dr. Sedan-4P	$2,226	2,700 lbs.	----
----	71A	4-dr. Station Wagon-6P	$2,643	3,110 lbs.	----

Falcon (V-8)

----	54A	4-dr. Sedan-6P	$2,431	2,735 lbs.	22,719
----	62A	2-dr. Sedan-4P	$2,381	2,700 lbs.	29,263
----	71A	4-dr. Station Wagon-6P	$2,733	3,110 lbs.	11,568

Note: Total Falcon output was 63,550 units in 1969. Ford did not indicate the numbers of sixes or V-8s made. All production figures were the total of each body style with both engines.

Futura (6)

----	54B	4-dr. Sedan-6P	$2,481	2,748 lbs.	----
----	62B	2-dr. Sedan-4P	$2,444	2,715 lbs.	----
----	62C	2-dr. Sport Coupe	$2,581	2,738 lbs.	----
----	71B	4-dr. Station Wagon-6P	$2,754	3,120 lbs.	----

Futura (V-8)

----	54B	4-dr. Sedan-6P	$2,571	2,748 lbs.	11,850
----	62B	2-dr. Sedan-4P	$2,534	2,715 lbs.	6,482
----	62C	2-dr. Sport Coupe	$2,671	2,738 lbs.	5,931
----	71B	4-dr. Station Wagon-6P	$2,844	3,120 lbs.	7,203

Note: Total series output was 31,466 units. Ford did not indicate the number of sixes or V-8s produced. All production figures were the totals for each body style.

Maverick (6)

----	91	2-dr. Sedan-6P	$1,995	2,411 lbs.	127,833

Fairlane (6)

----	54A	4-dr. Sedan-6P	$2,471	3,010 lbs.	27,296
----	65A	2-dr. Hardtop Coupe-6P	$2,482	3,025 lbs.	85,630
----	71B	4-dr. Station Wagon-6P	$2,824	3,387 lbs.	10,882

Fairlane (V-8)

----	54A	4-dr. Sedan-6P	$2,561	3,120 lbs.	27,296
----	65A	2-dr. Hardtop Coupe-6P	$2,572	3,133 lbs.	85,630
----	71B	4-dr. Station Wagon-6P	$2,914	3,387 lbs.	10,882

Note: Total series output was 123,808 units. Ford did not indicate the number of models produced with sixes and V-8s. All production figures were the total production of each body style with both engines.

Fairlane 500 (6)

----	54B	4-dr. Sedan-6P	$2,551	3,029 lbs.	40,888
----	65B	2-dr. Formal Hardtop Coupe-6P	$2,609	3,036 lbs.	28,179
----	63B	4-dr. Fastback Coupe-6P	$2,584	3,083 lbs.	29,849
----	76B	2-dr. Convertible-6P	$2,834	3,220 lbs.	2,264
----	71B	4-dr. Station Wagon-6P	$2,934	3,415 lbs.	12,869

Fairlane 500 (V-8)

----	54B	4-dr. Sedan-6P	$2,641	3,135 lbs.	40,888
----	65B	2-dr. Formal Hardtop Coupe-6P	$2,699	3,143 lbs.	28,179
----	63B	4-dr. Fastback Coupe-6P	$2,674	3,190 lbs.	29,849
----	76B	2-dr. Convertible-6P	$2,924	3,336 lbs.	2,264
----	71B	4-dr. Station Wagon-6P	$3,024	3,523 lbs.	12,869

Note: Total series output was 114,049 units including 3,379 Formal Hardtop coupes, 7,345 Sportsroof fastback coupes and 219 convertibles, all produced with bucket seats. Ford did not indicate the number of sixes or V-8s produced, only total production figures for each body style.

Fairlane Torino (6)

----	54C	4-dr. Sedan-6P	$2,716	3,075 lbs.	11,971
----	65C	2-dr. Fastback Coupe-6P	$2,737	3,090 lbs.	20,789
----	71E	4-dr. Squire Station Wagon-6P	$3,090	3,450 lbs.	14,472

Fairlane Torino (V-8)

----	54C	4-dr. Sedan-6P	$2,806	3,180 lbs.	11,971
----	65C	2-dr. Fastback Coupe-6P	$2,827	3,195 lbs.	20,789
----	71E	4-dr. Squire Station Wagon-6P	$3,180	3,556 lbs.	14,472

Note: Total series output was 47,232 units. Ford did not indicate the number of models produced with sixes or V-8s. All production figures were totals for each body style.

Fairlane Torino GT (V-8)

----	65D	2-dr. Formal Hardtop Coupe-5P	$2,848	3,173 lbs.	17,951
----	63D	2-dr. Fastback Coupe-5P	$2,823	3,220 lbs.	61,319
----	76D	2-dr. Convertible-5P	$3,073	3,356 lbs.	2,552

Fairlane Torino GT Cobra (V-8)

----	65A	2-dr. Hardtop Coupe-5P	$3,208	3,490 lbs.	------
----	63B	2-dr. Fastback Coupe-5P	$3,183	3,537 lbs.	------

Note: Total series output was 81,822 units, including the unrecorded numbers of Cobra models. Ford did not indicate the number of each model produced. Totals are production numbers of each body style with both sixes and V-8s.

Custom (6)

----	54E	4-dr. Sedan-6P	$2,674	3,608 lbs.	45,653
----	62E	2-dr. Sedan-6P	$2,632	3,585 lbs.	15,439
----	71D	4-dr. Ranch Wagon-6P	$3,074	4,069 lbs.	17,489

Custom (V-8)

----	54E	4-dr. Sedan-6P	$2,779	3,648 lbs.	45,653
----	62E	2-dr. Sedan-6P	$2,737	3,625 lbs.	15,439
----	71D	4-dr. Ranch Wagon-6P	$3,179	4,109 lbs.	17,489

Note: Total series output was 78,581 units. Ford did not indicate the number of each model with sixes or V-8s. All production figures were total figures for each body style with both engines.

Custom 500 (6)

----	54B	4-dr. Sedan-6P	$2,773	3,620 lbs.	45,761
----	62B	2-dr. Sedan-6P	$2,731	3,570 lbs.	7,585
----	71H	4-dr. Ranch Wagon-6P	$3,138	4,082 lbs.	16,432
----	71J	4-dr. Ranch Wagon-10P	$3,251	4,132 lbs.	11,563

1969 Fairlane Torino four-door sedan

1969 Fairlane Torino Formal two-door hardtop

Custom 500 (V-8)

----	54B	4-dr. Sedan-6P	$2,878	3,660 lbs.	45,761
----	62B	2-dr. Sedan-6P	$2,836	3,610 lbs.	7,585
----	71H	4-dr. Ranch Wagon-6P	$3,243	4,122 lbs.	16,432
----	71J	4-dr. Ranch Wagon-10P	$3,556	4,172 lbs.	11,563

Note: Total series output was 81,341 units. Ford did not indicate the models produced with sixes or V-8s. All production figures were totals for each body style with both engines.

Galaxie 500 (6)

----	54A	4-dr. Sedan-6P	$2,897	3,670 lbs.	104,606
----	64B	2-dr. Fastback Coupe-6P	$2,913	3,680 lbs.	63,921
----	65C	2-dr. Formal Hardtop Coupe-6P	$2,965	3,635 lbs.	71,920
----	57B	4-dr. Hardtop Sedan-6P	$2,966	3,705 lbs.	64,031
----	76A	2-dr. Convertible-6P	$3,142	3,840 lbs.	6,910
----	71B	4-dr. Country Sedan-6P	$3,257	4,067 lbs.	36,287
----	71C	4-dr. Country Sedan-10P	$3,373	3,092 lbs.	11,563

Galaxie 500 (V-8)

----	54A	4-dr. Sedan-6P	$3,002	3,710 lbs.	104,606
----	63B	2-dr. Fastback Coupe-6P	$3,018	3,720 lbs.	63,921
----	65C	2-dr. Formal Hardtop Coupe-6P	$3,070	3,675 lbs.	71,920
----	57B	4-dr. Hardtop Sedan-6P	$3,071	3,745 lbs.	64,031
----	76A	2-dr. Convertible-6P	$3,247	3,880 lbs.	6,910
----	71B	4-dr. Country Sedan-6P	$3,362	4,107 lbs.	36,287
----	71C	4-dr. Country Sedan-10P	$3,487	4,132 lbs.	11,563

Note: Total series output was 359,238 units. Ford didn't indicate the models produced with sixes or V-8s. All production figures were total production of each body style with both engines.

Galaxie 500XL (V-8)

----	63C	2-dr. Fastback Coupe-5P	$3,052	3,785 lbs.	54,557
----	76B	2-dr. Convertible-5P	$3,280	3,935 lbs.	7,402

Note: Total series output was 61,959 units. Ford did not indicate the number of model produced with sixes or V-8s. All production figures were the totals with both engines.

LTD (V-8)

----	54C	4-dr. Sedan-6P	$3,192	3,745 lbs.	63,709
----	57F	4-dr. Sedan-6P	$3,261	3,840 lbs.	113,168
----	65A	2-dr. Formal Hardtop Coupe-6P	$3,234	3,745 lbs.	111,565
----	71E	4-dr. Country Sedan-6P	$3,644	4,202 lbs.	46,445
----	71A	4-dr. Country Sedan-10P	$3,721	4,227 lbs.	82,790

Note: Total series output was 417,677 units.

Engines:

Falcon and Maverick Base Six: Overhead valve. Cast-iron block. Displacement: 170 cid. B & S: 3.50 x 2.94 in. Compression ratio: 8.7:1. Brake hp: 100 at 4000 rpm. Carburetor: Holley one-barrel. Seven main bearings. Code U.

Fairlane Base Six (Falcon and Maverick Optional): Overhead valve. Cast-iron block. Displacement: 200 cid. B & S: 3.68 x 3.13 in. Compression ratio: 8.8:1. Brake hp: 115 at 3800 rpm. Carburetor: Motorcraft one-barrel. Seven main bearings. Code T.

Ford Base Six: Overhead valve. Cast-iron block. Displacement: 240 cid. B & S: 4.00 x 3.18 in. Compression ratio: 9.2:1. Brake hp: 150 at 4000 rpm. Carburetor: Motorcraft one-barrel. Seven main bearings. Code V. (Police code B and taxi code E.)

Ford Optional Six: Overhead valve. Cast-iron block. Displacement: 250 cid. B & S: 3.68 x 3.91 in. Compression ratio: 9.0:1. Brake hp: 155 at 4000 rpm. Carburetor: Motorcraft one-barrel. Seven main bearings. Code L.

Torino GT Base 302 V-8: Overhead valve. Cast-iron block. Displacement: 302 cid. B & S: 4.00 x 3.00 in. Compression ratio: 9.5:1. Brake hp: 220 at 4600 rpm. Carburetor: Motorcraft two-barrel. Five main bearings. Code F. (Police and taxi code D.)

1969 Fairlane Torino GT Cobra two-door hardtop

1969 Torino GT two-door convertible

1969 Torino GT two-door hardtop, Sportsroof

1969 Torino GT Talladega Special two-door, Sportsroof

1969 Falcon Futura two-door Sports Coupe

1969 Falcon four-door sedan

1969 Falcon Futura station wagon

Boss 302 V-8: Overhead valve. Cast-iron block. Displacement: 302 cid. B & S: 4.00 x 3.00 in. Compression ratio: 10.5:1. Brake hp: 290 at 5600 rpm. Carburetor: Holley four-barrel. Five main bearings. Code G.

Falcon, Fairlane and Torino Optional 351 V-8: Overhead valve. Cast-iron block. Displacement: 351 cid. B & S: 4.00 x 3.50 in. Compression ratio: 9.5:1. Brake hp: 250 at 4600 rpm. Carburetor: Motorcraft two-barrel. Five main bearings. Code H.

351 Four-Barrel V-8: Overhead valve. Cast-iron block. Displacement: 351 cid. B & S: 4.00 x 3.50 in. Compression ratio: 10.7:1. Brake hp: 290 at 4800 rpm. Carburetor: Motorcraft four-barrel. Five main bearings. Code M.

Ford Optional Interceptor V-8: Overhead valve. Cast-iron block. Displacement: 390 cid. B & S: 4.05 x 3.78 in. Compression ratio: 9.5:1. Brake hp: 265 at 4400 rpm. Carburetor: Motorcraft two-barrel. Five main bearings. Code Y.

Ford Optional 390 V-8: Overhead valve. Cast-iron block. Displacement: 390 cid. B & S: 4.05 x 3.78 in. Compression ratio: 10.5:1. Brake hp: 320 at 4600 rpm. Carburetor: Holley four-barrel. Five main bearings. Code S.

Cobra GT Optional Cobra Jet 428 V-8: Overhead valve. Cast-iron block. Displacement: 428 cid. B & S: 4.13 x 3.98 in. Compression ratio: 10.6:1. Brake hp: 335 at 5200 rpm. Carburetor: Holley four-barrel. Five main bearings. Code Q.

Cobra GT Optional Super Cobra Jet 428 V-8: Overhead valve. Cast-iron block. Displacement: 428 cid. B & S: 4.13 x 3.98 in. Compression ratio: 10.5:1. Brake hp: 360 at 5400 rpm. Carburetor: Holley four-barrel. Five main bearings. Code P.

Ford Optional Thunder Jet 429 V-8: Overhead valve. Cast-iron block. Displacement: 429 cid. B & S: 4.36 x 3.59 in. Compression ratio: 10.5:1. Brake hp: 320 at 4500 rpm. Carburetor: Motorcraft two-barrel. Five main bearings. Code K.

Ford Optional Thunder Jet 429 Four Barrel V-8: Overhead valve. Cast-iron block. Displacement: 429 cid. B & S: 4.36 x 3.59 in. Compression ratio: 10.5:1. Brake hp: 360 at 4600 rpm. Carburetor: Motorcraft four-barrel. Five main bearings. Code N.

Boss 429 V-8: Overhead valve. Cast-iron block. Displacement: 429 cid. B & S: 4.36 x 3.59 in. Compression ratio: 11.3:1. Brake hp: 375 at 5600 rpm. Carburetor: Holley four-barrel. Five main bearings. Code Z.

Chassis:

Falcon: Wheelbase: 113 in., station wagons and 110.9 in., other models Overall length: 184.3 in. and 198.7 in., station wagons. Tires: 7.75 x 14 four-ply tubeless blackwall, station wagon; 7.35 x 14 four-ply tubeless blackwall, Sports Coupe and 6.95 x 14 four-ply tubeless blackwall, other models.

Maverick: Wheelbase: 103 inches. Overall length: 179.4 inches. Tires: 6.00 x 13 four-ply tubeless blackwall.

Fairlane: Wheelbase: 116.0 in. and 113 in., station wagons. Overall length: 201 in. and 203.9 in., station wagons. Tires: 7.35 x 14 four-ply tubeless blackwall, 7.50 x 14 four-ply blackwall, convertibles and F70-14, Cobra.

Ford: Wheelbase: 121 in. Overall length: 213.9 in. and 216.9 in., station wagons. Tires: 8.25 x 15 four-ply tubeless blackwall and 9.00 x 15 four-ply tubeless blackwall, station wagons.

Options:

Falcon: 200-cid six-cylinder engine ($26). 302-cid V-8 engine ($79). Cruise-O-Matic automatic transmission ($175). Power steering ($89). Power tailgate window, station wagons ($35). Tinted windshield ($32). AM radio ($61). Wheel covers ($21).

Maverick: 200-cid six-cylinder engine. Selectaire air conditioning. Tinted glass. Day/night rearview mirror. Cruise-O-Matic automatic transmission ($175). AM radio ($61). White sidewall tires ($34). Accent seat trim. Grabber group package.

Fairlane and Torino: 302-cid, 220-hp V-8, standard on Torino GT. 351-cid V-8 engine ($84). Cruise-O-Matic automatic transmission ($222). Four-speed manual transmission ($194, standard on Cobra). AM radio ($61). Power steering ($100). Power tailgate window on station wagons ($35). Luggage rack on station wagons ($47). Two-tone paint ($27). White sidewall tires ($34). Vinyl roof on two-door hardtops and four-door sedans ($90).

Ford: 390-cid, 265-hp V-8 engine ($58). 429-cid, 320-hp V-8 ($163). 429-cid, 360-hp V-8 ($237). Cruise-O-Matic automatic transmission ($222). Power steering ($100). Power front disc brakes ($65). Tinted windshield ($45). Air conditioning ($369). AM radio ($61). AM/FM stereo radio ($181). Vinyl roof ($100). White sidewall tires ($33).

History:

The 1969 Ford lines were publicly introduced on Sept. 27, 1968. Calendar year production for America's number two automaker hit the 1,743,442 unit level this year. A total of 1,880,384 Fords were registered as new cars during calendar year 1969. Semon E. (Bunkie) Knudsen remained as president of the company and continued to actively pursue a strong

1969 Torino Squire station wagon

high-performance image. Stock car driver Richard Petty was enticed to drive for Ford in 1969, after a long and successful association with Plymouth. He captured the checkered flag in the Riverside 500 Grand National Race. David Pearson, also driving Fords, won the NASCAR championship with 26 Grand National victories. They drove streamlined Torino Talladega Specials that sold for $3,680. A total of 754 were built during January and February of 1969. It was the next to last season for the compact Falcon, which could not be modified to meet federal safety regulations at reasonable cost. Ford called its fastback cars "Sportsroof" models and used the name "Squire" on its fanciest station wagons. The Maverick was designed to be direct competition for the Volkswagen and was intended to influence those who liked a small and economical car. With a base price of $1,995 it was the only Ford under $2,000.

1970 Ford

Maverick — 6: The Maverick was introduced on April 17, 1969 as a 1970 model. Ford Motor Co. chose the date, as close as possible to the introductory date of the Mustang, with the skyrocketing success of that midyear Ford's sales beginning in April 1964. Maverick didn't set Mustang type sales records but it was a sales success and was back for the full 1970 model year. It used a Falcon chassis and 170-cid six-cylinder engine and came only as a two-door sedan. Essentially, it replaced the economy minded Falcon, in its last year and this time as a Fairlane sub series. The Maverick Grabber package was enhanced in 1970 with plenty of options including distinctive black hood and body stripes, a three-spoke wooden steering wheel and C78 x 14 tires. Five Grabber colors also were introduced in 1970: Brite Yellow, Grabber Yellow, Vermillion, Grabber Green and Grabber Blue. In December 1970, the 302 V-8 was offered as an option for the Maverick series in addition to the 250-cid six cylinder engine.

Fairlane — 6 and V-8: The base trim level of the intermediate Fairlane series was simply called the Fairlane and included a chrome windshield, rear window and rain gutter moldings plus front and rear door armrests and nylon carpeting. The Fairlane 500 had that name in script, on the rear fenders above the side marker lights, two chrome "hash marks" on the front fenders, behind the front wheel opening and the Ford name, in block letters, on the driver's side of the hood and across the escutcheon panel. The Fairlane series was completely restyled, with a sleek body shell and rounded fender contours. The midyear 1969 introduction of the 1970 Maverick drew attention was from the aging Falcon series and its sales plummeted. For the first half of 1970, the 1969 Falcon Futura was again offered as a 1970 series in two-door and four-door sedan versions as well as a station wagon. At mid model year, the revised Falcon, sans the Futura name completely, was repositioned as the lowest-price Fairlane model. It was available only as a two-door sedan, although all the high-performance engine options were offered in it. The Falcon continued to be produced by Ford Motor Co. as a popular series in such overseas markets as South America and Australia.

Torino — 6 and V-8: The Torino was now considered to be a separate series from the Fairlane and offered an intermediate trim level. Yet it still was based on the Fairlane and included all the Fairlane 500 trim plus a single horizontal chrome strip along the body side. The Torino name appeared, in script, on the driver's side of the hood and in block letters on the side of the front fenders, behind the front wheel opening.

1970 Galaxie 500 four-door sedan

Torino Brougham — V-8: The Torino Brougham was the top trim level of the 1970 Torino series and included all the Torino trim plus polished aluminum wheel well and rocker panel moldings, retractable headlights, wheel covers and the 302-cid, 220-hp V-8. The station wagon version included all of the above features plus simulated wood grain appliqués and power front disc brakes.

Torino GT and Cobra — V-8: The Torino GT was the sport version of the Torino series and included all the Torino trim plus hood scoop, trim rings with hubcaps, courtesy lights, carpeting, padded seats, GT emblems, the 302-cid, 220-hp V-8 engine and E70-14 fiberglass-belted white sidewall tires. There were F70-14 tires on convertible versions. The Torino Cobra was the high-performance version of the Torino series and included all of the Torino trim plus the 429-cid, 360-hp V-8, a four-speed manual transmission, competition suspension, seven-inch wide wheels with hubcaps, black center hood, hood locking pins, bright exterior moldings, courtesy lights, Cobra emblems and F70-14 fiberglass-belted black sidewall tires with raised white letters. The Cobra package included a functional hood scoop and rear window louvers.

Custom — 6 and V-8: The full-size Fords were only slightly restyled for 1970, with a revamped rear end treatment. The taillights of the new model were positioned lower in the body and the grille was updated. The Custom series was the base trim level and included chrome windshield and rear window moldings, nylon carpeting, the script Custom name on the rear fenders and the Ford name, in block letters, across the front of the hood and in the rear escutcheon panel. The Custom 500 models offered Custom trim plus a horizontal chrome strip along the mid-section of the body and a brushed aluminum trim strip at the front of the hood.

Galaxie 500 — 6 and V-8: The Galaxie 500 was the intermediate trim level for 1970 and included all the Custom trim plus a pleated vinyl interior, chrome side window and rain gutter moldings and polished aluminum wheel opening moldings.

XL — V-8: The Ford XL was the sport trim version of the full-size two-door convertible and two-door fastback models and included the Galaxie 500's features plus the 302-cid V-8, bucket seats, special wheel covers, LTD-style die-cast grille, retractable headlights, pleated, all-vinyl interior trim and the XL designation, in block letters and in the center of the front of the hood.

LTD — V-8: The LTD was the top trim level full-size Ford for 1970 and included all the Galaxie 500 trim plus the 351-cid, 250-hp V-8 engine, Cruise-O-Matic automatic transmission, electric clock, bright exterior moldings and dual accent paint stripes. The LTD station wagon models, essentially Country Squires also included simulated wood grain appliqués on the body. All LTDs also included retractable headlights and a die-cast grille. The absolute top trim level for 1970 was the LTD Brougham two- and four-door hardtops and four-door sedan. These were LTDs with more lavish interiors than the regular LTD offered. Exterior trim remained the same as the standard LTD.

VIN: Falcon, Fairlane, Ford, Maverick and Torino

The serial number code was broken down in the following manner. First symbol indicated the year: 0 = 1970. The second symbol identified assembly plant, as follows: A = Atlanta, Georgia, B = Oakville, Ontario, Canada, E = Mahwah, New Jersey, F = Dearborn, Michigan, G = Chicago, Illinois, H = Loraine, Ohio, J = Los Angeles, California, K = Kansas City, Missouri, N = Norfolk, Virginia, P = Twin Cities (Minneapolis and St. Paul, Minnesota), R = San Jose, California, S = Allen Park Pilot Plant, T = Metuchen, New Jersey, U = Louisville, Kentucky, W = Wayne, Michigan, X = St. Thomas, Ontario, Canada, Y = Wixom, Michigan and Z = St.

1970 XL convertible

1970 XL Sportsroof two-door hardtop

Louis, Missouri. The third and fourth symbols identified the body series. The fifth symbol identified the engine code, as follows: C = 429-cid V-8, F = 302-cid V-8, G = 302-cid Boss V-8 with four barrel carb, H = 351-cid V-8, J = 429-cid V-8, K = 429-cid V-8, L = 250-cid six-cylinder, M = 351-cid V-8 with four-barrel carb, N = 429-cid V-8 with four-barrel carb, R = 428-cid Super Cobra Jet V-8 with four-barrel carb, S = 390-cid V-8 with four-barrel carb, T = 200-cid six-cylinder, U = 170-cid six-cylinder, V = 240-cid six-cylinder, X = 390-cid V-8; Y = 390-cid V-8 and Z = 429-cid Boss V-8 with four-barrel carb. The last six digits were the unit's production number, beginning at 100001 and up at each of the assembly plants.

Maverick (6)

Model No.	Body/ Style No.	Body Type & Seating	Factory Price	Shipping Weight	Production Total
----	91	2-dr. Sedan-6P	$1,995	2,411 lbs.	451,081

Note: Total series output was 451,081 units.

Falcon Sub-Series (6)

----	54A	4-dr. Sedan-6P	$2,500	3,116 lbs.	Note 1
----	62A	2-dr. Sedan-6P	$2,460	3,100 lbs.	Note 1
----	71D	4-dr. Station Wagon-6P	$2,767	3,155 lbs.	Note 1

Fairlane 500 (6)

----	54B	4-dr. Sedan-6P	$2,627	3,116 lbs.	Note 1
----	65B	2-dr. Hardtop -6P	$2,660	3,128 lbs.	Note 1
----	71B	4-dr. Station Wagon-6P	$2,957	3,508 lbs.	Note 1

Fairlane 500 (V-8)

----	54A	4-dr. Sedan-6P	$2,528	3,216 lbs.	30,443
----	62A	2-dr. Sedan-6P	$2,479	3,200 lbs.	26,071
----	71D	4-dr. Station Wagon-6P	$2,856	3,255 lbs.	10,539
----	54B	4-dr. Sedan-6P	$2,716	3,216 lbs.	25,780
----	65B	2-dr. Hardtop-6P	$2,750	3,228 lbs.	70,636
----	71B	4-dr. Station Wagon-6P	$3,047	3,608 lbs.	13,613

Note 1: Fairlane series production was 177,091 units. Ford did not indicate the number of sixes or V-8s produced so the production figures are totals for each body style with both engines.

Torino (6)

----	54C	4-dr. Sedan-6P	$2,689	3,158 lbs.	Note 1
----	57C	4-dr. Hardtop-6P	$2,795	3,189 lbs.	Note 1
----	65C	2-dr. Hardtop-6P	$2,722	3,173 lbs.	Note 1
----	63C	2-dr. Fastback-6P	$2,810	3,211 lbs.	Note 1
----	71C	4-dr. Station Wagon-6P	$3,074	3,553 lbs.	Note 1

Torino (V-8)

----	54C	4-dr. Sedan-6P	$2,778	3,258 lbs.	30,117
----	57C	4-dr. Hardtop-6P	$2,885	3,289 lbs.	14,312
----	65C	2-dr. Hardtop-6P	$2,812	3,273 lbs.	49,826
----	63C	2-dr. Fastback-6P	$2,899	3,311 lbs.	12,490
----	71C	4-dr. Station Wagon-6P	$3,164	3,653 lbs.	10.613

Note 1: Total Torino series output was 117,358 units. Ford did not indicate the number of sixes or V-8s produced so the production figures are totals for each body style with both engines.

Torino Brougham (V-8)

----	57E	4-dr. Hardtop-6P	$3,078	3,309 lbs.	14,543
----	65E	2-dr. Hardtop-6P	$3,006	3,293 lbs.	16,911
----	71E	4-dr. Squire Station Wagon-6P	$3,379	3,673 lbs.	13,166

Note: Total series output was 44,620 units.

Torino GT (V-8)

----	63F	2-dr. Fastback-5P	$3,105	3,366 lbs.	56,819
----	76F	2-dr. Convertible-5P	$3,212	3,490 lbs.	3,939

Torino GT Cobra (V-8)

----	63H	2-dr. Fastback-5P	$3,270	3,774 lbs.	7,675

Note: Total series output was 68,433 units.

1970 LTD Brougham two-door hardtop

Custom (6)

----	54E	4-dr. Sedan-6P	$2,771	3,527 lbs.	Note 1
----	54B	4-dr. Sedan-6P	$2,872	3,567 lbs.	Note 1

Custom (V-8)

----	54E	4-dr. Sedan-6P	$2,850	3,563 lbs.	42,849
----	71D	4-dr. Ranch Wagon-6P	$3,305	4,079 lbs.	15,086
----	54B	4-dr. Sedan-6P	$2,951	3,603 lbs.	41,261
----	71H	4-dr. Ranch Wagon-6P	$3,368	4,049 lbs.	15,304
----	71J	4-dr. Ranch Wagon-10P	$3,481	4,137 lbs.	9,943

Note: Total Custom series output was 124,443 units. Ford did not indicate the number of sixes or V-8s produced so the production figures are totals for each body style with both engines.

Galaxie 500 (6)

----	54A	4-dr. Sedan-6P	$3,026	3,540 lbs.	Note 1
----	57B	4-dr. Hardtop-6P	$3,096	3,611 lbs.	Note 1
----	65C	2-dr. Formal Hardtop Coupe-6P	$3,094	3,550 lbs.	Note 1
----	63B	2-dr. Fastback-6P	$3,043	3,549 lbs.	Note 1

Galaxie 500 (V-8)

----	54A	4-dr. Sedan-6P	$3,137	3,661 lbs.	101,784
----	57B	4-dr. Hardtop-6P	$3,208	3,732 lbs.	53,817
----	65C	2-dr. Formal Hardtop Coupe-6P	$3,205	3,671 lbs.	57,059
----	63B	2-dr. Fastback-6P	$3,154	3,670 lbs.	50,825
----	71B	4-dr. Country Sedan-6P	$3,488	4,089 lbs.	32,209
----	71C	4-dr. Country Sedan-10P	$3,600	4,112 lbs.	22,645

Note: Total Galaxie series output was 318,339 units. Ford did not indicate the number of sixes or V-8s produced so the production figures are totals for each body style with both engines.

XL (V-8)

----	63C	2-dr. Fastback-5P	$3,293	3,750 lbs.	27,251
----	76B	2-dr. Convertible-5P	$3,501	3,983 lbs.	6,348

Note: Total XL series output was 33,599 units.

LTD (V-8)

----	54C	4-dr. Sedan-6P	$3,307	3,701 lbs.	78,306
----	57F	4-dr. Hardtop-6P	$3,385	3,771 lbs.	90,390
----	65A	2-dr. Hardtop-6P	$3,356	3,727 lbs.	96,324
----	71E	4-dr. Country Squire Wagon-6P	$3,832	4,139 lbs.	39,837
----	71A	4-dr. Country Squire Wagon-10P	$3,909	4,185 lbs.	69,077

LTD Brougham (V-8)

----	54	4-dr. Sedan-6P	$3,502	3,829 lbs.	Note 1
----	57	4-dr. Hardtop-6P	$3,579	4,029 lbs.	Note 1
----	65	2-dr. Hardtop-6P	$3,537	3,855 lbs.	Note 1

Note: Total series output was 373,934 units. Production was not broken down by LTD and LTD Brougham models.

Engines:

Maverick Base Six: Overhead valve. Cast-iron block. Displacement: 170 cid. B & S: 3.50 x 2.94 in. Compression ratio: 9.0:1. Brake hp: 105 at 4400 rpm. Carburetor: Holley one-barrel. Seven main bearings. Code U.

Maverick Optional Six: Overhead valve. Cast-iron block. Displacement: 200 cid. B & S: 3.68 x 3.13 in. Compression ratio: 8.0:1. Brake hp: 120 at 4400 rpm. Carburetor: Motorcraft one-barrel. Seven main bearings. Code T.

Ford Base Six: Overhead valve. Cast-iron block. Displacement: 240 cid. B & S: 4.00 x 3.18 in. Compression ratio: 9.2:1. Brake hp: 150 at 4000 rpm. Carburetor: Motorcraft one-barrel. Seven main bearings. Code V.

Ford and Maverick Optional Six: Overhead valve. Cast-iron block. Displacement: 250 cid. B & S: 3.68 x 3.91 in. Compression ratio: 9.0:1. Brake hp: 155 at 4400 rpm. Carburetor: Motorcraft one-barrel. Seven main bearings. Code L.

Torino GT Base 302 V-8: Overhead valve. Cast-iron block. Displacement: 302 cid. B & S: 4.00 x 3.00 in. Compression ratio: 9.5:1. Brake hp: 220 at 4600 rpm. Carburetor: Motorcraft two-barrel. Five main bearings. Code F.

Boss 302 V-8: Overhead valve. Cast-iron block. Displacement: 302 cid. Compression ratio: 10.6:1. Brake hp: 290 at 5800 rpm. Carburetor: Holley four-barrel. Five main bearings. Code: G.

Falcon, Fairlane and Torino Optional 351 V-8: Overhead valve. Cast-iron block. Displacement: 351 cid. B & S: 4.00 x 3.50 in. Compression ratio: 9.5:1. Brake hp: 250 at 4600 rpm. Carburetor: Motorcraft two-barrel. Five main bearings. Code H.

1970 LTD four-door hardtop

1970 LTD two-door hardtop

1970 Country Squire station wagon

351 Four-Barrel V-8: Overhead valve. Cast-iron block. Displacement: 351 cid. B & S: 4.00 x 3.50 in. Compression ratio: 11.0:1. Brake hp: 300 at 5400 rpm. Carburetor: Motorcraft four-barrel. Five main bearings. Code M.

Ford Optional 390 V-8: Overhead valve. Cast-iron block. Displacement: 390 cid. B & S: 4.05 x 3.78 in. Compression ratio: 9.5:1. Brake hp: 270 at 4400 rpm. Carburetor: Motorcraft two-barrel. Five main bearings. Code X.

Cobra GT Optional Cobra Jet 428 V-8: Overhead valve. Cast-iron block. Displacement: 428 cid. B & S: 4.13 x 3.98 in. Compression ratio: 10.6:1. Brake hp: 335 at 5200 rpm. Carburetor: Holley four-barrel. Five main bearings.

Cobra GT Optional Super Cobra Jet 428 V-8: Overhead valve. Cast-iron block. Displacement: 428 cid. B & S: 4.13 x 3.98 in. Compression ratio: 10.5:1. Brake hp: 360 at 5400 rpm. Carburetor: Holley four-barrel. Five main bearings. Code R.

Ford Optional Thunder-Jet 429 V-8: Overhead valve. Cast-iron block. Displacement: 429 cid. B & S: 4.36 x 3.59 in. Compression ratio: 10.5:1. Brake hp: 320 at 4400 rpm. Carburetor: Motorcraft two-barrel. Five main bearings. Code K.

Ford Optional Thunder-Jet 429 Four-Barrel V-8: Overhead valve. Cast-iron block. Displacement: 429 cid. B & S: 4.36 x 3.59 in. Compression ratio: 10.5:1. Brake hp: 360 at 4600 rpm. Carburetor: Motorcraft four-barrel. Five main bearings. Code N.

Ford Optional Police Interceptor 429 V-8: Overhead valve. Cast-iron block. Displacement: 429 cid. B & S: 4.36 x 3.59 in. Compression ratio: 11.3:1. Brake hp: 370 at 5400 rpm. Carburetor: Holley four-barrel. Five main bearings.

Boss 429 V-8: Overhead valve. Cast-iron block. Displacement: 429 cid. B & S: 4.36 x 3.59 in. Compression ratio: 11.3:1. Brake hp: 375 at 5600 rpm. Carburetor: Holley four-barrel. Five main bearings. Code Z.
Note: The Ram Air Boss 429-cid V-8 had the same specifications as the Boss 429.

Chassis:

Falcon: Wheelbase: 110.9 in. and 113 in., station wagons. Overall length: 184.3 in. and 198.7 in., station wagons. Tires: 6.95 x 14 four-ply tubeless blackwall and 7.75 x 14 four-ply tubeless blackwall, station wagons.

Maverick: Wheelbase: 103 in. Overall length: 179.4 in. Tires: 6.00 x 13 four-ply tubeless blackwall.

Fairlane/Torino: Wheelbase: 117.0 in. and 114 in., station wagons. Overall length: 206.2 in. and 209 in., station wagons. Tires: E78 x 14, G78 x 14, station wagons and F70 x 14, convertibles. The GT used E70 x 14 tires.

Ford: Wheelbase: 121 in. Overall length: 213.9 in. and 216.9 in., station wagons. Tires: F78 x 15 four-ply blackwall, G78 x 15 four-ply tubeless blackwall, Custom and Custom 500 V-8 and H78 x 15 four-ply tubeless blackwall, Galaxie 500 and LTD.

Options:

Maverick: 200-cid six-cylinder engine. 250-cid six cylinder engine. 302-cid V-8 [after December 1970]. Selectaire air conditioning. Tinted glass. Day/night rearview mirror. Cruise-O-Matic automatic transmission ($175). AM radio ($61). White sidewall tires ($34). Accent seat trim. Grabber package with 200-cid six, three-speed manual transmission, black grille and black hood and side body stripes, 14-inch wheels with trim rings, deck-lid spoiler, dual racing mirrors, C78 x 14 tires, three-spoke wood trim steering wheel and black vinyl interior trim.

Fairlane and Torino: Power steering ($100). Air conditioning ($389). Cruise-O-Matic automatic transmission ($201 to $222). Four-speed manual transmission ($194). AM radio ($61). Station wagon power tailgate window ($35). Station wagon rooftop luggage rack ($46). White sidewall tires ($34). Vinyl roof on two- and four-door hardtops and sedan ($95). 250-hp 351-cid V-8 engine ($45).

Ford: Power disc brakes ($65). Power steering ($105). Air conditioning ($389). Cruise-O-Matic automatic transmission ($201 to $222). Tinted windshield ($45). AM radio ($61). AM/FM radio ($240). Vinyl roof ($105). White sidewall tires ($34). Custom 390-cid, 265-hp V-8 ($131). Galaxie 500/XL/LTD 390-cid, 265-hp V-8 ($86). Custom 429-cid, 320-hp V-8 ($213). Galaxie 500/XL/LTD 429-cid, 320-hp V-8 ($168). LTD Luxury trim package ($104).

1970-1/2 Falcon two-door sedan

1970 Falcon Futura two-door sedan

1970 Falcon Futura sedan

1970 Falcon Futura station wagon

The full-size Fords were introduced in September 1969. The Falcon and Torino appeared in dealer showrooms at midyear. Model year production peaked at 1,326,533 units and a calendar year production of 1,647,918 cars was recorded. The new reverse-curve Torino rear window design was influenced by Ford's involvement in racing. These cars competed with the aerodynamic Dodge Daytona and Plymouth Superbird. Only six checkered flags were taken by FoMoCo stock car drivers. The DeTomaso Pantera, an Italian-built specialty sports car powered by a 351-cid, 310-hp Ford "Cleveland" V-8 debuted in 1970. Early in the 1970 model year, the Falcon compact was marketed in three styles: two- and four-door sedans and station wagons. It was replaced by the Fairlane-based 1970-1/2 Falcon later in the 1970 model year.

1970 Torino Brougham four-door hardtop

1970 Fairlane 500 two-door hardtop

1970 Torino GT Sportsroof two-door hardtop

1970 Torino two-door hardtop

1970 Torino GT convertible

1970-1/2 Torino Sportsroof two-door hardtop

1970 Torino GT Cobra Sportsroof two-door hardtop

1970 Torino Brougham two-door hardtop

1970 Torino Brougham Squire station wagon

1970-1/2 Maverick Grabber

1970 Maverick

1971 Ford

Pinto — Four: The Pinto was Ford's new sub-compact offering, built to serve the ever-growing small car market and compete with imports and domestic sub-compacts such as Chevrolet's Vega and the American Motor's Gremlin. It came only as a two-door sedan at first. Standard equipment included ventless door windows, high back slim line bucket seats, all-vinyl upholstery, two-pod instrument cluster, glove box, interior dome light, floor-mounted transmission controls, rack and pinion steering, hot water heater, Direct-Aire ventilation system and 6.00 x 13 rayon blackwall tires. In mid-season, a three-door Pinto Runabout was added. Its standard equipment was the same as the above with a fold-down rear seat, load floor color-keyed carpeting and passenger compartment color-keyed carpeting. Pintos were available with either a British-built 1600cc overhead valve four-cylinder engine, or a second, more powerful and more popular German-built 2000cc four-cylinder engine. Both engines used a four-speed manual transmission, but only the larger engine was available with the three-speed Cruise-O-Matic transmission. While good fuel economy was the main objective of the new Pinto, those equipped with the larger engine and four-speed manual transmission provided quite brisk performance by any standards.

Maverick 6 and V-8: The 1971 Maverick added a four-door sedan to the model choices and the Grabber, which had been an option package, now became another version of the two-door sedan. Also the 210-hp, 302-cid V-8 engine was available for the first time. The 302 proved to be a brisk performer in the small bodied Maverick and the perfect combination with the Grabber two-door sedan. The Maverick continued its list of standard features from the 1970 model including the economy-minded 170-cid six cylinder engine and three-speed transmission as standard equipment. The Grabber edition included a simulated hood scoop, grille-mounted road lamps, trim rings and hub caps, special stripes on the sides plus fender decals, blackout paint on the hood, grille and lower back panel plus color-keyed dual racing mirrors with the left side a remote-controlled mirror. The Grabber also offered bright window frames and a deluxe steering wheel.

Torino and Torino 500 — 6 and V-8: The 1971 Torinos were merely 1970 bodies with updated trim and a slightly revised grille. Standard equipment on the base Torino series included a chrome-trimmed windshield, rear window and rain gutter moldings, front and rear armrests and the Torino name, in block letters, on the rear fenders. The Torino 500 series had all the base Torino trim plus color-keyed carpeting, cloth and vinyl interior trim, an Argent-painted egg crate grille and polished aluminum wheel well and rocker panel moldings.

Torino Brougham, Torino GT and Torino Cobra — V-8: The Torino Brougham was the top trim level Torino for 1971 and included all the Torino 500 equipment plus wheel covers, chrome exterior moldings, soundproofing, Brougham ornamentation, cloth interior trims in four colors and a 210-hp, 302-cid V-8. The Squire wagon also included power front disc brakes, simulated wood grain paneling on the body and G78-14 belted black sidewall tires. The Torino GT was the sporty version of the Brougham series and included all the basic Brougham trim plus color-keyed outside racing mirrors with a remote-controlled left-hand mirror. GT identification was on the grille and rocker panels and it also included simulated hood scoop, hubcaps with trim rings, chrome-trimmed foot pedals, a full-width taillight and E70-14 white sidewall Wide-Oval tires. The convertible also had a power top. The Torino Cobra was the high-performance version of the Brougham series and included all the Brougham trim plus the 285-hp, 351-cid "Cleveland" V-8, four-speed manual transmission with a Hurst shifter, special Cobra identification, heavy-duty suspension, seven-inch wide, Argent-painted wheels with chrome hubcaps, a black grille and lower escutcheon panel, a black-finished hood with non-reflective paint, polished aluminum wheel well moldings, F70-14 white sidewall Wide-Oval tires and a 55-amp heavy-duty battery. The cars also had dual exhausts and pleated vinyl seat trim.

Custom — 6 and V-8: The full-size Fords received a total restyling. The grille was a full-width horizontal unit, with a larger, vertical center section that protruded forward. The hood peaked at the center section of the

grille and became wider toward the windshield. The Custom series was the base trim level full-size 1971 Ford and included a chrome-trimmed windshield and rear window moldings, nylon carpeting and the Custom name, in block letters, on the rear fenders and rear escutcheon panel. The Custom 500 models included the Custom trim plus polished aluminum wheel well moldings, argent and chrome appliqués on the instrument panel plus rear deck moldings and Custom 500 ornamentation. The Custom and Custom 500 models were available with either the 140-hp, 240 cid six-cylinder or the 210-hp, 302-cid V-8 as standard equipment.

Galaxie 500 — 6 and V-8: The Galaxie 500 was the intermediate trim level full-size 1971 Ford and included all the Custom trim plus wood grain appliqués on the interior doors and instrument panel black-painted inserts, polished aluminum wheel well moldings, chrome window frames, deck and rear quarter extension moldings, additional Galaxie 500 ornamentation, the 351-cid, 240-hp V-8 and F78-15 belted black sidewall tires. The Country Sedan used H78-15 tires.

LTD — V-8: A more formal roof line was used in the LTD series and the interiors were completely restyled, with the emphasis on a luxury appearance. The taillights were rectangular and were located at either end of the rear escutcheon panel. The LTDs featured an additional red plastic center reflector that gave the illusion of a full-width taillight. The LTD included all the Galaxie 500 trim plus power front disc brakes, an electric clock, luxury seat trim on all but convertibles, a left-hand outside rearview mirror, nylon carpeting, a power top on convertibles and G78-15 belted tires. The LTD Country Squire station wagons also included wheel covers, a power tailgate window, simulated wood grain appliqués on the body, pleated vinyl trim and H78-15 belted black sidewall tires. The LTD Brougham series included the LTD trim plus wheel covers, Brougham seat trim, a deluxe steering wheel, a front door courtesy light, cut-pile carpeting, a front seat center armrest and polished seat side shields, rear door courtesy light switches, LTD "C" pillar ornamentation and high back bucket seats on the two-door hardtop.

VIN:

The 1971 Ford serial number code was broken down as follows: The first symbol indicated the year: 1 = 1971. The second symbol identified the assembly plant: A = Atlanta, Georgia; B = Oakville, Ontario, Canada, E = Mahwah, New Jersey, F = Dearborn, Michigan, G = Chicago, Illinois, H = Lorain, Ohio, J = Los Angeles, California, K = Kansas City, Missouri; N = Norfolk, Virginia, P = Twin Cities (Minneapolis and St. Paul, Minnesota), R = San Jose, California, S = Allen Park Pilot Plant, T = Metuchen, New Jersey, U = Louisville, Kentucky, W = Wayne, Michigan, X = St. Thomas, Ontario, Canada, Y = Wixom, Michigan and Z = St. Louis, Missouri. The third and fourth symbols identified the body series: 64B=Pinto Runabout. The fifth symbol identified the engine codes: C = 429-cid V-8, D = 302-cid high-output V-8, F = 302-cid V-8, G = 302-cid Boss V-8 with four-barrel

1971 Galaxie 500 four-door hardtop

1971 LTD Country Squire station wagon

1971 LTD Brougham two-door hardtop

1971 LTD Brougham four-door hardtop

1971 LTD two-door hardtop

carb, H = 351-cid V-8, J = 429-cid V-8, K = 429-cid V-8, L = 250-cid six-cylinder, M = 351-cid V-8 with four-barrel carb, N = 429-cid V-8 with four-barrel carb, P = 429-cid V-8, Q = 351-cid V-8, R = 351-cid Boss V-8, S = 400-cid V-8, T = 200-cid six-cylinder, U = 170-cid six-cylinder, V = 240-cid six-cylinder, W = 98-cid four-cylinder, X = 122-cid four-cylinder and Y = 390-cid V-8. The last six digits were the unit's production number, beginning at 100001 and up.

Pinto (Four)

Model No.	Body/ Style No.	Body Type & Seating	Factory Price	Shipping Weight	Production Total
---	62B	2-dr. Sedan-4P	$1,919	1,949 lbs.	288,606
---	64BD	2-dr. Runabout-4P	$2,062	1,994 lbs.	63,796

Note: Total series output was 352,402 units.

Maverick (6)

---	54A	4-dr. Sedan-6P	$2,235	2,610 lbs.	Note
---	62B	2-dr. Runabout-6P	$2,175	2,478 lbs.	Note
---	62D	2-dr. Grabber-6P	$2,354	2,570 lbs.	Note

Maverick (V-8)

---	54A	4-dr. Sedan-6P	$2,404	2,803 lbs.	73,208
---	62B	2-dr. Runabout-6P	$2,344	2,671 lbs.	159,726
---	62D	2-dr. Grabber-6P	$2,523	2,763 lbs.	38,963

Note: Total series output was 271,697 units.

Torino (6)

---	54A	4-dr. Sedan-6P	$2,672	3,141 lbs.	-----
---	62A	2-dr. Hardtop-6P	$2,706	3,151 lbs.	-----
---	71D	2-dr. Station Wagon-6P	$3,023	3,498 lbs.	-----

Torino (V-8)

---	54A	4-dr. Sedan-6P	$2,767	3,220 lbs.	29,501
---	62A	2-dr. Hardtop-6P	$2,801	3,230 lbs.	37,518
---	71D	2-dr. Station Wagon-6P	$2,950	3,577 lbs.	21,570

Note: Total series output was 261,349 units.

Torino Brougham (V-8)

---	57E	4-dr. Brougham Hardtop-6P	$3,248	3,345 lbs.	4,408
---	65E	2-dr. Brougham Hardtop-6P	$3,175	3,390 lbs.	8,593
---	71E	2-dr. Squire Station Wagon-6P	$3,560	3,663 lbs.	15,805

Torino GT and Torino Cobra (V-8)

---	63F	2-dr. GT Sport Coupe-5P	$3,150	3,346 lbs.	31,641
---	76F	2-dr. GT Convertible-5P	$3,408	3,486 lbs.	1,613
---	63E	2-dr. Cobra Hardtop-5P	$3,295	3,594 lbs.	3,054

Note: Total series output was 65,114 units.

Custom (6)

| --- | 54B | 4-dr. Sedan-6P | $3,288 | 3,683 lbs. | Note 1 |

Custom (V-8)

| --- | 54B | 4-dr. Sedan-6P | $3,363 | 3,724 lbs. | 41,062 |
| --- | 71B | 4-dr. Ranch Wagon-6P | $3,890 | 4,190 lbs. | 16,696 |

Custom 500 (6)

| --- | 54D | 4-dr. Sedan-6P | $3,426 | 3,688 lbs. | Note 1 |

Custom 500 (V-8)

| --- | 54D | 4-dr. Sedan-6P | $3,501 | 3,729 lbs. | 33,765 |
| --- | 71D | 4-dr. Ranch Wagon-6P | $3,982 | 4,215 lbs. | 25,957 |

Note 1: Total Custom and Custom 500 series output was 117,480 units. Six and V-8 production figures were not broken out by Ford.

Galaxie 500 (6)

---	54F	4-dr. Sedan-6P	$3,246	3,668 lbs.	Note 1
---	57F	4-dr. Hardtop-6P	$3,665	3,723 lbs.	Note 1
---	65F	2-dr. Hardtop-6P	$3,628	3,668 lbs.	Note 1

Galaxie 500 (V-8)

---	54F	4-dr. Sedan-6P	$3,367	3,826 lbs.	98,130
---	57F	4-dr. Hardtop-6P	$3,786	3,881 lbs.	46,595
---	65F	2-dr. Hardtop-6P	$3,749	3,826 lbs.	117,139
---	71F	4-dr. Country Sedan-6P	$4,074	4,241 lbs.	60,487
---	71D	4-dr. Country Sedan-10P	$4,188	4,291 lbs.	-----

Note: Total series output was 322,351 units. Production figures for the 10-passenger Country Sedan were not available. Six and V-8 production figures were not broken out by Ford.

LTD (V-8)

---	53H	4-dr. Sedan-6P	$3,931	3,913 lbs.	92,260
---	57H	4-dr. Hardtop-6P	$3,969	3,908 lbs.	48,166
---	65H	2-dr. Formal Hardtop-6P	$3,923	3,853 lbs.	103,896
---	76H	2-dr. Convertible-6P	$4,094	4,091 lbs.	5,750
---	71H	4-dr. Country Squire-6P	$4,308	4,308 lbs.	130,644
---	71H	4-dr. Country Squire-10P	$4,496	4,358 lbs.	------

LTD Brougham (V-8)

---	53K	4-dr. Sedan-6P	$4,094	3,949 lbs.	26,186
---	57K	4-dr. Hardtop-6P	$4,140	3,944 lbs.	27,820
---	65K	2-dr. Hardtop-6P	$4,097	3,883 lbs.	43,303

Note: Total series output was 478,025 units. Production figures for the 10-passenger Country Sedan were not available.

Engines:

Pinto Four: Overhead cam. Cast-iron block. Displacement: 98 cid. B & S: 3.19 x 3.06 in. Compression ratio: 8.4:1. Brake hp: 75 at 5000 rpm. Carburetor: one-barrel. Five main bearings. Code W.

Pinto Alternate Four: Overhead cam. Cast-iron block. Displacement: 122 cid. B & S: 3.58 x 3.03 in. Compression ratio: 9.0:1. Brake hp: 100 at 5600 rpm. Carburetor: Ford/Weber two-barrel. Five main bearings. Code X.

Maverick Base Six: Overhead valve. Cast-iron block. Displacement: 170 cid. B & S: 3.50 x 2.94 in. Compression ratio: 8.7:1. Brake hp: 100 at 4200 rpm. Carburetor: Motorcraft one-barrel. Seven main bearings. Code U.

Maverick Optional Six: Overhead valve. Cast-iron block. Displacement: 200 cid. B & S: 3.68 x 3.13 in. Compression ratio: 8.7:1. Brake hp: 115 at 4000 rpm. Carburetor: Motorcraft one-barrel. Seven main bearings. Code T.

Ford Base Six: Overhead valve. Cast-iron block. Displacement: 240 cid. B & S: 4.00 x 3.18 in. Compression ratio: 8.9:1. Brake hp: 140 at 4000 rpm. Carburetor: Motorcraft one-barrel. Seven main bearings. Code V.

Ford and Maverick Optional Six: Overhead valve. Cast-iron block. Displacement: 250 cid. B & S: 3.68 x 3.91 inches. Compression ratio: 9.0:1. Brake hp: 145 at 4000 rpm. Carburetor: Motorcraft one-barrel. Seven main bearings. Code L.

Torino GT Base 302 V-8: Overhead valve. Cast-iron block. Displacement: 302 cid. B & S: 4.00 x 3.00 in. Compression ratio: 9.0:1. Brake hp: 210 at 4600 rpm. Carburetor: Motorcraft two-barrel. Five main bearings. Code F.

1971 Torino 500 four-door hardtop

1971 Torino Brougham four-door hardtop

1971 Torino Brougham Squire station wagon

1971 Torino GT Sportsroof two-door hardtop

1971 Torino Cobra two-door hardtop

Fairlane and Torino Optional 351 "Cleveland" two-barrel V-8: Overhead valve. Cast-iron block. Displacement: 351 cid. B & S: 4.00 x 3.50 in. Compression ratio: 9.0:1. Brake hp: 240 at 4600 rpm. Carburetor: Motorcraft two-barrel. Five main bearings. Code H.

351 "Cleveland" four-barrel V-8: Overhead valve. Cast-iron block. Displacement: 351 cid. B & S: 4.00 x 3.50 in. Compression ratio: 10.7:1. Brake hp: 285 at 5400 rpm. Carburetor: Holley four-barrel. Five main bearings. Code M.

Boss 351 V-8: Overhead valve. Cast-iron block. Displacement: 351 cid. B & S: 4.00 x 3.50 in. Compression ratio: 11.1:1. Brake hp: 330 at 5400 rpm. Carburetor: Holley four-barrel. Five main bearings. Code R.

Ford Optional 390 V-8: Overhead valve. Cast-iron block. Displacement: 390 cid. B & S: 4.05 x 3.78 in. Compression ratio: 8.6:1. Brake hp: 225 at 4400 rpm. Carburetor: Motorcraft two-barrel. Five main bearings. Code Y.

Ford Optional 400 "Cleveland" V-8: Overhead valve. Cast-iron block. Displacement: 400 cid. B & S: 4.00 x 4.00 in. Compression ratio: 9.0:1. Brake hp: 260 at 4400 rpm. Carburetor: Motorcraft two-barrel. Five main bearings. Code S.

Ford Thunder Jet 429 four-barrel V-8: Overhead valve. Cast-iron block. Displacement: 429 cid. B & S: 4.36 x 3.59 in. Compression ratio: 10.5:1. Brake hp: 360 at 4600 rpm. Carburetor: Motorcraft four-barrel. Five main bearings. Code N.

Ford Cobra Jet 429 V-8: Overhead valve. Cast-iron block. Displacement: 429 cid. B & S: 4.36 x 3.59 in. Compression ratio: 11.3:1. Brake hp: 370 at 5400 rpm. Carburetor: Holley four-barrel. Five main bearings. Code C.

Super Cobra Jet 429 V-8: Overhead valve. Cast-iron block. Displacement: 429 cid. B & S: 4.36 x 3.59 in. Compression ratio: 11.3:1. Brake hp: 375 at 5600 rpm. Carburetor: Holley four-barrel with Ram-Air induction. Five main bearings. Code J.

Chassis:

Pinto: Wheelbase: 94 in. Overall length: 163 in. Tires: 6.00 x 13 belted black sidewall.

Maverick: Wheelbase: 103 in. Overall length: 179.4 in. Tires: 6.45 x 14 and 6.50 x 14 on V-8s.

Torino: Wheelbase: 117 in. and 114 in. on station wagons. Overall length: 206.2 inches and 209 in. on station wagons. Tires: E78-14 belted blackwall.

Ford: Wheelbase: 121 in. Overall length: 216.2 in. and 219.2 in. on station wagons. Tires: F78-15 belted black sidewall, G78-15 on Galaxie 500s and LTDs and H78-15 on station wagons.

Options:

Pinto: 122-cid, 100-hp four-cylinder overhead cam engine ($50). Cruise-O-Matic automatic transmission ($175). AM radio ($61). Chrome window moldings ($60). White sidewall tires ($33).

Maverick: 200-cid, 115-hp six ($39). 250-cid, 145-hp six ($79). 302-cid, 210-hp V-8. Cruise-O-Matic automatic transmission ($183). AM radio ($61). Power steering ($95). White sidewall tires ($34). Rear window defroster. Tinted glass. Vinyl roof. Deluxe seat belts. Heavy duty

1971 Maverick four-door sedan

suspension. Heavy duty battery. Consolette with storage. Consolette with storage plus an electric clock. Protection group with black vinyl body moldings and front and rear bumper guards.

Torino: 351-cid, 240-hp V-8 ($45). 351-cid, 285-hp V-8 ($93). 429-cid, 370-hp Cobra Jet V-8, Cobra ($279) and in other Torinos ($372). Cruise-O-Matic automatic transmission, Torino ($217) and Cobra ($238). Four-speed manual transmission ($250). AM radio ($66). Power steering ($115). Power tailgate window on station wagons ($35). Luggage rack on station wagon ($52). Vinyl roof ($95). White sidewall tires ($34).

Ford: 400-cid, 260-hp V-8. 390-cid, 255-hp V-8 ($98). 429-cid, 320-hp V-8 ($168). 429-cid, 360-hp V-8 ($268). Cruise-O-Matic automatic transmission, price varies with engine choice ($217 to $238). Power steering ($115). Power front disc brakes ($52). Tinted windshield ($54). Air conditioning ($420). Cruise control ($84). AM radio ($66). AM/FM radio ($240). Vinyl roof on passenger cars ($113) and $142, station wagons ($142). White sidewall tires ($34).

History:

The 1971 Fords were introduced on Sept. 18, 1970. Model year production peaked at 1,910,924 units. Calendar year production of 2,176,425 cars was recorded. (Note: The model year figure includes only Fords, Torinos, Mavericks, Pintos and Thunderbirds while the calendar year figure covers all passenger car and station wagon models.) The more expensive full-size Ford four-door sedans were advertised as "pillared hardtops" in 1971. Fords captured only three NASCAR races as the performance era wound to its close. Lee Iacocca became the president of Ford Motor Co. The "FE" series big-block V-8 was dropped and the Fairlane name ceased to exist with the end of the 1970 model year. The big-block, 390-cid and 428-cid V-8s were gradually phased-out during the 1971 production run. They were replaced by a new 400-cid "Cleveland" V-8 and the 429-cid V-8.

1971 Maverick four-door sedan

1971 Maverick Grabber two-door sedan

1971 Pinto two-door hatchback

1972 Galaxie 500 four-door hardtop

1972 LTD Country Squire station wagon

1972 LTD convertible

1972 Ford

Pinto — Four: The Pintos were unchanged from the 1971 models. The big news was the addition of a two-door station wagon. The Runabout received a larger rear window. Once again in 1972, the Pinto standard equipment included vent less door windows, high back slim line bucket seats, all-vinyl upholstery, two-pod instrument cluster, glove box, interior dome light, floor-mounted transmission controls, rack and pinion steering, hot water heater, Direct-Aire ventilation system and 6.00 x 13 rayon blackwall tires. Pintos were available with either a standard British-built 1600cc (98 cid) 54-hp overhead valve four-cylinder engine, or a second, more powerful and more popular German-built 2000cc (122 cid) 86 hp four-cylinder engine. Both engines used a four-speed manual transmission, but only the larger engine was available with the three-speed Cruise-O-Matic transmission. While good fuel economy was the main objective of the new Pinto, those equipped with the larger engine and four-speed manual transmission provided quite brisk performance by any standards.

Maverick 6 and V-8: Back again for 1972 was the Maverick in standard two-door and four-door versions along with the two-door Grabber version. The basic Mavericks came with the 170-cid six and three-speed manual transmission plus 6.45 x 14 blackwall tires. Other standard features in 1972 included cowl intake ventilation, center rear fuel filler, curved vent less side glass with flip-style rear windows on the two-door, full-width seats in cloth and vinyl trim, color-keyed floor mats, door-operated courtesy lights, a two-spoke steering wheel and a three-speed blower and blend-air heater. Again in 1972, the Grabber edition was available with simulated hood scoops, grille-mounted road lamps, trim rings and hub caps, black or two-color hood stripes and body stripes with the Grabber logo, dual racing mirrors with the left side a remote-controlled mirror, full-width seats in Ruffino vinyl or Manston cloth, a deck lid spoiler and

quarter panel extension moldings, blackout paint on the grille, headlamp surrounds and stone deflector. The Grabber also offered bright window frames and a deluxe steering wheel. Once again, Maverick buyers could opt for the 200 or 250-cid six or the 302-cid V-8.

Torino — 6 and V-8: Two basic lines of intermediate-size Ford Torinos remained. Both the base Torino models and the top-line Gran Torinos were restyled from end-to-end. The Torino models featured a chrome-trimmed windshield, rear window and rain gutter moldings, highback bench seats, all-vinyl seat and door trim, floor mats, hubcaps with trim rings, a 250-cid six-cylinder engine and a three-speed manual transmission. The Torino station wagon also included power front disc brakes and a three-way tailgate. The Gran Torino was the top trim level for 1972 and included all the Torino trim plus manual front disc brakes, cloth and vinyl trim on seats and interior door panels, carpeting, lower body, wheel well and deck lid moldings, dual-note horn, trunk mat, deluxe steering wheel and chrome trim on the foot pedals. The Gran Torino Squire station wagon also included the 302-cid, 140-hp V-8, deluxe pleated vinyl interior trim, wheel covers and wood grain appliqués on the body, tailgate and instrument panel. The Gran Torino Sport was the rakish version of the Gran Torino line and included all the Gran Torino features plus the 302-cid, 140-hp V-8 engine, pleated all-vinyl trim, hood scoops, color-keyed dual racing mirrors and a unique grille. The Torino's "Coke bottle" shape was even more pronounced for 1972. There were rounded front fender profiles, and a rear fender that swept up toward the roof "C" pillar, then tapered toward the rear of the car. Behind the car was a massive rear bumper that housed rectangular taillights at each end. The grille was slightly reminiscent of the Cobra with its large oval between the quad headlights. Automotive writer Tom McCahill observed that the 1972 Torinos looked like "land-locked tunas sucking air." The top profile of the four-door sedans was rounder than in previous years, and the two-door fastback "Sportsroof" featured an extremely low roofline.

Ford Custom and Custom 500 — 6 and V-8: The 1972 full-size Fords received only minor trim updating with a slightly restyled grille set within the same grille opening. There was a slightly more protective front bumper. The rest of the body styling remained unchanged. The Custom was the base trim level for 1971 and included a chrome-trimmed windshield and rear window moldings; nylon carpeting, an ignition key warning buzzer, a 351-cid V-8 and Cruise-O-Matic automatic transmission. Six-cylinder versions were available for fleet and taxi use as well. Power steering and F78-15 belted black sidewall tires were also standard. The Custom 500 versions included all the Custom trim plus lower back panel and wheel lip moldings, and cloth and vinyl seating surfaces. Station wagons also included H78-15 belted black sidewall tires and power tailgate window.

Galaxie 500 — 6 and V-8: The Galaxie 500 was the intermediate trim level full-size Ford for 1972 and included all the Custom 500 trim plus wheel lip and deck lid moldings, rocker panel moldings and wood grain appliqués on the instrument panel.

Ford LTD — V-8: The LTD was the top trim level full-size Ford for 1972 and included all the Galaxie 500 trim plus power front disc brakes, electric clock, luxury seat trim except convertibles, rear bumper guards, wood grain accents on interior door panels, front door courtesy lights, chrome trim on foot pedals, chrome armrest bases, F78-15 belted black sidewall tires on two-door hardtops and G78-15 tires on all others, except station wagons. Country Squire station wagons also included full wheel covers and reflective rear wood grain paneling, in addition to the wood grain paneling on the body. LTD Brougham included all the standard LTD features plus full wheel covers, rocker panel moldings, unique Brougham seat and door trim, highback, flight-bench seats with center armrest, cut-pile carpeting, rear door courtesy light switches, front end rear dual armrests and G78-15 belted black sidewall tires.

VIN:

The 1972 Ford serial number code was broken down as follows: The first symbol indicated the year: 2 = 1972. The second symbol identified the assembly plant: A = Atlanta, Georgia; B = Oakville, Ontario, Canada, E = Mahwah, New Jersey, F = Dearborn, Michigan, G = Chicago, Illinois, H = Lorain, Ohio, J = Los Angeles, California, K = Kansas City, Missouri; N = Norfolk, Virginia, P = Twin Cities (Minneapolis and St. Paul, Minnesota), R = San Jose, California, S = Allen Park Pilot Plant, T = Metuchen, New Jersey, U = Louisville, Kentucky, W = Wayne, Michigan, X = St. Thomas, Ontario, Canada, Y = Wixom, Michigan and Z = St. Louis, Missouri. The third and fourth symbols identified the body series: 62D=Maverick Grabber two-door. The fifth symbol identified the engine codes: A=460 V-8, F = 302-cid V-8, H = 351-cid V-8, L = 250-cid six-cylinder, N = 429-cid V-8 with four-barrel carb, Q = 351-cid V-8, R = 351-cid Boss V-8, S = 400-cid V-8, T = 200-cid six-cylinder, U = 170-cid six-cylinder, V = 240-cid six-cylinder, W = 98-cid four-cylinder and X = 122-cid four-cylinder. The last six digits were the unit's production number, beginning at 100001 and up.

Pinto (Four)

Model No.	Body/ Style No.	Body Type & Seating	Factory Price	Shipping Weight	Production Total
---	62B	2-dr. Sedan-4P	$1,960	1,968 lbs.	181,002
---	64B	2-dr. Runabout-4P	$2,078	2,012 lbs.	197,920
---	73B	2-dr. Station Wagon-4P	$2,265	2,293 lbs.	101,483

Note: Total series output was 480,405 units.

Maverick (6)

---	54A	4-dr. Sedan-6P	$2,245	2,833 lbs.	Note
---	62A	2-dr. Runabout-6P	$2,190	2,538 lbs.	Note
---	62D	2-dr. Grabber-6P	$2,359	2,493 lbs.	Note

Maverick (V-8)

---	54A	4-dr. Sedan-6P	$2,406	2,826 lbs.	73,686
---	62A	2-dr. Runabout-6P	$2,350	2,731 lbs.	145,931
---	62D	2-dr. Grabber-6P	$2,519	2,786 lbs.	35,347

Note: Total series output was 254,964 units.

Torino (6)

---	53B	4-dr. Hardtop-6P	$2,641	3,469 lbs.	Note
---	65B	2-dr. Hardtop-6P	$2,673	3,369 lbs.	Note
---	71B	4-dr. Station Wagon-6P	$2,955	3,879 lbs.	Note
---	53D	4-dr. Sedan-6P	$2,856	3,476 lbs.	Note

Torino (V-8)

---	53B	4-dr. Hardtop-6P	$2,731	3,548 lbs.	33,486
---	65B	2-dr. Hardtop-6P	$2,762	3,448 lbs.	33,530
---	71B	4-dr. Station Wagon-6P	$3,045	3,958 lbs.	22,204
---	53D	4-dr. Sedan-6P	$2,947	3,555 lbs.	102,300

1972 LTD Brougham two-door hardtop

Gran Torino (6)

---	65D	2-dr. Hardtop-6P	$2,878	3,395 lbs.	Note 1
---	71D	4-dr. Station Wagon-6P	$3,096	3,881 lbs.	Note 1

Gran Torino (V-8)

---	65D	2-dr. Hardtop-6P	$2,967	3,474 lbs.	132,284
---	71D	4-dr. Station Wagon-6P	$3,186	3,960 lbs.	45,212
---	63R	2-dr. Fastback-6P	$3,094	3,496 lbs.	60,794
---	65R	2-dr. Sport Hardtop-6P	$3,094	3,474 lbs.	31,239
---	71K	4-dr. Squire Station Wagon-6P	$3,486	4,042 lbs.	35,595

Note: Total series output was 496,645 units. Six and V-8 production was not documented by Ford Motor Co.

Custom (6 and V-8)

---	54B	4-dr. Sedan-6P	$3,288	3,759 lbs.	33,014
---	71B	4-dr. Ranch Wagon-6P	$3,806	4,317 lbs.	13,064

Custom 500 (6 and V-8)

---	54D	4-dr. Sedan-6P	$3,418	3,764 lbs.	24,870
---	71D	4-dr. Ranch Wagon-6P	$3,895	4,327 lbs.	16,834

Note: Total series output was 87,782 units. Six and 10-passenger station wagon production was not broken out.

Galaxie 500 (6 and V-8)

---	54F	4-dr. Sedan-6P	$3,685	3,826 lbs.	104,167
---	57F	4-dr. Hardtop-6P	$3,720	3,881 lbs.	28,939
---	65F	2-dr. Hardtop-6P	$3,752	3,826 lbs.	80,855
---	71F	4-dr. Country Sedan-6P	$4,028	4,308 lbs.	55,238

Note: Total series output was 269,199 units. Six and 10-passenger station wagon production was not broken out

LTD (V-8)

---	53H	4-dr. Sedan-6P	$3,906	3,913 lbs.	104,167
---	57H	4-dr. Hardtop-6P	$3,941	3,908 lbs.	33,742
---	65H	2-dr. Hardtop-6P	$3,898	3,853 lbs.	101,048
---	76H	2-dr. Convertible-6P	$4,073	4,091 lbs.	4,234
---	71H	4-dr. Country Squire-6P	$4,318	4,308 lbs.	121,419

LTD Brougham (V-8)

---	53K	4-dr. Sedan-6P	$4,047	3,949 lbs.	36,909
---	57K	4-dr. Hardtop-6P	$4,090	3,944 lbs.	23,364
---	65K	2-dr. Hardtop-6P	$4,050	3,883 lbs.	50,409

Note: Total series output was 475,292 units. Station wagon production was not broken out between six- and 10-passenger models.

Engines:

Pinto Base Four: Overhead cam. Cast-iron block. Displacement: 98 cid. B & S: 3.19 x 3.06 in. Compression ratio: 8.0:1. Net hp: 54 at 4600 rpm. Carburetor: Motorcraft one-barrel. Five main bearings. Code W.

Pinto Optional Four: Overhead cam. Cast-iron block. Displacement: 122 cid. B & S: 3.58 x 3.03 in. Compression ratio: 8.2:1. Net hp: 86 at 5400 rpm. Carburetor: Ford/Weber two-barrel. Five main bearings. Code X.

Maverick Base Six: Overhead valve. Cast-iron block. Displacement: 170 cid. B & S: 3.50 x 2.94 in. Compression ratio: 8.3:1. Net hp: 82 at 4400 rpm. Carburetor: Motorcraft one-barrel. Seven main bearings. Code U.

1972 LTD two-door hardtop with moon roof

Ford Base Six: Overhead valve. Cast-iron block. Displacement: 240 cid. B & S: 4.00 x 3.18 in. Compression ratio: 8.5:1. Net hp: 103 at 3800 rpm. Carburetor: Motorcraft one-barrel. Seven main bearings. Code V.

Torino Base and Maverick Optional Six: Overhead valve. Displacement: 250 cid. B & S: 3.68 x 3.91 in. Compression ratio: 8.0:1. Net hp: 98 at 3400 rpm. Carburetor: Motorcraft one-barrel. Seven main bearings. Code L.

Torino and Gran Torino Base 302 V-8: Overhead valve. Cast-iron block. Displacement: 302 cid. B & S: 4.00 x 3.00 in. Compression ratio: 8.5:1. Net hp: 140 at 4000 rpm. Carburetor: Motorcraft two-barrel. Five main bearings. Code F.

351 "Windsor" V-8: Overhead valve. Cast-iron block. Displacement: 351 cid. B & S: 4.00 x 3.50 in. Compression ratio: 8.3:1. Net hp: 153 at 3800 rpm. Carburetor: Motorcraft two-barrel. Five main bearings.

Torino and Gran Torino Optional V-8, 351 "Cleveland" two-barrel: Overhead valve. Cast iron block. Displacement: 351 cid. B & S: 4.00 x 3.50 in. Compression ratio: 8.6:1. Net hp: 163 at 3800 rpm. Carburetor: Motorcraft two-barrel. Five main bearings. Code H.

Torino and Gran Torino Optional V-8, 351 "Cleveland" four-barrel: Overhead valve. Cast-iron block. Displacement: 351 cid. B & S: 4.00 x 3.50 in. Compression ratio: 8.6:1. Net hp: 248 at 5400 rpm. Carburetor: Holley four-barrel. Five main bearings.

351 HO "Cleveland" V-8: Overhead valve. Cast-iron block. Displacement: 351 cid. B & S: 4.00 x 3.50 in. Compression ratio: 8.6:1. Net hp: 266 at 5400 rpm. Carburetor: Holley four-barrel. Five main bearings. Code Q.

Ford Optional 400 "Cleveland" V-8: Overhead valve. Cast-iron block. Displacement: 400 cid. B & S: 4.00 x 4.00 in. Compression ratio: 8.5:1. Net hp: 172 at 4000 rpm. Carburetor: Motorcraft two-barrel. Five main bearings. Code S.

Ford Optional Thunderbird 429 V-8: Overhead valve. Cast-iron block. Displacement: 429 cid. B & S: 4.36 x 3.59 in. Compression ratio: 8.5:1. Net hp: 212 at 4400 rpm. Carburetor: Motorcraft four-barrel. Five main bearings. Code N.

Thunderbird 460 V-8: Overhead valve. Cast-iron block. Displacement: 460 cid. B & S: 4.36 x 3.85 in. Compression ratio: 8.5:1. Net hp: 224 at 4400 rpm. Carburetor: Motorcraft four-barrel. Five main bearings. Code A.

1972 Torino two-door hardtop

1972 Gran Torino Sport fastback

1972 Gran Torino Squire station wagon

Chassis:

Pinto: Wheelbase: 94 in. Overall length: 163 in. Tires: 6.00 x 13 rayon black sidewall. A78-13, A70-13 and 175-R13 tires were optional.

Maverick: Wheelbase: 103 in. Overall length: 179.4 in. Tires: C78-14 tubeless blackwall, V-8 and 6.45 x 14 tubeless blackwall, six.

Torino and Gran Torino: Wheelbase: 118 in., four-door sedan and 114 in., other models. Overall length: 203.7 in., two-door, 207.3 in., four-door and 211.6 in., station wagon. Tires: E78-14. Torino two-door, F78-14, Gran Torino and Torino four-door and H78-14, station wagons. E70-14, Gran Torino Sport hardtop and F70-14, Gran Torino Sport Sportsroof. All tires were belted black sidewall.

Ford: Wheelbase: 121 in. Overall length: 216.2 in. and 219.2 in., station wagons. Tires: F78-15 belted black sidewall, G78-15, Galaxie 500 and LTD and H78-15, station wagons.

Options:

Pinto: 122-cid, 86-hp overhead cam four ($49). Cruise-O-Matic automatic transmission ($170). AM radio ($59). Chrome window moldings, part of Luxury Decor Group ($137). Wheel covers ($23). White sidewall tires ($42). Other Pinto options in 1972 included air conditioning, a consolette with electric clock, a compass, a rear window

1972 Gran Torino fastback

1972 Maverick four-door sedan

1972 Maverick two-door sedan

1972 Maverick "Grabber" two-door sedan

1972 Maverick two-door sedan with Sprint Décor option

1972 Pinto Runabout two-door hatchback

1972 Pinto Runabout two-door hatchback

1972 Pinto Squire station wagon

1972 Pinto two-door sedan

defogger, vinyl or rubber front and rear floor mats, AM push button radio, an AM/FM radio, a two-way citizen's band radio and a rear speaker. A traveling and camping package included a luggage rack, heavy-duty shock absorbers, a trailer hitch, trailer light wiring harness and mirrors. A protective equipment package included air horns, front and rear bumper guards, a locking gas cap, body moldings, a spotlight, a remote trunk release and wheel covers. Available safety equipment included tot guard child safety seats, a fire extinguisher and an emergency flare kit. Other options included a fog lamp, a fold-down rear seats for the base Pinto, pivoting quarter windows and a day-night rear view mirror.

Maverick: 200-cid six-cylinder ($38). 250-cid six-cylinder ($77). 302-cid V-8 engine. Cruise-O-Matic automatic transmission ($177). AM radio ($59). Power steering ($92). White sidewall tires ($34). Other 1972 Maverick options included a floor-mounted three speed manual shifter, Selectaire air conditioning, rear window defogger, tinted glass, power steering, deluxe seat belts, bumper guards, door edge guards, a heavy duty battery, heavy duty suspension, an electric clock, lockable storage consolette, two-tone paint and a vinyl roof. Packages included the Luxury and Décor group which added a vinyl roof, front and rear bumper guards with color-keyed inserts, C78 x 14 whitewall tires, color keyed wheel covers, remote control left-hand exterior mirror, deluxe gas cap and road lamp inserts outside also added a tan interior with cut pile carpeting, padded door trim panels, all-vinyl seats, reclining front bucket seats and a wood grain appliqué on the instrument panel. The convenience group included a color-keyed left side exterior racing mirror and a day-night inside mirror. The protection group offered such items as black vinyl body moldings and front and rear bumper guards.

Torino and Gran Torino: 351-cid, 163-hp "Cleveland" V-8 ($44). 351-cid, 248-hp "Cleveland" V-8, two-door models only ($127). 429-cid, 205-hp V-8 ($99). Cruise-O-Matic automatic transmission, $21 to $211, depending on engine chosen. Four-speed manual transmission ($200). AM radio ($64). AM/FM stereo radio ($208). Power steering ($112). Power tailgate window on station wagons ($34). Luggage rack on station wagons ($77). Vinyl roof ($93). White sidewall tires ($34).

Ford: 400-cid, 172-hp V-8 ($95). 429-cid, 205-hp V-8 ($222). Power front disc brakes, standard on LTDs ($50). Tinted windshield ($53). Air conditioning ($409). Air conditioning with Climate Control ($486). Cruise Control ($99). AM radio ($64). AM/FM stereo radio ($234). Vinyl roof ($110). Vinyl roof on station wagons ($148). White sidewall tires ($34).

History:

The 1972 Ford line was introduced Sept. 24, 1971. New options for 1972 included electric sliding sunroofs, an electric deck lid release, tailgate power lock and body moldings with vinyl inserts. Sun roofs, which Ford referred to consistently as moon roofs, were installed on 0.6 percent of all 1972 Ford Motor Co products, including Lincolns and Mercurys. Engines were no longer rated at brake horsepower. Beginning in 1972, all engines were rated in SAE net horsepower or the theoretical power, deducting for drain caused by the accessories and transmission. Pollution requirements and rising insurance rates, plus the lower compression ratios, meant considerably restricted performance. As a result, 1971 is almost universally considered to be the end of the Ford muscle car era. The Ford model year output peaked at 1,855,201 vehicles this year. The calendar year production total was counted as 1,868,016 units. Henry Ford II was Ford Motor Co. board chairman and Lee Iacocca was the firm's president. Ford Division (also called Ford Marketing Corp.) was headed by J. B. Naughton, who held the title of vice-president and divisional general manager. The model year 1972 was a sales record-breaker and marked the first time in history that Ford dealers sold more than three million cars and trucks.

1973 Ford

Pinto — Four: The Pinto exterior remained basically the same as in the 1972 model year with the exception of front and rear bumpers. Front bumper guards were made standard equipment this year (but deleted in later years). The new bumper treatment lengthened the Pintos by 1.5 inches. Styles included the two-door or three-door, depending on your preference, Runabout. It had a large rear hatch with gas-operated springs. Other body styles continued to be the original two-door Pinto sedan and the station wagon, in its second year. In 1972, Pinto owners could add a larger four-cylinder engine and could add a limited number of options.

Maverick — 6 and V-8: The Maverick series was basically unchanged from the 1972 models. There was, however, a slightly new appearance up front because of the flatter, reinforced bumper. Standard features on the base Maverick again were the 200-cid six, three-speed manual transmission, 14-inch blackwall tires, cowl air induction, curved side glass with rear quarter flip-style windows on two-door models, recessed door handles, a locking glove box, full-width seats with a random striped cloth and vinyl trim, steel guard rails in the side doors, locking steering column with a key reminder buzzer, uni-lock shoulder and lap belts, sound insulation, color-keyed carpeting and a color-keyed steering wheel.

Torino and Gran Torino — 6 and V-8: The 1973 Torino and Gran Torino models were slightly modified from 1972 specifications. A revised grille had a more rectangular opening than the 1972 version and blended well with the large front bumper. Improvements included larger standard rear brakes, an interior hood release and optional spare tire lock. The Torino models were the base trim level and featured chrome-trimmed windshield, rear window and rain gutter moldings, highback bench seats, all-vinyl seat and door trim, floor mats, hubcaps, a 250-cid six-cylinder engine and three-speed manual transmission. The Torino station wagon also included power front disc brakes and Ford's famous three-way tailgate. The Gran Torino was the top trim level for 1973 and included all the Torino trim plus manual front disc brakes, cloth and vinyl trim on seats and interior door panels, carpeting, lower body, wheel well and deck lid moldings, dual note horns, a trunk mat, a deluxe two-spoke steering wheel and chrome trim on the foot pedals. The Gran Torino Squire station wagon also included the 302-cid, 138-hp V-8, deluxe pleated vinyl interior trim, wheel covers and wood grain appliqués on the body, tailgate and instrument panel. The Gran Torino Sport was the daring version of the Gran Torino and included all the Gran Torino features plus the 302-cid, 138-hp, V-8, pleated, all-vinyl trim, hood scoops, color-keyed dual racing mirrors and a unique grille

Ford — V-8: Full-size Fords were restyled for the 1973 model year. The emphasis was placed on a more rounded profile, similar to the Torino series. The "Mercedes" grille was the current craze at Ford Motor Co. and big Fords had their own version, complete with a spring-loaded hood ornament on the high trim-level models. At the rear, two rectangular taillights were used on all models and were similar to those used on the lower-priced lines of the 1972 full-size Fords. The Custom 500 was the base trim level Ford in 1973 and included chrome-trimmed windshield and rear window moldings, nylon carpeting, ignition key warning buzzer, the 351-cid V-8, Cruise-O-Matic automatic transmission, power steering and G78-15 belted black sidewall tires. The Galaxie 500 was the intermediate trim level and included all the Custom 500 features plus lower back panel wheel lip moldings, cloth and vinyl seating surfaces, rocker panel moldings and wood grain appliqués on the instrument panel. The LTD was the top trim level and included all the Galaxie 500 features plus deep-cushioned low-back bench seats, an electric clock, a deluxe two-spoke steering wheel, chrome trim on the foot pedals, polished aluminum trim around the rear edge of the hood, body moldings with vinyl inserts and HR78-15 steel-belted radial tires. The LTD Brougham added Flight-Bench seats with center armrests, front door courtesy lights, full wheel covers, cut-pile carpeting, carpeted lower door panels, polished rocker panel moldings and extensions, an automatic seatbelt release on two-door models, a vinyl roof and color-keyed seat belts. The Ranch Wagon contained all the features of the Galaxie 500 models plus J78-15 tires. The Country Sedan contained Ranch Wagon features plus a dual note horn, wood grain appliqués on the instrument panel and front and rear door panels, a special sound package, body moldings and a chrome-plated grille. The Country Squires contained all the features found in the LTDs plus J78-15 tires and the 400-cid V-8.

The 1973 Ford serial number code was broken down as follows: The first symbol indicated the year: 3 = 1973. The second symbol identified the assembly plant: A = Atlanta, Georgia; B = Oakville, Ontario, Canada, E = Mahwah, New Jersey, F = Dearborn, Michigan, G = Chicago, Illinois, H = Lorain, Ohio, J = Los Angeles, California, K = Kansas City, Missouri; N = Norfolk, Virginia, P = Twin Cities (Minneapolis and St. Paul, Minnesota), R = San Jose, California, S = Allen Park Pilot Plant, T = Metuchen, New Jersey, U = Louisville, Kentucky, W = Wayne, Michigan, X = St. Thomas, Ontario, Canada, Y = Wixom, Michigan and Z = St. Louis, Missouri. The third and fourth symbols identified the body series: 63R=Gran Torino Sport fastback. The fifth symbol identified the engine codes: A=460 V-8, F = 302-cid V-8, H = 351-cid V-8, L = 250-cid six-cylinder, N = 429-cid V-8 with four-barrel carb, Q = 351-cid V-8, R = 351-cid Boss V-8, S = 400-cid V-8, T = 200-cid six-cylinder, W=98-cid four-cylinder and X = 122-cid four-cylinder. The last six digits were the unit's production number, beginning at 100001 and up.

1973 LTD four-door hardtop

The Ford Motor Co. body plate changed slightly in 1973. The VIN was on the left side adjacent to the type, Passenger. Along the bottom were six codes from left to right. The first was the body type code, the same as in the VIN. The second was the color code: 6F=Gold Glow. The third code symbol was the trim: BF= Light Ginger with standard cloth and vinyl bench seat. The fourth code was the transmission: W = C4 automatic. The fifth space was the rear axle with 6 = 3.00:1 ratio. Last was the DSO code which listed one of the 33 U. S. Ford districts 74=Seattle or one of the Ford special codes 84 = Home office reserve.

Escort (Four)

Model No.	Body/ Style No.	Body Type & Seating	Factory Price	Shipping Weight	Production Total
20	61D	2-dr. Pony Hatchback-4P	$6,436	2,180 lbs.	Note 1
21	61D	2-dr. GL Hatchback-4P	$6,801	2,187 lbs.	Note 1
25	58D	4-dr. GL Hatchback-4P	$7,022	2,222 lbs.	Note 1
28	74D	4-dr. GL Station Wagon-4P	$7,312	2,274 lbs.	Note 1
23	61D	2-dr. GT Hatchback-4P	$8,724	2,516 lbs.	Note 1

Note 1: For the model year, a total of 206,729 two-door hatchbacks. 102,187 four-door hatchback sedans, and 65,849 station wagons were built.

Pinto (Four)

---	62B	2-dr. Sedan-4P	$1,997	2,124 lbs.	116,146
---	64B	2-dr. Runabout-4P	$2,120	2,162 lbs.	150,603
---	73B	2-dr. Station Wagon-4P	$2,319	2,397 lbs.	217,763

Note: Total Pinto output was 484,512 units.

Maverick (6)

---	54A	4-dr. Sedan-6P	$2,297	2,737 lbs.	Note 1
---	62A	2-dr. Sedan-6P	$2,240	2,642 lbs.	Note 1
---	62D	2-dr. Grabber sedan-6P	$2,419	2,697 lbs.	Note 1

Maverick (V-8)

---	54A	2-dr. Sedan-6P	$2,419	2,900 lbs.	110,382
---	62A	2-dr. Sedan-6P	$2,362	2,800 lbs.	148,943
---	62D	2-dr. Grabber Sedan-6P	$2,541	2,855 lbs.	32,350

Note: Total Maverick output was 291,675 units.

Torino (6)

---	53B	4-dr. Sedan-6P	$2,701	3,597 lbs.	Note 1
---	65B	2-dr. Hardtop-6P	$2,732	3,528 lbs.	Note 1

Torino (V-8)

---	53B	4-dr. Sedan-6P	$2,796	3,683 lbs.	37,524
---	65B	2-dr. Hardtop-6P	$2,826	3,615 lbs.	28,005
---	71B	4-dr. Station Wagon-6P	$3,198	4,073 lbs.	23,982

Gran Torino (6)

---	53D	4-dr. Sedan-6P	$2,890	3,632 lbs.	Note 1
---	65D	2-dr. Hardtop-6P	$2,921	3,570 lbs.	Note 1

1973 Galaxie 500 four-door pillared hardtop

1973 LTD Brougham two-door hardtop

1973 LTD Country Squire station wagon

1973 Gran Torino two-door hardtop

Gran Torino (V-8)

---	53D	4-dr. Sedan-6P	$2,984	3,719 lbs.	98,404
---	65D	2-dr. Hardtop-6P	$3,015	3,656 lbs.	138,962
---	71D	4-dr. Station Wagon-6P	$3,344	4,096 lbs.	60,738
---	71K	4-dr. Squire Station Wagon-6P	$3,559	4,124 lbs.	40,023
---	63R	2-dr. Sport Fastback-6P	$3,154	3,670 lbs.	51,853
---	65R	2-dr. Sport Hardtop-6P	$3,154	3,652 lbs.	17,090

Gran Torino Brougham (6)

---	53K	4-dr. Sedan-6P	$3,051	3,632 lbs.	------
---	65K	2-dr. Hardtop-6P	$3,071	3,590 lbs.	------

Gran Torino Brougham (V-8)

---	53K	4-dr. Sedan-6P	$3,140	3,719 lbs.	------
---	65K	2-dr. Hardtop-6P	$3,160	3,656 lbs.	------

Note: Torino and Gran Torino series output was 496,581 units. Ford Motor Co. didn't break out six or V-8 installations nor did they break out Gran Torino Broughams. Styles 53B, 53D and 53K were called four-door pillared hardtops in 1973.

Custom 500 (V-8)

---	53D	4-dr. Sedan-6P	$3,606	4,078 lbs.	42,549
---	71D	4-dr. Ranch Wagon-6P	$4,050	4,550 lbs.	22,432

Galaxie 500 (V-8)

---	53F	4-dr. Sedan-6P	$3,771	4,110 lbs.	85,654
---	57F	4-dr. Hardtop-6P	$3,833	4,120 lbs.	25,802
---	65F	2-dr. Hardtop-6P	$3,778	4,059 lbs.	70,808
---	71F	4-dr. Country Sedan-6P	$4,164	4,581 lbs.	51,290

LTD (V-8)

---	53H	4-dr. Sedan-6P	$3,958	4,150 lbs.	122,851
---	57H	4-dr. Hardtop-6P	$4,001	4,160 lbs.	28,608
---	65H	2-dr. Hardtop-6P	$3,950	4,100 lbs.	120,864
---	71H	4-dr. Country Squire-6P	$4,401	4,642 lbs.	142,933

LTD Brougham (V-8)

---	53K	4-dr. Sedan-6P	$4,113	4,179 lbs.	49,553
---	57K	4-dr. Hardtop-6P	$4,103	4,189 lbs.	22,268
---	65K	2-dr. Hardtop-6P	$4,107	4,128 lbs.	68,901

Note: Total series output was 941,054 units. The LTD four-door sedan was called a "pillared hardtop."

Engines:

Pinto Base Four: Overhead cam. Cast-iron block. Displacement: 98 cid. B & S: 3.19 x 3.06 in. Compression ratio: 8.0:1. Net hp: 54 at 4800 rpm. Carburetor: Motorcraft one barrel. Five main bearings. Code W.

Pinto Optional Four: Overhead cam. Cast-iron block. Displacement: 122 cid. B & S: 3.58 x 3.03 in. Compression ratio: 8.2:1. Net hp: 86 at 5400 rpm. Carburetor: Ford/Weber two-barrel. Five main bearings. Code X.

Maverick Base Six: Overhead valve. Cast-iron block. Displacement: 200 cid. B & S: 3.68 x 3.13 in. Compression ratio: 8.3:1. Net hp: 84 at 3800 rpm. Carburetor: Motorcraft single-barrel. Seven main bearings. Code T.

Torino Base and Maverick Optional Six: Overhead valve. Cast-iron block. Displacement: 250 cid. B & S: 3.68 x 3.91 in. Compression ratio: 8.0:1. Net hp: 88 at 3200 rpm. Carburetor: Motorcraft single-barrel. Seven main bearings. Code L.

Torino and Gran Torino Base 302 V-8: Overhead valve. Cast-iron block. Displacement: 302 cid. B & S: 4.00 x 3.00 in. Compression ratio: 8.0:1. Net hp: 135 at 4200 rpm. Carburetor: Motorcraft two-barrel. Five main bearings. Code F.

351 "Windsor" V-8: Overhead valve. Cast-iron block. Displacement: 351 cid. B & S: 4.00 x 3.50 in. Compression ratio: 8.0:1. Net hp: 156 at 3800 rpm. Carburetor: Motorcraft two-barrel. Five main bearings.

1973 Gran Torino Squire station wagon

Torino and Gran Torino 351 "Cleveland" V-8: Overhead valve. Cast-iron block. Displacement: 351 cid. B & S: 4.00 x 3.50 in. Compression ratio: 8.0:1. Net hp: 154 at 4000 rpm. Carburetor: Motorcraft two-barrel. Five main bearings. Code H.

351 "Cobra Jet Cleveland" V-8: Overhead valve. Cast-iron block. Displacement: 351 cid. B & S: 4.00 x 3.50 in. Compression ratio: 8.0:1. Net hp: 266 at 5400 rpm. Carburetor: Holley four-barrel. Five main bearings. Code Q.

Ford Optional 400 "Cleveland" V-8: Overhead valve. Cast-iron block. Displacement: 400 cid. B & S: 4.00 x 4.00 in. Compression ratio: 8.0:1. Net hp: 163 at 3800 rpm. Carburetor: Motorcraft two-barrel. Five main bearings. Code S.

Ford Optional Thunderbird 429 V-8: Overhead valve. Cast-iron block. Displacement: 429 cid. B & S: 4.36 x 3.59 in. Compression ratio: 8.0:1. Net hp: 201 at 4400 rpm. Carburetor: Motorcraft four-barrel. Five main bearings. Code N.

Thunderbird 460 V-8: Overhead valve. Cast-iron block. Displacement: 460 cid. B & S: 4.36 x 3.85 in. Compression ratio: 8.0:1. Net hp: 219 at 4400 rpm. Carburetor: Motorcraft four-barrel. Five main bearings. Code A.

Note: Beginning in 1973, Ford rated each engine with two or three different hp ratings, depending on the model each engine was installed in. We show lowest rating for each engine, except the "460's" highest rating. As body size and weight increased, horsepower ratings increased correspondingly. Most engine ratings varied between one and five horsepower. The 460-cid V-8 varied by 17 hp.

Chassis:

Pinto: Wheelbase: 94 in. Overall length: 163 in. Tires: 6.00 x 13 rayon blackwall. A78-13, A70-13 and 175-R13 tires were optional.

Maverick: Wheelbase: 103 in. Overall length: 179.4 in. Tires: 6.45 x 14 tubeless blackwall and C78-14 tubeless blackwall, V-8.

Torino and Gran Torino: Wheelbase: 114 in., two-door sedan and 118 in., four-door sedan. Overall length: 203.7 in., two-door, 207.3 in., four-door and 211.6 in., station wagons. Tires: E78-14, Torino two-door, F78-14, Gran Torino and Torino four-door and H78-14, station wagons. The Gran Torino Sport hardtop used E70-14 tires while the Gran Torino Sport fastback had size F70-14. All tires were belted blackwalls.

Ford: Wheelbase: 121 in. Overall length: 216.2 in. and 219.2 in., station wagons. Tires: F78-15 belted black sidewall and G78-15, Galaxie 500 and LTD as well as H78-15, station wagons.

Options:

Pinto: 122-cid four ($48.53). Cruise-O-Matic automatic transmission ($170). AM radio ($59). Luxury decor group ($137). Wheel covers ($23). White sidewall tires ($42). Sports accent group with radial whitewall tires, a vinyl roof, lower body paint, wheel covers, bright exterior moldings, cut pile carpeting, deluxe seat and door trim and wood tone accents. Four speed transmission. Convenience group ($18). Manual front disc brakes ($31). Electric rear window defroster ($42). AM/FM stereo radio ($190). Color-keyed racing-style mirrors ($12). Tinted glass, all windows ($36). Flip-style quarter windows ($28). Handling suspension ($12).

1973 Gran Torino Brougham four-door sedan

1973 Gran Torino Sport fastback

Maverick: 200-cid six-cylinder engine ($77). 302-cid, 135-hp V-8. Cruise-O-Matic automatic transmission ($177). AM radio ($59). Power steering ($92). White sidewall tires ($33). Luxury décor option with grain vinyl roof, body and wheel well moldings, front and rear bumper guards with rubber inserts, bright pillar appliqué, color-keyed wheel covers, deluxe gas cap and DR78 x 14 steel belted whitewall tires. The Luxury décor interior included reclining seats, tan soft vinyl interior, cut pile carpeting, color-keyed instrument panel with wood tone appliqué, deluxe two-spoke steering wheel, sound package and handling package. Other Maverick options included Selectaire air conditioning, high back bucket seats, an AM/FM stereo radio, a vinyl roof, dual racing mirrors, a rear window defogger, a locking jack, tinted glass, heavy-duty suspension, a heavy-duty battery and varied axle ratios. Additional options included an appearance group with door edge guards and floor mats, a deluxe bumper group and forged aluminum wheels. Floor shifts were available with both the three-speed manual and automatic transmission, the latter with bucket seats as well. Wide oval blackwall or raised-white letter tires also were available.

Torino and Gran Torino: 351-cid, 159-hp "Cleveland" V-8 ($44). 400-cid, 168-hp "Cleveland" V-8 ($127). 429-cid, 197-hp V-8 ($99). Cruise-O-Matic automatic transmission ($211). Four-speed manual transmission ($200). AM radio ($64). AM/FM stereo radio ($206). Power steering ($112). Power tailgate window, station wagons ($34). Luggage racks, station wagons ($77). Vinyl roof ($93). White sidewall tires ($34).

Ford: 400-cid, 172-hp V-8 ($95). 429-cid, 205-hp V-8 ($222). 460-cid, 202-hp V-8 ($222). Power front disc brakes, standard on LTDs ($50). Tinted windshield ($53). Air conditioning ($409). Air conditioning with Climate Control ($486). Cruise Control ($99). AM radio ($64). AM/FM stereo radio ($234). Vinyl roof ($110). Vinyl roof on station wagons ($148). White sidewall tires ($34).

History:

The 1973 Ford line was publicly introduced on Sept. 22, 1972. Highlights for 1973 included the new impact-absorbing bumpers and an increased emphasis on making cars theft and vandal-proof. A new fixed-length radio antenna was adopted along with inside hood release mechanisms. A spare tire lock was a new, extra-cost option. The Ford LTD was honored, by *Motor Trend* magazine, as the "Full-size Sedan of the Year" while *Road Test* magazine called it their "Car of the Year." The full-size Fords were the only models to receive significant restyling. The rest of the Ford lines received only minor trim updating. More federally-mandated safety requirements were initiated. They were reflected in massive "park bench" safety bumpers. These were supposed to tolerate a direct impact at five mph without damage. Pollution standards were tightened. The existing engines were further de-tuned or more emissions control equipment was added. Manufacturers began striving for improved mileage at the expense of performance and efficiency in

1973 Maverick Grabber two-door sedan

1973 Maverick two-door sedan

1973 Maverick four-door sedan

1973 Pinto Squire station wagon

1973 Pinto Runabout hatchback

1973 Pinto Runabout hatchback

1974 Gran Torino Brougham two-door hardtop

1974-1/2 Gran Torino Elite two-door hardtop

the face of further federal regulations. The Arab embargo of oil products imported from the Middle East also brought fuel economy into the spotlight. Ford Motor Co. executives included Board Chairman Henry Ford II, corporate president Lee Iacocca and Ford Marketing Corp. vice-president and Ford Division general manager B. E. Bidwell.

1974 Ford

Pinto — Four: This was the year that energy-absorbing bumpers were added to the Pinto. This brought an obvious change to the front of the car, as the air slot opening in the gravel pan could no longer be seen. Also eliminated was the center-mounted license plate holder. It didn't look right with the massive new bumper, but then, hardly anything else did either. The bumper was plain on the base trim models, but came with rubber-faced vertical guards and a black vinyl impact strip on models with the Deluxe decor package. Pinto station wagons could be outfitted with optional trim packages that included simulated wood grain exterior paneling and roof luggage racks. The Pinto was now in its third full model year and had weathered questions about its gas tank, which in some cases caught fire when punctured in rear impact collisions. While that controversy cast a shadow of doubt over Ford's small car, newer Pintos, especially the station wagon, were popular and versatile cars, especially with growing families.

Maverick — 6 and V-8: The Maverick had a slight frontal restyling for 1974 as energy-absorbing bumpers were adopted this year. A horizontal slot appeared in the center of the face bar, where the license plate indentation had formerly been positioned. Deluxe models featured side moldings with vinyl inserts; wheel cutout trim moldings and, on cars with vinyl roofs, a Maverick nameplate on the rear roof pillar. On all models, a similar nameplate was carried at the left-hand side of the grille. Again in 1974, Maverick was packaged in base trim as an economy model with its 200-cid six-cylinder engine and three-speed manual transmission. Two-door Mavericks came with such no-nonsense features as a cloth and vinyl bench seat, flip-style rear quarter windows, a heater-defroster, locking glove box and a waiting list of options. The four-door Maverick was much the same. The options available were growing as many members of the Baby Boom generation were buying their first cars and wanted a little customization and personalization for the money. It was the fourth full model year for the Maverick, introduced in April 1969.

Torino and Gran Torino — V-8: New grilles, front bumpers and some optional revisions in roof pillar treatments characterized the 1974 Torino editions. The grille used a finer mesh and was now segmented by seven vertical division bars. The bumper had a slightly more prominent center protrusion. Opera window treatments could be ordered, at extra cost, for a fancier looking coupe. Side trim was revised to eliminate the wide, horizontally ribbed decorative panels used on high-trim models the previous season. The Gran Torino Elite arrived at midyear featuring full-length side trim with vinyl inserts; a chrome center molding across the grille; single headlamps in square bezels and parking lamps notched into the corners of the front fenders.. The Torino was the base trim level and featured windshield, rear window and rain gutter moldings, high back bench seats, vinyl upholstery and trim, floor mats, three-speed manual transmission, HR78-14 tires or G78-14 tires on hardtops and a base 302-cid V-8. The Torino station wagon included power front disc brakes, H78-14 tires and a three-way tailgate. The top-level Gran Torino added manual front disc brakes, cloth and vinyl seat trim, carpeting, lower body, wheel well and deck lid moldings, a dual note horn, deluxe two-spoke steering wheel and chrome foot pedal trim. The Gran Torino Squire station wagon added the deluxe pleated vinyl interior trim, wheel covers, wood grain body appliqués and tailgate trim and plus wood grain dashboard inserts. The Gran Torino Sport included all-vinyl trim, hood scoops, color-keyed dual outside racing mirrors and a unique grille.

Ford — V-8: The full-size Fords were slightly re-trimmed versions of the 1973 restyle. The main difference appeared at the front where extension caps were no longer used on the front fender corners, so that the vertical parking lamp lens was taller than the previous type and had a ribbed appearance. The overall shape of the grille was the same but used finer mesh inserts. The central section was surrounded by a rectangular housing that segmented it from the rest of the grille. This hinted at the trendy "Mercedes-Benz" look. Some called it neo-classical styling. To heighten this image, a stand-up hood ornament was added to high-trim Fords. The Custom 500 was the base trim level and included chrome windshield and rear window moldings, nylon carpeting, an ignition key warning buzzer, power steering, automatic transmission, G78-15 belted black sidewall tires and the 351-cid engine. The intermediate Galaxie 500 added wheel lip moldings, cloth and vinyl seats, rocker panel moldings and instrument panel wood grain appliqués. The top-level LTD featured deep cushioned, low-back bench seats, an electric clock, deluxe two-spoke steering wheel, chrome trim on the foot pedals, polished aluminum trim for the rear hood edge; and HR78-15 steel-belted radial tires. The LTD Brougham came with high back Flight-Bench seats with a center armrest, front door courtesy lights, full wheel covers, cut-pile carpeting and carpeted lower door panels, as well as polished rocker panel moldings, an automatic seatback release in two-door styles, a vinyl roof and color-keyed seat belts. The Ranch Wagon rode on J78-15 tires. The Country Sedan added a dual note horn, wood grain instrument panel appliqué, wood grain front and rear door panel trim, special sound insulation, body moldings and a special chrome-plated grille. The Country Squire came with J78-15 tires and the 400-cid V-8.

VIN:

The 1974 Ford serial number code was broken down as follows: The first symbol indicated the year: 4 = 1974. The second symbol identified the assembly plant: A = Atlanta, Georgia; B = Oakville, Ontario, Canada, E = Mahwah, New Jersey, F = Dearborn, Michigan, G = Chicago, Illinois, H = Lorain, Ohio, J = Los Angeles, California, K = Kansas City, Missouri; N = Norfolk, Virginia, P = Twin Cities (Minneapolis and St. Paul, Minnesota), R = San Jose, California, S = Allen Park Pilot Plant, T = Metuchen, New Jersey, U = Louisville, Kentucky, W = Wayne, Michigan, X = St. Thomas, Ontario, Canada, Y = Wixom, Michigan and Z = St. Louis, Missouri. The third and fourth symbols identified the body series: 73B=Pinto station wagon. The fifth symbol identified the engine codes: A=460 V-8, F = 302-cid V-8, H = 351-cid V-8, L = 250-cid six-cylinder, Q = 351-cid Cobra Jet V-8, S = 400-cid V-8, T = 200-cid six-cylinder, X = 122-cid four-cylinder and Y=139-cid four. The last six digits were the unit's production number, beginning at 100001 and up.

Pinto

Model No.	Body/ Style No.	Body Type & Seating	Factory Price	Shipping Weight	Production Total
---	62B	2-dr. Sedan-4P	$2,527	2,372 lbs.	132,061
---	64B	2-dr. Hatchback-4P	$2,631	2,402 lbs.	174,754
---	73B	2-dr. Station Wagon-4P	$2,771	2,576 lbs.	237,394

Note: Total Pinto output was 544,209 units. The two-door hatchback coupe was called the Runabout.

Maverick (6)

---	54A	4-dr. Sedan-6P	$2,824	2,851 lbs.	Note 1
---	62A	2-dr. Sedan-6P	$2,742	2,739 lbs.	Note 1
---	62A	2-dr. Grabber sedan-6P	$2,923	2,787 lbs.	Note 1

Maverick (V-8)

---	54A	4-dr. Sedan-6P	$2,982	3,014 lbs.	137,728
---	62A	2-dr. Sedan-6P	$2,949	2,902 lbs.	139,818
---	62A	2-dr. Grabber sedan-6P	$3,081	2,950 lbs.	23,502

Note: Total Maverick output was 301,048 units. Ford Motor Co. did not break out six and V-8 production.

Torino

---	53B	4-dr. Sedan-6P	$3,176	3,793 lbs.	31,161
---	65B	2-dr. Hardtop-6P	$3,310	3,509 lbs.	22,738
---	71B	4-dr. Station Wagon-6P	$3,755	4,175 lbs.	15,393

Gran Torino

---	53D	4-dr. Sedan (Pillared HT)-6P	$3,391	3,847 lbs.	72,728
---	65D	2-dr. Hardtop-6P	$3,485	3,647 lbs.	76,290
---	71D	4-dr. Station Wagon-6P	$3,954	4,209 lbs.	29,866

Gran Torino Sport and Squire

| --- | 71K | 4-dr. Squire Station Wagon-6P | $4,237 | 4,250 lbs. | 22,837 |
| --- | 65R | 2-dr. Sport Hardtop-5P | $3,761 | 3,771 lbs. | 23,142 |

Gran Torino Brougham

| --- | 53K | 4-dr. Sedan (Pillared HT)-6P | $3,903 | 3,887 lbs. | 11,464 |
| --- | 65K | 2-dr. Hardtop-5P | $3,912 | 3,794 lbs. | 26,402 |

Gran Torino Elite

| --- | 65M | 2-dr. Hardtop-6P | $4,374 | 4,092 lbs. | 96,604 |

Note: Total series output was 426,086 units. Styles 53D and 53K were called four-door pillared hardtops.

Custom 500

| --- | 53D | 4-dr. Sedan-6P | $3,911 | 4,180 lbs. | 128,941 |
| --- | 71D | 4-dr. Ranch Wagon-6P | $4,417 | 4,654 lbs. | 12,104 |

Galaxie 500

---	53F	4-dr. Sedan (Pillared HT)-6P	$4,093	4,196 lbs.	49,661
---	57F	4-dr. Hardtop-6P	$4,166	4,212 lbs.	11,526
---	65F	2-dr. Hardtop-6P	$4,140	4,157 lbs.	34,214
---	71F	4-dr. Country Sedan-6P	$4,513	4,690 lbs.	22,400

LTD

---	53H	4-dr. Sedan (Pillared HT)-6P	$4,299	4,262 lbs.	72,251
---	57H	4-dr. Hardtop-6P	$4,367	4,277 lbs.	12,375
---	65H	2-dr. Hardtop-6P	$4,318	4,215 lbs.	73,296
---	71H	4-dr. Country Squire-6P	$4,827	4,742 lbs.	64,047

LTD Brougham

---	53K	4-dr. Sedan (Pillared HT)-6P	$4,576	4,292 lbs.	30,203
---	57K	4-dr. Hardtop-6P	$4,646	4,310 lbs.	11,371
---	65K	2-dr. Hardtop-6P	$4,598	4,247 lbs.	39,084

Note: Total full-size Ford output was 519,916 units. Styles 53F, 53H and 53K were called four-door pillared hardtops. An LTD station wagon was offered but there are production numbers available for it.

Engines:

Pinto Base Four: Overhead cam. Cast-iron block. Displacement: 122 cid. B & S: 3.58 x 3.03 in. Compression ratio: 8.2:1. Net hp: 86 at 5400 rpm. Carburetor: Ford/Weber two-barrel. Five main bearings. Code X.

Pinto Optional Four: Overhead cam. Cast-iron block. Displacement: 139 cid. B & S: 3.78 x 3.13 in. Compression ratio: 8.6:1. Net hp: 80. Carburetor: Motorcraft two-barrel. Five main bearings. Code Y.

Maverick Base Six: Overhead valve. Cast-iron block. Displacement: 200 cid. B & S: 3.68 x 3.13 in. Compression ratio: 8.3:1. Net hp: 84 at 3800 rpm. Carburetor: Motorcraft one-barrel. Seven main bearings. Code T.

Maverick Optional Six: Overhead valve. Cast-iron block. Displacement: 250 cid. B & S: 3.68 x 3.91 in. Compression ratio: 8.0:1. Net hp: 91 at 3200 rpm. Carburetor: Motorcraft one-barrel. Seven main bearings. Code L.

Base Torino and Maverick Optional 302 V-8: Overhead valve. Cast-iron block. Displacement: 302 cid. B & S: 4.00 x 3.00 in. Compression ratio: 8.0:1. Net hp: 140 at 3800 rpm. Carburetor: Motorcraft two-barrel. Five main bearings. Code F.

Torino and Gran Torino Optional 351 "Cleveland" V-8: Overhead valve. Cast-iron block. Displacement: 351 cid. B & S: 4.00 x 3.50

1974 LTD four-door pillared hardtop

1974 Maverick four-door sedan with Luxury package

in. Compression ratio: 8.0:1. Net hp: 162 at 4000 rpm. Carburetor: Motorcraft two-barrel. Five main bearings. Code H.

Torino and Gran Torino Optional 351 "Cobra Jet Cleveland" Four-Barrel V-8: Overhead valve. Cast-iron block. Displacement: 351 cid. B & S: 4.00 x 3.50 in. Compression ratio: 7.9:1. Net hp: 255 at 5600 rpm. Carburetor: Motorcraft four-barrel. Five main bearings. Code Q.

Ford, Torino and Gran Torino Optional 400 V-8: Overhead valve. Cast-iron block. Displacement: 400 cid. B & S: 4.00 x 4.00 in. Compression ratio: 6.0:1. Net hp: 170 at 3400 rpm. Carburetor: Motorcraft two-barrel. Five main bearings. Code S.

Ford, Torino and Gran Torino Optional Thunderbird 460 V-8: Overhead valve. Cast-iron block. Displacement: 460 cid. B & S: 4.36 x 3.85 in. Compression ratio: 8.0:1. Net hp: 220 at 4000 rpm and 215 hp when used in other Ford products. Carburetor: Carter four-barrel. Five main bearings. Code A.

Chassis:

Pinto: Wheelbase: 94.2 inches. Overall length: 169 in and 179 in., station wagon. Tires: 6.00 x 13 and A78-13, station wagon.

Maverick: Wheelbase: 103 in., two-door and 109.9 in., four-door. Overall length: 187 in., two-door and 194 in., four-door. Tires: 6.45 x 14, two-door, C78-14, four door and D70-14, Grabber.

Torino: Wheelbase: 114 in., two-door and 118 in., four-door. Overall length: 212 in., two-door, 216 in., four-door and 222 in., station wagon. Tires: G78-14 belted blackwall on hardtops and H78-14 on other models.

Ford: Wheelbase: 121 in. Overall length: 223 in. and 226 in., station wagons. Tires: G78-15 belted blackwalls, Custom 500, HR78-15 steel-belted radials on LTD and J78-15 belted blackwall tires on station wagons.

Options:

Pinto: 140-cid, 90-hp four ($52). Cruise-O-Matic transmission ($212). AM radio ($61). AM/FM stereo radio ($222). Luxury Decor Group ($137). Full wheel covers ($23). Forged aluminum wheels ($154). White sidewall tires ($44). Vinyl top ($83). Air conditioning ($383). Squire station wagon package ($241).

Maverick: 250-cid six ($42). 302-cid, 140-hp V-8 ($122). Cruise-O-Matic transmission ($212). AM radio ($61). Power steering ($106). White sidewall tires ($33). Vinyl top ($83). Air conditioning ($383). Luxury Decor Group, except Grabber ($332). Leather-wrapped steering wheel. High back bucket seats. Dual color-keyed outside mirrors. Heavy-duty suspension. Heavy-duty battery. Bumper guards with rubber inserts. Metallic glow paints. Manual front disc brakes. Three-speed manual floor shifter with 200-cid six, 302-V-8 and on cars with bucket seats or the Luxury décor option. Option packages included the Protection, Convenience, Deluxe bumper, Exterior décor and Light groups. There also was an all-vinyl seat trim option that was standard on the Grabber and optional on the base two and four-door Mavericks. It was available in Black, Blue Avocado or Tan. Steel-belted radials. Wide-oval tires with raised white letters, standard on Grabber. Steel belted whitewall radial tires. Trim rings and hub caps, standard on Grabber. Forged aluminum wheels.

1974 Pinto Runabout with Luxury package

Torino: 351-cid, 162-hp "Cleveland" V-8 ($46). 400-cid, 170-hp V-8 ($140). 460-cid, 215-hp V-8 ($245). 351 cid, 225-hp "Cleveland" four-barrel V-8 ($132). Cruise-O-Matic transmission; with small V-8 ($219) and with 460 V-8 ($241). AM radio ($67). AM/FM stereo radio ($217). Power steering ($117). Power disc brakes, station wagons and standard on other Torinos ($71). Power tailgate window ($35). Station wagon luggage rack ($80). Vinyl roof ($96). White sidewall tires ($33). Station wagon third passenger seat ($67). Moon roof ($490). AM/FM stereo radio with tape player ($378).

Ford: 400-cid, 170-hp V-8, standard in Country Squire ($94). 460-cid, 215-hp V-8 ($304). Tinted glass ($55). Air conditioning ($426). Climate Control air conditioning ($506). Cruise Control ($103). AM radio ($67). AM/FM radio ($243). Vinyl roof on passenger cars ($115). Vinyl roof on station wagons ($148). Vinyl roof on LTD Brougham, standard. White sidewall tires ($33). AM/FM stereo with tape player ($378). Power seats ($106). Power windows ($134). Moon roof ($516). Country Squire Brougham option ($202). Country Squire Luxury package option ($545). Brougham Luxury Package option ($380).

Note: Cruise-O-Matic automatic transmission and power front disc brakes were standard on Torino station wagons. Automatic transmission, power steering and power front disc brakes were standard on the LTD, Custom 500, Galaxie and Thunderbird. Air conditioning, power windows and an AM radio were also standard in Thunderbirds.

History:

Ford's 1974 model year resulted in 1,843,340 assemblies, including Falcon Club Wagons. Calendar year output was 1,716,975 units again including the Falcon Club Wagon. More federally mandated safety requirements were initiated, primarily in the form of massive rear 'safety' bumpers designed to withstand direct impact, at five mph, without damage. When combined with the front safety bumpers adopted in 1973, the weight of a typical car was up nearly 350 pounds! Pollution standards were also further tightened, which, when combined with the weight increases, made 1974 models generally more sluggish than any available in the recent past. Model year declines of 130,000 units were caused by lagging buyer interest in the larger Fords and Thunderbirds.

1975 Ford

Pinto — 4 and V-6: Changes to the Pinto were minor for 1975. There was little reason to make many changes since the Pinto's good fuel economy was helping to sell the car. The optional 2.8-liter V-6 was available only with Cruise-O-Matic transmission and that combination only in the hatchback and station wagon. Perhaps those limitations made a healthy 84 percent of Pinto buyers avoid it in what would have been a landslide in an election. The unpopular V-6 received only 16 percent of the "vote" of buyers. New accessories for the Pinto included power steering, power front disc brakes and a fuel-economy warning light. The bulwark of the Pinto line was the standard 2.3-liter inline four-cylinder engine, usually equipped with either a four-speed manual or a three-speed automatic transmission.

Maverick — 6 and V-8: Originally scheduled to be replaced by the new Granada, the Maverick's existence was extended after the energy scare of 1973 and 1974. The sedans and the sporty Grabber featured refinements to interior and exterior trim and also had thicker, cut-pile carpeting, a deluxe steering wheel plus the customary 200-cid base six and three-speed manual transmission. Ford block lettering was added along the hood lip and the width of the center slot in the front bumper was slightly decreased. New options included power disc brakes and a deck lid-mounted luggage rack. A catalytic converter was required with the base engine, while the optional 250-cid six or 302-cid V-8 came without the converters. Radial tires were also added to the regular equipment list. Buyers were given a choice of blue, black or tan interior

1975 LTD Landau two-door hardtop coupe with opera windows

1975 Gran Torino Brougham four-door sedan

1975 Elite two-door hardtop

combinations plus a new, light green trim. The base Maverick and more upscale Grabber continued their basic features while more options were available in 1975.

Granada — 6 and V-8: Ford referred to the Granada as a "precision-sized" compact car. Using the four-door platform of the humble Maverick, the Granada emphasized a more upscale look and feel. It came as a two-door coupe and four-door sedan. The luxury inspired styling was heavily influenced by European design themes. Even as a base model, it was quite elegant among cars in its class. The super-rich Ghia-optioned Granada went a step further where luxury was concerned. The 200-cid inline six was the base Granada power plant and was mated with a three-speed manual gearbox. Ghias came standard with a 250-cid inline six, digital clock, deluxe sound package and a wide range of seating surfaces. The base model could be ordered with the bigger six. Two-barrel 302-cid or 351-cid V-8s were offered in both levels. Dealer sales of Granadas in the United States peaked at 241,297 cars, cutting into the popularity of the Mustang II.

Torino, Gran Torino and Elite — V-8: The Torino was the same as the previous year. Torino models were the base trim level and featured chrome-trimmed windshield, rear widow and rain gutter moldings, high back bench seats, all-vinyl seat and door trim, floor mats, hubcaps, a 302-cid V-8 and three-speed manual transmission. The Torino station wagon included power front disc brakes and Ford's three-way tailgate. The 1975 Gran Torino was the intermediate trim level and included manual front disc brakes, cloth and vinyl trim on seats and interior door panels plus carpeting, lower body, wheel well and deck lid moldings, a dual note horn, a trunk mat, deluxe two-spoke steering wheel and chrome trim on the foot pedals. The Gran Torino Squire station wagon used the 351-cid, 148-hp V-8, Cruise-O-Matic automatic transmission, deluxe pleated vinyl interior trim, wheel covers and wood grain appliqués on the body, tailgate and instrument panel. The top level Gran Torino Brougham also had power front disc brakes, power steering; cloth seats, body moldings and a padded vinyl top. The Elite continued to offer its 1974 features for another year.

Ford — V-8: The Custom 500 was the base trim level Ford and it included chrome-trimmed windshield and rear window moldings, nylon carpeting, an ignition key warning buzzer, the 351-cid V-8 engine, Cruise-O-Matic automatic transmission, power steering and G78-15 belted blackwall tires. The LTD included wheel lip moldings, cloth and vinyl seating surfaces, rocker panel moldings and wood grain appliqués on the instrument panel. The top level LTD Brougham had deep-cushioned low back bench seats, an electric clock, deluxe two-spoke steering wheel, chrome trim on the foot pedals, polished aluminum

1975 Maverick two-door sedan

1975 Pinto Runabout two-door hatchback

trim around the rear edge of the hood, body moldings with vinyl inserts and HR78-15 steel-belted radial tires. The LTD Landau added high back Flight Bench seats with center armrests and front door courtesy lights, full wheel covers, cut-pile carpeting, carpeted lower door panels, polished rocker panel moldings, automatic seatback release on two-door models, a vinyl roof and color-keyed seat belts. The Ranch Wagon rode on JR78-15 steel-belted radial tires. The Country Sedan added a dual note horn, wood grain appliqués on the instrument panel and front and rear door panels, a special sound package, body moldings and a chrome-plated grille. The Country Squires added JR78-15 steel-belted radial tires and the 400-cid V-8.

VIN:

The 1975 Ford serial number code was broken down as follows: The first symbol indicated the year: 5 = 1975. The second symbol identified the assembly plant: A = Atlanta, Georgia; B = Oakville, Ontario, Canada, E = Mahwah, New Jersey, F = Dearborn, Michigan, G = Chicago, Illinois, H = Lorain, Ohio, J = Los Angeles, California, K = Kansas City, Missouri; P = Twin Cities (Minneapolis and St. Paul, Minnesota), R = San Jose, California, S = Allen Park Pilot Plant, T = Metuchen, New Jersey, U = Louisville, Kentucky, W = Wayne, Michigan, X = St. Thomas, Ontario, Canada, Y = Wixom, Michigan and Z = St. Louis, Missouri. The third and fourth symbols identified the body series: 66K=Granada Ghia two-door. The fifth symbol identified the engine codes: A=460 V-8, F = 302-cid V-8, H = 351-cid V-8, L = 250-cid six-cylinder, S = 400-cid V-8, T = 200-cid six-cylinder, Y= 139-cid four and Z=169-cid V-6. The last six digits were the unit's production number, beginning at 100001 and up.

Pinto (Four)

Model No.	Body/Style No.	Body Type & Seating	Factory Price	Shipping Weight	Production Total
---	64B	2-dr. Hatchback-4P	$2,967	2,528 lbs.	Note 1
---	73B	2-dr. Station Wagon-4P	$3,094	2,692 lbs.	Note 1

Pinto (V-6)

---	62B	2-dr. Sedan-4P	$2,769	2,495 lbs.	64,081
---	64B	2-dr. Hatchback-4P	$3,220	2,710 lbs.	68,919
---	73B	2-dr. Station Wagon-4P	$3,347	2,874 lbs.	90,763

Note: Total Pinto output was 223,763 units. Ford Motor Co. did not break out the four and V-6 production for the Pinto.

Maverick (Six)

---	54A	4-dr. Sedan-6P	$3,025	2,820 lbs.	Note 1
---	62A	2-dr. Sedan-6P	$3,061	2,943 lbs.	Note 1
---	62D	2-dr. Grabber-6P	$3,224	2,827 lbs.	Note 1

Maverick (V-8)

---	54A	4-dr. Sedan-6P	$3,147	2,971 lbs.	90,695
---	62A	2-dr. Sedan-6P	$3,183	3,094 lbs.	63,404
---	62D	2-dr. Grabber-6P	$3,346	2,979 lbs.	8,473

Note: Total Maverick output was 162,572 units. Ford Motor Co. did not break out production numbers among six and V-8 editions,

Granada (Six)

---	54H	4-dr. Sedan-6P	$3,756	3,293 lbs.	Note 1
---	66H	2-dr. Sedan-6P	$3,698	3,230 lbs.	Note 1

Granada (V-8)

---	54H	4-dr. Sedan-6P	$3,784	3,355 lbs.	118,168
---	66H	2-dr. Sedan-6P	$3,826	3,306 lbs.	100,810

Granada Ghia (Six)

---	54K	4-dr. Sedan-6P	$4,240	3,361 lbs.	Note 1
---	66K	2-dr. Sedan-6P	$4,182	3,311 lbs.	Note 1

Granada Ghia (V-8)

---	54K	4-dr. Sedan-6P	$4,326	3,423 lbs.	43,652
---	66K	2-dr. Sedan-6P	$4,268	3,373 lbs.	40,028

Note: Total Granada output was 302,649 units. Ford Motor Co. did not break out production numbers among six and V-8 editions,

Torino

---	53B	4-dr. Sedan-6P	$3,957	4,059 lbs.	22,928
---	65B	2-dr. Opera Window Coupe-6P	$3,954	3,987 lbs.	13,394
---	71B	4-dr. Station Wagon-6P	$4,336	4,412 lbs.	13,291

Gran Torino

---	53D	4-dr. Sedan-6P	$4,258	4,090 lbs.	53,161
---	65D	2-dr. Opera Window Coupe-6P	$4,234	3,998 lbs.	35,324
---	71D	4-dr. Station Wagon-6P	$4,593	4,456 lbs.	23,951

Torino Brougham

---	53K	4-dr. Sedan-6P	$4,791	4,163 lbs.	5,929
---	65K	2-dr. Opera Window Coupe-6P	$4,759	4,087 lbs.	4,849

Torino Sport

---	65R	2-dr. Sport Hardtop-5P	$4,744	4,044 lbs.	5,126

Elite

---	65M	2-dr. Hardtop-6P	$4,721	4,160 lbs.	123,372

Note: Total Torino, Gran Torino and Elite production was 318,482 units.

Custom 500

---	53D	4-dr. Sedan-6P	$4,380	4,377 lbs.	31,043
---	71D	4-dr. Ranch Wagon-6P	$4,970	4,787 lbs.	6,930

LTD

---	53H	4-dr. Sedan-6P	$4,615	4,408 lbs.	82,382
---	60H	2-dr. Opera Window Coupe-6P	$4,656	4,359 lbs.	47,432
---	71H	4-dr. Country Sedan-6P	$5,061	4,803 lbs.	22,935

LTD Brougham

---	53K	4-dr. Sedan-6P	$5,016	4,419 lbs.	32,327
---	60K	2-dr. Opera Window Coupe-6P	$5,050	4,391 lbs.	24,005
---	71K	4-dr. Country Squire-6P	$5,340	4,845 lbs.	41,550

LTD Landau

---	53L	4-dr. Sedan-6P	$5,370	4,446 lbs.	32,506
---	60L	2-dr. Opera Window Coupe-6P	$5,401	4,419 lbs.	26,919

Note: Total full-size Ford output was 348,029 units.

Engines:

Pinto Base Four: Overhead cam. Cast-iron block. Displacement: 139 cid. B & S: 3.78 x 3.13 in. Compression ratio: 8.6:1. Net hp: 83. Carburetor: Motorcraft two-barrel. Five main bearings. Code Y.

Pinto Optional V-6: Overhead valve. Cast-iron block. Displacement: 169 cid. B & S: 3.50 x 2.70 in. Compression ratio: 8.0:1. Net hp: 97. Carburetor: Holley two-barrel. Four main bearings. Code Z.

Maverick Base Six: Overhead valve. Cast-iron block. Displacement: 200 cid. B & S: 3.68 x 3.13 in. Compression ratio: 8.3:1. Net hp: 75 at 3200 rpm. Carburetor: Motorcraft one-barrel. Seven main bearings. Code T.

Granada Base and Maverick Optional Six: Overhead valve. Cast-iron block. Displacement: 250 cid. B & S: 3.68 x 3.91 in. Compression ratio: 8.0:1. Net hp: 72 at 2900 rpm. Carburetor: Motorcraft one-barrel. Seven main bearings. Code L.

Torino, Gran Torino and Elite Base 302 V-8: Overhead valve. Cast-iron block. Displacement: 302 cid. Bore and stroke: 4.00 x 3.00 in. Compression ratio: 8.0:1. Net hp: 129 at 3800 rpm. Carburetor: Motorcraft two-barrel. Five main bearings. Code F.

Torino, Gran Torino and Elite Optional 351 "Modified" V-8: Overhead valve. Cast-iron block. Displacement: 351 cid. B & S: 4.00 x

1975 Granada Ghia four-door sedan

1975 Granada four-door sedan

1975 Granada Ghia two-door hardtop

3.50 in. Compression ratio: 8.0:1. Net hp: 148 at 3800 rpm. Carburetor: Motorcraft two-barrel. Five main bearings. Code H.

Ford and Torino, Gran Torino and Elite Optional 400 V-8: Overhead valve. Cast-iron block. Displacement: 400 cid. B & S: 4.00 x 4.00 in. Compression ratio: 8.0:1. Net hp: 158 at 3800 rpm. Carburetor: Motorcraft two-barrel. Five main bearings. Code S.

Ford and Torino, Gran Torino and Elite Optional Thunderbird 460 V-8: Overhead valve. Cast-iron block. Displacement: 460 cid. B & S: 4.36 x 3.65 in. Compression ratio: 8.0:1. Net hp: 218 at 4000 rpm. Carburetor: Motorcraft four-barrel. Five main bearings. Code A.

Chassis:

Pinto: Wheelbase: 94.4 in. and 94.7 in., station wagons. Overall length: 169 in. and 179 in., station wagons. Tires: BR78-13B.

Maverick: Wheelbase: 103 in., two-door and 109.9 in., four-door. Overall length: 187 in., two-door and 194 in., four-door Tires: BR78-14m two-door, CR78-14, four-door and DR70-14, Grabber.

Granada: Wheelbase: 109.9 in. Overall length: 198 in. and 200 in., Ghia. Tires: DR78-14 and ER78-14, Ghia four-door.

Torino, Gran Torino and Elite: Wheelbase: 114.0 in., Torino and Elite and 118.0 in., station wagon. Overall length: 216.0 in., Elite, 217.6 in., Torino and 222.6 in., wagons. Tires: HR78 x 14, Torino and XR78 x 15, Elite.

Ford: Wheelbase: 121 in. Overall length: 224 in. and 226 in., station wagon. Tires: HR78-15.

Options:

Pinto: 169-cid V-6 ($229). Cruise-O-Matic automatic transmission ($212). AM radio ($61). AM/FM stereo radio ($222). Luxury Decor Group ($137). Forged aluminum wheels ($154). White sidewall tires ($33).

Maverick: 302-cid, 129-hp V-8. Cruise-O-Matic automatic transmission ($212). AM radio ($61). Power steering ($106). Luxury decor package ($392). White sidewall tires ($33). Appearance and comfort package. Also packages for the interior, lights, exterior, security and convenience. Selectaire air conditioning. Leather-wrapped steering wheel. AM/FM HiFi stereo. Tinted glass. Metallic glow paint. Power front disc brakes. Space saver spare tire.

Granada: 302-cid, 129-hp V-8 ($85). 351-cid, 143-hp V-8 engine. Cruise-O-Matic automatic transmission ($222). Power steering ($106). Power brakes ($45). AM radio ($61). AM/FM stereo radio ($222). Vinyl roof ($83). Air conditioning ($426). White sidewall tires ($33).

Torino, Gran Torino and Elite: 400-cid, 158-hp V-8 ($54). 460-cid, 218-hp V-8 ($245). AM radio ($67). AM/FM stereo radio ($217). Power steering ($117). Power front disc brakes ($71) and standard on station wagons. Power tailgate window, station wagons ($35). Luggage rack, station wagons ($80). Vinyl top ($96). Air conditioning ($426). White sidewall tires ($33).

Ford: 400-cid, 158-hp V-8 ($94) and standard on Country Squires. 460-cid, 218-hp V-8 ($304). Tinted glass ($55). Air conditioning ($426). Climate Control air conditioning ($506). Cruise control ($103). AM radio ($67). AM/FM stereo radio ($243). Vinyl roof ($115). Vinyl roof on station wagons ($148), Vinyl roof, standard on LTD Landau. White sidewall tires ($33).

History:

The 1975 Ford line was introduced Sept. 27, 1974. Model year sales, by United States dealers, included 282,130 Pintos, 142,964 Mavericks, 241,297 Granadas, 158,798 Torinos, 102,402 Elites, 297,655 LTDs and 37,216 Thunderbirds. The production of 1975 Ford models, in U.S. factories, hit 1,302,205 cars. Calendar year production of Fords, in this country, peaked at 1,302,644 units. The big Fords were attractively face lifted with the addition of a larger Mercedes-style grille and new taillights. The most significant change occurred with the two-door hardtop model. The true pillarless hardtop was replaced by a coupe with fixed quarter windows and large opera windows. The Granada was a new intermediate size car offered in four-door sedan and two-door

sedan versions. As Ford was proud to point out, the four-door had more than a passing resemblance to the Mercedes-Benz. Granadas could be fitted with options that created anything from a taxi to a mini-limousine. They came powered by engines ranging from the sedate 250-cid six-cylinder to the 351-cid V-8, the latter making it one of the fastest Fords. Pollution standards were stiffened once again and, in 1975, all cars were required to burn unleaded gasoline. The majority of the new models came with catalytic converters on the exhaust systems, to help reduce emissions and contaminates. Top executives influencing Ford Division policy were Henry Ford II, Lee Iacocca and B.E. Bidwell. It was the final season for the long-lasting Custom 500 nameplate.

1976 Ford

Pinto — Four and V-6: Ford's subcompact, introduced in 1971, had a new front-end look this year. Appearance changes included a new argent-painted egg-crate grille of one-piece corrosion-resistant plastic, bright bezels for the single round headlamps, bright front lip hood molding, and "Ford" block letters centered above the grille. That new grille was peaked and angled forward slightly, with a tighter crosshatch pattern than before, and held square inset parking lamps. Backup lights were integral with the horizontal tail lamps. Bodies held front and rear side marker lights. For the first time, standard interiors had a choice of all vinyl or sporty cloth-and-vinyl. Four new interior trim fabrics were offered, along with a new bright red interior color. Three four-passenger bodies were offered: two-door sedan, "three-door" Runabout hatchback, and two-door wagon. Wagons had flip-out rear compartment windows and a lift gate-open warning light, as well as tinted glass. Major fuel economy improvements resulted from catalysts, new carburetor calibrations, and a lower (3.18:1) rear axle ratio with the standard 140 cid (2.3-liter) OHC four and fully synchronized four-speed manual gearbox with floor shift lever. Pinto had front disc/rear drum brakes, rack-and-pinion steering, and unibody construction. New this year was a low-budget Pony MPG two-door, wearing minimal chrome trim and plain hubcaps. It had new calibrations for the 2.3-liter engine and a 3.00:1 axle ratio. Pinto standard equipment included a heater/defroster with DirectAire ventilation, bucket seats, mini-console, inside hood release, dome light, glove box, dual padded sun visors, and B78x13 tires. Runabouts and wagons had a fold-down back seat and deluxe seatbelts. Runabouts had a carpeted load area. A new Squire option for Runabouts added simulated wood grain vinyl paneling on body side and the lower back panel, similar to the Squire wagon. Squire also displayed bright surround and B-pillar moldings as well as belt, drip and window frame moldings.

Maverick — Six and V-8: Initially scheduled for disappearance when the new Granada arrived in 1975, Maverick hung on as concern about the fuel crisis continued. This year's grille was a forward-slanting horizontal-bar design, split into two sections by a center vertical divider bar. Rectangular park/signal lamps were mounted in the bright argent plastic grille and backup lights integral with the tail lamps. Single round headlamps continued. The front bumper held twin slots, and the hood showed a sculptured bulge. Front disc brakes were now standard. The base engine was the 200-cid (3.3-liter) inline six with one-barrel carburetor. Options were a 250-cid six or the 302 V-8. All three came with either three-speed manual or automatic transmissions. Maverick's fuel tank had grown from 16 to 19.2 gallons during the 1975 model year.

1976 Pinto Squire hatchback coupe

1976 Pinto Stallion hatchback

Gas mileage was improved with a rear axle ratio at 2.79:1, recalibrating engines and adding back-pressure modulation on the EGR system. Standard equipment included fully-synchronized three-speed column shift, C78 x 14 bias-ply tires, hubcaps, ventless windows with curved glass, front/rear side marker lights. The Maverick had a European-type armrest with door pull assist handle, and lockable glove box. A padded instrument panel held two round cluster pods for gauges. Standard bench seats were trimmed in Random stripe cloth and vinyl. Two-doors had a flipper rear quarter window.

Granada — Six and V-8: For 1976, Granada's fuel economy improved and the "precision-size" compact held a new standard vinyl bench seat and door trim. On each side of the single round headlamps were small, bright vertical sections patterned like the grille. Wide-spaced "Ford" letters stood above the grille. On the fender extensions were wraparound front parking lights and signal/marker lenses. Hoods held a stand-up ornament. Each wraparound tri-color horizontal-style tail lamp was divided into an upper and lower section, with integral side marker lights. Backup lamps sat inboard of the tail lamps. Sporting a tall, squared-off roofline and European-influenced design, the five-passenger Granada strongly resembled a Mercedes up front. Ford bragged: "Its looks and lines remind you of the Mercedes 280 and the Cadillac Seville." Bodies featured bright wraparound bumpers, plus bright moldings on windshield, backlight, drip rail, door belt, doorframe, and wheel lip. Two-door Granadas had distinctive opera windows. Four-doors had a bright center pillar molding with color-keyed insert. Two- and four-door sedans were offered, in base or Ghia trim. Standard equipment included a three-speed manual transmission, front disc/rear drum brakes, heater/defroster, inside hood release. DR78 x 14 black wall steel-belted radials, anti-theft decklid lock, buried walnut wood tone instrument panel appliqués, a locking glove box, two rear seat ashtrays, lighter, and full wheel covers. The base engine was the 200 cid (3.3-liter) inline six.

Granada Ghia — Six and V-8: The Ghia included an ornament on the opera window glass, a color-keyed body side molding with integral wheel lip molding, left-hand remote-control mirror, dual accent paint stripes on the body sides, hood and decklid, trunk carpeting and a lower back panel appliqué, color-keyed to the vinyl roof. Inside Ghia was a "floating pillow" design on independent reclining or flight bench seats, map pockets and an assist handle on back of front seats, a day/night mirror, and a luxury steering wheel with woodnote appliqué on the rim. Under Ghia's hood was the larger 250 cid six-cylinder engine.

Torino — V-8: Nine models made up the mid-size Torino lineup this year; base, Gran Torino and Brougham two- and four-doors, and a trio of wagons. Two-doors rode a 114 in. wheelbase; four-doors measured 118 in. between hubs. Fuel economy was improved by recalibrating engine spark and back-pressure EGR, and lowering the rear axle ratio to 2.75:1. Five body colors were new. Torino got a new saddle interior. Side-by-side quad round headlamps flanked a one-piece plastic grille with tiny crosshatch pattern, divided into six sections by vertical bars. Clear vertical parking/signal lamps hid behind twin matching outer sections,

making eight in all. "Ford" block letters stood above the grille. Two-door Torinos retained the conventional pillarless design, while four-doors were referred to as "pillared hardtops." Bodies held frameless, ventless curved side glass. Standard engine was the 351 cid (5.8-liter) V-8 with two-barrel carburetor and solid-state ignition, SelectShift Cruise-O-Matic, power front disc/rear drum brakes, power steering, and HR78 x 14 steel-belted radial tires were standard. Standard equipment included a cloth/vinyl front bench seat with adjustable head restraints, vinyl door trim panels, recessed door handles, day/night mirror, heater/defroster, and inside hood release. Wagons had a three-way tailgate and locking storage compartment. Squire wagons added a power tailgate window, full wheel covers, and wood grain paneling with side rails.

Gran Torino — V-8: The Gran Torino was the intermediate trim level as the Gran Torino Sport was dropped for 1976. The Gran Torino shared the saddle interior with the Torino. Torino and Gran Torino wore hubcaps.

Torino Brougham — V-8: Broughams had a split bench seat. Broughams added wheel covers, as well as opera windows and a vinyl roof to the Torino and Gran Torino list of standard equipment.

Elite — V-8: The Elite nameplate arrived in 1975 but its body had been called Gran Torino. Appearance changes were slight this year on the pillarless two-door hardtop body, which rode a 114 in. wheelbase. Elite sported a "luxury" sectioned grille with vertical bars and horizontal center bar. A stand-up hood ornament held the Elite crest. Single round headlamps in square housings had bright bezels, while vertical parking/signal lamps sat in front fender tip extensions. Wide vinyl-insert body side moldings were color-keyed to the vinyl roof. Large wraparound tail lamps had bright bezels and integral side marker lights. On the rear roof pillar were two tiny side-by-side opera windows. Bodies also displayed bright tapered wide wheel lip moldings. A standard gold vinyl roof replaced the former brown. Either a full vinyl roof or a new half-vinyl version was available, at no extra charge. The standard axle changed from 3.00:1 to 2.75:1. Standard equipment included the 351 cid (5.8-liter) two-barrel V-8 with SelectShift Cruise-O-Matic, power steering and brakes, four-wheel coil springs, and HR78 x 15 SBR tires. The standard bench seat had Westminster pleated knit cloth and vinyl trim. Woodnote accented the instrument cluster/panel, steering wheel and door panels. Also standard were front bumper guards, heater/defroster, DirectAire ventilation, clock, full wheel covers, and bright window moldings.

LTD/Custom 500 — V-8: LTD was the only full-size Ford available to private buyers this year, as the Custom 500 badge went on fleet models only. The ten-model lineup included two- and four-door base, Brougham and Landau LTD models; Custom 500 four-door and wagon; and base and Country Squire LTD wagons. Four-doors were called "pillared hardtops." Landau and Country squire models had hidden headlamps. Brougham and Landau two-doors carried half-vinyl roofs; four-doors got a "halo" vinyl roof. Front-end appearance changed slightly with a switch to dark argent paint on the secondary surface of the chromed grille. There was a new wheel cover design. LTD's crosshatch grille peaked slightly forward. Headlamp doors held a horizontal emblem. Tri-section wraparound front parking/signal lenses stood at fender tips. On the hood was a stand-up ornament. Two-doors had a six-window design, with narrow vertical windows between the front and rear side windows. Vinyl-insert body side moldings were standard. All models had a reflective rear appliqué. Six body colors were new. At mid-year, Country Squire lost the long horizontal chrome strip along its wood grain side panel. The base engine was the two-barrel 351 cid (5.8-liter) V-8. Wagons carried the 400-cid engine. Standard equipment included power steering and brakes, SelectShift Cruise-O-Matic, steel-belted radials, power ventilation system, and front bumper guards. Brougham, Landau and wagon also had rear guards. Police models with the 460 V-8 and three-speed automatic had first-gear lockout. Rear axle ratios changed to 2.75:1 and engines were recalibrated, in an attempt to boost gas mileage. Wagons had a fuel tank of only 21 gallons, versus 24.3 gallons on hardtops. Wagons now had standard hydro-boost rear brakes. A parking brake warning light became standard on all models. Decklid and ignition switch locks offered improved anti-theft protection.

I.D. Data:

Ford's 1976 11-symbol Vehicle Identification Number (VIN) was stamped on a metal tab on the instrument panel, visible through the windshield. The first digit was a model year code (6=1976). The second letter indicated the assembly plant: A=Atlanta, Georgia, B=Oakville, Ontario, Canada, E=Mahwah, New Jersey, G=Chicago, Illinois, H=Lorain; Ohio, J=Los Angeles, California, K= Kansas City, Missouri, P=Minneapolis-St. Paul, Minnesota, R=San Jose, California, T=Metuchen, New Jersey, U=Louisville, Kentucky, W=Wayne, Michigan and Y=Wixom, Michigan. Digits three and four were the body serial code, which corresponded to the Model Numbers, such as 10=Pinto 2-dr. The fifth symbol was an engine code: Y=140-cid four-cylinder, Z= 170-cid V-6, T=200-cid six-cylinder, L=250-cid six-cylinder, F=302-cid V-8, H=351-cid V-8, S=400-cid V-8, A=460-cid V-8 and C=Police 460-cid V-8. Digits six through 11

1976 Granada Ghia sedan

1976 Gran Torino two-door hardtop

made up the consecutive unit number of cars built at each assembly plant, beginning with 100001. A Vehicle Certification Label on the left front door lock face panel or door pillar showed the manufacturer, month and year of manufacture, GVW, GAWR, certification statement, VIN, body code, color code, trim code, axle code, transmission code, and domestic (or foreign) special order code.

Pinto (Four)

Model No.	Body Style No.	Body Type & Seating	Factory Price	Shipping Weight	Production Total
10	62B	2-dr. Sedan-4P	$3,025	2,452 lbs.	92,264
10	62B	2-dr. Pony Sedan	$2,895	2,450 lbs.	Note 1
11	64B	2-dr. Hatchback- 4P	$3,200	2,482 lbs.	92,540
11	64B	2-dr. Squire Hatch-4P	$3,505	2,518 lbs.	Note 2
12	73B	2-dr. Station Wagon-4P	$3,365	2,635 lbs.	105,328
12	73B	2-dr. Squire Wag-4P	$3,671	2,672 lbs.	Note 2

Pinto V-6

10	62B	2-dr. Sedan-4P	$3,472	2,590 lbs.	92,264
11	64B	2-dr. Hatchback- 4P	$3,647	2,620 lbs.	92,540
11	64B	2-dr. Squire Hatch-4P	$3,592	2,656 lbs.	Note 2
12	73B	2-dr. Station Wagon-4P	$3,865	2,773 lbs.	105,328
12	73B	2-dr. Squire Wag-4P	$4,171	2,810 lbs.	Note 2

Note 1: Pony production included in base sedan figure.
Note 2: Squire Runabout hatchback and Squire Wagon production was included with the standard Runabout and station wagon totals.

Maverick (Six)

91	62A	2-dr. Sedan-4P	$3,117	2,763 lbs.	60,611
92	54A	4-dr. Sedan-5P	$3,189	2,873 lbs.	79,076

Maverick (V-8)

91	62A	2-dr. Sedan-4P	$3,265	2,930 lbs.	60,611
92	54A	4-dr. Sedan-5P	$3,337	3,040 lbs.	79,076

Granada (Six)

82	66H	2-dr. Sedan-5P	$3,707	3,119 lbs.	161,618
81	54H	4-dr. Sedan-5P	$3,798	3,168 lbs.	287,923

Granada (V-8)

82	66H	2-dr. Sedan-5P	$3,861	3,226 lbs.	161,618
81	54H	4-dr. Sedan-5P	$3,952	3,275 lbs.	287,923

Granada Ghia (Six)

84	66K	2-dr. Sedan-5P	$4,265	3,280 lbs.	48,796
83	54K	4-dr. Sedan-5P	$4,355	3,339 lbs.	52,457

Granada Ghia (V-8)

84	66K	2-dr. Sedan-5P	$4,353	3,387 lbs.	48,796
83	54K	4-dr. Sedan-5P	$4,443	3,446 lbs.	52,457

Torino (V-8)

25	65B	2-dr. Hardtop-6P	$4,172	3,976 lbs.	34,518
27	53B	4-dr. Hardtop-6P	$4,206	4,061 lbs.	17,394
40	71B	4-dr. Station Wagon-6P	$4,521	4,409 lbs.	17,281

Gran Torino (V-8)

30	65D	2-dr. Hardtop-6P	$4,461	3,999 lbs.	23,939
31	53D	4-dr. Hardtop-6P	$4,495	4,081 lbs.	40,568
42	71D	4-dr. Station Wagon-6P	$4,769	4,428 lbs.	30,596
43	71K	4-dr. Squire Wagon-6P	$5,083	4,454 lbs.	21,144

Gran Torino Brougham (V-8)

32	65K	2-dr. Hardtop-6P	$4,883	4,063 lbs.	3,183
33	53K	4-dr. Hardtop-6P	$4,915	4,144 lbs.	4,473

Elite (V-8)

21	65H	2-dr. Hardtop-6P	$4,879	4,169 lbs.	146,475

Custom 500 (V-8)

52	60D	2-dr. Pillar Hardtop-6P	----	----	7,037
53	53D	4-dr. Pillar Hardtop-6P	$4,493	4,298 lbs.	23,447
72	71D	4-dr. Ranch Wagon-6P	$4,918	4,737 lbs.	4,633

LTD (V-8)

62	60H	2-dr. Pillar Hardtop-6P	$4,780	4,257 lbs.	62,844
63	53H	4-dr. Pillar Hardtop-6P	$4,752	4,303 lbs.	108,168
74	71H	4-dr. Station Wagon-6P	$5,207	4,752 lbs.	30,237
74	71H	4-dr. DF Rear Seat Wagon-10P	$5,333	4,780 lbs.	Note 3
76	71K	4-dr. Country Squire Wagon-6P	$5,523	4,809 lbs.	47,329
76	71K	4-dr. DF Seats Squire-10P	$5,649	4,837 lbs.	Note 3

Note 3: Wagons with dual-facing rear seats (a $126 option) are included in standard station wagon and Country Squire wagon totals.

LTD Brougham (V-8)

68	60K	2-dr. Pillar Hardtop-6P	$5,299	4,299 lbs.	20,863
66	53K	4-dr. Pillar Hardtop-6P	$5,245	4,332 lbs.	32,917

LTD Landau (V-8)

65	60L	2-dr. Pillar Hardtop-6P	$5,613	4,346 lbs.	29,673
64	53L	4-dr. Pillar Hardtop-6P	$5,560	4,394 lbs.	35,663

Engines:

Pinto Four: Inline with overhead cam. Cast-iron block and head. Displacement: 140 cid (2.3 liters). B&S: 3.78 x 3.13 in. Compression ratio: 9.0:1 Brake hp: 92 at 5000 rpm. Torque: 121 lbs.-ft. at 3000 rpm. Five main bearings. Hydraulic valve lifters. Carburetor: Holley-Weber 9510 two-barrel. VIN Code: Y.

Pinto Optional V-6: 60-degree, overhead-valve. Cast-iron block and head. Displacement: 170.8 cid (2.8 liters). B&S: 3.66 x 2.70 in. Compression ratio: 8.7:1. Brake hp: 103 at 4400 rpm. Torque: 149 lbs.-ft. at 2800 rpm. Four main bearings. Solid valve lifters. Carburetor: Motorcraft 9510 (D6ZE-BA) two-barrel. VIN Code: Z.

Maverick/Granada Base Six: Inline. Overhead valve. Cast-iron block and head. Displacement: 200 cid (3.3 liters). B & S: 3.68 x 3.13 in. Compression ratio: 8.3:1. Brake hp: 81 at 3400 rpm. Torque: 151 lbs.-ft. at 1700 rpm. Seven main bearings. Hydraulic valve lifters. Carburetor: Carter YFA 9510 one-barrel. VIN Code: T.

Granada Ghia Base Six: (Optional in Maverick and Granada) Inline. Overhead valve. Cast-iron block and head. Displacement: 250 cid (4.1 liters). B & S: 3.68 x 3.91 in. Compression ratio: 8.0:1 Brake hp: 87 at 3600 rpm. (Maverick/Ghia, 90 at 3000). Torque: 190 lbs.-ft. at 2000 rpm. (Ghia, 187 at 1900). Seven main bearings. Hydraulic valve lifters. Carburetor: Carter YFA 9510 one-barrel. VIN Code: L.

Optional V-8 (Maverick, Granada): 90-degree, overhead valve. Cast-iron block and head. Displacement: 302 cid (5.0 liters). B & S: 4.00 x 3.00 in. Compression ratio: 8.0:1. Brake hp: 138 at 3600 rpm. (Granada, 134 at 3600). Torque: 245 lbs.-ft. at 2000 rpm. (Granada, 242 at 2000). Five main bearings. Hydraulic valve lifters. Carburetor: Ford 2150A 9510 two-barrel. VIN Code: F.

Torino, Elite and LTD Base V-8: (Optional Granada) 90-degree, overhead valve. Cast-iron block and head. Displacement: 351 cid (5.8 liters). B & S: 4.00 x 3.50 in. Compression ratio: 8.0:1. (Torino, 8.1:1). Brake hp: 152 at 3800 rpm. (Torino, 154 at 3400). Torque: 274 lbs.-ft. at 1600 rpm. (Torino, 286 at 1800). Five main bearings. Hydraulic valve lifters. Carburetor: Ford 2150A two-barrel. VIN Code: H.

500/LTD wagon Base V-8: (Optional Torino, Elite and LTD) 90-degree, overhead valve. Cast-iron block and head. Displacement: 400 cid (6.6 liters). B & S: 4.00 x 4.00 in. Compression ratio: 8.0:1. Brake hp: 180 at 3800 rpm. Torque: 336 lbs.-ft. at 1800 rpm. Five main bearings. Hydraulic valve lifters. Carburetor: Ford 2150A two-barrel. VIN Code: S.

1976 Maverick four-door with luxury decor option

Thunderbird Base V-8: (Optional Torino, Elite and LTD) 90-degree, overhead valve. Cast-iron block and head. Displacement: 460 cid (7.5 liters). B & S: 4.36 x 3.85 in. Compression ratio: 8.0:1. Brake hp: 202 at 3800 rpm. Torque: 352 lbs.-ft. at 1600 rpm. Five main bearings. Hydraulic valve lifters. Carburetor: Motorcraft 9510 or Ford 4350A9510, both four-barrel. VIN Code: A.

Note: A Police 460-cid V-8 was also available for the LTD.

Chassis:

Pinto: Wheelbase: 94.5 in. and 94.8 in. on station wagon. Overall length: 169.0 in. and 178.8 in. on station wagon. Tires: A78 x 13 or B78 x 13.

Maverick: Wheelbase: 103.0 in. and 109.9 in. on sedan. Overall length: 187.0 in. and 193.9 in. on sedan. Tires: C78 x 14 and DR78 x 14 with V-8 engine.

Granada: Wheelbase: 109.9 in. Overall length: 197.7 in. Tires: DR78 x 14.

Torino: Wheelbase: 114.0 in. and 118.0 in. on station wagon. Overall length: 213.6 in., 217. 6 on the sedan and 222.6 in. on the station wagon. Tires: HR78 x 14.

Elite: Wheelbase: 114.0 in. Overall length: 216.1 in. Tires: HR78 x 15.

LTD/Custom 500: Wheelbase: 121.0 in. Overall length: 223.9 in. and 225.6 in. on the station wagon. HR78 x 15 and JR78 x 15 on station wagon.

Options:

Pinto: A sporty new Stallion option featuring special silver body paint and taping, black window and door moldings, and blacked-out wiper arms, hood, grille and lower back panel. Black tape treatment went on rocker panel and wheel lip areas with Stallion decals on front fenders. Stallion also included dual racing mirrors, styled steel wheels with trim rings, A70 x 13 tires with raised white letters, and a "competition" handling suspension ($283). A Luxury Decor Group included woodnote instrument panel appliqué, custom steering wheel, passenger door courtesy light switch, and rear seat ashtray. ($241). Convenience light group ($70 to $102). Protection group ($73 to $134). Air conditioner ($420). Rear defroster, electric ($70). Tinted glass ($46). Leather-wrapped steering wheel ($33). Dual color-keyed mirrors ($42). Entertainment: AM radio ($71); w/stereo tape player ($192). AM/FM radio ($129). AM/FM stereo radio ($173). Sunroof, manual ($230). Half vinyl roof ($125). Metallic glow paint ($54). Roof luggage rack ($52 to $75). Rocker panel moldings ($19). Wheels: Forged aluminum wheels ($82 to $172). Styled steel wheels ($92 to $119). Wheel covers ($28). Trim rings ($29). SelectShift Cruise-O-Matic: ($186). Power steering: ($117). Power brakes: ($54).

Maverick: A Stallion dress-up package, similar to Pinto's, included black grille and moldings; unique paint/tape treatment on hood, grille, decklid, lower body, and lower back panel; plus large Stallion decal on front quarter panel. The package also included dual outside mirrors, raised white-letter steel-belted radials on styled steel wheels, and "competition" suspension option ($329). Exterior decor group ($99). Interior decor group ($106). Luxury decor group ($508). Luxury interior decor ($217). Deluxe bumper group ($28 to $61). Convenience group ($34 to $64). Protection group ($24 to $39). Light group ($22 to $34). Security lock group ($16). Air conditioning ($420). Rear defogger ($40). Tinted glass ($45 to $59). Dual color-keyed mirrors ($13 to $25). AM radio ($71); w/tape player ($192). AM/FM radio ($128). AM/FM stereo radio ($210); w/tape player ($299). Vinyl roof ($94). Metallic glow paint ($54). Decklid luggage rack ($51). Rocker panel moldings ($19). Bumper guards, front or rear ($17). Reclining bucket seats ($147). Cloth bucket seat trim ($24). Vinyl seat trim ($25). Color-keyed deluxe seatbelts ($17). Forged aluminum wheels ($98 to $187). Styled steel wheels ($59 to $89). Hubcap trim rings ($35), no charge with decor group. Space-saver spare ($13) but no charge with radial tires. Automatic transmission: ($245). Power brakes: ($53). Sure-Track brakes ($124). Heavy duty suspension ($16). 250-cid six cylinder engine: ($96).

1976 Ford Elite

1976 Gran Torino Brougham four-door pillared hardtop

Granada: Sports sedan option ($482). Exterior decor group ($128). Interior decor group ($181). Luxury decor group ($642). Convenience group ($31 to $75). Deluxe bumper group ($61). Light group ($25 to $37). Protection group ($24 to $39). Visibility group ($30 to $47). Security lock group ($17). Air conditioning ($437). Rear defogger ($43). Rear defroster, electric ($76). Fingertip speed control ($96). Power windows ($95 to $133). Power door locks ($63 to $88). Power four-way seat ($119). Tinted glass ($47). Leather-wrapped steering wheel ($14 to $33). Luxury steering wheel ($18). Tilt steering wheel ($54). Fuel monitor warning light ($18). Digital clock ($40). Dual-note horn ($6). Color-keyed outside mirrors ($29 to $42). Lighted visor vanity mirror ($40). AM radio ($71); w/tape player ($192). AM/FM radio ($142). AM/FM stereo radio ($210); w/tape player ($299). Power moon roof ($786). Power sun roof ($517). Vinyl or half vinyl roof ($102). Metallic glow paint ($54). Rocker panel moldings ($19). Decklid luggage rack ($33). Console ($65). Reclining seats ($60). Leather seat trim ($181). Deluxe cloth seat trim ($88). Trunk carpeting ($20). Trunk dress-up ($33). Color-keyed seatbelts ($17). Styled steel wheels ($41 to $60); w/trim rings ($76 to $95). Lacy spoke aluminum wheels ($112 to $207). 250-cid six ($96). 302-cid V-8 ($154) or ($88), Granada Ghia. 351-cid V-8 ($200) or ($134), Granada Ghia. Automatic transmission ($245). Power brakes ($57). Four-wheel power disc brakes ($210). Sure-Track brakes ($227). Heavy duty suspension ($29). Trailer towing package ($42).

Torino/Elite: Squire Brougham option ($184). Interior decor group: Elite ($384). Accent group: Torino ($45). Deluxe bumper group ($50 to $67). Light group ($41 to $43). Convenience group: Torino ($33 to $84); Elite ($49). Protection group ($26 to $42). Security lock group ($18). Auto-temp control air conditioning ($88). Anti-theft alarm system ($84). Rear defroster, electric ($99). Windshield/rear window defroster, Power windows ($104 to $145). Power tailgate wagon window: ($43). Power door locks ($68 to $109). Electric decklid release ($17). Six-way power seat ($130). Automatic seatback release ($30). Reclining passenger seat ($70). Leather-wrapped steering wheel ($36). Luxury steering wheel ($20). Tilt steering wheel ($59). Fuel sentry vacuum gauge ($13 to $32). Fuel monitor warning light ($20). Electric clock ($18). Dual-note horn ($7). Remote driver's mirror, chrome ($14). Remote-control color-keyed mirrors ($32 to $46). Lighted visor vanity mirror ($43). AM radio ($78). AM/FM stereo radio ($229); w/tape player ($326). AM/FM stereo search radio: Elite ($386). Dual rear speakers ($39). Exterior: Power moon roof: Elite ($859). Power sunroof ($545). Vinyl roof: Torino ($112); Elite. no charge. Opera windows: Torino ($50). Fender skirts: Torino ($41). Rocker panel moldings ($26). Bumper guards, front or rear: Torino ($18). Luggage rack: Torino ($82 to $91). Bucket seats ($146). Rear-facing third seat, station wagon ($104). Vinyl bench seat trim: Torino ($22). Pleated vinyl bench seat trim ($22 to $28). Duraweave vinyl seat trim: Torino ($55). Color-keyed seatbelts ($18). Trunk trim ($36). Deluxe wheel covers: Torino ($37). Luxury wheel covers ($58 to $95). Wire wheel covers: Elite ($99). Magnum 500 wheels w/trim rings: Torino ($141 to $178). Turbine spoke cast aluminum wheels: Elite ($226). 400-cid V-8 ($100). 460-cid V-8 ($292). Heavy duty handling and suspension ($18 to $32), Torino and ($92), Elite. Heavy duty electrical system ($29), Torino and Elite ($80). Medium trailer and towing package ($59). Heavy duty trailer and towing package ($87 to $121), Torino and ($121), Elite.

1976 Maverick Stallion coupe

1976 Granada sedan (with Exterior Decor Group option)

LTD: Landau luxury group including concealed headlamps, a convenience group, half vinyl roof (on two-door), front cornering lamps, wide color-keyed body moldings, and unique narrow center pillar windows, padded door panels with woodnote accents, fold-down center armrests, and a digital clock ($472 to $708). Brougham option: wagon ($396); Squire ($266). Harmony color group ($99). Convenience group ($97-$104). Light group ($76 to $79). Deluxe bumper group ($41 to $59). Protection group ($47 to $78). Security lock group ($18). Air conditioning ($353); w/auto-temp control ($486). Anti-theft alarm system ($566). Rear defogger ($43). Rear defroster, electric ($83). Fingertip speed control ($87 to $107). Power windows ($108 to $161). Power mini-vent and side windows ($232). Power door locks ($68-$109). Six-way power driver's seat ($132) or driver and passenger ($259). Automatic seatback release ($30). Tinted glass ($64). Luxury steering wheel ($20). Tilt steering wheel ($59). Fuel monitor warning light ($20). Electric clock ($18). Digital clock ($25 to $43). Cornering lamps ($43). Dual-note horn ($6). Driver's remote mirror ($14). AM radio ($78). AM/FM stereo radio ($229); w/tape player ($326). AM/FM stereo search radio ($386). Dual rear speakers ($39). Sunroof, manual ($632). Full vinyl roof ($126) exc. wagon ($151). Half vinyl roof ($126). Fender skirts ($42). Metallic glow paint ($59). Dual accent paint stripes ($29). Rocker panel moldings ($26). Vinyl-insert body side moldings ($41). Rear bumper guards ($18). Luggage rack ($82 to $96). Dual-facing rear seats, wagon ($126). Split bench seat w/passenger recliner ($141). Leather interior trim ($222). All-vinyl seat ($22). Duraweave vinyl trim ($55). Recreation table ($58). Color-keyed seatbelts ($18). Deluxe cargo area ($83 to $126). Lockable side stowage compartment ($43). Luggage area trim ($36). Full wheel covers ($30). Deluxe wheel covers ($63 to $93). 400-cid V-8 ($100). 460-cid V-8 ($353) and $251 on the LTD station wagon. Four-wheel power disc brakes ($170). Heavy duty suspension ($18). Adjustable air shock absorbers ($43). Extended-range fuel tank ($99). Light duty trailer towing package ($53). Medium duty trailer towing package ($46 to $145). Heavy duty trailer towing package ($132 to $230).

History:

The 1967 Fords were introduced on October 3, 1975. Model year production was 1,861,537, including Mustangs. Calendar year sales by U.S. dealers were 1,682,583, including Mustangs. The total sales gave Ford a 19.9 percent share of the market. Ford sales had declined sharply in the 1975 model year, down over 21 percent. Full-size models had sold best. Even the success of the Granada (new for 1975) wasn't as great as anticipated. Ford had introduced Pinto Pony and Mustang II MPG models late in the 1975 model year. Sales swung upward again for the 1976 model year, even though few major changes were evident in the lineup. Part of the reason was Ford's new "California strategy," that offered special option packages for West Coast buyers to take sales away from the imports. It proved quite successful in 1976. Prices jumped as the model year began, then were cut back in January. Production fell for Pinto, Mustang II and Maverick in 1976, but overall production increased nearly 19 percent, especially due to Granada sales. Model year sales followed a similar pattern, up 18.5 percent. Henry Ford II, Lee Iacocca and B.E. Bidwell were the top Ford executives. Pinto was once described as "a car nobody loved, but everybody bought." This was the last year for the unsafe Pinto gas tank and filler neck. The faulty components had

1976 LTD Landau four-door pillared hardtop

caused a number of highly publicized fires resulting in massive product-liability lawsuits. Granada had proven to be one of the fastest Fords, at least with a "Windsor" 351 cid V-8 under its hood.

1977 Ford

Pinto — Four and V-6: Revised front and rear styling hit Ford's subcompact, offered again in two-door sedan, "three-door" Runabout and station wagon form. A new "soft" nose with sloping hood and flexible fender extension and deflector assembly were up front. At the rear of the two-door sedan and three-door Runabout were new, larger horizontal dual-lens tail lamps. There were new extruded anodized aluminum bumpers front and rear. A new vinyl roof grain was available. Runabouts had a new optional all-glass third door. Inside was new cloth trim, optional on the base high-back bucket seats. A new lower (2.73:1) rear axle ratio went with the standard OHC 140 cid (2.3-liter) four-cylinder engine and a wide-ratio four-speed manual gearbox. The low-budget Pony came with rack-and-pinion steering, front disc brakes, all-vinyl or cloth/vinyl high-back front bucket seats, a mini-console, color-keyed carpeting, and argent hubcaps. The base two-door sedan included a color-keyed instrument panel and steering wheel, bright backlight trim, plus bright drip and belt moldings. Runabouts had a fold-down rear seat, rear lift gate, and rubber load floor mat. All models except the Pony could have a 170.8 cid (2.8-liter) V-6. A new Sports option included a tachometer, ammeter and temperature gauge, new soft-rim spots steering wheel, front stabilizer bar, higher-rate springs, and higher axle ratio. A new Cruising Wagon was aimed at youthful buyers. It included a front spoiler, styled wheels, Sports Rallye equipment, and carpeted rear section.

Maverick — Six and V-8: For its final season, Maverick changed little except for some new body and interior colors, two new vinyl roof colors, and a new vinyl-insert body side molding. New options included wire wheel covers, four-way manual bucket seats, and high-altitude option. The optional 302 V-8 got a variable-Venturi carburetor. All engines gained Dura-Spark ignition. There was also a new wide-ratio three-speed manual shift. Revised speedometers showed miles and kilometers. The Decor Group added a halo vinyl roof. The standard engine was the 200 cid (3.3-liter) six. Standard equipment included front disc brakes (manual), three-speed column-shift manual transmission, a foot parking brake with warning light, and 19.2-gallon gas tank. Also standard were color-keyed carpeting, armrests with a door pull assist handle, flip-open rear quarter windows, bright hubcaps and bright drip rail and wheel lip moldings.

Granada — Six and V-8: Styling of the Mercedes-emulating Granada remained similar to 1976, with nine new body colors available. A new full-synchronized four-speed manual transmission with overdrive fourth gear became standard. That made Granada the first domestic model to offer an overdrive four-speed as standard equipment (except in California, where it was unavailable). The base engine was the 200-cid (3.3-liter) inline six with Dura-Spark ignition. Also standard were front disc brakes, an inside hood release, wiper/washer control on the turn signal lever. The body sported window, drip, belt and wheel lip moldings. Two-doors displayed opera lamps. The Granada Ghia

1977 Pinto three-door Runabout (with optional wire wheels)

added a left-hand remote-control mirror, wide color-keyed vinyl-insert body side moldings (integral with wheel lip moldings), flight bench seats, and unique wire-style wheel covers. A new variable-Venturi carburetor for the 302 V-8 was used only in California. Four models were offered: Granada and Ghia two- and four-door sedans. New Granada options included four-way manual bucket seats, automatic-temperature-control air conditioning, illuminated entry, front cornering lamps, simulated wire wheel covers, white lacy-spoke cast aluminum wheels, wideband whitewall radials, electric trunk lid release, and a high-altitude option.

LTD II — V-8: Serving as a replacement for the abandoned Torino, the new A-bodied LTD II had similar dimensions, and long-hood styling that wasn't radically different. The goal, according to Ford, was to combine "LTD's traditional high level of workmanship with Mustang's sporty spirit." A wide choice of models were offered: S, base and Brougham in the two-door hardtop, a four-door pillared hardtop or a four-door wagon. The wagons were offered only this year, and LTD II would last only into the 1979 model year. Among the more noticeable styling features were vertically-stacked quad rectangular headlamps, and doors with a straight beltline. Sharply-tapered opera windows on the wide roof pillars stood to the rear of the regular quarter windows of two-doors, except the "S" model. Four-doors were also a six-window design. Inside, the LTD II had new seat trim and new-look door trim. The standard engine dropped to a 302 V-8, now with Dura-Spark ignition and a lower axle ratio. Standard equipment on the budget-priced "S" included SelectShift automatic transmission, power steering and brakes and a Kirsten cloth/vinyl bench seat. The basic LTD II had an Ardmore cloth/vinyl flight bench seat, deluxe door trim, rear panel appliqué, hood ornament, and rocker panel and wheel lip moldings. The top-line Brougham added Doral cloth/vinyl split bench seats, dual horns, an electric clock, and wide color-keyed vinyl-insert side moldings. The standard engine was the 302 cid V-8 hooked to SelectShift Cruise-O-Matic.

LTD/Custom 500 — V-8: Rivals may have shrunk their big cars, but the Ford remained full-size once again. According to the factory, that gave LTD a "wider stance, and more road-hugging weight." New colors and fabrics entered LTD interiors this year, but not much else was different. Power train changes included improved 351 and 400 cid V-8s with new Dura-Spark ignition, as well as lower rear axle ratios. New options included illuminated entry, Quadra sonic tape player, simulated wire wheel covers, forged aluminum wheels, and wide whitewall radial tires. The LTD Brougham was dropped, but the top-rung Landau model took its position in the lineup. Six basic models were available: LTD and Landau two- and four-door, LTD wagon, and Country Squire wagon. The Custom 500 was for fleet buyers only. Standard LTD equipment included a 351 cid (5.8-liter) V-8 with Dura-Spark ignition, SelectShift automatic transmission, power brakes and steering, a Redondo cloth/vinyl bench seat, a hood ornament and bright hubcaps. Landau models added concealed headlamps, an Ardmore cloth/vinyl flight bench seat, electric clock, half or full vinyl roof, rear bumper guards, full wheel covers, color-keyed side moldings, and a dual-note horn. A Landau Creme and Blue package was announced for the mid-year, with choice of color combinations. A Creme body color came with a creme or blue vinyl roof. Inside was a Creme super-soft vinyl luxury group, and split bench seats with blue welts.

I.D. Data:

As before, Ford's 11-symbol Vehicle Identification Number (VIN) was stamped on a metal tab fastened to the instrument panel and was visible through the windshield. Coding was similar to 1976. The model year code was 7 = 1977. The Code Y for the Wixom. Michigan, assembly plant was dropped. One engine code was added: Q = the modified 351-cid two-barrel V-8.

Pinto (Four)

Model No.	Body Style No.	Body Type & Seating	Factory Price	Shipping Weight	Production Total
10	62B	2-dr. Sedan-4P	$3,237	2,315 lbs.	48,863
10	62B	2-dr. Pony Sedan-4P	$3,099	2,313 lbs.	Note 1
11	64B	2-dr Hatchback-4P	$3,353	2,351 lbs.	74,237
12	73B	2-dr. Station Wagon-4P	$3,548	2,515 lbs.	79,449
12	73B	2-dr. Squire Wagon-4P	$3,891	2,552 lbs.	Note 2

Pinto (V-6)

10	62B	2-dr. Sedan-4P	$3,519	2,438 lbs.	48,863
11	64B	2-dr. Hatchback- 4P	$3,635	2,414 lbs.	74,237
12	73B	2-dr. Station Wagon-4P	$3,830	2,638 lbs.	79,449
12	73B	2-dr. Squire Wagon-4P	$4,172	2,675 lbs.	Note 2

Note 1: Pony production is included in the base sedan figure.
Note 2: Squire Wagon production is included in the standard station wagon total.
Note: Totals included 22,548 Pintos produced as 1978 models but sold as 1977 models. There were 6,599 two-door sedans, 8,271 hatchback Runabouts and 7,678 station wagons.

Maverick (Six)

| 91 | 62A | 2-dr. Sedan-4P | $3,322 | 2,782 lbs. | 40,086 |
| 92 | 54A | 4-dr. Sedan-5P | $3,395 | 2,887 lbs. | 58,420 |

Maverick (V-8)

| 91 | 62A | 2-dr. Sedan-4P | $3,483 | 2,947 lbs. | 40,086 |
| 92 | 54A | 4-dr. Sedan-5P | $3,556 | 3,052 lbs. | 58,420 |

Granada (Six)

| 82 | 66H | 2-dr. Sedan-5P | $4,022 | 3,124 lbs. | 157,612 |
| 81 | 54H | 4-dr. Sedan-5P | $4,118 | 3,174 lbs. | 163,071 |

Granada (V-8)

| 82 | 66H | 2-dr. Sedan-5P | $4,209 | 3,219 lbs. | 157,612 |
| 81 | 54H | 4-dr. Sedan-5P | $4,305 | 3,269 lbs. | 163,071 |

Granada Ghia (Six)

| 84 | 66K | 2-dr. Sedan-5P | $4,452 | 3,175 lbs. | 34,166 |
| 83 | 54K | 4-dr. Sedan-5P | $4,548 | 3,229 lbs. | 35,730 |

Granada Ghia (V-8)

| 84 | 66K | 2-dr. Sedan-5P | $4,639 | 3,270 lbs. | 34,166 |
| 83 | 54K | 4-dr. Sedan-5P | $4,735 | 3,324 lbs. | 35,730 |

LTD II (V-8)

30	65D	2-dr. Hardtop-6P	$4,785	3,789 lbs.	57,449
31	53D	4-dr. Pillar Hardtop-6P	$4,870	3,904 lbs.	56,704
42	71D	4-dr. Station Wagon-6P	$5,064	4,404 lbs.	23,237
43	71K	4-dr. Squire Wagon-6P	$5,335	4,430 lbs.	17,162

LTD II S (V-8)

25	65B	2-dr. Hardtop-6P	$4,528	3,789 lbs.	9,531
27	53B	4-dr. Pillar Hardtop-6P	$4,579	3,894 lbs.	18,775
40	71B	4-dr. Station Wagon-6P	$4,806	4,393 lbs.	9,636

LTD II Brougham (V-8)

| 32 | 65K | 2-dr. Hardtop-6P | $5,121 | 3,898 lbs. | 20,979 |
| 33 | 53K | 4-dr. Pillar Hardtop-6P | $5,206 | 3,930 lbs. | 18,851 |

Custom 500 (V-8)

52	60D	2-dr. Pillar Hardtop-6P	-----	-----	4,139
53	53D	4-dr. Pillar Hardtop-6P	-----	-----	5,582
72	71D	4-dr. Station Wagon-6P	-----	-----	1,406

LTD (V-8)

62	60H	2-dr. Pillar Hardtop-6P	$5,128	4,190 lbs.	73,637
63	53H	4-dr. Pillar Hardtop-6P	$5,152	4,240 lbs.	160,255
74	71H	4-dr. Station Wagon-6P	$5,415	4,635 lbs.	90,711
76	71K	4-dr. Country Squire-6P	$5,866	4,674 lbs.	Note 3

Note 3: Country Squire and wagons with dual-facing rear seats are included in basic wagon totals.

LTD Landau (V-8)

| 65 | 60L | 2-dr. Pillar Hardtop-6P | $5,717 | 4,270 lbs. | 44,396 |
| 64 | 53L | 4-dr. Pillar Hardtop-6P | $5,742 | 4,319 lbs. | 65,030 |

Engines:

Pinto Four: Inline with overhead cam. Cast-iron block and head. Displacement: 140 cid (2.3 liters). B & S: 3.78 x 3.13 in. Compression ratio: 9.0:1. Brake hp: 89 at 4800 rpm. Torque: 120 lbs.-ft. at 3000 rpm. Five main bearings. Hydraulic valve lifters. Carburetor: Motorcraft 5200 two-barrel. VIN Code: Y.

Pinto Optional V-6: 60-degree, overhead-valve. Cast-iron block and head. Displacement: 170.8 cid (2.8 liters). B & S: 3.66 x 2.70 in. Compression ratio: 8.7:1. Brake hp: 93 at 4200 rpm. Torque: 140 lbs.-

1977 Maverick coupe

1977 Maverick sedan

1977 Granada Sports Coupe

1977 Granada sedan

1977-1/2 Granada Sports Coupe (with opera-window louvers)

ft. at 2600 rpm. Four main bearings. Solid valve lifters. Carburetor: Motorcraft 2150 two-barrel. VIN Code: Z.

Maverick, Granada Base Six: Inline and overhead valve. Cast-iron block and head. Displacement: 200 cid (3.3 liters). B & S: 3.68 x 3.13 in. Compression ratio: 8.5:1. Brake hp: 96 at 4400 rpm. Torque: 151 lbs.-ft. at 2000 rpm. Seven main bearings. Hydraulic valve lifters. Carburetor: Carter YFA one-barrel. VIN Code: T.

Granada Ghia Base Six (Optional: Maverick, Granada): Inline. Overhead valve. Cast-iron block and head. Displacement: 250 cid (4.1 liters). B & S: 3.68 x 3.91 in. Compression ratio: 8.1:1. Brake hp: 98 at 3400 rpm. Torque: 182 lbs.-ft. at 1800 rpm. Seven main bearings. Hydraulic valve lifters. Carburetor: Carter YFA one-barrel. VIN Code: L.

LTD II Base V-8 (Optional: Maverick, Granada): 90-degree, overhead valve. Cast-iron block and head. Displacement: 302 cid (5.0 liters). B & S: 4.00 x 3.00 in. Compression ratio: 8.4:1. Brake hp: 130 to 137 at 3400 to 3600 rpm. Torque: 243 to 245 lbs.-ft. at 1600 to 1800 rpm. Five main bearings. Hydraulic valve lifters. Carburetor: Motorcraft 2150 two-barrel. VIN code: F.

Note: Horsepower and torque ratings of the 302 V-8 varied slightly, according to model.

LTD Optional V-8: 90-degree, overhead valve, Cast-iron block and head. Displacement: 351 cid (5.8 liters). B & S: 4.00 x 3.50 in. Compression ratio: 8.3:1. Brake hp: 149 at 3200 rpm. Torque: 291 lbs.-ft. at 1600 rpm. Five main bearings. Hydraulic valve lifters. Carburetor: Motorcraft 2150 two-barrel. Windsor engine. VIN Code: H.

Optional Granada V-8: Same as 351 cid V-8 above, but 135 hp at 3200 rpm. Torque: 275 lbs.-ft. at 1600 rpm.

LTD and LTD II wagon V-8 (Optional Granada Ghia and LTD II): Same as 351 cid V-8 above, but the compression ratio is 8.0:1, the brake hp is 161 at 3600 rpm and the torque is 285 lbs.-ft. at 1800 rpm. VIN Code: Q.

LTD wagon Base V-8 (Optional LTD and LTD II): 90-degree, overhead valve. Cast-iron block and head. Displacement: 400 cid (6.6 liters). B & S: 4.00 x 4.00 in. Compression ratio: 8:0.1. Brake hp: 173 at 3800 rpm. Torque: 326 lbs.-ft. at 1600 rpm. Five main bearings. Hydraulic valve lifters. Carburetor: Motorcraft 2150 two-barrel. VIN Code: S.

LTD Optional V-8: 90-degree, overhead valve. Cast-iron block and head. Displacement: 460 cid (7.5 liters). B & S: 4.36 x 3.85 in. Compression ratio: 8.0:1. Brake hp: 197 at 4000 rpm. Torque: 353 lbs.-ft. at 2000 rpm. Five main bearings. Hydraulic valve lifters. Carburetor: Motorcraft 4350 four-barrel. VIN Code: A.

Note: A Police 460-cid V-8 was also available for the LTD.

Chassis:

Pinto: Wheelbase: 94.5 and 94.8, wagon. Overall length: 169.0 in. and 178.8 in., wagon. Tires: A78 x 13.

Maverick: Wheelbase: 103.0 in. and 109.9 in., sedan. Overall length: 187.0 in. and 193.9 in., sedan. Tires: C78 x 14 and DR78 x 14 with V-8.

Granada: Wheelbase: 109.9 in. Overall length: 197.7 in. Tires: DR78 x 14 steel belted radials.

LTD II: Wheelbase: 114.0, two door and 118.0 in, sedan and station wagon. Overall length: 215.5 in., two door, 219.5 in., sedan and 223.1 in. station wagon. Tires: HR78 x 14 steel belted radials.

LTD/Custom 500: Wheelbase: 121.0 in. Overall length: 224.1 in. and 225.6 in., station wagon. Tires: HR78 x 15 and JR78 x 15, station wagon.

Options:

Pinto: Cruising wagon package, including body side tape stripe ($416). Sports Rallye package ($89). Exterior decor group ($122 to $128). Interior decor group ($160). Convenience light group ($73 to $108). Deluxe bumper group ($65). Protection group ($122 to $142). Air conditioner ($446) Rear defroster, electric ($73). Tinted glass ($48). Dual sport mirrors ($45). AM radio ($76), w/stereo tape player ($204). AM/FM radio ($135). AM/FM stereo radio ($184). Sunroof, manual ($243). Flip-up open air roof ($147). Half vinyl roof ($133). Glass third door ($13). Metallic glow paint ($58). Special paint/tape w/luggage rack: cruising wagon ($58). Black narrow vinyl-insert side moldings ($37). Roof luggage rack ($80). Rocker panel moldings ($20). Four-way driver's seat ($33). Load floor carpet ($23). Cargo area cover ($30). Wire wheel covers ($79 to $119). Forged aluminum wheels ($57 to $183). Styled steel wheels ($98 to $127). Wheel covers ($29). 170-cid V-6 ($289). SelectShift Cruise-O-Matic ($196). Optional axle ratio ($14). Power brakes ($58). Power steering ($124). Heavy duty battery ($16). High altitude option ($39).

Maverick: Exterior decor group ($105). Interior decor group ($112). Deluxe bumper group ($65). Convenience group ($49 to $67). Protection group ($34 to $41). Light group ($36). Air conditioning ($446). Rear defogger ($42). Tinted glass ($47 to $63). Dual sport mirrors ($14 to $27). AM radio ($76); w/tape player ($204). AM/FM radio ($135). AM/FM stereo radio ($222); w/tape player ($317). Vinyl roof ($100). Metallic glow paint ($58). Wide vinyl-insert side moldings ($64). Bumper guards, front and rear ($36). Four-way reclining driver's bucket seat ($33). Reclining vinyl bucket seats ($129). Cloth reclining bucket seats ($25). Vinyl seat trim ($27). Wire wheel covers ($86 to $119). Lacy spoke aluminum wheels ($218 to $251). Styled steel wheels ($100 to $131). C78 x 14 white sidewall tires ($33). CR78 x 14 steel belted radial tires ($89). CR78 x 14 white sidewall steel belted tires ($121). DR78 x 14 white sidewall steel belted radial tires ($89 to $112). DR78 x 14 steel-belted white sidewall tires ($121 to $144). Space-saver spare ($14). 250-cid six ($102). 302-cid V-8 ($161). SelectShift Cruise-O-Matic ($259). Power brakes ($57). Power steering ($131). Heavy duty suspension ($17). Heavy duty battery ($16). High altitude option ($39).

LTD II: Squire Brougham option ($203). Sports instrumentation group ($103 to $130). Exterior decor group ($225 to $276). Accent group ($58). Deluxe bumper group ($72). Light group ($46 to $49). Convenience group ($101 to $132). Power lock group ($92 to $125). Air conditioning ($505); w/auto-temp control ($546). Rear defroster, electric ($87). Fingertip speed control ($93 to $114). Illuminated entry system ($51). Tinted glass ($57). Power windows ($114 to $158). Power station wagon tailgate window: ($43). Six-way power seat ($143). Leather-wrapped steering wheel ($39 to $61). Tilt steering wheel ($63). Day/date clock ($20 to $39). Cornering lamps ($43). Remote driver's mirror, chrome ($14). Dual sports mirrors ($51). AM radio ($72). AM/FM radio ($132). AM/FM stereo radio ($192); w/tape player ($266); w/Quadra sonic tape player ($399). AM/FM stereo search radio ($349). Dual rear speakers ($43). Full vinyl roof ($111 to $162). Half vinyl roof ($111). Opera windows ($51). Vinyl-insert side moldings ($39). Rear-facing third seat station wagon ($100). Vinyl seat trim ($22). Color-keyed seatbelts ($18). Deluxe wheel covers ($36). Luxury wheel covers ($59 to $95). Wire wheel covers ($99). Turbine

1977 LTD Landau four-door pillared hardtop

1977 LTD II hardtop coupe

1977 LTD II Brougham pillared hardtop

spoke cast aluminum wheels ($234 to $270). H78 x 14 steel-belted white sidewalls ($45). HR78 x 14 wide-band white sidewall tires ($16 to $61). JR78 x 14 steel-belted white sidewalls ($26 to $71). HR78 x 15 steel-belted white sidewalls ($45). 351-cid V-8 ($66). 400-cid V-8 ($155) and $100, LTD station wagon. Heavy duty handling and suspension ($9 to $33). Heavy duty battery ($17). Heavy duty alternator ($45). Heavy duty trailer towing package ($93 to $111).

LTD: Landau luxury group ($403 to $563). Convenience group ($88 to $136). Light group ($36 to $38). Deluxe bumper group ($43 to $63). Protection group ($50 to $59). Air conditioning ($514), with auto-temp control ($600). Rear defogger ($46). Rear defroster, electric ($88). Fingertip speed control ($92 to $113). Illuminated entry system ($54). Power windows ($114 to $170). Power mini-vent and side windows ($246). Power door locks ($72 to $116) Six-way power driver's seat ($139); driver and passenger seats ($275). Tinted glass ($68). Tilt steering wheel ($63). Electric clock ($20). Digital clock ($26 to $46). Cornering lamps ($46). Driver's remote mirror ($16). AM radio ($83). AM/FM radio ($147). AM/FM stereo radio ($242); with tape player ($346); with Quadra sonic tape player ($450). AM/FM stereo search radio ($409). Dual rear speakers ($42). Full vinyl roof ($134), Landau two-door, no charge. Half vinyl roof ($134). Fender skirts ($45). Rocker panel moldings ($28). Vinyl-insert side moldings ($43). Rear bumper guards ($20). Luggage rack ($101). Dual-facing station wagon rear seats ($134). Split bench seat with passenger recliner ($149). Leather seat trim ($236). All-vinyl seat trim ($23). Duraweave vinyl trim ($59). Color-keyed seatbelts ($20). Lockable side storage compartment ($46). Full wheel covers ($32). Deluxe wheel covers ($67 to $99) Wire wheel covers ($105 to $137). Deep-dish aluminum wheels ($251 to $283). 460-cid V-8 ($297) and ($189) LTD station wagon. Traction-Lok differential ($57). Optional axle ratio ($16). Heavy duty suspension ($20). Heavy duty battery ($18). Heavy duty trailer towing package ($125). High altitude option ($42).

History:

The 1977 Fords were introduced on October 1, 1976. Model year production: 1,840,427, including Mustangs. Calendar year sales by U.S. dealers were 1,824,035, including Mustangs. Both the new LTD II and the shrunken Thunderbird were meant to rival Chevrolet's Monte Carlo and the Pontiac Grand Prix. The LTD cost nearly 7 percent more than in 1976. Since gasoline prices weren't rising, Ford's lineup of relatively small cars wasn't doing as well as hoped. Slight price cuts of smaller models, after their 1977 introduction, didn't help. Plants producing smaller Fords shut down nearly two months earlier for the

1977 LTD Country Squire wagon

'78 changeover than did those turning out full-sized models. During the model year, Maverick production halted and was replaced by the new Fairmont compact. A UAW strike against Ford during the model year didn't affect production. It was nearly identical to the 1976 output. Ford continued the successful California strategy during 1977, offering special models available on the West Coast.

1978 Ford

Pinto — Four and V-6: New body and interior colors made up most of the changes in Ford's rear-drive subcompact Pinto. In 1978, they carried split-cushion bucket rear seats. New options included white-painted forged aluminum wheels and an accent stripe treatment in four color combinations. Seven body colors were available, as well as vinyl roofs in jade or chamois. Pinto's model lineup still included the two-door sedan, three-door hatchback Runabout and station wagon. The base engine remained the 140-cid (2.3-liter) overhead-cam four plus a four-speed manual gearbox. Optional power rack-and-pinion steering added a new variable-ratio system similar to one used on the new Fairmont and Zephyr series. A Sports Rallye Package included a tachometer, sport steering wheel, front stabilizer bar, heavy-duty suspension, and 3.18:1 axle. The Rallye Appearance package contained dual racing mirrors, black front spoiler, gold accent stripes, and blacked-out exterior moldings. The Cruising Wagon option returned, with front spoiler, graphic multi-colored paint striping, cargo area carpeting, styled steel wheels, dual sport mirrors, and steel side panels with round tinted porthole windows. At mid-year a panel delivery Pinto was added. Most regular production options were available on the panel Pinto plus a rear-window security screen.

Fairmont — Four, Six and V-8: A new, more modern compact model, the Fairmont, and its Mercury Zephyr corporate twin, debuted for 1978. They shared the new unitized Fox body/chassis platform that eventually carried a number of other Ford models. Fairmont was designed with an emphasis on efficiency and fuel economy, achieved by means of reduced weight and improved aerodynamics. Ford also made the best use of interior space and offered easy maintenance. The clean styling was influenced by Ford's Ghia design studios in Turin, Italy. Zephyr differed only in grille design and trim details. Under the chassis was a new suspension with MacPherson struts and coil springs up front, and four-link coil spring design at the rear. Front coil springs were mounted on the lower control arms. Rack-and-pinion steering had a power assist available at extra cost. The base engine was the 140 cid (2.3-liter) "Lima" four, also used in Pintos and Mustangs. It was the first four-cylinder in a domestic Ford compact. A four-speed manual gearbox was standard, but V-8 models required automatic. Four-cylinder models had standard low-back bucket seats, while sixes and eights held a bench seat. Standard equipment included B78 x 14 black tires and hubcaps. The Fairmont's wheelbase was 105.5 inches. The opening model lineup included two- and four-door sedans and a station wagon. A Euro styled (ES) option was added later. It included a blacked-out grille, rear quarter window louvers, black window frames and turbine-spoked wheel covers. The Futura Sport Coupe, with roofline reminiscent of Thunderbird, joined the

1978 Pinto station wagon (with Exterior Decor Package)

1978 Pinto three-door hatchback

1978 Pinto three-door Runabout (with Rallye Appearance Package)

original sedans and wagon in December. The coupe borrowed its name from the 1960s Falcon. Inside, the five-passenger Futura were pleated vinyl bucket seats, wood tone appliqué on the dash, and color-keyed seatbelts. William P. Benton, Ford's vice-president (and Ford Division General Manager) said Fairmont Futura "has the best fuel economy in its class, leg, shoulder and hip room of a mid-size car, and responsive handling, plus a rich new look and an array of luxury touches."

Granada Six and V-8: Granada and its twin, the Mercury Monarch, took on a fresh look this year with new bright grilles, rectangular headlamps, parking lamps, a front bumper air spoiler, wide wheel lip moldings, new wraparound tail lamps, and lower back panel appliqués. Also new on two-doors were "window" opera windows split by a bright center bar. This was the first major restyle since 1974 and the first quad rectangular headlamps in the Ford camp. The spoiler and hood-to-grille-opening panel seal, and revised decklid surface, helped reduce aerodynamic drag. A Ford badge went on the lower driver's side of the grille. Rectangular headlamps stood above nearly-as-large rectangular parking lamps, both in a recessed housing. Two-door and four-door sedans were offered again, in base or Ghia trim. Granada Ghia had wide side moldings. A new European Sports Sedan (ESS) option package included a blackout vertical grille texture as well as black rocker panels, door frames and side moldings, black rubber bumper guards and wide rub strips and a unique interior. ESS had color-keyed wheel covers, a heavy-duty suspension, dual sport mirrors, decklid and hood pin striping. It rode on FR78 x 14 steel belted radial tires. The car also had individual reclining bucket seats. Distinctive was the ESS half-covered, louvered quarter windows. Low on the cowl was an ESS badge, above the Granada script. Other options included an AM/FM stereo with cassette tape player, and a 40-channel CB transceiver. Five new Granada colors were offered this year, and a valino vinyl roof came in three new color choices. The base 200 cid six from 1977 was replaced by a 250 cid (4.1-liter) version.

LTD II — V-8: Station wagons left the LTD II lineup this year, since the new Fairmont line included a wagon. Other LTD II models continued with the S base and Brougham series. Broughams had a full-length body trim strip. The standard engine was again the 302 cid (5.0-liter) V-8 with Cruise-O-Matic transmission, power front disc brakes, and power steering. Options included the 351-cid and 400-cid V-8 engines, a heavy-duty trailer towing package (for the 400 V-8), and a Sports Appearance package. Two-doors could either have a solid panel at the rear, or the extra rear coach-style window. A new bumper front spoiler, hood-to-grille-opening panel seal, revised decklid surface, and new fuel tank air deflector were supposed to cut aerodynamic drag and boost economy. Bumper-to-fender shields were new, too. A revised low-restriction fresh-air intake went on V-8 engines. A new mechanical spark control system was limited to the 351M and 400 cid V-8s. Newly optional this year was a 40-channel CB radio. The Mercury Cougar was the corporate twin to the LTD II.

LTD/Custom 500 — V-8: Full-sized Fords were carried over for 1978, with new body colors available but little change beyond a new front bumper spoiler, rear floor pan air deflector, and other aerodynamic additions. The decklid also was new. The LTD still came in two-door or four-door pillared hardtop form, as well as plain-side and Country Squire (simulated wood paneled) station wagons. The Custom 500 was the fleet model and was sold in Canada. Station wagons could now have optional removable auxiliary cushions for the dual facing rear seats. Among the more than 70 options were new two-tone body colors for the LTD Landau. Air conditioners now allowed the driver to control heating and cooling. A downsized LTD arrived for 1979. The 1978 model was the final full-sized version.

I.D. Data:

Just as in 1976 and 1977, Ford's 11-symbol Vehicle Identification Number (VIN) was stamped on a metal tab fastened to the instrument panel and was visible through the windshield. The model year coding changed with the year: 8 = 1978.

Pinto (Four)

Model No.	Body Style No.	Body Type & Seating	Factory Price	Shipping Weight	Production Total
10	62B	2-dr. Sedan-4P	$3,336	2,337 lbs.	62,317
10	62B	2-dr. Pony Sedan-4P	$2,995	2,321 lbs.	Note 1
11	64B	2-dr. Hatchback-4P	$3,451	2,381 lbs.	74,313
12	73B	2-dr. Station Wagon-4P	$3,794	2,521 lbs.	52,269
12	73B	2-dr. Squire Wag-4P	$4,109	2,555 lbs.	Note 2

Pinto (V-6)

Model No.	Body Style No.	Body Type & Seating	Factory Price	Shipping Weight	Production Total
10	62B	2-dr. Sedan-4P	$3,609	2,463 lbs.	62,317
11	64B	3-dr. Hatchback-4P	$3,724	2,507 lbs.	74,313
12	73B	2-dr. Station Wagon-4P	$4,067	2,637 lbs.	52,269
12	73B	2-dr. Squire Wag-4P	$4,382	2,672 lbs.	Note 2

Note 1: Pony production was included in the base sedan figure.
Note 2: The Squire Wagon production was included in the standard station wagon total.
Pinto Production Note: Totals do not include 22,548 Pintos produced in 1978 but sold as 1977s.

Fairmont (Four)

Model No.	Body Style No.	Body Type & Seating	Factory Price	Shipping Weight	Production Total
93	36R	2-dr. Sport Coupe-5P	$4,044	2,605 lbs.	116,966
91	66B	2-dr. Sedan-5P	$3,589	2,568 lbs.	78,776
92	54B	4-dr. Sedan-5P	$3,663	2,610 lbs.	136,849
94	74B	4-dr. Station Wagon-5P	$4,031	2,718 lbs.	128,390

Fairmont (Six)

Model No.	Body Style No.	Body Type & Seating	Factory Price	Shipping Weight	Production Total
93	36R	2-dr. Sport Coupe-5P	$4,164	2,648 lbs.	116,966
91	66B	2-dr. Sedan-5P	$3,709	2,611 lbs.	78,776
92	54B	4-dr. Sedan-5P	$3,783	2,653 lbs.	136,849
94	74B	4-dr. Station Wagon-5P	$4,151	2,770 lbs.	128,390

Note: Prices shown are for four-cylinder and six-cylinder engines. A V-8 cost $199 more than the six.

Granada (Six)

Model No.	Body Style No.	Body Type & Seating	Factory Price	Shipping Weight	Production Total
81	66H	2-dr. Sedan-5P	$4,264	3,087 lbs.	110,481
82	54H	4-dr. Sedan-5P	$4,342	3,122 lbs.	139,305

Granada (V-8)

Model No.	Body Style No.	Body Type & Seating	Factory Price	Shipping Weight	Production Total
81	66HR	2-dr. Sedan-5P	$4,445	3,177 lbs.	110,481
82	54H	4-dr. Sedan-5P	$4,523	3,212 lbs.	139,305

Granada Ghia (Six)

Model No.	Body Style No.	Body Type & Seating	Factory Price	Shipping Weight	Production Total
81	66K	2-dr. Sedan-5P	$4,649	3,147 lbs.	Note 3
82	54K	4-dr. Sedan-5P	$4,728	3,230 lbs.	Note 3

Granada Ghia (V-8)

Model No.	Body Style No.	Body Type & Seating	Factory Price	Shipping Weight	Production Total
81	66K	2-dr. Sedan-5P	$4,830	3,237 lbs.	Note 3
82	54K	4-dr. Sedan-5P	$4,909	3,320 lbs.	Note 3

Granada ESS (Six)

Model No.	Body Style No.	Body Type & Seating	Factory Price	Shipping Weight	Production Total
81	----	2-dr. Sedan-5P	$4,836	3,145 lbs.	Note 3
82	----	4-dr. Sedan-5P	$4,914	3,180 lbs.	Note 3

Granada ESS (V-8)

Model No.	Body Style No.	Body Type & Seating	Factory Price	Shipping Weight	Production Total
81	----	2-dr. Sedan-5P	$5,017	3,235 lbs.	Note 3
82	----	4-dr. Sedan-5P	$5,095	3,270 lbs.	Note 3

Note 3: Granada Ghia and ESS production was included in the base Granada totals.

LTD II (V-8)

Model No.	Body Style No.	Body Type & Seating	Factory Price	Shipping Weight	Production Total
30	65D	2-dr. Hardtop-6P	$5,069	3,773 lbs.	76, 285
31	53D	4-dr. Pillared Hardtop-6P	$5,169	3,872 lbs.	64, 133

LTD II S (V-8)

Model No.	Body Style No.	Body Type & Seating	Factory Price	Shipping Weight	Production Total
25	65B	2-dr. Hardtop-6P	$4,814	3,746 lbs.	9,004
27	53B	4-dr. Pillared Hardtop-6P	$4,889	3,836 lbs.	21,122

LTD II Brougham (V-8)

Model No.	Body Style No.	Body Type & Seating	Factory Price	Shipping Weight	Production Total
30	65K	2-dr. Hardtop-6P	$5,405	3,791 lbs.	Note 4
31	53K	4-dr. Pillared Hardtop-6P	$5,505	3,901 lbs.	Note 4

Note 4: Brougham production was included in the LTD II totals.

LTD Landau (V-8)

| 64 | 60L | 2-dr. Pillared Hardtop-6P | $5,898 | 4,029 lbs. | 27,305 |
| 65 | 53L | 4-dr. Pillared Hardtop-6P | $5,973 | 4,081 lbs. | 39,836 |

Custom 500 (V-8)

52	60D	2-dr. Pillared Hardtop-6P	----	----	1,359
53	53D	4-dr. Pillared Hardtop-6P	----	----	3,044
72	71D	4-dr. Ranch Wagon-6P	----	----	1,196

Note: The Custom 500 was produced for sale in Canada. Totals included an LTD "S" two-door and Ranch wagon for sale in the U.S.

LTD (V-8)

62	60H	2-dr. Pillared Hardtop-6P	$5,335	3,972 lbs.	57,446
63	53H	4-dr. Pillared Hardtop-6P	$5,410	4,032 lbs.	112,392
74	71H	4-dr. Station Wagon-6P	$5,797	4,532 lbs.	71,285
74	71K	4-dr. Country Squire-6P	$6,207	4,576 lbs.	Note 5

Note 5: Country Squire production, and wagons produced with dual-facing rear seats, was included in basic wagon totals.

Engines:

Pinto and Fairmont Base Four: Inline with overhead cam. Cast-iron block and head. Displacement: 140 cid (2.3 liters). B & S: 3.78 x 3.13 in. Compression ratio: 9.0:1. Brake hp: 88 at 4800 rpm. Torque: 118 lbs.-ft. at 2800 rpm. Five main bearings. Hydraulic valve lifters. Carburetor: Motorcraft 5200 two-barrel. VIN Code: Y.

Pinto Optional V-6: 60-degree, overhead-valve. Cast-iron block and head. Displacement: 170.8 cid (2.8 liters). B & S: 3.66 x 2.70 in. Compression ratio: 8.7:1. Brake hp: 90 at 4200 rpm. Torque: 143 lbs.-ft. at 2200 rpm. Four main bearings. Solid valve lifters. Carburetor: Motorcraft 2150 two-barrel. VIN Code: Z.

Fairmont Optional Six: Inline. Overhead valve. Cast-iron block and head. Displacement: 200 cid (3.3 liters). B & S: 3.68 x 3.13 in. Compression ratio: 8.5: 1. Brake hp: 85 at 3600 rpm. Torque: 154 lbs.-ft. at 1600 rpm. Seven main bearings. Hydraulic valve lifters. Carburetor: Carter YFA one-barrel. VIN Code: T.

Granada Base Six: Inline. Overhead valve. Cast-iron block and head. Displacement: 250 cid (4.1 liters). B & S: 3.68 x 3.91 in. Compression ratio: 8.5: 1. Brake hp: 97 at 3200 rpm. Torque: 210 lbs.-ft. at 1400 rpm. Seven main bearings. Hydraulic valve lifters. Carburetor: Carter YFA one-barrel. VIN Code: L.

LTD and LTD II Base V-8 (Optional in Fairmont and Granada): 90-degree, overhead valve. Cast-iron block and head. Displacement: 302 cid (5.0 liters). B & S: 4.00 x 3.00 in. Compression ratio: 8.4:1. Brake hp: 134 at 3400 rpm. (Fairmont is 139 hp at 3600 rpm.) Torque: 248 lbs.-ft. at 1600 rpm. (Fairmont is 250 lbs.-ft. at 1600 rpm). Five main bearings. Hydraulic valve lifters. Carburetor: Motorcraft 2150 two-barrel. VIN Code: F.

LTD wagon Base V-8 (Optional in LTD and LTD II): 90-degree, overhead valve. Cast-iron block and head. Displacement: 351 cid (5.8 liters). B & S: 4.00 x 3.50 in. Compression ratio: 8.3:1. (LTD compression ratio is 8.0:1.) Brake hp: 144 at 3200 rpm. (The LTD was 145 hp at 3400 rpm.) Torque: 277 lbs.-ft. at 1600 rpm. (The LTD was 273 lbs.-ft. at 1800 rpm.) Five main bearings. Hydraulic valve lifters. Carburetor: Motorcraft 2150 two-barrel. Windsor engine. VIN Code: H.

LTD II Optional V-8: Modified version of the 351-cid V-8 with a compression ratio of 8.0:1 and brake hp of 152 at 3600 rpm. Torque: 278 lbs.-ft. at 1800 rpm. VIN Code: Q.

LTD and LTD II Optional V-8: 90-degree, overhead valve. Cast-iron block and head. Displacement: 400 cid (6.6 liters). B & S: 4.00 x 4.00 in. Compression ratio: 8.0:1. Brake hp: 166 at 3800 rpm. (The LTD was 160 hp at 3800 rpm.) Torque: 319 lbs.-ft. at 1800 rpm. (The LTD was 314 lbs.-ft. at 1800 rpm.) Five main bearings. Hydraulic valve lifters. Carburetor: Motorcraft 2150. VIN Code: S.

LTD Optional V-8: 90-degree, overhead valve. Cast-iron block and head. Displacement: 460 cid (7.5 liters). B & S: 4.36 x 3.85 in. Compression ratio: 8.0:1. Brake hp: 202 at 4000 rpm. Torque: 348 lbs.-ft. at 2000 rpm. Five main bearings. Hydraulic valve lifters. Carburetor: Motorcraft 4350 four-barrel. VIN Code: A.

Note: A Police 460-cid V-8 was also available for the LTD series.

Chassis:

Pinto: Wheelbase: 94.5 in. and 94.8 in. on station wagon. Overall length: 169.3 in. and 179.1 in. on station wagon. Tires: A78 x 13.

Fairmont: Wheelbase: 105.5 in. Overall length: 193.8 in. and 195.8 in. on Futura. Tires: B78 x 14 and CR78 x 14 on the station wagon.

Granada: Wheelbase: 109.9 in. Overall length: 197.7 in. Tires: DR78 x 14 steel-belted white sidewall tires and ER78 x 14 on the Granada Ghia.

LTD II: Wheelbase: 114.0 in. and 118.0 in. on the LTD II sedan. Overall length: 215.5 in. and 219.5 in. on the LTD II sedan. Tires: HR78 x 14 steel-belted black wall.

LTD/Custom 500: Wheelbase: 121.0 in. Overall length: 224.1 in., 225.7 in. on the LTD station wagon and 226.8 in. on the LTD Landau. Tires: HR78 x 15, JR78 x 15 on station wagon and GR78 x 15 with the 302-cid V-8.

Options:

Pinto: Cruising wagon option ($365 to $401). Cruising wagon paint/ tape treatment ($59). Sports Rallye package ($76 to $96). Rallye appearance package ($176 to $201). Exterior decor group ($30 to $40). Interior decor group ($149 to $181). Interior accent group ($28 to $40). Convenience/light group ($81 to $143). Deluxe bumper group ($70). Protection group ($83 to $135). Air conditioner ($459). Rear defroster, electric ($77). Tinted glass ($53); windshield only ($25). Trunk light ($5). Driver's sport mirror ($16). Dual sport mirrors ($49). Day/night mirror ($7). AM radio ($65); w/digital clock ($47 to $119); with stereo tape player ($119 to $192). AM/FM radio ($48 to $120). AM/FM stereo radio ($89 to $161). Flip-up open air roof ($167). Half vinyl roof ($125). Glass third door ($25). Bumper guards ($37). Roof luggage rack ($59). Rocker panel moldings ($22). Lower body protection ($30). Four-way driver's seat ($33). Load floor carpet ($23). Cargo area cover ($25). Wire wheel covers ($90). Forged aluminum wheels ($173 to $252) and white wheels ($187 to $265). Styled steel wheels ($78). 170-cid V-6 ($273). SelectShift Cruise-O-Matic ($281). Optional axle ratio ($13). Power brakes ($64). Power steering ($131).

Fairmont: ES option: sedan ($300). Squire option ($365). Exterior decor group ($214). Exterior accent group ($96). Interior decor group ($176 to $301). Interior accent group ($89 to $94). Deluxe bumper group ($70). Convenience group ($29 to $60). Appearance protection group ($36 to $47). Light group ($35 to $40). Air conditioning ($465). Floor shift lever ($30). Rear defogger ($47). Rear defroster, electric ($84). Tinted glass ($52); windshield only ($25). Sport steering wheel ($36). Electric clock ($18). Interval wipers ($29). Lift gate wiper/washer for station wagon ($78). Trunk light ($4). Left remote mirror ($19). Dual bright mirrors ($13

1978 Granada Ghia two-door sedan

1978 Fairmont four-door sedan

1978 Granada ESS sedan

1978 Fairmont Futura Sport Coupe

to $36). Day/night mirror ($8). AM radio ($72); with an eight-track tape player ($192). AM/FM radio ($120). AM/FM stereo radio ($176); with 8-track or cassette player ($243). Vinyl roof ($89 to $124). Pivoting front vent windows ($37 to $60). Rear quarter vent louvers ($33). Bumper guards, front and rear ($37). Luggage rack ($72). Lower body protection ($30 to $42). Bucket seat, non-reclining ($72). Bench seat ($72 credit). Cloth seat trim ($19-$37). Vinyl seat trim ($22). Lockable side storage box ($19). Hubcaps with trim rings ($34), no charge on Futura. Deluxe wheel covers ($33). Turbine wheel covers ($33 to $66). Wire wheel covers ($48 to $114). Cast aluminum wheels ($210 to $276). 200-cid six ($120). 302-cid V-8 ($319). SelectShift Cruise-O-Matic ($368) and ($281) on the Fairmont station wagon. Power brakes ($63). Power steering ($140). Handling suspension ($30). Heavy duty battery ($17).

Granada: Luxury interior group ($476). Interior decor group ($211). Convenience group ($30 to $89). Deluxe bumper group ($70). Light group ($30 to $43). Cold weather group ($37 to $54). Heavy-duty group ($37 to $54). Protection group ($25 to $43). Visibility group ($4 to $58). Air conditioning ($494); auto-temp ($535). Rear defogger ($47). Rear defroster, electric ($84). Fingertip speed control ($55 to $102). Illuminated entry system ($49). Power windows ($116 to $160). Power door locks ($76 to $104). Power decklid release ($19). Automatic parking brake release ($8). Power four-way seat ($90). Tinted glass ($54); windshield only ($25). Tilt steering wheel ($58). Digital clock ($42). Cornering lamps ($42). Trunk light ($4). Left remote mirror ($14). Dual remote mirrors ($31 to $46). Dual sport mirrors ($42 to $53). Day/night mirror ($8). Lighted right visor vanity mirror ($34). AM radio ($72); w/tape player ($192). AM/FM radio ($135). AM/FM stereo radio ($176); with 8-track or cassette player ($243); w/ Quadrasonic tape ($365). AM/FM stereo search radio ($319). CB radio ($270). Power moon roof ($820). Full or half vinyl roof ($102). Console ($75). Four-way driver's seat ($33). Leather seat trim ($271). Cloth flight bench seat ($54). Deluxe cloth seat/door trim: Ghia/ESS ($99). Color-keyed seatbelts ($19). Deluxe wheel covers ($37) No charge on Ghia and ESS. Wire wheel covers ($59 to $96). Styled steel wheels w/trim rings ($59 to $96). Lacy spoke aluminum wheels ($205 to $242) and white wheels ($218 to $255). 302 V-8 ($181). SelectShift Cruise-O-Matic ($193). Floor shift lever ($30). Power brakes ($63). Four-wheel power disc brakes ($300). Power steering ($148). Heavy duty suspension ($27).

LTD II: Sports appearance package ($216 to $363). Sports instrumentation group ($111 to $138). Sports touring package ($287 to $434). Deluxe bumper group ($76). Light group ($49 to $54). Convenience group ($107 to $139). Power lock group ($100 to $132). Front protection group ($46 to $58). Air conditioning ($543); w/auto-temp control ($588). Rear defroster, electric ($93). Fingertip speed control ($104 to $117). Illuminated entry system ($54). Tinted glass ($62); windshield only ($28). Power windows ($126 to $175). Power door locks ($71 to $101). Six-way power seat ($149). Automatic parking brake release ($9). Leather-wrapped steering wheel ($51 to $64). Tilt steering wheel ($70). Electric clock ($20). Day/date clock ($22 to $42). Cornering lamps ($46). Trunk light ($4). Dual-note horn ($7). Remote driver's mirror ($16). Dual chrome mirrors ($7). Dual sport mirrors ($29 to $58). Lighted visor vanity mirror ($33 to $37). AM radio ($79). AM/FM radio ($132). AM/FM stereo radio ($192); with tape player ($266); with Quadrasonic tape player ($399). AM/FM stereo search radio ($349). CB radio ($295). Dual rear speakers ($46). Full or half vinyl roof ($112). Opera windows ($51). Bucket seats with console ($211), on Brougham ($37). Vinyl seat trim ($24). Cloth/vinyl seat trim ($24). Front floor mats ($20). Heavy-duty floor mats ($9). Color-keyed seatbelts ($21). Deluxe wheel covers ($38). Luxury wheel covers ($62 to $100). Wire wheel covers ($105 to $143), no charge with sports package. Cast aluminum wheels ($196 to $301). HR78 x 14 steel-belted radial white sidewall tires ($46). HR78 x 14 wide-band white sidewalls ($66). HR78 x 14 steel-belted radials ($62). HR78 x 15 steel-belted radials with white sidewalls ($68). Inflatable spare (NC). 351-cid V-8 ($157). 400-cid V-8 ($283). Heavy duty handling suspension ($36). Heavy duty battery ($18). Heavy-duty alternator ($50). Heavy-duty trailer towing package ($184).

LTD: Landau luxury group ($457 to $580). Convenience group ($96 to $146). Light group ($26 to $38). Deluxe bumper group ($50 to $72). Protection group ($45 to $53). Air conditioning ($562), with auto-temp control ($607). Rear defogger ($50). Rear defroster, electric ($93). Fingertip speed control ($104 to $117). Illuminated entry system ($54). Power windows ($129 to $188). Power door locks ($82 to $153). Six-way power driver's seat ($149) or driver and passenger ($297). Tinted glass ($75); windshield only ($28). Tilt steering wheel ($70). Automatic parking brake release ($8). Electric clock ($21). Digital clock ($28 to $49). Cornering lamps ($46). Trunk light ($4). Dual-note horn ($7). Driver's remote mirror ($16). Dual remote mirrors ($32 to $37). Lighted visor vanity mirror ($33 to $37). AM radio ($79). AM/FM radio ($132). AM/FM stereo radio ($192); w/tape player ($266); with Quadrasonic tape player ($399). AM/FM stereo search radio ($349). Dual rear speakers ($46). Power moon roof ($896). Full vinyl roof ($141), no charge on Landau two-door. Half vinyl roof ($141). Rear bumper guards ($22). Luggage rack ($80). Dual-facing rear seats: wagon ($143). Split

bench seat with passenger recliner ($141 to $233). Leather seat trim ($296). All-vinyl seat trim ($24). Duraweave vinyl trim ($50). Color-keyed seatbelts ($21). Lockable side stowage compartment ($33). Full wheel covers ($38). Deluxe or color-keyed wheel covers ($61 to $99). Wire wheel covers ($99 to $137). Deep-dish aluminum wheels ($263 to $301). 351-cid V-8 ($157). 400-cid V-8 ($283). 460-cid V-8 ($428) or ($271) on LTD wagon. Traction-Lok differential ($62). Optional axle ratio ($14). Four-wheel power disc brakes ($187 to $197). Semi-metallic front disc pads ($8). Heavy duty suspension ($65). Adjustable air shock absorbers ($50). Heavy duty battery ($18). Heavy duty alternator ($50). Heavy duty trailer towing package ($139).

History:

The 1978 Fords were introduced on October 7, 1977. The Fairmont Futura premiered December 2, 1977. Model year production was 1,929,254 including Mustangs. Calendar year sales by U.S. dealers were 1,768,753, including Mustangs. The model year sales increased for 1978, though production slipped a bit. Major recalls of more than four million vehicles bruised Ford's reputation. Pintos were recalled for gas tanks that might burst into flame. Many Ford automatic transmissions had a problem with jerking suddenly from park to reverse, a situation that never was resolved. Philip Caldwell replaced Ford president Lee Iacocca. Iacocca emerged within a few months as the new head of Chrysler Corporation. The new compact Fairmont was more popular than the Maverick. There were 417,932 Fairmonts sold versus just 105,156 Mavericks sold in 1977. Fairmont was a better seller than Mustang in its first year. Granada and LTD II sales plummeted for the model year. Fairmont was "the most successful new-car nameplate ever introduced by a domestic manufacturer and Ford's top selling car line in 1978," said Walter S. Walla, Ford Division General Manager. It was also highly rated by the auto magazines. Readers of *Car and Driver* called it "the most significant new American car for 1978." Computer-assisted design techniques were used to develop the Fairmont/Zephyr duo, along with more than 320 hours of wind-tunnel testing. Corporate Average Fuel Economy (CAFE) standards began in 1978. Automakers' fleets were required to meet a specified average miles-per-gallon rating each year for the next decade, with 27.5 mpg the ultimate goal. Fairmont was designed with the CAFE ratings in mind, which required that Fords average 18 mpg. This year's model introduction meetings had been held in the Detroit and Dearborn area for the first time since 1959. More than 15,000 dealers, general managers and spouses attended. The international emphasis was highlighted by a "flags of the world of Ford" display at the world headquarters, in a special ceremony. Ford began to import the front-wheel drive Fiesta from its German plant.

1978 LTD II "S" hardtop coupe

1978 LTD Landau pillared hardtop

1978 Fairmont two-door sedan

1978 Fairmont ES Sport Coupe

1978 Fairmont station wagon

1979 Ford

Pinto — Four and V-6: Restyling brought the subcompact Pinto a new front-end look with single rectangular headlamps in bright housings, as well as a new sloping hood and fenders, and horizontal-style argent grille. New sculptured-look front and rear aluminum bumpers had black rub strips and end sections. Full wheel covers took on a new design. Inside, a new instrument panel and pad held rectangular instrument pods. The redesigned cluster now included a speedometer graduated in miles and kilometers, a fuel gauge and warning lights with symbols. New body and interior colors were available. The two-door sedan, "three-door" hatchback Runabout and station wagon still were offered. A Cruising Package was optional on both Runabouts and wagons, featuring multi-color side paint and tape treatment and black louvers on the wagon's lift gate window. There was also a new ESS option for sedans and Runabouts, with black grille and exterior accents, a black-hinged glass third door, wide black side moldings, and sports-type equipment. Pinto's standard equipment list grew longer this year, adding an AM radio, power brakes, electric rear defroster, and tinted glass. The low-budget Pony lacked some of these extras. The standard engine remained the 140 cid (2.3-liter) overhead-cam four, with a four-speed gearbox. Oil-change intervals were raised to 30,000 miles. The V-6 added a higher-performance camshaft, while the V-6 automatic transmissions offered higher rpm shift points to improve acceleration.

Fairmont — Four, Six and V-8: Appearance of the year-old compact didn't change this year. Model lineup included two-door and four-door sedans, a station wagon, and the Futura coupe. Seven new body colors and four new vinyl roof colors were available. Availability of the distinctive two-tone paint treatment was expanded to sedans, as well as the Futura. A four-speed overdrive manual transmission with new single-rail shifter design replaced the former three-speed, coupled with either the 200 cid (3.3-liter) inline six or 302 cid (5.0-liter) V-8. It was the first time a V-8 was mated with a manual transmission in the Fairmont series. The base engine remained the 140 cid (2.3-liter) four with a non-overdrive

four-speed manual transmission. The six was now offered on wagons sold in California. Ignition and door locks were modified to improve theft-resistance. A lower axle ratio (2.26:1) came with the V-8 and automatic. Inside was a new dark walnut woodtone instrument cluster appliqué. The Fairmont ES package also was offered again. It included a blackout grille, black window frames, dual black sail-mount sport mirrors and turbine wheel covers plus special suspension with rear stabilizer bar.

Granada — Six and V-8: Billed as "An American Classic" and playing on its perceived Mercedes styling origins, Granada changed little for 1979. Few customers had chosen four-wheel disc brakes, so that option was dropped. Both the standard 250 cid (3.3-liter) inline six and 302 cid (5.0-liter) V-8 came with a four-speed overdrive manual gearbox that used a new enclosed single-rail shift mechanism. As before, two- and four-door sedans were produced, in base, Ghia or ESS trim. Base models got all-bright versions of the 1978 Ghia wheel cover. Ghia seats had a new sew style plus all-vinyl door trim with carpeted lower panels. Leather/vinyl trim was now available with bucket seats. New soft Rossano cloth and Wilshire cloth luxury trim also was available. Ignition locks offered improved theft-resistance. New options included tone-on-tone paint in five color combinations. Dropped were white lacy-spoke aluminum wheels, Traction-Lok axle, and the Luxury Interior Group. This year's ESS option was identified by "Granada" script above the "ESS" badge. The Granada ESS had a blacked-out grille, color-keyed wheel covers and dual mirrors, individually reclining bucket seats with Euro headrests and a leather-wrapped steering wheel. Optional speed control for the ESS included a black leather-wrapped steering wheel.

LTD II — V-8: Not enough buyers had found LTD II appealing, so this would be its final season. Not much was new this year, except for a redesigned front bumper spoiler, corrosion-resistant plastic battery tray, and an electronic voltage regulator. Seven body colors were new, as were front and full vinyl roofs. Broughams had new interior fabric selections. All models had standard flight bench seating with a fold-down center armrest. The base engine remained the 302 cid (5.0-liter) V-8, with the 351-cid V-8 optional. The 400-cid V-8 option was discontinued. Automatic transmission was standard. A newly optional 27.5 gallon gas tank suggested LTD II's economy problems hadn't been corrected with either a lighter weight front bumper or by carburetor refinements. Rear bumper guards became standard, and the ignition lock was modified. The Sports Touring Package included two-tone paint, a grille badge and Magnum 500 wheels with HR78 x 14 raised-white-letter tires. A Sports Appearance Group for two-doors had bold tri-color tape stripes. Two-door hardtop and four-door pillared hardtop bodies were offered again. They came in base, Brougham or "S" trim.

LTD — V-8: Substantial downsizing made the 1979 LTD the ninth new full-size model in the company's history. Still built with body-on-frame construction, it was intended to be space-efficient and fuel-efficient. It resulted from more than 270 hours of wind-tunnel testing. Riding a 114.4-inch wheelbase, with seven inches cut, the LTD increased its interior space. A conventional sedan design replaced the pillared hardtop. Door openings were larger and the doors were thinner. Overall, the new design was slightly taller and squarer. Inside, LTD's seating position was higher. A tall, narrow ornament adorned the hood. Two-doors were four-window design with a slim coach-style quarter window. Landaus had new rear-pillar coach lamps. Country Squire wagons showed a new woodtone appliqué treatment. Inside were thin-back seats with foam padding over flex-o-lator cushion support, and a four-spoke soft-rim steering wheel. A steering-column stalk held the dimmer, horn and wiper/washer controls. Door-lock plungers moved to the armrests to improve theft-resistance. Lockable side stowage compartments were standard on wagons. The base engine, except on wagons with California emissions, was the 302 cid (5.0-liter) V-8. That engine had a new single accessory-drive belt operating the fan/water pump, alternator, and power steering pump. A variable-venturi carburetor became standard on both the 302 and the optional 351 V-8 engines. Up front was a new short/long arm coil spring front suspension with link-type stabilizer bar and at the rear was a new four-bar link coil spring setup. Front disc brakes used a new pin-slider design.

1979 Pinto three-door Runabout

1979 Pinto ESS three-door hatchback

I.D. Data:

Ford's 11-symbol Vehicle Identification Number (VIN) was stamped on a metal tab fastened to the instrument panel and was visible through the windshield. The first digit was the model year code, 9= 1979. The second letter indicated the assembly plant: A=Atlanta, Georgia; B=Oakville, Ontario, Canada; E=Mahwah, New Jersey; G=Chicago, Illinois; H=Lorain, Ohio; J=Los Angeles, California; K=Kansas City, Missouri; S=St. Thomas, Ontario, Canada; T=Metuchen, New Jersey; U=Louisville, Kentucky; W=Wayne, Michigan. Digits three and four corresponded to the Model Numbers: (10=Pinto 2-dr. sedan). The fifth symbol was an engine code: Y=140-cid six, Z=170-cid V-6, T=200-cid six, L=250-cid six, F=302-cid V-8 and H=351 V-8. Digits 6 through 11 made up the unit number of cars built at each assembly plant, beginning with 100001. A Vehicle Certification Label on the left front door lock face panel or door pillar showed the manufacturer, month and year of manufacture, GVW. GAWR, certification statement, VIN, body code, color code, trim code, axle code, transmission code, and special order code.

Pinto (Four)

Model No.	Body Style No.	Body Type & Seating	Factory Price	Shipping Weight	Production Total
10	62B	2-dr. Sedan-4P	$3,629	2,346 lbs.	75,789
10	41E	2-dr. Pony Sedan-4P	$3,199	2,329 lbs.	Note 1
11	64B	3-dr. Hatchback-4P	$3,744	2,392 lbs.	69,383
12	73B	2-dr. Station Wagon-4P	$4,028	2,532 lbs.	53,846
12	41E	2-dr. Pony Wagon-4P	$3,633	----	Note 1
12	73B	2-dr. Squire Wag-4P	$4,343	2,568 lbs.	Note 2

Pinto (V-6)

10	62B	2-dr. Sedan-4P	$3,902	2,446 lbs.	75,789
11	64B	3-dr. Hatchback-4P	$4,017	2,492 lbs.	69,383
12	73B	2-dr. Station Wagon-4P	$4,301	2,610 lbs.	53,846
12	73B	2-dr. Squire Wag-4P	$4,616	2,646 lbs.	Note 2

Note 1: Pony production was included in the base sedan and wagon figures.
Note 2: Squire Wagon production was included in the standard station wagon total.

Fairmont (Four)

93	36R	2-dr. Sport Coupe-5P	$4,071	2,546 lbs.	106,065
91	66B	2-dr. Sedan-5P	$3,710	2,491 lbs.	54,798
92	54B	4-dr. Sedan-5P	$3,810	2,544 lbs.	133,813
94	74B	4-dr. Station Wagon-5P	$4,157	2,674 lbs.	100,691

Pinto (Six)

93	36R	2-dr. Sport Coupe-5P	$4,312	2,613 lbs.	106,065
91	66B	2-dr. Sedan-5P	$3,951	2,558 lbs.	54,798
92	54B	4-dr. Sedan-5P	$4,051	2,611 lbs.	133,813
94	74B	4-dr. Station Wagon-5P	$4,398	2,741 lbs.	100,691

Note: Prices shown are for the four- and six-cylinder engines. A V-8 cost $283 more than the six.

Granada (Six)

81	66H	2-dr. Sedan-5P	$4,342	3,051 lbs.	76,850
82	54H	4-dr. Sedan-5P	$4,445	3,098 lbs.	105,526

Granada (V-8)

81	66H	2-dr. Sedan-5P	$4,625	3,124 lbs.	76,850
82	54H	4-dr. Sedan-5P	$4,728	3,169 lbs.	105,526

Granada Ghia (Six)

81	66K	2-dr. Sedan-5P	$4,728	3,089 lbs.	Note 3
82	54K	4-dr. Sedan-5P	$4,830	3,132 lbs.	Note 3

Granada Ghia (V-8)

602	66K	2-dr. Sedan-5P	$5,011	3,160 lbs.	Note 3
602	54K	4-dr. Sedan-5P	$5,113	3,203 lbs.	Note 3

Granada ESS (Six)

81	----	2-dr. Sedan-5P	$4,888	3,105 lbs.	Note 3
82	----	4-dr. Sedan-5P	$4,990	3,155 lbs.	Note 3

Granada ESS (V-8)

433	----	2-dr. Sedan-5P	$5,161	3,176 lbs.	Note 3
433	----	4-dr. Sedan-5P	$5,273	3,226 lbs.	Note 3

Note 3: Granada Ghia and ESS production totals were included with the base Granada totals.

LTD II (V-8)

30	65D	2-dr. Hardtop-6P	$5,445	3,797 lbs.	18,300
31	53D	4-dr. Pillar Hardtop-6P	$5,569	3,860 lbs.	19,781

LTD II "S" (V-8)

25	65B	2-dr. Hardtop-6P	$5,198	3,781 lbs.	834
27	53B	4-dr. Pillar Hardtop-6P	$5,298	3,844 lbs.	9,649

Note: The LTD "S" was for fleet sales only.

LTD II Brougham (V-8)

.30	65K	2-dr. Hardtop-6P	$5,780	3,815 lbs.	Note 4
31	53K	4-dr. Pillar Hardtop-6P	$5,905	3,889 lbs.	Note 4

Note 4: Brougham production was included in the LTD II totals.

LTD (V-8)

62	66H	2-dr. Sedan-6P	$5,813	3,421 lbs.	54,005
63	54H	4-dr. Sedan-6P	$5,913	3,463 lbs.	117,730
74	74H	4-dr. Station Wagon-6P	$6,122	3,678 lbs.	37,955
74	74K	4-dr. Country Squire-6P	$6,615	3,719 lbs.	29,932

Note: Production of wagons with dual-facing rear seats was included in the basic wagon totals. Totals also included Custom 500 production for the Canadian market (2,036 two-doors, 4,567 four-doors and 1,568 wagons).

LTD Landau (V-8)

64	66K	2-dr. Sedan-6P	$6,349	3,472 lbs.	42,314
65	54K	4-dr. Sedan-6P	$6,474	3,527 lbs.	74,599

Engines:

Pinto/Fairmont Four: Inline. Overhead cam. Cast-iron block and head. Displacement: 140 cid (2.3 liters). B & S: 3.78 x 3.13 in. Compression ratio: 9.0:1. Brake hp: 88 at 4800 rpm. Torque: 118 lbs.-ft. at 2800 rpm. Five main bearings. Hydraulic valve lifters. Carburetor: Motorcraft 5200 two-barrel. VIN Code: Y.

Pinto Optional V-6: 60-degree, overhead-valve V-6. Cast-iron block and head. Displacement: 170.8 cid (2.8 liters). B & S: 3.66 x 2.70 in. Compression ratio: 8.7:1. Brake hp: 102 at 4400 rpm. Torque: 138 lbs.-ft. at 3200 rpm. Four main bearings. Solid valve lifters. Carburetor: Motorcraft 2150 or 2700VV two barrel. VIN Code: Z.

1979 Pinto Squire station wagon

1979 Pinto Cruising Wagon

1979 Fairmont Squire wagon

1979 Fairmont Futura sedan

1979 Fairmont two-door sedan

1979 Granada sedan (with optional two-tone paint and cast aluminum wheels)

1979 Granada Ghia coupe

Fairmont Optional Six: Inline. Overhead valve. Cast-iron block and head. Displacement: 200 cid (3.3 liters). B & S: 3.68 x 3.13 in. Compression ratio: 8.5: 1. Brake hp: 85 at 3600 rpm. Torque: 154 lbs.-ft, at 1600 rpm. Seven main bearings. Hydraulic valve lifters. Carburetor: Carter YFA or Holley 1946 single -barrel. VIN Code: T.

Granada Six: Inline. Overhead valve. Cast-iron block and head. Displacement: 250 cid (4.1 liters). B & S: 3.68 x 3.91 in. Compression ratio: 8.6:1. Brake hp: 97 at 3200 rpm. Torque: 210 lbs.-ft. at 1400 rpm. Seven main bearings. Hydraulic valve lifters, Carburetor: Carter YFA single barrel. VIN Code: L.

LTD and LTD II V-8 (Optional Fairmont and Granada): 90-degree, overhead valve. Cast-iron block and head. Displacement: 302 cid (5.0 liters). B & S: 4.00 x 3.00 in. Compression ratio: 8.4:1. Brake hp: 129 at 3600 rpm. in the LTD and 133 at 3400 in the LTD II. It was 140 at 3600 in the Fairmont and 137 at 3600 in the Granada. Torque: 223 lbs.-ft. at 2600 rpm, LTD; 245 at 1600. LTD II; 250 at 1800, Fairmont and 243 at 2000 for the Granada. Five main bearings. Hydraulic valve lifters. Carburetor: Motorcraft 2150 or 2700VV two-barrel. VIN Code: F.

LTD Optional V-8: 90-degree, overhead valve. Cast-iron block and head. Displacement: 351 cid (5.8 liters). B & S: 4.00 x 3.50 in. Compression ratio: 8.3:1. Brake hp: 135 or 142 at 3200 rpm. Torque: 286 lbs.-ft. at 1400 rpm. Five main bearings. Hydraulic valve lifters. Carburetor: Motorcraft 7200VV two-barrel. Windsor engine. VIN Code: H.

LTD and LTD II Optional V-8: The modified version of the 351-cid V-8. Compression: 8.0:1. Brake hp: 151 at 3600 rpm. Torque: 270 lbs.-ft. at 2200 rpm. Carb: Motorcraft 2150 two-barrel. Code: H.

Chassis:

Pinto: Wheelbase: 94.5 in. and 94.8 in. on station wagon. Overall length: 168.8 in. and 178.6 in. on the station wagon. Tires: A78 x 13.

Fairmont: Wheelbase: 105.5 in. Overall length: 193.8 in. and Futura, 195.8 in. Tires: B78 x 14 and CR78 x 14, station wagon.

Granada: Wheelbase: 109.9 in. Overall length: 197.8 in. Tires: DR78 x 14 steel-belted black wall and ER78 x 14 on the Granada Ghia.

LTD II: Wheelbase: 114.0 in., two-door sedan and 118.0 in., four door sedan. Overall length: 217.2 in., two-door sedan and 221.2 in., four-door sedan. Tires: HR78 x 14 steel-belted black wall.

LTD: Wheelbase: 114.4 in. Overall length: 209.0 in. and 212.9 in., LTD station wagon. Tires: FR78 x 14 steel-belted white sidewalls and GR78 x 14 on the LTD station wagon.

Options:

Pinto: ESS package ($236 to $261). Cruising package ($330 to $566); tape delete ($55 credit). Sport package ($96 to $110). Exterior decor group ($20 to $40). Interior decor group ($137 to $207). Interior accent group ($5 to $40). Convenience group ($24 to $61). Deluxe bumper group ($52). Protection group ($33 to $36). Light group ($25 to $37). Air conditioner ($484). Rear defroster ($84). Tinted glass ($59). Trunk light ($5). Driver's sport mirror ($18). Dual sport mirrors ($52). Day/night mirror ($10). AM radio: Pony ($65). AM radio w/digital clock ($47 to $119); w/stereo tape player ($119 to $192). AM/FM radio ($48 to $120). AM/FM stereo radio ($89 to $161); w/cassette player ($157 to $222). Radio flexibility option ($90). Flip-up open air roof ($199). Glass third door ($25). Rear bumper guards ($19). Roof luggage rack ($63). Mud/

stone deflectors ($23). Lower side protection ($30). Interior: Four-way driver's seat ($35). Load floor carpet ($24). Cargo area cover ($28). Wire wheel covers ($99). Forged aluminum wheels ($217 to $289); white wheels ($235 to $307). Lacy spoke aluminum wheels ($217 to $289). Styled steel wheels ($54). A78 x 13 white sidewalls ($43). BR78 x 13 black walls ($148); white sidewalls ($191). BR70 x 13 raised white lettering ($228). 170-cid V-6 ($273). Cruise-O-Matic automatic transmission ($307). Optional axle ratio ($13). Power brakes ($70). Power steering ($141).

Fairmont: Option Packages: ES option, including a blackout grille, black window frames, dual black sail-mount sport mirrors (left remote) and turbine wheel covers ($329). Futura sports group, included unique tape striping, a charcoal argent grille and color-keyed turbine wheel covers ($102). Ghia package ($207 to $498). Squire option ($399). Exterior decor group ($223). Exterior accent group ($82). Interior decor group ($170 to $311). Interior accent group ($80 to $84). Instrumentation group ($77). Deluxe bumper group ($57). Convenience group ($33 to $65). Appearance protection group ($36 to $47). Light group ($27 to $43). Air conditioning ($484). Rear defogger ($51). Rear defroster, electric ($90). Fingertip speed control ($104 to $116). Power windows ($116 to $163). Power door locks ($73 to $101). Power deck lid release ($22). Power seat ($94). Tinted glass ($59); windshield only ($25). Sport steering wheel ($39). Tilt steering ($69 to $81). Electric clock ($20). Interval wipers ($35). Rear wiper/washer ($63). Map light ($7). Trunk light ($7). Left remote mirror ($17). Dual bright mirrors ($37-$43). Day/night mirror ($10). AM radio ($72); with eight-track tape player ($192). AM/FM radio ($120). AM/FM stereo radio ($176); with eight-track or cassette player ($243). Premium sound system ($67). Radio flexibility ($93). Flip-up open air roof ($199). Full vinyl roof ($90). Luggage rack ($76). Lower body protection ($30 to $42). Vinyl bucket seats, non-reclining ($72). Bench seat ($72 credit). Cloth/vinyl seat trim ($20 to $42). Vinyl seat trim ($24). Front floor mats ($18). Lockable side storage box ($20). Hubcaps and trim rings ($37). Deluxe wheel covers ($37). Turbine wheel covers ($39 to $76). Wire wheel covers ($50 to $127). Styled steel wheels ($40 to $116). Cast aluminum wheels ($251 to $327). 200-cid six ($241). 302-cid V-8 ($524). Cruise-O-Matic automatic transmission ($401), Fairmont and ($307) on the Fairmont station wagon. Floor shift lever ($31). Power brakes ($70). Power steering ($149). Heavy duty suspension ($19 to $25). Handling suspension ($41).

Granada: Interior decor group ($211). Convenience group ($35 to $94). Deluxe bumper group ($78). Light group ($41 to $46). Cold weather group ($30 to $60). Heavy-duty group ($18 to $60). Protection group ($24 to $47). Visibility group ($5 to $70). Air conditioning ($514); auto-temp ($555). Rear defogger ($51). Rear defroster, electric ($90). Fingertip speed control ($104 to $116). Illuminated entry system ($52). Power windows ($120 to $171). Power door locks ($78 to $110). Power deck lid release ($22). Automatic parking brake release ($8). Power four-way seat ($94). Tinted glass ($64); windshield only ($25). Tilt steering wheel ($69). Digital clock ($47). Cornering lamps ($43). Trunk light ($5). Left remote mirror ($17). Dual remote mirrors ($37 to $54). Dual sport mirrors ($46 to $63). Day/night mirror ($11). Lighted right visor vanity mirror ($36). AM radio ($72); with tape player ($192). AM/FM radio ($135). AM/FM stereo radio ($176); with eight-track or cassette player ($243); with Quadrasonic tape ($365). AM/FM stereo search radio

1979 Granada ESS sedan

1979 LTD II hardtop coupe (with Sports Appearance Package)

1979 LTD Landau sedan

1979 LTD Country Squire station wagon

($319). CB radio ($270). Radio flexibility ($93). Power moon roof ($899). Full or half vinyl roof ($106). Lower body protection ($31). Console ($99). Four-way driver's seat ($34). Reclining seats (NC). Leather seat trim ($271). Flight bench seat (NC). Cloth/vinyl flight bench seat ($54). Deluxe cloth/vinyl trim (NC). Front floor mats ($18). Color-keyed seatbelts ($19). Deluxe wheel covers ($41), non charge on the Ghia and ESS. Wire wheel covers ($108), except no charge on the Ghia and ESS ($67). Styled steel wheels with trim rings ($83 to $124). Cast aluminum wheels ($248 to $289). 302-cid V-8 ($283). Cruise-O-Matic automatic transmission ($309). Floor shift lever ($31). Power brakes ($70). Power steering ($155). Heavy duty suspension ($20).

LTD II: Sports appearance package (2-dr.) ($301 to $449). Sports instrumentation group ($121 to $151). Sports touring package (2-dr.) ($379 to $526). Deluxe bumper group ($63). Light group ($51 to $57). Convenience group ($120 to $155). Power lock group ($111 to $143). Protection group ($49 to $61). Air conditioning ($562); with auto-temp control ($607). Rear defrester, electric ($99). Fingertip speed control ($113 to $126). Illuminated entry system ($57). Tinted glass ($70); windshield only ($28). Power windows ($132 to $187). Six-way power seat ($163). Tilt steering wheel ($75). Electric clock ($22). Day/date clock ($22 to $45). Cornering lamps ($49). Dual-note horn ($9). Remote driver's mirror ($18). Dual sport mirrors ($9 to $68). Lighted visor vanity mirror ($34 to $39). AM radio ($79). AM/FM radio ($132). AM/FM stereo radio ($192); with tape player ($266); with Quadrasonic tape player ($399). AM/FM stereo search radio ($349). CB radio ($295). Dual rear speakers ($46). Radio flexibility ($105). Full or half vinyl roof ($116). Opera windows ($54). Front bumper guards ($26). Mud/stone deflectors ($25). Lower body protection ($33 to $46). Bucket seats with console ($211), ($37) for Brougham. Vinyl seat trim ($26). Cloth/vinyl seat trim ($26). Front floor mats ($20). H.D. floor mats ($9). Color-keyed seatbelts ($22). Deluxe wheel covers ($45). Luxury wheel covers ($66 to $111). Wire wheel covers ($116 to $161). no charge with sports package. Cast aluminum wheels ($200 to $361). 351-cid V-8 ($263). Traction-Lok differential ($64). Heavy duty suspension ($41). Heavy duty battery ($18-$21). Heavy duty alternator ($50). Engine block heater ($13 to $14).

LTD: Interior luxury group: Landau ($705); Country Squire ($758). Exterior accent group ($29 to $66). Convenience group ($68 to $99). Light group ($32 to $41). Protection group ($46 to $55). Air conditioning ($597); with auto-temp control ($642). Rear defogger ($57). Rear defroster, electric ($100). Fingertip speed control ($113 to $126). Illuminated entry system ($57). Power windows ($137 to $203). Power door locks ($87 to $161). Power driver's seat ($164); or driver and passenger ($329). Tinted glass ($83); windshield only ($28). Tilt steering wheel ($76). Automatic parking brake release ($8). Electric clock ($24). Digital clock ($32 to $55). Cornering lamps ($49). Trunk light ($4). Dual-note horn ($9). Driver's remote mirror, door or sail mount ($18). Dual remote mirrors ($37 to $55). Lighted visor vanity mirror ($36 to $41). AM radio ($79). AM/FM radio ($132). AM/FM stereo radio ($192); with tape player ($266); with AM/FM stereo search radio with Quadrasonic tape player ($432). CB radio ($295). Power antenna ($47). Dual rear speakers ($46). Deluxe sound package ($55); luxury package ($42). Premium sound system ($74 to $158). Radio flexibility ($105). Full or half vinyl roof ($143). Bumper guards, front or rear ($26). Bumper rub strips ($54). Luggage rack ($113).

Lower body protection ($33 to $46). Dual-facing rear seats: wagon ($145 to $149). Flight bench seat ($99). Dual flight bench seat recliner ($58). Split bench seat with passenger recliner ($187 to $233). All-vinyl seat trim ($26). Duraweave vinyl trim ($52). Front floor mats ($20). Trunk trim ($41-$46). Color-keyed seatbelts ($24). Full wheel covers ($39). Luxury wheel covers ($64). Wire wheel covers ($145). FR78 x 14 white sidewalls ($47). GR78 x 14 black walls ($30). GR78 x 14 white sidewalls ($47 to $77). HR78 x 14, station wagon, black ($30) or white sidewalls ($77). Conventional spare ($13). 351-cid V-8 ($263). Optional axle ratio ($18). Heavy duty suspension ($22). Handling suspension ($42). Adjustable air shock absorbers ($54). Heavy duty battery ($18 to $21). Heavy duty alternator ($50). Engine block heater ($13 to $14). Heavy duty trailer towing package ($161 to $192).

History:

The 1979 Fords were introduced to the public on Oct. 6, 1978. Model year production was 1,835,937 vehicles including Mustangs. Calendar year sales were 1,499,098. Ford dealers also sold 77,733 German Ford-made Fiestas in 1979. To attempt to meet the CAFE requirement of 19 mpg this year, Ford pushed sales of the new downsized LTD. Buyers seemed to want the big V-8 rather than economical fours and sixes, prompting Ford to increase the price of the V-8 model. LTD sales fell rather sharply, putting the smaller LTD far behind Caprice and Impala. LTD II production ceased in January 1979, amid flagging sales. Sales declined considerably for model year 1979, down 15 percent. A gasoline crisis in mid-year didn't help. Ford had lagged behind other companies in downsizing its big-car lineup. Pinto sales were good, even though the outmoded design rival the new subcompacts. Sales of the new Mustang were impressive — nearly 70 percent above the final figure for its second-generation predecessor. A replacement for the Pinto was scheduled for 1981, dubbed "Erika." That was changed to Escort by the time the new front-drive subcompact was introduced. Ford would have to wait for a true rival to Chevrolet's Chevette. Philip Caldwell was president of Ford Motor Co.

1980 Ford

Pinto — Four: All Pintos had four-cylinder engines for 1980, as the optional V-6 disappeared. The standard 140-cid (2.3-liter) four received improvements to boost its highway gas mileage. Styling was virtually identical to 1979, with seven new body colors and three new interior trim colors available. The low-budget Pony now wore steel-belted radial tires. Batteries were maintenance-free, and the Pintos carried a restyled scissors jack. Radios played a Travelers' Advisory band, and the station wagon's Cruising Package option was revised. This was Pinto's final season, to be replaced by the new front-drive Escort. The Rallye Pack option, introduced late in 1979 on hatchback and wagon, was expanded

1980 Pinto three-door hatchback (with Rallye Pack option)

1980 Fairmont two-door sedan (turbocharged)

this year. The model lineup for the final year included the two-door sedan, three-door hatchback Runabout, two-door station wagon, and Pony sedan or wagon. The Pony lacked the base model's tinted glass, rear window defroster, AM radio, bumper rub strips, and vinyl-insert body moldings, as well as bright window frame, belt and B-pillar moldings.

Fairmont — Four/Six and V-8: The power plants were the major news in the Fairmont line this year. Most notable was the announcement of a turbocharged four. Though it was interesting speculation, it never made production. A new 255-cid (4.2-liter) V-8 did and replaced the former 302 option. It was available only with automatic transmission. Both the 255 and the 200-cid (3.3-liter) inline six had a new lightweight starter. The base engine remained the 140-cid (2.3-liter) four, with a four-speed manual gearbox. Manual-shift transmissions had a new self-adjusting clutch. New high-pressure, P-metric steel-belted radial tires were standard on all models. A mini-spare tire and maintenance-free battery were standard. All radios added a Travelers' Advisory band. Fairmont came in nine new body colors and two new two-tone color schemes (with accent color in the bodyside center). A four-door sedan joined the Futura coupe at mid-year, wearing the unique Futura crosshatch grille. Futuras had standard halogen headlamps (except where prohibited by state laws). Styling was similar to 1978 and 1979. The Futura coupe had a wood grain dash appliqué, quad halogen headlamps, a trunk light, bright window frame moldings, vinyl body moldings, and wheel lip and door belt moldings. The optional sport steering wheel switched from brushed aluminum to black finish.

Granada — Six and V-8: Apart from seven new body colors and three new vinyl roof colors, little changed on the compact Granada sedans. A new lightweight starter went under the hood, a better scissors jack in the trunk, and Ardmore cloth upholstery on the seats. Maintenance-free batteries were standard. Joining the option list were a heavy-duty 54-amp battery, mud/stone guards, and revised electronic search stereo radios and tape players. Ford's "Tu-tone" paint cost $180. The standard engine was the 250-cid (4.1-liter) inline six with a 302-cid (5.0-liter) V-8 optional. California Granadas required the new 255-cid V-8. Granada came in two- or four-door sedan form again with the base, Ghia or ESS trim. Granada Ghia carried dual body/hood/decklid accent stripes, black/argent lower back panel appliqué, a left remote mirror, wide vinyl-insert body moldings, and burled walnut wood tone door trim. The sporty Granada ESS had a blacked-out grille, dual remote mirrors, black rocker panel paint, hood and deck lid paint stripes, bucket seats with chain-mail vinyl inserts, a leather-wrapped steering wheel and louvered opera windows.

LTD — V-8: Reshuffling of the model lineup hit the full-size line for 1980. This year's selections included the budget-priced LTD "S," the base LTD, and the LTD Crown Victoria sedans. An "S" edition also joined the LTD (plain-body) and Country Squire station wagon choices. The Crown Victoria, the same name as the stylish mid-1950s Ford,

1980-1/2 Fairmont Futura sedan

replaced the Landau as the top model. A new four-speed automatic transmission with overdrive top gear became optional on all models. New in 1980 were standard P-metric radial tires with higher pressure, standard maintenance-free battery, and halogen headlamps except the LTD "S." The Crown Victoria and Country Squire carried a new wide hood ornament design, while standard LTDs had no ornament at all. Country Squire wagons had simulated wood panels with planking lines. A new rear half vinyl roof with "frenched" seams and brushed aluminum roof wrap over moldings was on the Crown Victoria. Front bumper guards were standard. The "S" had a different front end and grille, with round headlamps and parking lamps inset into the grille. Other models showed quad headlamps. Two-door opera windows had a more vertical look. The LTD had three police packages available including the 302-cid V-8, the regular 351-cid V-8, and the high-output 351-cid V-8. Police packages included heavy-duty alternators, a 2.26:1 axle for the 5.0 liter or 3.08:1 for the 5.8 liter, a 71 ampere-hour battery, heavy-duty power brakes, 140-mph speedometer, heavy-duty suspension and GR70 x 15 black sidewall police radials. The police automatic transmissions had a first-gear lockout and oil cooler.

I.D. Data:

Ford's 11-symbol Vehicle Identification Number (VIN) was stamped on a metal tab fastened to the instrument panel, visible through the windshield. Coding was the same as 1979, except engine codes (symbol five) changed to: A=140-cid four-cylinder, B=200-cid six-cylinder, C=250-cid six-cylinder, D=255-cid V-8, F=302-cid V-8 and G=351-cid V-8. The model year code was O=1980.

Pinto (Four)

Model No.	Body Style No.	Body Type & Seating	Factory Price	Shipping Weight	Production Total
10	62B	2-dr. Sedan-4P	$4,223	2,385 lbs.	84,053
10	41E	2-dr. Pony Sedan-4P	$3,781	2,377 lbs.	Note 1
11	64B	3-dr. Hatchback-4P	$4,335	2,426 lbs.	61,842
12	73B	2-dr. Station Wagon-4P	$4,622	2,553 lbs.	39,159
12	41E	2-dr. Pony Wagon-4P	$4,284	2,545 lbs.	Note 1
12/604	73B	2-dr. Squire Wagon-4P	$4,937	2,590 lbs.	Note 2

Note 1: Pony production was included in base sedan and wagon figures. Panel delivery Pintos also were produced.
Note 2: Squire Wagon production was included in the standard station wagon total.

Fairmont (Four)

91	66B	2-dr. Sedan-5P	$4,435	2,571 lbs.	45,074
92	54B	4-dr. Sedan-5P	$4,552	2,599 lbs.	143,118
94	74B	4-dr. Station Wagon-5P	$4,721	2,722 lbs.	77,035

Fairmont (Six)

91	66B	2-dr. Sedan-5P	$4,604	-----	45,074
92	54B	4-dr. Sedan-5P	$4,721	-----	143,118
94	74B	4-dr. Station Wagon-5P	$4,890	-----	77,035

Fairmont Futura (Four)

| 93 | 36R | 2-dr. Sport Coupe-5P | $4,837 | 2,612 lbs. | 51,878 |
| 92 | ---- | 4-dr. Sedan-5P | $5,070 | ----- | 5,306 |

Fairmont Futura (Six)

| 93 | 36R | 2-dr. Sport Coupe-5P | $5,006 | ----- | 51,878 |
| 92 | ---- | 4-dr. Sedan-5P | $5,239 | ----- | 5,306 |

Note: Prices shown are for four- and six-cylinder engines. A 255-cid V-8 cost $119 more than the six.

Granada (Six)

| 81 | 66H | 2-dr. Sedan-5P | $4,987 | 3,063 lbs. | 60,872 |
| 82 | 54H | 4-dr. Sedan-5P | $5,108 | 3,106 lbs. | 29,557 |

Granada (V-8)

| 81 | 66H | 2-dr. Sedan-5P | $5,025 | 3,187 lbs. | 60,872 |
| 82 | 54H | 4-dr. Sedan-5P | $5,146 | 3,230 lbs. | 29,557 |

Granada Ghia (Six)

| 81/602 | 66K | 2-dr. Sedan-5P | $5,388 | 3,106 lbs. | Note 3 |
| 82/602 | 54K | 4-dr. Sedan-5P | $5,509 | 3,147 lbs. | Note 3 |

Granada Ghia (V-8)

| 81/602 | 66K | 2-dr. Sedan-5P | $5,426 | 3,230 lbs. | Note 3 |
| 82/602 | 54K | 4-dr. Sedan-5P | $5,547 | 3,271 lbs. | Note 3 |

Granada ESS (Six)

| 81/933 | ---- | 2-dr. Sedan-5P | $5,477 | 3,137 lbs. | Note 3 |
| 82/933 | ---- | 4-dr. Sedan-5P | $5,598 | 3,178 lbs. | Note 3 |

Granada ESS (V-8)

| 81/933 | ---- | 2-dr. Sedan-5P | $5,515 | 3,261 lbs. | Note 3 |
| 82/933 | ---- | 4-dr. Sedan-5P | $5,636 | 3,302 lbs. | Note 3 |

Note 3: Granada Ghia and ESS production is included in the base Granada totals above.

Note: Prices shown are for the six-cylinder and 255-V-8 engines. A 302-cid V-8 cost $150 more than the 255-cid V-8.

LTD (V-8)

62	66H	2-dr. Sedan-6P	$6,549	3,447 lbs.	15,333
63	54H	4-dr. Sedan-6P	$6,658	3,475 lbs.	51,630
74	74H	4-dr. Station Wagon-6P	$7,007	3,717 lbs.	11,718

LTD "S" (V-8)

----	66D	2-dr. Sedan-6P	-----	-----	553
61	54D	4-dr. Sedan-6P	$6,320	2,464 lbs.	19,283
72	74D	4-dr. Station Wagon-6P	$6,741	3,707 lbs.	3,490

LTD Crown Victoria (V-8)

64	66K	2-dr. Sedan-6P	$7,070	3,482 lbs.	7,725
65	54K	4-dr. Sedan-6P	$7,201	3,524 lbs.	21,962
76	74K	4-dr. Country Squire-6P	$7,426	3,743 lbs.	9,868

Note: Production of wagons with dual-facing rear seats was included in the basic wagon totals.

Engines:

Pinto and Fairmont Base Four: Inline. Overhead cam. Cast-iron block and head. Displacement: 140-cid (2.3 liters). B & S: 3.78 x 3.13 in. Compression ratio: 9.0:1. Brake hp: 88 at 4600 rpm. Torque: 119 lbs.-ft. at 2600 rpm. Five main bearings. Hydraulic valve lifters. Carburetor: Motorcraft 5200 two-barrel. VIN Code: A.

Fairmont Six: Inline. Overhead valve. Cast-iron block and head. Displacement: 200-cid (3.3 liters). B & S: 3.68 x 3.13 in. Compression ratio: 8.6:1. Brake hp: 91 at 3800 rpm. Torque: 160 lbs.-ft. at 1600 rpm. Seven main bearings. Hydraulic valve lifters. Carburetor: Holley 1946 two-barrel. VIN Code: B.

Granada: Inline. Overhead valve. Cast-iron block and head. Displacement: 250 cid (4.1 liters). B & S: 3.68 x 3.91 in. Compression

1980 Fairmont Futura Sport Coupe (turbocharged)

1980 Fairmont Squire station wagon

1980 Granada Ghia sedan

1980 Granada sedan

ratio: 8.6:1. Brake hp: 90 at 3200 rpm. Torque: 194 lbs.-ft. at 1660 rpm. Seven main bearings. Hydraulic valve lifters. Carburetor: Carter YFA one-barrel. VIN Code: C.

Fairmont and Granada Optional V-8: 90-degree, overhead valve. Cast-iron block and head. Displacement: 255 cid (4.2 liters). B & S: 3.68 x 3.00 in. Compression ratio: 8.8:1. Brake hp: 119 at 3800 rpm, Fairmont. Torque: 194 lbs.-ft. at 2200 rpm, Fairmont. Five main bearings. Hydraulic valve lifters. Carburetor: Motorcraft 2150 two-barrel. VIN Code: D.

LTD Base V-8 (Optional Granada): 90-degree, overhead valve. Cast-iron block and head. Displacement: 302 cid (5.0 liters). B & S: 4.00 x 3.00 in. Compression ratio: 8.4:1. Brake hp: 130 at 3600 rpm, LTD and 134 at 3600, Granada. Torque: 230 lbs.-ft. at 1600 rpm, LTD and 232 at 1600, Granada. Five main bearings. Hydraulic valve lifters. Carburetor: Motorcraft 2150 or 2700VV two-barrel. VIN Code: F.

LTD Optional V-8: 90-degree, overhead valve. Cast-iron block and head. Displacement: 351 cid (5.8 liters). B & S: 4.00 x 3.50 in. Compression ratio: 8.3:1. Brake hp: 140 at 3400 rpm. Torque: 265 lbs.-ft. at 2000 rpm. Five main bearings. Hydraulic valve lifters. Carburetor: Motorcraft 7200VV two barrel. Windsor engine. VIN Code: G.

Note: A high-output version of the 351 cid V-8 was available for police use.

Chassis:

Pinto: Wheelbase: 94.5 in. and 94.8 in. on station wagon. Overall length: 170.8 in. and 180.6 in., station wagon. Tires: BR78 x 13 steel-belted radials and A78 x 13, Pony.

Fairmont: Wheelbase: 105.5 in. and 197.4 in. on Futura coupe. Overall length: 195.5 in. and 197.4 in., Futura. Tires: P175/75-R14.

Granada: Wheelbase: 109.9 in. Overall length: 199.7 in. Tires: DR78 x 14 steel-belted radials. ER78 x 14, Ghia and FR78 x 14, ESS.

LTD: Wheelbase: 114.3 in. Overall length: 209.3 in. and 215.0 in., LTD wagon. Tires: P205/75-R14 and P215/75-R14, station wagon.

Options:

Pinto: ESS package, including a charcoal grille and headlamp doors, black windshield and backlight moldings, dual black racing mirrors, glass third door with black hinges, blackout paint treatment, black wheel lip moldings and ESS fender insignia ($281 to $313). Cruising package ($355-$606); tape delete ($70 credit). Rally pack: hatch ($369) or wagon ($625). Sport package ($103 to $118). Exterior decor group ($24 to $44). Interior decor group ($165 to $238). Interior accent group ($5 to $50). Convenience group ($26 to $118). Protection group ($36 to $40). Light group ($41). Air conditioner ($538). Rear defroster, electric ($96). Tinted glass ($65). Trunk light ($5). Driver's remote mirror ($18). Dual sport mirrors ($58). Day/night mirror ($11). AM radio: Pony ($80). AM/FM radio ($65 to $145). AM/FM stereo radio ($103 to $183); with cassette player ($191 to $271). Radio flexibility option ($60). Flip-up open air roof ($206 to $219). Glass third door ($31). Metallic glow paint ($45). Roof luggage rack ($71). Mud/stone deflectors ($25). Lower body protection ($34). Four-way driver's seat ($38). Load floor carpet ($28). Cargo area cover ($30). Front floor mats ($19). Wire wheel covers ($104). Forged aluminum wheels ($225 to $300); white wheels ($256

1980 LTD four-door sedan

1980 LTD Country Squire station wagon

to $331). Lacy spoke aluminum wheels ($225 to $300). Styled steel wheels ($56). BR78 x 13 white sidewall tires ($50). BR70 x 13 raised-white letter tires ($87). Select-Shift automatic transmission ($340). Optional axle ratio ($15). Power brakes ($78). Power steering ($160). Heavy duty battery ($20 to $21). Engine block heater ($15).

Fairmont: ES option, including a blackout grille, dual black remote sport mirrors, turbine wheel covers, black sport steering wheel, rear bumper guards, handling suspension, and black lower back panel ($378). Futura sports group, with color-keyed turbine wheel covers, charcoal/argent grille, and youth-oriented tape stripes ($114). Ghia package: ($193) Futura coupe and standard sedan ($566). Squire option ($458). Exterior decor group ($260). Exterior accent group ($95). Interior decor group ($184 to $346). Interior accent group ($110 to $115). Instrument cluster ($85). Convenience group ($29 to $51). Appearance protection group ($46 to $53). Light group ($30 to $48). Air conditioning ($571). Rear defroster, electric ($101). Fingertip speed control ($116 to $129). Power windows ($135 to $191). Power door locks ($88 to $125). Power deck lid release ($25). Power seat ($111). Tinted glass ($71). Sport steering wheel ($43). Leather-wrapped steering wheel ($44). Tilt steering ($78 to $90). Interval wipers ($39). Rear wiper/washer ($79). Left mirror ($19). Dual bright remote mirrors ($54 to $60). AM radio ($93). AM/FM radio ($145). AM/FM stereo radio ($183); with eight-track player ($259); with cassette player ($271). Premium sound system ($94). Radio flexibility ($63). Flip-up open air roof ($219). Full or half vinyl roof ($118). Pivoting front vent windows ($50). Luggage rack ($88). Mud/stone deflectors ($25). Non-reclining bucket seats ($31 to $50). Bench seat ($50 credit). Cloth/vinyl seat trim ($28 to $44). Vinyl seat trim ($25). Front floor mats ($19), Lockable side storage box ($23). Hubcaps with trim rings ($41). Deluxe wheel covers ($41). Turbine wheel covers ($43) and argent color ($43 to $84). Wire wheel covers ($74 to $158). Styled steel wheels ($49 to $133). Cast aluminum wheels ($268 to $351). P175/75-R14 WSW ($50). P185/75-R14 ($31) and white sidewall ($81). Raised white letter tires ($96). Conventional spare ($37). Turbo 140-cid four cylinder ($481). 200-cid six cylinder ($169). 255-cid V-8 ($288). Select-Shift automatic transmission ($340). Floor shift lever ($38). Optional axle ratio ($15). Power brakes ($78). Power steering ($165). Handling suspension ($44). Heavy duty battery ($20 to $21). Engine block heater ($15).

Granada: Interior decor group ($243). Convenience group ($39 to $108). Light group ($46 to $51). Cold weather group ($31 to $65). Heavy-duty group ($20 to $65). Protection group ($29 to $53). Visibility group ($6 to $66). Air conditioning ($571); auto-temp ($634). Rear defroster, electric ($101). Fingertip speed control ($116 to $129). Illuminated entry system ($58). Power windows ($136 to $193). Power door locks ($89 to $125). Power deck lid release ($25). Power four-way seat ($111). Tinted glass ($71). Tilt steering wheel ($78). Digital clock ($54). Cornering lamps ($50). Dual remote mirrors ($41 to $60). Dual sport mirrors ($50 to $69). Lighted right visor vanity mirror ($41). AM radio ($93). AM/FM radio ($145). AM/FM stereo radio ($183); with eight-track player ($259); with cassette ($271). AM/FM stereo search radio ($333); with eight-track ($409); with cassette and Dolby ($421).

Radio flexibility ($63). Power moon roof ($998). Full or half vinyl roof ($118). Mud/stone deflectors ($25). Console ($110). Four-way driver's seat ($38). Reclining bucket seats, no charge. Deluxe cloth/vinyl seat, no charge. Flight bench seat, no charge. Cloth/vinyl flight bench seat ($60). Leather seat trim ($277). Front floor mats ($19). Color-keyed seatbelts ($23). Luxury wheel covers ($46), except Ghia, no charge. Wire wheel covers ($119), except. Ghia and ESS ($73). Styled steel wheels with trim rings ($91 to $138). Cast aluminum wheels ($275 to $321). Inflatable spare ($37). 255-cid V-8 ($38). 302-cid V-8 ($188). Select-Shift automatic transmission ($340). Floor shift lever: ($38). Power brakes ($78). Power steering ($165). Heavy duty suspension ($23). Heavy duty battery ($20 to $21). Engine block heater ($15).

LTD: Interior luxury group ($693 to $741). Convenience group ($68 to $98). Power lock group ($114 to $166). Light group ($33 to $43). Protection group ($48 to $58). Air conditioning ($606); w/auto-temp control ($669). Rear defroster, electric ($103). Fingertip speed control ($116). Illuminated entry system ($58). Power windows ($140 to $208). Power door locks ($89 to $120). Power driver's seat ($168); or driver and passenger ($335). Tinted glass ($85). Autolamp on/off delay ($63). Leather-wrapped steering wheel ($44). Tilt steering wheel ($78). Automatic parking brake release ($10). Electric clock ($24). Digital clock ($38 to $61). Seatbelt chime ($23). Interval wipers ($40). Cornering lamps ($48). Trunk light ($5). Dual-note horn ($10). Driver's remote mirror ($19). Dual remote mirrors ($38 to $56). Lighted right visor vanity mirror ($35 to $41); pair of mirrors ($42 to $83). AM radio ($93). AM/FM radio ($145). AM/FM stereo radio ($183); with eight-track tape player ($259): with cassette ($271). AM/FM stereo search radio ($333); with eight-track ($409); with cassette ($421). CB radio ($316). Power antenna ($49). Dual rear speakers ($40). Premium sound system ($94). Radio flexibility ($66). Full or half vinyl roof ($145). Bumper guards, rear ($26). Bumper rub strips ($56). Luggage rack ($115). Dual-facing rear seats: wagon ($146 to $151). Flight bench seat ($56). Leather split bench seat ($349). Dual flight bench seat recliners ($55). Split bench seat with recliners ($173 to $229). All-vinyl seat trim ($28). Duraweave vinyl trim ($50). Front floor mats ($19); front/rear ($30). Trunk trim ($46 to $51). Trunk mat ($14). Color-keyed seatbelts ($24). Luxury wheel covers ($70). Wire wheel covers ($138). Cast aluminum wheels ($310). P205/75-R14 white sidewall tires ($50). P215/75-R14 blackwall tires ($29); white sidewall tires ($50 to $79). P225/75-R14 white sidewall tires ($79 to $107). P205/75-R15 white sidewalls ($55 to $87). Conventional spare ($37). 351-cid V-8 ($150). Four-speed overdrive automatic transmission ($138). Traction-Lok differential ($69). Optional axle ratio ($19). Handling suspension ($43). Adjustable air shock absorbers ($55). Heavy duty battery ($20 to $21). Engine block heater ($15). Heavy duty trailer towing package ($164 to $169).

History:

The 1980 Fords were introduced on October 12, 1979. Model year production was 1,167,581, including Mustangs. Calendar year sales by U. S. dealers was 1,074,675, including Mustangs. Dealers also sold 68,841 imported Fiestas, made by Ford of Germany. Early in 1980, the "Erika" subcompact was renamed Escort (and Mercury Lynx). Overall Ford sales for the model year fell more than 28 percent, touching every car in the lineup but headed by LTD's 43 percent drop. LTD was advertised during this period as rivaling Rolls-Royce for smooth, quiet ride qualities. The restyled and downsized Thunderbird didn't find many buyers either. Two assembly plants closed during 1980, at Mahwah, New Jersey, and at Los Angeles, California. Ford expected to spend $2 billion for expansion and retooling at other domestic facilities. Foremost hope for the future was the new Escort being readied for 1981 introduction. Philip E. Benton became head of the Ford Division, following the retirement of Walter S. Walla. The 1980 CAFE goal for automakers' fleets was 20 mpg (up from 19 mpg in 1979). Thunderbird was the star of the lineup in its new downsized form. On the power plant front, a turbocharged four was announced as a Fairmont option, but didn't quite materialize, presumably due to mechanical difficulties.

1980 LTD Crown Victoria sedan

1981 Ford

Escort — Four: Ford's international experience influenced the new "world car," the front-wheel-drive Escort. A $3 billion development program had been initiated in the early 1970s to produce Escorts for both the U.S. and Europe. The engine alone cost $1 billion to develop. The U.S. version of the all-new overhead-cam, Compound Valve Hemispherical (CVH) engine had to meet federal emissions standards.. The transverse-mounted engine displaced just 97.6 cid. The cylinder head and intake manifold were aluminum. The CVH design put the spark plug close to the center of the combustion chamber. Escort's maintenance-free features included self-adjusting brakes, lubed-for-life wheel bearings and front suspension, preset carb mixtures, hydraulic valve lifters, fixed caster and camber settings at the front end, and self-adjusting clutches. Three-door hatchback and four-door lift gate bodies were offered. Five trim levels included base, L, GL, GLX and sporty SS. Escort's four-speed manual transaxle was fully synchronized, with wide-ratio gearing. Escort had four-wheel independent suspension, rack-and-pinion steering, standard halogen headlamps and a maintenance-free battery. Front suspension used MacPherson struts with strut-mounted coil springs and a stabilizer bar. At the rear were independent trailing arms with modified MacPherson struts and coil springs, mounted on stamped lower control arms. P-metric (P155/80R) radial tires rode on 13 in. steel wheels. Cast aluminum wheels were optional. Standard equipment included an AM radio, two-speed wipers, three-speed heater/defroster, inside hood release, high-back vinyl front bucket seats, a bench-type folding rear seat, a door-mounted driver's mirror, a day/night mirror, courtesy lights, and semi-styled steel wheels. Options included a console with graphic display module, intermittent wipers, and pivoting front vent windows. Gas mileage estimates reached 30 mpg city and 44 mpg highway. Early criticisms prompted Ford to continually refine the Escort. First-year versions suffered several recalls. Mercury Lynx was Escort's corporate twin.

Fairmont — Four/Six/V-8: In addition to the usual sedans and the Futura coupe, Fairmont delivered a station wagon in 1981 under the Futura badge. The four-door, steel-sided wagon had Futura's bright work and an upgraded interior. Squire (wood grain) trim was available at extra cost. Fairmonts also added new standard equipment, including power front disc brakes, bucket seats, a deluxe sound package, dual-note horn, bright window frames, visor vanity mirror and a glove box lock. The option list expanded to include a console with diagnostic warning lights and digital clock, an illuminated entry system, Traction-Lok rear axle (V-8 only), lighted visor vanity mirror, and Michelin TR type tires. Both the 200-cid (3.3-liter) six and 255-cid (4.2-liter) V-8 now had a viscous-clutch fan drive. The base engine remained the 140-cid (2.3-liter) four, with a four-speed manual gearbox. The four-speed transmission had a self-adjusting clutch. Fairmont's base four-cylinder produced EPA estimates of 34 mpg highway and 23 mpg city. Wide (non-wraparound) tail lamps had vertical ribbing, with backup lenses at inner ends. Four-doors had a six-window design with narrow quarter windows that tapered to a point at the top. Wagons carried vertical wraparound tail lamps.

Granada — Four/Six/V-8: Granada received an aerodynamic restyle that was supposed to deliver a 21 percent improvement in fuel economy. Ford called it "the industry's most changed American-built sedan for 1981." This Granada was three inches shorter than its predecessor, but with more leg, hip and shoulder room inside, and more luggage space. Granada's chassis was based on the familiar "Fox" platform, with coil springs all around. The fully unitized body weighed 400 pounds less than the 1980 version. Drag coefficient rated a low 0.44. Standard was the 140-cid (2.3-liter) OHC four, as in Fairmont and Mustang, with four-speed manual shift. Automatic transmission was standard with the bigger engines. New for 1981 was a MacPherson strut front suspension, a pin-slider front disc brake system, front bucket seats, a revised instrument panel and stalk-mounted controls for turn signals, horn, dimmer, and wiper. P-metric steel-belted radial tires rode on 14 in. stamped steel wheels. Granada also sported halogen headlamps. Three Granada series were offered: L, GL and GLX (replacing base, Ghia and ESS). Body styles included only the two-and four-door sedans. Wide tail lamps had backup lamps toward the center. There was a see-through hood ornament. A square badge was mounted ahead of the front door. Mercury Cougar was Granada's corporate companion.

LTD — V-8: Full-size Fords no longer carried a standard full-size engine. LTD's new standard power train consisted of the 255-cid (4.2-liter) V-8 and automatic overdrive transmission, which had been introduced in 1980 as an option on the LTD and the Thunderbird. That transmission also featured a lockup clutch torque converter. The three-speed automatic was abandoned. A high-output 351-cid V-8, delivering 20 more horsepower, was available only for police cars. LTD's lineup included four-door sedans in base, "S" and Crown Victoria trim. There were two-door sedans in base and Crown Victoria trim and four-door

1981 Escort GLX three-door hatchback

1981 Escort GLX four-door liftgate

wagons in all three series. Switching to a smaller base power plant didn't seem to help mileage that was estimated at just 16 mpg. Standard equipment included halogen headlamps on "S" models, and separate ignition and door keys. Remote mirrors were now door-mounted rather than sail-mounted. Appearance was the same as 1980.

I.D. Data:

Ford had a new 17-symbol Vehicle Identification Number (VIN), again stamped on a metal tab fastened to the instrument panel. It was visible through the windshield. Symbols one to three indicated the manufacturer, make and vehicle type: 1FA=Ford passenger car. The fourth symbol B=the restraint system. The letter P plus two digits that indicated the body type such as 91=Fairmont two-door sedan. Symbol eight indicated the engine type: 2=a 98-cid four cylinder engine, A=the 140-cid four cylinder, B=a 200c-cid six, D= a 255-cid V-8, F=a 302-cid V-8, G=351-cid V-8. The ninth digit was a check digit. Symbol 10 indicated the model year: B=1981. Symbol 11 was the assembly plant: A=Atlanta, Georgia; B=Oakville, Ontario, Canada; G=Chicago, Illinois; H=Lorain, Ohio; K=Kansas City, Missouri; X=St. Thomas, Ontario, Canada; T= Metuchen, New Jersey; U=Louisville, Kentucky and W=Wayne, Michigan. The final six digits made up the sequence number, starting with 100001. A Vehicle Certification Label on the left front door lock face panel or door pillar showed the manufacturer, month and year of manufacture, GVW, GAWR, certification statement, VIN, and codes for such items as body type, color, trim, axle, transmission, and special order information.

Escort (Four)

Model No.	Body Style No.	Body Type & Seating	Factory Price	Shipping Weight	Production Total
05	61D	3-dr. Hatchback-4P	$5,158	1,962 lbs.	Note 1
08	74D	4-dr. Liftgate-4P	$5,731	2,074 lbs.	Note 1
05/60Q	61D	2-dr. L Hatchback-4P	$5,494	1,964 lbs.	Note 1
08/60Q	74D	4-dr. L Liftgate-4P	$5,814	2,075 lbs.	Note 1
05/60Z	61D	2-dr. GL Hatchback-4P	$5,838	1,987 lbs.	Note 1
08/60Z	74D	4-dr. GL Liftgate-4P	$6,178	2,094 lbs.	Note 1
05/602	61D	3-dr. GLX Hatchback-4P	$6,476	2,029 lbs.	Note 1
08/602	74D	4-dr. GLX Liftgate-4P	$6,799	2,137 lbs.	Note 1
05/936	61D	3-dr. SS Hatchback-4P	$6,139	2,004 lbs.	Note 1
08/936	74D	4-dr. SS Liftgate-4P	$6,464	2,114 lbs.	Note 1

Note 1: Escort production totaled 192,554 three-door hatchbacks and 128,173 four-door lift backs. Breakdown by trim levels was not available. Hatchbacks are called two- or three-door and liftgate models also are called station wagons.

Fairmont (Four)

20	66	2-dr. S Sedan-5P	$5,701	-----	-----
20	66B	2-dr. Sedan-5P	$6,032	2,564 lbs.	23,066
21	54B	4-dr. Sedan-5P	$6,151	2,614 lbs.	104,883
23	74B	4-dr. Station Wagon-5P	$6,384	2,721 lbs.	59,154

Fairmont (Six)

20	66	2-dr. S Sedan-5P	$5,914	-----	-----
22	66B	2-dr. Sedan-5P	$6,245	2,617 lbs.	23,066
21	54B	4-dr. Sedan-5P	$6,364	2,667 lbs.	104,883
23	74B	4-dr. Station Wagon-5P	$6,597	2,788 lbs.	59,154

Fairmont Futura (Four)

22	36	2-dr. Coupe-5P	$6,347	2,619 lbs.	24,197
21/605	54B	4-dr. Sedan-5P	$6,361	2,648 lbs.	Note 2
21/605	74B	4-dr. Station Wagon-5P	$6,616	2,755 lbs.	Note 2

Fairmont Futura (Six)

20	36R	2-dr. Coupe-5P	$6,560	2,672 lbs.	24,197
20	54B	4-dr. Sedan-5P	$6,574	2,701 lbs.	Note 2
21	74B	4-dr. Station Wagon-5P	$6,829	2,822 lbs.	Note 2

Note 2: Production totals listed under the base Fairmont sedan and wagon also include Futura models.

Granada (Four)

26	66D	2-dr. L Sedan-5P	$6,474	2,707 lbs.	35,057
27	54D	4-dr. L Sedan-5P	$6,633	2,750 lbs.	86,284
26/602	66D	2-dr. GL Sedan-5P	$6,875	2,728 lbs.	Note 3
27/602	54D	4-dr. GL Sedan-5P	$7,035	2,777 lbs.	Note 3
26/933	66D	2-dr. GLX Sedan-5P	$6,988	2,732 lbs.	Note 3
27/933	54D	4-dr. GLX Sedan-5P	$7,148	2,784 lbs.	Note 3

Granada (Six)

26	66D	2-dr. L Sedan-5P	$6,687	2,797 lbs.	35,057
27	54D	4-dr. L Sedan-5P	$6,848	2,840 lbs.	86,284
26/602	66D	2-dr. GL Sedan-5P	$7,088	2,818 lbs.	Note 3
27/602	54D	4-dr. GL Sedan-5P	$7,248	2,867 lbs.	Note 3
26/933	66D	2-dr. GLX Sedan-5P	$7,201	2,822 lbs.	Note 3
27/933	54D	4-dr. GLX Sedan-5P	$7,361	2,874 lbs.	Note 3

Note 3: Granada GL and GLX production is included in base Granada totals above.
Note: Prices shown are for four-and six-cylinder engines. A 255-cid V-8 cost $50 more than the six.

LTD (V-8)

32	66H	2-dr. Sedan-6P	$7,607	3,496 lbs.	6,279
33	54H	4-dr. Sedan-6P	$7,718	3,538 lbs.	35,932
38	74H	4-dr. Station Wagon-6P	$8,180	3,719 lbs.	10,554
39	74K	4-dr. Country Squire-6P	$8,640	3,737 lbs.	9,443

LTD S (V-8)

31	54D	4-dr. Sedan-6P	$7,522	3,490 lbs.	17,490
37	74D	4-dr. Station Wagon-6P	$7,942	3,717 lbs.	2,465

LTD Crown Victoria (V-8)

34	66K	2-dr. Sedan-6P	$8,251	3,496 lbs.	11,061
35	54K	4-dr. Sedan-6P	$8,384	3,538 lbs.	39,139

Note: Production of wagons with dual-facing rear seats (a $143 option) was included in the basic wagon totals. A prefix P precedes the model number in many reports of 1981 Ford production.

Engines:

Escort Base Four: Inline. Overhead cam. Cast-iron block and aluminum head. Displacement: 97.6 cid (1.6 liters). B & S: 3.15 x 3.13 in. Compression ratio: 8.8:1. Brake hp: 65 at 5200 rpm. Torque: 85 lbs.-ft. at 3000 rpm. Five main bearings. Hydraulic valve lifters. Carburetor: Holley-Weber 5740 two-barrel. VIN Code: 2.

Fairmont and Granada Base Four: Inline. Overhead cam. Cast-iron block and head. Displacement: 140 cid (2.3 liters). B & S: 3.78 x 3.13 in. Compression ratio: 9.0:1. Brake hp: 88 at 4600 rpm. Torque: 118 lbs.-ft. at 2600 rpm. Five main bearings. Hydraulic valve lifters. Carburetor: Holley 6500 two barrel. VIN Code: A.

Fairmont and Granada Optional Engine: Inline. Overhead valve. Cast-iron block and head. Displacement: 200 cid (3.3 liters). B & S: 3.68 x 3.13 in. Compression ratio: 8.6:1. Brake hp: 88 at 3800 rpm. Torque: 154 lbs.-ft. at 1400 rpm. Seven main bearings. Hydraulic valve lifters. Carburetor: Holley 1946 single barrel. VIN Code: B.

LTD Base V-8 (Optional on Fairmont and Granada): 90-degree, overhead valve. Cast-iron block and head. Displacement: 255 cid (4.2 liters). B & S: 3.68 x 3.00 in. Compression ratio: 8.2:1. Brake hp: 115 at 3400 rpm, Fairmont and Granada, and 120 at 3400, LTD. Torque: 195 lbs.-ft. at 2200 rpm, Fairmont and Granada and 205 at 2600, LTD. Five main bearings. Hydraulic valve lifters. Carburetor: Motorcraft 2150 or 7200VV two-barrel. VIN Code: D.

LTD Optional V-8: 90-degree, overhead valve. Cast-iron block and head. Displacement: 302 cid (5.0 liters). B & S:: 4.00 x 3.00 in. Compression ratio: 8.4:1. Brake hp: 130 at 3400 rpm. Torque: 235 lbs.-ft. at 1800 rpm. Five main bearings. Hydraulic valve lifters. Carburetor: Motorcraft 2150 or 7200VV two-barrel. VIN Code: F.

LTD Optional V-8: 90-degree, overhead valve. Cast-iron block and head. Displacement: 351 cid (5.8 liters). B & S: 4.00 x 3.50 in.

1981 Fairmont sedan

1981 Fairmont Futura Squire station wagon

Compression ratio: 8.3:1. Brake hp: 145 at 3200 rpm. Torque: 270 lbs.-ft. at 1800 rpm. Five main bearings. Hydraulic valve lifters. Carburetor: Motorcraft 7200VV two-barrel. Windsor engine. VIN Code: G.

Note: A high-output 351-cid V-8 was available with 165 brake hp at 3600 rpm and 285 lbs.-ft. of torque at 2200 rpm.

Chassis:

Escort: Wheelbase: 94.5 in. Overall length: 163.9 in., hatchback and 165.0 in., lift back. Tires: P155/80-R13 steel-belted radial blackwalls.

Fairmont: Wheelbase: 105.5 in. Overall length: 195.5 in. and Futura coupe, 197.4 in. Tires: P175/75-R14 steel-belted blackwalls.

Granada: Wheelbase: 105.5 in. Overall length: 196.5 in. Tires: P175/75-R14 steel-belted blackwalls.

LTD: Wheelbase: 114.3 in. Overall Length: 209.3 in. and 215.0 in., LTD station wagon. Tires: P205/75-R14 steel-belted white sidewalls and P215/75-R14, LTD station wagon.

Options:

Escort: Squire wagon package ($256). Instrument group ($77). Protection group ($49). Light group ($39). Air conditioner ($530). Rear defroster, electric ($102). Fingertip speed control ($132). Tinted glass ($70); windshield only ($28). Digital clock ($52). Intermittent wipers ($41). Rear wiper/washer ($100). Dual remote sport mirrors ($56). AM/FM radio ($63). AM/FM stereo radio ($100); with cassette player ($187). Dual rear speakers ($37). Premium sound ($91). AM radio delete ($61 credit). Flip-up open air roof ($154 to $228). Front vent windows, pivoting ($55). Remote quarter windows ($95). Vinyl-insert body moldings ($41). Bumper guards, front or rear ($23). Bumper rub strips ($34). Roof luggage rack ($74). Roof air deflector ($26). Lower body protection ($60). Console ($98). Low-back reclining bucket seats ($30). Reclining front seatbacks ($55). Cloth/vinyl seat trim ($28) or vinyl, no charge. Deluxe seatbelts ($23). Wheel trim rings ($44). Aluminum wheels ($193 to $330). P155/80-R13 white sidewall tires ($55). P165/80-R13 blackwalls($19) or white sidewalls ($55 to $74). Optional axle ratio ($15). Power brakes ($79). Power steering ($163). Handling suspension ($37). Extended-range gas tank: Escort ($32). Engine block heater ($16). Automatic transaxle ($344).

Fairmont: Squire option ($200). Interior luxury group ($232 to $256). Instrument cluster ($88). Appearance protection group ($50). Light group ($43). Air conditioning ($585). Rear defroster, electric ($107). Fingertip speed control ($132). Illuminated entry ($60). Power windows ($140 to $195). Power door locks ($93 to $132). Remote deck lid release ($27). Power seat ($122). Tinted glass ($76); windshield only ($29). Leather-wrapped steering wheel ($49). Tilt steering ($80 to $93). Electric clock ($23). Interval wipers ($41). Rear wiper/washer ($85). Map light ($9); dual-beam ($13). Trunk light ($6). Left remote mirror ($15). Dual bright remote mirrors ($55). Lighted visor vanity mirror ($43). AM/FM radio ($51). AM/FM stereo radio ($88); with eight-track player ($162); with cassette player ($174). Twin rear speakers ($37). Premium sound system ($91). Radio flexibility ($61). AM radio delete ($61 credit). Flip-up open air roof ($228). Full or half vinyl roof ($115). Pivoting front vent windows ($55). Lift gate assist handle for station wagon ($16). Rocker panel moldings ($30). Bumper guards, rear ($23). Bumper rub strips ($43). Station wagon luggage rack ($90). Lower body protection ($37 to $49) Interior Console ($168). Bench seat ($24 credit). Cloth seat trim ($28 to $54). Flight bench seat, no charge but

1981 Granada GLX sedan

1981 Escort three-door hatchback

1981 Granada GL coupe

1981 Escort GLX Squire wagon

with vinyl trim ($26). Front floor mats ($18-$20). Locking storage box ($24). Deluxe seatbelts ($23). Wire wheel covers ($76 to $117). Styled steel wheels ($52 to $94). P175/75-R14 whitewall tires($55). P185/75-R14 white sidewalls($86). P190/65-R390 blackwalls on TRX aluminum wheels ($470 to $512). Conventional spare ($39). 200-cid six-cylinder engine ($213). 255-cid V-8 ($263). Floor shift lever ($43). Traction-Lok differential ($67). Select-Shift automatic transmission ($349). Power steering ($168). Heavy-duty suspension ($22). Handling suspension ($45). Heavy-duty battery ($20). Engine block heater ($16).

Granada: Interior sport group ($282 to $295). Light group ($45). Cold weather group ($67). Protection group ($51). Air conditioning ($585). Rear defroster ($107). Fingertip speed control ($89 to $132). Illuminated entry system ($60). Power windows ($140 to $195). Power door locks ($93 to $132). Power deck lid release ($27). Power flight bench seat ($122); split bench ($173). Tinted glass ($76) and windshield only ($29). Sport steering wheel ($26 to $39); leather-wrapped ($49); tilt ($80 to $94). Electric clock ($23). Interval wipers ($41). Cornering lamps ($51). Map light ($13). Trunk light ($6). Remote right mirror ($52). Lighted right visor vanity mirror ($43). AM/FM radio ($51). AM/FM stereo radio ($88); with eight-track player ($162); with cassette ($174). Premium sound ($91). Radio flexibility ($61). AM radio delete ($61 credit). Flip-up open-air roof ($228). Full or half vinyl roof ($115). Pivoting front vent windows ($55). Mud/stone deflectors ($26). Console ($168). Split bench seat: GL/GLX ($178). Cloth seat trim ($45 to $62). Flight bench seat, no charge. Front floor mats ($18 to $20). Color-keyed seatbelts ($23). Luxury wheel covers: L ($43) and GL/GLX, no charge. Wire wheel covers ($124); GL/GLX ($80). Cast aluminum wheels ($308 to $350). P175/75-R14 whitewalls ($55). P185/75-R14 SSW ($32); white sidewalls($86); raised white letters ($102). 190/65-R390 blackwalls on TRX aluminum wheels ($468 to $512). Conventional spare ($39). 200-cid six ($213). 255-cid V-8 ($263). Select-Shift automatic transmission ($349). Floor shift lever ($43). Traction-Lok differential ($67). Optional axle ratio ($16). Power steering ($168). Heavy-duty suspension ($22). Heavy-duty battery ($20). Engine block heater ($16).

LTD: Interior luxury group ($693 to $765). Convenience group ($70 to $101). Power lock group ($93 to $176). Light group ($37). Protection group ($57). Air conditioning ($624); w/auto-temp control ($687). Rear defroster, electric ($107). Fingertip speed control ($135). Illuminated entry system ($59). Power windows ($143 to $211). Power driver's seat ($173) or driver and passenger ($346). Tinted glass ($87); windshield only ($29). Autolamp on/off delay ($65). Leather-wrapped steering wheel ($45). Tilt steering wheel ($80). Automatic parking brake release ($10). Electric clock ($23). Digital clock ($40 to $63). Seatbelt chime ($23). Cornering lamps ($48). Remote right mirror ($39). Lighted right visor vanity mirror ($38) or a pair ($43 to $80). AM/FM radio ($51). AM/FM stereo radio ($88); with eight-track tape player ($162) and Crown Victoria ($74); with cassette ($174) and Crown Victoria ($87). AM/FM stereo search radio ($234) and Crown Victoria ($146); with eight-track ($221 to $309); with cassette ($233 to $321). Power antenna ($48). Dual rear speakers ($39). Premium sound system ($116 to $146).

Radio flexibility ($65). AM radio delete ($61 credit). Full or half vinyl roof ($141). Luggage rack ($84). Dual-facing rear seats on station wagon ($146). Cloth/vinyl flight bench seat ($59). Leather seating ($361). Dual flight bench seat recliners ($56). Cloth/vinyl split bench seating ($178 to $237). All-vinyl seat trim on Crown Victoria and Country Squire ($28) and Duraweave vinyl ($54). Front floor mats ($20). Trunk trim ($45). Luxury wheel covers ($72). Wire wheel covers ($135). Cast aluminum wheels ($338). P215/75-R14 white sidewalls($30). P225/75-14 whitewalls ($30 to $61). P205/75-15 whitewalls ($10 to $40). Puncture-resistant tires ($95 to $125). Conventional spare ($39). 302-cid V-8 ($41). 351-cid V-8 ($83) and ($41) on the LTD wagon. High Output 351-cid V-8 ($139 to $180).). Four-speed overdrive automatic transmission ($162). Traction-Lok differential ($71). Heavy duty suspension ($23). Handling suspension ($45). Adjustable air shock absorbers ($57). Heavy duty battery ($20). Heavy duty alternator ($46). Engine block heater ($16). Heavy duty trailer towing package ($176).

Note: Ford body colors for 1981 were: Black, Bright Bittersweet, Candy Apple Red, Medium or Bright Red, Light Medium Blue, Medium Dark Brown, Bright Yellow, Cream, Chrome Yellow, Tan, Antique Cream, Pastel Chamois, Fawn, and White. Also available was a selection of metallics including: Silver, Medium Gray, Light Pewter, Medium Pewter, Maroon, Dark Blue, Bright Blue, Medium Dark Spruce, Dark Brown, Dark Pine, and Dark Cordovan. Some Ford products were available with nine "Glamour" colors and 16 clear coat paint selections.

History:

The 1981 Fords were introduced on October 3, 1980. The model year production was 1,054,976, including Mustangs. Calendar year sales by U.S. dealers were 977,220, including Mustangs. Dealers also sold 47,707 German-Ford made Fiestas. Escort quickly managed to become the best-selling Ford, selling 284,633 examples. Escort was primed to compete with Chevrolet's five-year-old Chevette. Other Ford sales slumped. The downsized Granada sold better than in 1980, finding 105,743 buyers. Total model year sales were down more than 7 percent. Mustang didn't sell as well as the predictions. It dropped by 29.5 percent for the model year. Calendar year production and sales both fell but not to a shocking level. This was a bad year all around for the industry. Car prices and interest rates rose steadily during this inflationary period, while the country also remained in a recession.

1981 LTD Crown Victoria sedan

Escort evolved from the "Erika" project, first begun in 1972. Both a 1.3-liter and 1.6-liter engine were planned, but only the larger one found its way under North American Escort hoods. Ford spent some $640 million to renovate its Dearborn, Michigan, plant to manufacture Escort's 1.6-liter CVH engine. They were also built at a Ford facility in Wales. Additional future production was planned for Lima, Ohio, and for a Mexican plant.

1982 Ford

Escort — Four: A new four-door hatchback sedan joined Escort's initial "three-door" (actually a two-door) hatchback and four-door liftback wagon. Base and SS wagons were dropped. The L, GL and GLX Escorts now had bright headlamp housings. New stainless steel wheel trim rings (formerly stamped aluminum) arrived on the GL, GLX and GT models. Escort had a new low-restriction exhaust and larger tires (P165/80-R13) in all series. Ford's oval script emblem now appeared on the front and back. An electric hatch release was now standard on GLX hatchbacks. Air-conditioned models included a switch that disconnected the unit for an instant when the gas pedal was floored. Base Escorts included single rectangular halogen headlamps, short black bumper end caps, semi-styled steel wheels with black and argent hub covers, and black wheel nut covers. Inside were vinyl high-back front bucket seats, a black two-spoke steering wheel and color-keyed soft-feel pad. Escort L included bright headlamp doors, an "L" badge on the liftgate, and blackout front end. Escort GL included added deluxe bumper end caps and rub strips and a "GL" badge in back. Inside, the GL had high-back reclining bucket seats and a four-spoke soft-feel color-keyed steering wheel. GLX included dual color-keyed remote sport mirrors, a "GLX" badge and a console with graphic warning display. Escort GT included a front air dam, roof grab handles and a black grille. Escorts had a larger, 11.3-gallon gas tank this year. EPA ratings reached 31 mpg and 47 mpg highway on the base Escort with four-speed.

EXP — Four: First shown at the Chicago Auto Show, then introduced in April as an early 1982 model, EXP was the first two-seater Ford offered in 25 years. Ford Division General Manager Louis E. Lataif said: "We're introducing another two-seater [like the early Thunderbird] but the EXP will be a very affordable, very fuel-efficient car matched to the lifestyles of the '80s." The sporty coupe weighed 1,000 lbs. less than the original Thunderbird. EXP was also two inches lower and five inches shorter. EXP's rakish body rode an Escort/Lynx 94.2-inch wheelbase, with that car's front-drive running gear, four-wheel independent suspension, and dashboard. EXP was longer, lower and narrower than Escort. The EXP weighed about 200 lbs. more than Escort but carried the same small engine. Standard features included steel-belted radial tires, power front disc/rear drum brakes, halogen headlamps, rack-and-pinion steering, reclining high-back bucket seats, four-spoke sport steering wheel, easy-to-read instrument panel and console with full instrumentation. Under the hood was the 97.6 cid (1.6-liter) CVH engine with standard four-speed overdrive manual transaxle. Ford's coupe was a notchback while Mercury's LN7 had a "bubble back" window. The EXP carried an ample list of standard equipment. It included power brakes, tachometer,

1982 LTD two-door sedan

full carpeting, power hatchback release, digital clock, and cargo area security shade. An optional TR handling package included special wheels and Michelin TRX tires in P165/70R365 size, and a larger-diameter front stabilizer bar. Ford offered an optional (no-extra-cost) 4.05:1 final drive ratio for better performance. In March 1982, an 80-hp edition of the CVH four became available. It included a higher (9.0:1) compression, a bigger air cleaner intake, larger carburetor venturis and a higher-lift camshaft.

Fairmont Futura — Four/Six/V-8: All Fairmont models acquired the Futura name this year as the lineup shrunk to a single series: just a two- and four-door sedan, and sport coupe. The station wagon was dropped, and the 255-cid (4.2-liter) V-8 was available only in police and taxi packages. The base engine was the 140-cid (2.3-liter) four, with the 3.3-liter inline six optional. The optional SelectShift automatic with the six included a new lockup torque converter. Quad rectangular headlamps now stood above quad park/signal lamps, like LTD, but without its wraparound side marker lenses. Fairmont had small marker lenses set low on front fenders. Front fenders held a Futura badge. Interiors held new high-gloss wood tone door trim and instrument panel appliqués. A new deep-well trunk was featured. AM radios added dual front speakers, and a new flash-to-pass feature was added to the headlamp lever. There was also a new gas cap tether. The once optional sweep-hand electric clock was switched to quartz-type, and the available extended-range fuel tank was increased to 20 gallons from 16.

Granada — Four/Six/V-6: Following its major restyle and downsizing for 1981, Granada looked the same this year but added a pair of station wagons (L and GL series). New station wagon options included a luggage rack, two-way liftgate (with flip-up window), rear wiper/washer, and Squire package. Fuel filler caps were now tethered. Flash-to-pass control on the steering column was new this year. Sedans could get an optional extended-range fuel tank. No more V-8s went under Granada hoods. A new optional "Essex" 232-cid (3.8-liter) 112-hp V-6 was said to offer V-8 power. It weighed just four pounds more than the base 140-cid (2.3-liter) four. An inline six also remained available and was standard on wagons. The V-6 got an EPA rating of 19 mpg, city and 26 mpg, highway. A new torque converter clutch that provided a direct connection became standard on the SelectShift automatic for the six and V-6 engines. This would be Granada's final season, but its basic design carried on in the form of a restyled LTD.

LTD — V-8: After a long history, the 351 cid (5.8-liter) V-8 no longer was available for private full-size Fords, but continued as an option for police models. Little changed on this year's LTD lineup, apart from seven new body colors. Ford ovals were added to front grilles and rear deck lids (or tailgates). All monaural radios had dual front speakers and wiring for rear speakers. The sweep-hand clock added quartz operation. A new medium-duty trailer towing option replaced the former heavy-duty one. New optional wire wheel covers incorporated a locking feature. The base engine was a 255-cid (4.2-liter) V-8. Optional was the 302-cid (5.0-liter) V-8. Also optional for 1982 was a Tripminder computer that combined a trip odometer with quartz clock to show vehicle speed, real or elapsed time, and fuel flow. The LTD was the largest Ford with its 114.3-inch wheelbase.

1982 Escort GLX five-door hatchback

1982 EXP three-door hatchback

I.D. Data:

Ford's 17-symbol Vehicle Identification Number (VIN) was stamped on a metal tab fastened to the instrument panel, visible through the windshield. The first three symbols: 1FA= manufacturer, make and vehicle type. The fourth symbol: B=the restraint system. The letter "P" plus the model number was the body type, such as P05=Escort two-door hatchback. Symbol eight indicated the engine type: 2=98-cid four-cylinder, A=140-cid four-cylinder, B or T=200-cid six, 3=232-cid V-6, D=255-cid V-8, F=302-cid V-8 and G=351-cid V-8. Next was a check digit. Symbol 10 indicated the model year: C=1982. Symbol 11 was the assembly plant: A=Atlanta, Georgia; B=Oakville, Ontario, Canada; G=Chicago, Illinois; H=Lorain, Ohio; K=Kansas City, Missouri; R=San Jose, California; T=Edison, New

Jersey; W=Wayne, Michigan X=St. Thomas, Ontario, Canada and Z=St. Louis, Missouri. The final six digits made the sequence number, starting with 100001. A Vehicle Certification Label on the left front door lock face panel or door pillar showed the manufacturer, month and year of manufacture as well as the GVW, GAWR, certification statement, VIN, and codes for such items as body type, color, trim, axle, transmission, and special order information.

Escort (Four)

Model No.	Body Style No.	Body Type & Seating	Factory Price	Shipping Weight	Production Total
05	61D	2-dr. Hatchback-4P	$5,462	1,920 lbs.	Note 1
06	58D	4-dr. Hatchback-4P	$5,668	-----	Note 1
05	61D	2-dr. L Hatchback-4P	$6,046	1,926 lbs.	Note 1
06	58D	4-dr. L Hatchback-4P	$6,263	2,003 lbs.	Note 1
08	74D	4-dr. L Station Wagon-4P	$6,461	2,023 lbs.	Note 1
05	61D	2-dr. GL Hatchback-4P	$6,406	1,948 lbs.	Note 1
06	58D	4-dr. GL Hatchback-4P	$6,622	2,025 lbs.	Note 1
08	74D	4-dr. GL Station Wagon-4P	$6,841	2,043 lbs.	Note 1
05	61D	2-dr. GLX Hatchback-4P	$7,086	1,978 lbs.	Note 1
06	58D	4-dr. GLX Hatchback-4P	$7,302	2,064 lbs.	Note 1
08	74D	4-dr. GLX Station Wagon-4P	$7,475	2,079 lbs.	Note 1
05	61D	2-dr. GT Hackback-4P	$6,706	1,963 lbs.	Note 1

Note 1: Total Escort production came to 165,660 two-door hatchbacks, 130,473 four-door hatchbacks, and 88,999 station wagons. Trim level breakdown was not available. Bodies were sometimes called three-door and five-door.

EXP (Four)

01	67D	3-dr. Hackback-2P	$7,387	2,047 lbs.	98,256

Fairmont Futura (Four)

22	36R	2-dr. Sport Coupe-5P	$6,517	2,597 lbs.	17,851
20	66B	2-dr. Sedan-5P	$5,985	2,574 lbs.	8,222
21	54B	4-dr. Sedan-5P	$6,419	2,622 lbs.	101,666

Fairmont Futura (Six)

22	36R	2-dr. Sport Coupe-5P	$7,141	2,682 lbs.	17,851
20	66B	2-dr. Sedan-5P	$6,619	2,659 lbs.	8,222
21	54B	4-dr. Sedan-5P	$7,043	2,707 lbs.	101,666

Granada (Four)

26	66D	2-dr. L Sedan-5P	$7,126	2,673 lbs.	12,802
27	54D	4-dr. L Sedan-5P	$7,301	2,705 lbs.	62,339
28	74D	4-dr. L Station Wagon-5P	-----	-----	45,182
26	66D	2-dr. GL Sedan-5P	$7,543	2,699 lbs.	Note 2
27	54D	4-dr. GL Sedan-5P	$7,718	2,735 lbs.	Note 2
28	74D	4-dr. GL Station Wagon-5P	-----	-----	Note 2
26	66D	2-dr. GLX Sedan-5P	$7,666	2,717 lbs.	Note 2
27	54D	4-dr. GLX Sedan-5P	$7,840	2,753 lbs.	Note 2

Granada (Six and V-6)

26	66D	2-dr. L Sedan-5P	$7,750	2,791 lbs.	12,802
27	54D	4-dr. L Sedan-5P	$7,925	2,823 lbs.	62,339
28	74B	4-dr. L Station Wagon-5P	$7,983	2,965 lbs.	45,182
26	66D	2-dr. GL Sedan-5P	$8,167	2,817 lbs.	Note 2
27	54D	4-dr. GL Sedan-5P	$8,342	2,853 lbs.	Note 2
28	74D	4-dr. GL Station Wagon-5P	$8,399	2,995 lbs.	Note 2
26	66D	2-dr. GLX Sedan-5P	$8,290	2,835 lbs.	Note 2
27	54D	4-dr. GLX Sedan-5P	$8,464	2,871 lbs.	Note 2

Note 2: Granada GL and GLX production is included in basic Granada L totals above.

Prices shown are for four- and six-cylinder engines. The six-cylinder price includes $411 for the required automatic transmission. A 232-cid V-6 cost $70 more than the inline six.

LTD (V-8)

32	66H	2-dr. Sedan-6P	$8,455	3,496 lbs.	3,510
33	54H	4-dr. Sedan-6P	$8,574	3,526 lbs.	29,776
38	74H	4-dr. Station Wagon-6P	$9,073	3,741 lbs.	9,294

LTD S (V-8)

31	54D	4-dr. Sedan-6P	$8,312	3,522 lbs.	22,182
37	74D	4-dr. Station Wagon-6P	$8,783	3,725 lbs.	2,973

LTD Crown Victoria (V-8)

34	66K	2-dr. Sedan-6P	$9,149	3,523 lbs.	9,287
35	54K	4-dr. Sedan-6P	$9,294	3,567 lbs.	41,405
39	74K	4-dr. Country Squire-6P	$9,580	3,741 lbs.	9,626

Engines:

Escort and EXP Base Four: Overhead cam. Cast-iron block and aluminum head. Displacement: 97.6 cid (1.6 liters). B & S: 3.15 x 3.13 in. Compression ratio: 8.8:1. Brake hp: 70 at 4600 rpm. Torque: 89 lbs.-ft. at 3000 rpm. Five main bearings. Hydraulic valve lifters. Carburetor: Motorcraft 740 two-barrel. VIN Code: 2.
Note: An 80-hp high-output version of the 1.6-liter four arrived later in the model year.

Fairmont and Granada Base Four: Inline. Overhead cam. Cast-iron block and head. Displacement: 140-cid (2.3 liters). B & S: 3.78 x 3.13 in. Compression ratio: 9.0:1. Brake hp: 86 at 4600 rpm. Torque: 117 lbs.-ft. at 2600 rpm. Five main bearings. Hydraulic valve lifters. Carburetor: Holley 6500 or Motorcraft 5200 two barrel. VIN Code: A.

Granada Base Six (Optional Fairmont): Inline. Overhead valve. Cast-iron block and head. Displacement: 200 cid (3.3 liters). B & S: 3.68 x 3.13 in. Compression ratio: 8.6:1. Brake hp: 87 at 3800 rpm. Torque: 151 to 154 lbs.-ft. at 1400 rpm. Seven main bearings. Hydraulic valve lifters. Carburetor: Single-barrel Holley 1946. VIN Code: B or T.

Optional Granada V-6: 90-degree, overhead valve. Cast-iron block and aluminum head. Displacement: 232 cid (3.8 liters). B & S: 3.80 x 3.40 in. Compression ratio: 8.65:1. Brake hp: 112 at 4000 rpm. Torque: 175 lbs.-ft. at 2000 rpm. Four main bearings. Hydraulic valve lifters. Carburetor: Motorcraft 2150 two-barrel. VIN Code: 3.

LTD Base V-8: 90-degree, overhead valve. Cast-iron block and head. Displacement: 255 cid (4.2 liters). B & S: 3.68 x 3.00 in. Compression ratio: 8.2:1. Brake horsepower: 122 at 3400 rpm. Torque: 209 lbs.-ft. at 2400 rpm. Five main bearings. Hydraulic valve lifters. Carburetor: Two-barrel Motorcraft 2150 or 7200VV. VIN Code: D.
Note: The 255 cid V-8 was also offered in Fairmont police cars.

LTD Wagon Base V-8 (Optional LTD sedan): 90-degree, overhead valve. Cast-iron block and head. Displacement: 302 cid (5.0 liters). B & S: 4.00 x 3.00 in. Compression ratio: 8.4:1. Brake hp: 132 at 3400 rpm. Torque: 236 lbs.-ft. at 1800 rpm. Five main bearings. Hydraulic valve lifters. Carburetor: Motorcraft 2150A or 7200VV two barrel. VIN Code: F.

LTD High-Output Police V-8: 90-degree, overhead valve. Cast-iron block and head. Displacement: 351 cid (5.8 liters). B & S: 4.00 x 3.50 in. Compression ratio: 8.3:1. Brake hp: 165 at 3600 rpm. Torque: 285 lbs.-ft. at 2200 rpm. Five main bearings. Hydraulic valve lifters. Carburetor: VV two barrel. VIN Code: G.

Chassis:

Escort: Wheelbase: 94.2 in. Overall length: 163.5 in., hatchback and 165.0 in., wagon. Tires: P65/80-R13 steel-belted radial blackwalls.

EXP: Wheelbase: 94.2 in. Overall length: 170.3 in. Tires: P65/80-R13 steel-belted radial blackwalls.

Fairmont: Wheelbase: 105.5 in. Overall length: 195.5 in. and 197.4 in., Futura. Tires: P175/75-R14 steel-belted blackwalls.

Granada: Wheelbase: 105.5 in. Overall length: 196.5 in. Tires: P175/75-R14 steel-belted blackwalls.

LTD: Wheelbase: 114.3 in. Overall Length: 209.3 in., LTD; 215.0 in., LTD wagon and 211.0 in., LTD Crown Victoria. Tires: P205/75-R14 steel-belted white sidewall radials and P215/75-R14, LTD wagon.

Options:

Escort: Squire wagon package ($293). Instrument group ($87). Appearance protection group ($55). Light group ($30). Air conditioner ($611). Rear defroster, electric ($120). Remote liftgate release ($30). Tinted glass ($82); windshield only ($32). Digital clock ($57). Interval wipers ($48). Rear wiper/washer ($117). Dual remote sport mirrors ($66). AM radio ($61). AM/FM radio ($76) and base ($137). AM/FM stereo radio ($106); with cassette or eight-track player ($184) and base ($245). Dual rear speakers ($39). Front vent windows, pivoting ($60). Remote quarter windows ($109). Bumper guards front or rear ($26). Bumper rub strips ($41). Luggage rack ($93). Roof air deflector ($29). Lower body protection ($68). Console ($111). Low-back reclining bucket seats ($33 to $98). High-back reclining bucket seats ($65). Cloth/vinyl seat trim ($29) and vinyl only, no charge. Shearling/leather seat trim ($109 to $138). Deluxe seatbelts ($24). Wheel trim rings ($48). Aluminum wheels ($232 to $377). P165/80R13 WSW ($58). High Output 1.6-liter four ($57). Fuel-saver 1.6-liter four, no charge. Automatic transaxle ($411). Optional axle ratio (no charge). Power brakes ($93). Power steering ($190). Handling suspension ($139 to $187) and ($41), GLX. Heavy-duty battery ($22 to $26). Engine block heater ($17 to $18).

EXP: Appearance protection group ($48). Air conditioner ($611). Fingertip speed control ($151). Tinted glass ($82). Right remote mirror ($41). AM/FM radio ($76). AM/FM stereo radio ($106); with cassette or eight-track player ($184). Premium sound ($105). AM radio delete ($37 credit). Flip-up open air roof ($276). Luggage rack ($93). Lower body protection ($68). Low-back bucket seats ($33). Cloth/vinyl seat trim ($29) and vinyl, no charge.

1982 Fairmont Futura sedan

Leather seat trim ($138). Shearling/leather seat trim ($138). Cast aluminum wheels ($232). P165/80-R13 raised-white letter tires ($72). Automatic transaxle ($411). Optional axle ratio: No charge. Power steering ($190). TR performance suspension package: with TR sport aluminum wheels ($405) or with steel wheels ($204). Heavy-duty battery ($22 to $26). Heavy-duty alternator ($27). Engine block heater ($17 to $18).

Fairmont: Interior luxury group ($282). Instrument cluster ($100). Appearance protection group ($57 to $59). Light group ($49 to $51). Air conditioning ($676). Rear defroster, electric ($124). Fingertip speed control ($155). Illuminated entry ($68). Power windows ($165 to $235). Power door locks ($106 to $184). Remote deck lid release ($32). Power seat ($139). Tinted windshield ($32). Tilt steering ($95). Quartz clock ($32). Interval wipers ($48). Map light ($10). Trunk light ($7). Left remote mirror ($22). Dual bright remote mirrors ($65). AM/FM radio ($39 to $54). AM/FM stereo radio ($85) and with eight-track or cassette player ($172). Twin rear speakers ($39). Premium sound system ($105). AM radio delete ($61 credit). Flip-up open-air roof ($276). Full or half vinyl roof ($137 to $140). Pivoting front vent windows ($63). Rocker panel moldings ($33). Console ($191). Vinyl flight bench seat ($29). Cloth/vinyl seat trim ($29). Flight bench seat, no charge. Front floor mats ($13 to $22). Turbine wheel covers ($54). Styled steel wheels ($54 to $107). P175/75-R14 white sidewall tires ($66). Conventional spare ($51). 200-cd six ($213). Automatic transmission ($411). Floor shift lever ($49). Traction-Lok differential ($76). Power steering ($195). Handling suspension ($52). Heavy-duty battery ($22 to $26). Extended-range gas tank ($46). Engine block heater ($17 to $18).

Granada: Granada Squire option ($282). Cold weather group ($77). Appearance protection group ($57 to $59). Light group ($49 to $51). Air conditioning ($676). Rear defroster, electric ($124). Fingertip speed control ($155). Illuminated entry ($68). Power windows ($165 to $235). Power door locks ($106 to $184). Power split bench seat ($196). Tinted glass ($88). Tinted windshield ($32). Leather-wrapped steering wheel ($55). Tilt steering ($95). Quartz clock ($32). Interval wipers ($48). Liftgate wiper/washer: wagon ($99). Cornering lamps ($59). Map light, dual-beam ($15). Trunk light ($7). Lighted right visor vanity mirror ($46) and pair ($91). AM/FM radio ($39-$54). AM/FM stereo radio ($85); with eight-track or cassette player ($172). Premium sound system ($105). AM radio delete ($61 credit). Flip-up open air roof ($276). Full or half vinyl roof ($137 to $140). Two-way liftgate, wagon ($105). Protective body moldings ($49). Luggage rack ($115). Console ($191). Vinyl seat trim ($29). Flight bench seat (NC). Split bench seat ($230). Front floor mats ($13 to $22). Luxury wheel covers ($49) and GL and GLX, no charge. Wire wheel covers ($80 to $152). Cast-aluminum wheels ($348 to $396). P185/75-R14 blackwalls ($38). P185/75-R14 white walls ($104) and wagon, ($66). P185/75-R14 raised white letter tires ($121) and ($83), wagon. P190/65-R390 blackwalls on TRX aluminum wheels ($529 to $583). Conventional spare ($51). 200-cid six ($213). 232-cid V-6 ($283) exc. wagon ($70). Automatic transmission ($411). Floor shift lever ($49). Traction-Lok differential ($76). Optional axle ratio, no charge. Power steering ($195). Power steering ($195). Heavy-duty suspension ($24). Heavy-duty battery ($22 to $26). Extended-range gas tank ($46). Engine block heater ($17 to $18).

LTD: Interior luxury group ($727 to $807). Convenience group ($90 to $116). Power lock group ($106 to $201). Light group ($43). Protection group ($67). Air conditioning ($695); w/auto-temp control ($761). Rear defroster, electric ($124). Fingertip speed control ($155). Illuminated entry system ($68). Power windows ($165 to $240). Power driver's seat ($198) or driver and passenger ($395). Tinted glass ($102); windshield only ($32). Autolamp on/off delay ($73). Leather-wrapped steering wheel ($51). Tilt steering wheel ($95). Automatic parking brake release ($12). Tripminder computer ($215 to $293). Quartz clock ($32). Digital clock ($46 to $78). Seatbelt chime ($27). Interval wipers ($48). Cornering lamps ($55). Lighted right visor vanity mirrors ($46 to $91). AM/FM radio ($41 to $54). AM/FM stereo radio ($85) and with eight-track or cassette tape player ($172) and Crown Victoria ($87). AM/FM stereo search radio ($232) and Crown Victoria ($146). With eight-track or cassette ($233 to $318). Power antenna ($55). Dual

1982 Granada GL Squire station wagon

rear speakers ($41). Premium sound system ($133 to $167). Full or half vinyl roof ($165). Pivoting front vent windows ($63). Rocker panel moldings ($32). Luggage rack ($104). Dual-facing rear seats, wagon ($167). Leather seating ($412). Dual flight bench seat recliners ($65). Split bench seating ($139 to $204). All-vinyl seat trim ($28); Duraweave vinyl ($62). Front floor mats ($15-$21). Trunk trim ($49). Luxury wheel covers ($82). 15 in. wheel covers ($49). Wire wheel covers ($152). Cast aluminum wheels ($384). P215/75-R14 white sidewalls ($36). P225/75-R14 white sidewalls ($36 to $73). P205/75-15 white sidewalls ($11 to $47). Puncture-resistant tires ($112 to $148). Conventional spare ($51). 302-cid V-8 ($59). Traction-Lok differential ($80). Heavy-duty suspension ($26). Handling suspension ($49). Heavy-duty battery ($22 to $26): Heavy-duty alternator ($52). Engine block heater ($17 to $18). Medium duty trailer towing package ($200 to $251).

History:

The 1982 Fords were introduced on Sept. 24, 1981. The EXP was introduced earlier, on April 9, 1981. Total model year production was 1,035,063, including Mustangs. Calendar year sales by U.S. dealers was 925,490, including Mustangs). The Escort became the best selling domestic car during the model year, finding 321,952 buyers, up more than 13 percent from 1981. Total Ford Division sales for the model year declined by close to 20 percent. The Ford Motor Co. market share held at the 16.5 percent level of the prior year. *Car and Driver* readers had voted Escort "Most Significant New Domestic Car" for 1981, and it beat Chevrolet's Chevette. Granada gained sales but other models did not. Mustang dropped by almost one-third, with Fairmont and Thunderbird dropping by more than 40 percent. EXP did not sell as well as hoped for after its spring 1981 debut. Within a couple of months, incentives were being offered. Sales rose a bit later, partly due to a high-output EXP 1.6-liter engine that debuted in mid-year. Two new plants (San Jose, California, and St. Thomas, Ontario) were assigned to assemble the Escort/EXP subcompacts. Escort was also assembled at Wayne, Michigan, and Edison, New Jersey. As the 1983 model year began, Ford offered low-interest financing (a 10.75 percent rate) to customers who would buy one of the leftover 1982 models. In January 1982, the UAW agreed to an alternating-shift arrangement at certain plants. Workers would work 10 days, then take 10 days off. Ford's advertising theme at this time was: "Have you driven a Ford lately?"

1983 Ford

Escort — Four: America's best selling car in 1982 lost its base model, dropping to four series. That made Escort L the new base model with GL, GLX, and a sporty GT. The new GT was said to be more akin to the high-performance XR3, the image car of the European Escort line. Its 1.6-liter four had multi-port fuel injection. GT also carried five-speed manual shift with 3.73:1 final drive, a TR performance suspension with Michelin TRX tires, functional front and rear spoilers, molded wheel lip

1983 Escort GT three-door hatchback

flares and a tailpipe extension. GT standards also included fog lamps, unique tail lamp treatment, a reclining sport seat, a specially-tuned exhaust, special steering wheel, and console and full instrumentation. The high-output carbureted 97.6-cid (1.6-liter) four was introduced late in the 1982 model year as an option on any Escort except the GT. The 1983 Escort might have any of three suspension levels: base, handling, and TRX performance. All Escorts had all-season steel-belted radial tires and a larger, 13-gallon gas tank. A five-speed gearbox was available with either the high output or EFI engine. Escort's Fuel-Saver package came with economy 3.04:1 final drive and wide-ratio four-speed gearbox. The GLX no longer had front and rear bumper guards. The GL now had standard low-back reclining bucket seats. All except L had a new locking gas filler door with inside release. Optional knit vinyl seat trim replaced regular vinyl on GL and GLX.

EXP — Four: This year's EXP looked the same, but had a wider choice of engines and transaxles. The standard power train was a 97.6-cid (1.6-liter) four with two-barrel carburetor and fast-burn capability. It was hooked to a four-speed manual transaxle with overdrive fourth gear. The high-output 1.6-liter was available with either automatic or a new optional five-speed gearbox. That engine produced 80 hp, versus 70 for the base four. Newly optional this year was a multi-port fuel-injected version of the four. Acceleration to 60 mph was supposed to be cut by three seconds with the new power plant. Five-speed gearboxes came with 3.73:1 final drive ratio. Shift control for the optional automatic transaxle was revised to a straight-line pattern. The EXP had a larger, 13-gallon gas tank. Seats had a new sew style and more porous knit vinyl that would be cooler in summer. A remote-control locking fuel filler door was now standard. New options included a remote fuel door release, sport performance bucket seats, and P175/80-R13 tires. Michelin TRX tires and TR wheels were now available with base suspension.

LTD — Four/Six/V-6: The familiar LTD nameplate took on two forms for 1983: a new, smaller five-passenger model, and the old (larger) LTD Crown Victoria (listed below). This new LTD was built on the "L" body shell. Among its features were gas-pressurized shocks and struts, as introduced in 1982 on the new Continental. LTD came in a single well-equipped series: just a four-door sedan and wagon. Sedans carried the 140 cid (2.3-liter) four with four-speed as base power train; wagons, the 250 cid (3.3-liter) inline six with three-speed automatic. A 3.8-liter "Essex" V-6 became optional, with four-speed overdrive automatic. So was a propane-powered four, intended to attract fleet buyers. The base 2.3-liter engine had a new single-barrel carburetor and fast-burn technology. LTD had rack-and-pinion steering and a wheelbase that was 105.5 inches. It used the Fairmont platform and its aerodynamic design features included a 60-degree rear-window angle and an aero-styled decklid. Its drag coefficient was claimed to be just 0.38. Quad rectangular headlamps were deeply recessed. The sloping rear end held horizontal tri-color wraparound tail lamps with upper and lower segments. The instrument panel evolved from the 1982 Thunderbird. Mercury Marquis was LTD's corporate twin and each was between compact and mid-size.

Fairmont Futura — Four/ Six: For its final season, Fairmont continued with little change. The lineup had been simplified into a single series for the 1982 model year. The 4.2-liter V-8 was dropped completely, leaving only a base four and optional inline-six. The 140-cid (2.3-liter) switched to two-barrel carburetion and added fast-burn technology and a redesigned exhaust manifold. Two- and four-door sedans were offered, along with a two-door coupe. A low-budget "S" series was introduced. The Traction-Lok axle was now available with TR-type tires. One new option was a 100-amp alternator. Flight bench seating and a headlamp-on warning buzzer were added to the interior luxury group. Dual rear speakers were discontinued as an option. Radios got a new look and graphics. In 1984, the rear-drive Fairmont would be replaced by the new front-drive Tempo.

LTD Crown Victoria — V-8: Full-size Fords carried on with little change and a longer name. Initially, the model lineup consisted of two- and four-door sedans and a Country Squire station wagon in just one luxury level. Later came low budget "S" sedans and a plain-bodied wagon. The

1983 EXP HO Sport Coupe

base engine was the fuel-injected 302-cid (5.0-liter) V-8 with four-speed overdrive automatic. The Country Squire now had a standard AM/FM radio. All models had a new fuel cap tether. Quad rectangular headlamps stood above rectangular parking lamps, and the assembly continued around the fender tips to enclose signal/marker lenses. Sedans also had a new tail lamp design. The Country Squire had a revised wood tone appearance without the former planking lines. New options included a remote-control locking fuel door, locking wire wheel covers, and new-generation electronic radios. Two trailer-towing packages were offered.

I.D. Data:

Ford's 17-symbol Vehicle Identification Number (VIN) again was stamped on a metal tab fastened to the instrument panel and was visible through the windshield. The first three symbols, 1FA= manufacturer, make and vehicle type. The fourth symbol, B=the restraint system. Next came letter P followed by two digits that indicated the body type. P04=Escort L two-door hatchback. Symbol eight indicated the engine type: 2=98-cid four cylinder; 4=H.O. 98-cid four cylinder; 5=98-cid EFI four cylinder; A=140-cid four cylinder; D=140-cid turbo four cylinder; X=200-cid six; 3=232-cid V-6; F=302-cid V-8 and G=351-cid V-8. Next was a check digit. Symbol 10 indicated the model year: D=1983. Symbol 11 was the assembly plant: A=Atlanta, Georgia; B=Oakville, Ontario, Canada; G=Chicago, Illinois; H=Lorain, Ohio; K=Kansas City, Missouri; R=San Jose, California; T= Edison, New Jersey; W=Wayne, Michigan; X=St. Thomas, Ontario, Canada and Z=St. Louis, Missouri. The final six digits were the sequential number that began with 100001. A Vehicle Certification Label on the left front door lock face panel or door pillar showed the manufacturer, month and year of manufacture, GVW, GAWR, certification statement, VIN, and codes for such items as body type, color, trim, axle, transmission, and special order information.

Escort (Four)

Model No.	Body Style No.	Body Type & Seating	Factory Price	Shipping Weight	Production Total
04	61D	2-dr. L Hatchback-4P	$5,639	1,932 lbs.	Note 1
13	58D	4-dr. L Hatchback-4P	$5,846	1,998 lbs.	Note 1
09	74D	4-dr. L Station Wagon-4P	$6,052	2,026 lbs.	Note 1
05	61D	2-dr. GL Hatchback-4P	$6,384	1,959 lbs.	Note 1
14	58D	4-dr. GL Hatchback-4P	$6,601	2,025 lbs.	Note 1
10	74D	4-dr. GL Station Wagon-4P	$6,779	2,052 lbs.	Note 1
06	61D	2-dr. GLX Hatchback-4P	$6,771	1,993 lbs.	Note 1
15	58D	4-dr. GLX Hatchback-4P	$6,988	2,059 lbs.	Note 1
11	74D	4-dr. GLX Station Wagon-4P	$7,150	2,083 lbs.	Note 1
07	61D	2-dr. GT Hatchback-4P	$7,339	2,020 lbs.	Note 1

Note 1: Total Escort production was 151,386 two-door hatchbacks, 84,649 four-door hatchback sedans, and 79,335 station wagons. Trim level breakdown is not available. Bodies were sometimes called three-door and five-door.

EXP (Four)

01	67D	3-dr. Hatchback-2P	$6,426	2,068 lbs.	19, 697
01/301B	67D	3-dr. HO Coupe-2P	$7,004	------	Note 2
01/302B	67D	3-dr. HO Sport Coupe-2P	$7,794	------	Note 2
01/303B	67D	3-dr. Luxury Coupe-2P	$8,225	------	Note 2
01/304B	67D	3-dr. GT Coupe-2P	$8,739	------	Note 2

Note 2: Production of step-up models is included in basic EXP total above.

Fairmont Futura (Four)

37	36R	2-dr. Coupe-4P	$6,666	2,601 lbs.	7,882
35	66B	2-dr. Sedan-5P	$6,444	2,582 lbs.	3,664
36	54B	4-dr. Sedan-5P	$6,590	2,626 lbs.	69,287

Fairmont Futura (Six)

37	36R	2-dr. Coupe-4P	$7,344	2,720 lbs.	7,882
35	66B	2-dr. Sedan-5P	$7,122	2,701 lbs.	3,664
36	54B	4-dr. Sedan-5P	$7,268	2,745 lbs.	69,287

Fairmont "S" (Four)

35/41K	66B	2-dr. Sedan-5P	$5,985	2,569 lbs.	Note 3
36/41K	54B	4-dr. Sedan-5P	$6,125	2,613 lbs.	Note 3
35/41K	66B	2-dr. Sedan-5P	$6,663	2,688 lbs.	Note 3
36/41K	54B	4-dr. Sedan-5P	$6,803	2,732 lbs.	Note 3

Note 3: Fairmont "S" production is included in Futura sedan totals above.

LTD (Four)

39	54D	4-dr. Sedan-5P	$7,777	2,788 lbs.	111,813
39/60H	54D	4-dr. Brougham-5P	$8,165	2,802 lbs.	Note 4
40	74D	4-dr. Station Wagon-5P	------	------	43,945

1983 LTD four-door sedan

1983 LTD Country Squire station wagon

LTD (Six)

39	54D	4-dr. Sedan-5P	$8,455	2,874 lbs.	111,813
39/60H	54D	4-dr. Brougham-5P	$8,843	2,888 lbs.	Note 4
40	74D	4-dr. Station Wagon-5P	$8,577	2,975 lbs.	43,945

Note 4: Brougham production is included in basic sedan total.
Note: Prices shown are for four-and six-cylinder engines. The six-cylinder price includes $439 for the automatic transmission. A 232-cid V-6 cost $70 more than the inline-six.

LTD Crown Victoria (V-8)

42	66K	2-dr. Sedan-6P	$10,094	3,590 lbs.	11,414
43	54K	4-dr. Sedan-6P	$10,094	3,620 lbs.	81,859
44	74K	4-dr. Country Squire-6P	$10,253	3,773 lbs.	20,343
43/41K	54K	4-dr. S Sedan-6P	$ 9,130	------	Note 5
44/41K	74K	4-dr. S Station Wagon-6P	$ 9,444	------	Note 5
44/41E	74K	4-dr. Station Wagon-6P	$10,003	------	Note 5

Note 5: Production of S models and the basic station wagon was included in the sedan and Country Squire totals.

Engines:

Escort and EXP Base Four: Inline and overhead cam. Cast-iron block and aluminum head. Displacement: 98 cid (1.6 liters). B & S: 3.15 x 3.13 in. Compression ratio: 8.8:1. Brake hp: 70 at 4600 rpm. Torque: 88 lbs.-ft. at 2600 rpm. Five main bearings, Hydraulic valve lifters. Carburetor: Motorcraft 740 two-barrel. VIN Code: 2.

Escort and EXP Optional Four: High-output 1.6-liter. Hp: 80 at 5400 rpm. Torque: 88 lbs.-ft. at 3000 rpm. VIN Code: 4.

Escort GT Base Four (Optional in Escort and EXP: Fuel-injected 1.6-liter. Compression ratio: 9.5:1. Hp: 88 at 5400 rpm. Torque: 94 lbs.-ft. at 4200 rpm. VIN Code: 5.

Fairmont and LTD Base Four: Inline. Overhead cam. Cast-iron block and head. Displacement: 140 cid (2.3 liters). B & S: 3.78 x 3.13 in. Compression ratio: 9.0: 1. Brake hp: 90 at 4600 rpm. Torque: 122 lbs.-ft. at 2600 rpm. Five main bearings. Hydraulic valve lifters. Carburetor: Carter YFA single-barrel. VIN Code: A.

Note: A 140-cid (2.3-liter) propane-powered four was also available for LTD.

Fairmont and LTD Optional Six: Inline. Overhead valve. Cast-iron block and head. Displacement: 200 cid (3.3 liters). B & S: 3.68 x 3.13 in. Compression ratio: 8.6:1. Brake hp: 92 at 3800 rpm. Torque: 156 lbs.-ft. at 1400 rpm. Seven main bearings. Hydraulic valve lifters. Carburetor: Holley 1946 single-barrel. VIN Code: X.

LTD Optional V-6: 90-degree, overhead valve. Cast-iron block and aluminum head. Displacement: 232 cid (3.8 liters). B & S: 3.80 x 3.40 in. Compression ratio: 8.65:1. Brake hp: 110 at 3800 rpm. Torque: 175 lbs.-ft. at 2200 rpm. Four main bearings. Hydraulic valve lifters. Carburetor: Motorcraft 2150 or 7200VV two-barrel. VIN Code: 3.

Crown Victoria Base V-8 (Optional LTD): 90-degree, overhead valve. Cast-iron block and head. Displacement: 302 cid (5.0 liters). B & S: 4.00 x 3.00 in. Compression ratio: 8.4:1. Brake hp: 130 at 3200 rpm. Torque: 240 lbs.-ft. at 2000 rpm. Five main bearings. Hydraulic valve lifters. Electronic fuel injection. VIN Code: F.

Note: Crown Victoria also announced a high-output V-8 with 145-hp at 3600 rpm and 245 lbs.-ft. at 2200 rpm.

Crown Victoria High-Output Police V-8: 90-degree, overhead valve. Cast-iron block and head. Displacement: 351 cid (5.8 liters). B & S: 4.00 x 3.50 in. Compression ratio: 8.3:1. Brake hp: 165 at 3600 rpm. Torque: 290 lbs.-ft. at 2200 rpm. Five main bearings. Hydraulic valve lifters. Carburetor: VV two-barrel. VIN Code: G.

Chassis:

Escort: Wheelbase: 94.2 in. Overall length: Escort, 163.9 in. and wagon, 165.0 in. Tires: P165/80-R13 steel-belted blackwalls and P165/70-R365 Michelin TRX on Escort GT.

EXP: Wheelbase: 94.2 in. Overall length: 170.3 in. Tires: P165/80-R13 steel-belted blackwalls and EXP luxury coupe, P165/70-R365 Michelin TRX.

Fairmont: Wheelbase: 105.5 in. Overall length: 195.5 in. and 197.4, Futura coupe. Fairmont: P175/75-R14 steel-belted blackwalls.

LTD: Wheelbase: 105.5 in. Overall length: 196.5 in. Tires: P185/75-R14 steel-belted blackwalls.

Crown Victoria: Wheelbase: 114.3 in. Overall length: 211.1 in. and 215.0 in., station wagon. Tires: P215/75-R14 steel-belted whitewalls.

Options:

Escort: Squire wagon package ($350). Instrument group ($87). Appearance protection group ($39). Light group ($43). Air conditioner ($624). Rear defroster, electric ($124). Fingertip speed control ($170). Tinted glass ($90); windshield only ($40). Digital clock ($57). Interval wipers ($49). Rear wiper/washer ($117). Dual remote sport mirrors ($67). AM radio: L ($61). AM/FM radio ($82) and ($143) on L. AM/FM stereo radio ($109) and ($170) on base. With cassette or eight-track player ($199) and ($260) on L. Premium sound ($117). Flip-up open-air roof ($217 to $310). Pivoting front vent windows ($60). Remote quarter windows ($109). Luggage rack ($93). Lower body protection ($68). Console ($111). Fold-down center armrest ($55). Low-back reclining bucket seats: L ($98). High-back reclining bucket seats: L ($65). Vinyl low-back reclining bucket seats: GL/GLX ($24). Vinyl high-back bucket seats: L ($24). Wheel trim rings ($54). Cast-aluminum wheels ($226 to $383). TR sport aluminum wheels ($568) and ($411) on GLX or ($201), GT. TR styled steel wheels ($210 to $367). H.O. 1.6-liter four ($70 to $73). Close-ratio four-speed trans, no charge. Five-speed manual transmission ($76). Automatic transaxle ($439) and GT ($363). Power brakes ($95). Power steering ($210). Handling suspension ($199) and GLX ($41). Performance suspension: Escort ($41) and with Michelin TRX tires on GT ($41). Heavy duty battery ($26).

EXP: Air conditioner ($624). Rear defroster: base ($124). Tinted glass: H.O. ($90). AM/FM radio ($82). AM/FM stereo radio ($109) and ($199) with cassette or eight-track player or ($90) on luxury coupe. Premium sound ($117). AM radio delete ($37 credit). AM/FM stereo delete: luxury coupe ($145 credit). AM/FM stereo/cassette delete: GT ($235 credit). Flip-up open air roof ($310). Lower body protection ($68). Low-back sport cloth or knit vinyl bucket seats, no charge. Low-back sport performance seats ($173). Leather/vinyl seat trim ($144). Shearling low-back bucket seats ($227). TR sport aluminum wheels on GT, no charge. H.O. 1.6-liter four on GT ($70). Automatic transaxle, base EXP ($439) and ($363), other EXP. Power steering ($210). TR performance suspension with Michelin TRX tires ($41) EXP luxury. Heavy-duty battery ($26). Heavy-duty alternator ($27). Engine block heater ($17 to $18).

Fairmont: Interior luxury group ($294). Instrument cluster ($100). Appearance protection group ($32 to $60). Light group ($55). Air conditioner ($724). Rear defroster, electric ($135). Fingertip speed control ($170). Illuminated entry ($82). Power windows ($180 to $255). Power door locks ($120 to $170). Remote deck lid release ($40). Four-way power seat ($139). Tinted glass ($105). Tinted windshield ($38). Tilt steering ($105). Quartz clock ($35). Interval wipers ($49). Dual bright remote mirrors on S ($68). Lighted visor vanity mirrors, pair ($100). AM radio: S ($61). AM/FM radio ($59 to $120). AM/FM stereo radio ($109 to $170) and ($199 to $260) with eight-track or cassette player. Premium sound system ($117). AM radio delete ($61 credit). Flip-up open air roof ($310). Full or half vinyl roof ($152). Pivoting front vent windows ($63). Console ($191). Cloth/vinyl seat trim ($35). Front floor mats ($15 to $24). Wire wheel covers ($87 to $152). Turbine wheel covers for S ($66). Styled steel wheels ($60 to $126). 200-cid six ($239). Select-Shift automatic transmission ($439). Floor shift lever ($49). Traction-Lok differential ($95). Heavy duty suspension ($24). Heavy-duty battery ($26). Extended-range gas tank ($46).

1983 LTD Brougham sedan

LTD: Squire option ($282). Brougham decor option: wagon ($363). Power lock group ($170 to $210). Cold weather group ($77). Appearance protection group ($60). Light group ($38). Air conditioner ($724) with auto-temp ($802). Electric rear defroster ($135). Fingertip speed control ($170). Illuminated entry ($76). Autolamp on-off delay ($73). Power windows ($255). Six-way power driver's seat ($207) or dual ($415). Tinted glass ($105). Leather-wrapped steering wheel ($59). Tilt steering ($105). Electronic instrument cluster ($289 to $367). Tripminder computer ($215 to $293). Digital clock ($78). Diagnostic warning lights ($59). Interval wipers ($49). Liftgate wiper/washer, wagon ($99). Cornering lamps ($60). Map light: fleet ($15). AM/FM radio ($59). AM/FM stereo radio ($109) or ($199) with eight-track or cassette player. Electronic-tuning AM/FM stereo radio ($252) and ($396) with cassette. Premium sound system ($117 to $151). AM radio delete ($61 credit). Flip-up open air roof ($310). Full vinyl roof ($152). Two-way liftgate, wagon ($105). Luggage rack, wagon ($126). Console ($100). Individual seats with console ($61). Leather seat trim ($415). Front floor mats ($23). Luxury wheel covers ($55). Wire wheel covers ($159 to $198). Styled wheels ($178). Cast aluminum wheels ($402). Turbo 140-cid four ($896). 200-cid six ($239). 232-cid V-6 ($309) and ($70) on wagon. Select-Shift automatic transmission ($439). Overdrive automatic transmission ($615) and ($176) on wagon. Floor shift lever ($49). Traction-Lok differential ($95). Heavy-duty battery ($26). Extended-range gas tank ($46). Engine block heater ($17 to $18).

Crown Victoria: Interior luxury group ($830 to $911). Convenience group ($95 to $116). Power lock group ($123 to $220). Light group ($48). Protection group ($68). Air conditioning ($724) and ($802) with auto-temp control. Electric rear defroster ($135). Fingertip speed control ($170). Illuminated entry system ($76). Power windows ($180 to $255). Power driver's seat ($210) or driver and passenger ($420). Remote fuel door lock ($24). Tinted glass ($105). Autolamp on/off delay ($73). Leather-wrapped steering wheel ($59). Tilt steering wheel ($105). Tripminder computer ($215 to $261). Quartz clock: S ($35). Digital clock ($61 to $96). Interval wipers ($49). Cornering lamps ($60). Remote right mirror ($43). Lighted visor vanity mirrors ($100). AM/FM stereo radio: S ($106) and ($112 to $218) with eight-track or cassette tape. AM/FM stereo search radio ($166 to $272) or ($310 to $416) with eight-track or cassette. Power antenna ($60). Premium sound system ($145 to $179). AM/FM delete ($152 credit). Luggage rack, Country Squire ($110). Dual-facing rear seats, Country Squire ($167). Leather seat trim ($418). Split bench seating ($139). All-vinyl seat trim ($34); Duraweave vinyl on wagon ($96). Carpeted floor mats ($33). Trunk trim ($49). Luxury wheel covers ($88). Wire wheel covers ($159 to $198). Cast-aluminum wheels ($390). Conventional spare ($63). Traction-Lok differential ($95). Heavy-duty suspension ($26). Handling suspension ($49). Heavy-duty battery ($26). Engine block heater ($17 to $18). Medium-duty trailer towing package ($200 to $251). Heavy-duty trailer towing package ($251 to $302).

History:

The 1983 Fords were introduced on Oct. 14, 1982. The Thunderbird was introduced later, on Feb. 17, 1983. Model year production was 928,146, including Mustangs. Calendar year sales by U.S. dealers was 1,060,314, including Mustangs. Once again, Escort was the best-selling car in the country. That helped Ford's model year sales to rise 12 percent over 1982. Next in line in terms of sales were the new smaller LTD and full-size LTD Crown Victoria. Ford still ranked number two in domestic auto sales with Oldsmobile a potent contender for that spot. Ford was judged second in the industry in quality, behind the Lincoln-Mercury division but ahead of rival GM and Chrysler. Low 10.75 percent financing was extended in December 1982 to include 1983 and leftover 1982 models. Continuing demand kept the big rear-drive Ford alive, as did improved fuel supplies. Tempo was introduced in May 1983 as a new 1984 model.

1984 Ford

Escort — Four: Diesel power was news under Ford subcompact hoods, as the company's first passenger-car diesel engine was available on both Escort and Tempo. The Mazda 2.0-liter diesel four came with a five-speed manual (overdrive) transaxle. A little later, a turbocharged, fuel-injected 97.6-cid (1.6-liter) four was ready for the GT model. Turbos hooked up to a five-speed manual gearbox, a package that included firmer suspension and special wheels and tires. Carbureted, high-output and fuel injected versions of the 1.6-liter engines were available. In addition to the carryover L, GL and sporty GT, the LX replaced the GLX. It included the fuel-injected four, TR suspension, an overhead console with digital clock and a five-speed transaxle. Escort GT now sported black polycarbonate bumpers. Inside was a new instrument panel with integral side-window demisters, and a new steering wheel. A new fold-down rear seat was standard on GL, GT and LX. Power ventilation replaced the "ram air" system.

EXP — Four: Turbocharged power brought EXP a strong performance boost for 1984. The new turbo model had a unique front air dam and rear deck lid spoiler. The turbo version included a tighter suspension with Koni shock absorbers, Michelin P185/65-R365 TRX tires on new cast aluminum wheels, and a five-speed manual transaxle. Base power train was upgraded to the high-output 1.6-liter engine, also mated to five-speed manual. EXP had a completely revised exterior. The silhouette was altered dramatically by adding a "bubble back" liftgate. EXP also had new blackout tail lamps, color-keyed bumper rub strips and mirrors, and a revised front air dam. Both the liftgate and tail lamps came from Mercury's former LN7, discontinued for 1984. Inside was a standard overhead console with digital clock and a new instrument panel with performance cluster and tachometer. Styled steel wheels were a new design. New options included a tilt steering wheel, electronic radios with graphic equalizer, clear coat paint, and illuminated visor vanity mirror. Both EXP and Escort had a new clutch/starter interlock system.

Tempo — Four: Ford's replacement for the departed rear-drive Fairmont arrived as an early 1984 model, wearing Ford's "rakish contemporary styling." Aircraft-type door configurations were shared with the 1983 Thunderbird. Door tops extended into the roof to create a wraparound effect. Two- and four-door sedans were offered on a 99.9-inch wheelbase. The four-door sedan had a six-window design and rounded window corners. Tempo came in L, GL and GLX trim. A new 140-cid (2.3-liter) HSC (high swirl combustion) four-cylinder engine was developed specially for Tempo. Displacement was identical to the familiar 2.3-liter four used in the Fairmont and LTD, but the bore and stroke dimensions differed in this OHV design. This was the first production fast-burn engine, controlled by an EEC-IV onboard computer, also used in the Thunderbird Turbo Coupe. Tempo could have either a close-ratio five-speed manual or automatic transaxle. A Fuel Saver four-speed was standard. Tempo had fully independent quadra-link rear suspension using MacPherson struts, a MacPherson strut front suspension and stabilizer bar. Power front disc brakes were standard. Inside, Tempo had low-back bucket seats with cloth trim; color-keyed molded door trim panels with integral storage bins; a storage bin above the radio; color-keyed vinyl sun visors; a carpeted package tray; and a consolette. An optional TR handling package included Michelin

1984 EXP Turbo coupe

1984 Escort GL five-door hatchback

1984 Escort LX station wagon

1984 LTD Brougham sedan

P185/65-R365 TRX tires on new-design cast aluminum wheels, and a special handling suspension. Mercury's Topaz was nearly identical except for trim and the list of options available.

LTD — Four/V-6/V-8: LTD received a few fresh touches that included argent accents on body moldings and optional bumper rub strips plus a revised instrument panel appliqué. A new A-frame steering wheel with center horn button replaced the four-spoke design. Headlamp doors now had dark argent paint, instead of light argent. Parking and turn lamp lenses switched from clear white to amber, and bulbs from amber to clear. The most noteworthy new body feature was the unique formal roof treatment added to the Brougham four-door sedan. It had a distinctive solid rear pillar and "Frenched" back window treatment, and included a full Cambria cloth roof. The inline six-cylinder engine finally disappeared. Manual transmission with the base 140-cid (2.3-liter) four was dropped. A 302-cid (5.0-liter) EFI high-output V-8 was available only on police sedans. That made the fuel-injected 232-cid (3.8-liter) V-6 the only regular option. It was standard on wagons. All engines added EECIV controls. Propane power was available but found few takers. Base and Brougham sedans were offered, along with a station wagon. Power steering and three-speed automatic were standard, with four-speed automatic available in V-6 models. New LTD options included a flight bench seat, the single most requested feature.

LTD Crown Victoria — V-8: The Crown Victoria's new grille featured a light argent second surface, and a new optional Brougham roof for the formal looking, four-door sedan. It included a padded full vinyl top, an upright rear window with "Frenched" treatment, and electro-luminescent coach lamps on the center pillar. Interiors had a new vinyl grain pattern. The full-size Ford was a carryover, available again as a two- or four-door sedan, plus pair of wagons. The Crown Victoria station wagon was just a Country Squire without simulated wood trim. The wide grille had a 12 x 4 hole crosshatch pattern (plus a 2 x 2 pattern within each segment). Amber signal/marker lenses consisted of a large lens above a small one. "LTD Crown Victoria" lettering went ahead of the front door, just above the crease line. The standard engine was the 302-cid (5.0-liter) fuel-injected V-8. The high-performance 351-cid (5.8-liter) V-8 with variable-venturi carburetor was available only with police package.

I.D. Data:

Ford's 17-symbol Vehicle Identification Number (VIN) was stamped on a metal tab fastened on the instrument panel and was visible through the windshield. The first three symbols, 1FA=manufacturer, make and vehicle type. The fourth symbol B=the restraint system. Next came the letter P followed by two digits that indicated the body type. P04=Escort L two-door hatchback. Symbol eight indicated the engine type: 2=98-cid carbureted four cylinder; 4=High Output four; 5=fuel-injected four; 8=98-cid turbo FI four; H=121-cid diesel; A=140-cid four; R or J=HSC four; 6=140-cid propane-fueled four; W=140-cid EFI four; 3=232-cid V-6; F=302-cid V8 and G=351-cid V-8l. Next was a check digit. Symbol 10 indicated the model year: E=1984. Symbol 11 was the assembly plant: A=Atlanta, Georgia; B=Oakville, Ontario, Canada; G=Chicago, Illinois; H=Lorain, Ohio; K=Kansas City, Missouri; T=Edison, New Jersey; W=Wayne, Michigan; X=St. Thomas, Ontario, Canada and Z=St. Louis, Missouri. The final six digits were the sequential number, starting with 100001. A Vehicle Certification Label on the left front door lock face panel or door pillar showed the manufacturer, month and

year of manufacture, GVW, GAWR, certification statement, VIN, and code for body type and color, trim, axle ratio, transmission, and special order data.

Escort (Four)

Model No.	Body Style No.	Body Type & Seating	Factory Price	Shipping Weight	Production Total
04	61D	2-dr. Hatchback-4P	$5,629	1,981 lbs.	Note 1
13	58D	4-dr. Hatchback-4P	$5,835	2,024 lbs.	Note 1
04	61D	2-dr. L Hatchback-4P	$5,885	1,981 lbs.	Note 1
13	58D	4-dr. L Hatchback-4P	$6,099	2,034 lbs.	Note 1
09	74D	4-dr. L Station Wagon-4P	$6,313	2,066 lbs.	Note 1
05	61D	2-dr. GL Hatchback-4P	$6,382	2,033 lbs.	Note 1
14	58D	4-dr. GL Hatchback-4P	$6,596	2,086 lbs.	Note 1
10	74D	4-dr. GL Station Wagon-4P	$6,773	2,115 lbs.	Note 1
15	58D	4-dr. LX Hatchback-4P	$7,848	2,137 lbs.	Note 1
11	74D	4-dr. LX Station Wagon-4P	$7,939	2,037 lbs.	Note 1

Escort GT (Four)

07	61D	2-dr. Hatchback-4P	$7,593	2,103 lbs.	Note 1
07	61D	2-dr. Turbo Hatchback-4P	------	2,239 lbs.	Note 1

Note 1: Total Escort production was 184,323 two-door hatchbacks, 99,444 four-door hatchbacks, and 88,756 station wagons. Trim level breakdown not available. Bodies are referred to as three-door and five-door.

Diesel Note: Diesel-powered Escorts came in L and GL trim, priced $558 higher than gasoline models.

EXP (Four)

01/A80	67D	3-dr. Hatchback-2P	$6,653	2,117 lbs.	23,016
01/A81	67D	3-dr. Luxury Coupe-2P	$7,539	2,117 lbs.	Note 2
01/A82	67D	3-dr. Turbo Coupe-2P	$9,942	2,158 lbs.	Note 2

Note 2: Production of luxury and turbo coupe models is included in basic EXP total above.

Tempo (Four)

18	66D	2-dr. L Sedan-5P	$6,936	2,249 lbs.	Note 3
21	54D	4-dr. L Sedan-5P	$6,936	2,308 lbs.	Note 3
19	66D	2-dr. GL Sedan-5P	$7,159	2,276 lbs.	Note 3
22	54D	4-dr. GL Sedan-5P	$7,159	2,339 lbs.	Note 3
20	66D	2-dr. GLX Sedan-5P	$7,621	2,302 lbs.	Note 3
23	54D	4-dr. GLX Sedan-5P	$7,621	2,362 lbs.	Note 3

Note 3: Total Tempo production came to 107,065 two-doors and 295,149 four-doors.

Diesel note: Diesel-powered Tempos cost $558 more than equivalent gasoline models.

LTD (Four)

39	54D	4-dr. Sedan-5P	$8,605	2,804 lbs.	154,173
39/60H	54D	4-dr. Brougham-5P	$9,980	2,812 lbs.	Note 4
40	74D	4-dr. Station Wagon-5P	------	------	59,569

LTD (V-6)

39	54D	4-dr. Sedan-5P	$9,014	2,881 lbs.	154,173
39/60H	54D	4-dr. Brougham-5P	$10,389	2,889 lbs.	Note 4
40	74D	4-dr. Station Wagon-5P	$9,102	2,990 lbs.	59,569

Note 4: Brougham production is included in basic sedan total.

LTD Crown Victoria (V-8)

42	66K	2-dr. Sedan-6P	$10,954	3,546 lbs.	12,522
43	54K	4-dr. Sedan-6P	$10,954	3,587 lbs.	130,164
44	74K	4-dr. Country Squire-6P	$11,111	3,793 lbs.	30,803
43/41	54K	4-dr. S Sedan-6P	$ 9,826	------	Note 5
44/41K	74K	4-dr. S Station Wagon-6P	$10,136	------	Note 5
44/41E	74K	4-dr. Station Wagon-6P	$10,861	------	Note 5

Note 5: Production of S models and the station wagon was included in the basic sedan and Country Squire totals.

Engines:

Escort Base Four: Inline. Overhead cam. Cast-iron block and aluminum head. Displacement: 97.6 cid (1.6 liters). B & S: 3.15 x 3.13 in. Compression ratio: 9.0:1. Brake hp: 70 at 4600 rpm. Torque: 88 lbs.-ft. at 2600 rpm. Five main bearings. Hydraulic valve lifters. Carburetor: Motorcraft 740 two-barrel. VIN Code: 2.

EXP Base Four (Optional Escort): High-output 1.6-liter. Hp: 80 at 5400 rpm. Torque: 88 lbs.-ft. at 3000 rpm. VIN Code: 4.

Escort LX and GT Base Four (Optional in Escort and EXP): Fuel-injected version of 1.6-liter. Hp: 84 at 5200 rpm. Torque: 90 lbs.-ft. at 2800 rpm. VIN Code: 5.

1984 LTD sedan

1984 LTD Crown Victoria sedan

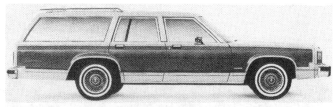

1984 LTD Country Squire station wagon

1984 Tempo L sedan (with diesel engine)

1984 Tempo GLX coupe

Escort and EXP Turbo Four: 1.6-liter with fuel injection and turbocharger. Compression ratio: 8.0:1. Hp: 120 at 200 rpm. Torque: 120 lbs.-ft. at 3400 rpm. VIN Code: 8.

Escort and Tempo Diesel Four: Inline. Overhead cam. Cast-iron block and aluminum head. Displacement: 121 cid (2.0 liters). B & S: 3.39 x 3.39 in. Compression ratio: 22.5:1. Brake hp: 52 at 4000 rpm. Torque: 82 lbs.-ft. at 2400 rpm. Five main bearings. Solid valve lifters. Fuel injection. VIN Code: H.

Tempo Base Four: Inline. Overhead valve. Cast-iron block and head. Displacement: 140 cid (2.3 liters). B & S: 3.70 x 3.30 in. Compression ratio: 9.0:1. Brake hp: 84 at 4400 rpm. Torque: 118 lbs.-ft. at 2600 rpm. Five main bearings. Hydraulic valve lifters. Carburetor: Holley 6149 single-barrel. High Swirl Combustion (HSC) design. VIN Code: R (U.S.) or J (Mexico).

LTD Base Four: Inline. Overhead cam. Cast-iron block and head. Displacement: 140 cid (2.3 liters). B & S: 3.78 x 3.13 in. Compression ratio: 9.0:1. Brake hp: 88 at 4000 rpm. Torque: 122 lbs.-ft. at 2400 rpm. Five main bearings. Hydraulic valve lifters. Carburetor: Carter YFA single-barrel. VIN Code: A.

LTD Propane Four: 140-cid four for propane fuel. Compression ratio: 10.0:1. Brake hp: 88 at 4000 rpm. Torque: 122 lbs.-ft. at 2400 rpm. VIN Code: 6.

LTD Optional V-6: 90-degree, overhead valve. Cast-iron block and aluminum head. Displacement: 232 cid (3.8 liters). B & S: 3.80 x 3.40 in. Compression ratio: 8.7:1. Brake hp: 120 at 3600 rpm. Torque: 205 lbs.-ft. at 1600 rpm. Four main bearings. Hydraulic valve lifters. Throttle-body fuel injection. VIN Code: 3.

Crown Victoria Base V-8: 90-degree, overhead valve. Cast-iron block and head. Displacement: 302 cid (5.0 liters). B & S: 4.00 x 3.00 in. Compression ratio: 8.4:1. Brake hp: 140 at 3200 rpm. Torque: 250 lbs.-ft. at 1600 rpm. Five main bearings. Hydraulic valve lifters. Electronic fuel injection (TBI). VIN Code: F.

Note: Crown Victoria wagons had a high-output 302-cid, 155-hp V-8 with 265 lbs.-ft. of torque at 2000 rpm.

Crown Victoria High-Output Police V-8: 90-degree, overhead valve. Cast-iron block and head. Displacement: 351 cid (5.8 liters). B & S: 4.00 x 3.50 in. Compression ratio: 8.3:1. Brake hp: 180 at 3600 rpm. Torque: 285 lbs.-ft. at 2400 rpm. Five main bearings. Hydraulic valve lifters. Carburetor: VV two-barrel. VIN Code: G.

Chassis:

Escort Wheelbase: 94.2 in. Overall length: 163.9 in. and 165.0 in., station wagon. Tires: P165/80-R13 steel-belted blackwalls, P165/70-R15 Michelin TRX, Escort GT and P185/65-R15 Michelin TRX, Escort Turbo GT.

EXP Wheelbase: 94.2 in. Overall length: 170.3 in. Tires: P165/80-R13 steel-belted blackwalls.

Tempo Wheelbase: 99.9 in. Overall length: 176.2 in. Tires: P175/80-R13 steel-belted blackwalls.

LTD Wheelbase: 105.9 in. Overall length: 196.5 in. Tires: P185/75-R14 steel-belted blackwalls.

Crown Victoria Wheelbase: 114.3 in. Overall length: 211.1 in. and 215.0 in., station wagon. Tires: P215/75-R14 steel-belted whitewalls.

Options:

Escort: Squire wagon package ($373). Instrument group ($87). Power door lock group ($124 to $176). Light group ($67). Air conditioner ($643). Electric rear defroster ($130). Fingertip speed control ($176). Tinted glass ($95). Tilt steering ($104). Overhead console w/digital clock ($82). Interval wipers ($50). Rear wiper/washer ($120) and LX ($46). Dual remote sport mirrors ($68). AM radio: L ($39). AM/FM radio ($82) and L ($121). AM/FM stereo radio ($109) and L ($148). With cassette player ($204) and L ($243). Electronic-tuning AM/FM stereo ($252 to $291) and w/cassette ($396 to $435). Graphic equalizer ($176). Premium sound ($117). Flip-up open-air roof ($315). Luggage rack ($100). Lower body protection ($68). Console ($111). Vinyl seat trim ($24). Color-keyed front mats ($22). Wheel trim rings ($54). Cast aluminum wheels ($279). TR aluminum wheels ($201). Styled steel wheels ($104 credit). P165/80-R13 steel-belted whitewalls ($59). Fuel-saver 1.6-liter four, no charge. Five-speed manual transmission ($76). Automatic transaxle ($439) and LX and GT ($363). Power brakes ($95). Power steering ($215). Handling suspension: L ($199) and GL ($95). Heavy duty battery ($27).

EXP: Air conditioner ($643). Fingertip speed control ($176). Tinted glass ($95). Tilt steering ($104). Lighted visor vanity mirror ($50). AM/FM stereo radio ($109). With cassette player ($204) and ($95), luxury coupe. Electronic-tuning AM/FM stereo ($252). Luxury coupe ($144) and Turbo ($49). With cassette ($396), luxury coupe ($288) and Turbo ($193). Graphic equalizer ($176). Premium sound ($117). AM radio delete ($39 credit). AM/FM stereo delete: luxury coupe ($148 credit). AM/FM stereo/cassette delete: Turbo ($243 credit). Flip-up open air roof ($315). Lower body protection ($68). Low-back knit vinyl bucket seats, no charge. Sport performance seats ($173). Front floor mats ($22). Wheels: TR aluminum wheels ($369). TR styled steel wheels ($168). Cast aluminum wheels ($238). P165/80-R13 raised white letter tires ($90). P165/70-R365 TRX tires, no charge. Power steering ($215). Heavy duty battery ($27). Heavy duty alternator ($27). Engine block heater ($18).

Tempo: TR performance package with aluminum wheels ($366 to $424). Sport appearance group: GL 2-dr. ($299). Power lock group ($202 to $254). Appearance protection group ($71). Light/convenience group ($50 to $85). Air conditioning ($743). Electric rear defroster, electric ($140). Fingertip speed control ($176). Illuminated entry ($82). Anti-theft system ($159). Power windows ($272). Power deck lid release ($41). Six-way power seat ($224). Tinted glass ($110). Tilt steering ($110). Sport instrument cluster ($71 to $87). Digital clock ($61). Interval wipers ($50). Dual sport remote mirrors ($93). Lighted visor vanity mirrors, pair ($100-$112). AM/FM radio ($59). AM/FM stereo radio ($109) and ($204) with cassette player ($204). Electronic-tuning AM/FM stereo ($252) and with cassette ($396). Premium sound system ($117). AM radio delete ($39 credit). Flip-up open air roof ($315). Console ($111). Fold-down front armrest ($55). Vinyl seat trim ($35). Carpeted front floor mats ($13). Trunk

1984 Tempo GLX sedan

trim ($30). Luxury wheel covers ($59). Styled steel wheels ($59) and no charge, GL and GLX. P175/80-R13 whitewall tires ($72). Five-speed manual transmission ($76). Automatic transaxle ($439). Power steering ($223). Heavy duty suspension, no charge. Soft ride suspension package, no charge. Heavy duty battery ($27). Engine block heater ($18).

LTD: Squire option ($282). Brougham décor, wagon ($363). Interior luxury group ($388). Power lock group ($213 to $254). Cold weather group ($77). Light group ($38). Police package ($859 to $1,387). Taxi pkg. ($860). Fleet package ($210). Air conditioner ($743) and with auto-temp ($809). Electric rear defroster ($140). Fingertip speed control ($176). Illuminated entry ($82). Autolamp on-off delay ($73). Power windows ($272). Six-way power driver's seat ($224) and dual seats ($449). Tinted glass ($110). Leather-wrapped steering wheel ($59). Tilt steering ($110). Electronic instrument cluster ($289 to $367). Tripminder computer ($215 to $293). Interval wipers ($50). Liftgate wiper and washer for wagon ($99). AM/FM stereo radio ($109) and ($204) with cassette player. Electronic-tuning AM/FM stereo radio with cassette ($396). Premium sound system ($151). Full vinyl roof ($152). Luggage rack, wagon ($126). Vinyl seat trim ($35). Split or flight bench seat, no charge. Individual seats with console ($61). Leather seat trim ($415). Luxury wheel covers ($55). Wire wheel covers ($165) and locking ($204). Styled wheels ($178). Styled steel wheels with trim rings ($54). P185/75-R14 whitewalls ($72). P195/75-R14 blackwalls ($38) or whitewalls ($116). Puncture-sealant tires ($240). Conventional spare ($63). Propane 140-cid four ($896). 232-cid V-6 ($409). Overdrive automatic transmission ($237) Heavy-duty battery ($27). Heavy-duty alternator ($52). Extended-range gas tank ($46). Engine block heater ($18). Trailer towing package ($398).

Crown Victoria: Interior luxury group ($954 to $1,034). Convenience group ($109 to $134). Power lock group ($140 to $238). Light group ($48). Protection group ($68). Police package ($279 to $398). Air conditioning ($743) and ($809) with auto-temp control. Electric rear defroster ($140). Fingertip speed control ($176). Illuminated entry system ($82). Power windows ($198 to $272). Power driver's seat ($227) or driver and passenger ($454). Remote fuel door lock ($35). Tinted glass ($110). Autolamp on/off delay ($73). Leather-wrapped steering wheel ($59). Tilt steering wheel ($110). Auto. parking brake release ($12). Tripminder computer ($215 to $261). Digital clock ($61). Interval wipers ($50). AM/FM stereo radio, S ($106) or ($112 to $204) with cassette tape player. Electronic-tuning AM/FM stereo radio with/cassette ($166) and ($416), S. Power antenna ($66). Premium sound system ($151 to $179). Radio delete ($148 credit). Luggage rack ($110). Dual-facing rear seats: Country Squire ($167). Leather seat trim ($418). Split bench seating ($139). All-vinyl seat trim ($34) or Duraweave vinyl ($96). Carpeted front floor mats ($21). Trunk trim ($49). Wire wheel covers ($165) and locking ($204). Cast aluminum wheels ($390). P225/75-R14 whitewalls ($42 to $43). P205/75R15 whitewalls ($17). Puncture-sealant ($178). Conventional spare ($63). Traction-Lok differential ($95). Heavy duty suspension ($26). Heavy duty battery ($27). Engine block heater ($18). Trailer towing package ($200-$251).

History:

The 1984 Fords were introduced on Sept. 22, 1983, except Tempo that debuted in May 1983. Model year production was 1,496,997, including Mustangs. Calendar year sales by U.S. dealers was 1,300,644, including Mustangs. Sales hit their highest mark since 1979 during the 1984 model year, a 27-percent jump over 1983. Escort lost its title as the nation's top-selling car to Chevrolet's Cavalier. EXP sales declined again in 1984. The Escort and Tempo 2.0-liter diesel, from Mazda Motors, showed sluggish sales as well. Edsel B. Ford II was named advertising manager in late 1983. Tempo design had begun in 1979 as the Topaz project. That name ultimately was given to the Mercury version.

1985 Ford

Escort — Four: Reverse gear on the four-and five-speed manual transaxle moved to a new position this year, intended to make shifting easier. Radios had a new flat-face design. Starting in mid-year 1984, clear coat paints were made available on the Escort L and GL. Little was new on Ford's subcompact two- and four-door hatchbacks as the model

1985 Tempo GL coupe (with Sports option package)

year began. Later, a restyled 1985-1/2 Escort appeared, powered by a new 1.9-liter four-cylinder engine. The standard engine for the first series was the CVH 97.6 cid (1.6-liter) carbureted four, with four-speed gearbox. A high-output version was available, as well as one with electronic fuel injection and another with a turbocharger. The 2.0-liter diesel was offered again. Five-speed manual and three-speed automatic transmissions were available. Escort L had a brushed aluminum B-pillar appliqué. Wagons and diesels had standard power brakes. Escort GL added AM radio, low-back seats, and additional bright moldings. Escort LX included power brakes, blackout body treatment, digital clock, fog lamps, TR performance suspension and styled steel wheels. GT models carried wide black body moldings with argent striping, dual black remote racing mirrors, power brakes, TR performance suspension, five-speed transaxle, remote liftgate release, fog lamps, and sport-tuned exhaust. Turbo GT had aluminum TR wheels and standard power steering.

EXP — Four: The two-seater EXP got a revised location for reverse gear (below fifth gear). Radios and cassette players showed a new flat-face design. The base engine was the fuel-injected 97.6-cid (1.6-liter) four. The Turbo Coupe was available again, wearing aluminum wheels with low-profile performance tires and Koni shock absorbers. This was EXP's final season in its original form. Standard equipment included an AM radio, tinted rear-window glass, halogen headlamps, power brakes, tachometer, handling suspension, remote locking fuel door and black moldings. Inside were low-back cloth/vinyl reclining bucket seats. EXP's Luxury Coupe added an AM/FM stereo radio, interval wipers, luxury cloth seats with four-way (manual) driver's side adjuster, dual remote mirrors, rear defroster, and tinted glass. Turbo Coupe included a front air dam, black rocker panel moldings, AM/FM stereo with cassette, power steering, TR suspension and aluminum wheels, wheel spats, and a rear spoiler.

Tempo — Four: Throttle-body fuel injection was added to Tempo's 2300 HSC (High Swirl Combustion) engine after a year of carburetion. A new high-output version had a new cylinder head and intake manifold, and drove a special 3.73:1 final drive ratio. Five-speed manual overdrive transaxles were standard in all Tempo series, with revised reverse gear position (now below fifth gear). GLX Tempos now had a sport instrument cluster, power lock group, light convenience group, tinted glass, AM/FM stereo radio, power steering and tilt steering wheel. There were new see-through reservoirs for brake, power steering and washer fluid levels. The 1985 instrument panel included side window demisters, plus contemporary flat-face radio design and a storage shelf. Tempo again came in three series: L, GL and GLX. Base Tempos came with an AM radio, cloth/vinyl reclining low-back bucket seats, body accent stripes, dual deck lid stripes on two-doors, power brakes, bright bumpers with black end caps, and a black left-hand mirror. GL added a blackout back panel treatment, digital clock, black body moldings, styled wheels, interval wipers, and dual striping on four-door deck lids. A high-performance Sport GL performance option included the high-output (HSO) engine, seven-spoke aluminum wheels with locking lug nuts, improved suspension components, dual remote mirrors and sport performance cloth seats.

LTD — Four/V-6/V-8: Modest restyling gave LTD a new horizontal grille for its third season, plus new sedan tail lamps. Only minor trim changes were evident. Base models wore new deluxe wheel covers. The base 140-cid (2.3-liter) engine added low-friction piston rings, with a boost in compression. Wagons had a standard 232-cid (3.8-liter) V-6. New options included dual electric remote mirrors and black vinyl rocker panel moldings. Joining the base and Brougham sedan and LTD wagon later in the model year was a new high-performance LX touring sedan. It carried a high-output, fuel-injected 302-cid (5.0-liter) V-8 with a four-speed overdrive automatic transmission. The performance sedan also had a special handling suspension with rear stabilizer bar, 15:1 steering gear, and Goodyear Eagle GT performance tires. LX had a body-colored grille, charcoal and red-orange accents, twin chromed exhaust extensions and styled road wheels. Inside was a center console with floor shifter, tachometer, and unique front bucket seats with inflatable lumbar support. Both base and Brougham sedans had an AM radio, Select Shift automatic transmission, locking glove box, power brakes and steering and a reclining split-bench seating with cloth upholstery,. Brougham added a digital clock, light group, seatback map pockets, lighted visor vanity passenger-side mirror and luxury cloth upholstery.

LTD Crown Victoria — V-8: Except for an aluminum front bumper on station wagons and some new body and vinyl roof colors, full-size Fords showed no significant body change. The Crown Victoria got new gas-filled shock absorbers, pressurized with nitrogen. An ignition diagnostics monitor was added to the EEC-IV electronic engine controls. A single key was now used for door and ignition locks. Lower body panels now had urethane coating for extra corrosion protection. The model lineup for the biggest rear-wheel drives remained: two- and four-door sedan (standard or S, with plain-bodied and Country Squire wagons. The 302-cid (5.0-liter) V-8 engine had fuel injection and came with four-speed automatic overdrive transmission. A new optional automatic load leveling suspension was available later in the model year. With a heavy-duty trailer towing package, Crown Victoria and Country Squire could again tow trailers up to 5,000 lbs. Standard equipment included chrome bumpers, dual-note horn, cloth/vinyl reclining flight bench seating, power steering and brakes, and deluxe wheel covers. The budget-priced S models lacked the padded half (rear) vinyl roof, dual accent tape striping, quartz clock, brushed lower deck lid appliqué and various moldings but had an AM radio. Other models got an AM/FM stereo.

I.D. Data:

Ford's 17-symbol Vehicle Identification Number (VIN) again was stamped on a metal tab that was fastened to the instrument panel and was visible through the windshield. Coding was similar to 1984. The model year code changed to F=1985. The engine code W=HSC 140-cid FI four was added. The 6=propane four was dropped. A Vehicle Certification Label on the left front door lock face panel or door pillar showed the manufacturer, month and year of manufacture, GVW, GAWR, certification statement, VIN, and codes for body type, color, trim, axle, transmission, and special order information.

Escort (Four)

Model No.	Body Style No.	Body Type & Seating	Factory Price	Shipping Weight	Production Total
04/41P	61D	2-dr. Hatchback-4P	$5,620	1,981 lbs.	Note 1
13/41P	58D	4-dr. Hatchback-4P	$5,827	2,034 lbs.	Note 1
04	61D	2-dr. L Hatchback-4P	$5,876	1,981 lbs.	Note 1
13	58D	4-dr. L Hatchback-4P	$6,091	2,034 lbs.	Note 1
09	74D	4-dr. L Station Wagon-4P	$6,305	2,066 lbs.	Note 1
05	61D	2-dr. GL Hatchback-4P	$6,374	2,033 lbs.	Note 1
14	58D	4-dr. GL Hatchback-4P	$6,588	2,086 lbs.	Note 1
10	74D	4-dr. GL Station Wagon-4P	$6,765	2,115 lbs.	Note 1
15	58D	4-dr. LX Hatchback-4P	$7,840	2,137 lbs.	Note 1
11	74D	4-dr. LX Station Wagon-4P	$7,931	2,073 lbs.	Note 1

Escort GT (Four)

07	61D	2-dr. Hatchback-4P	$7,585	2,103 lbs.	Note 1
07/935	61D	2-dr. Turbo Hatchback-4P	$8,680	2,239 lbs.	Note 1

1985-1/2 Escort — Second Series (Four)

31	----	2-dr. Hatchback-4P	$5,856	2,089 lbs.	Note 1
31	----	2-dr. L Hatchback-4P	$6,127	2,096 lbs.	Note 1
36	----	4-dr. L Hatchback-4P	$6,341	2,154 lbs.	Note 1
34	----	4-dr. L Station Wagon-4P	$6,622	2,173 lbs.	Note 1
32	----	2-dr. GL Hatchback-4P	$6,642	2,160 lbs.	Note 1
37	----	4-dr. GL Hatchback-4P	$6,855	2,214 lbs.	Note 1
35	----	4-dr. GL Station Wagon-4P	$7,137	2,228 lbs.	Note 1

Note 1: Ford said the second series production was 100,554 two-door hatchbacks, 48,676 four-door hatchbacks and 36,998 station wagons. Other sources report total Escort production was 112,960 two-doors, 111,385 four-doors, and 82,738 wagons. Trim breakdown was not available. Bodies also called three-door and five-door.

Diesel Note: Diesel-powered Escorts came in L and GL trim and were $558 higher than gasoline models.

1985 EXP Luxury Coupe

EXP (Four)

01/A80	67D	3-dr. Hatchback-2P	$6,697	2,117 lbs.	26,462
01/A81	67D	3-dr. Luxury Coupe-2P	$7,585	2,117 lbs.	Note 2
01/A82	67D	3-dr. Turbo Coupe-2P	$9,997	------	Note 2

Note 2: Production of luxury and turbo coupe models was included in the basic EXP totals.

Tempo (Four)

18	66D	2-dr. L Sedan-5P	$7,052	2,249 lbs.	Note 3
21	54D	4-dr. L Sedan-5P	$7,052	2,308 lbs.	Note 3
19	66D	2-dr. GL Sedan-5P	$7,160	2,276 lbs.	Note 3
22	54D	4-dr. GL Sedan-5P	$7,160	2,339 lbs.	Note 3
20	66D	2-dr. GLX Sedan-5P	$8,253	2,302 lbs.	Note 3
23	54D	4-dr. GLX Sedan-5P	$8,302	2,362 lbs.	Note 3

Note 3: Tempo production was 72,311 two-doors and 266,776 four-doors. A turbocharged Tempo GTX, priced at $9,870, was announced but apparently not produced.

Diesel Note: Diesel-powered Tempos cost $479 more than equivalent gasoline models.

LTD (Four)

39	54D	4-dr. Sedan-5P	$8,874	2,804 lbs.	162,884
39/60H	54D	4-dr. Brougham-5P	$9,262	2,812 lbs.	Note 4
40	74D	4-dr. Station Wagon-5P	-----	------	42,642

LTD (V-6)

39	54D	4-dr. Sedan-5P	$9,292	2,881 lbs.	162,884
39/60H	54D	4-dr. Brougham-5P	$9,680	2,889 lbs.	Note 4
40	74D	4-dr. Station Wagon-5P	$9,384	2,990 lbs.	42,642

LTD LX Brougham (V-8)

39/938	54D	4-dr. Sedan-5P	$11,421	------	Note 4

Note 4: Brougham production was included in the basic sedan total.

LTD Crown Victoria (V-8)

42	66K	2-dr. Sedan-6P	$11,627	3,546 lbs.	13,673
43	54K	4-dr. Sedan-6P	$11,627	3,587 lbs.	154,612
44	74K	4-dr. Country Squire-6P	$11,809	3,793 lbs.	30,825
43/41K	54K	4-dr. S Sedan-6P	$10,609	-----	Note 5
44/41K	74K	4-dr. S Station Wagon-6P	$10,956	-----	Note 5
44/41E	74K	4-dr. Station Wagon-6P	$11,559	-----	Note 5

Note 5: Production of S models and basic station wagon was included in sedan and Country Squire totals above.

Police Model: Crown Victoria S police models were $10,929 with the 302-cid V-8 and $11,049 with 351 cid V-8.

Engines:

Escort Base Four: Inline. Overhead cam. Cast-iron block and aluminum head. Displacement: 97.6 cid (1.6 liters). B & S: 3.15 x 3.13 in. Compression ratio: 9.0:1. Brake hp: 70 at 4600 rpm. Torque: 88 lbs.-ft. at 2600 rpm. Five main bearings. Hydraulic valve lifters. Carburetor: Holley 740 two-barrel. VIN Code: 2.

Note: Second Series Escorts carried a 1.9-liter engine. See 1986 listing for specifications.

EXP Base Four (Optional Escort): High-output 1.6-liter. Hp: 80 at 5400 rpm. Torque: 88 lbs.-ft. at 3000 rpm. VIN Code: 4.

Escort LX and GT Base Four (Optional Escort): Fuel-injected 1.6-liter. Hp: 84 at 5200 rpm. Torque: 90 lbs.-ft. at 2800 rpm. VIN Code: 5.

Escort and EXP Turbo Four: Same as 1.6-liter four above, with fuel injection and turbocharger Compression ratio: 8.0:1. Horsepower: 120 at 5200 rpm. Torque: 120 lbs.-ft. at 3400 rpm. VIN Code: B.

Escort and Tempo Diesel Four: Inline. Overhead cam. Cast-iron block and aluminum head. Displacement: 121 cid (2.0 liters). B & S: 3.39 x 3.39 in. Compression ratio: 22.5:1. Brake hp: 52 at 4000 rpm. Torque: 82 lbs.-ft. at 2400 rpm. Five main bearings. Solid valve lifters. Fuel injection. VIN Code: H.

1985 Ford Tempo GLX sedan

1985 Escort (1st series) **GL five-door hatchback** (with diesel engine)

1985 LTD LX Brougham sedan

Tempo Base Four: Inline. Overhead valve. Cast-iron block and head. Displacement: 140 cid (2.3 liters). B & S: 3.70 x 3.30 in. Compression ratio: 9.0:1. Brake hp: 86 at 4000 rpm. Torque: 124 lbs.-ft. at 2800 rpm. Five main bearings. Hydraulic valve lifters. Throttle-body fuel injection. High Swirl Combustion (HSC) design. VIN Code: X.

Tempo Optional Four: High-output version of HSC. Hp: 100 at 4600 rpm. Torque: 125 lbs.-ft. at 3200 rpm. VIN Code: S.

LTD Base Four: Inline. Overhead cam. Cast-iron block and head. Displacement: 140 cid (2.3 liters). B & S: 3.78 x 3.13 in. Compression ratio: 9.5:1. Brake hp: 88 at 4000 rpm. Torque: 122 lbs.-ft. at 2400 rpm. Five main bearings. Hydraulic valve lifters. Carburetor: Carter YFA single-barrel. VIN Code: A.

LTD Propane Four: 140-cid engine with propane fuel. Compression ratio: 10.0:1. Brake hp: 88 at 4000 rpm. Torque: 122 lbs.-ft. at 2400 rpm. VIN Code: 6.

LTD Wagon Base V-6 (Optional LTD): 90-degree: overhead valve. Cast-iron block and aluminum head. Displacement: 232 cid (3.8 liters). B & S: 3.80 x 3.40 in. Compression ratio: 8.7:1. Brake hp: 120 at 3600 rpm. Torque: 205 lbs.-ft. at 1600 rpm. Four main bearings. Hydraulic valve lifters. Throttle-body fuel injection. VIN Code: 3.

Crown Victoria Base V-8: 90-degree, overhead valve. Cast-iron block and head. Displacement: 302 cid (5.0 liters). B & S: 4.00 x 3.00 in. Compression ratio: 8.4:1. Brake hp: 140 at 3200 rpm. Torque: 250 lbs.-ft. at 1600 rpm. Five main bearings. Hydraulic valve lifters. Electronic fuel injection (TBI). VIN Code: F.

LTD LX Base V-8: 302 cid V-8 with compression ratio: 8.3:1. Hp: 165 at 3800 rpm. Torque: 245 lbs.-ft. at 2000 rpm.

Crown Victoria Optional High-Output V-8: 302-cid V-8 with 155 hp at 3600 rpm. Torque: 265 lbs.-ft. at 2000 rpm.

Crown Victoria High-Output Police V-8: 90-degree, overhead valve. Cast-iron block and head. Displacement: 351 cid (5.8 liters). B & S: 4.00 x 3.50 in. Compression ratio: 8.3:1. Brake hp: 180 at 3600 rpm. Torque: 285 lbs.-ft. at 2400 rpm. Five main bearings. Hydraulic valve lifters. Carburetor: 7200VV two-barrel. VIN Code: G.

Chassis:

Escort: Wheelbase: 94.2 in. Overall length: 163.9 in. and 165.0 in., station wagon. Tires: P165/80-R13 steel-belted blackwalls; P175/80-R13, Escort L; P165/70R365 Michelin TRX Escort LX and GT.

EXP: Wheelbase: 94.2 in. Overall length: 170.3 in. EXP P165/80-R13 steel-belted blackwalls and P185/65-R365 Michelin TRX, EXP Turbo.

Tempo: Wheelbase: 99.9 in. Overall length: 176.2 in. Tires: P175/80-R13 steel-belted blackwalls.

LTD: Wheelbase: 105.6 in. Overall length: 196.5 in. Tires: P195/75-R14 SBR BSW and P205/70-HR14 Goodyear Eagle blackwalls for LX and police versions.

Crown Victoria: Wheelbase: 114.3 in. Overall length: 211.0 in. and 215.0 in., station wagon. Tires: P215/75-R14 steel-belted whitewalls.

Options:

Escort: Squire wagon package ($373). Instrument group ($87). Convenience group ($206 to $341). Light group ($67). Air conditioner ($643). Electric rear defroster ($139). High-capacity heater ($76). Fingertip speed control ($176). Power door locks ($124 to $176). Tinted glass ($95). Tilt steering ($104). Overhead console w/digital clock ($82). Interval wipers ($50). Rear wiper/washer ($120) and LX ($46). Dual remote sport mirrors ($68). AM radio: base/L ($39). AM/FM radio ($82) and ($121) base/L. AM/FM stereo radio ($109) and ($148) base/L. With cassette player ($148) and ($295), base/L. Electronic-tuning AM/FM stereo with cassette ($409 to $448). Premium sound ($138). Flip-up open-air roof ($315). Luggage rack, wagon ($100). Console ($111). Vinyl seat trim ($24). Cloth/vinyl low-back bucket seats: L ($33). Color-keyed front mats ($22). Wheel trim rings ($54). Cast aluminum wheels ($279). TR aluminum wheels on LX and GT ($201). Styled steel wheels fleet only ($104 credit). P165/80-R13 steel-belted whitewall tires ($59). High-Output 1.6-liter four ($73) Five-speed manual transmission ($76). Automatic transaxle ($439). Power brakes: Escort ($95). Power steering: Escort ($215) Handling suspension, L ($199) and GL ($95). Heavy duty battery ($27). Heavy duty alternator ($27). Engine block heater ($18).

EXP: Air conditioner ($643). Fingertip speed control ($176). Tinted glass ($95). Tilt steering ($104). Lighted visor vanity mirror ($50). AM/FM stereo radio: base ($109) and with cassette player ($256). On luxury coupe ($148). Electronic-tuning AM/FM stereo w/cassette ($409) and ($300) on luxury coupe. On Turbo ($152). Premium sound ($138). AM radio delete ($39 credit). AM/FM stereo delete, luxury coupe ($148 credit). AM/FM stereo/cassette delete, Turbo ($295 credit). Flip-up open-air roof ($315). Four-way driver's seat, base ($55). Low-back vinyl bucket seats, base, no charge. Cloth sport performance seats, luxury coupe ($173). TR aluminum wheels, luxury coupe ($370). TR styled steel wheels, luxury coupe ($168). Cast aluminum wheels, luxury coupe ($238). P165/80-R13 raised white letter tires ($90). P165/70-R365 Michelin TRX, no charge. Automatic transaxle ($363). Power steering ($215). Heavy duty battery ($27). Heavy duty alternator: ($27). Engine block heater ($18).

Tempo: Sport performance package, GL ($900 to $911). Power lock group ($202 to $254). Luxury option group, GL and LX ($755 to $855). Select option group, GL ($401). Air conditioning ($743). Electric rear defroster ($140). Fingertip speed control, GL and GLX ($176). Power windows ($272). Power deck lid release ($40). Remote fuel door release ($26). Six-way power driver's seat ($224). Tinted glass ($110). Tilt steering, GL ($110). Sport instrument cluster ($87). Dual sport remote mirrors ($93). AM/FM stereo radio, L and GL ($109) and ($148 to $256 with cassette player. Electronic-tuning AM/FM stereo with cassette ($152 to $409). Graphic equalizer ($107 to $218). AM radio delete ($39 credit). Vinyl seat trim ($35). Leather seat trim, GLX ($300). Styled wheels, L ($73). P175/80-R13 white sidewalls ($72). Power steering ($223). Automatic transaxle ($266 to $363). Engine block heater ($18).

LTD: Squire option ($282). Interior luxury group, wagon ($388). Power lock group ($213 to $254). Light group ($38). Police package ($901 to $1,429). Taxi package ($860). Air conditioning ($743) and auto-temp ($809). Fingertip speed control ($176). Illuminated entry ($82). Autolamp on-off delay ($73). Power windows ($272). Six-way power driver's seat ($224) and dual ($449). Tinted glass ($110). Leather-wrapped steering wheel ($59). Tilt steering ($110). Tripminder computer ($215 to $293). Digital clock ($78). Diagnostic warning lights ($89). Auto. parking brake release LPO ($12). Interval wipers ($50). Liftgate wiper/washer, wagon ($99). Dual electric remote mirrors ($96). Lighted visor vanity mirrors ($57 to $106). AM/FM stereo radio ($109) and with cassette player ($256). Electronic-tuning AM/FM stereo radio with cassette ($409). Premium sound system ($138). Formal roof, cloth or vinyl ($848). Full vinyl roof ($152). Two-way lift gate, wagon ($105). Luggage rack, wagon ($126). Lower body protection ($41). Vinyl seat trim ($35). Flight bench seat, no charge. Luxury wheel covers ($55). Wire wheel covers, locking ($204). Cast aluminum wheels, LX ($224). Styled wheels ($178). Styled steel wheels w/trim rings, fleet ($54). P195/75R14 whitewalls ($72). P205/70-R14 whitewalls ($134). Puncture-sealant P195/75-14 whitewalls ($202). Conventional spare LPO ($63). 232-cid V-6 ($418). First gear lockout delete ($7). Traction-Lok differential ($95). Extended-range gas tank ($46). Engine block heater ($18).

Note: Many LTD options listed above were not available for the LX Brougham.

LTD Crown Victoria: Interior luxury group ($949 to $1,022). Convenience group ($109 to $134). Power lock group ($140 to $238). Light group ($48). Air conditioning ($743) and with auto temp control ($809). Electric rear defroster ($140). Fingertip speed control ($176). Illuminated entry system ($82). Power windows ($198 to $272). Power driver seat ($227) or driver and passenger ($454). Remote fuel door lock ($35). Tinted glass ($110). Autolamp on/off delay ($73). Leather-wrapped steering wheel ($59). Tilt steering wheel ($110). Auto. parking brake release ($12). Tripminder computer ($215 to $261). Quartz clock: S ($35). Digital clock ($61 to $96). Interval wipers ($50). Cornering lamps ($68). Remote right mirror ($46). Lighted visor vanity mirrors ($106). AM/FM stereo radio: S ($109) and with cassette tape Player ($148 to $256). Electronic-

1985 LTD Crown Victoria two-door sedan

tuning AM/FM stereo radio with cassette ($300). Power antenna ($66). Premium sound system ($168). Fully padded Brougham vinyl roof ($793). Luggage rack: wagon ($110). License frames ($9). Dual-facing rear seats: wagon ($167). Leather split bench seat ($418). Cloth/vinyl split bench seating ($139). All-vinyl seat trim ($34) and Duraweave vinyl, wagon ($96). Carpeted front/rear floor mats ($33). Trunk trim ($37). Wire wheel covers, locking ($204). Cast-aluminum wheels ($390). P205/75-R15 whitewalls ($17). Puncture-sealant tires ($178). P215/70-R15 whitewalls ($79). Conventional spare ($63). First gear lockout delete, S ($7). Traction-Lok differential ($95). Heavy-duty suspension ($26). Handling suspension ($49). Automatic load leveling ($200). Engine block heater ($18). Trailer towing package ($251 to $302).

History:

The 1985 Fords were introduced on Oct. 4, 1984. Model year production was 1,265,221, including Mustangs but with incomplete Escort totals from Ford. That total included 24,708 turbo fours, 10,246 diesels, 828,320 four-cylinder engines, 270,461 sixes and 290,322 V-8s. Calendar year sales by U.S. dealers was 1,386,195, including Mustangs. Ford sales rose 14 percent for 1985, partly resulting from incentive programs late in the season. Ford's market share rose to a healthy 17.2 percent, up from 16 percent in the 1984 model year. All seven series showed an increase, led by Escort with a 21 percent rise. Tempo did well, too. Ford raised prices only 1.3 percent on average in 1985, though Crown Victoria had a six percent price increase. Mustangs were actually cheaper.

1986 Ford

Escort — Four: The 1986 Escort actually arrived as a 1985-1/2 model, carrying a bigger (1.9-liter) four-cylinder engine. The model lineup included the LX series replacing the GL, and the temporarily-abandoned GT reintroduced. Pony was the name for the base hatchback. The 2.0-liter diesel engine remained only as an option. Inside was a new black four-spoke steering wheel. Options included tilt steering, speed control, and an instrumentation group. Escort's base engine was carbureted, hooked to a four-speed manual transaxle. Automatic shift was optional. Escort had four-wheel independent suspension. Pony had standard power brakes, day/night mirror, dome light, cloth/vinyl low-back reclining bucket seats, and P175/80-R13 tires. Escort L added an AM radio and load floor carpet. LX included remote fuel door lock, remote lift-gate release, wide vinyl body moldings and styled steel wheels. Escort GT had a high-output 1.9-liter engine with port fuel injection and five-speed manual transaxle plus performance suspension with new front and rear stabilizer bars and eight-spoke aluminum wheels. Also included were fog lamps, a console with graphic display, a leather-wrapped steering wheel, body-color wheel spats with integral rocker panel moldings, a rear spoiler and body-color body moldings. One easy-to-spot styling feature was GT's offset grille. A GT decal sat on the solid passenger side of the grille.

EXP — Four: After a brief absence from the lineup, the two-seater EXP returned in restyled form with a sleek new front-end design, including air dam and aero headlamps. Also new was a bubble-back styled rear hatch with integral spoiler. Large "EXP" recessed lettering was easy to spot on the wide C pillar. Wraparound full-width tail lamps (split by the license plate's recessed housing) were divided into upper/lower segments, and tapered downward to a point on each quarter panel. Luxury Coupe

1986 Escort LX wagon

1986 Tempo LX coupe

1986 Taurus LX sedan

and Sport Coupe versions were offered, with 1.9-liter fast-burn four, five-speed manual transaxle, and four-wheel independent suspension. Luxury Coupe had the carbureted engine, along with a tachometer and trip odometer, reclining low-back bucket seats trimmed in cloth/vinyl (or all vinyl), AM/FM stereo radio, overhead console, and left remote mirror. A fuel-injected high-output version of the four went into the Sport Coupe, which also had special handling components, performance bucket seats, center console with graphic systems monitor, fog lamps and low-profile 15 in. handling tires on cast aluminum wheels.

Tempo — Four: After only two seasons in the lineup, Tempo got new front and rear styling. Tempo also had a color-keyed lower front valence panel. Wide, dark gray body moldings held bright inserts. Completing the look were aero-style mirrors. Inside was a new-design four-spoke deep-dish steering wheel. A push-pull headlamp switch replaced the toggle unit. New door sill scuff plates were added. A new LX series replaced the GLX. Both GL and LX tires were upgraded to 14-inch size. Sport GL went to 15 inchers, and had red interior accent colors. In addition to the basic GL and LX models, Select GL and Sport GL packages were offered. GL included full cloth reclining front bucket seats, power front disc/rear drum brakes, interval wipers and a digital clock. Tempo LX included styled wheels, tilt steering, power door locks, a full array of courtesy lights, bright argent lower back panel appliqué and AM/FM stereo radio. A Select GL package added power steering, tinted glass, dual sail-mounted remote electric mirrors, and AM/FM stereo radio. Sport GL had a special handling suspension, as well as a high specific output (HSO) version of the standard 2300 HSC (high swirl combustion) four. All had a standard five-speed manual transaxle. Automatic was optional on GL and Select GL. So was the 2.0-liter diesel.

Taurus — Four/V-6: The aerodynamic new mid-size, front-drive Taurus lacked a grille up front. At the rear were wraparound tail lamps. Taurus wagons had narrow vertical tail lamps, and center high-mount stop lamps above the lift gate. Taurus had flush-mounted glass all around. Aero styling gave an impressive drag coefficient, as low as 0.33 for the sedan. Series offered were the L, GL, LX, and, later, a sporty MT5. The base engine was a new 153-cid (2.5-liter) fuel-injected HSC four. Sedans had fully independent MacPherson strut suspension, front and rear. Wagons had independent short and long arm rear suspension. Polycarbonate bumpers were corrosion-proof. The driver-oriented instrument panel featured three analog backlit instrument clusters. Windshield wipers had 20-in. blades and an articulated driver's side arm for a full wipe all the way to the pillar. Standard equipment included power brakes and steering, gas-filled shocks and struts, all-season steel-belted radials, AM radio, and reclining cloth flight bench seats. Wagons had a 60/40 split fold-down rear seat and cargo tie-downs. MT5 came with five-speed manual transaxle and floor shift lever, and included interval wipers, tinted glass, tachometer and bucket seats. The LX included air conditioning, power locks, cloth split bench seats, tilt steering, power windows, and lighted visor vanity mirrors. Taurus looked much like the related Mercury Sable but the sedans shared no sheet metal. They shared drive trains and running gear, plus most equipment.

LTD — Four/V-6: Ford's rear-drive mid-size was scheduled for abandonment at mid-year, now that the front-drive Taurus had arrived.

1986 LTD Crown Victoria Country Squire station wagon

1986 Escort GT hatchback

For its final partial season, the 232-cid (3.8-liter) V-6 became standard (though the four was listed as a credit option). The high-performance LX sedan didn't make the lineup this year, and not much was new apart from the required center high-mount stop lamp. Quite a few low-rate options were dropped. Four-speed automatic overdrive became optional. LTD was virtually identical to Mercury Marquis. Models included base and Brougham sedans, and the base wagon.

LTD Crown Victoria — V-8: Big rear-drives had more than a spark of life remaining in Ford's plans. Crown Victoria added the top-level LX sedan and Country Squire LX wagon. Each incorporated a previously optional interior luxury group. LX had reclining split bench seats upholstered in velour cloth or vinyl. Leather seating was optional. Equipment included power windows and a variety of luxury trim. Sequential multi-port fuel injection was now used on the 302-cid (5.0-liter) V-8 engine coupled with four-speed overdrive automatic. Changes to the 302 engine included fast-burning combustion chambers, higher compression, roller tappets and low-tension piston rings. Wagons now had a mini spare tire rather than the conventional one. Standard equipment included an AM/FM stereo radio with four speakers, quartz clock, front/rear courtesy lights, cloth flight bench seat with dual recliners, and remote driver's mirror. Seven exterior colors were new, along with five vinyl roof colors. Country Squire's simulated wood grain panels switched from cherry to dark cherry. Quad rectangular headlamps stood above amber park/signal lenses. The front end showed a straight, symmetrical design.

I.D. Data:

Ford's 17-symbol Vehicle Identification Number (VIN) was stamped on a metal tab fastened to the instrument panel and was visible through the windshield. The first three symbols 1FA=manufacturer, make and vehicle type. The fourth symbol B=the restraint system. Letter P followed by two digits indicated the body type such as P31=Escort L two-door hatchback. Symbol eight indicated the engine type: 9=113-cid four; J=113-cid H.O four; H=121-cid diesel; X=140-cid HSC four; S=H. O. 140-cid FI four; W=140-cid EFI turbo four; D=153-cid FI four; U=163-cid V-6; 3=232-cid V-6; F=302-cid V-8 and G=351-cid V-8. Next was a check digit. Symbol 10 indicated the model year: G=1986. Symbol 11 was the assembly plant: A=Atlanta, Georgia; B=Oakville, Ontario, Canada; G=Chicago, Illinois; H=Lorain, Ohio; K=Kansas City, Missouri; T=Edison, New Jersey; W=Wayne, Michigan and X=St. Thomas, Ontario, Canada. The final six digits made up the sequential number, starting with 100001. A Vehicle Certification Label on the left front door lock face panel or door pillar showed the manufacturer, month and year of manufacture, GVW, GAWR, certification statement, VIN, and body type, color, trim, axle, transmission, and special order information.

Escort (Four)

Model No.	Body Style No.	Body Type & Seating	Factory Price	Shipping Weight	Production Total
31/41P	------	2-dr. Pony Hatchback-4P	$6,052	2,089 lbs.	Note 1
31	------	2-dr. L Hatchback-4P	$6,327	2,096 lbs.	Note 1
36	------	4-dr. L Hatchback-4P	$6,541	2,154 lbs.	Note 1
34	------	4-dr. L Station Wagon-4P	$6,822	2,173 lbs.	Note 1
32	------	2-dr. LX Hatchback-4P	$7,284	2,160 lbs.	Note 1
37	------	4-dr. LX Hatchback-4P	$7,448	2,214 lbs.	Note 1
35	------	4-dr. LX Station Wagon-4P	$7,729	2,228 lbs.	Note 1
33	------	2-dr. GT Hatchback-4P	$8,112	2,282 lbs.	Note 1

Note 1: A total of 228,013 two-door hatchbacks, 117,300 four-door hatchback sedans, and 84,740 station wagons were produced in 1986. Trim level breakdown is not available. Bodies often called three-door and five-door.

EXP (Four)

01	------	2-dr. Sport Coupe-2P	$7,186	-----	Note 2
01/931	------	2-dr. Luxury Coupe-2P	$8,235	-----	Note 2

Note 2: Total EXP production was 30,978.

Tempo (Four)

19	66D	2-dr. GL Sedan-5P	$7,358	2,363 lbs.	Note 3
22	54D	4-dr. GL Sedan-5P	$7,508	2,422 lbs.	Note 3
20	66D	2-dr. GLX Sedan-5P	$8,578	2,465 lbs.	Note 3
23	54D	4-dr. GLX Sedan-5P	$8,777	2,526 lbs.	Note 3

Note 3: Total Tempo production came to 69,101 two-doors and 208,570 four-doors.

Taurus (Four)

29	54D	4-dr. L Sedan -6P	$9,645	2,749 lbs.	Note 4
30	74D	4-dr. L Station Wagon-6P	-----	-----	Note 4
29/934	54D	4-dr. MT5 Sedan-6P	$10,276	2,154 lbs.	Note 4
30/934	74D	4-dr. MT5 Wagon-6P	$10,741	2,173 lbs.	Note 4
29/60D	54D	4-dr. GL Sedan-6P	------	2,160 lbs.	Note 4
30/60D	74D	4-dr. GL Station Wagon-6P	------	2,214 lbs.	Note 4
29/60H	54D	4-dr. LX Sedan-6P	------	2,228 lbs.	Note 4
30/60H	74D	4-dr. LX Station Wagon-6P	------	2,282 lbs.	Note 4

Taurus (V-6)

29	54D	4-dr. L Sedan -6P	$10,256	2,749 lbs.	Note 4
30	74D	4-dr. L Station Wagon-6P	$10,763	3,097 lbs.	Note 4
29/934	54D	4-dr. MT5 Sedan-6P	-------	-------	Note 4
30/934	74D	4-dr. MT5 Wagon-6P	-------	-------	Note 4
29/60D	54D	4-dr. GL Sedan-6P	$11,322	2,909 lbs.	Note 4
30/60D	74D	4-dr. GL Station Wagon-6P	$11,790	3,108 lbs.	Note 4
29/60H	54D	4-dr. LX Sedan-6P	$13,351	3,001 lbs.	Note 4
30/60H	74D	4-dr. LX Station Wagon-6P	$13,860	3,198 lbs.	Note 4

Note 4: Taurus production came to 178,737 sedans and 57,625 station wagons for 1986.

LTD (Four)

39	54D	4-dr. Sedan-5P	$ 9,538	2,801 lbs.	58,270
39	54D	4-dr. Brougham-5P	$ 9,926	2,806 lbs.	Note 5
40	74D	4-dr. Station Wagon-5P	------	------	14,213

LTD (V-6)

39	54D	4-dr. Sedan-5P	$10,032	2,878 lbs.	58,270
39	54D	4-dr. Brougham-5P	$10,420	2,883 lbs.	Note 5
40	74D	4-dr. Station Wagon-5P	$10,132	2,977 lbs.	14,213

Note 5: Brougham production was included in the basic sedan total.

LTD Crown Victoria (V-8)

42	66K	2-dr. Sedan-6P	$13,022	3,571 lbs.	6,559
43	54K	4-dr. Sedan-6P	$12,562	3,611 lbs.	97,314
44	74K	4-dr. Country Squire-6P	$12,655	3,834 lbs.	20,164
44/41E	74K	4-dr. Station Wagon-6P	$12,405	3,795 lbs.	Note 6
43/41K	54K	4-dr. S Sedan-6P	$12,188	3,591 lbs.	Note 5
44/41K	74K	4-dr. S Station Wagon-6P	$12,468	3,769 lbs.	Note 6

LTD Crown Victoria LX (V-8)

42/60H	66K	2-dr. Sedan-6P	$13,752	3,608 lbs.	Note 6
43/60H	54K	4-dr. Sedan-6P	$13,784	3,660 lbs.	Note 6
44/41E	74K	4-dr. Station Wagon-6P	$13,567	3,834 lbs.	Note 6
44/60H	74K	4-dr. Country Squire-6P	$13,817	3,873 lbs.	Note 6

Note 6: S and LX models and the station wagon are included in the basic sedan and Country Squire totals.
Note: A Police model (P43/41K/55A) S sedan was $11,813 with the 302-cid V-8 or $11,933 with the 351-cid V-8.

Engines:

Escort Base Four: Inline. Overhead cam. Cast-iron block and aluminum head. Displacement: 113 cid (1.9 liters). B & S: 3.23 x 3.46 in. Compression ratio: 9.0:1. Brake hp: 86 at 4800 rpm. Torque: 100 lbs.-ft. at 3000 rpm. Five main bearings. Hydraulic valve lifters. Carburetor: Holley 740 two-barrel. VIN Code: 9.

Escort GT Base Four (Optional Escort): High-output, multi-port fuel-injected 1.9-liter. Hp: 108 at 5200 rpm. Torque: 114 lbs.-ft. at 4000 rpm. VIN Code: J.

Escort and Tempo Diesel Four: Inline. Overhead cam. Cast-iron block and aluminum head. Displacement: 121 cid (2.0 liters). B & S: 3.39 x 3.39 in. Compression ratio: 22.7:1. Brake hp: 52 at 4000 rpm. Torque: 82 lbs.-ft. at 2400 rpm. Five main bearings. Solid valve lifters. Fuel injection. VIN Code: H.

Tempo Base Four: Inline. Overhead valve. Cast-iron block and head. Displacement: 140 cid (2.3 liters). B & S: 3.70 x 3.30 in. Compression ratio: 9.0:1. Brake hp: 86 at 4000 rpm. Torque: 124 lbs.-ft. at 2800 rpm. Five main bearings. Hydraulic valve lifters. Throttle-body fuel injection. High Swirl Combustion (HSC) design. VIN Code: X.

Tempo Optional Four: High-output HSC four. Hp: 100 at 4600 rpm. Torque: 125 lbs.-ft. at 3200 rpm. VIN Code: S.

Taurus (Late) Base Four: Inline. Overhead valve. Cast-iron block and head. Displacement: 153 cid (2.5 liters). B & S: 3.70 x 3.60 in. Compression ratio: 9.0:1. Brake hp: 88 at 4600 rpm. Torque: 130 lbs.-ft. at 2800 rpm. Five main bearings. Hydraulic valve lifters. Electronic fuel injection. VIN Code: D.

Taurus LX and Wagon Base V-6 (Optional Taurus): 60-degree, overhead valve. Cast-iron block and head. Displacement: 183 cid (3.0 liters). B & S: 3.50 x 3.10 in. Compression ratio: 9.25:1. Brake hp: 140 at 4800 rpm. Torque: 160 lbs.-ft. at 3000 rpm. Four main bearings. Hydraulic valve lifters. Multi-port fuel injection. VIN Code: U.

LTD Base V-6: 90-degree, overhead valve. Cast-iron block and aluminum head. Displacement: 232 cid (3.8 liters). B & S: 3.80 x 3.40 in. Compression ratio: 8.7:1. Brake hp: 120 at 3600 rpm. Torque: 205 lbs.-ft. at 1600 rpm. Four main bearings. Hydraulic valve lifters. Throttle-body fuel injection. VIN Code: 3.

Crown Victoria Base V-8: 90-degree, overhead valve. Cast-iron block and head. Displacement: 302 cid (5.0 liters). B & S: 4.00 x 3.00 in. Compression ratio: 8.9:1. Brake hp: 150 at 3200 rpm. Torque: 270 lbs.-ft. at 2000 rpm. Five main bearings. Hydraulic valve lifters. Sequential (port) fuel injection. VIN Code: F.

Crown Victoria High-Output Police V-8: 90-degree, overhead valve. Cast-iron block and head. Displacement: 351 cid (5.8 liters). B & S: 4.00 x 3.50 in. Compression ratio: 8.3:1. Brake hp: 180 at 3600 rpm. Torque: 285 lbs.-ft. at 2400 rpm. Five main bearings. Hydraulic valve lifters. Two-barrel carburetor. VIN Code: G.

Chassis:

Escort: Wheelbase: 94.2 in. Overall length: 166.9 in. and 168.0 in., wagon. Tires: P165/80-R13 steel-belted blackwalls, P175/80-R13, L wagon and LX and P195/60-HR15 blackwalls, Escort GT.

EXP: Wheelbase: 94.2 in. Overall length: 168.4 in. Tires: P185/70-R14 steel-belted blackwalls.

Tempo: Wheelbase: 99.9 in. Overall length: 176.2 in. Tires: P185/80-R14 steel-belted blackwalls.

Taurus: Wheelbase: 106.0 in. Overall length: 188.4 in. and 191.9 in., station wagon. Tires: P195/70-R14 blackwalls and P205/70-R14, GL and LX.

LTD: Wheelbase: 105.6 in. Overall length: 196.5 in. Tires: P195/75-R14 blackwalls.

Crown Victoria: Wheelbase: 114.3 in. Overall length: 211.0 in. and 215.0 in., wagon. Tires: P205/75-R15 steel-belted whitewalls.

Options:

Escort: Instrument group ($87). Climate control/convenience group ($742 to $868). Premium convenience group ($306 to $390). Protection convenience group ($131 to $467). Select L pkg. ($397). Light group ($67). Air conditioner ($657). Electric rear defroster ($135). Fingertip speed control ($176). Tinted glass ($99). Tilt steering ($115). Overhead console with digital clock ($82). Interval wipers ($50). Rear wiper/washer ($126). Dual remote sport mirrors ($68). AM radio ($39). AM/FM stereo radio ($109) and ($148) base. With cassette player ($256) and ($295) base and L. ($148) on the GT ($148). Premium sound ($138). Front vent windows, pivoting ($63). Wide vinyl body moldings ($45). Luggage rack: wagon ($100). Console ($111). Vinyl seat trim ($24). Bright wheel trim rings ($54). Styled wheels ($128 to $195). P165/80-R13 steel-belted whitewalls ($59). Full-size spare ($63). 2.0-liter diesel four ($591). Five-speed manual transmission ($76). Automatic transaxle ($466) and ($390) LX and GT. Power steering ($226). Heavy duty suspension ($26). Heavy duty battery ($27). Heavy duty alternator ($27). Engine block heater ($18).

1986 EXP Sport Coupe

1986 Taurus GL station wagon

EXP: Climate control/convenience group ($841 to $868). Sun/Sound group ($612). Convenience group ($300 to $455). Air conditioner ($657). Rear defroster ($135). Fingertip speed control ($176). Console w/graphic systems monitor ($111). Tinted glass ($99). Tilt steering ($115). Interval wipers ($50). Dual electric remote mirrors ($88). Lighted visor vanity mirror ($50). AM/FM stereo radio with cassette player ($148). Premium sound ($138). Flip-up open-air roof ($315). Cargo area cover ($59). Vinyl seat trim ($24). Automatic transaxle ($390). Power steering ($226). Heavy duty battery ($27). Heavy duty alternator ($27). Engine block heater ($18).

Tempo: Sport GL package ($934). Select GL package ($340 to $423). Power lock group ($207 to $259). Power equipment group ($291 to $575). Convenience group ($224 to $640). Air bag restraint system ($815). Air conditioning ($743). Electric rear defroster ($145). Fingertip speed control ($176). Power windows ($207 to $282). Six-way power driver's seat ($234). Tinted glass ($113). Tilt steering ($115). Sport instrument cluster ($87). Dual electric remote mirrors ($111). AM/FM stereo radio ($109) and with cassette player ($148 to $256). Electronic-tuning AM/FM stereo with cassette ($171 to $279) and ($23) with Sport GL pkg. Premium sound ($138). Deck lid luggage rack ($100). Console ($116). Front center armrest ($55). Vinyl seat trim ($35). Leather seat trim ($300). Styled wheels ($72). P185/70-R14 whitewalls ($72). 2.0-liter diesel four ($509). Automatic transaxle ($448). Power steering ($223). Heavy duty battery ($27). Engine block heater ($18).

Taurus: Exterior accent group ($49 to $99). Power lock group ($180 to $221). Light group ($48 to $51). Air conditioning ($762). Electronic climate control air conditioning: GL ($945) and LX ($183). Rear defroster ($145). Insta-clear windshield ($250). Fingertip speed control ($176). Illuminated entry ($82). Keyless entry ($202). Power windows ($282). Six-way power driver's seat ($237) or dual ($473). Tinted glass: L ($115). Leather-wrapped steering wheel ($59). Tilt steering ($115). Electronic instrument cluster ($305). Autolamp on/off delay ($73). Diagnostic warning lights ($89). Digital clock: L ($78). Interval wipers: L ($50). Rear wiper/washer, wagon ($124). Cornering lamps ($68). Dual electric remote mirrors: L ($59 to $96). Dual lighted visor vanity mirrors ($104-$116). Electronic-tuning AM/FM stereo radio ($157), L and MT5. Electronic-tuning AM/FM stereo with cassette/Dolby ($127 to $284). Power antenna ($71). Premium sound system ($168). Power moon roof ($701). Bucket seats, no charge. Split bench seating: L ($276). Vinyl seat trim ($39). Leather seat trim: LX sedan ($415). Rear-facing third seat: wag ($155). Reclining passenger seat ($45). Luxury wheel covers ($65). Styled wheels, 14 in. ($113 to $178). Cast aluminum wheels, 15 in. ($326 to $390). Conventional spare ($63). 182-cid V-6 ($611). Heavy duty suspension ($26). Heavy duty battery ($27). Extended-range gas tank ($46).

LTD: Squire option ($282). Interior luxury group ($388). Power lock group ($218 to $259). Light group ($38). Air conditioning ($762). Rear defroster ($145). Fingertip speed control ($176). Autolamp on-off delay ($73). Power windows ($282). Six-way power driver's seat ($234). Tinted glass ($115). Leather-wrapped steering wheel ($59). Tilt steering ($115). Overdrive automatic transmission ($245). Digital clock ($78). Auto. parking brake release ($12). Interval wipers ($50). Cornering lamps ($68). Dual electric remote mirrors ($96). Lighted visor vanity mirrors ($57 to $106). AM/FM stereo radio ($109) and ($256) with cassette player. Premium sound system ($138). Pivoting front vent windows ($79). Two-way liftgate, wagon, ($105). Luggage rack, wagon ($126). Vinyl seat trim ($35). Flight or split bench seat, no charge. Luxury wheel covers ($55). Wire wheel covers, locking ($212). Styled wheels ($178). Styled steel wheels w/trim rings ($54). Conventional spare ($63). 140-cid four ($494 credit). Heavy duty suspension ($43). Heavy duty battery ($27). Extended-range gas tank ($46). Engine block heater ($18).

LTD Crown Victoria: Convenience group ($109 to $134). Power lock group ($143 to $243). Light group ($48). Police package ($291 to

1986 LTD Crown Victoria sedan

$411). Air conditioning ($762) and ($828) with auto-temp control. Rear defroster, electric ($145). Fingertip speed control ($176). Illuminated entry system ($82). Power windows ($282). Power six-way driver's seat ($237) or driver and passenger ($473). Tinted glass ($115). Autolamp on/off delay ($73). Leather-wrapped steering wheel ($59). Tilt steering wheel ($115). Tripminder computer ($215 to $261). Digital clock ($61 to $96). Interval wipers ($50). Cornering lamps ($68). Remote right convex mirror ($46). Dual electric remote mirrors ($100). AM/FM stereo radio, S ($109) and with cassette tape player ($148-$256). Electronic-tuning AM/FM stereo radio with cassette ($300). Power antenna ($73). Premium sound system ($168). Brougham vinyl roof ($793). Luggage rack, wagon ($110). Dual-facing rear seats, wagon ($167). Leather seat trim ($433). Reclining split bench seats ($144). Duraweave vinyl ($100). Wire wheel covers, locking ($205). Cast aluminum wheels ($390). P205/75-R15 puncture-sealant tires ($161). Conventional spare ($63). Traction-Lok differential ($100). Heavy duty suspension ($26). Handling suspension ($49). Automatic load leveling ($200). Heavy duty battery ($27). Heavy duty alternator ($54). Engine block heater ($18). Trailer towing package ($377-$389).

History:

The 1986 Fords were introduced on Oct. 3, 1985. The Taurus premiered on Dec. 26, 1985. Model year production was 1,559,959, including the Mustangs. Calendar year sales by U.S. dealers was 1,397,141, including Mustangs. The new front-drive, mid-size Taurus was the big news for 1986. Its aerodynamic styling went considerably beyond the Tempo design, taking its cue from European Fords. Taurus hardly resembled the rear-drive LTD that it was meant to replace. Mercury's Sable was similar, but with its own set of body panels and features.

1987 Ford

Escort — Four: Fuel injection replaced the carburetor on Escort's base 1.9-liter four-cylinder engine. As before, Escort GT was powered by a high-output version of the four, with multi-point injection. Some shuffling of model designations and the deletion of the LX series meant this year's offering consisted of Pony, GL and GT models. Automatic motorized front seat belts were introduced during the model year. Joining the option list: a fold-down center armrest and split fold-down rear seat.

EXP — Four: Ford's tiny two-seater came in two forms: Luxury Coupe with the base 1.9-liter four-cylinder engine, or Sport Coupe with the high-output power plant. EXP enjoyed a restyling for reintroduction as

1987 Escort GL four-door hatchback

1987 Taurus LX sedan

a 1986-1/2 model, after a brief departure from the lineup. Rather than a distinct model, EXP was now considered part of the Escort series.

Tempo — Four: Front-drive only through its first three seasons, the compact Tempo added a part-time four-wheel-drive option this year. "Shift-on-the-fly" capability allowed engagement of 4WD while in motion, simply by touching a dashboard switch. Models with that option, which was intended for use only on slippery roads, got an "All Wheel Drive" nameplate. 4WD models also included the high-output version of the 2.3-liter four-cylinder engine. Power steering was now standard on all Tempos, while the driver's airbag became a regular production option (RPO) instead of a limited-production item. A revised three-speed automatic transmission contained a new fluid-linked converter, eliminating the need for a lockup torque converter.

Taurus — Four/V-6: Sales of the aero-styled front-drive Taurus began to take off soon after its mid-1986 debut and little change was needed for the 1987 model year. The basic engine for the L and MT5 series, and the GL sedan, was a 2.5-liter four. A 3.0-liter V-6 was optional in all except the MT5. Other models had the V-6 standard with four-speed overdrive automatic transmission. The MT5 came with a standard five-speed gearbox and the L and GL had a three-speed automatic. Similar Mercury Sables all had V-6 power.

LTD Crown Victoria — V-8: Only a few equipment changes arrived with the 1987 full-size Fords. Air conditioning, tinted glass and a digital clock were now standard equipment. Two- and four-door sedans and a four-door station wagon, in base and LX trim levels, were all powered by a 5.0-liter V-8 with four-speed overdrive automatic transmission.

I.D. Data:

Ford's 17-symbol Vehicle Identification Number (VIN) was stamped on a metal tab fastened to the instrument panel, visible through the windshield. The first three symbols 1FA=manufacturer, make and vehicle type. The fourth symbol B=restraint system. Next came letter P followed by the two-digit model number: P20=Escort Pony two-door hatchback. Symbol eight indicated the engine type. Next was a check digit. Symbol 10 indicated the model year: H=1987. Symbol 11=assembly plant. The final six digits made up the sequence number, starting with 100001.

Escort (Four))

Model No.	Body/ Style No.	Body Type & Seating	Factory Price	Shipping Weight	Production Total
20	61D	2-dr. Pony Hatchback-4P	$6,436	2,180 lbs.	Note 1
21	61D	2-dr. GL Hatchback-4P	$6,801	2,187 lbs.	Note 1
25	58D	4-dr. GL Hatchback-4P	$7,022	2,222 lbs.	Note 1
28	74D	4-dr. GL Station Wagon-4P	$7,312	2,274 lbs.	Note 1
23	61D	2-dr. GT Hatchback-4P	$8,724	2,516 lbs.	Note 1

Note 1: For the model year, a total of 206,729 two-door hatchbacks. 102,187 four-door hatchback sedans, and 65,849 station wagons were built.

EXP (Four)

18	----	2-dr. Sport Coupe-2P	$8,831	2,388 lbs.	Note 2
17	----	2-dr. Luxury Coupe-2P	$7,622	2,291 lbs.	Note 2

Note 2: Total EXP production was 25,888.

Tempo (Four)

31	66D	2-dr. GL Sedan-5P	$8,043	2,462 lbs.	Note 3
36	54D	4-dr. GL Sedan-5P	$8,198	2,515 lbs.	Note 3
32	66D	2-dr. LX Sedan-5P	$9,238	2,562 lbs.	Note 3
37	54D	4-dr. LX Sedan-5P	$9,444	2,617 lbs.	Note 3
33	66D	2-dr. Sport GL Sedan-5P	$8,888	2,667 lbs.	Note 3
38	54D	4-dr. Sport GT Sedan-5P	$9,043	2,720 lbs.	Note 3
34	66D	2-dr. AWD Sedan-5P	$9,984	2,667 lbs.	Note 3
39	54D	4-dr. AWD Sedan-5P	$10,138	2,720 lbs.	Note 3

Note 3: Total Tempo production came to 70,164 two-doors and 212,468 four-doors.

Taurus (Four)

50	54D	4-dr. L Sedan-6P	$10,491	-----	Note 4
51	54D	4-dr. MT5 Sedan-6P	$11,966	2,886 lbs.	Note 4
56	74D	4-dr. MT5 Station Wagon-6P	$12,534	3,083 lbs.	Note 4
52	54D	4-dr. GL Sedan-6P	$11,498	-----	Note 4

Taurus (V-6)

50	54D	4-dr. L Sedan-6P	$11,163	2,982 lbs.	Note 4
55	74D	4-dr. L Station Wagon-6P	$11,722	3,186 lbs.	Note 4
52	54D	4-dr. GL Sedan-6P	$12,170	3,045 lbs.	Note 4
57	74D	4-dr. GL Station Wagon-6P	$12,688	3,242 lbs.	Note 4
53	54D	4-dr. LX Sedan-6P	$14,613	3,113 lbs.	Note 4
58	74D	4-dr. LX Station Wagon-6P	$15,213	3,309 lbs.	Note 4

Note 4: Total Taurus production came to 278,562 sedans and 96,201 station wagons.

LTD Crown Victoria (V-8)

70	66K	2-dr. Sedan-6P	$14,727	3,724 lbs.	5,527
73	54K	4-dr. Sedan-6P	$14,355	3,741 lbs.	105,789
78	74K	4-dr. Country Squire-6P	$14,507	3,920 lbs.	17,652
76	74K	4-dr. Station Wagon-6P	$14,235	3,920 lbs.	Note 5
72	54K	4-dr. S Sedan-6P	$13,860	3,708 lbs.	Note 5
75	74K	4-dr. S Station Wagon-6P	$14,228	3,894 lbs.	Note 5

LTD Crown Victoria LX (V-8)

71	66K	2-dr. Sedan-6P	$15,421	3,735 lbs.	Note 5
74	54K	4-dr. Sedan-6P	$15,454	3,788 lbs.	Note 5
77	74K	4-dr. Station Wagon-6P	$15,450	4,000 lbs.	Note 5
79	74K	4-dr. Country Squire-6P	$15,723	4,000 lbs.	Note 5

Note 5: The S, LX and basic station wagons were included in the basic sedan and Country Squire totals.

Engines:

Escort Base Four: Inline. Overhead cam. Cast iron block and aluminum head. Displacement: 113 cid (1.9 liters). B & S: 3.23 x 3.46 in. Compression ratio: 9.0:1. Brake hp: 90 at 4600 rpm. Torque: 106 lbs.-ft. at 3400 rpm. Five main bearings. Hydraulic valve lifters. Throttle-body fuel injection.

Escort GT and EXP Sport Coupe Base Four: High-output, multi-port fuel injection of 1.9-liter. Hp: 115 at 5200 RPM. Torque: 120 lbs.-ft. at 4400 rpm.

Escort Diesel Four: Inline. Overhead cam. Cast iron block and aluminum head. Displacement: 121 cid (2.0 liters). B & S: 3.39 x 3.39 in. Compression ratio: 22.7:1. Brake hp: 58 at 3600 rpm. Torque: 84 lbs.-ft. at 3000 RPM. Five main bearings. Solid valve lifters. Fuel injection.

Tempo Base Four: Inline. Overhead valve. Cast iron block and head. Displacement: 140 cid (2.3 liters). B & S: 3.70 x 3.30 in. Compression ratio: 9.0:1. Brake hp: 86 at 3800 RPM. Torque: 120 lbs.-ft. at 3200 rpm. Five main bearings. Hydraulic valve lifters. Throttle-body fuel injection. High Swirl Combustion (HSC) design.

Tempo AWD or Sport Base Four: High-output version of HSC four. Hp: 94 at 4000 RPM. Torque: 126 lbs.-ft. at 3200 rpm.

Taurus Base Four: Inline. Overhead valve. Cast iron block and head. Displacement: 153 cid (2.5 liters). B & S: 3.70 x 3.60 in. Compression ratio: 9.0:1. Brake hp: 90 at 4400 rpm. Torque: 140 lbs.-ft. at 2800 rpm. Five main bearings. Hydraulic valve lifters. Throttle-body fuel injection.

Taurus LX Base V-6 (Optional Taurus): 60-degree, overhead valve. Cast iron block and head. Displacement: 182 cid (3.0 liters). B & S: 3.50 x 3.10 in. Compression ratio: 9.3:1. Brake hp: 140 at 4800 rpm. Torque: 160 lbs.-ft. at 3000 rpm. Four main bearings. Hydraulic valve lifters. Multi-port fuel injection.

LTD Crown Victoria Base V-8: 90-degree, overhead valve. Cast iron block and head. Displacement: 302 cid (5.0 liters). B & S: 4.00 x 3.00 in. Compression ratio: 8.9:1. Brake hp: 150 at 3200 rpm. Torque: 270 lbs.-ft. at 2000 rpm. Five main bearings. Hydraulic valve lifters. Sequential-port fuel injection.

Chassis:

Escort: Wheelbase: 94.2 in. Overall length: 166.9 in. and 168.0 in., station wagon. Tires: Pony, P165/80-R13; GL 4-dr and station wagon, P165/80-R13 and GT, P195/60-HR15.

EXP: Wheelbase: 94.2 in. Overall length: 168.4 in. Tires: P185/70-R14.

Tempo: Wheelbase: 99.9 in. Overall length: 176.5 in. Tires: P185/70-R14.

Taurus: Wheelbase: 106.0 in. Overall length: 188.4 in. and 191.9 in., station wagon. Tires: P195/70-R14 and P205/70-R14, GLX.

Crown Victoria: Wheelbase: 114.3 in. Overall length: 211.0 in. and 215.0 in, station wagon. Tires: P205/75-R15.

Options:

Escort: Overhead console with digital clock, tachometer, trip odometer and coolant temperature gauge, dual power mirrors, power steering on GL w/gas engine ($496). GL with diesel engine ($409). Overhead console w/clock ($82). Tachometer, trip odometer & coolant temp gauge ($87). Dual power mirrors ($88). Power steering ($235). Air conditioning, heavy-duty battery, rear defogger, tinted glass, intermittent wipers; GL with gas engine ($920). GL with diesel or GT ($893). Air conditioning ($688). Heavy-duty battery ($27). Rear defogger ($145). Tinted glass ($105). Intermittent wipers ($55). Light/Security Group plus front center armrest, cruise control, split folding rear seatback, tilt steering column; GL ($395). Light/Security Group, GL ($91). GT ($67). Front center armrest, Escort ($55). Cruise control ($176). Split folding rear seat ($49). Tilt steering column ($124). Premium Sound System ($138). Luggage rack ($110). AM radio ($39). AM/FM Stereo, Pony ($159). GL ($120). AM/FM Stereo with cassette, AM/FM stereo, Pony ($306). GL ($267). GT ($148). Cast aluminum wheels ($293). Styled road wheels ($195). Rear wiper/washer

1987 LTD Crown Victoria LX sedan

1987 Tempo All-Wheel-Drive sedan

($126). 2.0-liter diesel four, no charge. Five-speed manual transmission ($76). Automatic transaxle, GL ($490). Power steering ($235).

EXP: Overhead console w/clock ($82). Tachometer, trip odometer & coolant temp gauge ($87). Dual power mirrors ($88). Power steering ($235). Air conditioning plus heavy-duty battery, rear defogger, tinted glass, intermittent wipers - Luxury Coupe ($920). Sport Coupe ($893). Air conditioning ($688). Heavy-duty battery ($27). Rear defogger ($145). Tinted glass ($105). Intermittent wipers ($55). Cruise control ($176). Tilt steering column ($124). Cargo area cover, dual power mirrors, dual visor mirrors, (lighted right), cruise control, power steering, tilt steering column, Luxury Coupe ($473). Sport Coupe ($309). Cargo area cover, ($59). Dual power mirrors, ($88). Visor mirrors (lighted right) ($50). Overhead console w/graphic systems monitor, removable sunroof, AM/FM ST w/cassette, premium Sound System, Luxury Coupe ($597). Sport Coupe ($566). Console w/graphic systems monitor ($56). Removable sunroof ($355). AM/FM ST with cassette ($148). Premium Sound System ($138). Luggage rack ($110). Clear coat paint ($91). AM/FM stereo ($148). Cast aluminum wheels ($293). Styled road wheels ($195). Rear wiper/washer ($126). Automatic transaxle ($415). Power steering ($235).

Tempo: Select GL Package with tinted glass, dual power mirrors and AM/FM Stereo ($191). Without radio ($124). Tinted glass ($120). Dual power mirrors ($111). AM/FM Stereo ET radio ($93). Power Lock Group, includes remote fuel filler and trunk releases, power driver's seat, power windows: 2-door GL, Sport or All Wheel Drive ($560). 4-door GL, Sport or All Wheel Drive ($635). LX 2-door ($323). LX 4-door ($347). Power Lock Group, 2-doors ($237). 4-doors ($288). Power driver's seat ($251). Power windows, 2-doors ($222). 4-doors ($296). Front center armrest, Premium Sound System, AM/FM ST ET cassette, speed control, tilt steering column: GL ($643). Select GL ($565). Sport GL ($418). LX ($371). All Wheel Drive ($510). Front center armrest ($55). Premium Sound System ($138). AM/FM Stereo ET cassette, GL ($250). LX or Select GL ($157). Speed control ($176). Tilt steering column ($124). Air conditioning ($773). Console ($116). Rear defogger ($145). Sport instrument cluster ($87). Deck lid luggage rack ($115). AM/FM Stereo ($93). AM/FM Stereo ET cassette, GL ($250). LX, Select GL or All Wheel Drive ($157). Styled road wheels ($178). All vinyl seat trim ($35). Automatic transaxle ($482).

Taurus: Automatic air conditioning, LX ($183). GL ($945). Manual air conditioning ($788). Autolamp system ($73). Heavy-duty battery ($27). Digital clock ($78). Rear defogger ($145). Engine block heater ($18). Remote fuel door and deck lid release ($91) Remote liftgate release, wagons ($41). Extended range fuel tank ($46). Tinted glass ($120). Illuminated entry system ($82). Electronic instrument cluster ($351). Keyless entry system ($202). Power door locks ($195). Dual power mirrors, L sedan ($96). L wagon ($59). Power moon roof ($741). AM/FM Stereo ET radio ($141). AM/FM Stereo w/cassette, L ($268). GL, MT5 & LX ($137). Premium sound system ($168). Power antenna ($76). Rear-facing third seat, wagons ($155). Reclining passenger seat ($45). Power driver's seat ($251). Dual power seats, LX ($502). Others ($251). Speed control ($176). Tilt steering column ($124). Leather-wrapped steering wheel ($59). Rear wiper and washer, wagons ($126). Finned wheel covers, L, GL & MT5 ($65). Locking spoked wheel covers L, GL & MT5 ($205). LX ($140). Aluminum wheels, L, GL & MT5 ($390). LX ($326). Styled road wheels, L, GL & MT5 ($178). LX ($113). Power windows ($296). Intermittent wipers ($55). Split bench seats ($276). Leather seat trim ($415). Vinyl seat trim ($39). 3.0-liter V-6 on L and GL ($672). Heavy duty handling suspension ($26).

1987 LTD Country Squire station wagon

1987 Escort GL station wagon

1987 Taurus LX station wagon

LTD Crown Victoria: Automatic A/C and rear defogger ($211). Autolamp system ($73). Heavy-duty battery ($27). Convenience group with remote deck lid or tailgate release, intermittent wipers, trip odometer, low fuel and oil warning lights (except LX $135) and with Power Lock Group ($85). Cornering lamps ($68). Rear defogger ($145). Engine block heater ($18). Illuminated entry system ($82). Light group ($48). Power lock group: Power door locks, remote fuel door release, two-doors ($207). sedans and wagons ($257). Deluxe luggage rack ($115). AM/FM Stereo w/cassette ($137). Power antenna ($76). Premium Sound System ($168). Power driver's seat ($251). Dual power seats ($502). Dual facing rear seats, wagon ($173). Cruise control ($176). Leather-wrapped steering wheel ($59). Tilt steering column ($124). Tripminder computer ($215). Locking wire wheel covers ($212). Cast aluminum wheels ($390). Power windows & mirrors ($393). Intermittent wipers ($55). Brougham half vinyl roof ($665). Split bench seat ($139). Duraweave vinyl seat trim ($96). Leather seat trim ($418). Traction-Lok differential ($100). Heavy duty handling suspension ($26). Automatic load leveling ($200). Trailer towing package ($387 to $399).

History:

The 1987 Fords were introduced on Oct. 2, 1986. Model year production was 1,474,116, including Mustangs. Calendar year sales by U.S. dealers were 1,389,886 cars, including Mustangs. Once again, Ford's subcompact Escort ranked number one in sales for the model year. Taurus became the second best-selling passenger car in the country. As soon as the mid-size Taurus began its rise to become a hot seller, Ford's LTD left the lineup for good. Sales of the full-size, rear-drive LTD Crown Victoria slid this year, but its place in the lineup was assured.

1988 Ford

Escort — Four: For the first half of the model year, Escort continued with little change except an automatic transmission became optional for the base Pony. The diesel engine option had been dropped. During the model year, motorized automatic front shoulder belts were made standard. A face-lifted Second Series Escort arrived at mid-year. Changes included new fenders, tail lamps, body moldings, quarter panels and plastic bumpers, plus a switch to 14-inch tires. The upgraded GT got a new grille and rear spoiler.

EXP — Four: Only one model remained for the first half of the model year, the Luxury Coupe, as the Sport Coupe was dropped. A Second Series EXP arrived at mid-year, the final season for the subcompact.

Tempo — Four: Restyling of Ford's compact sedans included aero-styled headlamps (integrated with parking lamps and side marker

lenses), wraparound tail lamps, and new bumpers. The four-door also got new body panels and window designs. A new analog instrument panel contained a standard temperature gauge. Under the hood, multi-point fuel injection was used on both the standard and high-output 2.3-liter four-cylinder engines. The standard four got a boost of 12 hp. All Wheel Drive was now available only in the four-door model. The high-output engine was standard in the GLS series and the AWD this year.

Taurus — Four and V-6: Performance fans had a new 3.8-liter V-6 to choose this year. Horsepower was the same as the 3.0-liter V-6, but the engine developed 55 more lbs.-ft. of torque. All models, except the base L and MT5 sedans, could get the 3.8-liter engine. It came only with four-speed overdrive automatic transmission. The MT5 wagon was dropped leaving only the MT5 sedan with the four-cylinder engine and five-speed manual transmission. L and GL sedans also had the four but with three-speed automatic. All station wagons (and the LX sedans) had a standard 3.0-liter V-6 with four-speed automatic.

LTD Crown Victoria — V-8: No two-doors remained in the full-size Ford lineup for 1988. The four-door sedans and wagons got a front and rear restyle (including a new grille and hood, bumpers with rub strips, and trunk lid). Sedans also gained wraparound tail lamps. P215/70-R15 whitewall tires became standard, along with intermittent wipers, a trip odometer, low fuel and oil-level warning lights, an automatic headlamp on/off system, and front-door map pockets. Both base and LX models were powered by a 150-hp, 5.0-liter V-8 engine with four-speed overdrive automatic.

I.D. Data:

Ford's 17-symbol Vehicle Identification Number (VIN) was stamped on a metal tab fastened to the instrument panel and was visible through the windshield. The first three symbols 1FA=manufacturer, make and vehicle type. The fourth symbol=restraint system. Next came letter P followed by two digits that indicated the model number, such as P20=Escort Pony two-door hatchback. Symbol eight indicated the engine type. Next was a check digit. Symbol 10 indicated the model year: J=1988. Symbol 11 was the assembly plant. The final six digits made up the sequence number, starting with 100001.

1988-1/2 Escort GT hatchback coupe

1988 Escort GL three-door hatchback

1988-1/2 Escort LX station wagon

1988 Escort hatchback sedan

Escort (Four))

Model No.	Body/ Style No.	Body Type & Seating	Factory Price	Shipping Weight	Production Total
20	61D	2-dr. Pony Hatchback-4P	$6,632	2,180 lbs.	Note 1
21	61D	2-dr. GL Hatchback-4P	$6,649	2,187 lbs.	Note 1
25	58D	4-dr. GL Hatchback-4P	$7,355	2,222 lbs.	Note 1
28	74D	4-dr. GL Station Wagon-4P	$7,938	2,274 lbs.	Note 1
23	61D	2-dr. GT Hatchback-4P	$9,055	2,516 lbs.	Note 1
90	61D	2-dr. Pony Hatchback-4P	$6,747	------	Note 1
91	61D	2-dr. LX Hatchback-4P	$7,127	2,258 lbs.	Note 1
95	58D	4-dr. LX Hatchback-4P	$7,457	2,295 lbs.	Note 1
98	74D	4-dr. LX Station Wagon-4P	$8,058	2,307 lbs.	Note 1
93	61D	2-dr. GT Hatchback-4P	$9,093	------	Note 1

Note 1: A total of 206,729 two-door hatchbacks. 102,187 four-door hatchback sedans, and 65,849 station wagons were built.

EXP (Four)

17	----	2-dr. Luxury Coupe-2P	$8,073	2,291 lbs.	Note 1

EXP Second Series (Four)

88	----	2-dr. Luxury Coupe-2P	$8,201	2,359 lbs.	Note 1

Tempo (Four)

31	66D	2-dr. GL Sedan-5P	$8,658	2,536 lbs.	Note 2
36	54D	4-dr. GL Sedan-5P	$8,808	2,585 lbs.	Note 2
37	54D	4-dr. LX Sedan-5P	$9,737	2,626 lbs.	Note 2
39	54D	4-dr. AWD Sedan-5P	$10,413	2,799 lbs.	Note 2
33	66D	2-dr. GLS Sedan-5P	$9,249	2,552 lbs.	Note 2
38	54D	4-dr. GLS Sedan-5P	$9,400	2,601 lbs.	Note 2

Note 2: Total Tempo production came to 313,262 or 49,930 two-door and 263,332 four-door sedans.

Taurus (Four)

50	54D	4-dr. L Sedan-6P	$11,699	------	Note 3
51	54D	4-dr. MT5 Sedan-6P	$12,385	2,882 lbs.	Note 3
52	54D	4-dr. GL Sedan-6P	$12,200	------	Note 3

Taurus (V-6)

50	54D	2-dr. L Sedan-6P	$12,731	3,005 lbs.	Note 3
55	74D	4-dr. L Station Wagon-6P	$12,884	3,182 lbs.	Note 3
52	54D	4-dr. GL Sedan-6P	$12,872	3,049 lbs.	Note 3
57	74D	4-dr. GL Station Wagon-6P	$13,380	3,215 lbs.	Note 3
53	54D	2-dr. LX Sedan-6P	$15,295	3,119 lbs.	Note 3
58	74D	4-dr. LX Station Wagon-6P	$15,905	3,288 lbs.	Note 3

Note 3: Total Production was 387,577 (294,576 sedans and 93,001 wagons.)

LTD Crown Victoria (V-8)

73	54K	4-dr. Sedan-6P	$15,218	3,779 lbs.	Note 4
72	54K	4-dr. S Sedan-6P	$14,653	3,742 lbs.	Note 4
76	74K	4-dr. Station Wagon-8P	$15,180	3,991 lbs.	Note 4
78	74K	4-dr. Country Squire-8P	$15,613	3,998 lbs.	Note 4

LTD Crown Victoria LX (V-8)

74	54K	4-dr. Sedan-6P	$16,134	3,820 lbs.	Note 4
77	74K	4-dr. Station Wagon-8P	$16,210	3,972 lbs.	Note 4
79	74K	4-dr. Country Squire-8P	$16,643	4,070 lbs.	Note 4

Note 4: Total production came to 110,249 sedans and 14,940 station wagons.

Engines:

Escort Base Four: Inline. Overhead cam. Cast-iron block and aluminum head. Displacement: 113 cid (1.9 liters). B & S: 3.23 x 3.46 in. Compression ratio: 9.0:1. Brake hp: 90 at 4600 rpm. Torque: 106 lbs.-ft. at 3400 rpm. Five main bearings. Hydraulic valve lifters. Throttle-body duel injection.

1988 Tempo sedan with all-wheel-drive

1988 Tempo GLS sedan

Escort GT Base Four: High-output. MFI version of 1.9-liter. Hp: 115 at 5200 rpm. Torque: 120 lbs.-ft. at 4400 rpm.

Tempo Base Four: Inline. Overhead valve. Cast-iron block and head. Displacement: 140 cid (2.3 liter). B & S: 3.70 x 3.30 in. Compression ratio: 9.0:1. Brake hp: 98 at 4400 rpm. Torque: 124 lbs.-ft. at 2200 rpm. Five main bearings. Hydraulic valve lifters. Multi-point fuel injection. High Swirl Combustion (HSC) design.

Tempo AWD and Sport Base Four: High-output version of HSC engine. Hp: 100 at 4400 rpm. Torque: 130 lbs.-ft. at 2600 rpm.

Taurus Base Four: Inline. Overhead valve. Four-cylinder. Cast-iron block and head. Displacement: 153 cid. (2.5 liters). B & S: 3.70 x 3.60 in. Compression ratio: 9.0:1. Brake hp: 90 at 4000 rpm. Torque: 130 lbs.-ft. at 2600 rpm. Five main bearings. Hydraulic valve lifters. Throttle-body fuel injection.

Taurus LX and Wagons V-6 (Optional Taurus L sedan): 60-degree, overhead valve. Cast-iron block and head. Displacement: 182 cid (3.0 liters). B & S: 3.50 x 3.10 in. Compression ratio: 9.3:1. Brake hp: 140 at 4800 rpm. Torque: 160 lbs.-ft. at 3000 rpm. Four main bearings. Hydraulic valve lifters. Multi-port fuel injection.

Taurus Optional V-6: 90-degree, overhead valve. Cast-iron block and aluminum head. Displacement: 232 cid (3.8 liters). B & S: 3.80 x 3.40 in. Compression ratio: 9.0:1. Brake hp: 140 at 3800 rpm. Torque: 215 lbs.-ft. at 2200 rpm. Four main bearings. Hydraulic valve lifters. Multi-point fuel injection.

LTD Crown Victoria Base V-8: 90-degree, overhead valve. Cast-iron block and head. Displacement: 302 cid (5.0 liters). B & S: 4.00 x 3.00 in. Compression ratio: 8.9:1. Brake hp: 150 at 3200 rpm. Torque: 270 lbs.-ft. at 2000 rpm. Five main bearings. Hydraulic valve lifters. Sequential (port) fuel injection.

Chassis:

Escort: Wheelbase: 94.2 in. Overall length: 166.9 in. and 168.0 in. station wagon. Tires: Pony, P175/80-Rl3; GL 4-dr and wagon, P165/80-R13. Second Series Escort: P175/70-Rl4 and GT P195/60-HR15.

EXP: Wheelbase: 94.2 in. Overall length: 168.4 in. Tires: P185/70-R14.

Tempo: Wheelbase: 99.9 in. Overall length: 176.5 in. Tires: P185/70-R14.

Taurus: Wheelbase: 106.0 in. Overall length: 188.4 in. and wagon, 191.9 in. Tires: P195/70-R14 and Taurus LX, P205/70-R14.

Crown Victoria: Wheelbase: 114.3 in. Overall length: 211.0 in. and 216.0 in., station wagon. Tires: P205/70-R15.

Options:

Escort: Escort GT Special Value Pkg. ($815). Four-speed manual Transaxle Package with four-speed manual transaxle, wide vinyl body moldings, electronic AM/FM stereo, electronic digital clock/overhead console, power steering, tinted glass, interval wipers, bumper guards, bumper rub strips and rear window defroster plus instrumentation group, light/security group, dual electric remote control mirrors and trim rings with center hubs ($582). Automatic transaxle package with wide vinyl body moldings, electronic AM/FM stereo radio, digital clock and overhead console, tinted glass, interval wipers, the instrumentation group, the light and security group, dual electric remote-control mirrors

1988 Taurus LX station wagon

1988 Taurus LX sedan

and trim rings with center hubs ($823). Console with graphic systems monitor ($56). Flip-up open-air roof ($355). Electronic AM/FM stereo radio ($137). Premium sound system ($138). Manual air conditioning ($688). Front center arm rest ($55). Heavy duty battery ($27). Electronic digital clock and overhead console ($82). Rear window defroster ($145). Tinted glass ($105). Instrumentation group ($87). Light and security group, GL ($91) or GT ($67). Deluxe luggage rack ($115). Color-keyed remote-control mirrors ($88). Wide vinyl body moldings ($50). Clear coat paint on GL ($91). AM radio ($39). Electronic AM/FM stereo, Pony ($206) and GL ($167). Electronic AM/FM radio with cassette, Pony ($343); GL ($304) and GT ($137). Premium sound system ($138). Speed control ($182). Split fold down rear seat ($49). Tilt wheel ($124). Styled road wheels ($195). Interval windshield wipers ($55). Rear window wiper and washer ($126). Heavy duty alternator ($27). Engine block heater ($18). Full size spare tire ($73). Five-speed manual transmission ($76). Automatic transaxle, GL ($490). Power steering ($235). Heavy duty handling suspension ($26).

EXP: EXP Special value package ($961). Four-speed manual transaxle package with four-speed manual, vinyl body moldings, AM/FM stereo, digital clock and overhead console, power steering, tinted glass, interval wipers, rear window defroster, instrumentation group, light and security group, dual remote control mirrors and trim rings with center hubs ($582). Automatic transaxle package with vinyl body moldings, AM/FM stereo, digital clock and overhead console, tinted glass, interval wipers, dual remote-control mirrors and trim rings with center hubs ($823). Sun and sound group including console with graphic systems monitor ($56). Flip-up open air roof ($355). AM/FM stereo ($137). Premium sound system, Luxury Coupe ($586). Manual air conditioner ($688). Heavy-duty battery ($27). Rear window defroster ($145). Tinted glass ($105). Instrumentation group ($87).). AM/FM stereo with cassette ($137). Premium sound system ($138). Speed control ($182). Tilt wheel ($124). Trim rings with center hubs ($67). Styled road wheels ($195). Rear window wiper and washer ($126). Heavy-duty alternator ($27). Automatic transaxle ($415). Power steering ($235).

Tempo: Preferred equipment packages: 2-door GL ($245); 4-door GL ($295); 4-door GL ($1,013); 4-door LX ($748) and 4-door LX ($984). Manual air conditioner ($773). Front center armrest ($55). Rear window defroster ($145). Sport instrument cluster ($87). Deck lid luggage rack ($115). Power lock group, 2-door ($237) and 4-door ($287). Dual electric remote control mirrors ($111). AM/FM stereo radio with cassette ($141). Power driver's seat ($251). Premium sound system ($138). Speed control ($182). Tilt steering wheel ($124). Polycast wheels ($176). Power side windows, 4-door ($296). Clear coat metallic paint ($91). All vinyl seat and trim ($37). Heavy duty battery ($27). Engine block heater ($94). Automatic transaxle. ($482).

Taurus: Preferred equipment packages: L, 201A=$1,203, 4-door GL sedan, 203A=$1,366, 204A=$1,808, 4-door GL station wagon, 203A=$1,316 and 204A=$1,758. LX, 207A=$559 and 208A=$1,495. MT5 four-door sedan, 212A=$972. Electronic climate control air conditioning, L or GL ($971). LX or Packages 201A, 203A or 204A ($183). Manual air conditioning ($788). Autolamp system ($73). Heavy-duty battery ($27). Cargo area cover ($66). Electronic digital clock ($78). Cornering lamps ($68). Rear window defroster ($145). Engine block heater ($18). Remote fuel door and deck lid release, sedans ($91). Remote fuel door release, station wagons ($41). Extended range fuel tank ($46). Illuminated entry system ($82). Diagnostic ($89). Electronic, LX ($239) and others, except MT5 ($351). Light group ($59).

1988 LTD Country Squire station wagon

Load floor ("picnic table") extension ($66). Power door locks ($195). Dual illuminated visor mirrors: L ($116) and GL or MT5 ($104). Power moon roof ($741). Clear coat paint ($183). High level audio system, package 207A ($167) and package 212A ($335). All other Taurus ($472). Electronic AM/FM stereo search radio with cassette ($137). Premium sound system ($168). Power antenna ($76). Rear facing third seat ($155). Six-way power driver's seat ($251). Six-way dual power seats, LX and packages 204A or 212A ($251). All other Taurus ($502). Speed control ($182). Tilt steering column ($124). Leather-wrapped steering wheel ($59). Rear window washer and wiper ($126). Leather seat trim, LX ($415); GL and MT5 ($518). Vinyl seat trim, L ($51) and others ($37). Bolt-on luxury wheel covers with packages 203A or 204A ($21). All other Taurus ($85). Finned wheel covers ($65). Custom 15-inch locking wheel covers, L or GL ($212), LX or packages 203A or 204A ($148) or with packages 207A or 208A ($34) and on the MT5 ($127). Cast aluminum wheels, L or GL ($227), MT5 ($141), LX or packages 203A or 204A ($162) and packages 207A or 208A ($49). Styled road wheels: L or GL ($178), MT5 ($93), LX or packages 203A or 204A ($113). Power side windows ($296). Insta-clear windshield ($250). Interval windshield wipers ($55). 3.0-liter V-6, L ($672). 3.8-liter V-6: LX, L and GL wagons ($396) and other Taurus models ($1,068). Heavy duty handling suspension ($26).

LTD Crown Victoria: Preferred equipment packages: LTD Crown Victoria 4-door, 110A ($472); LTD Crown Victoria LX 4-door, 111A ($699), 112A ($988) and 113A ($1,564); LTD Crown Victoria LTD 4-door and Country Squire station wagon, 130A ($587) and 131A ($1,385); LTD Country Squire 4-door station wagon, 130A ($472) and 131A ($1,270); LTD Country Squire LX 4-door station wagon and LTD Crown Victoria LX 4-door, 132A ($756) and 133A ($1,191) and LTD Crown Victoria S, 120A ($352) and 121A ($1,085). Automatic temperature control air conditioning with packages 110A, 111A, 112A, 130A, 131A or 132A ($66) and all others ($211). High level audio system with package 112A or 132A ($335) and with package 113A or 133A ($167). All other Crown Victorias ($472). Heavy duty battery ($27). Cornering lamps ($68). Rear window defroster ($145). Engine block heater ($18). Illuminated entry system ($82). Light group ($59). Power lock group ($245). Deluxe luggage rack ($115). Vinyl insert body moldings ($66). Electronic AM/FM stereo search radio with cassette and Dolby noise reduction system ($137). Power antenna ($76). Premium sound system ($168). Power six-way driver's seat ($251). Dual control power seats with packages 111A, 112A, 113A, 131A, 132A or 133A ($2,511) and ($502) other models. Dual facing rear seats ($173). Speed control ($182). Leather-wrapped steering wheel ($59). Tilt steering wheel ($124). Tripminder computer ($215). Locking wire wheel covers ($212). Cast aluminum wheels ($390). Power side windows with dual remote mirrors ($379). Insta-clear windshield ($250). Brougham vinyl roof ($665). All vinyl seat trim ($37). Duraweave vinyl seat trim ($96). Leather seat trim ($415). 100 ampere alternator ($52). Remote deck lid release ($50). Deluxe 15-inch wheel covers ($49). Traction-Lok differential ($100). Heavy-duty handling suspension ($26). Auto load leveling ($195). Trailer towing package ($387 to $399).

History:

The 1988 Fords were introduced on Oct. 1, 1987. The Tempo was introduced in November 1987 and the Second Series Escort and EXP debuted on May 12, 1988. Total model year production was 1,606,531, including Mustangs. The calendar year sales by U.S. dealers was 1,527,504, including Mustangs. Escort and EXP started off the year in the same form, but were replaced by a modestly modified Second Series in the spring. For the first time in nearly a decade, the full-size LTD Crown Victoria got a notable restyling. Tempo earned a more

1988 LTD Crown Victoria sedan

modest restyle, while Taurus added some performance with a new engine choice. During 1987, Taurus had become Ford's top seller, displacing the Escort. In addition to the domestic models, Ford now offered a Korean-built Festiva subcompact, designed by Mazda.

1989 Ford

Escort — Four: Following its mild face lift during the 1988 model year, the Escort entered 1989 with little change. With the EXP two-seater gone, the remaining Escort lineup included only the Pony and GT (both in two-door hatchback form only), and the LX (in three body styles). The 1989 models had gas-charged struts. The base 1.9-liter four produced 90 hp, while the GT's high-output version, with its multi-port fuel injection, delivered 115 hp.

Tempo — Four: Little change was evident on this year's compact Tempo sedan. It received a notable aero facelift a year earlier. GL models added nitrogen-pressurized shock absorbers. GLS had a new standard front center armrest. All models got an emissions-system warning light. A stretchable cargo tie-down net went into GLX, LX and All-Wheel-Drive models.

Probe — Four: The new Probe was a separate model with its two-door hatchback body and interior designed by Ford. Its chassis and power train were shared with the Mazda MX-6 coupe, also produced at the Flat Rock, Michigan, plant. The base and GL, powered by a 110-hp Mazda 2.2-liter (12-valve) four and the GT, with a turbocharged/intercooled 145 hp four variant were available. A five-speed manual gearbox was standard while four-speed automatic was optional on the GL/LX. Standard equipment included cloth reclining front bucket seats, power brakes and steering, tachometer, gauges, AM/FM stereo radio and a tinted backlight and quarter windows. The LX added such items as full tinted glass, a tilt steering column, power mirrors and a rear defogger. The sporty GT added front and rear disc brakes, alloy wheels, automatically-adjustable performance suspension and P195/60-VR15 tires on alloy wheels.

Taurus — Four and V-6: Most of the attention this year went to the new Taurus SHO, a high-performance model with special dual-overhead-cam 3.0-liter V-6 (four valves per cylinder) that churned out 220 hp. The engine was built by Yamaha, and the only transmission was a Mazda-built five-speed manual (designed by Ford). SHO also included disc brakes on all four wheels, a special handling suspension, dual exhausts, and P215/65-R15 performance tires on aluminum alloy wheels. The SHO added a set of subtle ground-effects body panels headed by a front air dam with fog lamps. Interior touches included a leather-wrapped steering wheel, analog gauges, power front sport seats with lumbar adjustment, 140-mph speedometer, 8000-rpm tachometer, a rear defogger, console with cup holders and armrest, and power windows. With the demise of the MT5, SHO was the only Taurus with manual shift.

LTD Crown Victoria — V-8: Since it enjoyed a significant facelift a year earlier, the full-size rear-drive Ford returned with few changes for 1989.

1989 Escort GT hatchback coupe

Base and LX trim levels were offered, a four-door sedan and station wagon body styles, all powered by a 150-hp 5.0-liter V-8 with four-speed overdrive automatic. Standard equipment included air conditioning, tinted glass and automatic headlamp on and off. On the dashboard, an engine-systems warning light replaced the former low-oil indicator.

I.D. Data:

Ford's 17-symbol Vehicle Identification Number (VIN) was stamped on a metal tab fastened to the instrument panel and was visible through the windshield. The first three symbols indicated the manufacturer, make and vehicle type. The fourth symbol denoted the restraint system. Next came letter P followed by two digits that indicated the model number, such as P90=Escort Pony two-door hatchback. Symbol eight indicated the engine type. Next was a check digit. Symbol 10 indicated the model year: K=1989. Symbol 11 denoted the assembly plant. The final six digits made up the sequence numbers, starting with 000001 (except Probe, 500001).

Escort (Four))

Model No.	Body/Style No.	Body Type & Seating	Factory Price	Shipping Weight	Production Total
90	------	2-dr. Pony Hatchback-4P	$6,964	2,235 lbs.	Note 1
91	------	2-dr. LX Hatchback-4P	$7,349	2,242 lbs.	Note 1
95	------	4-dr. LX Hatchback-4P	$7,679	2,313 lbs.	110,631
98	------	4-dr. LX Station Wagon-4P	$8,280	2,312 lbs.	30,888
93	------	2-dr. GT Hatchback-4P	$9,315	2,442 lbs.	Note 1

Note 1: Production of two-door hatchbacks totaled 201,288 with no further breakout available.

Tempo (Four)

31	66D	2-dr. GL Sedan-5P	$9,057	2,529 lbs.	Note 1
36	54D	4-dr. GL Sedan-5P	$9,207	2,587 lbs.	Note 2
37	54D	4-dr. LX Sedan-5P	$10,156	2,628 lbs.	Note 2
39	54D	4-dr. AWD Sedan-5P	$10,860	2,787 lbs.	Note 2
33	66D	2-dr. GLS Sedan-5P	$9,697	2,545 lbs.	Note 1
38	54D	4-dr. GLS Sedan-5P	$9,848	2,603 lbs.	Note 2

Note 1: Production of two-door sedans totaled 23,719 with no further breakout available.
Note 2: Production of four-door sedans totaled 217,185 with no further breakout available.

Probe (Four)

20	------	2-dr. GL Coupe-4P	$10,459	2,715 lbs.	Note 1
21	------	2-dr. LX Coupe-4P	$11,443	2,715 lbs.	Note 1
21	------	2-dr. GT Coupe-4P	$13,593	2,870 lbs.	Note 1

Note 1: Production of two-door coupes totaled 162,889 with no further breakout available.

Taurus (Four)

50	54D	4-dr. L Sedan-6P	$11,778	2,901 lbs.	Note 1
52	54D	2-dr. GL Sedan-6P	$12,202	2,927 lbs.	Note 1

Taurus (V-6)

50	54D	4-dr. L Sedan-6P	$12,450	3,020 lbs.	Note 1
55	74D	4-dr. L Station Wagon-6P	$13,143	3,172 lbs.	Note 2
52	54D	4-dr. GL Sedan-6P	$12,874	3,046 lbs.	Note 1
57	74D	4-dr. GL Station Wagon-6P	$13,544	3,189 lbs.	Note 2
53	54D	2-dr. LX Sedan-6P	$15,282	3,076 lbs.	Note 1
58	74D	4-dr. LX Station Wagon-6P	$16,524	3,220 lbs.	Note 2
54	54D	4-dr. SHO Sedan-6P	$19,739	3,078 lbs.	Note 1

Note 1: Production of four-door sedans totaled 284,175 with no further breakout available.
Note 2: Production of station wagons totaled 87,013 with no further breakout available.

LTD Crown Victoria (V-8)

73	54K	4-dr. Sedan-6P	$15,851	3,730 lbs.	Note 1
72	54K	4-dr. S Sedan-6P	$15,434	3,696 lbs.	Note 1
76	74K	4-dr. Station Wagon-6P	$16,209	3,941 lbs.	Note 2
78	74K	4-dr. Country Squire-6P	$16,527	3,935 lbs.	Note 2

Note 1: Production of four-door sedans totaled 110,437 with no further breakout available.
Note 2: Production of station wagons totaled 12,549 with no further breakout available.

LTD Crown Victoria LX (V-8)

74	54K	4-dr. Sedan-6P	$16,767	3,770 lbs.	Note
77	74K	4-dr. Station Wagon-8P	$17,238	3,915 lbs.	Note
79	74K	4-dr. Country Squire-8P	$17,556	4,013 lbs.	Note

Note: See production figures for Crown Victoria models above.

1989 Taurus SHO sedan

Engines:

Escort Base Four: Inline. Overhead cam. Cast-iron block and aluminum head. Displacement: 113 cid (1.9 liters). B & S: 3.23 x 3.46 in. Compression ratio: 9.0:1. Brake hp: 90 at 4600 rpm. Torque: 106 lbs.-ft. at 3400 rpm. Five main bearings. Hydraulic valve lifters. Throttle-body fuel injection.

Escort GT Base Four: High-output. Multi-port fuel-injected version of 1.9-liter four with 110 hp at 5400 rpm. Torque: 115 lbs.-ft. at 4200 rpm.

Probe Base Four: Inline. Overhead cam. Cast-iron block. Displacement: 133 cid (2.2 liters). B & S: 3.39 x 3.70 in. Compression ratio: 8.6:1. Brake hp: 110 at 4700 rpm. Torque: 130 lbs.-ft. at 3000 rpm. Hydraulic valve lifters. Port fuel injection.

Probe GT Turbocharged Four: Same as 2.2-liter but with turbocharger and intercooler: Compression ratio: 7.8:1. Brake hp: 145 at 4300 rpm. Torque: 190 lbs.-ft. at 3500 rpm.

Tempo Base Four: Inline. Overhead valve. Cast-iron block and head. Displacement: 140 cid (2.3 liters). B & S: 3.70 x 3.30 in. Compression ratio: 9.0:1. Brake hp: 98 at 4400 rpm. Torque: 124 lbs.-ft. at 2200 rpm. Five main bearings. Hydraulic valve lifters. Multi-point fuel injection. High Swirl Combustion (HSC) design.

Tempo AWD and Sport Base Four: High-output version of HSC four with Brake hp: 100 at 4400 rpm. Torque: 130 lbs.-ft. at 2600 rpm.

Taurus Base Four: Inline. Overhead valve. Cast-iron block and head. Displacement: 153 cid (2.5 liters). B & S: 3.70 x 3.60 in. Compression ratio: 9.0:1. Brake hp: 90 at 4400 rpm. Torque: 130 lbs.-ft. at 2600 rpm. Five main bearings. Hydraulic valve lifters. Throttle body fuel injection.

Taurus LX and Taurus wagon Base V-6 (Optional Taurus): 60-degree, overhead valve. Cast-iron block and head. Displacement: 182 cid (3.0 liters). B & S: 3.50 x 3.10 in. Compression ratio: 9.3:1. Brake hp: 140 at 4800 rpm. Torque: 160 lbs.-ft. at 3000 rpm. Four main bearings. Hydraulic valve lifters. Multi-port fuel injection.

Taurus SHO Base V-6: Duel-overhead-cam with 24 valves. Cast-iron block and head. Displacement: 182 cid (3.0 liters). B & S: 3.50 x 3.10 in. Compression ratio: 9.8:1. Brake hp: 220 at 6000 rpm. Torque: 200 lbs.-ft. at 4800 rpm. Four main bearings. Hydraulic valve lifters. Sequential port fuel injection.

Taurus Optional V-6: 90-degree, overhead valve. Cast-iron block and aluminum head. Displacement: 232 cid (3.8 liters). B & S: 3.80 x 3.40 in. Compression ratio: 9.0:1. Brake hp: 140 at 3800 rpm. Torque: 215 lbs.-ft. at 2200 rpm. Four main bearings. Hydraulic valve lifters. Port fuel injection.

1989 LTD Crown Victoria sedan

1989 Taurus LX station wagon

LTD Crown Victoria Base V-8: 90-degree, overhead valve. Cast-iron block and head. Displacement: 302 cid (5.0 liters). B & S: 4.00 x 3.00 in. Compression ratio: 8.9:1. Brake hp: 150 at 3200 rpm. Torque: 270 lbs.-ft. at 2000 rpm. Five main bearings. Hydraulic valve lifters. Sequential port fuel injection.

Chassis:

Escort: Wheelbase: 94.2 in. Overall length: 166.9 in. and 168.0 in., wagon. Tires: Pony, P175/70-R14 and GT P195/60-HR15.

Tempo: Wheelbase: 99.9 in. Overall length: 176.5 in. Tires: P185/70-R14.

Probe: Wheelbase: 99.0 in. Overall length: 177.0 in. Tires: P185/70-SR14 and GT P195/60-VR15.

Taurus: Wheelbase: 106.0 in. Overall length: 188.4 in. and 191.9 in., wagon. Tires: P195/70-R14; LX, P205/70-R14 and SHO, P215/65-R15.

Crown Victoria: Wheelbase: 114.3 in. Overall length: 211.0 in. and 216.0 in., wagon. Tires: P215/70-R15.

Options:

Escort: Escort GT special value package, 330A ($815). Five-speed manual transaxle package with power steering, electronic digital clock, overhead console, rear window defroster, tinted glass plus instrumentation group, light security group, dual electric remote control mirrors, wide vinyl body moldings, electronic AM/FM stereo radio, luxury wheel covers, interval windshield wipers, 2- and 4-door LX hatchback, 320A ($560) and 4-door LX Wagon ($484). Automatic transaxle package includes all of 320A with automatic transaxle replacing five-speed manual, 2- & 4-door LX hatchback, 321A ($938) and 4-door LX wagon ($863). Manual air conditioner ($720). Heavy duty battery ($27). Digital clock and overhead console ($82). Rear window defroster ($150). Tinted glass ($105). Instrumentation group ($87). Light and security group, LX ($91) and GT ($67). Deluxe luggage rack ($115). Color-keyed electronic remote control mirrors ($98). Wide vinyl body moldings ($50). Clear coat paint, LX ($91) and GT, including Tu-Tone ($183). Tu-Tone Paint ($91). AM Radio ($54). Electronic AM/FM stereo, Pony ($206) and LX ($152). Electronic AM/FM with cassette, Pony ($343), LX ($289) and GT ($137). Premium sound system ($138). Speed control ($191). Split fold-down rear seat ($50). Power steering ($235). Tilt steering ($124). Luxury wheel covers ($71). Vinyl trim ($37). Polycast wheels ($193). Interval windshield wipers ($55). Rear window wiper and washer ($126). Heavy duty alternator ($27). Engine block heater ($20). Full size spare tire ($73). P175/70-R14 whitewalls, LX ($73). Five-speed manual transmission, LX sedan ($76). Automatic transaxle ($490) and LX wagon ($415). Power steering ($235).

Tempo: Preferred equip packages: 226A, 2-door GL ($449) and 4-door GL ($499); 227A 4-door GL ($1,250); 229A, 2-door GLS ($1,220); 229A, 4-door GLS ($1,270); 233A 4-door LX ($863); 234A 4-door LX ($1,099) and 232A, 4-door AWD ($352). Manual air conditioner ($807). Rear window defroster ($150). Sport instrument cluster ($87). Deck lid luggage rack ($115). Power lock group, 2-door ($246) and 4-door ($298). Dual electronic remote control mirrors ($121). AM/FM stereo radio with cassette ($137). Power driver's seat ($261). Premium sound system ($138). Speed control ($191). Sports appearance group ($1,178). Tilt steering wheel ($124). Supplemental air bag restraint system, GL ($815) and LX ($751). Polycast wheels ($193). Power side windows, 4-door ($306). Clear coat metallic paint ($91). Lower accent paint treatment ($159). All vinyl Seat and trim ($37). Engine block heater ($20). P185/70-R14 whitewalls ($82). Automatic transaxle ($515).

Probe: Preferred equipment packages: Tinted glass, interval wipers, light group, dual electric remote group, tilt steering column and cluster, rear window defroster, 251A ($334). Electronic instrument cluster, electronic control air conditioner, illuminated entry, leather-wrapped steering wheel and transaxle shift knob, power driver's seat, trip computer, rear washer and wiper, walk-in passenger seat, power windows, speed control, power door locks, AM/FM electronic cassette with premium sound and power antenna, 253A ($2,214). Anti-lock braking system, electronic air conditioning, illuminated entry, leather-wrapped steering wheel and transaxle shift knob, power driver's seat, trip computer, vehicle maintenance monitor with overhead console, rear washer and wiper, walk-in passenger seat, power windows, speed control, power door locks, AM/FM electronic cassette with premium sound system and power antenna, 261A ($2,621). Manual air conditioner with package 250A, including tinted glass ($927). Other Probe models ($807). Rear window defroster ($150). Power door locks ($155). Speed control ($191). Flip-up open-air roof ($355). Aluminum wheels, with GL ($290) and with LX ($237). AM/FM electronic stereo radio w/ premium sound system ($168). AM/FM electronic cassette with premium sound system and power antenna ($344). AM/FM premium electronic cassette with premium sound system, CD player, power antenna, with packages 251A, 252A, or 260A ($1,052; with packages 253A or 261A ($708). Engine block heater ($20). Automatic transaxle ($617).

Taurus: Preferred packages: GL, 204A ($1,749); LX, 207A ($777); 208A, Sedan ($1,913) and wagon ($1,513); SHO, 211A ($533). Electronic

1989 Escort LX station wagon

1989 Tempo AWD sedan

1989 Probe GT

climate control air conditioning package, 202A ($971) and SHO, LX or package 204A ($183). Manual air conditioning ($807). Autolamp system ($73). Heavy duty battery ($27). Cargo area cover ($66). Cornering lamps ($68). Rear window defroster ($150). Engine block heater ($20). Remote fuel door, deck lid or liftgate release ($91). Extended range fuel tank ($46). Illuminated entry system ($82). Diagnostic instrument cluster ($89). Electronic instruments, LX ($239) and GL ($351). Keyless entry system with package 207A or 211A ($137) and on other Taurus models ($218). Light group ($59). Load floor "picnic table" extension ($66). Power door locks ($205). Dual illuminated visor mirrors ($100). Power moon roof ($741). Clear coat paint ($183). Auto parking brake release ($12). High level audio system with package 204A ($335) or package 207A ($167). Other Taurus models ($472). Electronic AM/FM stereo search radio with cassette ($137). Premium sound system ($168). Power radio antenna ($76). JBL audio system ($488). Rear facing third seat ($155). Six-way power driver's seat ($261). Dual six-way power seats, LX or package 204A or 211A ($261). Other Taurus models ($502). Speed control ($191). Tilt steering column ($124). Leather-wrapped steering wheel ($63). Rear window washer and wiper ($126). Finned wheel covers ($65). Custom 15-inch locking wheel covers, with package 202A ($212) or with package 204A ($148). Cast aluminum wheels, L or GL ($279), LX or package 204A ($215) and packages 207A or 208A ($49). Styled road wheels, GL ($193), LX or 204A ($128). Power windows ($306). Insta-clear windshield ($250). Interval windshield wipers ($55). Leather seat trim, LX and SHO ($489) and GL ($593). Vinyl seat trim, L ($51) or GL ($37). Bolt-on luxury wheel covers with package 204A ($21) and other models ($85). P205/70-R14 whitewalls ($82). P205/65-R15 blackwalls ($65). P205/65-R15 whitewalls ($146). Conventional spare tire ($73). Engines: 3.0-liter V-6, L and GL sedan ($672). 3.8-liter V-6: Taurus GL wagon ($400) and other Taurus ($1,072). Heavy duty handling and suspension ($26).

Crown Victoria: Preferred packages: 4-door LTD Crown Victoria LX, 111A ($383); 4-door LTD Crown Victoria LX, 112A ($938); 4-door LTD Crown Victoria LX, 113A ($1,514); 4-door LTD Crown Victoria wagon and Country Squire wagon, 131A ($1,280); 4-door LTD Crown Victoria LX wagon and Country Squire LX wagon, 132A ($688); 4-door LTD Crown Victoria LX Wagon and Country Squire LX wagon, 133A ($1,191); 4-door LTD Crown Victoria S, 120B ($66) and 4-door LTD Crown Victoria S, 121A ($802). Auto temperature control air conditioning with packages 111A, 112A, 131A or 132A ($66). Other Crown Victoria models ($216). High level audio system with packages 112A or 132A ($335) or with packages 113A or 133A ($167). Other Crown Victoria models ($472). Heavy duty battery ($27). Cornering lamps ($68). Rear window defroster ($150). Engine block heater ($20). Illuminated entry system ($82). Light group ($59). Power lock group ($255). Vinyl insert body moldings ($66). Clear coat paint ($226). Electronic AM/FM stereo search radio with cassette tape player and Dolby noise reduction system ($137). Power radio antenna ($76). Premium sound system ($168). Power six-way driver's seat ($261). Dual control power seats with packages 112A, 131A, or 132A ($251) and with other models ($522). Power facing rear seat, wagons ($173). Speed control ($191). Leather-wrapped steering wheel ($63). Tilt steering wheel ($124). Tripminder computer ($215). Style locking wire wheel covers ($228). Cast aluminum wheels ($40). Power windows and dual electronic remote mirrors ($389). Insta-clear windshield ($250). Brougham half vinyl roof ($665). Duraweave vinyl

seat trim ($96). Leather seat trim ($489). 100 ampere alternator ($52). Electronic digital clock ($96). Remote deck lid release ($50). Deluxe 15-inch wheel covers ($49). Traction-Lok differential ($100). Heavy duty handling and suspension ($26). Auto load leveling ($195). Trailer towing package ($387 to $399).

History:

The 1989 Fords were introduced on Oct. 6, 1988. The Thunderbird premiered on Dec. 26, 1988 and Probe appeared on May 12, 1988. The model year production was 1,505,908, including Mustangs. Calendar year sales by U.S. dealers were 1,433,550, including Mustangs. The sporty new Probe coupe arrived, a product of a joint venture between Ford and Mazda, but built in Michigan. The Thunderbird was restyled, including a Super Coupe with a supercharged V-6 engine. That SC was named *Motor Trend* magazine's "Car Of The Year." Taurus also jumped on the performance bandwagon with the "Super High Output" (SHO) engine in its SHO edition. The car ran the 0-60 mph standard test in the eight-second neighborhood.

1990 Ford

Escort — Four: Not much was new in the Ford subcompact for 1990, since an all-new version was expected for 1991. Rear shoulder belts became standard this year, to complement the motorized front belts. The model lineup was unchanged with a Pony two-door hatchback, the LX in three body styles, and the sporty GT two-door hatchback. The GT version of the 1.9-liter four-cylinder engine produced 110 hp, versus 90 hp for the base power plant.

Tempo — Four: Little was new this year for the popular compact Ford sedans, except the addition of standard floor mats and both foot well and trunk lights. Polycast wheels got a fresh look. Two versions of the 2.3-liter four-cylinder engine were available, and Tempo came in three trim levels plus the All Wheel Drive four-door. A five-speed manual gearbox was standard. The AWD had standard three-speed automatic.

Probe — Four and V-6: The Probe got a new V-6 engine choice. Only the GL came with a standard Mazda-built four-cylinder engine. Probe's GT again carried a turbocharged and intercooled four, and the LX got the 140-hp, 3.8-liter V-6. A GT choice was the four-speed overdrive automatic transmission. Four-wheel disc brakes were standard on the LX and anti-lock brakes were optional. All Probes got new front and rear fascias. New body moldings and cladding adorned the GT. Its alloy wheels were restyled. The GT also got a new soft-feel steering wheel and other models got leather on the wheel and gearshift knob.

1990 Escort GT three-door hatchback